Irene C. Fountas **&** Gay Su Pinnell

# LEADING *for* LITERACY

## What Every **School Leader** Needs to Know

**HEINEMANN**
Portsmouth, NH

**Heinemann**
145 Maplewood Avenue, Suite 300
Portsmouth, NH 03801
www.heinemann.com

*Offices and agents throughout the world*

Library of Congress Cataloging-in-Publication Data is on file.
ISBN: 978-0-325-09233-1

*Editor:* Jeff Byrd, Debra Doorack
*Production:* Angel Lepore
*Cover design:* Ellery Pierce Harvey, Kelsey Roy
*Interior designs:* Kelsey Roy
*Typesetter:* Technologies 'N Typography, Inc.
*Manufacturing:* Jaime Spaulding

Printed in Dongguan, China
1  2  3  4  5  TP  26  25  24  23  22
February 2022 Printing

# Contents

# Acknowledgments

IN MANY WAYS THIS book is the centerpiece of our body of work. Assuring that every child leads a literate life in and out of school requires strong leadership capacity in every school, every year. And, producing a book like this one requires leadership and collaboration among a dedicated team of professionals.

We have leaned on the considerable talents of a remarkable editorial team. We express our gratitude to Jeff Byrd who led this project with passion and energy as the Editorial Director for several years. From the beginning, he has contributed his clear thinking and constructive feedback, showing a deep understanding of our work. He has worked tirelessly to bring this volume to completion, and we couldn't have done this without him. We also thank Debra Doorack, editor, who stepped in to assist in the final phase and made outstanding contributions, as did Betsy Sawyer who reviewed all drafts and provided her editorial expertise. We also thank Lupe Ortiz who reviewed and improved upon content related to English learners and Cindy Nguyen-Pham who offered editorial support. Kerry Crosby, a generous colleague, reviewed the assessment and writing content and also helped to provide wonderful examples to illustrate. Sue Paro and David Pence were always there to provide source material and guidance as needed. We thank you all.

Our dear friend and colleague at Heinemann Wendy Mattson provided examples, assisted with photographs, and critiqued important sections of the book. She was always there to help in any way she could. Along with Wendy, Jessica Sherman graciously made suggestions, helped with examples, and reviewed materials. Together, their deep knowledge of school settings has been invaluable.

The design and production of this book have been complex. We owe the spectacular visual product to an outstanding design and production team. First, we thank Kelsey Roy who was responsible for the book's beautiful interior design. Kelsey brought unique talent to the team, and her conceptual understanding of the content was invaluable. Thanks also go to Ellery Harvey. When we look at the books we have published, we are reminded of his artistic sense and his ability to reflect our concepts and messages in the design. We are especially thankful for his work with Kelsey on the book's arresting cover. And what is a book without engaging photos? We thank Michael Grover, for his special skills in photography.

On the production side, we thank Angel Lepore for her patience, grace, and expert management of the entire production process. She kept the bar high for all and the project on track. We are also thankful for the support of Mark Tricca, who handled the always challenging matters of budgeting and big-picture scheduling. Thanks also to Jaime Spaulding and the manufacturing team for their skill in seeing that this book was printed and distributed as efficiently as possible.

We express our heartfelt appreciation to Sam Garon, Marketing Director, who deeply understands our work and advocates relentlessly for teachers and children. Thank you also to Doria Turner and Alana Jeralds, Sam's colleagues in the marketing department who offered copywriting and logistical support.

Two people work with us every day to organize, communicate, and prepare the initial manuscripts. We are especially grateful to Cheryl Wasserstrom and Andrea Lelievre for supporting every detail to bring this publication to completion. We could not have moved forward without their coordination and timely support.

And, as always, we thank the leaders of the Heinemann team—Vicki Boyd, President, our publisher Mary Lou Mackin, and editorial director Betsy Sawyer. They are examples of leadership every day.

The content of this book rests on the people who have inspired us and taught us for decades. To Anthony Bryk and his team, whose work in improvement science elevated our thinking, we express our sincere gratitude. We also thank a real leader in elementary education, Kim Marshall, for his thoughtful and often courageous work in advocating for bold leadership moves that assure schools of excellence for all children. Our Literacy Collaborative colleagues at Lesley University and The Ohio State University inspire us continuously as they work with schools to increase teacher expertise and support innovations that lead to equitable student outcomes. We also thank our Reading Recovery colleagues around the world for their passion and commitment to addressing systemic issues that are obstacles to the success of the lowest achieving children in schools. We are especially grateful to Cindy Downend, Linda Murphy, and Wendy Vaulton for their visionary leadership and invaluable feedback, their insightful suggestions about content and processes, and their skillful collaboration in developing and providing impactful training for school-based and central office school leaders over the past decades.

Finally, we thank all the teachers, teacher leaders, coaches, principals, and other educators who lift the lives of children through dynamic, skillful, and joyful literacy. They continually inspire us to think more, learn more, and do better so that together we can change systems, transform the status quo, and assure every child a bright, healthy, and successful future.

*Irene          Gay*

# Introduction

## The Journey Ahead

*A journey of a thousand miles must begin with a single step.*
—Lao-tzu

HAVE YOU EVER BEEN on a trip and found yourself spending time with a stranger because you were, at least for a while, headed in the same direction? Perhaps you shared a ride, passed the time while waiting for a flight, sat beside one another on a bus, or buddied up during a tour. Your separate journeys brought you together and, for a period of time, you traveled side by side. You may have enjoyed some pleasant conversation, laughed at a few jokes, recommended a new book, shared photos of the family or friends, and told stories from the road and of home. Maybe you discovered that you shared lots in common, or (more exciting!) you found companionship in someone very different from you.

We think of this book as an opportunity to join your journey as a school leader for a short time. We are coming from different places and bring with us different experiences, perspectives, and understandings, but in these pages our professional lives as educators converge. We're companions who get to think together, reflect on our roles and responsibilities, take up some challenging ideas, and dive into the important work of school leadership.

It's an important time for us to join together, because the stakes couldn't be any higher for the children and families we serve. As an education leader, you are surrounded by passionate, dedicated, and well-meaning professionals who  are working very hard and doing admirable work. And yet, despite the best intentions and the tremendous efforts, you witness the educational system failing too many students. The system's flaws are revealed, painfully, in the unevenness of the intellectual, social, and emotional outcomes for the children who live so many hours of their lives in your schools. The system fails to deliver on the promise of equitable, high-quality learning experiences and academic opportunity for every single child.

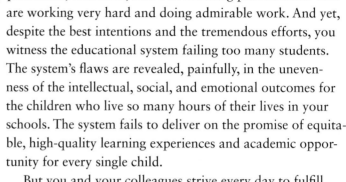

But you and your colleagues strive every day to fulfill that promise. You believe the schools you lead can make the lives of children better. You are determined that the outcomes for all of your students be positive and equitable. You want educational systems to improve, for children and for the quality of life in our society.

We've written this book to support you in your efforts. We believe *your leadership* is the primary factor that can spark and sustain improvements to the system. Through the quality and strength of your leadership, you can cast a vision and communicate a clear rationale for meaningful change. You can harness the collective efficacy of the educators with whom you work to create a system that produces strong, equitable learning outcomes that enable children to meet the literacy demands of the twenty-first century. Your collaboration with other leaders at every level—from the central office to the classroom—can cultivate a culture of continuous improvement. This work is challenging but has important, lasting consequences. The effects of your leadership will impact generations of children and families. And that is the most important reward for an educator.

## Leadership Throughout the System

Let's begin our journey together by thinking about two questions. Who are the leaders in your educational system? And what roles do they play? As you consider these questions, maybe a particular leadership role comes to mind, such as "principal" or "coach" or "curriculum coordinator." Or perhaps you think of a particular responsibility, such as "to supervise teachers" or "to lead data analysis." As a leader yourself, you may immediately think of your own role and your own responsibilities. Or maybe you think of a place, such as the central office or the school office, that is associated with a variety of leadership positions. Or perhaps, in your experience, leaders are just titles on the district website, seemingly detached from the accountability felt by classroom teachers. Your experiences as an education leader and your work with other leaders in the system are important, for they may narrow or expand how you think about who leaders are and what roles they play.

Over the past thirty years, we have spent time with many different leaders in many different schools and districts. Our experiences and work have led us to think of these professionals in this way: as educators in a *variety of roles* who are responsible for *improving the educational system* in order to ensure *positive, equitable outcomes for each child.* Let's spend a moment unpacking that idea, beginning at the end.

As an education leader, you direct all of your professional energy toward ensuring *positive, equitable outcomes for each child.* You have an enormous responsibility for the intellectual, social, emotional, and physical well-being and growth of the children in your school and district. Many leaders with whom we have worked—and we are sure this also describes you—desperately want every child, every day, in every classroom to experience the joys of living a literate life in and out of school. You want each child to become a member of an inclusive, equitable learning community—one in which learning is relevant and meaningful and the unique perspectives, experiences, and knowledge of each child are valued. You want every student to make progress because of responsive, culturally sustaining teaching that is provided by observant, informed, and supportive teachers who are growing and learning as professionals.

Creating healthy, highly productive learning communities and supporting effective teaching can be daunting. That's especially true if you attempt to fix issues in isolation, issue by issue, classroom by classroom, or school by school, while larger processes, policies, and practices in the system may be working against your efforts. As a leader, your focus on *improving the educational system* holds the most promise. And the system is incredibly complex. Processes, policies, schedules, personnel, budgets, digital infrastructure, local and state funding, learning materials, instructional practices, teaching resources, approaches to intervention, school culture, and whole communities are but some of the interrelated factors that need to be examined and grappled with when analyzing the system of educating students in your district. And those factors are notoriously resistant to meaningful, lasting improvements. Working for systemic change is demanding, and the challenges are complex.

Fortunately, in your system, leaders are at work in a *variety of roles* (Figure 1). Central office leaders have the responsibilities of focusing on system issues that are relevant to all the schools in a district. Superintendents, assistant superintendents, and curriculum directors work toward effective, equitable learning opportunities for students across schools by developing processes and systems of support that elevate the expertise of teachers and result in success for students in every discipline at every grade level.

School-based leaders play a critical role at the school level. While many

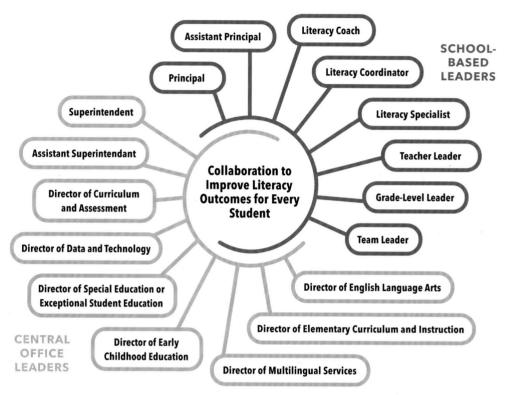

**SYSTEM LEADERSHIP**

**SCHOOL-BASED LEADERS**

**CENTRAL OFFICE LEADERS**

Assistant Principal

Literacy Coach

Principal

Literacy Coordinator

Superintendent

Literacy Specialist

Assistant Superintendant

Teacher Leader

Director of Curriculum and Assessment

Grade-Level Leader

Director of Data and Technology

Team Leader

Director of Special Education or Exceptional Student Education

Director of English Language Arts

Director of Elementary Curriculum and Instruction

Director of Early Childhood Education

Director of Multilingual Services

**Collaboration to Improve Literacy Outcomes for Every Student**

**Figure 1.** System Leadership

educators and families think first and foremost of principals and assistant principals—the administrative roles in which school leadership has traditionally been concentrated—school-based leaders can be found throughout schools where there has been intentional development of shared leadership. These leaders include coaches, team leaders, literacy specialists, and other building-level instructional leaders who work collaboratively with colleagues to support professional learning and effective teaching practices. They can also include teacher leaders and grade-level leaders who have responsibility for both teaching children and supporting the professional growth of their colleagues.

Education leaders have a variety of roles and titles and different scopes of responsibility. Each of you is most effective when using your influence—wherever you are positioned in the system—to lift the collective efficacy of your team, to champion positive change, and to take action that is linked to improvements in teacher expertise and positive outcomes for all students.

## Literacy Changes Lives

This book is our way of supporting you in that important work. And because of our years of research and experience in supporting school improvement, we focus on helping you reflect on and improve the systems to produce high literacy outcomes for every child. We believe literacy is freedom. When children attain a high level of literacy, they have access to voices, ideas, and perspectives that can bring joy, offer guidance, inform decisions, and change minds. They can pursue learning that is personally meaningful. They have the ability to share their unique voices, ideas, and perspectives through texts they create. They can advocate for a more just society and challenge inequities in our systems. Literacy doesn't inoculate children from every hardship, but with a high level of literacy, children's potential to move beyond harmful or unhealthy conditions increases significantly. Literacy brings the freedom of new and positive choices, offering hope and the promise of a fulfilling, productive life.

Because of this belief, we work to create and improve educational systems through high-quality literacy teaching and learning, which together assure the basic human right of every child to grow up literate. As we think about assuring children their right to literacy, an important question to ask is: *What are the barriers that stand in the way of every child's right to success in literacy?* Spend some time considering the answer based on your work in your school or district. In this book, we'll think together about the strengths you can build on, obstacles you face, and ways to approach and address them through systemic improvements, one small step at a time.

In our experience *there is no quick fix*. You will have to address the complexities of the system, so throughout these chapters, we will need to get comfortable with the complexity. Our goal is not to reduce or simplify the important work before you, but rather to offer ways of thinking about your work that we hope will help you begin to plan for, study, and take actions that address the challenges that exist.

As a leader in an education system, you are the most powerful lever for systemic change. And the way you *think* about your role and responsibilities matters greatly. Your effectiveness as a leader is not just about *what* you do in your role; your impact and influence will be enlarged or diminished based on how you *think* about what you do. Rationales rooted in evidence will provide a strong foundation for your leadership. Therefore, we will focus on the *thinking* part of *doing*, which is where the greatest potential for sustained, systemic change lies.

## Who Is This Book For?

We have written this book for all leaders in the education system who have a responsibility for assuring successful literacy outcomes for students. They include central office and school-based leaders. The information in the chapters is directed specifically to leaders at the school level—teacher leaders, team leaders, literacy coaches, literacy specialists, principals, and more. Throughout the book, we'll refer to these leaders as *school leaders*.

Since the ideas in this book have critical implications for central office leaders in their role of leading and coordinating the work of all personnel in the system, we have included notes in each chapter with information specifically for central office leaders (more on that soon). When central office leaders and school-based leaders work collaboratively toward common goals, their leadership provides coherence for educators throughout the system, and the students benefit as a result.

## A Look at the Map

As we journey onward from here, let's take a look at the organization of the content so that you can get the most from the information provided.

In section 1 we discuss the foundations of inspirational school leadership. We'll examine the qualities of effective school leaders and invite you to reflect on how you're viewed as a leader. Then, we'll discuss the importance of creating the common vision and shared values that will help you nurture and sustain a healthy, collaborative school culture. Finally, we'll look at how to build effective teams that deliver high outcomes for all students.

In the middle of the book, we focus on important aspects of literacy teaching and learning. Think of these chapters as your go-to guide for observing, understanding, and supporting systems that produce strong student outcomes in your school. We focus on big ideas about effective learning, how children learn to read and write, the importance of a healthy learning community, and the important role of language in literacy teaching. Then we describe a curriculum based on the observable behaviors and understandings of readers, writers, and language users. We think together about effective systems for assessing chil-

dren's literacy learning. And then we dig into research-based instructional practices; explore contexts for reading, writing, and word study; and learn what to listen and look for when observing lessons. We share ideas for teaching English learners and designing effective systems for intervention. From there, we look at the importance of high-quality books and text collections for literacy learning.

In the last section of the book, we discuss the responsibilities and opportunities you have as a school leader. We'll think together about how to build the leadership capacity of your system by lifting teachers into leadership roles and creating new leadership opportunities throughout the system. We'll reimagine professional learning as a continuous, sustained characteristic of the school culture, and we'll look at coaches and teacher leaders as important agents of change.

## SPECIAL FEATURES IN THIS BOOK

SIDEBARS                                TOOLS

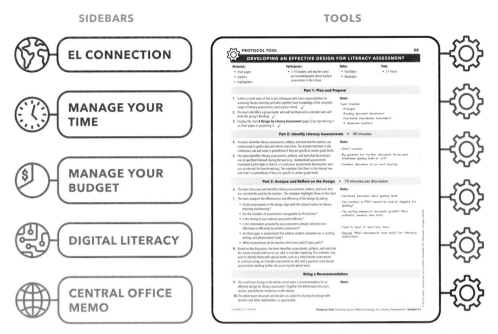

**Figure 2.** Special Features in this Book

Finally, as we part ways in the last chapter, we'll offer ideas for sustaining and scaling up systemic improvements as you continue on the journey of school leadership.

Throughout each chapter, you'll find special features that are designed to support your work in practical ways (Figure 2). The side columns of pages contain key ideas and useful guidance to help you support English learners in your school, manage your time and budget effectively, and use digital tools and resources with greater impact. A special note in each chapter offers implications of the chapter content for central office leaders. You'll also find a variety of tools throughout the book, such as protocols, templates, and observation tools. These practical resources have been helpful to many of the school leaders with whom we've worked. The tools will support you across many aspects of your work,

### A SPECIAL NOTE ABOUT OBSERVATION TOOLS

Observation tools (also known as look-for tools) are designed to help you, as a school leader, notice and reflect on important aspects of the education system–from the physical space in classrooms to teacher talk to the various instructional contexts. Observation tools also offer an important opportunity for teacher professional learning.

To maximize professional learning, we suggest engaging teachers in the construction of tools for observation and reflection. We suggest a process that helps teachers see tools as valuable for their own learning. We suggest you begin your use of a tool by working with teachers to discuss the topic and identify the essential elements for observation and reflection. Use *The Literacy Continuum* (see Chapter 9) and other articles or professional readings as the basis for the content of the discussion. For example, before observing interactive read-aloud lessons, talk with teachers about the lesson structure and what they would see and hear in an effective interactive read-aloud lesson and co-create the look-for tool.

When you give time and opportunity for teachers to contribute their understandings, engage in the thinking, and develop the criteria that is important to look for, they understand the tool from the inside instead of simply looking at a list of phrases they may not understand. You could type up your list and use it for your observations. You might also decide to distribute the observation tool we have provided and discuss how the criteria compare. Talk about criteria they may want to add or change. If you decide to use the tool we have provided, you will do so within a context in which the teachers already understand the tool from their engagement in the process. This collaborative process supports the professional learning of the teachers who will use the tool for reflection and contributes to the collective efficacy of the whole team.

For more information about using observation tools, see Chapter 21.

from welcoming new teachers with a letter that introduces your school's values and priorities, to assessing your school culture, to observing and talking to a teacher about a literacy lesson. The last chapter contains *The Fountas & Pinnell LIFT: Literacy Improvement Facilitation Tool,* a comprehensive tool that brings together many of the important ideas in the book and can help you and your school team make a plan for moving toward a coherent and sustainable system for literacy improvement. We provide an example of how each tool has been effectively used, and you'll be able to copy or download blank tools as often as you need. We will continue to refine and improve these tools over time, so the documents that you find online will always reflect our most current version.

As we mentioned earlier, we will take a thinking, noticing, and reflective stance toward the work of school leadership. At the end of each chapter, you'll find a summary, called the Takeaway, of the big ideas we explored as well as questions that can prompt deeper thinking about your school and possible actions that can move your school forward. If you're reading this book with your colleagues, you may find it helpful to discuss the questions and reflect on the ideas together.

## Essentials for the Journey

As we embark on this journey, what do we need to pack (or perhaps repack)? There are a few essentials we would suggest: a willingness to ask questions, an openness to self-reflection, a commitment to listening to the voices of educators around you, and a tentative stance toward all of the work. We've discovered that leaders who are honest, vulnerable, collaborative, and reflective have the capacity to lead significant and sustained improvements in their schools and districts.

We have written this book with the belief that yesterday's or even today's schools will not meet the needs of tomorrow's children. Our educational systems need to change for the good of our children as they live into the challenges and opportunities of the twenty-first century. We'll have given you a lot of information and support to accomplish your goals by the time you finish reading this book. By then, we hope that you'll have shifted your lens and that you'll be feeling energized and empowered to do the visionary work of school leadership. Bring everything you've learned and be willing to add on to your learning. Think with us so that you can build on your understandings. We hope you will celebrate what's working well, reflect, and grow. Armed with a wealth of information and practical tools, you will become a more effective school leader and the children and families you serve will benefit.

Our journey has begun, so let's take the next step together.

*Irene*       *Gay*

# SECTION 1    *Leading and Learning Together*

# SECTION 1

## *Leading and Learning Together*

School leaders experience the urgency of providing high-quality, engaging literacy experiences to every child, *this year*, in every school. It is tempting to plunge into a new curriculum or new set of standards. Teachers have become accustomed to being inundated with new programs every few years, some requiring a complete change in what they do and believe. It is no wonder that many wait them out or apply them in a half-hearted and superficial way.

We believe change is essential and ongoing. But each change must have deep roots in rationales and values so that it can flourish and grow in quality over time. So, in this first section, we lay a foundation for excellent literacy education in the shared values and common understandings that all educators in the school believe will make a difference in the lives of the children they teach. These chapters can help you create your common vision and values and move the teaching team toward greater collaboration, with the common goal of improving student outcomes. The teaching team never loses sight of that priority.

One good year of instruction benefits individual children, but it is *not enough*. All children, especially those who are vulnerable for some reason, need year after year of strong education in literacy. That means everyone has to be effective, and everyone has to help each other. To the school leader, it means creating teams that are committed to common goals and who can solve problems together. It may sound like a daunting task, but building a culture of collaboration and teamwork is worth the effort. Take time to examine the ideas in these four chapters and think about your own school and district. This is the first step of the journey.

# Chapter 1

## Leaders Who Inspire

*There are only three ways to generate human
connection and conduct: You can coerce,
motivate, or inspire.*
—Stronge, Richard, and Catano

EACH OF US TAKES on many different roles in our lives. We are grandparents, daughters and sons, scout leaders, soccer coaches, committee chairs, volunteers, professional educators, after-school chess coaches, helpful neighbors, best friends. On most days, we take on multiple roles, sometimes simultaneously.

Think for a moment about the role that brought you to this book: your role as a school leader. Picture yourself standing in front of a mirror and think about your reflection. How do you see yourself as a school leader? How would others describe you in that role? Now check your profile from a few different angles: your attitude when interacting with families, your ability to listen actively and empathetically, the quality of your feedback when talking with teachers, the messages you send when communicating with your team, your enthusiasm for learning alongside your colleagues, your current level of knowledge about literacy learning and teaching. What are your strengths? What are areas of growth for you as a leader?

We hope you saw in that mirror a leader who commits to building the professional capacity of your team, creates a positive environment in which students and adults can learn, and succeeds in creating sustainable improvements that make a positive difference in the literacy lives of children. If not, you still can become the kind of leader your students and teachers need you to be, whether you are a coach, a teacher leader, a principal, or other leader. It can help to name and reflect on the stance, dispositions, attitudes, and competencies most often found in inspirational school leaders.

The skills and personal characteristics discussed in this chapter are the product of our work with many different leaders in varying leadership roles in schools and districts around the world. Although there have been important differences in their personalities and circumstances, we have noticed that those who are most effective share certain strengths that we believe contribute to their success as school leaders.

Of course, no one leader possesses all these qualities or embodies them all the time. There is no such thing as a perfect leader. But we do know that those who possess more of these qualities than not have a strong potential to create and sustain systemic improvement. And the quality of their leadership infuses the culture of their schools with energy and shared purpose.

# Characteristics of Effective School Leaders

As you consider each of the following ten characteristics, keep an eye on that mirror. Reflect on your own characteristics as a school leader and how you see your role. Which qualities do you feel are most important in your current role? And how many of these descriptors would others use to describe you?

## Visionary

As a visionary school leader, you have the responsibility of inspiring your team and harnessing their collective expertise to accomplish your common goal of educating all the children in your school and preparing them for productive lives in the future. You lead the team in co-creating an ambitious vision and set of values that form the foundation of their collective work and guide their decisions—from the kinds of materials to purchase to how teachers view their responsibilities toward all students in the school. A visionary leader understands that the mission of a school is to provide effective teaching and equitable learning opportunities to all children so each one of them grows up as a

**FROM MANAGER TO DESIGNER: THE CHANGING ROLE OF LEADERSHIP**

Historically, school leaders have often been seen as "managers," leading some to suggest that business managers should perform the leadership roles in schools. School leaders have also been seen as "protectors" of teachers. But an emerging role is more aptly labeled "designer." The school leader is guiding a design team in a process of constant development. Different leaders may work at different levels and on different goals, but the visionary leader assures that the progress is undertaken with coherence. Everything and everyone work together toward the vision. Changes in one area are examined for potential unintended consequences in other areas. Always the questions are asked: *Does this action fit with our vision? Does it benefit our students? How will we know?*

joyfully literate person. A visionary leader inspires action so that others on the team want to do whatever it takes to achieve the school's vision. The leader is not content with the status quo but works constantly, with passion, to continuously improve the social, emotional, and intellectual outcomes for all the children in the school.

## Collaborative

A single leader cannot create and sustain school improvement. The improvement is a shared, inclusive effort. In fact, the shelf life of most school improvement initiatives lasts only until the leader who initiated them leaves the school. No matter how charismatic, knowledgeable, and committed you are, sustainable, systemic improvement in schools requires a team approach that builds collective efficacy—the belief that if you work together you can accomplish more than any one person can accomplish alone. You are part of a team and need not attempt all the work yourself, for we are smarter and more capable together. Therefore, an important part of your job is to foster a culture of teamwork. As an effective school leader, you invite dialogue and encourage people to work together rather than legislating and handing down decisions.

Collaboration fosters transparency and trust. There is more transparency because individuals know what they are doing and why they are doing it. No one is left out. This is *our* vision, *our* values and beliefs, *our* work, *our* school, *our* data, *our* resources, *our* students. It's challenging sometimes. And although you cannot delay improvement until everyone is on board, it is worth the extra effort because it makes everything else possible. Aim for a thoughtful process to achieve a consensus in which everyone agrees to take the first step. With visible progress, work for continuous improvement, one small step at a time.

## Committed

Take a long view, realizing that improvement always takes time, and you never arrive at a state of "all goals achieved." Improvement needs breadth (widespread involvement) and depth (many individuals with expertise). Your commitment is broader than yourself as a single leader or even yourself as a leader with a small group of people supporting you. You sow the seeds so that progress may still be made toward the mission even if you are not present. You build a team with many levels of expertise

### DO YOU HAVE A GROWTH MINDSET?

Mindsets are powerful beliefs that affect how you behave. Your mindset consists of what you believe about yourself. In order to inspire others, you must believe that you can produce desired outcomes through persistence, even if the goals are high. The motivation for that persistence may come from a "growth mindset" (Dweck 2006), which you can think of as a sense of "self-efficacy."

In her influential book *Mindset: The New Psychology of Success,* Dweck contrasts a "fixed mindset" and a "growth mindset." A fixed mindset suggests that you are pretty much who you are with the qualities you now possess and that those qualities can't change appreciably. People with a fixed mindset know they can learn some new things but believe that their basic ability doesn't change over time. As leaders, they tend to stay on the "safe side" and may be anxious about what others think.

People with a growth mindset believe that they can change and become more effective through learning and effort. They see a future that holds higher levels of expertise and achievement for themselves because they know they are always improving. Leaders with a growth mindset seek learning. They take chances and are willing to try something hard because they believe they can make good things happen.

Do you lead from a fixed or a growth mindset? The way you answer that question might be telling. But take heart. According to Dweck, people with fixed mindsets *can* change. If you work hard at developing your skills, you will become increasingly more effective.

and with high commitment. When hiring new members of the team, you consider how their experience and expertise contribute to the common vision. Enculturation of new teachers has everything to do with acquiring skills and beliefs that will contribute to the vision. The process of design takes continuous effort but is highly rewarding. Design provides for a coherent, long-term effort with layers of action, all related to the vision. In order to inspire others, you must believe that you can produce desired outcomes, even if the goals are high. Visionary goals are achievable over time with persistence. Committed leaders recognize that the road to improvement is long, but they never stray from their core work of ensuring that students and teachers are learning.

## Inclusive

An effective school leader actively includes people with different perspectives, experiences, and identities in the work of the school. They seek out perspectives and ideas that haven't been considered, draw in voices that are heard less often, and take time to understand the experiences of educators whose journeys are different from their own. Inclusive leaders invite families into decisions and respect the funds of knowledge that they can contribute about children's histories, cultures, and identities. They value people's differences for how they sharpen and strengthen the work of the school. And they make consistent efforts to foster and promote culturally sustaining practices among other school leaders, teachers, and support staff.

## Analytical

*Why are we doing this? How can we do it better? Why weren't we successful the last time we tried?* Effective school leaders ask analytical questions—questions aimed at identifying persistent problems of practice or process—like these all the time, deeply understanding their roots, analyzing previous attempts to solve them, and assembling the team most likely to succeed the next time around. Inquisitive and analytical by nature, these leaders know that knowledge leads to understanding— and that complex problems must be fully understood before they can be solved (see Figure 1-1).

### FROM SMALL STEPS COME GIANT LEAPS

You know all too well how difficult it can be for people to accept change and how often change is met with fear, resistance, and negativity. When a new initiative hits a wall, it can be helpful to scale back and remember that iterative improvements always add up and often can lead to significant and more palatable changes. Not only that, but when you *start* with small steps, you can test them out, solicit feedback, and make corrections as needed before an idea gets too far down the road. In a school, this might look like testing a new initiative in one classroom first, analyzing the results before extending it to a second classroom or grade, and refining again until you have enough evidence to show that the improvement can work on a broader scale. Bryk and colleagues recommend this approach to school improvement in their book *Learning to Improve* (2021). And for a variation on the idea of starting small, see the *Inc.* article "Why Brilliant Leadership Minds Embrace the Rule of 1 Percent" (2021) in which Haden advocates for making big improvements by leveraging lots of small, simple changes.

**INQUIRY CYCLE**

**Figure 1-1.** Inquiry Cycle

Information is the product of analysis, and effective school leaders use information to make thoughtful decisions about the way the school operates. They value evidence of progress and improvement in individual classrooms and take time to observe the evidence firsthand whenever possible. They base their decisions on data that have a meaningful connection to the values of their school. Their decisions are not a quick reaction to the loudest voice or the longest email, but the result of deep and considered analysis of data and anecdotal evidence and their own understanding of literacy teaching and learning. And because they are constantly improving, they regularly consult sources to expand their knowledge, for examaple, sound theory and research on learning, data from students in the school or district, teachers' knowledge and expertise, and the characteristics of children's homes and communities. With the help of a strong team and the time to collect and analyze evidence and sort through data sources, analytical school leaders can make decisions that lead to strong outcomes for students.

## Equity-Focused

As a school leader, you work relentlessly to create a system that produces equitable outcomes for all students. You ask the questions that reveal and challenge implicit biases, oppression, racist policies, and systemic inequities: Which

Effective leaders inspire collaborative inquiry into problems that can affect student learning.

students are thriving using this approach and which are not? Who sits on the leadership team? Which families are taking part, which are not, and why? Are certain groups of students underrepresented in the gifted and talented program, and if so, what does that indicate about the screening and admission process? What percentage of new hires in the last five years have been teachers of color? If the results are disaggregated, do any patterns of inequity emerge? Does the quality and quantity of teacher feedback differ depending on the gender (race, class, culture, level) of the student? And you take action to disrupt inequities in the system using every available resource: budget, allocation of space, policies and processes, materials, staffing, schedules, and professional learning.

## Inquisitive

You're probably familiar with the concept of a lead learner—one who models continuous learning and makes it possible for others to learn continuously too (Fullan 2020). Whether or not they embrace the moniker *lead learner*, we have found that effective school leaders naturally assume a learning stance. They tend to create the kind of school culture in which good questions are welcomed and answers are found through collaborative inquiry and the evidence that confirms them. In a learning culture like this, everyone feels safe to admit what they do not know and free to share what they do. Everyone in the school is a learner who actively seeks out professional learning opportunities for themselves and others. Effective leaders put their own learning, growth, and development on full display, and they provide ample time and resources for all members of the school community to learn alongside them. A sense of continuous, meaningful inquiry can be felt—and seen—throughout the building because school leaders put a premium on knowledge.

It's not enough, though, for leaders to model and facilitate learning in a broad sense—you also must act as curators of specific knowledge, steering learning opportunities in directions that target identified problem areas in the school or address hot topics that have come up repeatedly in discussion with other leaders or classroom teachers. In this way, you'll distribute information that can help others solve real problems affecting student learning in a single classroom or across the board.

## Reflective

As a busy school leader, your days are always full. From the time you enter the building to the time you leave, you are constantly in motion, moving through a sea of meetings, classroom observations, conversations, and encounters as you juggle priorities and stamp out fires. Sometimes it feels like there is no time to breathe, much less to reflect on the day's setbacks or triumphs. But effective leaders *do* find—or make—the time to reflect on their experiences because they know that reflection leads to a level of self-awareness that enables them to think about experiences from different perspectives and in new ways.

Through reflection, school leaders are better able to evaluate their expectations against the reality of the outcomes. They reflect on all parts of the elaborate system of interrelated parts that is their school: student data, conversations with teachers, the effects of new policies, the inclusion of all families within the school community, the impressions one has when walking down the school's hallways, and the level of teachers' engagement during staff meetings.

Management consultant, educator, and author Peter Drucker said: "Follow effective action with quiet reflection. From the quiet reflection will come even more effective action." While it may seem like a luxury at first, setting aside time for even just a few moments of reflection each day can yield important insights you might not otherwise discover.

## Vulnerable

An effective school leader can be vulnerable with other members of the team. You are honest with the team about what you are trying to accomplish and are willing to admit when you've made a mistake or when you don't know. You are willing to take risks that contribute to the values and goals of the school and share them publicly, knowing that if you do not succeed, you will still learn and grow from the experience. Your vulnerability communicates that the school is a professional safe space where it is acceptable to take a risk and okay to be unsure. Your transparency builds trust, promotes a culture of collegiality, and ensures that professional learning is the norm.

## Courageous

It's one thing to have a good design and a vision; it's another to take action. And action is essential if you want to accomplish your mission. Action requires courage. Some decisions and actions are hard. They may take extra energy, courageous conversations, honest argument, and even some courteous confrontation of the realities. And sometimes you'll have to make some decisions that work for children and families but do not fully please your colleagues. The higher the level of trust and the greater the team investment, the easier it will be to make hard decisions. As Rosalynn Carter once expressed, being a leader means more than leading people where they want to go; it sometimes means leading people where they *ought* to go. Courageous school leaders are willing to go to some uncomfortable places to achieve equitable outcomes for all children. And they are strong enough to demand full participation in the school improvement process, driving home the point as often as necessary that improvement is *not* optional.

**Central Office Memo**

**Supporting School-Based Leaders**
Reflect on your own characteristics as a leader who inspires others. How do school-based leaders regard you in relationship to their teams? Consider how you can support the recruitment, hiring, development, and retention of central office and school-based personnel who show evidence of these characteristics. When you take this stance and invest in the capacity of the team, the visionary work will have deep roots and it will survive a change in personnel at both the central office and school levels. Have a discussion with the school-based leaders about the expertise and supports you can offer their work and solicit the supports they feel they need. Be sure to document your meetings and set a few action steps or priorities to accomplish so the journey of improvement will continue to move forward.

In a culture of collegiality and trust, courageous conversations are valued.

# The Takeaway

We hope you have seen in yourself at least some of the personal characteristics we've explored in this chapter, but it's worth remembering that nobody is a born leader. Great leaders are shaped by their knowledge and experiences. Your future experiences will highlight qualities you don't yet know you possess and make the characteristics you already exhibit even stronger. And you'll have the support of strong colleagues who have been shaped and strengthened by their own past experiences. Nobody expects you to go it alone.

The vision of school leadership put forth in this book is about teamwork, not leading from the "top" down. It's about seeing the educators in your school as a group of professionals with a variety of strengths and skills who all want the same great things for students. In Chapter 2 we discuss how to establish a vision and a set of values and beliefs that all members of the school community can embrace and use as the foundation for decision-making. On that bedrock you will build the kind of culture in which teamwork can flourish.

## Think About Your School

- How do you see yourself as a leader? What do you see as your strengths?
- If you were to ask your colleagues, how would they describe you as a leader? What qualities are they likely to name?

## Move Your School Forward

- Identify one or two areas related to your role as a school leader that you'd like to learn more about, and make it a priority to carve out time for inquiry.
- Identify two or three specific supports you need to grow as a leader. Then, make a plan for acquiring those supports from other leaders in the school, your partners in the district office, or research and reading you can do on your own.

# Chapter 2

## Creating a Common Vision and Values

*Vision without action is merely a dream. Action
without vision just passes the time. Vision with
action can change the world.*
—Joel A. Barker

LITTLE CAN BE ACHIEVED without your vision of what might be—the possibilities, the dreams. A vision is deeply and communally held; it is concrete in terms of what you expect to see when your goals are achieved. It springs from your own beliefs as a leader about how children and educators in your school live and what you want their experiences to be. It rests on your faith in the expertise and continual growth of colleagues in the school, with whom you must create the vision so that you hold it in common. It depends on the collective and collaborative work of the educators within the school and their support for each other. The vision guides what you will do together and rests on your core beliefs, so it is wise to sort out, over time, what you collectively value. What do you want to see in classrooms and in the ways that adults work together? The articulation of values and beliefs is a commitment to the ways your team will behave in order to achieve its vision and will provide the guiding principles for decision-making. This is what you really think, believe, and want to have happen for children.

An aspirational vision has the power to prompt action. Such a vision brings coherence to seemingly unrelated pursuits. Too often we leap straight to determining a solution for a single problem without first analyzing it and imagining how it fits with the broader picture of school improvement. There's a tendency to "just try something," which often results in a hodgepodge of practices that sometimes get in the way of one another. Your common vision will support and bring coherence to everything you do. It will guide decisions, help determine solutions, and offer critical questions to ask every time you make a new move.

You can begin the process of creating a vision for literacy learning by doing something very simple. Think about what students will need to know and be able to do when they graduate high school. Be sure to take a long view as you imagine prekindergarten or kindergarten students leaving your system thirteen or fourteen years from now. What competencies will they need to live and work productively in the twenty-first-century world?

Today's children will be required to collaborate rather than compete, to show kindness and empathy to others, and to live in and appreciate a global, diverse society. They will need to think quickly and deeply, listen and read critically, and write and speak with clarity and power to solve important problems. They are going to be the collaborative leaders of industries, charities, and governments, and we hope, in the process, they will make the world a better place. To ensure that the children in your school or district are prepared for the future, you need a clear vision of how that can happen.

What are the skills and competencies that the youngest children in your school will need by the time they leave your education system?

## A Process for Developing a Shared Vision

Over the years, we have helped many school leaders and their teams develop a shared vision for literacy learning in their schools. When facilitating the process in person, we use a three-column chart to support educators in co-constructing their vision. We encourage you to download the blank three-column chart from Online Resources (or make your own) and participate in the process with your colleagues. We find the process to be revealing and invigorating, and we hope you do too.

The process begins with a simple exercise. Imagine yourself observing in a classroom during literacy time. *Ideally*, what would you see and hear the children doing? Take a few moments to jot down some descriptions in the first column of the chart (Figure 2-1). Be as specific as you can. Just focus on what the children are doing, not the teacher. Keep asking yourself: *What would I see? What would I hear?*

**Figure 2-1.** Ideal Literacy Classroom

When you complete your list, you'll have some very concrete, observable evidence of what you most want to see happening in the literacy classrooms across your school. The descriptions you listed in the first column are what you would ideally see and hear the children doing during literacy time in the classroom. What do you notice as you review the descriptors? Like many of the school leaders with whom we have worked, you have probably described a classroom in which children are engaged in authentic literacy learning that is characterized by real reading, real books, real talk, and real writing. The children are doing in school what they do in life outside of school. Take a moment to compare your list to the descriptors that other school leaders have shared during this process (Figure 2-2).

In an ideal literacy classroom, children choose books they want to read, share their thinking about books they have read, and reflect on their reading.

# IDEAL LITERACY CLASSROOM

| What do you see and hear the children doing? | What materials are needed in the classroom? | |
|---|---|---|
| <ul><li>listening to books and poems the teacher is reading aloud</li><li>reading books independently</li><li>sitting in comfortable places to enjoy their independent reading</li><li>reading and talking about books in a small group with the teacher</li><li>recommending books to each other</li><li>choosing books from a classroom library</li><li>talking with each other about their books and their unique perspectives (in pairs, in small groups, and as a whole group)</li><li>sharing their thinking about texts through drawing, writing, performance</li><li>keeping a record of books they have read and a list of books they want to read in their reader's notebook</li><li>using a variety of manipulatives, magnetic letters, and word sorts to work with sounds, letters, and words</li><li>writing for a variety of real purposes and audiences</li><li>playing games with letters, sounds, and word parts</li><li>listening to books individually at a listening center</li><li>reading enlarged-print books, poems, and songs with the support of the teacher</li><li>reading print and digital texts</li><li>writing in a variety of genres or forms</li><li>writing in a reader's notebook to express their thinking about books</li><li>collecting their writing ideas in writer's notebooks</li><li>making sketches in their writer's notebooks</li><li>creating multimodal presentations</li><li>gluing artifacts in their writer's notebooks</li><li>using printed and digital research tools to learn about a topic</li></ul> | | |

**Figure 2-2.** Ideal Literacy Classroom: What You See and Hear Children Doing

Now, imagine you have an unlimited budget to purchase all the materials needed for this ideal classroom. What are the children reading? What do they need to support their work as writers? What materials are they using for word study? What resources are they referencing to build their knowledge of the world? Reflect for a moment and then list the materials in the second column.

You now have two important lists that will help you create a shared vision for literacy learning in your school: a description of what you would want to see and hear children doing in an ideal literacy classroom and a list of materials that would be needed in the literacy classroom and school you have described. Look over your list of materials. How do the materials that are currently used in literacy classrooms in your school compare to the materials on your list? The reality is that many schools have accumulated decades of stuff that contributes to clutter but doesn't contribute to students' literate lives. What would you need to purchase so that literacy classrooms in your school are supplied with the materials needed to support authentic literacy learning? If you had unlimited financial resources or if you were going to purchase the materials over several years, where would you begin? Figure 2-3 lists materials that many other school leaders have recorded during this process. Notice what types of materials are listed. They're the artifacts of a literate life—the very same things that readers and writers need outside of school to lead a literate life. Is there anything that you would add to your list?

What materials are needed to support authentic literacy teaching and learning in the classroom?

| AUTHENTIC LITERACY CLASSROOM | | |
|---|---|---|
| **What do you see and hear the children doing?** | **What materials are needed in the classroom?** | **What will teachers need to teach this way?** |
| • listening to books and poems the teacher is reading aloud | • beautiful picture books for reading aloud | |
| • reading books independently | • multiple copies of books for book clubs | |
| • sitting in comfortable places to enjoy their independent reading | • multiple copies of leveled books for guided reading | |
| • reading and talking about books in a small group with the teacher | • enlarged-print versions of books, poems, and songs for shared reading | |
| • recommending books to each other | • hundreds of books in the classroom for the children to choose from, arranged by titles, genres, authors, and topics | |
| • choosing books from a classroom library | | |
| • talking with each other about their books and their unique perspectives (in pairs, in small groups, and as a whole group) | • baskets or tubs for a classroom library | |
| | • high-quality books and other media that represent a variety of people and their backgrounds, interests, and lived experiences | |
| • sharing their thinking about texts through drawing, writing, performance | | |
| • keeping a record of books they have read and a list of books they want to read in their reader's notebook | • personal book boxes for each student | |
| | • devices for collaboration, research, reading, writing, creating, and presenting | |
| • using a variety of manipulatives, magnetic letters, and word sorts to work with sounds, letters, and words | • a reader's notebook and a writer's notebook for each child | |
| | • two easels; unlined chart paper | |
| • writing for a variety of real purposes and audiences | • pocket charts | |
| • playing games with letters, sounds, and word parts | • individual whiteboards and dry-erase markers for each child | |
| • listening to books individually at a listening center | • pocket folders to organize and store word study activities | |
| • reading enlarged-print books, poems, and songs with the support of the teacher | • letters in a variety of textures, styles, and sizes | |
| • reading print and digital texts | • sticky notes | |
| • writing in a variety of genres or forms | • long, thin pointers for shared reading | |
| • writing in a reader's notebook to express their thinking about books | • magnetic letters and word cards | |
| • collecting their writing ideas in writer's notebooks | • various writing tools | |
| • making sketches in their writer's notebooks | • variety of paper for writing | |
| • creating multimodal presentations | • pocket folders to collect and organize pieces of writing | |
| • gluing artifacts in their writer's notebooks | • markers, pens, art paper | |
| • using printed and digital research tools to learn about a topic | • bookmaking materials | |
| | • rug for meeting area | |
| | • comfortable seating for meeting area | |
| | • tables that can be arranged flexibly | |
| | • movable seating (e.g., chairs on wheels) | |

**Figure 2-3.** Authentic Literacy Classroom: Materials Needed

At this point in the process, we change the title of our co-constructed chart from *Ideal Literary Classroom* to *Authentic Literacy Classroom*, a name that communicates what is distinctive about the ideal literacy learning experience you have described so far. Step again into the authentic literacy classroom that you have imagined, and this time reflect on the teacher. If you value authentic literacy experiences, what will teachers need to be able to teach this way and for children to engage in this kind of learning? List your ideas in the third column.

The ideas you have listed in the third column are likely to be very revealing. In all the times we have talked with school leaders about this topic, not one of them ever said that teachers need a program. No program can substitute for teacher expertise. That's because they—and you—know that no program can substitute for thoughtful, informed, responsive teaching. Of course, high-quality resources are essential, but they are only effective in the hands of a knowledgable teacher. The completed chart in Figure 2-4 lists supports that school leaders *have* said that teachers need. Notice how many of the supports rely on your leadership and a healthy culture of collaboration and teamwork.

What are the experiences, resources, and supports that teachers need in order to teach this way?

## AUTHENTIC LITERACY CLASSROOM

| What do you see and hear the children doing? | What materials are needed in the classroom? | What will teachers need to teach this way? |
|---|---|---|
| • listening to books and poems the teacher is reading aloud | • beautiful picture books for reading aloud | • a written document that clearly articulates the literacy competencies that children need to be successful (curriculum goals) |
| • reading books independently | • multiple copies of books for book clubs | |
| • sitting in comfortable places to enjoy their independent reading | • multiple copies of leveled books for guided reading | • a clearly articulated vision of every students' literacy learning opportunities |
| • reading and talking about books in a small group with the teacher | • enlarged-print versions of books, poems, and songs for shared reading | • a collaborative culture that supports risk-taking and continuous improvement |
| • recommending books to each other | • hundreds of books in the classroom for the children to choose from, arranged by titles, genres, authors, and topics | • professional books and resources |
| • choosing books from a classroom library | | • many professional learning opportunities: workshops, institutes, seminars |
| • talking with each other about their books and their unique perspectives (in pairs, in small groups, and as a whole group) | • baskets or tubs for a classroom library | |
| | • high-quality books and other media that represent a variety of people and their backgrounds, interests, and lived experiences | • opportunities to observe each other teach and reflect with each other |
| • sharing their thinking about texts through drawing, writing, performance | | • opportunities to work with a literacy coach or teacher leader |
| • keeping a record of books they have read and a list of books they want to read in their reader's notebook | • personal book boxes for each student | • time to plan and reflect together |
| | • devices for collaboration, research, reading, writing, creating, and presenting | • assessments that measure students' authentic reading and writing |
| • using a variety of manipulatives, magnetic letters, and word sorts to work with sounds, letters, and words | • a reader's notebook and a writer's notebook for each child | • collegial partnerships with school leaders |
| • writing for a variety of real purposes and audiences | • two easels; unlined chart paper | • expertise for making instructional decisions that are responsive to students' needs |
| • playing games with letters, sounds, and word parts | • pocket charts | |
| • listening to books individually at a listening center | • individual whiteboards and dry-erase markers for each child | • tools for reflecting on teaching |
| • reading enlarged-print books, poems, and songs with the support of the teacher | • pocket folders to organize and store word study activities | • time to collaborate |
| • reading print and digital texts | • letters in a variety of textures, styles, and sizes | |
| • writing in a variety of genres or forms | • sticky notes | |
| • writing in a reader's notebook to express their thinking about books | • long, thin pointers for shared reading | |
| • collecting their writing ideas in writer's notebooks | • magnetic letters and word cards | |
| • making sketches in their writer's notebooks | • various writing tools | |
| • creating multimodal presentations | • variety of paper for writing | |
| • gluing artifacts in their writer's notebooks | • pocket folders to collect and organize pieces of writing | |
| • using printed and digital research tools to learn about a topic | • markers, pens, art paper | |
| | • bookmaking materials | |
| | • rug for meeting area | |
| | • comfortable seating for meeting area | |
| | • tables that can be arranged flexibly | |
| | • movable seating (e.g., chairs on wheels) | |

**Figure 2-4.** Authentic Literacy Classroom: What Teachers Need to Teach This Way

This exercise has not been wishful thinking. You have described a classroom in which children actually engage in meaningful literacy learning and have the artifacts with which to live a reading life and a writing life in school. And you have described what teachers will need if they are to develop confidence and competence in teaching this way.

Through this process, you and your colleagues have also gained valuable insights into what you truly value and want to support. And those insights lead to the next step: articulating a set of values and beliefs for literacy teaching and learning.

## Creating Your Core Values

It is important to develop a set of shared values with your team. The values help teachers think about teaching and learning in a way that reflects your common vision. You might say your values operationalize your vision.

When working with school leaders, we've shared our own core values. We identified five core values that we hold for students and five core values that we hold for literacy educators (see Figure 2-5). Our vision statement appears alongside the values. We recommend creating your core values and then drafting a vision statement that summarizes the big ideas.

Our beliefs and values underlie our own work in schools. We have revisited them many times over and revise them periodically. As you read each value, ask yourself:

- *Do I agree or disagree?*
- *Is the value reflected in my school? If so, how?*

Many of our values may resonate with your own. You can use our core values as a starting point for a discussion of examples of aspirational values. Make your own set of values or modify and adapt ours. Begin by asking:

- *What must students know to live productive lives in the future?*
- *What do we want literacy learning to look like for our students?*
- *What will be important for the educators?*

Then ask: *If this is what we want students to experience, to know, and to be able to do, then what values and beliefs do we want literacy educators to hold?* Use the protocol tool **Developing Your Core Values and Vision with Your Team** (see page 30) to support your work.

The values you create are the shared understandings that you and your team agree will guide decisions about assessment, curriculum, instruction, intervention, and professional learning. The values align your decisions with your vision. The values become a shared document that everyone on the team has contributed to and owns. Teams will want to revisit the values each year to ground themselves in their beliefs. You will also want to share the values

*continued on page 30*

**Creating Clarity and Coherence**
Evaluate how information about the district's overarching vision and core values is communicated, discussed, and revisited with all stakeholders—teachers, leaders, children, and families. Be sure the understandings are in written form with dates so there is clarity and coherence that transcends word of mouth and can be revisited each year.

Think about the authentic literacy opportunities all children deserve and reflect on the ability of the central office team to advocate for the materials and professional learning opportunities that will be needed. Spend time in the school buildings, particularly in the classrooms, so you can have firsthand experience and foster collaborative relationships and shared goals.

# FOUNTAS & PINNELL CORE VALUES

## SCHOOLS ARE PLACES WHERE *ALL STUDENTS*:

**OUR VISION** The schools we envision recognize every child's right to grow up literate as a member of a dynamic learning community. Every child, every day, in every classroom experiences the joy of being part of an inclusive, equitable classroom community in which learning is relevant and meaningful and the unique perspectives, experiences, and knowledge of each child are valued. Teaching is responsive and culturally sustaining, and teachers are observant, informed, and responsive to the strengths and needs of each child. The educators take the stance of learning professionals, and school leaders foster a collaborative and innovative culture that benefits from the expertise of the team and assures equitable outcomes for students. This vision is supported by a set of common values and beliefs that we describe on these pages.

**(1)** **Are members of an inclusive, equitable community in which their identities, families, cultures, and languages are valued.**

All students feel like they belong and actively contribute to the classroom and school culture by treating everyone with kindness and respect. They take responsibility for their own learning and support the learning of others.

**(2)** **Learn about themselves and their world through authentic, collaborative inquiry.**

A culture of inquiry honors and supports each student's thinking, perspective, voice, and thirst for knowledge. As students experience and construct a wide variety of texts and pursue lines of inquiry that interest and engage them as learners, their pursuits help them build knowledge and communicate their thinking across a range of disciplines in a variety of media.

**(3)** **Believe in their own ability to acquire and use language and literacy for learning and enjoyment.**

With the belief that they can make decisions independently and act on those decisions, students have a strong sense of agency that enhances their learning. Actively involved in their own literacy growth, students think about texts, read texts, talk about texts, and write for a variety of authentic purposes and audiences. They develop strong knowledge of the alphabetic system so they can process information accurately and fluently.

**(4)** **Read, think about, talk about, and write about relevant content that engages their hearts and minds.**

Every day, students spend time reading, thinking about, talking about, and writing about content that they enjoy and that has significance in their world. As students read and write about topics and issues that matter to them, they engage with a wide range of ideas that expand their knowledge, broaden their perspectives, nurture empathy, and deepen their commitment as global citizens of their future world.

**(5)** **Engage with texts that are culturally relevant, reflect the diversity in our world, and vary in genre, content, and perspective.**

A rich and varied text base is the foundation for a multitext approach to literacy learning. Students learn how to notice aspects of the writer's and the illustrator's craft and apply what they have learned to their reading and writing. They make connections across texts, to their own selves, and to the world. Students think critically about texts and learn to question aspects of the craft as well as accuracy and authenticity.

**Figure 2-5.** Our Vision and Core Values

# FOUNTAS & PINNELL CORE VALUES

## SCHOOLS ARE PLACES WHERE *ALL LITERACY EDUCATORS:*

**(6) Are members of a community with a strong belief that their work can transform children's lives through literacy.**

Educators view themselves as members of a collaborative and innovative professional community with common expectations for themselves, their colleagues, and their students. They support each other as learners and believe that the success of students is dependent on the work they do together. They value a culture of clarity, transparency, respect, innovation, and collegiality, with strong literacy outcomes for every student as a shared goal.

**(7) Work as a team to take collective responsibility for the high achievement of each student in a widely diverse population.**

With common understandings and language, educators work collaboratively to ensure coherence and positive student outcomes across the learning experiences in the school. They engage families and guardians and the community as valued partners in each child's literacy journey.

**(8) Implement a set of evidence-based instructional practices in whole-class, small-group, and individual contexts to assure coherence within and across grade levels.**

Students read, think about, talk about, and write about texts across many different instructional contexts that take place with their whole class, in small groups, and as individuals. Each instructional context is reciprocally connected to the others, improving student outcomes and creating equitable literacy opportunities for every child in the school.

**(9) Make sound instructional decisions based on evidence gained from systematic observation and ongoing assessment data.**

Teachers notice and build on children's strengths. Teachers observe and assess the effects of their teaching on student learning moment by moment, day by day, and week by week across the school year and use the evidence to continually inform their instructional decisions. As a school team, educators review data to identify patterns and to consider the collective impact of their work on student outcomes.

**(10) Demonstrate a commitment to their own professional learning and to supporting the learning of their colleagues.**

All educators commit to continued growth in their expertise. Through ongoing, sustainable professional learning, educators refine their craft, increase their cultural awareness, and strengthen their instructional decision-making. They reflect upon their understandings and perspectives, and they challenge one another's thinking to promote positive, equitable outcomes for all students. The expansion of professional capacity through fostering teacher leadership, coaching, and teamwork within the school directly enhances the instructional excellence provided to each student.

## PROTOCOL TOOL

A common vision that is sustainable over time must be supported by a set of common values and beliefs that are clearly stated. Your core values might change over time as you incorporate new thinking and new ways of understanding the world around you and the world in which your students live. But it is important that you engage with colleagues to articulate your values, reach consensus, and create a shared written document that can be shared and revisited over time. For help in getting started, use the protocol tool **Developing Your Core Values and Vision with Your Team (01)**.

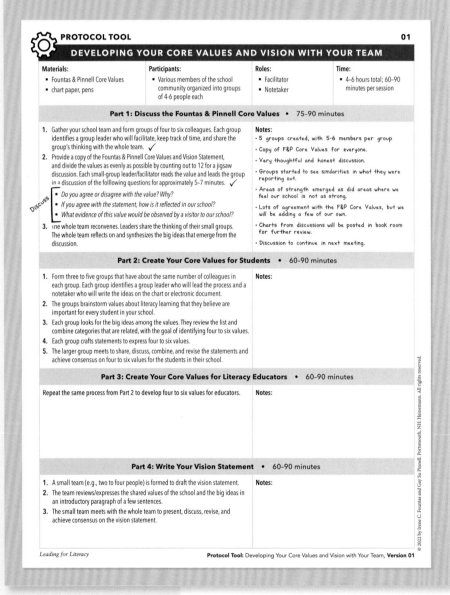

*continued from page 27*

with new teachers and families to help them understand what you are all about at your school. Once you have engaged your colleagues in this process, you will have modeled many important qualities of leadership. You will have collaborated, helped others construct their own thinking, and included a diversity of voices and perspectives. Through the process, you will have led your colleagues to articulate rationales for their beliefs and brought everyone together on the same page. Now you are ready for the last step: writing a broad summary of your school's vision so that you can move forward with coherence and common purpose.

# Writing a Vision Statement

The values and beliefs you've developed add up to a vision for teaching and learning in your school. Now you need to express that vision in a written statement.

Your vision statement should not be linguistically complicated or overly long. It will be of no use to anyone if its main points can't easily be held in minds and hearts or displayed around the school.

We have placed our vision statement alongside our core values in a sidebar (Figure 2-5). As with our core values, we invite you to use our vision statement as an example for your own. Part 4 of the protocol **Developing Your Core Values and Vision with Your Team (01)** provides a process for drafting and building consensus around your vision. The important thing is to express your vision in writing so that it can be shared, reflected upon, and discussed. It will be a touchstone for everything you do and every decision you make.

# The Takeaway

In this chapter we have helped you think about and articulate your ideal vision for literacy teaching and learning so that you can work with your colleagues to do the same for your school. Engaging in this work will provide the foundation for prioritizing actions and making decisions that are forward moving and coherent.

With a common vision for literacy learning and an embracing set of values, everyone can pull in the same direction. Nothing will be left to chance, as every member of the school community will have clarity on the literacy opportunities that all students will have, no matter the classroom or the specific teacher. The child's experiences across the grades will build on each other and have coherence. All educators will know what is essential in order to accomplish the school's mission and what role they play as a team member.

Effective communication and collaboration will require that you assess the culture in which the team can achieve their goals. In Chapter 3 we will discuss how to promote a collaborative culture in which strong, productive teams thrive and lead your visionary literacy implementation forward.

## Think About Your School

- What elements of authentic literacy learning are evident in the primary classrooms in your school?
- What elements of authentic literacy learning are evident in the intermediate classrooms?
- Which of the big ideas from this chapter do you believe are already reflected in your school?
- What could be one or two aspirational goals that are achievable within a reasonable time frame?
- Is your school engaged in innovation to adequately prepare students for their future world?

## Move Your School Forward

- Consider how you can build on the strengths that exist in classrooms. Think about first steps that will confirm the strengths and open doors for meaningful discussion of actions.
- Download the blank, three-column tool from Online Resources for imagining the ideal literacy classroom. Enlist other school leaders, a small group of teachers, and the instructional coach in working through the process described on pages 20–27.
- Engage with colleagues to articulate your values, reach consensus, and create a shared written document to share with the entire school community, including families and central office staff.

# Chapter 3

# Fostering a Culture of Collaboration and Teamwork

*Changing a toxic school culture into a healthy school culture
that inspires lifelong learning among students and adults is
the greatest challenge of instructional leadership.*
—Roland S. Barth

THE CULTURE OF A school includes the norms, values, and beliefs that exist within the school community. A school is a place where people teach and learn, so what people believe about that learning and about each other influences how they behave in the school environment. Your school's culture is revealed by:

- The way people speak and interact (what teachers say, think, and do).
- How decisions are made and by whom.
- The unspoken norms, assumptions, and customs.
- How educators see their own ability to effectively teach the children with whom they work.
- The environment that educators create for children.

- The level of ownership people take for performing their responsibilities.
- The belief that people can succeed.

The culture of a school can determine whether teachers can effectively teach students and support them in living productive and literate lives. A school's culture may be based on the belief that all students can learn and succeed, or it may be based on opposite assumptions. Some school cultures give permission for kids to fail when, in fact, the school has failed the kids. Whether we succeed or fail has everything to do with the culture—the (sometimes unarticulated) beliefs that are communicated by people throughout the school. Ladson-Billings has cautioned that we should not be talking about an "achievement gap." Rather, we should talk about "education debt" (2006). If the educators and leadership within a school believe that students can and will fail, or that failure is an option, then their thinking will permeate everything that happens within the school environment, leading students *away* from success.

Your school's culture depends on educators' personal belief systems. A negative culture, described by Cromwell (2002) as "toxic," can be truly chilling. No vision can be accomplished because communication is infrequent and sometimes negative. Teachers do not believe some children can learn or that they can teach them. There is a negative view toward the families and community, often disguised as pity. In this kind of toxic environment, the students themselves are often blamed for the lack of success. Students must comply with the regulations of the school. Imagine how discouraging and defeating it would feel to be part of an environment like this, for both students and teachers. Our firm belief is that a toxic school culture is the major cause of teacher burnout, as teachers become increasingly discouraged by a lack of success, and as the students they teach become casualties of the burnout.

## Toward a Positive School Culture

A positive culture, on the other hand, is one in which educators have an unwavering belief in themselves, their teams, and their students. They recognize the competencies each student possesses. They value the whole child. They value and promote the individual identities and diverse perspectives of students. They believe that students can succeed, and they create policies and procedures that support the belief that universal success is possible. They feel responsible; they believe in their responsibility to help their colleagues; they take risks; they innovate; they share. The interactions are characterized by mutual respect and by expressed pleasure at the accomplishments of students. They have confidence that their teaching will lead to positive outcomes for all of their students. And they make students' progress over time visible.

You can make real a positive vision for children only if you take into account the school culture that exists and then build a new culture, if needed, with any changes necessary to realize that vision. School culture *can* be changed, but such a transformation can be difficult to accomplish, because

In a positive school culture, teachers value and promote the identities and perspectives of each child.

the beliefs often are deeply held. They cross ethnic, racial, and socioeconomic lines. They are reinforced by conversations that often begin with "The kids from that neighborhood . . ." or "These kids. . . ." They are reinforced when teachers talk about how kids are "different today" or "how hard it is to work here." Commiseration simply drags down expectations, and the culture is in danger of becoming a toxic tide. And you can find this kind of feeling in *any* kind of community.

Both external and internal practices influence culture. The educators in your school may feel hammered by news coverage, state mandates, "turnovers" and "takeovers," new testing programs, or even general public accusations of incompetence. A natural tendency is not only to suspend belief in oneself but to take a defensive posture by blaming others (for example, the students and families). The most powerful internal influences are the school policies, the schedule, rules made for the convenience of adults, top-down authority with no opportunity to develop a collective voice, and, of course—the other teachers. Colleagues influence each other. A preponderance of positive leaders—teachers who believe in the vision and mission and who see themselves as instrumental in accomplishing them—can make a huge difference in the culture of the school. You can empower leaders to be drivers of improvement in your school by creating a culture in which all educators believe that all students can be successful and all teachers can grow.

School culture changes only when teachers and students experience success.

You can change school culture only when success becomes part of the teacher's life as well as the children's. This does not happen with one workshop or by lecturing. Belief is more likely to follow behavior than the other way around. Nothing helps raise a teacher's belief in students so much as seeing them succeed (and feeling her own power at being the critical supporter of that success). We have seen many teachers, both experienced and new, become transformed by achieving unexpected success as a result of their own actions. Sometimes, success means simply being able to look through a different lens, detect progress, though small, and work continuously to use those gains for further progress. We have seen this when teachers learn to work skillfully with children who are initially struggling to read and write. When children make leaps of progress, teachers' beliefs and practices are challenged or validated, and their self-efficacy is strengthened.

## Characteristics of a Strong, Collaborative Culture

A strong school culture supports the process of putting vision into action. The school is more than a place where people work. School is where many teachers come back "home" to a familiar classroom and professional community year after year. Most importantly, school is a place where children are learning how to live their lives. Home is, of course, the first influence, but school plays a significant and very important role, especially in the area of literacy and how it serves an individual throughout life. People learn the behaviors and norms of a place by spending time *in that place*. They develop beliefs about themselves and others in that same place. The culture of the school is reflected in the culture of *each classroom within it*. How adults work together in the school is mirrored in what we see in the lives of the children who share the same space every day. Below we discuss some characteristics of culture to incorporate into your design.

## A Culture of Common Goals

Your goal is to work with your school team to establish a common vision and articulate core values. The vision is to be shared among all people who influence the lives of students in schools. Team members are involved in articulating the goals and developing a shared and coherent language in order to talk about them and about student progress. It is helpful for educators to use a common assessment system and to track student progress over time. While decisions about individual students will vary and interactions will be different, educators can agree on and implement a shared and coherent set of instructional practices. The educators have a vision of progress—what they will expect of students over time as evidenced in data—and a common set of effective instructional practices that serve as a framework for individual student work. They share ways of communicating to families and members of the community. The common goals are shared across intervention teachers, classroom teachers, specialist teachers, and others. It takes work to develop common goals; teachers may need a high level of professional learning to give them the resources to create goals that are worthy of today's students and educators.

## A Culture of Collegiality and Trust

Your school's greatest resource is the expertise of its teachers. Take notice of the level of openness, collegiality, and trust within your school. With goodwill, teachers can work together to address problems and help each other improve. Taking time for careful analysis is critical; don't jump to the quickest solutions. Use self-reflection and student data (both scores and observational data) and adjust decision-making to address problems. Then study what happens (Bryk et al. 2021). This process of improvement science is best undertaken in small steps and places where people believe that they have the support and respect of their colleagues. Everyone has the responsibility to help everyone do better.

Trust is foundational to all of the concepts described in this chapter, and sometimes trust is difficult to achieve. "Trust gives school leaders the respect and credibility they need for educators to listen to, collaborate with, and fol-

---

### A GROWTH MINDSET IN TEACHERS

In Chapter 1 we mentioned Dweck's (2006) concept of a growth mindset and how it is important for school leaders. But a growth mindset also is important for teachers who need to hold the belief that they can make a difference for their students. No one really wants to do a poor job. But have you ever heard something like, "Well, I did everything in the manual, so it's not my fault." In a school with a toxic culture, blame usually falls on the students. In a school with a positive culture, the teacher can turn to colleagues, without blame, for help in examining the teaching, the method, or the materials. They can find solutions together to achieve what they know is possible. Marie Clay has said, "If a child has not learned, then we have not yet found the way to teach him."

low them." (Saphier 2018) Saphier says that building trust is not always easy because "teachers mostly work individually and often see themselves as artistic, solo practitioners rather than working side-by-side in teams and being members of an organization." A "trusting culture" is valuable and fuels an engine for continual improvement. For example, as a leader, you want teachers to place trust in you because of your:

- Competence and ability to manage specific operations of the school.
- Appreciation for them as unique individuals and professionals, shown by your interest in what they do.
- Ability to make it safe to make mistakes and willingness to examine your own mistakes.
- Honesty about how things are going.
- Transparency in your rationales and decisions.
- Actions that demonstrate a commitment to the welfare of students rather than your own advancement.
- Straight talk and honest feedback, delivered in a sensitive, constructive way.
- Advocacy for them as teachers.
- Consistency in seeking input on decisions that are a team effort and your ability to say "no."
- Celebration of small victories.
- Showing of respect by listening to understand, not judge.
- Caring and compassionate actions that show kindness in little things.

Many teachers have worked in highly competitive environments—so much so that the temptation to be secretive or even dishonest sometimes arises. Collective responsibility means something different. Trust is established through action, and you, as the school leader, are key in establishing the right environment for fostering trust:

- There is a sense that all participants support everyone being the best they can be.
- Teachers are not characterized. Progress and learning are appreciated, rather than characterizing teachers as "good" or "bad."
- School policies are examined to determine those that lead to and foster collaboration rather than competition.
- Formal and informal assessment takes place regularly and is shared.
- Daily work and decision-making are driven by agreements that are openly shared among team members.
- People feel free to share both successes and failures.
- People do not judge; rather, they problem-solve and assist.
- The leader models and expects respectful talk about colleagues, students, families, and communities.
- There is a dedicated time for professional collaboration (and directions that could be read or put online do not consume meetings).

Central Office Memo

**Collaborative Culture** It is equally important for you as a central office leader to reflect on its culture, as the culture in each school will likely be influenced by your example. Think about how the individuals relate to each other, trust each other, and work with each other toward shared goals. How would you describe the culture that exists in the central office?

Spend time reflecting on the unique culture of each school in the system. Think about how you and your team can celebrate the strengths and support the establishment of healthy cultures that reflect the mission and core values of the entire system.

The more that teachers and leaders work together, the easier it becomes to establish mutual trust.

- Data are provided in a timely way and thoughtfully considered rather than being used to assign blame.
- Participants have access to the professional learning experiences they need.
- Everyone participates in setting reasonable goals and is aware of the concrete evidence of progress.

Not everything depends on you as the school leader. We have noticed that, too often, the leader takes responsibility for everything and then fails or feels so stretched that she loses confidence. Team members may become dependent and critical. Your team members need to be actively involved in creating an atmosphere of trust. The National Center for Literacy Education (2012) offers an asset inventory for collaborative school teams to use to reflect on their collective work (download at ncte.org). Your team members can think about the collaborative group in which they are participating and ask some questions to help them reflect and improve. For example, they can rate the extent to which they:

- Value working together.
- Respect teachers' professional and personal lives.
- Are comfortable sharing evidence related to individual and collective efforts.
- Share successes and failures without being judged.
- Challenge each other and engage in hard conversations.
- Routinely monitor progress toward goals for students.
- Have the skills to use data effectively.
- Examine and discuss student work with each other.
- Have shared agreements that drive decisions and work.
- Share new learning with others.
- Have common understandings about learning.

Using an inventory such as this one (or creating your own) helps to shape the norms or the agreements with which your group operates. It will assist people in holding an honest conversation about trust and collaboration. It sharpens awareness of the critical factor of trust and helps people appreciate each other as individuals. Members will see the need to actively work to be honest with each other in a respectful way. They will see their work with students as a continuous process of inquiry and see their team members as colleagues.

Galinsky and Schweitzer (2015) claim encouragingly that winning trust doesn't have to be a long, slow process; however, we can't take it for granted that people just naturally trust people. "In an age where it's all too easy to get lured into a sense of false intimacy created through social media and email, real trust can be a rare commodity." They suggest that leaders who inspire trust the most demonstrate two traits—warmth and competence.

## A Culture of Collective Responsibility

A culture of collective responsibility is a culture of "we." Think about what language can tell you about the culture. Teachers need to work actively to create language that emphasizes "*our* kids" and "*our* school." Fifth-grade teachers should be eager to see younger children acquiring a strong foundation as readers and writers because they will be teaching them soon; primary teachers can appreciate and feel validated by stories of success from their students as they move up the grades. In some schools, teachers think only about "my class" or "my kids." There may be competition between teachers or grade levels or between primary and intermediate grades for recognition or resources.

The structure of our schools, whereby children "start over" again each year, has advantages, but it works against a feeling of collective ownership over time. A culture of collective responsibility creates a single community within the whole school.

Teachers need to feel accountable for creating access to learning for every child.

## A Culture of Accountability

True accountability to a school community means much, much more than high-stakes test scores or an annual school grade. Teachers are accountable to their students to feel the success and joy of reading, writing, talking, and inquiry every day. They are accountable for engaging and efficient teaching, for an organized classroom, and for creating access to learning for every child. Perhaps the person most accountable in the school is the principal, and this can cause enormous stress. Principals are accountable to the central office and to the community for student outcomes. They are accountable to parents and caregivers to provide their children the best school experience possible. And they are accountable to teachers as colleagues who are transparent, whose words match behaviors, who are fair, and who can be direct because there is mutual trust. But all the educators in the school need to recognize that as professionals they share in the principal's accountability. They need to be accountable to each other to give and receive help and to constantly grow as educators. They need to be accountable for their students' progress as learners, which includes accountability to families and the school community. Most of all, they need to hold themselves accountable for providing what children need in order to be successful.

## A Culture of Innovation and Inquiry

A "can do" attitude can go a long way toward solving problems. But equally important is your belief that the group can analyze problems, identify barriers, and work together to overcome them. It is everyone's responsibility. Every time a problem is solved, or an innova-

**Norms for Collaborative Inquiry**

- Effective use of time
- Professional Courtesy
- NO JUDGMENT - feel safe/environment
- Be flexible in teaching/day/on the spot teaching
- Support one another / help each other
- Open to constructive criticism
- Be positive - < successes, confirmation
- Be present - in the moment - the right now
- KEEP STUDENTS IN THE FOREFRONT
- Be reflective < what went well, what are the challenges
- Be prepared / plan

Norms for working together in a collaborative environment reflect what the school community values.

tion is adopted, it gives people the confidence to tackle more. If more expertise in teaching is needed, the group figures out how to get it; if student learning slows, the group uses evidence (data) as the basis for classroom improvement efforts; if materials are scarce, the group brainstorms to find sources. Large victories build upon smaller ones. Just as teachers see themselves as continual learners, they see the school as continually developing as an environment, a community, and a dynamic, innovative, and effective place for learning.

## A Culture of Teamwork

The origin of the word *team* refers to a team of horses or oxen as they "pull together." While no one wants to be thought of as a horse or an ox, we can all appreciate the powerful concept of uniting to pull together with common purpose in a common direction. The concept is fundamental to today's meaning of the term: a group of individuals with different but complementary skills and perspectives who collaborate and work closely together to achieve a shared goal. All members of the team consider the goal to be important and, with effort, achievable. They know that no one can opt out of the team's common goals, and they hold each other accountable. Each member contributes his specific skills, and each contribution is important. Team members believe they can accomplish far more together than they can by working alone.

You will likely find that creating an effective team in a school is much more nebulous and complex than creating teams in business, sports, or other organizations. Here are a few reasons why:

- Very often, educators do not realize that teamwork is even needed in their roles. The assumption in many schools is that each teacher will do her assigned jobs by following the curriculum and working hard, with no expectation that she will collaborate with, or support, her peers. This view fits with the old "factory" concept of schooling. Responsibilities are defined and divided, and jobs assigned.

- Often, teachers are hired to fill vacancies rather than chosen for all the ways their strengths and experiences can contribute to the overall effectiveness of the school team.

- It is rare for educators in a school to be conscious of a common vision—and rarer still in an entire school district. Vision statements are often created by people far removed from day-to-day teaching and handed down at the beginning of each school year during orientation.

- There is little flexibility in the way educators fulfill their roles. They work in "silos" with only perfunctory communication and a tendency to avoid conflict.

- Teachers often depend on "accidental" alliances that are formed as they seek support. Too often, new members of the staff are isolated;

some members make a habit of working alone. Or they communicate only in grade-level groups.

- Competition is fostered by incentive or punishment, using test scores and often controlled by someone outside the school.

- Little or no time is reserved for teachers to work together to plan, study their practice, or solve problems that impact student outcomes.

As a school leader, one of your most important goals is to create a culture in which your school staff becomes a real team, not just a collection of individual teachers with assigned roles.

## A Culture of Professional Learning

Your goal is to help educators in the school develop the expectation that every person in every role is a learner who is always evolving. Even the "more expert" literacy coach needs to hone his skills through professional learning. No one is an expert who has learned *all* there is to know and lived *every* possible experience. But, rather, everyone is respected as a learner. The environment is safe for people to take risks, make mistakes, and ask for help. Team members may focus on different areas of learning, or the staff may identify a problem of practice for the whole school to study. As new teachers enter the environment, set an expectation for commitment to continuous learning and share how you will support their learning.

# Fostering a Healthy Culture

As a leader, you play a critical role in fostering a culture that will support your school's mission and collective vision. To foster a healthy culture, you may need to create contrived structures that will support more collegial collaboration (Hargreaves 2012), such as book study groups and grade-level meetings.

## HOW TO FOSTER A HEALTHY CULTURE

1. Be sure you and your colleagues have a clear, articulated vision that everyone has contributed to and understands.

2. Be an example of respect, transparency, and other characteristics you want your colleagues to exhibit.

3. Listen to your colleagues; acknowledge their concerns and challenges before moving to solve them.

4. Develop professional relationships that also acknowledge people's individuality and life outside of school.

5. Take opportunities to review, share, and communicate your school's common values to current personnel, new personnel, and families.

6. Support clear, open communication channels.

7. Demonstrate an unwavering commitment to the success of all children in the school—in word and deed.

8. Establish clear norms around professional expectations—how we agree to work with each other in the school.

9. Acknowledge achievement and progress by individuals and by the team. (A little thank-you or congratulation goes a long way.)

10. Make student progress visible by returning regularly to accomplishments, expectations, assessment, and goals.

# The Takeaway

We have discussed the characteristics of strong leaders, how you can develop a common vision for literacy learning and establish a set of values that support the vision, and how to build a collaborative school culture that allows everyone to succeed.

## Think About Your School

- How would you describe the culture of your school?
- How do the educators relate to one another?
- What aspects of the culture are strengths?
- What aspects of the culture need to be strengthened to support continuous professional learning?
- What are some specific times when teamwork worked effectively in your school?
- Has there been a time when better teamwork would have helped?

## Move Your School Forward

- Review with your colleagues the ten key behaviors for fostering a healthy school culture presented in this chapter. Commit to making a conscious effort to exhibit these behaviors in your interactions with teachers, school staff, and other leaders in the building.
- Task a small group of teachers and school-based leaders with developing a set of norms for collaborative inquiry that can be shared with everyone in the school and with central office partners. See page 39 for a sample.

# Chapter 4

# Creating Effective Teams to Improve Student Outcomes

*Teamwork is the ability to work together toward a common
vision. The ability to direct individual accomplishments
toward organizational objectives. It is the fuel that allows
common people to attain uncommon results.*
—Andrew Carnegie

THE TEAM OF EDUCATORS in your school are your richest resource. When you
unite the whole group of educators—teachers, coaches, specialists, support
staff, administrators—around common goals, you can unleash the collective
expertise and energy of the group to create a culture of professional learning and improve student outcomes. Your ability to tap the expertise of every
educator in your building and bring together purposeful, effective, dynamic,
outcome-centered teams will play a critical role in achieving your school's
mission.

Creating and sustaining a team culture in your school *can* be achieved. Consider the five keys for building a team culture shown in Figure 4-1. With such
a culture, you will have the best chance for a "win." In the area of literacy, that
means inviting children to live a reading and writing life in school, achieving a
high level of competence in both, and finding real pleasure and expression in

| | 5 KEYS FOR BUILDING A TEAM CULTURE | |
|---|---|---|
| 1 | **Every educator is "on the team" and believes the team can improve student outcomes.** | Every team member feels responsible for the education and well-being of every child and makes decisions with that sense of responsibility in mind. By working together to increase effectiveness, solve problems, measure progress, and support each other's learning, team members continually grow in their belief that together they can make a difference in children's lives. |
| 2 | **Team members work together toward a shared vision.** | Members share a common vision to which they are committed. They see a greater purpose related to the difference the school is making in the lives of children. Accomplishing their work often means forming smaller teams as appropriate; however, strong efforts are made to foster cross-team communication so that the smaller teams work smoothly together rather than at cross purposes. |
| 3 | **Team members are learners and innovators who seek solutions to problems.** | Team members are willing to confront the reality of challenging situations. When team members recognize a problem, they speak up. They may not have the answers yet, but they are eager to study the issue and engage in collaborative problem-solving. They know there will be setbacks but there will be continuous and consistent improvement. They believe that they are part of a learning organization. |
| 4 | **Team members trust one another.** | Members appreciate and care about their teammates and strive to make their team better. The members of the team are proud of their work and can appreciate and build on the strengths of others. There is a tone of mutual respect in their interactions, even when disagreements arise. They accept that difficult conversations are part of the process and learn how to communicate with each other in a constructive way. They feel connected by the common purpose to which they aspire. The discourse is constructive, and problems are not avoided. The team works through challenges and conflict together. The environment is inclusive and characterized by trust. |
| 5 | **Team members hold themselves and each other accountable.** | We are all vulnerable when we submit our work to scrutiny, but that very act strengthens members of the team and makes it possible to do their collective work. Instructional processes are subjected to collaborative inquiry within which teachers work together for greater efficiency and effectiveness in implementing a set of research-based practices. Everyone learns from mistakes and failures. They understand that everyone has something to learn; everyone can grow and improve every year. The team members commit to getting better for each other. |

**Figure 4-1.** 5 Keys for Building a Team Culture

literacy. With a healthy culture you will be able to benefit from mutual commitment instead of what feels like coercion or compliance. Invest in the team culture throughout the year and communicate that it is an *expectation*, not a choice, that members will work together to achieve their shared goals.

## Learner-Centered Teams

An important product of building a team culture in a school is the creation of specific, learner-centered teams that do visible, coherent, action-oriented work each school year on behalf of the larger, schoolwide team. As you consider the types of smaller teams that might be beneficial at your school (Figure 4-2), a question such as this can help center your decision-making: *What teams are needed to carry forward and strengthen the school's vision and values this school year?* Teams aligned to your vision and values will naturally be learner-centered. Student outcomes, such as the quality of students' learning experiences, their social and emotional health, equitable access to learning opportunities for every student, and students' progress toward academic benchmarks, will be squarely at the center of every team's mission and goals.

To be effective and deliver impactful results, each team needs a clear purpose. Members must be selected with care and invited (strongly encouraged, although not ordered) to participate with the understanding that their experiences, expertise, and perspectives will be useful to a particular team. Teams remain sharply focused and in a learning mode by articulating and centering big questions that drive their work and inquiry. And teams are clear about the products they need to deliver or the outcomes they need to achieve to help improve student learning at the school. We'll talk more about the characteristics of effective teams a little later in this chapter.

You will have noticed that we suggest that an instructional coach or other teacher leader is present on almost every team. That would be wonderful, but if there is only one coach or teacher leader, you don't want to spread that person too thin. An instructional coach needs time to coach, and a teacher leader needs time to teach. Experienced team leaders can keep the coach or teacher leader informed of the work. In time, such teamwork will build many effective leaders within the school.

When all teams are learner-centered and aligned to the values of your school, their efforts complement each other. The work and products of one team will very often inform the decision-making and outcomes of other teams. For example, the School Advisory, Intervention, and Equity and Inclusion Teams will rely on trends and other analyses compiled by the Data Team. The English Learners Team may join with the Literacy Team on instructional rounds or walkthroughs (see Chapter 20) to observe how teachers adjust their literacy teaching for English learners who speak a particular home language. The School Library Team and the Digital Team may confer with Grade-Level Teams to discuss how to increase access to high-quality texts in a hybrid learning environment. Coherence of purpose among teams makes sharing and collaborating easier and increases their cumulative impact.

As teams accomplish their purposes and as the needs and opportunities at your school change, teams will disband. A flexible team structure that allows for the creation and dissolution of teams is healthy; it indicates that teams are doing productive work, are setting attainable goals, and are so clear about their purpose that they know when it's time to declare the mission "accomplished." When need and opportunity arise, teams may re-form, reaffirm their purpose, rearticulate questions that focus their work, agree to new products

*continued on page 50*

## HEALTHY TEAMS BEGIN WITH SCHOOL LEADERS

Your ability to create a culture of collaboration, innovation, communication, clarity, trust, and respect is important for sustaining teams in your school and allowing then to flourish. Solicit input, share priorities and rationales, and provide continuous professional learning opportunities to build the capacity of the schoolwide team. Then you and your team can hold each other accountable for your collective results.

# EXAMPLES OF LEARNER-CENTERED TEAMS IN SCHOOLS

| TEAMS | PURPOSES | MEMBERS | FOCUS QUESTIONS | OUTCOMES/PRODUCTS |
|---|---|---|---|---|
| **Grade-Level Teams** | To coordinate assessment, instruction, routines, and schedules that create a strong culture of learning, respect, and trust and result in positive outcomes for all students<br><br>To create effective, cohesive learning experiences for students across the grade levels | Teachers at each grade level<br><br>Instructional coach | *How can we work together as a team of teachers to improve the outcomes of the students in our classes?*<br><br>*What effective practices are my colleagues using that I can incorporate into my teaching and the learning experiences of my classroom?* | ▪ Clear and consistent instructional language<br>▪ Consistent routines<br>▪ Predictable schedules<br>▪ Coordinated experiences that strengthen the culture of the classroom and grade-level community |
| **Data Team** | To analyze individual and group data for needs, strengths, and patterns among students | Principal or assistant principal<br><br>One teacher from each grade<br><br>Instructional coach<br><br>Interventionist<br><br>Specialists | *Is classroom instruction producing positive learning outcomes for all students?*<br><br>*Are there disparities in the academic achievement of particular groups of students (e.g., boys, students of color, students at a particular grade, level) and if so, what actions are required to ensure that all children are academically successful?* | ▪ Share trends in data regularly with faculty, grade-level teams, and individual teachers<br>▪ Submit data-informed recommendations to other teams and school leaders that contribute to improved student outcomes |
| **Intervention Team** | To review the progress of students receiving intervention services and adjust instruction or intensity as needed<br><br>To review and improve the intervention services and processes for monitoring student progress | Interventionist<br><br>Instructional coach<br><br>Principal or assistant principal | *Are interventions helping students make accelerated progress toward grade-level understandings and behaviors?*<br><br>*How can student sustain their progress following the intervention?* | ▪ Modifications to teaching and learning experiences within interventions to help individual students take on new learning more efficiently and effectively |
| **School Library Team** | To plan services and instruction in the school library<br><br>To share newly published books and older titles that align to teaching goals<br><br>To increase the amount of high-quality books in the school library and classroom libraries that authentically represent a diversity of people and life experiences | Librarian/media specialist<br><br>Representative teachers from grades K–1, grades 2–3, and intermediate grades | *What kinds of experiences in the school library will most effectively support classroom teaching and contribute to positive student outcomes?*<br><br>*How can we increase students' access to diverse, high-quality books throughout the school?* | ▪ Publish a plan of school library services that support classroom teaching<br>▪ Share book recommendations with grade-level teams |
| **Literacy Team (or other disciplinary teams)** | To examine and improve literacy teaching and literacy learning experiences across grades | Literacy coach<br><br>One literacy/ELA teacher from each grade | *What practices of effective literacy teaching and learning are present within the school that need to be supported and amplified?*<br><br>*What practices of effective literacy teaching and learning do teachers need to begin to take on?* | ▪ Plan and lead one instructional round each month to observe and learn from the literacy teaching of colleagues<br>▪ Discuss one to two effective literacy practices at each faculty meeting |

**Figure 4-2.** Examples of Learner-Centered Teams in Schools

| EXAMPLES OF LEARNER-CENTERED TEAMS IN SCHOOLS | | | | |
|---|---|---|---|---|
| **TEAMS** | **PURPOSES** | **MEMBERS** | **FOCUS QUESTIONS** | **OUTCOMES/PRODUCTS** |
| **School Advisory Team (School Advisory Council, Principal's Advisory Council)** | To provide diverse perspectives and recommendations on school culture, student outcomes, and community partnerships<br><br>To assist in developing and evaluating annual school improvement plans | Principal and assistant principal<br><br>School psychologist<br><br>Teacher and support staff representatives<br><br>Head of parent-teacher organization<br><br>Family and community representatives | *How can the school more effectively help all students succeed academically?*<br><br>*How can the school best serve the emotional and social needs of students?*<br><br>*How can the school leverage family and community partnerships to improve student outcomes?* | ▪ School improvement plans required by the central office<br><br>▪ New initiatives that match community expertise with school needs |
| **Equity and Inclusion Team** | To analyze the educational outcomes and experiences of various groups of students<br><br>To identify and interrupt policies and practices within the school that contribute (even without intentional malice) to inequities in opportunities for particular groups of students | Educators and families working for equitable and inclusive practices and policies<br><br>Principal and assistant principal<br><br>Community leaders who are taking action for equity and access in the community | *What are the systemic inequities that exist in our school?*<br><br>*What actions can we take to interrupt the inequities?* | ▪ Professional learning opportunities to strengthen culturally responsive teaching practices<br><br>▪ Secure funding to provide digital access to all students, with extra support for families who have had less experience and access in the past (close the digital divide) |
| **Digital Team** | To help educators identify and plan for teaching and learning experiences that are effective in online and blended environments<br><br>To lead educators in developing the digital competency of all students<br><br>To identify and help implement digital tools that optimize teaching and learning experiences | Instructional technology specialist<br><br>Instructional coach<br><br>One teacher from each grade | *How can we effectively support all teachers and students in becoming proficient and confident with the digital resources and tools they will use to teach and learn?*<br><br>*What teaching practices and learning experiences are highly effective in an online learning environment?* | ▪ Guidelines for using digital resources and tools effectively in the classroom and remotely |
| **English Learners Team** | To identify and share instructional practices that improve the learning outcomes of English learners<br><br>To increase community support for English learners | English learner specialist<br><br>Instructional coach<br><br>One teacher from each grade<br><br>Family members from various cultures and home languages represented at the school | *What are effective practices for teaching English learners? Which practices are already present in classrooms and need to be supported? Which practices are not yet present and need to be introduced?*<br><br>*How can we increase culturally responsive teaching practices that support and honor the languages and cultures of the English learners at our school?* | ▪ Share effective classroom practices that support the learning of English learners<br><br>▪ Increased engagement of families of English learners in classrooms, schoolwide events, and teams |

Figure 4-2. (*continued*)

*continued from page 47*

and outcomes, and begin again. Promote a dynamic structure and plan for the amount and types of teams at your school to vary from year to year. Some years may require a greater number of teams because of evolving needs or new opportunities; other years may require fewer teams because educators are focused on putting into practice the ideas and outcomes that originated from the work of the previous year's teams. A few teams, such as grade-level teams and data teams, will continue year after year due to the ongoing relevance of their work.

## What Makes an Effective Team?

Don't leave the formation and functioning of teams to chance. Teams simply have too much potential for good. Think about and notice the characteristics of effective, high-performing teams (Figure 4-3) so that you can develop these qualities in the teams in your school. Effective teams come together for a clear **purpose** (that's the *why*), involve a diverse group of **people** pulling together with collective efficacy (that's the *who*), operate and communicate efficiently using a productive **process** (that's the *how*), and work toward the delivery of a specific, impactful **product** (that's the *what*).

### A Clear Purpose (the *Why*)

Few things raise the ire of busy professionals—teachers included—more than a meaningless meeting. Educators' time is the most valuable commodity in the school day, and they don't want to waste any part of it by participating in a group that doesn't know why it is gathered or what its goals are. On the other hand, many teachers are eager to join a team that has a clear, important purpose *and* the potential to have a positive impact on the outcomes of students.

Establishing a clear purpose for a team begins by making a connection to the shared vision and values of the school. Which of the school's values does the team support and advance? It's important to express the connection to one or more of the school's values in clear, precise, and compelling terms because the purpose will be the motivation and guiding principle for all of the team's work. The purpose will remind team members—especially on the hardest and longest of days—why their work matters. Consider this guidance:

> Surface the connection between what your team does and that larger entity and how your team's efforts serve the organization's mission and goals. This alignment is critical to secure commitment and buy-in from team members, and it gives the team a reason

---

### LEADING TEAMS

It's a good idea to ask a variety of educators who fulfill different roles in the school to lead teams. Asking the assistant principal or instructional coach to lead every team will diminish the school leader's effectiveness as a team leader and simultaneously deprive other educators of valuable experience leading a group of their peers. You might ask the interventionist to lead the intervention team, a teacher who is helping the staff take up antiracist practices to lead the equity team, and the instructional technology specialist to lead the digital team. If you regularly attend meetings of teams that you are not leading, you can show your support for their work and encourage the leaders in their role.

One last point. Often, innovation is a direct outcome of collaboration. Strive to have at least one out-of-the-box thinker on each team.

**The Elevator Speech Test** Try this exercise: describe in a few words the purpose of each team in your school and what it is presently working to achieve. If you find yourself wondering what a team is about or how it connects to the school's shared values, there's a good chance the team members are wondering too.

---

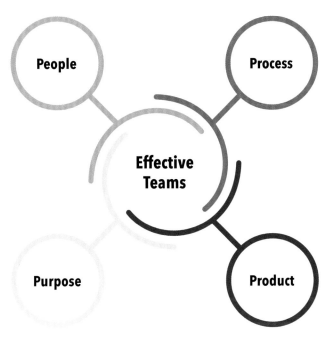

**Figure 4-3.** Characteristics of Effective Teams

for existing. If we want to produce transformational change in schools, we need to work strategically and be mission-aligned in all groups that work within larger units. Articulating purpose in relationship to other parts in the system is a critical action step for leaders. (Aguilar, p. 65)

Articulating a team's purpose may be work that you do alone, with other school leaders, or with teachers, specialists, and support staff who eventually become members of the team. The goal is to be crystal clear about the purpose so that you, other school leaders, and the team members can communicate why the team matters and how its work is relevant to the shared values of the school.

## A Diverse Group of People "Pulling Together" (the *Who*)

It's tempting to tap the same teachers, family members, community liaisons, and "super volunteers" again and again for multiple teams. But very few people can give their best to more than one or two groups at a time. And far more important than just "spreading out the work" is the intentional effort to include many different voices from your school and the community. Teams can serve to lift the concerns, ideas, and contributions of people and groups who have been underrepresented in decision-making and the meaningful work of local schools. A diverse group of members can bring fresh ideas, a jolt of energy,

**Look for Silos** Every organization is susceptible to "silos," and schools are no exception. In schools, silos are single teachers or small groups of teachers working hard but not collaborating. They work alone or with a small, set group of colleagues, without benefiting from the collective efficacy of the entire team. A silo mentality results in a lack of sharing effective practices or learning from one another. And when teachers aren't benefiting from the perspectives, expertise, and energy of their peers, students miss important benefits too.

and much-needed urgency to the work. Plan to invite new members into teams that continue from one year to the next so that you can incorporate new perspectives and expand the knowledge base of teachers, staff, and families.

As you consider team membership, keep in mind that assigning individuals to a team does not necessarily result in a collaborative group working efficiently toward a clear goal. A team may fail to "pull together" for many reasons. Sometimes subtle (or even overt and encouraged) competition exists. People may take or be assigned roles that don't maximize their talents or expertise. They may compete for a position of more influence. More value may be placed on individual accomplishments than on the team's collective achievements. Everyone on the team wants the "win," but their individual thoughts and actions may actually work against the goal. In the field of sports, owners and coaches consider more than individual skills and talent. In fact, they employ sports psychologists to help players realize that the "win" is possible only when the people on the team work as one. The role of the sports coach, then, is to observe individual abilities and consider how each person's skills can be used in a coordinated and effective way with others. As a school leader, you take on a similar role: assembling teams of educators whose skills, experiences, and perspectives come together in complementary ways to improve student outcomes.

**Collective Efficacy** When groups of teachers "pull together" on teams, they begin to develop a sense of *collective teacher efficacy*. While *self*-efficacy—an individual's belief in his own ability to accomplish something—is important,

## THE POWER OF COLLECTIVE EFFICACY

In a meta-analysis of 250 factors that influenced student achievement, Hattie (2016, 2017) revealed collective teacher efficacy as one of the top two greatest factors influencing improvements in student achievement (along with teacher estimates of achievement). In fact, Hattie discovered that the positive effects of collective efficacy on student academic performance more than outweigh the negative effects of low socioeconomic structures. Based on the results of Hattie's meta-analysis, collective efficacy as a predictor of student outcomes is:

- three times greater than socioeconomic status
- three times greater than classroom management
- three times greater than home environment and parent involvement
- two times greater than effects of prior achievement
- two times greater than feedback

a complex and hard-to-attain goal like ours is achievable only with the cumulative effect of a group working together with increasing effectiveness and agency. Effective teams who work together in a smooth, orchestrated way develop a belief in colleagues' ability to positively affect student outcomes. The educators in the building feel that "we can do it if we work together." That is *collective efficacy*. "Collective efficacy works because it influences student achievement indirectly through a constellation of productive patterns of behavior on the part of the adults in the building" (Donohoo and Katz 2017). The collective action has to go beyond words; it requires deep and personal commitment to actively work with the other members of the team. The team members are committed not only to the team's purpose but to each other; and that may mean working creatively and breaking with long-held customs or traditions to make things happen. It means recognizing that no one creates success alone, and it means committing to the school as a collaborative learning community. "Since collective efficacy influences how educators feel, think, motivate themselves, and behave (Bandura, 1993), it is a major contributor to the tenor of a school's culture" (Donohoo, Hattie, and Eells 2018).

Over the last two decades, a great deal of research has pointed to collective teacher efficacy as an important factor in improving student achievement. While the research reveals many complicated interrelationships, individual beliefs, and disparate skills, one thing is clear—the team is essential. Teachers can achieve more if they believe they can make a positive difference together and use evidence to measure the results. Cohesive, collaborative efforts based on evidence are a critical factor influencing the literacy outcomes of students. Schools in which teachers experience a sense of collective efficacy are characterized by the optimistic attitude held by teachers. They believe that they have support and can problem-solve together to meet the needs of all students. These school communities are likely to unite as a team to set challenging goals, pursue them tenaciously, and realize the continuous reward of their efforts in the evidence.

## A Productive Process (the *How*)

For many teams, ways of working together are figured out "on the fly." The process—where the team meets, how the members communicate and negotiate conflict, who does specific tasks such as leading or note-taking, and more—is deliberated and decided in moments of need. Some parts of the process happen to work well, others cause confusion, and some even set back the team's work. And after the job is done, team

Team meetings are a special opportunity to build a collaborative culture and include opportunities for professional learning and feedback. People tire of meetings that are not meaningful and don't appreciate sitting for long periods of time for little accomplishment. Consider how to communicate announcements via email or other means and make the small amount of time you meet as a team highly productive and efficient. Create a structure for the meeting, such as the structure shown in the **Team Meetings Template (03)** below, and begin and end on time to honor the team. To promote shared leadership, you might have teachers take turns soliciting agenda items and leading meetings while other teachers take notes and disseminate them afterward. Or you might have teachers alternate being responsible for the discussion of a journal article or a single agenda item instead of an entire meeting. And grade levels can share accomplishments or develop helpful professional-learning segments for small groups or the large group.

### ⚙ TEMPLATE TOOL                                                                03
### TEAM MEETINGS TEMPLATE

| Meeting Name or Team Name: Literacy Leadership Team | Date/Time: May 24, 3:30-4:30 | Location: Book Room |
|---|---|---|

Facilitator: Xiomara
Notetaker: Dana
Attendees: Zondwayo, Jasmine, Tom, Jess, Stacey, Julie, Britta

| Agenda/Action Items | | | |
|---|---|---|---|
| **Topic/Time** | **Purpose/Outcome** | **Person(s) Responsible** | **Action Steps with Timeframe** |
| Review Notes from Last Meeting (5 minutes) | Share feedback from team on proposal for Fall/Winter Professional Learning Plan | Xiomara | Dates for biweekly sessions TBD once teacher schedule draft is finalized |
| Professional Learning Plan (15 minutes) | Review and discuss returns, inventory, wish list | LLT | Xiomara will draft book return reminder and teacher wish list survey by 5/25 and share with LLT |
| Book Room Inventory (15 minutes) | What has worked this year? What can be improved? | Jasmine | Chart teacher input/feedback during faculty meeting on 6/1 |
| Schedules (20 minutes) | | Xiomara | See notes below |
| Review Actions (5 minutes) | | Xiomara | Consensus reached on draft plan |

**Notes:**

Follow-up on Professional Learning Plan
- Team shared their feedback on professional learning proposal from last meeting
- Consensus that plan is consistent with values/vision and priorities from Data Team
- Need to add dates/times for biweekly sessions once we have solid draft of fall teaching schedule

Book Room Inventory:
- Grade-level reps will remind Ts to make sure all GR books make their way back to bookroom
- Xiomara will draft email that:
  - Includes another reminder to return books
  - Includes a survey that asks Ts about the strengths and needs of the GR collection—texts levels, genre, representation, topics, etc.
  - Send draft to rest of LLT by 5/25
- LLT inventory of bookroom
  - Lily and Jesse (A-D)  • Tom (E-J)  • Stacey and Julie (K-M)
  - Dana (N-P)  • Britta (Q-S)  • Zon (T-V)
  - Xiomara (W-Z)

Schedules
- Jasmine wants teacher input on schedule for next year.
- Team agreed that it will be helpful to discuss during next faculty meeting (6/1) - teachers will chart strength, needs, and suggestions for improving schedule
- LLT wants feedback on intervention pull-out, IRA and Writer's Workshop in PM, specials rotations, lunch times

*Leading for Literacy*                              **Template Tool:** Team Meetings Template, **Version 01**

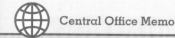

members often move on. No one pauses to reflect on what was learned about working together. In teams that remain intact from one school year to the next, the process of working together may have been established in the past but is now "invisible." New members are left to intuit the unspoken norms by which the team now operates.

You have the opportunity to guide teams to be intentional about establishing a productive process for working together. Draw attention to the many important aspects of process by leading team members to consider the following questions:

- When and where do we meet and for how long?
- Who facilitates our meetings?
- Who takes notes so there is a record of the meeting?
- How do we deliberate and reach a decision?
- How do we resolve conflicts about ideas?
- How do we communicate between meetings?
- How do we assign responsibilities related to our products or outcomes?
- How do we support one another and hold ourselves accountable to our purpose and products/outcomes?

Encourage team members to share what works well for them as individuals. Look for patterns of preferences and areas of agreement, and then build toward a consensus about the ways of working and communicating that are most effective for the team as a whole. Take time as a group to write and revise the norms that emerge from the discussion. You may also find it helpful to co-construct a meeting template that specifies agenda and action items for each meeting. You can download the **Team Meetings Template** (03) tool on the previous page from Online Resources. The effort is likely to produce a lot of goodwill and buy-in from members of the team.

It's valuable for established teams to revisit and reflect on their process periodically too. Team members who are doing the work are in the best position to reflect on the team's process and offer ways to strengthen it. Invite feedback by asking: *What is working well? What protocols and ways of interacting can be improved? Are there any norms that need to be revised to reflect how we've learned to work together?* Drawing attention to and reflecting on a team's process of working together encourages team members to learn from their experience and reinforces their collective efficacy.

## Specific, Impactful Products (the *What*)

Each team deserves to work toward a specific product or outcome that is worthy of the team's valuable time, energy, and expertise. The product or outcome flows from the team's purpose. For example, a grade-level team might produce descriptions of tools for supporting English learners. The same school's equity team might secure funding to provide digital access for all students. And the books and library team could develop, publish, and disseminate across the school an annotated list of library services that support teaching and learning.

An important way to assess the worthiness and relevance of a product or outcome is to ask: *Does the product or outcome of the team significantly impact the outcomes for learners at the school?* If a product or outcome is learner-centered, it is worthwhile. When the product is delivered or the outcome achieved, the team knows that it has fulfilled its purpose if the outcomes for learners are improved.

As to precisely *what* they will work toward, team members need to give input and, as often as possible, determine the product or outcome for themselves. Their input builds ownership in the product or outcome. People feel connected to and contribute to the outcome.

## NORMS OF COLLABORATION

*Thinking Collaborative* has published helpful norms for developing and sustaining productive group interaction (2017). To what extent are these norms reflected during team meetings at your school? Are there any norms that need to be introduced or strengthened in your team culture?

- **Pausing:** Pausing before responding or asking a question allows time for thinking and enhances dialogue, discussion, and decision-making.

- **Paraphrasing:** Using a paraphrase starter like "I thought I heard you say . . ." and providing an efficient paraphrase assists members of the group in hearing and understanding one another as they converse and make decisions.

- **Posing questions:** Using gentle, open-ended probes or inquiries increases the clarity and precision of the group's thinking. Questions may be posed to explore perceptions, assumptions, and interpretations and to invite others to inquire into their thinking.

- **Putting ideas on the table:** Ideas are the heart of meaningful dialogue and discussion. Label the intention of your comments. For example, "Here is one idea . . ." or "Another consideration might be . . ."

- **Providing data:** Providing data, both qualitative and quantitative, in a variety of forms supports group members in constructing shared understanding from their work. Data have no meaning beyond that which we make of them; shared meaning develops from collaboratively exploring, analyzing, and interpreting data.

- **Paying attention to self and others:** Meaningful dialogue and discussion are facilitated when all group members are conscious of themselves and others and aware of what they are saying *and* how they are saying it, as well as how others are responding. This includes paying attention to learning styles when planning, facilitating, and participating in group meetings and conversations.

- **Presuming positive intentions:** Assuming that others' intentions are positive promotes and facilitates meaningful dialogue and discussion and prevents unintentional put-downs.

You may need to help teams break their work into smaller steps. Encourage teams that are planning large-scale products or improvements to seek feedback on their work as they go along. They may need to test ideas in a classroom, refine their ideas, and test again. When ready, they can propose scaling up to a grade level or the school. A valuable product or outcome may be the result of an inquiry project that the team has decided to explore.

# The Takeaway

Strong learning teams are not simply assigned or created overnight. It takes time and energy, but the payoff is great. It is human nature to want to work collaboratively with others and to find true colleagues in the workplace. When you promote and insist on teamwork, you use the power of the group to improve the group. Accept different personalities but don't allow negative or divisive thinking. Strong learning teams are possible only if you engage in an inclusive process that communicates an unwavering commitment to continuous professional learning on behalf of the team's goal: equitable access to literacy success for every child.

In Section Two, we'll move from your aspirational vision to the nuts and bolts of teaching and learning. This section will provide you with an important foundation for how children learn and how they develop effective reading and writing processes that include strong phonics and spelling skills.

## Think About Your School

- What is the evidence that all educators in the school view themselves as a team?
- What teams exist in your school? Are they productive, innovative, and efficient? Why or why not?
- Are there teams in the school that are not really needed and exist only because of tradition?

## Move Your School Forward

- Review the chart on pages 48–49 with colleagues. Agree on a team you want to add. Decide when the new team will begin operating. Identify possible team members, extend invitations, describe the team's purpose in writing, and establish expectations for how often they will meet. Also identify work products they will share (and with whom), and decide whether the team's work will be continuous or short-term.
- As you and your colleagues assess existing teams and add new teams as needed, consider the resources each team will need to do their work. Ask a central office partner to attend team meetings occasionally to better understand the work and what resources and support the central office can offer.

# SECTION 2 · *Foundations for Effective Language and Literacy Learning*

# SECTION 2

## *Foundations for Effective Language and Literacy Learning*

Students' literacy learning rests on educators' understanding of several ideas: the way the learning brain expands understanding, the nature of the reading and writing processes, and the paths of progress learners take from early beginnings toward a high level of literacy with the expert support and guidance from the teacher. You and your school team have an advantage if you have a strong working understanding of the nature of learning and the processes of reading and writing. The teacher holds a tentative theory, one that is always ready to expand and change through observations of and experiences with children. Strong instruction can be guided by excellent materials, but it is the underlying understandings that make the difference in teacher effectiveness.

Talk is an all-important tool in learning. Classrooms where talk is intentional allows children to expand oral language, develop ideas, take on the language of texts, increase vocabulary, and turn talk into writing. Talk forms the social network of learning in the classroom. Talk builds self-identity but also a sense of community so that learners are supported by both the teacher and their peers.

Take a learning stance toward the literacy education in your school or district. Are people deepening their knowledge every year? Do they share new understandings and grow in the process? Do they notice the precision of their language while teaching? In these chapters we discuss essential principles of learning and becoming literate. We also recognize that there is a social element in learning both for students and teachers. We share the characteristics of healthy classroom communities, discuss the importance of student talk in the classroom, and offer suggestions as to how you can ensure that each classroom in your school is a community in which every child feels known and every child is supported so that literacy learning can flourish.

# Chapter 5

## How Children Think and Learn: Six Research-Based Principles

*Children's engagement, positive relationships, sense of agency, competence, and belonging are all causal predictors of academic achievement and well-being.*
—Peter Johnson et al.

HIGH-QUALITY CLASSROOM INSTRUCTION REFLECTS the way children learn—a simple statement on the surface, but one with deep implications. Decisions about the classroom environment, about materials, and about teaching rest on an understanding of the complex nature of learning and how it develops over time.

Over many years, we engaged in research on the conditions of learning that need to exist for students to achieve joy and success in learning. We have taught children, visited classrooms across the country, led seminars, and developed professional books, intervention systems, assessments, lessons, and classroom resources. Out of those many experiences, and with the help of school leaders like you, we have gained firsthand evidence of how children learn by observing them.

We believe that all instruction should take place in an inclusive classroom community of readers and writers where children are reading, thinking about, talking about, and writing about a wide range of beautiful, engaging texts; where children's curiosity drives authentic inquiry that builds a deep understanding of their world; and where all parts of the curriculum are thoughtfully connected to best support the learning interests and needs of individual children.

This kind of classroom community is not possible to attain unless the educators believe that all children can learn, that they are eager to learn about their world, and that they are capable of discovering and learning much more than what we teach them. Teachers who do not believe that every child can learn should not be teaching them. It's really that simple. When adults recognize that children are competent and curious and actively engage them in meaningful learning that is relevant and culturally sustaining, children become confident, active, self-initiating, self-regulating learners who find joy in a reading and writing life in and out of the classroom.

Related to the premise that all children can learn is the idea that no two children are the same and that teachers need to respond to children's individual strengths and needs. The teacher's moment-to-moment instructional decisions need to be based on observations and analysis of individual learners, not on what a simple, sequential program prescribes in the absence of knowledge about the particular children being taught. Some children can adapt to one-size-fits-all approaches to literacy learning, but it will cause many others to be left out, disengaged, and left behind.

Responsive teaching, on the other hand, recognizes and builds on each child's strengths and provides appropriate support to lead the learner forward. This kind of teaching is grounded in the teacher's detailed knowledge of each child's competencies, interacting to support the child's expansion of in-the-head processing systems for reading and writing.

Of course, it is not enough to believe that all children can learn and to embrace the idea of responsive teaching. Teachers' beliefs need to be operationalized in the classroom through the development of high levels of expertise and application of a coherent theory of human learning. Structure and sequence are indeed important, but the individual learner lies at the heart of the process.

On the pages that follow, we discuss six big ideas from the research about learning that have informed our specific beliefs about how children learn to read and write (Figure 5-1). For each big idea, we provide behaviors that you can look and listen for in classrooms. As we explore each of these ideas through the lens of children's experiences at school, we invite you to reflect on how they support the learning success of every student.

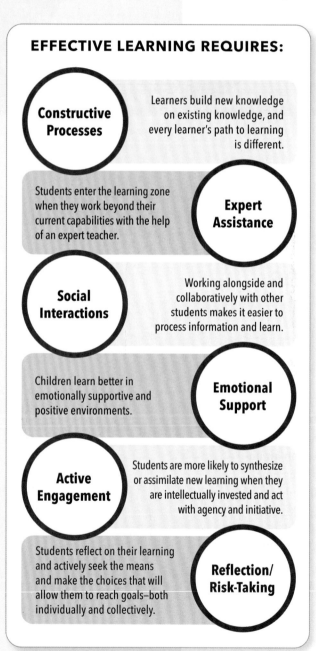

**EFFECTIVE LEARNING REQUIRES:**

**Constructive Processes**
Learners build new knowledge on existing knowledge, and every learner's path to learning is different.

Students enter the learning zone when they work beyond their current capabilities with the help of an expert teacher.
**Expert Assistance**

**Social Interactions**
Working alongside and collaboratively with other students makes it easier to process information and learn.

Children learn better in emotionally supportive and positive environments.
**Emotional Support**

**Active Engagement**
Students are more likely to synthesize or assimilate new learning when they are intellectually invested and act with agency and initiative.

Students reflect on their learning and actively seek the means and make the choices that will allow them to reach goals—both individually and collectively.
**Reflection/ Risk-Taking**

**Figure 5-1.** Conditions that lead to effective learning.

# Children Construct Their Learning

Children are not empty vessels to be filled with facts or knowledge. They bring to each learning task a wide range of assets—all the information and experience they already possess, the language they have acquired, funds of cultural knowledge, and the emotional and social mindsets they have developed over time. Like all humans, they are wired to ask questions, seek information, solve problems, and wonder about their world. By the time they get to school, their brain-based language and learning systems are already highly complex, and they have developed ways of learning that serve them well. The brain then works to make new understandings fit with what is already known or to change the current frame of understanding.

We have just described a *constructive* process of learning based on the well-known and well-tested idea that learners build new knowledge on existing knowledge. And because each learner is unique and brings a unique set of experiences and understandings to the learning process, every child's path to learning is different.

The constructive nature of learning is dramatically evident in young children's acquisition of language. Children learned the language of their environment without formal instruction. Through language examples and their interactions with others, they experience a truly amazing intellectual accomplishment, the acquisition of oral language. Of course, it is beginning language that throughout their lives they will elaborate, refine, and expand, but it is, nevertheless, a remarkable achievement.

Language learning is children's first self-extending system and is the foundation of their development of a literacy system. A child might say something like, "I throwed the ball" or "Me go too." Chances are that the child has never heard these actual statements from the adults around him; rather, he has constructed them based on some "rules" perceived in the language. Other users of the language can interpret the child's meaning, and gradually the child modifies the statements as he learns and shifts his understandings. In this way, the child's approximations become more standard over time. Language is constructed through many demonstrations of meaningful language, its constant use, feedback, and response from others. With strong and explicit teaching, the same is true for reading and writing.

Clay (2015) describes learning as "an act of construction rather than instruction." She explains that it is only the child who can build the "neurological power pack." Children who are constructing their learning use the scaffold that teachers provide to expand their competencies.

But does that mean children are always the ones in charge? Or that the understandings they construct must always be considered acceptable? And what about standards and assessments? In fact, constructivism *does not* mean "anything goes." Teachers need to balance learning that is constructed by the learner with that which is received by the learner. The idea is to guide students in the direction they need to go with instruction but grant them the freedom to get there with their own power and on their own path.

The supportive classroom offers high-quality teaching that provides opportunities for students to construct their understandings by doing the thinking and the figuring-out themselves instead of simply being told. The one who does the thinking is the one who learns. When children's innate sense of agency and self-efficacy is not nurtured and supported in the classroom they may disengage, and learning can slow.

In classrooms where students are actively engaged in the construction of their learning, as individuals and as a community, you might notice that:

- Everywhere you look there are co-constructed anchor charts that list students' "noticings," such as big ideas across texts, genre characteristics, authors' and illustrators' styles, and patterns in words. Anchor charts are constructed by the teachers and the students. The charts display the thinking that students are doing so that they can refer to them and build on their learning. New information is added over time as students actively search for and describe patterns and connections between texts, words, and concepts.

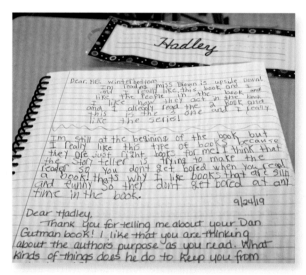

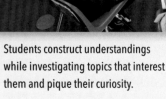

Students construct understandings while investigating topics that interest them and pique their curiosity.

- Teachers invite thinking and talking to prompt higher-level thinking and reflection, not just a mere recall of facts. High-quality questions and comments help students elevate and organize their thinking about a concept or text, consider how new learning integrates with their existing understandings, and reflect on not just *what* they know but *how* and *why* they know it and what they want to know more about. Teachers also promote a variety of perspectives.

- Students regularly explore topics of their own interest and participate in inquiry projects during which they conduct research individually, in pairs, or as a group. Students have time and resources to explore topics and real problems that are relevant to them so that new learning is meaningful and connected to previous learning experiences. Students are invested in the construction of knowledge and its application.

- Students articulate their observations and understandings. They write and talk about what they notice and pose "wonderings." Student talk is more frequent than teacher talk. When students talk, they share their thinking. The student who does the talking is the one who does the thinking and the learning. By expressing and exhibiting their understandings, students "own" the new knowledge and make it personally meaningful. They become aware of their learning and how they can apply it.

## Children Expand Their Capabilities Through Expert Assistance

Learning is faster and even more exciting when students work at a level just beyond their current capabilities. When learners enter the "learning zone," they reach beyond what they know and can do independently (Figure 5-2). It helps

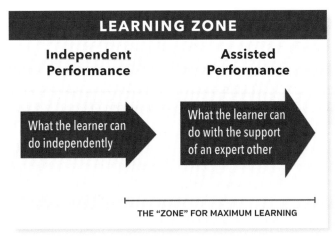

Figure 5-2. In the learning zone, students work at a level just beyond their current capabilities.

to have the assistance of another person with greater expertise and experience who gives just enough help to enable the learner to enter the zone and perform successfully (Vygotsky 1978). In schools, the teacher creates an environment and tasks, provides the materials and means, and uses language with intention and precision to help students reach beyond their current understandings and construct new knowledge *every day*. Sometimes called *cognitive guidance*, this assistance is especially important in the beginning, early, and intermediate stages of acquiring a new set of complex understandings.

With the support of a skilled teacher, children can stretch themselves to create new understandings.

Lev Vygotsky was a Russian psychologist who had a profound influence on our thinking about how children learn. He proposed the idea that learning is linked to social interrelationships. Supported by another with a higher level of expertise, individuals can perform at a level that is beyond what they can do alone, so they stretch themselves and construct new understandings and competencies in the process. Working in this "zone of proximal development," the individual constantly grows in knowledge and skills. As the individual acquires more, the scaffold extends to a new zone. The whole process is a challenge but is also highly satisfying to the learner.

In classrooms where teachers provide expert assistance to help children expand their capabilities in literacy, you might notice:

- Teachers think together with children as they read aloud high-quality text selections or facilitate book club discussions that build on and expand their knowledge of the world. Students do most of the talking, take risks, and share their perspectives.

- Teachers make comments, pose questions, and invite shared thinking.

- Teachers demonstrate fluent, phrased reading of texts and participation in discussions.

- Through prompts, teachers invite students to articulate what they notice about the text's meaning, language, and craft.

- Teachers revisit texts to help students notice more.

- When conferring with a student during readers' or writers' workshop, the teacher confirms the child's thinking and prompts the child to think more deeply and in different ways about the text or piece of writing.

- During guided writing lessons (as well as guided reading lessons), the teacher selects texts and instructs students in a way that builds on individuals' strengths and furthers their competencies.

- Teachers carefully select texts for different contexts and offer opportunities for children to problem-solve and stretch new understandings.

# Children Learn Through Social Interactions

Most human learning, particularly for children, takes place in a social context rather than in isolation. Even when students work alone, they do so within a context that is mediated by others. The seemingly solitary act of reading a book involves receiving and reacting to something that another person has created. When a task is performed within the social context of a classroom, social expectations and interactions have everything to do with the success of the learning. Human learning is a social act. Put simply, working alongside and collaboratively with other people makes it easier to process information and learn—and it certainly is more enjoyable.

Through social interactions, children learn to collaborate and work constructively as part of a group, acquire content knowledge, ask for and give help, and build understandings on the ideas of others. They also develop effective communications skills and practice using them every day.

When children talk with one another, they communicate and refine their ideas, reveal their understandings and perspectives, make meaning from texts and experiences, and learn from each other. Talk is thinking on display. From prekindergarten across the grades, the classroom is a place where children engage in productive talk and committed listening. The topics of conversation are rich and varied, centering on topics students are learning about, discoveries they are making, and shared work. They offer opportunities for children to expand their language and vocabulary through talk.

Much of the talk is what we call "text-based," which means that students are talking about books they have heard read or read for themselves. This kind of talk stretches their linguistic abilities as the literary language of texts becomes far more complex than the language we usually speak. They take on new vocabulary and more complex syntax as they consider and use language from texts. Over time, they take on academic language, beginning with words like *title* and *author* and moving toward terms such as *character development*, *plot*, and *solution*. They even learn some archaic words, such as *henceforth* or *perchance*.

Integral to the idea of social interaction are the human qualities of kindness, empathy, and respect for others. Within a supportive and inclusive classroom community, people enjoy real conversations, learn to take on other perspectives, expand their world view, and appreciate the diversity of backgrounds and cultures around them. Respecting others needs to be a way of life and is particularly important to foster in the school community. Personal connections with others help students associate positive emotions with learning. When social interactions are a planned part of the school day, students not only improve their own learning but also share responsibility for the learning of everyone in the class.

**Central Office Memo**

**Developing Teachers' Understandings** When you spend time in schools, think about how the six principles described in this chapter are reflected in the classrooms. Talk with the school leaders about how to provide opportunities for teachers to develop understandings of these principles and how they apply not only to language and literacy learning but to all subject areas. A strong understanding of the conditions of effective learning will be an important foundation for all learning.

In classrooms where children regularly work, think, and learn together through social interactions you might notice:

- Classroom norms for "how we work together" are posted in the classroom. A set of norms that are created with input from students helps the community of learners collaborate and work together successfully. It establishes a healthy, respectful learning culture and the collective efficacy of students as learners.
- Students look at and listen to others. They build on the ideas of others during discussion. When students actively and respectfully engage with

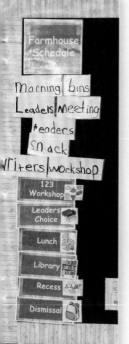

Opportunities for students to work, talk, and think together lead to better learning outcomes for all.

each other, they demonstrate that they value the ideas and contributions of others in their community. They understand that they can learn more when they seek multiple perspectives.

- Students discuss books in small groups as book clubs. In a book club, readers experience social learning at its richest. The experience of exchanging ideas with their peers and co-constructing deep understandings of a shared text is genuinely rewarding. It offers students an understanding that is deeper than any one reader could construct alone.

- The teacher and students use language that invites and reinforces a sense of community, such as "we," "our library," "our materials," and "our friend." The expectation that learning is a social, community experience is evident in the language used by members of the classroom community. The shared language of the community strengthens the sense of students' collective efficacy as learners.

- Lists of "texts we have shared" are posted in the classroom, and students share book recommendations. Students form a community of readers. Texts that students have read together as a class become a shared source of ideas, learning, and inspiration. Knowing the interests and preferences of their classmates, students recommend books to others in their community.

## Children Learn in Emotionally Supportive and Positive Environments

Human beings are fundamentally emotional as well as social creatures. Neuroscience reveals that there is a close relationship between the act of learning and the emotion connected to it (Immordino-Yang and Damasio 2007). Positive emotion must be a part of the experiences that children have in school if they are to be successful learners. If you fail day after day while trying to learn something, you experience no pleasure and you tend to avoid the task in the future. The real questions for us as educators are: *How can we create classrooms and schools that associate positive emotions with learning? How can we ensure that each student experiences the pleasures of living a literate life right now—in school and outside of it?*

In positive learning environments, sometimes there is comfortable silence, and other times a busy hum. The atmosphere is peaceful—not noisy or frenetic. The classroom is organized so that children can be in charge of their learning. It is not cluttered or stacked with never- or seldom-used materials. The look is clean and uncluttered, reducing stress for the teacher and students. Materials are easy to access. Students appear to be confident and competent in accessing materials and putting them away.

During the course of a school year, students will spend well over 1,000 hours in their classroom. Its organization, appearance, and artifacts show the culture that exists there and demonstrate that the classroom belongs to the students. They read books and discuss books that are relevant to their lives. The walls show individual and cooperative work with others. When you walk through a classroom, even when it is not filled with students, you can see what is valued there—a place where students see themselves and learn what it means to be human.

In classrooms that support and sustain the emotional well-being of learners, you might notice:

- The classroom is welcoming and visibly inclusive of the uniqueness of all students and their families. Students' names and work are prominently displayed. Students feel valued as people and as learners when they see evidence of their families, their languages, their heritage, and their learning in the classroom environment. They experience a sense of belonging.

- A daily schedule is posted in the classroom. A consistent schedule helps students feel secure in the classroom. When students know what they are to be doing now and what they will be doing next, they are able to focus attention on the learning experience at hand.

- Students use established routines as they learn individually, in small groups, and as a class. Predictable routines foster a healthy classroom community and make learning efficient. When expectations are clear and routines are well known, students feel confident and safe. They are able to take risks and optimize their time as learners.

- The classroom features warm, cozy areas and clean, tidy, organized workspaces. The physical space communicates a message of emotional safety. A classroom that is thoughtfully arranged can reduce stress, create calm, and promote productivity.

- Read-aloud books and classroom libraries reflect topics, authors, genres, and problems of interest to the age group; reflect the diversity of societies across the world, including cultural, gender, racial, and linguistic diversity; and appeal to the senses and emotions. When well-crafted, engaging texts are available in their learning environment, students experience the pleasure of story. They discover that the emotions they feel are universal.

- Children make personal connections with texts and express their feelings during discussions and in writing. Noticing, naming, and sharing emotions help children process new understandings more completely.

- Children are interested in and respect others. When children are respected as people who have valuable knowledge, lived experiences, and perspectives to share, every individual in the classroom becomes a teacher—a source of help, information, and new learning.

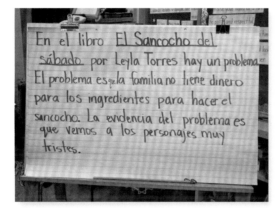

Welcoming and inclusive classroom environments promote positive emotions about learning.

## Children Learn Through Active Engagement

To feel the satisfaction—and most importantly, joy—of learning, an individual must act on the information, find it interesting, and find it relevant to life. They need to be disposed to inquiry and curiosity. This is not the same as being "on task," which is a form of compliance that has little to do with engagement.

Time on task does not necessarily mean that students are learning. Engagement, on the other hand, means that students are intellectually invested and acting with agency and initiative, not merely cooperating. Johnston and colleagues (2020) describe teaching as "creating conditions in which children will learn. We arrange for children to take the initiative in learning—to initiate literate activity, recognize problems, and generate solutions and knowledge both collaboratively and individually."

The principle of active engagement applies to all learning. Engagement and motivation are high when learners have a chance to initiate learning and to interact meaningfully with others around new concepts. A strong sense of agency and good self-regulation are characteristic of more successful students and adults. But the learning must be relevant.

Authentic engagement that embeds learning within a meaningful social context is much more effective than disconnected memorization. We have observed many students of all ages as they respond (or not) to the "word of the day" during morning announcements. We have also observed students of all ages actively take on new language and ideas by using them and even "borrowing" them for their own writing. They use academic language over and over for purposes that communicate to others. Authentic engagement increases the likelihood that children will synthesize or assimilate new learning. "Engagement leads *to more memorable learning and the propensity to reuse information*" (Keene 2018). It is the key to motivation and to building a sense of self-worth.

When students are actively learning, there is evidence of high engagement and high relevance of the content and experiences. Most of their learning is characterized by making connections, searching for patterns, solving problems, and grappling with big ideas. Each student sees herself as a literate person on a journey that is constantly changing.

In classrooms where students are actively engaged in their learning, you might notice:

- Students pose questions that reflect engagement with new ideas. When students generate their own questions, they explore ideas, discover the edges of their understanding, and make sense of new information. Students' questions reveal their stance as learners and their level of engagement.

- Students are busy about the work of learning: talking, conferring, reading, writing, drawing, sharing, imagining, researching, experimenting, playing. Rather than taking a passive, receptive stance, students initiate actions that lead to new learning. They show confidence that they can learn, know how to go about it, and are aware of their progress.

- Students make decisions about their own learning, including choosing their own books to read, pieces of writing to craft, and topics to research. Meaningful, authentic choices are critical to student engagement. Students are trusted to play an active role in the management of their own learning.

**Digital Literacy**

**Engaging Learners** Digital tools and resources can offer learning opportunities that are especially relevant to learners. Using technology, students can identify and investigate real-world problems that are of interest to them as individuals. They can collaborate online with other learners and experts by posting queries, sharing ideas, publishing tentative solutions, and receiving constructive feedback. Teachers can guide learners to digital resources that are pertinent to their interests and passions and facilitate the use of digital tools that help them collaborate, take risks, and experiment.

# Children Learn By Taking Risks and Reflecting on Their Learning

Productive learners take time to reflect. They have a type of growth mindset that enables them to see possibilities beyond the present; they have a positive view of themselves that motivates them to take risks; they are aware of learning and progress. It is this ability to anticipate and to be self-aware that helps them become active and reflect on their own learning. They actively seek the means and make choices that will allow them to reach goals—both individually and collectively. Children can demonstrate awareness of current skills and understanding of some of the complexities of the tasks they attempt. They can regulate their own behavior because they can recognize the rewards of sustained effort.

In many ways, risk-taking and reflection enable learners to stay with a task, trudging on even when it's a bit difficult. We know the pleasure of problem-solving, can anticipate ultimate success, and understand that we can learn from failures. When learning is reflective, students look back on what they are accomplishing and take charge of future learning. Michael Jordan, sometimes called the greatest basketball player of all time, sums up this idea of self-reflection neatly:

> "I've missed more than 9,000 shots in my career. I've lost almost 300 games. Twenty-six times, I've been trusted to take the game-winning shot and missed. I've failed over and over and over again in my life. And that is why I succeed."

While most of us cannot claim that level of expertise in our "game," we can point to the ability to learn from and value failures as the sign of effort. If we

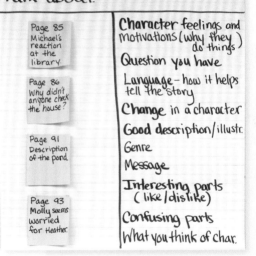

Classrooms that support active learning are busy, productive places where children act with initiative and purpose.

are lucky, we live or work within a culture that makes risk-taking safe and that values the self-reflection that makes self-regulation possible.

Teachers may find that students have difficulty reflecting on their work in productive ways. You might suggest that they post activities that guide children to reflect on their learning. Or, they might model thinking aloud about a book the class has read or a project or task they have completed. They can prompt students to consider a few questions:

- *What went well for you in your work?*
- *What do you want to do differently next time?*
- *How has your thinking changed?*

Reflection can be a group activity as well. After a whole-class minilesson on an aspect of reading—management of independent work, literary analysis, strategies and skills, or writing about reading—students might apply the principle to their own independent reading. At the end of the period they could engage in a quick share with the entire group to report discoveries and application. The same is true in writing as they share what they have learned and applied to their own pieces. Members of a book club can self-evaluate at the end of a discussion period and think about how they have changed and grown in their ability to talk about books with one another. Children can learn together how to take the reflective stance of a lifelong learner.

In classrooms where students take risks and continually reflect on their learning, you might notice:

- Students show a willingness to try new things and take risks. They seek new and challenging experiences that have the potential to lead to new understandings.
- Students choose their own books and record their thinking about books in a reader's notebook. When students write about their reading, they reflect on many aspects of books (such as characters, plot, and other narrative elements or new information learned from nonfiction) and their own experiences as a reader (for example, their opinions about different authors or genres). Readers revisit reader's notebooks to reflect on how they have changed as a reader.
- Students use writer's notebooks to jot ideas, collect artifacts, and record their observations of other writers' craft. Writing folders and portfolios showcase their growth as a writer. As students reflect on the craft of other writers, they expand their own repertoire of writing moves. As students look back at pieces of writing they have chosen to include in their portfolios, they notice and talk about specific ways their writing has changed over time.
- Students share discoveries they have made in reading, writing, word work, and research projects during group share. Group share brings students together as a community to reflect on what they are accomplishing as learners and to problem-solve together. The practice rein-

forces students' identity as a member of a collaborative community that takes time to reflect on its work.

- Members of a book club evaluate their discussions. Students engage in reflective learning when they self-evaluate their book club on characteristics such as turn-taking and keeping the talk centered on the text. As a group, they decide what they will work on the next time they meet, based on their reflection.

## The Takeaway

The six big ideas about learning that we've discussed in this chapter are intimately connected. They operate in concert. For example, social interaction supports emotional response and leads to construction of knowledge. All contribute together in a vital way to the individual who looks at the world as an exciting place, ripe with new chances to learn and full of opportunity.

Your beliefs about learning and the role of teachers and students influence the quality of the environment of the school, the materials and resources for

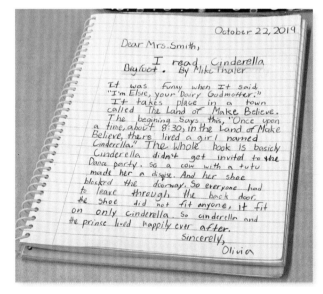

When children have regular opportunities to reflect on their learning, they are more inclined to want to learn more.

students, and the instruction in classrooms. As a school leader, you can bolster these important ideas about learning by looking for evidence of each one in your school. Where you find strong evidence, talk with teachers and other school leaders about what you notice. For example:

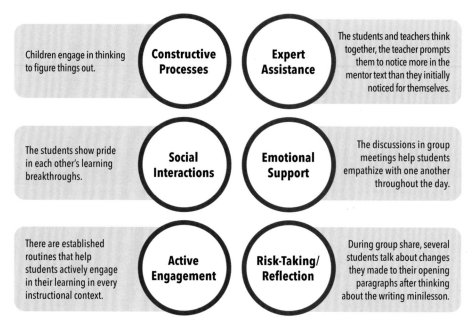

**Figure 5-3.** Six Big Ideas About Learning

## Think About Your School

- From your classroom observations, reflect on the underlying beliefs about teaching and learning that are held by the teachers and leaders in your school. Hold some informal conversations with experienced and new teachers to discuss observations.
- How does your school curriculum support or contradict the six big ideas of effective learning?

## Move Your School Forward

- What are opportunities for teachers to shift their thinking and practice toward the six big ideas?
- On learning walks or in professional learning sessions, focus on one big idea at a time, identifying how teacher decisions in each instructional context can support the learning prinicple.

# Chapter 6

# How Children Learn to Read and Write: Four Essential Principles

*Almost every child learns to read print and write print at the same time. Paying attention to print in these two activities surely has reciprocal effects, one affecting the other, whether we plan for this to occur or not.*
—Marie M. Clay

IN CHAPTER FIVE, WE examined six general principles that apply to all kinds of learning and all kinds of learners. In this chapter, we look at literacy learning specifically and describe four aspects of the theory of reading and writing that underpins our body of work. It is based in part on the research of Marie M. Clay as well as that of many others in the field of literacy learning and on our own observations of children in classrooms. All of these sources contribute to our longstanding view that children learn to read and write by actively engaging in the process of reading and writing meaningful text.

In this chapter, we examine four core principles in the theoretical frame that guides our work (Figure 6-1).

**READING AND WRITING ARE:**

| Complex | Reciprocal | Language-Based | Learned |
|---|---|---|---|
| **Reading and writing are complex processes.** Each learner builds an in-the-head literacy processing system in a unique way. | **Reading and writing are reciprocal processes.** Reading supports learning in writing, and writing supports learning in reading. | **Reading and writing are language-based processes.** Children use their knowledge of oral language to learn about written language and expand their oral language through their experiences with written language. | **Children learn to read and write by reading and writing.** The reading and writing processes are learned through early and continual use. Students learn by reading and writing for real purposes and audiences. |

**Figure 6-1.** Four Big Ideas About Reading and Writing

# Reading and Writing Are Complex Processes

It's impossible to determine whether literacy learning is one large and complex process or two separate but complementary processes—reading and writing. Either way, it is useful to consider the complexity of these processes one at a time. Reading involves sounds (from oral language) encoded, or mapped, onto letters that represent them. The reader connects sounds to the letters in words, says the words, and thus "decodes" the message. That is a simple view, but decoding, although very important, is only a small part of what happens when a person reads.

Reading is the process of bringing language and knowledge together to construct meaning from printed symbols arranged in regular patterns on a surface. It may be tempting to assume that reading is the simple task of looking at letters (arranged as words) and connecting the letters to the sounds of language—like cracking a secret code of abstract symbols. Connecting letters and sounds is indeed important and reading is processing language, but a large body of research indicates that reading is much more complex than decoding alone. When readers process a text, they are reading language, not simply saying individual words. The complex range of in-the-head strategic actions that readers employ simultaneously as they process a text expand their in-the-head neural network.

The visual scanning process requires coordination of the eye with the print. In English and many other languages, readers need to track print left to right and return to the left margin after finishing each line. They also need to move from the left to the right page and from the top line to the bottom line, and to turn (or swipe) pages to move through a volume, front to back.

A key concept in literacy learning is that as children engage in meaningful literacy activities, they build an effective in-the-head network that allows them to process texts and at the same time (given appropriate levels of challenge and support), to expand their literacy processing systems. They construct meaning as they read across sentences, problem-solving the words one at a time, and in the process, pulling together everything they know how to do. Processing a text means the reader's brain and eyes attend to several actions simultaneously:

- Scan the print from left to right and return to the left.
- Gather information from print and turn it into language.
- Search for and use more information if needed.
- Link sounds of language to the individual and groups of symbols that represent them.
- Self-monitor or check on their reading for accuracy and understanding.
- Notice when reading doesn't sound right, make sense, or look right and work to fix it.
- Anticipate the text that follows using their knowledge of syntax.
- Recognize known words and problem-solve new words.
- Adjust reading according to their own purposes and their appreciation for the text.
- Remember important information and carry it forward to read and interpret the rest of a text.
- Take action in flexible ways to connect meaning and fit new understandings with existing understandings.
- Anticipate what may happen next.
- Connect the meaning of the text to their lives.
- Make connections across texts.
- Think about what the writer might mean but has not directly stated.
- Notice aspects of the writer's or illustrator's craft, for example, literary characteristics, the way the text is organized, and how the illustrations support the story's meaning.
- Think critically about the meaning, purpose, or message of a text.

As a student reads a text, a complex neural network expands in her brain.

In other words, readers use everything they know to process a text, even from the beginning. The early reader works on continuous text, moving across the print, at first using the finger to assist the eyes. She has been building a reservoir of information almost from birth. Through interaction, she has learned language—the first example of a self-extending system, or a system that expands itself through using it. Children's brains are "hard wired" to acquire oral language. They learn it with seemingly unconscious effort. But reading and writing must be more intentionally learned.

Clay's (1991) definition of reading reflects this complexity: "Reading is *thinking,* powered by the language in the text." Readers develop *systems of strategic actions*; in other words, as children learn to read, they make complex and powerful connections in the brain. These connections allow them to operate on texts they have never seen before because they have developed in-the-head strategic actions that they can use on all texts. The information is in the print, but it is also in the understandings the students have in their heads and that they bring to the act of reading.

Writing, too, is more than simply encoding sounds and making appropriate letters. Writing is a recursive process, in which memory is helped by the fact that the individual can "hold still" what he has produced while he thinks of what he wants to say next. Writers simultaneously:

- Construct symbols from left to right, leaving space between words.
- Develop ideas.
- Choose language they want to use to express ideas.
- Identify their genre and purpose for writing.
- Write according to the purpose they intend.
- Organize their ideas in print.
- Draw from their experience with written and oral language in order to compose sentences, paragraphs, and longer texts.
- Self-monitor to be sure they are expressing what they intend.
- Keep the audience in mind while composing language.
- Put their own feelings and personalities (called "voice") into the writing.
- Give attention to grammar, capitalization, punctuation, and spelling so that the audience can read the piece for meaning.
- Give attention to the tone the piece expresses.
- Give attention to the print layout and other features they want to include.
- Are aware of the writing process and know how to engage in it (planning and rehearsing, drawing, drafting and revising, editing and proofreading, publishing the final product).

Even very young children put their personalities into their scribbles and early writing.

Children's first pieces of writing are simple and expressive, yet they still prompt reflection and revisiting. Given the chance to engage daily in the writing process, a rich experience in hearing written language read aloud, wide individual reading, and intentional instruction, children grow quickly into strong, articulate writers. They continually learn about being an effective writer from other writers. The back-and-forth lens on language and the writer's craft helps students learn new ways of thinking as readers and writers. And writing, like reading, allows them to articulate their thinking and at the same time helps them reflect on and evaluate their thinking. Maybe as an adult you make notes or write in a journal to help remember the moments of your life or to unravel problems. Writing is a tool for thinking, and it expands thinking.

In classrooms where children engage in the complex processes of reading and writing, you may notice:

- Teachers dedicate sustained time for reading and writing continuous text every day so students can learn how to process continuous text.

- Teachers support students' use of reading and writing to share thinking and learn new information across the curriculum.

- Teachers help students connect what they are attending to as readers to how they can use the knowledge as writers.

- Teachers share learning goals and accomplishments in ways that students understand.

- Students both solve words and comprehend a variety of texts and think how they can use the information as writers.

- The instruction provides continuous daily opportunities for students to attend to words in and out of text to build flexible systems for word analysis and constructing words.

- Students engage in talk that reveals critical thinking with peer and teacher support.

- Students make connections across a variety of texts by discussing and writing about plots, characters, settings, themes, and topics across books in a variety of instructional contexts and link the ideas to writing.

- Teachers support reading with accuracy, fluency, and comprehension.

- Teachers analyze reading behaviors to identify students' use of information from different sources in the text—the meaning, language, structure, sounds, and letters—and those that are neglected.

- Teachers systematically observe the aspects of processing that readers and writers control well and thus require little of their attention and arrange for new challenges to their learning.

# Reading and Writing Are Reciprocal Processes

Literacy power is built through a combination of reading and writing. Processes are built up and broken down in both endeavors, but writing "slows down" the process and makes it more visible. In early writing, children naturally and purposefully attend to the details of print, which provides strong support for early reading behaviors.

Very early writers may scribble, produce letter-like forms, strings of letters, or their names. They often combine drawing and writing and sometimes attach a message or "story" only after writing. But with experience, they recognize that print is different from pictures; it represents language that someone can read. And when written language is read aloud, it says the same thing every time.

Writing involves a complex series of actions. Children have to think of a message and hold it in the mind, think of the first word and how to start it, remember each letter form and its features, and manually reproduce the word letter by letter, left to right on a page. This immersion in the process begins to make literacy processing more visible.

Readers who are struggling to make progress benefit greatly from developing the processes of reading and writing together (Clay 2001; Anderson and Briggs 2011). And we believe it is essential for all students to have these advantages. Anderson and Briggs conclude, "When you teach reading and writing together, it is a two-for-one deal—a deal we simply cannot pass up."

From a student perspective, reading and writing are always connected. Children go smoothly from reading to writing, and writing to reading, always focusing on the uses of literacy for meaningful purposes. Shared writing is used in reading lessons and in writing lessons. In shared writing, the teacher acts as a scribe with a chart on an easel while the students contribute to composing the text. But sometimes, especially with younger children, the writing becomes interactive because the teacher invites children to come up to the easel to contribute a letter, a word part, or a word. The teacher also may have younger children say words slowly so they can hear the sounds and contribute their knowledge of letter/sound relationships as the teacher writes their thoughts in shared writing. The charts produced in shared and interactive writing can be reread over and over in a shared way by the group. This whole process brings reading and writing together for young children who are building a literacy processing system.

Students also use reader's notebooks to keep a record of their reading and write in response to reading. This includes their responses to books they encounter—in interactive

This student's writing reveals content knowledge gained from reading books.

read-aloud, guided reading, book clubs, and independent reading. They may record in their writer's notebooks interesting language in a poem that they might want to use in their own writing. In both notebooks, students move back and forth from a reader's lens to the lens of a writer. They learn to read like a writer and write like a reader. Allyn and Morrell (2016) described reading as breathing in and writing as breathing out.

In classrooms where literacy power is built through a combination of reading and writing, you may notice:

- Writing and reading lessons are connected with intention.
- Students engage daily in both writing and reading of authentic texts.
- Student writing shows that they are using understandings of the writer's and illustrator's craft gained through reading and listening to books in interactive read-aloud, shared reading, guided reading, independent reading, and book club.
- Students use familiar read-aloud and shared reading texts, and poetry, as mentor texts for reading and writing.
- While reading, students use knowledge of letters, sounds, and words that they developed during writing.
- Student writing reveals content knowledge gained from reading books.

# Reading and Writing Are Language-Based Processes

Language and human communication are at the heart of literacy learning. As students engage in meaningful language experiences through reading and writing, they are using language to learn and are learning more about how language is used. Over time, they expand their language through interactions with texts.

Clay (1991) was highly in tune with the research on language acquisition and development that was making breakthroughs when she was writing *Becoming Literate*. She considered language to be the first example of a self-extending system, one that grows, changes, and becomes more effective as it is used. When children engage in interactions with others, they are doing much more than "practicing." They are building knowledge by trying out the language according to their working hypotheses. For example, parents are sometimes taken aback when a child who has been saying "I ran" suddenly says "I runned." That's not a step backward. It signals that the child has learned through interaction that very often the past tense is signaled by *-ed* and is overgeneralizing and applying the rule to all verbs.

It is sometimes said that no one has to "teach" children to talk, yet they master the huge and complex body of knowledge needed to use language by about age five. That includes awareness of the phonological system (individual sounds that form words). The young child's accomplishments are amazing, when you stop and think about it. Every language has an infinite number of sentences, each with its own meaning, that are put together according to grammatical rules. By encountering and using language in the environment, children learn the rules that they can then use to generate an infinite number of sentences.

Even typical early statements by children ("More juice," "More cookie," "More TV") are not random utterances nor are they imitations of adult language. They are highly organized and meaningful statements that get responses from the adults with whom the child interacts. By using a "rule" and applying it to more and more examples, they refine the use of language. In this way language allows the learner to keep on learning by using it. Through learning language, children learn

Children learn language by using it.

- how the sounds of language are connected to graphic symbols (letters) and meaning;
- how to negotiate meaning with others;
- how to notice details in the sounds;
- how to form hypotheses about language and test them through interaction;
- how to search for more information, revise concepts, and connect sets of understanding.

In every culture, human beings need ways to communicate with others. Without a common language, people could not build the social systems they need for survival. Through language, children grow into the culture; and, through language, they can go beyond the "here and now" or the present geographical location.

In classrooms where students expand their language through literacy opportunities, you might notice:

- Students participate in meaningful interactions with print that build conceptual knowledge.
- Charts with phonics principles and examples are displayed in the classroom.
- Teachers and students study the language of texts in reading and writing minilessons.
- Teachers and students study the structure of both fiction and nonfiction texts.
- Vocabulary is built daily through explicit attention to words in interactive read-aloud, shared reading, guided reading, and reading minilessons, and students hear complex language daily in these same settings.
- Students are encouraged to use varied vocabulary and strong language in their own writing.

- In interactive read-aloud and book clubs, students have the opportunity to notice and use the written language with which they have engaged.

- Often, sections of text are revisited for close analysis of the writer's use of language.

- Students notice how punctuation reveals the structure of sentences.

- The teacher provides a daily phonics lesson on specific principles related to letters, sounds, words, word meanings, and word analysis.

- For students in intermediate grades, the teacher provides word study lessons on syllabication, meaningful parts of words, and word histories.

# Reading and Writing Are Learned Processes

Central Office Memo

**Guiding School Leaders** Your understanding of these essential principles will be important as you guide school leaders to select high-quality instructional materials and as you notice the way students engage in learning in every subject area. They also will be helpful as you support school-based or system-wide professional learning that is rooted in strong rationales for teaching.

Literacy is a relatively recent phenomenon in human history. Written language was developed independently in several countries going back to about 3100 BCE; but general use of written language is much more recent. In 1820, only about 12% of the world could read and write, while today that situation is largely reversed (Roser and Ortiz-Ospina 2016). As societies have grown more complex, the need for universal literacy has increased; literacy is seen not only as a tool for economic growth but one that adds to the quality of life for citizens.

Literacy is not a natural, inborn, human skill; it must be learned. It stems, however, from the natural human drive to communicate and create language. Most children need teaching in order to achieve the desired literacy levels, but they already have vast knowledge that they bring to the task of literacy learning. As with all human endeavors, literacy is best learned through use.

We are always amazed at reading and writing "programs" in which students spend very little time actually reading books or composing their own meaningful pieces of writing. How can they get good at something unless they have a chance to actively engage in doing it?

Although it may seem self-evident, it is important to note that:

- Reading is learned by engaging in the process of reading.
- Writing is learned by engaging in the process of writing.

Students' reading and writing processes need to be supported by skilled teaching. If necessary, you can help teachers identify needed lessons based on student assessments conducted individually and analyzed for the information that is essential for responsive teaching. The *Fountas & Pinnell Literacy Continuum* (see Chapter 9) guides teachers in selecting clear goals for teaching that engage the whole class, small groups, and individual students. Teachers can then

**If You Want to Know More** The *Fountas & Pinnell Literacy Continuum* is a tool for assessment and instructional planning of literacy lessons, experiences, and opportunities that are based on precise information about what proficient readers know and are able to do. It is used to identify instructional priorities based on the students' individual strengths and needs. We discuss the continuum in detail in Chapter 9.

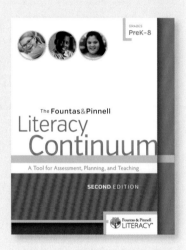

conduct ongoing assessments and keep records that show clear evidence of the unique paths of student progress.

Over time, students grow in realizing and monitoring their own progress. At the same time, the teaching is highly intentional. Teachers have explicitly laid out plans and goals so that lessons are efficient and direct and also invite students into the inquiry process to make their own discoveries.

In classrooms that foster a rich reading and writing life for students that is supported by expert teaching, you might notice:

- Children are actively engaged in interesting reading and writing across the day and week.
- The teaching decisions are based on students' precise reading and writing needs.
- Teachers use assessment data to plan and select goals. They compare these data to their accumulated knowledge of literacy learning over time.
- Teachers have clear goals expressed in behaviors and understandings that fit within a continuum of expected progress.
- Student and teacher records show concrete evidence of progress.
- Students are able to articulate new learning.

Students' reading and writing processes require support from a skilled teacher.

# The Takeaway

Learning is not a simple, linear, additive process. The learning brain is assembling complex networks of information. An important task of school leaders involves looking in classrooms for evidence that literacy teaching is based on how the human brain learns. Evidence exists in:

- Observations of the physical environment—wall displays, organization of student materials, displays of books, accessibility of supplies, evidence of exploration and learning, ambiance.
- Observations of student talk, reading, and writing behaviors—purposeful talk, independence and self-regulation, engagement.
- Examination of student artifacts—reader's notebooks, writer's notebooks, and portfolios.
- Examination of teacher records—benchmark assessment, ongoing assessment, plans, and goals.
- Observation of lessons—inclusion of both reading and writing connections across the curriculum.

Another important task for school leaders is assessing and supporting the health of classroom communities, which plays a crucial role in literacy learning. We examine the elements of healthy classroom communities in the next chapter.

## Think About Your School

- In what ways do teachers help children make connections between reading and writing?
- How consistently do teachers provide opportunities for the students to use their language knowledge as readers and writers?
- How do teachers systematically observe reading and writing so they can deepen their understanding of literacy?

## Move Your School Forward

- Bring together small groups of teachers to look at two to three artifacts such as student writing or reading records. Have them discuss how the artifacts reflect evidence of reading or writing as complex, interrelated, language-based, and learned processes.
- Teachers need to be systematic. Engage teachers in discussing their grade-level curriculum goals and how they tailor them for whole-class teaching. Talk about the implications for their small-group responsive teaching.

# Chapter 7

# Fostering a Strong Learning Community

*Our classrooms should be places of inquiry, joy, trial and
error, exploration, success and failure, and fascinations
revealed—where the process of discovery matters as
much (if not more than) the destination.*
—Ruth Culham

IN CHAPTERS FIVE AND SIX, we looked closely at important foundational understandings concerning how children learn and how they become literate. It's important to understand those principles and to advocate for their use in guiding instructional decisions, but learning also needs solid ground in which to grow. If you and your colleagues are to support every child on the path to proficient and joyful literacy, you also need to ensure that every classroom in the school is a healthy learning community.

In a healthy classroom community (Figure 7-1), all students feel a responsibility to help their peers accomplish great things. They feel safe to wrestle with difficult concepts and ideas, ask for help, take risks in their learning, and be honest about what's working for them as learners and what is not. Members feel that the classroom belongs to them, and they work together to create and sustain the physical spaces needed for their work. A classroom community

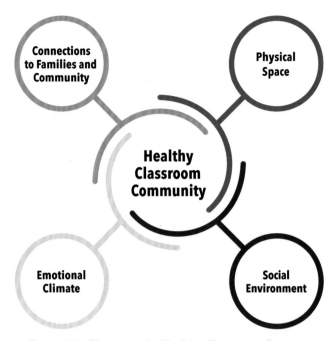

**Figure 7-1.** Elements of a Healthy Classroom Community

that works for everyone has norms and expectations for how its members will behave, and they are clearly expressed in writing and reviewed by the community as needed. Not only is the classroom a place where children learn to talk, read, and write; it also is a laboratory where they learn to be confident, self-determined, kind, and democratic members of a learning group. These characteristics will serve them well throughout their schooling.

When a classroom community is healthy, every element of it—the physical space, the social and emotional climate, partnerships with families—combine to create a place where learning grows and children soar. On the pages that follow we examine those individual elements in detail.

## The Physical Space

The classroom is designed to support a community of learners. It requires ownership and inclusiveness, and it includes practical spaces for students to work in different ways. It is important for teachers to establish quieter and noisier areas for different purposes. Traffic flow is also important, as teachers try to decrease the number of students who have to work in the same space at the same time. It is important to keep barriers (for example, shelving units and dividers) low so that teachers can see over them. Use as much natural light as possible.

Below are some general suggestions for helping teachers plan and organize classroom spaces that support the students as readers and writers. Of course, you will also need to support their planning and organizing for art, science, social studies, and mathematics. You'll find more detailed descriptions in *Guided Reading: Responsive Teaching Across the Grades,* Second Edition.

## Cozy and Calming Spaces

This is a workspace, so it is not necessary to fill the room with furniture, but some teachers have found it helpful to include some homey touches like a little table with a lamp, a carpet, and a rocking chair. You can include a variety of seating options, such as beanbag chairs, a yoga ball, cushions, stools, and wedges. Some cubes are both attractive and stackable.

A top priority is that the classroom is attractive and inviting to students. We have seen classrooms made cheerful with bright colors, but we have also seen some very effective classrooms that use more muted, neutral colors, which can be quite calming. Consider adding some green plants for an extra visual treat. A hodgepodge of color, however, with cluttered, disorganized areas and too much furniture and equipment will lead to inefficiency, stress, and discipline problems.

A calm and inviting classroom sets the tone for the work that children will do in it.

## Dedicated Workspaces

Students need the predictability and security of knowing where they can go to do certain types of work. They need spaces to work as individuals and in small groups and to meet as a community.

**Whole-class meeting space.** The physical layout includes a generous amount of space for the class library and a space where the entire group can meet together comfortably. Often this meeting space is defined by a rug, and students sit in a circle for group share or in a forward-facing group to listen to the teacher read aloud or to view an easel pocket chart. For a large class, a teacher may create two concentric circles of seating (some students sitting on chairs behind a circle of students sitting on the floor). It's important to have enough space to allow students to sit comfortably without touching each other.

**Small-group guided reading/writing space.** Groups engaged in guided reading or guided writing need to sit at a table with enough space that they can hold books comfortably or write in notebooks. Chairs should be available at the table rather than having to be carried around by students. We recommend a horseshoe table as it gives the teacher maximum access to students for observation and interaction, but a round table also works. Close to this area, the teacher needs space to keep books and materials for the week, for example, student folders, guided reading lessons, and other materials such as magnetic letters, a whiteboard, and markers. In addition, an easel and chart paper should be easily accessible.

A well-designed classroom includes a generous gathering space for whole-group teaching and learning.

**Meeting space for book clubs.** For book clubs, students meet in a circle without the barrier of a table. They can pull chairs into a circle in the meeting area or in any area of the room that is open.

**Independent workspaces.** Students can be assigned to particular seats at the tables (or at desks pushed together) so that the teacher can quickly get the group seated and ready for the next thing on the schedule. But the tables can also be used flexibly for students to work with partners on a variety of projects or play games related to phonics and word study.

**Computer and listening area.** Depending on the amount of technology in your school, teachers may need to establish an area where children can work with partners on devices and/or can listen to audio recordings. Even in classrooms where every child has a device, a designated area for recharging and working on laptops may be helpful.

**Classroom library.** The classroom library should be the most attractive and comfortable area of the room. Books are invitingly displayed, cover out, in labeled tubs or baskets. (Labels do not designate guided reading levels. Instead, books are grouped by title, author, genre, theme, and so on, as described in Chapter 11.) The library can be adjacent to or around the meeting area.

**Poetry display.** Teachers may want to post some favorite poems on the wall, have tubs of poetry books in the classroom library, and keep a basket for the personal poetry books that children have created and continue to add to over time. Teachers might also provide copies of favorite poems that children can glue into their own books and illustrate.

The classroom library needs to be a place that draws children in and invites them to browse and select books.

## Personal Spaces

In general, students are more efficient in retrieving their personal materials if they are neatly stored in a special box or cubby where they are organized in orderly ways. Personal materials might include a reader's notebook, a writer's notebook, a writing folder with completed writing projects, a word study folder, books for independent reading, a take-home portfolio for carrying books and other materials back and forth from home, and books being read. Containers are stored on a labeled shelf. This method is much more efficient than having students rummage in desks only to discover that they have lost materials. Alternatively, writing folders can be housed in crates in four corners of the room. This ensures only a few children go to retrieve their folders in each space.

## Storage Centers

Students need a place for getting and returning writing supplies—paper, markers, staplers, scissors, crayons, and so on. Labeling both the container and the place on the shelf where the supplies go will help even younger children become self-sufficient. It will also help younger children to place a cut-out shape on the shelf that identically matches the container. Centers with specific supplies include writing, art, math, phonics/word study, inquiry/science, and social studies inquiry. Classrooms for younger children would include blocks, puppets, and props for drama. A designated space where students leave materials for the teacher—for example, homework or their reader's notebook—is helpful. This might be a labeled basket, the corner of the teacher's desk, or a small table just inside the door where students stop to sign in. Students' "jobs" may include sharpening and sanitizing pencils.

## Using Wall Space Strategically

Teachers may start the year with some blank space. Initially the walls may contain only a poem or two or an alphabet chart in the early grades. A calendar and schedule will be useful. But the rest of the wall space is there to express children's thinking and reflect their lives. You see their names everywhere—on name charts for younger children, on labeled personal boxes, on poems with names inserted, on a work board for taking care of the classroom, on labeled self-portraits, and on other classroom artifacts. You will also see

Students' personal materials are neatly stored and easily accessed.

When supplies and materials are organized and visible, the message is clear: students will have what they need for their important work.

Use this **Physical Space Inventory (04)** tool as you evaluate the use of physical space in classrooms across the school. Be sure to share your findings with teachers afterward and discuss areas where improvement is needed.

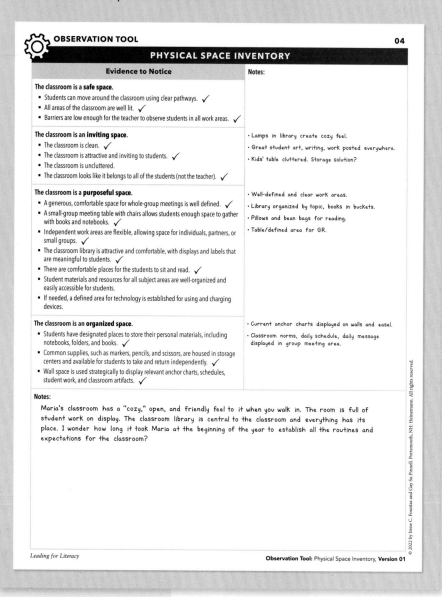

anchor charts from reading, writing, and phonics/word work minilessons that the teacher and children have created together. There are examples of student inquiry across content areas. There will also be reference materials such as a word wall in the early grades and a list of books students have shared in read-aloud lessons. The walls reflect the content of learning in the classroom. These materials reduce the memory load for students and help them recall routines and schedules, as well as what they have accomplished.

When the room is well organized and well stocked, encourage teachers to take out *all unnecessary or little-used furniture*. This might include bulky closed cabinets where it is tempting to store a lot of materials that are seldom used. Slim shelves are used instead when possible. Think hard about whether a large teacher's desk is really necessary! Teachers and students both will be inclined to stack (and leave) materials there. Some teachers use well-organized shelves for teaching materials or shelves on wheels along with a table to meet with students. The more the materials of the classroom are on display, the easier it will be to create a warm, uncluttered, welcoming space.

## The Social Environment

The moment children walk into the classroom, teachers want them to see it as a place where they will make friends and work cooperatively with others. Students need to see themselves as a *team*, a community of learners who have a culture of acceptance, kindness, and responsibility. Students need to view themselves as people who help others and who can look to others for help.

## Predictable Work Schedule

Predictability is reassuring to students, so while some disruptions are inevitable, it's important that classroom communities have a schedule that works and that they follow every day. Students can be of great help in sticking to time frames and making their work fit as needed. The more engaged they are, the more they can accomplish within the designated time period. Teachers can involve students in the construction of a schedule by asking for their input and suggestions for getting things done.

## Established Norms

Norms are the agreements that everyone in the community follows so that all can do their best work and enjoy the day. These norms are made with the participation of students. Even young children can help to make simple agreements related to using materials safely, not hurting themselves or others, taking care of the classroom, being kind, and listening and talking with respect. As they gain more experience in collaborative social environments, students learn more about how groups operate. They can establish norms, commit themselves to following them, and self-regulate their behavior. These norms will be posted in the classroom—not as teacher-created "rules" but as ways we work together in the classroom—and can be revisited, revised, and used for group reflection.

## Dependable Routines

The key to developing students' ability to regulate their learning is to establish and teach routines for each activity in the classroom. A routine is a set of actions or steps that an individual repeats for accomplishing something. Content may vary, but the routine stays the same and is well learned. There are routines for reading, for writing, and for word study, and the teacher introduces and promotes these routines in minilessons. Routines develop habits of mind and culture; students learn language that is positive. Students learn responsibility, problem-solving, and organizational skills that are productive in a group environment.

## Common Language

Over time, students learn the academic language they need to talk about their reading and writing, and that will serve them well. But they also learn many other things about

Taking part in creating classroom displays helps students feel known and appreciated.

Classroom norms can be posted prominently and all students can commit to honoring them.

using language in social interactions. They need the language of social discourse. They need to learn to talk together about what is happening in the classroom using language such as "our library," "our classroom," and "what we need to do." They learn social conventions for talking with each other about their ideas, for example:

"I disagree with what you said because . . ."

"I agree with ____ but not with _____ because . . ."

"Can you say more about that, because I understand it differently?"

"I understand what you are saying, but what about _____?"

"I'm thinking differently about that. May I explain what I think?"

"Can you help me understand why you think that?"

Instructional contexts like book clubs help students explicitly learn helpful language for social discourse, but the entire culture helps them learn productive language for positive interactions. The classroom is a place where people speak to each other with respect, are inclusive of all voices, and listen courteously to understand each other.

## Agreed-Upon Voice Tone and Volume

Students learn how to regulate their tone as appropriate for their homes. Tone and volume are taught as they interact with others. In some cultures, it is acceptable to speak more loudly, and among family members, a loud voice tone may be a conversational norm and enjoyed. But in a group of twenty-five other children, it can be distracting. The classroom is a place where the general tone of voice should be soft. It is true that if the teacher speaks softly, students will follow, but students may need more explicit instruction. Using a minilesson, teachers can teach young children the appropriate volumes they need to apply in different situations. Many older students will have habituated voice modulation but still need reminding of ways to be considerate of learning in a group environment.

A voice volume chart created with input from students can make community members aware of voice volume. They can even practice the tone of voice needed. Then teachers just need to say "zero voice" or "voice level two," for example, to encourage self-regulation.

## Empathy and Kindness

It's hard for young children—and even pre-adolescents—to take the perspectives of others. They need time to think about different perspectives. Read-aloud lessons and book clubs with text-set themes such as kindness and community help children learn through discussion, but so do the meetings about working in the classroom. In the classroom, they learn that kindness is valued and that they feel better about themselves if they help and care for others. We

**Central Office Memo**

**Fostering Learning Communities**
Learning will be optimal when students are supported by a strong school community and their learning is connected to their homes. You can help school leaders create the expectation that attention to building a strong learning community needs to happen promptly at the start of school.

Consider specific actions that can be initiated system-wide to connect families to the school and notice how each school creates an environment that signals a welcome to families when they enter the doors. Spend time walking through classrooms in the first few weeks of school to notice if they are student centered. Does each classroom feel like a space that belongs to the students, and do the students engage with each other in ways that show all of them are included?

are not talking about moralistic lectures (to which students don't respond very well). It is helpful when teachers work with children to help them use language to talk about their feelings and learn how to respect personal space. It is possible that some students in the school have had experiences that make it difficult for them to become positive members of the community. However, a majority feeling of collaborative ownership will go a long way toward establishing the norms of kindness in the classroom.

## Equity and Inclusivity

When they enter the classroom, all students are guaranteed equal treatment and access to learning opportunities. Equity may require that some students need even greater attention and teaching as well as peer support. Children understand that inclusiveness is not negotiable. Every member of the community—students, teachers, and school leaders—are expected to take action and use their voices to ensure that every member of the community has access to learning opportunities that promote academic success and intellectual, emotional, and social health.

A voice volume chart like this one helps children learn to use the right volume at the right time.

## The Emotional Climate

Students deserve to be happy and successful in school, day after day; otherwise, learning will not take place. They may not enjoy every single moment, but success will feed their emotional health. Here, we'll explore three concepts that are critical to emotional health in classrooms: belonging, choice, and self-efficacy.

Even preschool children can learn that kindness is not negotiable.

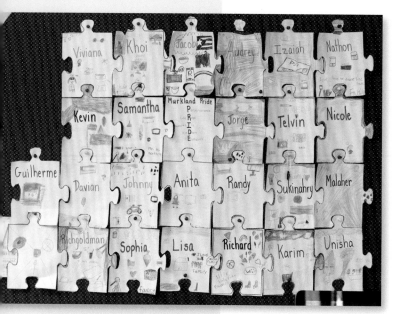

When students recognize themselves in images, names, and writings on the wall, they know they are part of a community.

Children need some opportunities during the day to choose what they do in the classroom.

## Belonging

Students need to feel that they belong to the community. They need to know their voice matters and that they will be listened to, as they listen to others. They will be included, as they include others. They will experience kindness and respect and will behave in ways that express these same feelings to others.

The community is characterized by sharing and by the use of positive, inclusive language and behavior. Children are taught how to use language to solve disputes using words, not physical actions. This feeling of belonging is built as children develop responsibility; problem-solving, organizational, and collaborative skills; and imagination.

Students will recognize themselves and their classmates in the images, names, and writings on the wall of the classroom, in the hallways, and everywhere in the physical environment. They see that they are all equally valued members of the community. In fact, everything works together—the physical environment and the social norms—to give students a sense of self.

## Choice

A critical element in emotional health is the ability to have some control over one's own environment and, in school, over one's own learning. Children need opportunities to choose for themselves. Within a systematic and rigorous instructional system, choice is not unlimited. Students cannot come into the classroom and choose everything they will do for the day. But they do need to make some real choices for themselves; and the opportunities for choice will expand as they gain experience and take on more responsibility. For example, even young children need to have choices in the books they read during independent reading. They may have a limited choice in the books they read for book clubs (the teacher introduces four or five possibilities), but there is choice. They choose topics for writing and drawing, subjects for biographies, topics for investigation in projects, and topics for argument and presentation.

## Self-Efficacy

Self-efficacy is the belief in one's own ability to take on new tasks and accomplish them. Individuals with a sense of self-efficacy believe that they can have power over their own learning. What they cannot do independently today, they will be able to do tomorrow.

Students build their self-efficacy by engaging in productive learning experiences and sharing what they have learned for meaningful purposes, day after day. The teacher is the one who facilitates successful learning, but this is not accomplished by making success too easy or giving students effusive praise for everything they do. It is by meeting challenging tasks that a sense of self-efficacy is built. The teacher creates the right elements for success, but the children accomplish it by making their voices heard, by having others listen, by making choices that contribute to the community, and because they get affirmation from their peers that what they do matters.

Children self-evaluate the quantity and quality of their work as they examine their own records in reader's and writer's notebooks. They become confident in their ability to produce a volume of work. Increasingly, over time, they become more self-reflective and able to direct their own learning in collaboration with the teacher.

# Connection to Families and the Community

Effective family and community partnerships also are essential to building and maintaining a healthy, productive classroom community of readers and writers. In fact, when schools engage families as valued partners in children's education, the learning outcomes for students improve.

Every family can contribute important information about their child: interests, habits, styles of learning, strengths, and areas of struggle. Families possess

The reflection tool **Reflecting on the Social and Emotional Climate (05)** can help you and the teachers in your school reflect on the social and emotional environment in classrooms. You may want to use the tool with grade-level groups or with groups of teachers from multiple grades.

**REFLECTION TOOL**     05

## REFLECTING ON THE SOCIAL AND EMOTIONAL CLIMATE

| Evidence to Think About | Notes: |
|---|---|
| **The community has established norms and guidelines for working together.** | • Turn & Talk routine strong—anchor chart visible |
| **The community:** | • "I agree/disagree" in 2/3 GR discussions |
| ▪ has routines | • Work board routine being used |
| ▪ has a predictable work schedule | • Kids moving quickly through rotation—all doing IR by end |
| ▪ has a common language for sharing thinking | • ? # of icons |
| ▪ has reached agreements about voice tone and volume | • ? quality of experience—do they know what work looks/sounds/feel for each icon |
| ▪ is characterized by empathy and kindness | • Kids working at appropriate volume—a little loud—ask T to reflect on her comfort |
| **The community is inclusive and equitable.** | |
| **Community members:** | • Pics of students all over classroom |
| ▪ feel welcomed | • Labels made using interactive writing (library, centers) |
| ▪ feel safe in expressing their needs | |
| ▪ have their needs met | |
| ▪ know their voices are valued | |
| **All students belong to the community.** | |
| **Students:** | • Ss have designated place to display WW books with their picture and name |
| ▪ take their classroom responsibilities/jobs seriously | • 2 interruptions at GR table - materials question and reporting other S for not following work board |
| ▪ are expected to solve disputes among themselves or with minimal facilitation by the teacher | |
| ▪ have their work and photos displayed throughout the classroom | |
| ▪ see themselves and their families reflected in the books they read | |
| **All students have opportunities to make meaningful choices about their learning.** | |
| **Students:** | • WW books show information and narrative writing |
| ▪ choose many of the books they read throughout the day and week | • Choice for IR - some Ss reading books, others reading poetry notebooks, other big books |
| ▪ choose topics for writing | |
| ▪ choose lines of inquiry and topics for investigation that they would like to pursue | |
| **All students have opportunities to reflect on how their actions impact the well-being of the community.** | |
| **Students:** | • Edwin said Rafi not following work board. |
| ▪ reflect on their participation in conversations or tasks. | • T. led kids through problem-solving sequence. Very well done! |
| ▪ reflect on their problem-solving skills. | |
| ▪ reflect on the ways in which they are providing feedback to their peers. | |
| ▪ reflect on the language and tone of their interactions. | |
| ▪ reflect on the ways in which they support their peers. | |
| ▪ reflect on the health and safety of other members of the community. | |
| **All students continuously build self-efficacy.** | |
| **Students:** | • Students moving from center to center freely (even if too quickly) |
| ▪ are given opportunities for independence and self-regulation. | • Share time - Tasked students to self-reflect |
| ▪ reflect on the quality of their work. | • ? could T be more specific in guiding reflections to these |
| ▪ reflect on their own time management. | |
| ▪ care for materials. | |
| ▪ reflect on their attitudes about taking on challenges. | |

*Leading for Literacy*     **Reflection Tool:** Reflecting on the Social and Emotional Climate, **Version 01**

*funds* of knowledge about their children that teachers and specialists can tap to create more effective and culturally relevant learning experiences (Gonzelez et al. 2005).

What do the educators at your school believe about the role of families in students' learning and in classroom communities? Do they view families as knowledgeable, helpful partners who can support and sustain a child's literacy success? Or do they treat families as uninvited guests in the classroom who complicate matters and take up time? Does the school culture convey that families are essential in helping students make progress in literacy learning? Or does it imply that teachers are the experts and families just passive recipients of information about their children's lives at school?

As a school leader, you can guide your colleagues to examine their beliefs and dispositions toward families. While sometimes uncomfortable, any honest examination includes recognizing and naming implicit biases that exist toward families of different racial, ethnic, socioeconomic, religious, or educational backgrounds. A teacher's previous experiences—positive or negative—with families from a particular group can impact and shape future interactions with families that share some of the same social identities. Past experiences can subtly influence the extent to which a teacher involves families in, or excludes them from, the classroom community.

The reality is that all families have hopes and dreams for their children. They are invested in their children's education and, despite the challenges that some families face, want to be meaningfully engaged as knowledgeable partners in their children's learning. This includes families for whom English is not their first language. While it may require more effort to communicate with some families of English learners, they are very interested in being engaged in their children's education.

How do you, as a school leader, show families and community partners that the school values their involvement and contributions—that they are an essential part of the classroom community? You may need to work on changing attitudes or simply insist on an open-door policy where families are concerned. Here are some other things you can do.

- Make sure all the educators in the school are aware of your strong belief that every family cares about their child's education, and all families want what's best for their children.

- Involve classroom teachers in developing a plan for reaching out to families at the beginning of the school year to build relationships and gather valuable information about students. You might plan with teachers to make phone calls, schedule home visits, and host back-to-school nights.

- Create structures for teachers to learn with and from families. For example, you may wish to develop a process for interviewing or surveying families to learn about their cultures; their understandings and

**Digital Literacy**

**Connecting to the Community**
When implemented thoughtfully, technology has the potential to connect communities of learners within the school with experts and organizations in the community beyond the school. Students can access online learning opportunities through libraries, science centers, museums, and other institutions of learning. With planning, educators might connect students with local librarians, government officials, curators, industry experts, writers, and artists through online collaboration platforms. As a school team, think about the knowledge, perspectives, and learning opportunities available in your community. In what ways can digital tools give students greater access to the opportunities?

expectations of school; the materials, resources, and access to technology in the home; and their preferences for communicating with the school, such as method (e.g., phone, video conference, email, text, etc.), language, time of day, and location for face-to-face meetings.

■ Ask families how much time and effort they can give to their child's education in school. Let them know that you respect any and all contributions they make because they are essential partners in their child's learning. As a school leader, you can guide colleagues to expand their definition of what successful engagement and partnerships with families mean and look like (Mapp, Carver, and Lander 2017).

■ As the school year progresses, check with teachers on their plans to cultivate and sustain family partnerships and provide support as needed. Building trust takes time and persistence. And when families don't communicate, urge teachers not to assume that they don't care. Keep trying, and make the relationship between homes and school a priority.

With your support and leadership, the family of every child can engage in classroom communities in ways that honor their diverse cultures, experiences, characteristics, and identities and their important contributions to their child's learning.

This classroom community expands to include members of the community surrounding the school.

## The Takeaway

It takes a village to raise a child—and a strong community to support a joyful reading and writing life in each classroom. Whatever the situation, children have a natural tendency toward inquiry. They bring to school their intelligence, curiosity, lived experiences, and ability to use language to communicate. Children respond to the opportunities the environment offers. When a classroom community is healthy and supportive of children's learning, readers and writers can flourish. As a school team, make time to talk about the physical spaces as well as the social and emotional supports for positive learning.

## Think About Your School

As you spend time in classrooms, get a feel for the social and emotional supports for each child:

- Are the unique qualities of each child confirmed and celebrated?
- How do children relate to and treat each other?
- What do you notice about the language students use as they interact with each other?

Consider the relationships with families and the community:

- Do the families feel like partners in the education of their children?
- How can the school team evaluate the strength of family partnerships?

## Move Your School Forward

- Identify one immediate action you can take with your team to strengthen an aspect of the classroom communities you have observed.
- Identify longer-term actions that would have the greatest impact on promoting healthy communities of readers and writers.

# Chapter 8

# The Talk Classroom: The Important Role of Language in Teaching and Learning

> *The dialogic classroom expands, among other things,*
> *students' ability to reason, communicate, collaborate,*
> *negotiate, take multiple perspectives, think critically,*
> *empathize, and build arguments and the likelihood they will*
> *behave socially in positive and responsible ways.*
> —Peter Johnston et al.

IN CHAPTER SEVEN, WE discussed the qualities of a healthy classroom community: the physical space, the social environment, the emotional climate, and the connections to families and the community. In this chapter, we turn to the importance of language within a learning community. Language expresses how we think and feel. Language makes us human, and we use it to share our memories, our thoughts, and our ideas with others.

When you enter a healthy classroom community that is alive with learning, you will see and hear children talking—with the teacher, with one or two other students, in small groups of four or five, and in larger groups. You'll see children discussing a story or nonfiction text they have read in guided reading; they will be making comments eagerly, one after another rather than just answering a teacher's questions. You'll see students in a circle, books on their laps, participating in a book club. They take turns and talk to each other, expressing and expanding their thinking and their opinions and backing them up with evidence from their experiences or from a text. You'll see students talking about their writing, giving one another feedback, and discussing their ideas with the teacher.

You will also see and hear teachers who value student talk. They want students to talk because their talk reveals their understandings and ideas. You'll notice teachers using structures that support student talk in pairs, small groups, and the whole group because they want students to listen to and understand others' thinking. You'll hear teachers using crisp, intentional language to facilitate students' thinking and the way they express it. They engage in genuine conversations with students and ask real questions to figure out what students are thinking about a book or a piece of writing.

Are the descriptions above what you typically see and hear when you go into a classroom during the literacy learning period in your school? If so, you are in a position to assess the quality of the talk by both students and teachers. In this chapter, we will discuss the types of talk to foster in the classroom, how teachers can create talk structures to support text-based talk, and how teachers' facilitative talk promotes learning. But let's first turn to the essential role that language plays in learning.

## The Importance of Language in Learning

From the beginning, language plays a critical part in conceptual development (Vygotsky 1962) and it is a tool for shaping literacy development. As a child hears and uses words, he begins to perceive order in what he is experiencing and recognizes experiences that have something in common. In this way the use of language helps the child classify objects, actions, and situations that make up his lived experiences. We recognize that there are many ways to communicate (for example, sign language, gestures, visual symbols), but all of these ways are typically part of the language that facilitates thought.

All children bring to school a rich store of oral language that they have learned in their homes and communities. With very few exceptions, children arrive at school having developed oral language skills that work effectively. Children have learned *how* to learn words. They have a vocabulary that they can use flexibly to express ideas. There may be differences in their repertoires of words (lexicon) and the syntactic structures they use, but children understand the sounds of language and the way words are put together to make meaning. The language of young children is appropriate for this point in their development, but all speakers need to expand their repertoire to acquire the thoughtful language that they use in school.

Over the six to seven years of elementary school, students' language expands greatly in complexity and in response to the talk they experience in classrooms. Talk reveals a treasure trove of information about individual students that informs teaching decisions. Teachers need a deep understanding of the ways that "talking helps us think, and thinking helps us talk" (Pranikoff 2017) and they need to work to make that understanding play out in their instruction. In a classroom that supports talking to learn, you will see students:

- Articulating their thinking about books.
- Discussing pieces of writing with their peers.
- Building on each other's ideas.
- Communicating and refining their ideas as they interact with others.
- Making meaning from the ideas and language they find in texts.
- Expressing connections to their own experiences.
- Using socially appropriate conventions of dialogue.
- Listening with commitment.
- Understanding and responding to different perspectives.
- Expressing friendship, sympathy, encouragement, and compassion.
- Asking questions to clarify understanding.
- Asking questions to gain others' perspectives.

Children bring to school a rich store of language and enjoy using and building on what they know to share their ideas.

Regardless of the age of the learners, talk is essential. Talk continuously shapes their thinking. Students learn different *ways* of talking. They learn to use language more effectively for social communication and to expand conceptual learning. As they engage with print, students draw upon their oral language as a resource and expand their control of oral language.

## Types of Talk to Foster in the Classroom

As you listen to students talk in the classroom, think about the content and the style they are using. Is it thoughtful and purposeful? Is there authentic dialogue? Is there a good volume of talk? What about the ratio between teacher talk and student talk? Do you find that students express themselves in different ways when talking about reading and talking about writing? Do students look at and listen to others with commitment? Listening is more than hearing someone talk; it's thinking about what the person said and responding in a thoughtful way. "We hear with our ears, but we listen with our minds" (Garman and Garman 1992). Let's look at each of these types of talk (Figure 8-1).

**TALK IS:**

**Figure 8-1.** Types of Talk to Foster in the Classroom

## Thoughtful Talk

Thoughtful talk is important across every area of the curriculum, but it is especially important in literacy learning. The *opposite* of thoughtful talk is:

- Answering questions that merely test whether you have read a book or understood the information in it.
- Retelling the whole story to prove you have read it.
- Reporting a list of facts.
- Repeating what the teacher says.
- Making comments unrelated to the text, often prompted by the teacher.

Thoughtful talk helps students think more deeply and in new ways.

Thoughtful talk moves toward deeper and more complex thinking. Thoughtful talk is:

- Articulating your *thinking* about a text, offering evidence from the text to support it.
- Analyzing plot, characters, and other aspects of text in fiction.
- Talking about what you notice in the organization and structure of a text, fiction or nonfiction.
- Talking about why a topic of nonfiction is important.
- Talking about the lessons from a text that you can take to your own life.
- Explaining the choices you made in your writing.

The actions above and hundreds of others listed in *The Literacy Continuum* show you the behaviors and understandings to notice, teach for, and support to expand students' thinking.

## Purposeful Talk

People use talk for a whole variety of purposes. Of course, they use language to communicate and, in the process, they grow their understanding and develop more complex language. They may not be consciously trying to expand language, but that happens from birth and throughout life. "Purposeful talk is also one of the main ways in which children develop their understandings of new concepts" (Fisher, Frey, and Rothenberg 2008). Students use talk purposefully to:

- Try out ideas.
- Assert leadership and persuade others.
- Argue for a point.
- Achieve consensus with others.
- Explore ideas with others.
- Build on the ideas of others.
- Try out different perspectives.
- Include others.
- Share opinions, likes, and dislikes.
- Disagree or agree with ideas in texts and comments of others.
- Ask questions and get help.

It's sometimes risky for students to speak up in class, and this is a real challenge for English learners, but it's important for them do so. Creating a safe environment for purposeful talk is an important goal for teachers. You can assist by creating a welcoming, safe, caring learning environment throughout the whole school.

## Authentic Talk

Think about the last time you engaged in a meaningful, thoughtful conversation. And then recall a time that you experienced "dialogue" that resembled an interrogation or a lecture from a dominant person. How did each experience make you feel? A strong, healthy learning community is characterized by real conversation. A real, meaningful conversation involves both or all people:

- Sharing ideas, perspectives, and feelings.
- Asking and answering real questions (not test questions to which someone already knows the answer).
- Responding to the other(s) and extending your own thinking in the process.
- Asking questions to understand what others mean.

In a personal conversation, Marie Clay once said, "Don't ask a question to which you already know the answer." Marie didn't mean that you couldn't assess a student's recall or comprehension of a story or nonfiction text, but that kind of activity should be as conversational as possible. During individual lessons and classroom conversations, teachers should be sharing their genuine comments and probing to learn what they really want to know about the student's thinking. Clay likened teaching to a conversation in which you first need to listen in order to reply. Others have called this type of education a *dialogic classroom,* " . . . one in which there are lots of open questions and extended exchanges among students. These are not classrooms based on the delivery of facts" (Johnston 2012).

Teachers can take a "dialogic stance," one that is informed by the purposes brought to classroom interactions over time. The teacher listens carefully to students' ideas rather than just searching for the one right answer. Remember that students quickly learn that teachers tend to ask questions of person after person and stop after they get the answer they want to hear. That's not conversation. A truly joyful, give-and-take dialogue—authentic talk—can invite students to enter and engage and build bigger ideas together.

## Accountable Talk

Accountability in talk means that students are accountable to the entire learning community to:

- Participate by sharing their own thinking.
- Listen with commitment to others.
- Respond with respect.

Text-based talk is vital to supporting literacy growth in students.

- Use respectful and socially appropriate ways to agree and disagree.
- Make an effort to include new voices in a conversation.
- Provide evidence for their statements and logical defense for their arguments.
- Engage in extended discussion that stays on a point as long as needed.
- Use accurate information.
- Keep their comments grounded in the text under discussion.

Notice that the descriptions above have mostly to do with the way students use language rather than answering questions with accuracy. In school, we have a great deal of accountability, and it usually means proving that you know or have learned something. But accountability in talk means that the individuals in the classroom are accountable to each other for purposeful, productive, and collaborative interactions.

## Academic Talk

The more classroom talk is based on texts, the higher the level of academic language that will be evident in students' talk. Usually, we think of academic language that is specific to disciplines of study. It includes technical language needed in the various content areas. In literacy education, it includes very specific vocabulary to talk about books, writer's and illustrator's craft, and pieces of writing. For a child in preschool or kindergarten, talking about an author or illustrator would represent academic language. But as students move up the grades, using all kinds of academic language becomes increasingly challenging and complex. High-level academic discussions about literature include references to concepts such as internal and external conflict, foreshadowing, and symbolism.

This language learning cannot happen all at once. Students can take on academic language and use it as part of the discussions they enter and enjoy with peers every day. In a literacy-rich classroom, academic talk is part of *conversation*—not something to be learned as an academic exercise but language that facilitates students' ability to talk with others about their thinking in response to books and their writing. *The Literacy Continuum* (see Chapter 9) lists academic language that students will exhibit at every level of learning, but it's not intended to be learned as a vocabulary list.

## Noticing Student Talk in the Classroom

Thoughtful, purposeful, authentic, accountable, and academic types of talk set a high standard for the oral language that is used in the classroom, and each type is vital to supporting literacy growth in students. During the school year, you can schedule walkthroughs that focus on the quantity and quality

## OBSERVATION TOOL

The observation tool **Quantity and Quality of Student Talk (06)** will support you in noticing student talk and discussing the types of talk with teachers.

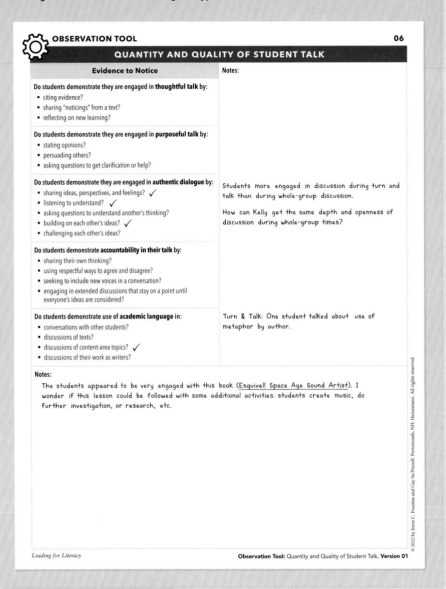

of student talk in the classroom. Use the observation tool **Quantity and Quality of Student Talk (06)** to identify and support talk that leads to effective learning. After an observation, invite the teacher to reflect on the quantity and quality of student talk in the classroom. Offer specific evidence that you observed, and ask questions that invite the teacher to imagine a classroom full of student talk, for example, *What do you do throughout the day to encourage students to talk about their ideas with one another?* You may also wish to invite a small group of teachers to join you on classroom walkthroughs that focus on student talk. As a group, observe in classrooms at multiple grades to identify effective practices that have the potential for promoting the quantity and quality of student talk. Collaborate with teachers to plan schoolwide professional learning opportunities focused on increasing high-quality student talk in classrooms.

If teachers support authentic, engaging, content-rich talk in the classroom every day, learning will be expanded exponentially, but that is a challenging thing to do. Many elements have to be in place—an orderly and well-supplied classroom, a healthy social-emotional culture that promotes risk-taking, and a teacher who can use language effectively to facilitate student learning. That is why professional, collaborative learning is so important in the school.

# The Importance of Text-Based Talk

Classrooms with high-quality, effective learning environments provide many opportunities for text-based talk in which children's thinking is grounded in text evidence and personal experiences related to the topics and themes in texts. The experience of talking about texts will influence students' identities as independent thinkers and productive members of a learning community.

## Understanding Multiple Perspectives

As we discussed in Chapter 5, children are naturally social in safe learning environments where they feel they are members of an inclusive community. They take risks by sharing their thinking and seek the thinking and perspectives of each other. These conditions promote children's sense of agency as they see themselves as valued members of a learning group. When children build meaningful social relationships through engagement with texts that reflect a wide range of culturally diverse authors and illustrators—those that represent a range in race, ethnicity, nationality, religion, gender, age, and geography—they develop positive identities as readers, writers, and thinkers and learn empathy for the diversity of the human race. In literacy as well as other subject areas, students benefit by reading and talking about several texts that present multiple perspectives on a variety of topics and issues.

## Connecting and Building on Ideas Among Texts

In a multitext approach to literacy learning, student talk varies in its form and focus across instructional contexts. (See Chapters 11–13 for a description of each instructional context.) In reading, students are talking about their thinking across five contexts. The use of related text sets (see Chapter 17) makes it almost impossible not to! What they discuss and notice in interactive read-aloud (for example, a writer's use of figurative language, the function of an author's note, or an interesting graphic), students will notice in shared, guided, and independent reading, as well as in book clubs. They will try it out in their own writing. What the teacher draws attention to in shared reading, the student will notice in independent reading. Ideas flow back and forth because texts for choice in book club are related to text sets in interactive read-aloud. In every context, students' noticings of the author's and illustrator's craft are woven into the fabric of the talk. Students discuss the big ideas and begin to see that the same essential human questions and issues come up repeatedly.

## Learning the Social Conventions of Text Talk

Effective text talk begins with the development of a strong learning community but also needs to include helping students develop social skills and processes for effective discussion of ideas with a partner or a group. To be successful and productive in their talk about texts, students need demonstration, scaffolds, and confirmation.

Explicit reading minilessons are an effective structure for helping children learn the social conventions and then apply them when talking with partners, in small groups, and in the whole group. Your students need to learn to look at the speaker, make eye contact with the speaker, talk one at a time, build on each other's comments, resist interrupting the speaker, and lean in toward the speaker. Talking in a group is different from talking to one person. Each principle of effective communication can be taught in a minilesson and applied during the talk structures that we discuss in the next section. Students' understanding and control of these social conventions will serve them well in all learning.

# Using Talk Structures to Expand Children's Thinking About Books

Talking as partners, in a small group, or as a whole group is valuable not only in developing children's voices in literary texts but also in engaging students in thinking about content and ideas across the curriculum. Teachers can build into daily lessons specific talk structures that work together to create more opportunities for students to talk about their thinking and to learn more about how to engage productively in discussion (Figure 8-2).

## Turn and Talk

In some classrooms, you might observe that only a few students do most of the talking during discussions. "Turn and talk" creates a structured opportunity for *all* students—not just those who lift their hands fastest—to share their thinking and learn from the thinking of their peers. Turn and talk is easy to teach and easy to use. It greatly increases the amount of student talk even in whole-class discussions.

A major benefit of turn and talk is that all students get a chance to express their thinking immediately to a partner or in a small group instead of waiting for a turn in the larger group. Turn and talk also encourages talk on the part of some students who may be shy of speaking in the large group; it provides "rehearsal" time for them and helps them feel more prepared for making comments. It is especially supportive to English learners who need this rehearsal

## TALK STRUCTURES ACROSS THE DAY

| IRA | SR | GR | IR | BC |
|---|---|---|---|---|
| **Interactive Read-Aloud** | **Shared Reading** | **Guided Reading** | **Independent Reading** | **Book Club** |
| Whole-Group Discussion | Whole-Group Discussion | Small-Group Discussion | Conferring | Small-Group Discussion |
| Turn and Talk | Turn and Talk | Turn and Talk | | Turn and Talk |

**Figure 8-2.** Talk Structures Across the Day

time and may benefit from interactions with a supportive partner before offering ideas in a whole-group setting.

Teaching the routine may be accomplished by preparing two to four children to demonstrate turn and talk with the rest as an audience. Arrange the students in a circle to watch the demonstration and talk about what they notice. They will notice that when the teacher says, "turn and talk," students immediately turn to another person. They take turns talking about a book the teacher has read. Each partner makes sure that the other has a turn to share thinking. The talk is based on the book. When the teacher signals "turn back," students quickly end their discussion and turn back ready for whole-class discussion or more reading. The teacher has been observing carefully and may invite several children to quickly share some of the ideas they have discussed. It all takes just a few minutes because students respond quickly and know what they are expected to do. When the whole class does turn and talk, they may need a little practice and direction in finding a nearby partner quickly. For an uneven number of students, the teacher serves as a partner for one student.

Once students have learned this routine, it can be used not just in interactive read-aloud but in many whole-class settings such as science, math, or social studies lessons when you want students to have a chance for more interaction. Usually there is no need for it in small-group settings such as guided reading or book club, but some teachers occasionally have children talk with a partner if they need more experience and confidence.

After turn and talk with a partner is firmly established, teachers can introduce iterations that expand discussions, such as turning and talking in threes, or partners turning to another pair to share what they talked about. When two

Fifth graders turn and talk to share their thinking about a book during an interactive read-aloud lesson.

pairs form a group of four, teachers will have prepared students for a small-group discussion. When the children talk in book clubs or guided reading, they have already learned how to participate effectively.

## Small-Group Discussion

Small-group discussions are commonplace in a classroom filled with authentic, meaningful student talk. Students gather again and again into various groupings throughout the day to discuss topics that are relevant and interesting to them. Brief small-group discussions are a part of guided reading lessons, but book club is the ideal instructional context to foster conversational skills of a substantive nature. The structure of book clubs provides for conscious attention to keeping a strand of discussion going, building on the ideas of others, agreeing and disagreeing politely and respectfully, asking questions to clarify, providing evidence from the text, and other discussion-based skills. All of these skills are learned and practiced over time.

The teacher's presence in the book club, or any other small group, is essential to lift the discussion and keep it rooted in the text, but you won't hear the teacher dominating the discussion. The teacher's role is to support the *students* in doing the thinking and in articulating it to each other.

A tool that may be helpful to teachers is the *Prompting Guide, Part 2, for Comprehension: Thinking, Talking, and Writing*. This document provides examples of precise, facilitative language that teachers have found helpful in accomplishing their goals without "taking over." The concise teacher statements support productive interactions without cluttering the discussion with extraneous words. Some examples of prompts that are appropriate to use in both book clubs and guided reading discussions are provided in Figure 8-3.

If teachers are using facilitative language like this, it will soon become part of the students' vocabulary. This thoughtful approach to discussion is far more affirming to students than effusive praise, which is often misplaced or inaccurate. In the next section, we will discuss the importance and impact of teachers' facilitative language in more depth.

## Conferring

*To confer* means to have a genuine conversation with a student about her work and her identity as a reader or writer. During readers' and writers' workshops,

Fourth graders look at the speaker as she shares her thinking about a book.

"*Create opportunities for them to talk, and then talk with them (not at them).*"

—**Marie M. Clay**

| PURPOSE | EXAMPLES OF PROMPTING LANGUAGE |
|---|---|
| **Get the Discussion Started** | • Who has an idea to start us off?<br>• Turn and talk to a partner and share your first thoughts about this book. |
| **Focus Thinking** | • Turn and talk to your partner about _____.<br>• Take us to parts of the story (book) that you want us to think about with you. |
| **Affirm Thinking** | • That helps me understand in a different way.<br>• I think we have two possible explanations.<br>• Help me understand why you think that. |
| **Agree/Disagree** | • I see your point, but I disagree that _____.<br>• I agree with what you are saying because _____. |
| **Ask for Thinking** | • What's another way to think about that?<br>• Can you explain your question?<br>• What was amazing to you? |
| **Change Thinking** | • How have your ideas changed?<br>• So, if that is true, then _____. |
| **Clarify Thinking** | • Do you mean _____?<br>• Say more about what you mean. |
| **Extend Thinking** | • Talk more about that.<br>• Building on what _____ said, I think _____. |
| **Focus on Big Ideas** | • What are big ideas that you took from this story?<br>• What are you taking with you from this story (book)? |
| **Make Connections** | • What does that remind you of?<br>• Do you recognize any similarities to your own life?<br>• How is this story (book) like _____? |
| **Paraphrase** | • I hear you saying that _____.<br>• Another way to say that is _____. |
| **Question/ Hypothesize** | • One possibility is _____.<br>• Some of the possible consequences might be _____.<br>• Imagine if _____. |
| **Redirect** | • Let's stay on our first issue before moving on.<br>• I'd like to return to our discussion of _____. |
| **Seek Evidence** | • What makes you think that?<br>• You're providing details to support your thinking.<br>• Can you find a passage that shows _____?<br>• On page _____, paragraph _____, line _____, the writer says _____. |
| **Share Thinking** | • It was surprising (sad, hopeful) when _____.<br>• This illustration makes me think _____.<br>• An unforgettable moment is when _____. |
| **Summarize** | • Let's sum up what we've said.<br>• Has everyone shared their thinking on this topic? |

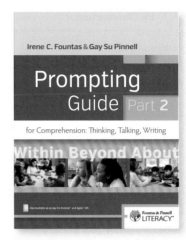

Irene C. Fountas & Gay Su Pinnell

**Prompting Guide** Part 2

for Comprehension: Thinking, Talking, Writing

Within Beyond About

Fountas & Pinnell
LITERACY

This guide provides precise, facilitative language that teachers can use directly with students.

**Figure 8-3.** Examples of Prompting Language for Small-Group Discussions

teachers confer with individual students to listen to their thinking, talk about their reading of a particular text or their work on a piece of writing, and provide brief, customized support and teaching that enables them to process texts and convey meaning more efficiently and effectively.

Conferences are conversational, with the student doing at least as much or more talking as the teacher. A student's talk during a reading or writing conference reveals his understandings and thinking and identifies the kind of support that will be helpful. Conferences also have an important instructional purpose. Conferences need to move the student forward as a reader or writer. While the teacher may focus briefly on a text-specific detail, the goal is to ensure that students learn something they can apply to any of their reading or writing in the future.

During workshops, teachers confer regularly with individual students about their work as readers and writers.

# How Facilitative Talk Promotes Learning

We now come to the importance of teacher talk in learning. The language that teachers choose to use has a powerful influence on students' learning and on their identities as learners. We use the term *facilitative talk* to describe the teacher's facilitative response to children's thinking. Facilitative talk is brief, clear, concise, intentional language the teacher uses to *facilitate* the type of thinking and talk by students that leads to new learning and strengthens their identities as capable, productive learners. When teachers are using facilitative talk, you won't see them correcting children's language, but you will see many opportunities for students to have conversations that *extend* their language through modeling or expanding upon the child's response. You won't hear effusive praise for everything students do, but you will notice thoughtful listening, confirmation, and extension of students' ideas by the teacher. You won't see the teacher dominating every discussion, but rather you'll see teachers and students sitting side by side and hear talk that centers on what the student is reading or writing or on the expression of thinking in the reader's or writer's notebook.

To illustrate what facilitative talk looks and sounds like in action, we present two examples of a small-group discussion of a book (Figures 8-4 and 8-5). While the scenarios are not actual taped examples, they reflect language moves that we have observed in many classrooms. The students' names are pseudonyms. As you read the discussions, think about what strikes you immediately.

### Welcome to the World!

The female arctic fox has her pups in the spring or early summer. If she's had plenty to eat that year, she usually has a big **litter**. Sometimes she has more than 15 wriggly pups. Good thing there is lots of room in a fox den.

The fox's newborn pups are blind and helpless. After about two weeks, their eyes begin to open. The mother fox stays in the den with her pups. The father brings her food and guards their home from hungry predators. An older sister fox may help take care of the many younger pups.

#### NEW FAMILIES, OLD DENS

Digging a new den is hard work. So arctic foxes use dens that may be hundreds of years old. Dens are often dug into the side of a hill or cliff. Some are as big as a football field, with more than one hundred entrances, or openings.

12

13

**Figure 8-4.** *Arctic Fox: Clever Hunter,* pp. 12–13 (Latta 2018)

## EXCERPTS FROM DISCUSSIONS OF *ARCTIC FOX: CLEVER HUNTER*

| | SCENARIO #1 | | SCENARIO #2 |
|---|---|---|---|
| **Teacher** | What did you learn about the Arctic fox? Donald, what did you learn? | **Teacher** | Who would like to start sharing your thinking? |
| **Donald** | I learned it lives in the Arctic. | **Donald** | I learned that foxes live in the Arctic. |
| **Teacher** | You learned it lives in the Arctic? Good. What else did you learn? Suri, what did you learn? | **Teacher** | Can you say more about that? |
| **Suri** | It's icy and cold there. | **Donald** | It's very cold and snowy and icy, and the fox has to keep warm. |
| **Teacher** | It's icy and cold there. Yes. It's covered with snow and ice. Who else learned something? David, what did you learn? | **Teacher** | Would anyone else like to add to Donald's comments about the fox's habitat or environment? |
| **David** | Its fur keeps it warm. | **Maya** | In winter there's no sun at all, and it's hard to survive there, but the fox has very warm fur. |
| **Teacher** | Its fur keeps it warm. Good thinking. Why is the Arctic called "the land of the midnight sun?" Maya, what do you think? | **David** | And he actually changes color in the winter, so he is white against the snow. It's hard to see him. Here on page 9, he's jumping in the snow to tunnel under. |
| **Maya** | It's got sun all the time. | **Suri** | That's how he catches an animal–like this little one on page 8–for dinner. |
| **Teacher** | Yes. It has sun all the time sometimes. Who else can say something about that? | **Teacher** | It's a very harsh environment, but you are saying the fox has some special ways of surviving. Have you noticed any other ways? |
| **David** | It's got sun setting on the snow, and it's very cold. | **Kaylie** | I loved the little pups on these pages (points to the images on pages 12 and 13). See; they dig down really deep and then have their babies. |
| **Teacher** | Uh-huh. It shines on snow. Anyone else? What about you, Suri? | **Suri** | Oh, I saw there could be fifteen of them. But the dens are also really old. They have to dig them, and it's hard. |
| **Suri** | There's no sun in the winter, but it shines all day in the summer, even all night. | **Donald** | But they are good diggers. |
| **Teacher** | Great! It shines all night and you can see it even at midnight–the midnight sun. Would you like that? | **Teacher** | They are so safe there. Does anyone have anything to add to what Kaylie and Suri are saying about the pups? |
| **Students** | Yes. | **Kaylie** | The mother stays with them, and the father is a guard. He also brings food back to them. They get bigger, and then they can go out and play. |

**Figure 8-5.** Excerpts from Discussions of *Arctic Fox: Clever Hunter*

# EXCERPTS FROM DISCUSSIONS OF *ARCTIC FOX: CLEVER HUNTER*

| | SCENARIO #1 | | SCENARIO #2 |
|---|---|---|---|
| **Teacher** | Everyone turn to page 9. At the top you see what the fox looks like in the summer and at the bottom you see what the fox looks like in the winter. What do you notice? Kaylie, you haven't said anything yet about the Arctic fox. What do you notice in this picture? | **Teacher** | You have noticed some ways that the Arctic fox survives a very harsh environment–one where it would be hard for people and most animals to live. What big ideas are you taking away from this book? |
| **Kaylie** | One fox is brown, and one is white. | **Maya** | You can look at animals and see that they all have good ways to survive. |
| **Teacher** | Right. One fox is brown, and one is white. But is it the same fox? Anybody? | **David** | Some of the ways that animals survive have to do with parts of their bodies; like, for example, the fox turns colors and is good at digging. |
| **Maya** | One is a summer fox, and one is a winter fox. | **Teacher** | Would it help to take a look at the picture on pages 4 and 5? |
| **Teacher** | It is summer and winter in color. Good thinking. But is it the same fox? David? | **Maya** | That's all the parts of the fox–the labels. Everything helps the fox stay warm. |
| **David** | It is the same fox that is brown in the summer and white in the winter. | **Donald** | The tail is like a blanket that she can wrap around her or lie on like a blanket. Or she can cover her nose with it. Everything is short, so the heat stays inside her body. |
| **Teacher** | Good. The same fox is brown in the summer and white in the winter. Is that good? | **Teacher** | I thought the labels were really helpful here. What about you? |
| **David** | It's good because he can dive in the snow and he is the same color. | **Students** | Yes. |
| **Teacher** | Great! You can't see him against the snow because he is white–like camouflage–and he can dive in and catch things. Anything else? | **Teacher** | Are there any more very important ideas about animals? |
| **Students** | [Silence] | **Kaylie** | I think it means we should respect the habitat and make sure it stays clean, so animals can use their ways to survive. |
| **Teacher** | Good job, everybody. | **Donald** | All animals have ways to survive. But I agree with Kaylie that people have to help them. Because if the Arctic gets warm, the foxes might not survive. |
| | | **Teacher** | Thumbs up if you think we had an interesting discussion. |

Figure 8-5. (*continued*)

Both scenarios are friendly. They are not "lectures," and students have a chance to talk. The teacher is interested in hearing the students share their understandings about the text. All of the students have processed the text. If you simply glance at both scenarios, you might think, "Oh, good, they are all engaged and interactive."

But you can't help noticing that the *nature* of student and teacher talk is quite different in the two scenarios. Sit down with a colleague and take a closer look. Have one person highlight all of the teacher talk in both scenarios; the other highlights all of the student talk in both scenarios. Now compare them. Scenario #1 shows far more teacher talk than student talk, while scenario #2 shows more of a balance. Because of the language choices of the teacher, the *quantity* of student talk is different.

Now, look again at the conversations. What does the teacher seem to do in each scenario? In scenario #1 the teacher repeats almost every answer that students give and makes an evaluative comment (usually "good"). He talks between every student and keeps going until a student produces the answer he wants and then he stops the line of questioning. He leads the talking all the way and never really gets to the larger ideas in the text. Scenario #2 presents an almost complete contrast.

In scenario #1, the teacher acts as chief evaluator, and in scenario #2, the teacher asks students to reflect. In scenario #1, students' talk is only in response to the teacher's questions. In scenario #2, students build on the ideas of other students. If we could look closely at the nonverbal behavior, we would see that in scenario #1, students either look at the teacher or down at their books. In scenario #2, we'd see that students look at the person who is talking or at the page he/she indicates. Because of the language choices of the teacher, the *quality* of student talk is different.

In case you think we have exaggerated these two scenarios, record some small-group discussions in classrooms in your school and transcribe them. You will find that there are some unconscious actions taking place. Teachers feel very responsible for what happens during lessons. They *want* students to learn, and they want them to come up with the right answers. They also want groups to function smoothly—without awkward pauses. They know there should be talking. There is a human tendency to fill silence in social situations, so that is just what teachers do.

A well-intentioned teacher can have a beautiful classroom with substantive and engaging materials. The routines of the community can be working smoothly, with groups forming and reforming. Children can be self-disciplined, choosing and reading books. Learning takes place. Yet lessons can be empty without the dynamics that lead to shifts in learning for both students *and* teachers. Talk needs to lead to bigger understandings that come about through the children's ability *to respond to each other*. High-progress students will learn in any environment, but most students need more precise instruction to make leaps in learning.

Hough and colleagues (2013) studied teachers within guided reading groups; hundreds of lessons were videotaped and analyzed by teams of researchers who did a close observation of the kinds of structures and interactions that went on. Hough et al. analyzed separately the "novice" and "expert" teachers; the factor that separated them was the ability to teach *responsively.* It's the hardest teaching skill to learn, and it requires high cognitive activity. It's developed over time and consists of an ability to observe behavior in detail "on the run" while teaching and to respond in a precise way that takes students forward day after day.

You might say that the students in scenario #2 take more initiative and offer greater insights than those in scenario #1. All the teacher has to do is ask for it! All of that is true, but it is learned behavior, *not* inborn. Day after day (and sometimes year after year) the students have learned to:

- Talk after reading (an expectation that actually builds in unconscious attention *while* reading to notice things to talk about).
- Build on the ideas of others.
- Follow a line of discussion.
- Look at and listen to the person who is talking.
- Take turns rather than waiting for the teacher to call on them.
- Use socially appropriate language. ("I agree because . . ." "I disagree because . . ." "Can I change the subject . . .")
- Get to the big ideas.
- Notice what's important in a text—not irrelevant details.

Scenario #2 is the product of *previous teaching.* Students have learned the behaviors that are appropriate in this social learning situation. They have practiced these behaviors over and over—not just as rote drill but as part of authentic interaction.

As a school leader, you can support teachers in learning and using facilitative language. You can provide a listening ear to help them become self-aware of the way they use language in instruction. As you observe teachers, use the observation tool **Teacher Talk in the Classroom (07)** on the next page to look and listen for the characteristics of teacher talk that support effective learning. After an observation, invite the teacher to share her perspectives on the language she uses to facilitate learning. Think collaboratively with the teacher about next steps you can take together to promote greater facilitative talk in the classroom.

## The Takeaway

It has been said that "learning floats on a sea of talk" (Britton 1983). Strong learning communities value talk, because talk is thinking. A talk-filled classroom that is grounded in real reading, real writing, and real inquiry provides

## OBSERVATION TOOL

The observation tool **Teacher Talk in the Classroom (07)** can support you in noticing and reflecting on teacher talk that facilitates students' thinking and learning. You may wish to share the tool with teachers as a common resource for professional learning and collaboration.

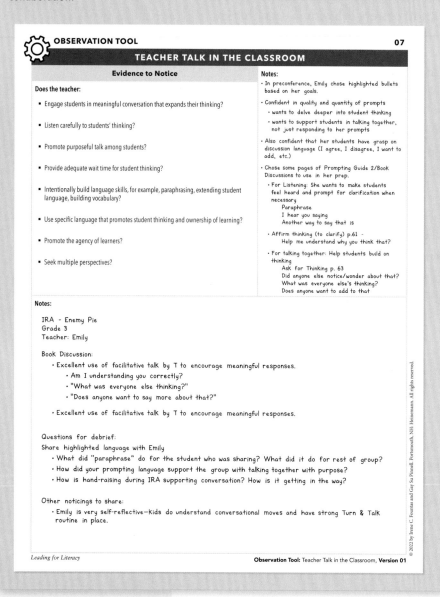

OBSERVATION TOOL                                                        07
### TEACHER TALK IN THE CLASSROOM

| Evidence to Notice | Notes: |
|---|---|
| **Does the teacher:** | • In preconference, Emily chose highlighted bullets based on her goals. |
| • Engage students in meaningful conversation that expands their thinking? | • Confident in quality and quantity of prompts |
| | • wants to delve deeper into student thinking |
| • Listen carefully to students' thinking? | • wants to support students in talking together, not just responding to her prompts |
| • Promote purposeful talk among students? | • Also confident that her students have grasp on discussion language (I agree, I disagree, I want to add, etc.) |
| • Provide adequate wait time for student thinking? | • Chose some pages of Prompting Guide 2/Book Discussions to use in her prep. |
| • Intentionally build language skills, for example, paraphrasing, extending student language, building vocabulary? | • For Listening: She wants to make students feel heard and prompt for clarification when necessary |
| |     Paraphrase |
| • Use specific language that promotes student thinking and ownership of learning? |     I hear you saying |
| |     Another way to say that is |
| • Promote the agency of learners? | • Affirm thinking (to clarify) p.61 - Help me understand why you think that? |
| • Seek multiple perspectives? | • For talking together: Help students build on thinking |
| |     Ask for Thinking p. 63 |
| |     Did anyone else notice/wonder about that? |
| |     What was everyone else's thinking? |
| |     Does anyone want to add to that |

**Notes:**

IRA - Enemy Pie
Grade 3
Teacher: Emily

Book Discussion:
• Excellent use of facilitative talk by T to encourage meaningful responses.
  • Am I understanding you correctly?
  • "What was everyone else thinking?"
  • "Does anyone want to say more about that?"

• Excellent use of facilitative talk by T to encourage meaningful responses.

Questions for debrief:
Share highlighted language with Emily
• What did "paraphrase" do for the student who was sharing? What did it do for rest of group?
• How did your prompting language support the group with talking together with purpose?
• How is hand-raising during IRA supporting conversation? How is it getting in the way?

Other noticings to share:
• Emily is very self-reflective—Kids do understand conversational moves and have strong Turn & Talk routine in place.

*Leading for Literacy*                     **Observation Tool:** Teacher Talk in the Classroom, **Version 01**

every student with powerful, sustained learning opportunities. By participating actively in conversations surrounding texts, students construct meaning, clarify ideas, and expand understandings. And they experience the joy of talking about important ideas with their peers. Ensuring classroom conditions and teaching practices that promote rich, text-based conversations among students is an important goal for you and other leaders in the school. When children's voices are genuinely valued, they will be interested, engaged and motivated to both articulate their thinking and benefit from the thinking of others. They will find meaning and satisfaction in learning from texts across a variety of disciplines. But most of all, the experience of talking about texts will influence their identities as independent thinkers and productive members of society.

Across all instructional contexts, teacher language is a critical factor in students' learning. Crafting effective learning interactions is the most sophisticated work that teachers can undertake, and here is where coaching can be extremely helpful. Many coaches find it helpful to explore areas of *The Literacy Continuum* together with colleagues, determining some priorities for a particular child or group of children. Then, they go to the prompting tools and select some possible language to try out. They can have key pages ready to use and/or note a few examples on a sticky note to make it less overwhelming. Over time, just looking at *The Literacy Continuum* will bring facilitative language to mind, and it will become more and more automatic. Just dropping the wordiness and constant stream of evaluative statements will leave room for carefully crafted language.

## Think About Your School

- How much student talk is grounded in texts?
- How do classroom conditions—the space, routines, practices—promote student talk?
- What strengths can you and your colleagues build on to expand student talk throughout the school?
- Do teachers use facilitative talk appropriately and powerfully?
- What is the impact of talk on students' learning and identities as learners?

## Move Your School Forward

- Share the two scenarios on pages 116 and 117 with teachers and guide a discussion about the important differences between the two.
- Follow up on the discussion by using the observation tool on page 120 to determine if teachers are using facilitative language to promote student talk. Note areas for improvement and share feedback with the teachers.

# SECTION 3

*Literacy by Design: Observing, Assessing, and Planning for Effective Teaching*

# SECTION 3

## *Literacy by Design: Observing, Assessing, and Planning for Effective Teaching*

Imagine starting a journey with only one piece of a map to guide your way. You'd know your starting point and where you would be at the point where the map ends, but how would you know what's beyond that point or how much progress you'd made toward your ultimate destination?

This is how teachers must feel when handed their grade-level slice of a school's curriculum and asked to implement it without a full sense of the bigger picture. To chart an efficient course, all teachers in the school need a *shared* vision of progress over many years of strong instruction. Every educator in the school needs to learn what to look for in the reading and writing behaviors their students demonstrate, as well as how those change in response to instruction. Holding such a vision helps teachers plan their teaching moves carefully and strategically. In Chapter 9, we discuss literacy progress over time across nine contexts for literacy learning and offer ready-to-use tools to assist you in supporting teachers' understanding of progress.

In Chapter 10, we turn to how students' progress in literacy learning is measured, and we walk you through the process of designing a comprehensive assessment system. Responsive teaching helps students move forward quickly, so assessment must be systematic and ongoing, and it must span every year of a child's schooling.

We hope that expert teachers supported by the school leadership will have a strong voice in designing the assessment system. This way, assessment can become a living process, one that educators constantly apply, share with colleagues, use to clarify goals, and draw support from in working together to inform instructional plans and daily interactions with students. Such a system also gives you and your team a valid and reliable way to assess and share the progress of grade-level cohorts in the school over time as teachers grow in their ability to use data to improve instruction.

# Chapter 9

# A Coherent Vision for Literacy Proficiency Across the Grades

*When we study how children work on texts (literacy processing) as they read and write irrespective of how teachers are teaching, we arrive at an alternative view of progress that measures what students are learning.*
—Marie M. Clay

No doubt, you have seen your share of standards and curriculum documents. You know that most only go so far, and few feel essential enough to use on a daily basis as a concrete plan for teaching and assessing learning. Too often we have seen these documents end up on shelves somewhere, gathering dust and failing to serve their intended purpose. In this chapter, we describe a different kind of literacy curriculum, *The Fountas & Pinnell Literacy Continuum: A Tool for Assessment, Planning, and Teaching*. This document is based on a detailed description of evidence of progress. It is a reminder that each child is proficient at a certain point in time, but each is always moving forward. Teachers need to think ahead of their students' present competencies so that they can create the most accelerative learning.

The continuum provides a detailed description of the competencies children need to achieve in language, reading, writing, phonics, oral language, and digital communication and how they develop over time. Teachers, instructional coaches, and literacy leaders in your school can refer to the continuum as they observe the readers, writers, and language users in their classrooms, plan lessons, identify specific teaching goals, and assess the effectiveness of their teaching and the progress of children's learning. Additionally, the continuum describes the characteristics of texts students should experience at each grade level and the behavioral goals for prekindergarten through middle school across the areas pertinent to the language arts.

Taken together, the eight continua present a broad picture of literacy and language learning that takes place during the important years of school (Figure 9-1). The progress of students across these continua, or even within each of them, is not an even, step-by-step process. Students learn as they have opportunities and give attention in different ways. Looking across the continua, educators can see patterns of progress over time. Learners progress in their individual ways, but ultimately they reach the same goal—they develop a complex and flexible literacy processing system.

*The Literacy Continuum* is both a standards document and a curriculum guide. Teachers and leaders can use it to set goals, observe for evidence of competence, guide instruction, work with individual children at the edge of what they need to learn next, look for evidence of learning (even small shifts), and reflect on progress.

In designing the continuum, we consulted current research on the reading process, literacy learning, and the unique needs of English learners. We closely observed readers and writers in classrooms across the country, analyzed texts and artifacts of learning, and noted how literacy behaviors shifted and advanced. We examined many sets of standards to determine how policy makers look at progress at the district, state, and national levels. We are confident that this continuum not only meets language and literacy standards (including the national and WEDA standards), but exceeds them. You may want to visit our website (*fp.pub/community*) to examine the various correlation documents we've provided to state and district boards of education.

## Descriptive, Not Prescriptive

The continuum does not prescribe a static scope and sequence of lessons, though it reflects small developmental changes over time. It provides a description of the characteristics of texts to use in various instructional reading contexts, specific genres and forms for use in writing and writing about reading, and the observable behaviors and understandings of proficient readers, writers, and language users. Teachers can use the tool to make decisions about which behaviors to notice, teach for, and support in the classroom based on the strengths and needs of their students.

# THE FOUNTAS & PINNELL LITERACY CONTINUUM

| Continuum | Brief Definition | Description of the Continuum |
|---|---|---|
| Interactive Read-Aloud and Literature Discussion | Students engage in discussion with the teacher and with one another about a text that they have heard read aloud or one they have read independently. | <ul><li>Year by year, grades PreK–8</li><li>Genres appropriate to grades PreK–8</li><li>Specific behaviors and understandings that are evidence of thinking within, beyond, and about the text</li></ul> |
| Shared and Performance Reading | Students read together or take roles in reading a shared text. They reflect the meaning of the text with their voices. | <ul><li>Year by year, grades PreK–8</li><li>Genres appropriate to grades PreK–8</li><li>Specific behaviors and understandings that are evidence of thinking within, beyond, and about the text</li></ul> |
| Writing About Reading | Students extend their understanding of a text through a variety of writing genres and sometimes with illustrations. | <ul><li>Year by year, grades PreK–8</li><li>Genres/forms for writing about reading appropriate to grades PreK–8</li><li>Specific evidence in the writing that reflects thinking within, beyond, and about the text</li></ul> |
| Writing | Students use their writers' notebooks to compose and write their own examples of a variety of genres, written for varying purposes and audiences. | <ul><li>Year by year, grades PreK–8</li><li>Genres/forms for writing appropriate to grades PreK–8</li><li>Aspects of craft, conventions, and processes that are evident in students' writing, grades PreK–8</li></ul> |
| Oral and Visual Communication | Students present their ideas through oral discussion and presentation. | <ul><li>Year by year, grades PreK–8</li><li>Specific behaviors and understandings related to listening and speaking, presentation</li></ul> |
| Digital Communication | Students learn effective ways of communicating and searching for information using digital devices; they learn to think critically about information and sources. | <ul><li>Year by year, grades PreK–8</li><li>Specific behaviors and understandings related to effective and ethical uses of digital communication tools</li></ul> |
| Phonics, Spelling, and Word Study | Students learn about the simple and complex relationships of letters to sounds as well as the structure and meaning of words to help them in reading and spelling. | <ul><li>Year by year, grades PreK–8</li><li>Specific behaviors and understandings in nine areas of understanding related to letters, sounds, and words, and how they work in reading and spelling</li></ul> |
| Guided Reading | Students read a teacher-selected text in a small group; the teacher provides explicit teaching and support for reading increasingly challenging texts. | <ul><li>Level by level, A to Z</li><li>Genres appropriate to grades K–8</li><li>Specific behaviors and understandings that are evidence of thinking within, beyond, and about the text</li><li>Specific suggestions for word work (drawn from the Phonics, Spelling, and Word Study continuum)</li></ul> |

**Figure 9-1.** The Fountas & Pinnell Literacy Continuum

## A THEORY OF PROFICIENT READING

The foremost researcher and theorist of literacy processing and literacy learning is New Zealander Marie Clay (1926–2000). Clay was a developmental psychologist who focused on cognitive growth. She studied children in great detail, documenting changes over time in their reading and writing behaviors. From her observations of how children's reading behaviors changed, she theorized changes in the way readers think. This was new territory in reading research at the time, and she referred to it as an "unusual lens." Unlike other investigators, Clay

- made a very large number of detailed observations of children across time as they encountered their first year of reading instruction;
- observed children's reading behaviors as they read continuous text (rather than single letters or words only);
- looked at the reading behaviors of proficient learners (rather than only children who were having difficulty; and
- identified multiple pathways to a fully integrated reading process.

She found that children can take many "different paths to common outcomes," depending on what they attend to at any given time and whether rich resources and adult support are available.

### Clay's Theory of Reading

**Sense, Meaning**
Does it make sense?

**Visual Information**
Does that look right?

**Sounds**
Say it. What can you hear?
What would you expect to see?

**Structure/Grammar**
Can we say it that way?

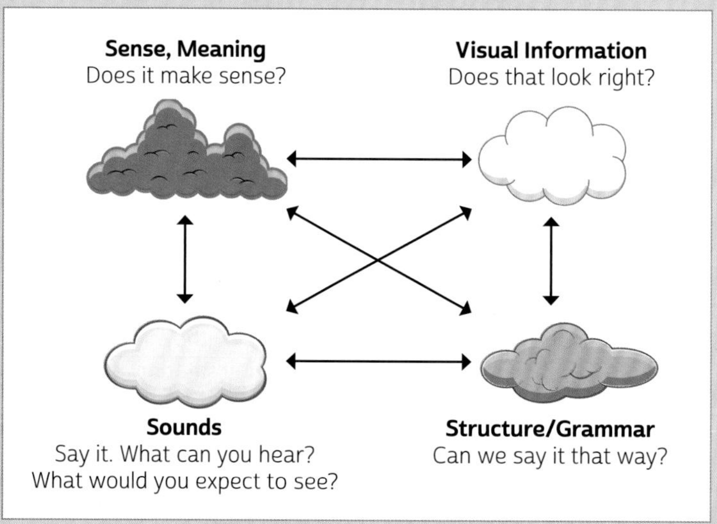

**Figure 9-2.** Four Sources of Information in Print

Clay's theory of reading suggests that early readers must learn to look for four different categories, or sources, of information in print and to check one against another to confirm a response (see Figure 9-2). They access what they know about the sounds of language, the visual features of letters and words (and their relationships to the sound system), and the structure of language. Very early in the acquisition of the reading process, we can see behavioral evidence of these cognitive processes as children read text, but they rapidly become unconscious as readers learn more.

## A Common Vision for Language and Literacy Learning

By examining the continuum together, you and your colleagues can discuss your common expectations for student achievement in each instructional area, grade by grade. Teachers can compare current expectations to those in the continuum and focus on goals that they want their students to achieve. For example, a coach and teachers at a grade level in an elementary school or middle school might work together over a few weeks or months. In grade-level groups they can examine one instructional area at a time and then share their perspectives with teachers of other grades. Looking across the grades will help them understand a long continuum of learning as well as work more effectively with students who are below or above their own grade levels. Working intensively with the continuum at their own grade levels (and perhaps the level below), they can make specific plans for instruction in particular areas and set long-term goals with precision.

As teachers consult *The Literacy Continuum* in order to teach for the same behaviors and understandings, students will benefit from the coherence of common goals and common language across the grades. The continuum also benefits teachers by helping them shift the lens through which they see their role—from teaching "the program" to teaching for effective literacy competencies. They learn that they are teaching for students to engage in reflective processes that they can apply to any book or any piece of writing. The result is teaching that is more thoughtful, intentional, precise, and rewarding and produces better outcomes for student learning.

*The Literacy Continuum* gives teachers a common language for discussing students' strengths and needs.

# Inferring Competencies by Observing Reading Behaviors

We will begin with important understandings about the reading process, as you will find that the goals for each instructional reading context on *The Literacy Continuum* are organized by these systems.

## Reading Is Thinking

Reading is a highly complex process that requires students to bring together their own language and background knowledge with the print on the page. By reading a text they can begin to build their neural network for processing written language. In this way, they bring invisible information (e.g., background information, language) together with information that is visible (the print). When students read, they use in-the-head systems of strategic actions to process texts, flexibly integrating many different kinds of information in order to construct meaning. These systems are displayed as a wheel in Figure 9-3 to express how

**Inside the Reading Brain** Writing for healthline.com (October 15, 2019), Rebecca Joy Stanborough explains that reading literally changes one's mind. "Using MRI scans, researchers have confirmed that reading involves a complex network of circuits and signals in the brain. As your reading ability matures, those networks also get stronger and more sophisticated." Stanborough goes on to say that in addition to strengthening the brain, reading increases empathy, builds vocabulary, prevents cognitive decline, reduces stress, aids sleep, alleviates depression, and lengthens a person's lifespan.

proficient readers engage in all of the strategic actions simultaneously in a smoothly orchestrated way as they read a text.

The reader builds an in-the-head network of strategic actions. For discussion, we developed a model of twelve systems that develop simultaneously as the reader processes texts. Each area lends itself to very simple actions in the early levels and to highly sophisticated actions at the higher levels of text. At every level, readers simultaneously employ all of them in an orchestrated way, usually without conscious attention.

Teachers need to infer the ways in which each student is becoming increasingly proficient by noticing the behavioral evidence of these systems of strategic actions in use. Teachers gain evidence of the reader's control of these in-the-head actions and understandings by observing their oral reading, their talk about texts, and their writing about reading. Students' oral reading is the

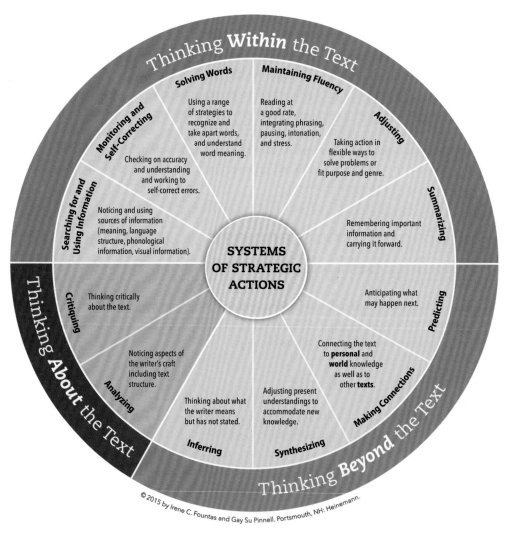

**Figure 9-3.** Systems of strategic actions and the contexts and evidence that serve as a resource for making teaching decisions.

best source of evidence of the first five systems of strategic actions. Their talk and writing about reading provide evidence of the last seven.

To describe the complexity of the reading process, the twelve systems of strategic actions are clustered into three categories that encompass how readers construct meaning as they process a text. On the wheel in Figure 9-3, the three categories are represented by three different colors in the wheel's outermost band: blue (thinking within the text), green (thinking beyond the text) and purple (thinking about the text). These categories are represented by colored bullets on the continuum. The systems of strategic actions that are grouped within each category are discussed below, with a focus on how teachers can find evidence of students engaging the strategic actions as they read.

## Thinking Within the Text

The reader processes the information that is provided in the text in order to gain the basic or literal meaning. Thinking within the text enables the reader to understand essential information that the writer wishes to convey. You'll find these strategic actions shown in the blue section of the wheel in Figure 9-3.

**Searching for and Using Information** As teachers observe students' oral reading behaviors they will notice behavioral evidence of searching for and using the information that is in the text. The reader attempts to use all sources of information to provide a response. For example, the student may say words using current knowledge of letters and sounds, take words apart, make several attempts, or reread to use language structure as a resource. The reader may reread to search for meaning or language or to notice information in illustrations or graphics.

**Monitoring and Self-Correcting** Teachers need to notice when a student stops at difficulty and does not self-initiate searching for more information. Even if the student does not read the word accurately, his behavior indicates an awareness of error. When the reader corrects the error for himself, he has demonstrated the important behaviors of monitoring and self-correcting. Accurate reading is, in itself, evidence that self-monitoring is going on and this behavior is noticed in all levels of reading.

**Solving Words** As a teacher notices a student's accurate reading, errors, substitutions, and self-corrections, she gains understanding of that student's ability to solve words. The student may recognize many words automatically and work at others by using word parts. In student talk and writing, teachers can form hypotheses about known vocabulary and also students' ability to derive the meaning of words from context.

**Maintaining Fluency** Listening to oral reading is the only way to understand a student's reading fluency. The criterion is not just "reading fast." The teacher needs to listen for a voice that moves along at an appropriate pace for the piece being read and reflects the meaning with intonation, pausing, phrasing, and word stress.

**Adjusting** Effective readers are flexible as they process texts. As teachers observe reading behaviors, they will notice when a reader slows down to problem-solve and then regains momentum. The student may search back to thoughtfully reconsider a difficult or challenging passage or examine a graphic. Readers read differently for different purposes and in different content disciplines and genres. Oral reading of nonfiction will actually sound different than oral reading of a suspenseful narrative.

**Summarizing** In students' talk and their writing about reading, teachers can look for evidence that they can concisely summarize the information and the big ideas in a text, leaving out irrelevant detail but including details that offer necessary evidence for thinking and understanding and reporting the larger messages.

## Thinking Beyond the Text

The reader applies analytical thinking to consider and critique the text as an object. Thinking about the text enables the reader to learn more about how texts are structured and crafted by writers. Applying analytic and critical thinking allows the reader to achieve a high level of understanding and enjoyment. These strategic actions are found in the green part of the wheel in Figure 9-3.

**Predicting** Teachers can find evidence in students' talk and writing about reading to show whether they can use the information they have to make predictions on such aspects as what characters will do, what might happen next in a story, or how problems might be resolved.

**Making Connections** Again, in talk and writing about reading, teachers will find evidence of the extent to which students can bring content knowledge, their own experience, or their understanding of other texts to the comprehension of texts they are reading.

By listening to students as they talk about their reading, teachers look for evidence that students are thinking analytically about texts.

**Synthesizing** In talk and writing, teachers can find evidence that students are taking on new learning—ideas and information—from their reading. They self-report new thinking and changes in perspectives.

**Inferring** By listening to students' talk and analyzing their writing about reading, teachers can look for evidence that students can think beyond the text to infer elements such as characters' feelings and motives, larger themes and ideas, causes of problems, and so on.

## Thinking About the Text

The reader applies analytical thinking to consider and critique the text as an object. Thinking about the text enables the reader to learn more about how texts are structured and crafted by writers. Applying analytic and critical thinking allows the reader to achieve a high level of understanding and enjoyment. Teachers gain evidence of their students' control of these behaviors and understandings by observing their oral reading, their talk about text, and their writing about reading. These strategic actions are found in the purple section of the wheel in Figure 9-3.

**Analyzing** By listening to students as they talk about their reading and by reading their writing, teachers look for evidence that students are thinking analytically about texts—that they are noticing aspects of the writer's craft, such as the plot structure, the use of figurative language, or the use of persuasion and argument.

| STRATEGIC ACTIONS | | EVIDENCE |
|---|---|---|
| **Thinking Within the Text** | • Searching for and Using Information<br>• Monitoring and Self-Correcting<br>• Solving Words<br>• Maintaining Fluency<br>• Adjusting<br>• Summarizing | • Code and analyze oral reading behaviors<br>• Notice evidence in talk and writing about reading |
| **Thinking Beyond the Text** | • Predicting<br>• Making Connections<br>• Synthesizing<br>• Inferring | • Notice evidence in talk after reading<br>• Notice evidence in writing about reading |
| **Thinking About the Text** | • Analyzing<br>• Critiquing | |

**Figure 9-4.** In Search of Evidence of Strategic Actions

**Critiquing** Talk and writing also reveal the extent to which students can think critically about their reading. Do they question the authenticity of the text or evaluate its quality? Do they think critically about the evidence offered to support an argument; do they consider alternative arguments?

We provide a summary of the strategic actions for reading and how to notice evidence of thinking within, beyond, and about the text in Figure 9-4.

# Inferring Competencies by Observing Writing Behaviors

Like reading, writing is a complex process in that it orchestrates thinking, language, and mechanics. The writing process can be described as a series of steps (getting an idea, drafting, revising, editing, and publishing), but it is in fact a recursive process in which all of these things happen not in a linear way but as a dynamic process, always in motion. Proficient writers constantly apply and reapply everything they know to successive attempts. They move forward, go back, redo, have sudden insights, and with opportunity and teaching they build effective—even powerful—writing systems over time.

Students need to develop a basic knowledge of the writing process and to know how to vary the process for different genres and purposes. Even young children can produce simple publications; as they write year after year, they engage in the same basic process but at more sophisticated levels. Their range becomes broader and their publications more complex.

The graphic in Figure 9-5 illustrates the process of writing as a system in which each element is closely related to others.

- **Purpose** and **audience** are near the center of the circle because they are the essential foundation of a piece of writing. Writers begin with a purpose and with awareness of a particular audience as they think about genre.

- Writers select a **genre**—such as functional, narrative, informational, persuasive, poetic, or hybrid—according to their purpose and audience.

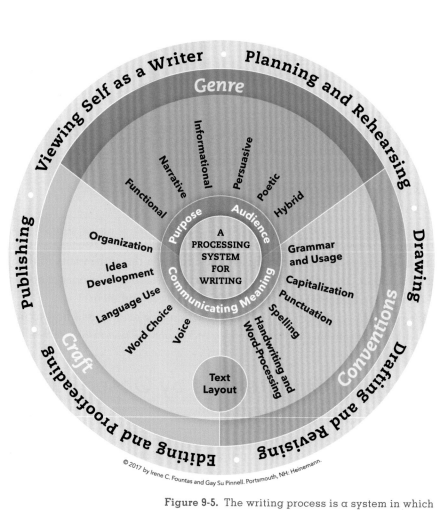

© 2017 by Irene C. Fountas and Gay Su Pinnell. Portsmouth, NH: Heinemann.

**Figure 9-5.** The writing process is a system in which each element is closely related to the others.

- Writers consider **genre, craft,** and **conventions** simultaneously as they write, although one aspect may have dominance at specific points in the process. All of these elements are in the service of **communicating meaning,** which is the reason it, too, is near the center of the circle.

- Writers use aspects of **craft** such as organization, idea development, language use, word choice, and voice to express well-developed ideas with an impactful style.

- To communicate their ideas clearly, writers also use **conventions** such as grammar and usage, capitalization, punctuation, spelling, and handwriting or word-processing.

- Both craft and conventions affect **text layout.** Writers use the layout of a text to contribute to and enhance meaning.

- The terms in the inside circle emphasize the recursive process of writing, from collecting ideas to **planning and rehearsing** to **publishing,** along with the important outcome for students—**viewing self as a writer.**

Students develop the range of competencies as they build an effective processing system across years of schooling and beyond. We view writing through different lenses: conventions, genre, and craft. All three are important, and all have component skills and understandings, which we discuss below.

## Conventions

All writers must be concerned about the conventions that help others read their ideas with ease. These conventions include grammar and usage, capitalization, punctuation, spelling, and handwriting. The conventions of writing have developed over centuries. For example, in the 1700s, spelling varied greatly and writers had their own idiosyncratic ways of going about it. But as the literacy levels of populations expanded and the printing press made written material more available, the need arose for standardized spelling so that messages were clear. Punctuation was invented for the same reasons.

Since it took so long for society to develop a wide range of conventions for writing, we should not expect young children to learn them immediately after they enter school. Insisting that everything they write be "correct" may put a damper on the expressive writing they need to do to get started as writers.

They may be afraid, for example, to try stronger and more interesting words just because they are unsure how to spell them. We want to foster the creativity in their writing. At the same time, we need a clear picture of what we need to teach them so that they steadily grow in the use of conventions over time.

## Genre

Just as there are genres in reading, young writers also need to write in a number of ways according to the purpose for writing (Figure 9-6). (This assumes that they actually have a purpose other than simply carrying out an assignment for the teacher to grade.) Very young children's writing will be expressive and need not be strongly categorized. They will "borrow" ideas, style, and language from the books they hear read aloud; they will tell their own personal stories. But as they write more and experience more texts, they will need to shape their writing according to the purpose it serves. Through interactive writing, shared writing, and minilessons, teachers can demonstrate these genres before children try to produce them for themselves. Six genres to explore are:

## SIX GENRES OF WRITING

1. Functional Writing
2. Narrative Writing
3. Informational Writing
4. Persuasive Writing and Argument
5. Poetic Writing
6. Hybrid Writing

**Figure 9-6.** Teachers can introduce, teach, reinforce, and expand any of these genres of writing for a range of purposes.

**Functional Writing** Writers learn the forms for letters, both "friendly" and formal. They make lists or write directions and procedures for doing something. Writing about reading, too, is required in school. Writing about reading helps readers organize their thinking and become more aware of it. It also helps them articulate their thinking to others. Finally, the reality of testing makes us aware that students need to do the "test writing" that convinces others of how much they know. They need to analyze a test prompt to discern the expectations and write to the point.

**Narrative Writing** A narrative tells a story. It is most often used in fiction writing, but is also useful in biography, memoir, and narrative nonfiction. These nonfiction texts, told in time order, do not necessarily have all the characteristics of a story. (For example, there may not be a story problem or a high point.) But what the writer is learning is how to put ideas into an organizational pattern; they discover that time order is one such pattern.

**Informational Writing** Much school writing is expository nonfiction, in which information is most often presented in categories. Students select a topic, do some research, make notes, and then prepare a report or presentation. In doing so, they use many aspects of the writer's craft—an interesting "lead," for example. They use underlying structures such as description, cause and effect, chronological sequence, temporal sequence, categorization, problem and solution, and question and answer. Students also write speeches, feature articles, and essays as they become more proficient. It's important to note that students will have had deep exposure to all kinds of expository writing through interactive read-aloud, and these mentor texts may be brought to their attention in writing minilessons.

**Persuasive Writing and Argument** Just as we want students to recognize, interpret, and think critically about persuasion and argument in the texts they read, we also want them to become proficient in producing those texts themselves. A high level of writing skill is needed to craft a good argument with a solid base of evidence and a series of logically organized and supported points. While persuasion seeks to convince the reader by appealing to emotions and tapping into beliefs, argument seeks to convince through logic. At times, though, both may be present in a speech or article.

**Poetic Writing** All students should have the opportunity to try some poetic writing. The language of poetry brings pleasure because it condenses ideas into a very few words. It is meant to be read and enjoyed over and over. Rhythm and rhyme characterize the first poems children experience, but as they collect poetry and read it, they will gradually become aware of the many forms poetry can take and use poetic description to convey sensory images and human feelings.

**Hybrid Writing** Some complex writing combines genres in the same text, and students will enjoy creating these unusual texts. For example, a nonfiction account of a historical period might have a fictional "diary" embedded in it. Or a report on insects might have a poem that shows the sounds they make.

As you can see, there is much for students to learn as they write every day. Not every one of these genres must be taught in isolation. If students experience a rich supply of read-aloud texts, carefully organized, then teachers can give them examples of high-quality writing daily. They can learn writing from writers. Over time, they will develop a way of approaching texts so that they notice aspects of genre and craft. They can read like writers!

## Craft

Looking across genres, proficient writers hone their craft. They collect and develop ideas, decide on the organization of those ideas, and select language that will best express them. All of this craft feeds into something writers call "voice," which is the individual's unique style as a writer. Young writers may try on different styles as they encounter them, but they eventually find ways of expressing their feelings and passion for a topic or story. This progression assumes that they are writing about something they care about.

Writing is a recursive process in which individuals engage again and again (see Figure 9-7). Every piece of writing that is worth reading has been subjected to a process of development.

Even young writers can plan and rehearse what to write. Often writers are assisted in this planning by reading and talking with others. Sometimes

Students develop a range of competencies in writing as they build an effective processing system across years of schooling.

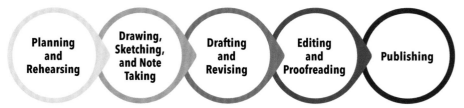

**Figure 9-7.** Writing is a nonlinear, recursive experience. The actions above occur as part of a dynamic process, always in motion.

they sketch or draw to capture some of their ideas, and sometimes they jot down notes. Many teachers give students a personal writer's notebook so they can record ideas, pieces of language, and sketches. The notebook becomes a resource for ideas. Writers start with what we have called a "discovery draft," which means getting ideas down on paper quickly and revisiting and rereading the draft to determine what fits, what to keep, and what to revise. Going back over the initial draft reveals "holes" in the story or logic of the piece. The revising process may lead to adding, deleting, or reorganizing the material.

When the piece has been revised to the writer's satisfaction, there is still editing and proofreading that will be needed. Here, the writer hones the language for precise meaning and evaluates it for conventions. With every piece they produce, young writers are expected to edit for the conventions they understand at the time. A very young writer, for example, might check to see that he has left spaces between words, that all the words he knows are written correctly, and that he ends a sentence with a period. Older writers would check punctuation and paragraphing and expect to produce a piece with conventional spelling. An excellent final draft that has been edited would be placed in the writing portfolio as "finished." As the writer collects pieces all year, she can look back on them to choose those that are most effective. She may even elect to revisit and expand a piece.

It's important to remember that the writing process is *recursive*. We have to lay it out in order to understand it, but the steps are not precisely linear. At any point in time, a writer may leap forward to edit or move back to redraft or rehearse with others. So, a writer may categorize a piece roughly as in the "revising stage" yet also incorporate some actions that belong to another phase.

## Inferring Competencies by Observing Phonics and Spelling Behaviors

The continuum for phonics, spelling, and word study is derived from three decades of work with teachers and students as well as reading research (of others and our own) on how children learn about sounds, letters, and words over time. Our work is based on the premise that not only do children need to acquire phonics and word analysis understandings, but they also need to apply these understandings daily to reading and writing continuous text. We believe *it is essential* for all readers and writers to have a wide range of word-solving strategies—possibly hundreds—that they can use rapidly, flexibly, and in a largely unconscious way as they move through a text, maintaining a focus on meaning.

## Grade-by-Grade Continuum

The grade-by-grade Phonics, Spelling, and Word Study continuum presents a general guide to the kinds of understandings students will need to acquire by the end of each grade. These understandings are related to the texts that they are expected to read at the appropriate levels. In presenting the grade-by-grade continuum, we are not suggesting that students should be held back because they do not know specific details about letters, sounds, and words. Instead, we are suggesting that specific teaching will be needed to support learners. The continuum can help classroom teachers and interventionist teachers work together to make decisions about the kind of support or extra services that will be most helpful to each learner.

## Nine Areas of Learning

Each grade level lists principles over which students will have developed control by the end of the school year. Across grades PreK–8, the principles are organized into nine broad categories of learning. These are related to the levels of texts that students are expected to read upon completing that grade. (The principles also are related to writing in that students use letter-sound relationships, spelling patterns, and word structure as they spell words while writing meaningful messages. Teachers will find much evidence of learning about phonics as they examine students' writing.) Some of the nine areas apply to all grades, while others phase out as students gain full control of them.

The nine areas of learning are listed below. It's important to note that the first three areas only apply to prekindergarten through grade one.

- **Early literacy concepts:** Very early understandings related to how written language or print is organized and used—how it works.
- **Phonological awareness:** The awareness of words, rhyming words, onsets and rimes, syllables, and individual sounds (phonemes).
- **Letter knowledge:** The ability to recognize and label the graphic symbols of language.
- **Letter-sound relationships:** The correspondence of letter(s) and sound(s) in written or spoken language.
- **Spelling patterns:** Beginning letters (onsets) and common phonograms (rimes), which form the basis for the English syllable.
- **High-frequency words:** Words that occur often in spoken and written language.
- **Word meaning/vocabulary:** *Word meaning* refers to the commonly accepted meaning of a word in oral or written language. *Vocabulary* often refers to the words one knows in oral language. *Reading vocabulary* refers to the words a person can read with understanding.

**If You Want to Know More**
*The Fountas & Pinnell Comprehensive Phonics, Spelling, and Word Study Guide* is a highly detailed companion to *The Literacy Continuum*. It specifies the appropriate letters/sounds at each grade level and includes all expectations related to phonics, spelling, and word study.

- **Word structure:** The parts that make up a word.
- **Word-solving actions:** The strategies a reader uses to recognize words and understand their meaning(s).

## Relationship to Strategic Actions

We place the behaviors and understandings included in the Phonics, Spelling, and Word Study continuum mainly in the "thinking about the text" category in the twelve systems for strategic actions. At the bottom line, readers must read the words at a high level of accuracy in order to do the kind of thinking necessary to understand the literal meaning of the text. In addition, the continuum focuses on word meanings, or vocabulary. Vocabulary development is an important factor in understanding the meaning of a text and has long been recognized as playing an important role in reading comprehension. As with other continua, keep in mind that the behaviors described here represent goals for a year of instruction.

*The Literacy Continuum* can help classroom teachers and interventionists make decisions about the kind of support or extra services that will be most helpful to each learner.

# Inferring Competencies by Observing Oral Language Behaviors

Within all the contexts that are part of a comprehensive language and literacy curriculum, learning is mediated by oral language. There are numerous references to oral language in every continuum presented in *The Literacy Continuum*. So, in a sense, oral communication is not only an integral part of every component of the curriculum but also a building block toward future communication. Oral language represents students' thinking. We need to intentionally develop the kind of oral language competencies that students need to take them into their future.

We created this continuum to focus on the broader areas of *communication* beyond the printed word. We cannot know exactly the kinds of communication skills that will be important in the future, but we can equip our students with the foundational competencies that will allow them to take advantage of new opportunities for communication.

In the Oral and Visual Communication continuum of *The Literacy Continuum*, we describe goals in specific terms for two large categories, Listening and Speaking and Presentation, for each grade level, PreK–8.

## Listening and Speaking

**Listening and Understanding** It is important that students develop the habit of listening with commitment, and that means with intent to understand

and respond. There's a lot to listen to—books read aloud daily, enlarged texts, the teacher and other students in discussion during guided reading and guided writing, book clubs, and reading and writing minilessons. All of the contexts involve listening to both the teacher and other students.

**Social Interaction** Constructive social interactions are basic to a happy life and also enable individuals to work collaboratively with others and, as a result, accomplish more. They are key to developing community both in school and in life. Throughout school, students need the opportunity to learn the social conventions that make productive dialogue work.

**Extended Discussion** The ability to participate in extended discussion is basic to expanding reading comprehension and participating in inquiry in the content areas and elsewhere. As they work together collaboratively, students need to learn to sustain a line of conversation and pursue ideas in a way that continually builds understanding. One student's comments may add to another's or provide a different perspective to consider, and everyone grapples with new ideas.

**Content** It's not a matter of just a lot of talk. Students need to talk *about* something important—ideas, subject matter, information—in other words, content. Talk without content can be empty and will not nourish learning. Over the years, students learn to articulate predictions, inferences, and arguments. They back up their points with evidence from the text and grow more skillful in the art of argument.

**Cultural Sensitivity** The school community is a place where students learn to respect cultural, linguistic, ethnic, racial, and gender differences. In an ideal world, all students would experience the process of learning a new language and have a shared experience of what this process is like. But that rarely happens. So it is essential that all students learn sensitive, respectful ways of interacting with emerging multilingual speakers who are learning English. Supportive interactions with peers in the classroom is the fastest and most pleasurable way for English learners to acquire the new language. At the same time, all students are given the opportunity to learn culturally sensitive language for talking about cultural differences.

Performance reading can be a first step toward helping children feel more comfortable when presenting in front of their peers.

## Presentation

Many adults are fearful about speaking in front of an audience—even to a small group—and some avoid presentations altogether. The likeliest reason for such fear is a lack of successful experiences speaking in front of groups, or even worse, bad experiences. In the literacy-rich classroom, students have many opportunities to speak in small and whole-class groups that are accepting and supportive of their efforts. The teacher and the other students do not speak in an evaluative way—thinking in terms of and using words like "good" or "bad." They listen in a committed way, ask questions, and tell what they found interesting. This careful consideration of the speaker's words is affirming, helps to extend the speaker's thinking and skill, and builds confidence. We describe goals for these qualities:

**Voice** If speakers have the opportunity to present in a safe environment, they develop a personal style, or "voice," that captures the interest of an audience. They begin to establish a speaking style of their own.

**Conventions** While we recognize that students are on a journey toward using language conventions, we also recognize that, ultimately, we do want students to enunciate clearly, talk at appropriate volume, and use conventional grammar. Conventions can be developed only by using oral language to communicate with others both in social interactions and in more formal presentations. In a literacy-rich classroom, students have opportunity to speak to the group every day and also to make more formal presentations to the class.

**Organization** Students need experience planning and organizing what they say. If they have experience making presentations that are clear and well-organized, that skill will spill over into all of their speaking experiences.

**Word Choice** Word selection is something that is learned through use over time. Students can plan effective word use for presentations; in the process, they borrow from all the literary language they have encountered in texts. As they use language, they incorporate appropriate words into the discussions they have with others. Making effective word choices depends on having a large vocabulary from which to choose, and in daily interactions, these words must be available on an unconscious level.

**Ideas and Content** Effective speakers can establish an argument using logic and evidence, influence others' point of view with persuasive language and relevant examples, and present ideas with elaboration that helps others understand them. Their interactions, discussion, and presentations are *substantive*. They are concise rather than rambling or repetitive.

**Media** Increasingly, speakers enhance their presentations with different kinds of visual displays—pictures, drawings, posters, electronic, or multimedia. Using a laptop, tablet, or smart phone, speakers can find and utilize videos, music, photo essays, sound effects, a variety of voices, and more to interest an audience.

## Using the Oral and Visual Communication Continuum

Teachers can use this continuum in connection with the Writing continuum. As in the Writing continuum, no texts are listed because the students themselves are producing the texts—oral, written, and visual. Often students will need to make outlines or notes for presentation, and sometimes they will need to write speeches. But most of the time, oral and written communication is a highly creative process that involves many ways of presenting one's ideas to others. The goals listed in this continuum can help teachers observe students' interactions and make decisions about how to help them become more effective in small- or large-group situations. If students have daily opportunities to present their ideas to others in a safe and supportive environment, they will grow in confidence and verbal ability.

# Inside *The Literacy Continuum*

The eight individual continua found in *The Literacy Continuum* are arranged according to instructional context to help teachers understand the goals for each kind of teaching (Figure 9-1). Each context begins with a general introduction that provides useful information to teachers. The eight continua are organized in the following ways.

## Grade by Grade

Seven continua are organized by grade level. Within each grade, you will find the continua for (1) interactive read-aloud and literature discussion, (2) shared and performance reading, (3) writing about reading, (4) writing, (5) oral and visual communication, (6) digital communication, and (7) phonics, spelling, and word study. These seven continua are presented at each grade level, PreK–8. You can turn to the section for a grade level and find all seven. If teachers have students who are working below grade level, they can consult the next lower grade continuum in the area of interest; if they have students working above grade level, they can consult for the continuum the grade above for ideas.

## Level by Level Organization

The guided reading continuum is organized according to the Fountas & Pinnell text gradient levels A to Z (see Chapter 17). These levels typically correlate to grades K–8, but students vary along them in their instructional levels. It is important for all students to receive guided reading instruction at a level that allows them to expand their ability to process text with a minimum of teacher support.

These levels represent categories of increasing complexity. Progressively, each level represents a small rise in challenge to the reader.

# *Continuum* Close-Up

Below we provide two excerpts from the Interactive Read-Aloud and Literature Discussion continuum for grade 2—a page from Selecting Texts, which includes characteristics of suitable texts (on the left), and a page from Selecting Goals, which includes behaviors to notice, teach, and support (on the right).

> When **selecting texts** for one of the reading instructional contexts, teachers need to consider the level of support they will need to provide to children to help them process and think about the text. This, of course, will vary both by book and over the course of the year—more support at the beginning and less at the end.

> **Red bullets** show new text characteristics introduced at the grade level–in this case at grade 2. Texts with these characteristics may require extra attention.

> The continuum describes the **characteristics of texts** suitable for students at each grade and in each of the reading instructional contexts. Together, the characteristics provide a broad look at the range and types of texts students should encounter over the course of a year. Teachers may also want to use these characteristics when choosing texts to add to their own classroom libraries.

GRADE **2**

*INTERACTIVE READ-ALOUD AND LITERATURE DISCUSSION*

## Selecting Texts  Characteristics of Texts for Reading Aloud and Discussion

Interactive Read-Aloud and Literature Discussion

### GENRE

#### ▶ Fiction

- Realistic fiction
- Traditional literature: e.g., folktale, tall tale, fairy tale, fable
- Fantasy
- Hybrid texts
- Special types of fiction: e.g., adventure story; animal story; family, friends, and school story; humorous story

#### ▶ Nonfiction

- Simple expository nonfiction
- Simple narrative nonfiction
- Simple biography
- Memoir
- Procedural texts
- Persuasive texts
- Hybrid texts

### FORMS

- Series books
- Picture books
- Chapter books
- Poems
- Nursery rhymes, rhymes, and songs
- Poetry collections
- Plays
- Types of poetry: lyrical poetry, free verse, limerick, haiku
- Letters

### TEXT STRUCTURE

- Simple narratives with straightforward structure (beginning, middle, several episodes, and ending) but more episodes included
- Many texts with repeating episodes or patterns
- Stories with simple plot (problem and solution)
- Informational texts related to a larger topic, sometimes with subtopics
- Underlying structural patterns: description, cause and effect, chronological sequence, temporal sequence (e.g., life cycles, how-to books), compare and contrast

- Informational texts with clearly defined overall structure and simple categories
- Simple biographical and historical texts with narrative structure
- Informational texts with some examples of simple argument and persuasion

### CONTENT

- Content that is appropriate for children's cognitive development, social and emotional maturity, and life experience
- Content that engages children's intellectual curiosity and emotions
- Language and word play related to concepts, parts of speech, and sound devices such as alliteration, assonance, onomatopoeia
- Familiar content that is authentic and relevant
- Humor that is easy to grasp: e.g., silly characters, funny situations, jokes, word play
- Content that reinforces and expands a child's experience and knowledge of self and the world
- Some content that may be beyond some children's immediate experiences
- Content that reflects a wide range of settings, languages, and cultures
- Some content linked to specific areas of study as described by the school curriculum or standards
- Realistic characters, settings, and events that occur in realistic fiction
- Imaginary characters, events (some nonsensical and funny), settings that occur in fantasy
- Content that reflects increasing understanding of the physical and social world

### THEMES AND IDEAS

- Themes reflecting everyday life
- Some books with multiple ideas that are easy to understand
- Ideas close to children's experiences

### LANGUAGE AND LITERARY FEATURES

- Elements of traditional literature and modern fantasy: e.g., the supernatural, imaginary and otherworldly creatures, gods and goddesses, talking animals
- Basic motifs of traditional literature and modern fantasy: e.g., struggle between good and evil, magic, the hero's quest, special character types, fantastic or magical objects, wishes, trickery, transformations
- Predictable story outcomes typical of traditional literature: e.g., good overcomes evil
- Some literary language typical of traditional literature: e.g., *once upon a time, long ago and far away, happily ever after*
- A few texts with settings distant in time and place from children's own experiences
- Main characters and supporting characters, some with multiple dimensions
- Multiple characters, each with unique traits
- Character development as a result of plot events
- Character dimensions (attributes) and relationships revealed through dialogue and behavior
- Variety in presentation of dialogue among multiple characters
- Predictable and static characters with simple traits typical of traditional literature
- Simple plot with problem and resolution
- Plot with a few episodes
- Most texts told from a single point of view
- Most texts written in first- or third-person narrative
- Language used to make comparisons
- Descriptive language conveying a range of human feelings: e.g., joy, sadness, anger, eagerness
- Descriptive language conveying sensory experiences (imagery)
- Poetic language
- Some figurative language
- Some procedural texts written in second person
- Mostly assigned dialogue
- Procedural language: e.g., step-by-step, directions, how-to
- Persuasive language

40  *The Fountas & Pinnell Literacy Continuum, Grades PreK–8*

In **Selecting Goals**, we list behaviors and understandings that are categorized for thinking *within*, *beyond*, and *about* texts.

## Selecting Goals  Behaviors and Understandings to Notice, Teach, and Support *(cont.)*

Interactive Read-Aloud and Literature Discussion

**INTERACTIVE READ-ALOUD AND LITERATURE DISCUSSION**

> Curriculum goals are included for both **fiction** and **nonfiction texts.**

### FICTION TEXTS *(continued)*

**Setting**
- Recall important details about setting after a story is read
- Recognize and understand that fiction texts may have settings that reflect a wide range of diverse places, languages, and cultures
- ◆ Notice and understand settings that are distant in time and place from students' own experiences
- ◆ Infer the importance of the setting to the plot of the story in realistic fiction and in fantasy

**Plot**
- Follow a plot with multiple events or episodes
- Notice and understand a simple plot with problem and solution
- Notice and remember the important events of a text in sequence
- Check understanding of plots with multiple events and ask questions if meaning is lost
- Tell the important events of a story using the pictures (after hearing the text read several times)
- Notice and understand when a problem is solved
- Include the problem and its resolution in telling what happened in a text
- ◆ Predict what will happen next in a story
- ◆ Predict story outcomes
- ◆ Infer the significance of events in a plot
- ◆ Give opinions about whether a problem seems real
- ■ Recognize and discuss aspects of narrative structure: e.g., beginning, series of events, high point of the story, problem resolution, ending

**Character**
- Recall important details about characters after a story is read
- Follow multiple characters, each with unique traits, in the same story
- Recognize that characters can have multiple dimensions: e.g., can be good but make mistakes, can change
- ◆ Infer characters' traits as revealed through thought, dialogue, behavior, and what others say or think about them and use evidence from the text to describe them
- ◆ Infer the character's traits from the physical details the illustrations include about them

- ◆ Infer characters' intentions, feelings, and motivations as revealed through thought, dialogue, behavior, and what others say or think about them
- ◆ Make predictions about what a character is likely to do and use evidence from the text to support predictions
- ◆ Notice character change and infer reasons from events of the plot
- ◆ Learn from vicarious experiences with characters in stories
- ◆ Notice predictable or static characters (characters that do not change) as typical in traditional literature
- ◆ Infer relationships between characters as revealed through dialogue and behavior
- ◆ Express opinions about the characters in a story (e.g., evil, dishonest, clever, sly, greedy, brave, loyal) and support with evidence
- ■ Understand that the same types of characters may appear over and over again in traditional literature: e.g., sly, brave, silly, wise, greedy, clever
- ■ Understand the difference between realistic characters and those that appear in fantasy
- ■ Express opinions about whether a character seems real

**Style and Language**
- Play with words or language orally: e.g., nonsense words or refrains from texts that are read aloud
- Follow and understand assigned and unassigned dialogue among multiple characters with a clear idea about who is speaking
- ■ Notice when a book has repeating episodes or language patterns
- ■ Notice a writer's choice of interesting words and language
- ■ Notice when a fiction writer uses poetic or descriptive language to show the setting, appeal to the five senses, or to convey human feelings such as loss, relief, or anger
- ■ Recognize how a writer creates humor
- ■ Understand the meaning of some literary language (language of books as opposed to typical oral language)
- ■ Notice and understand how the author uses literary language, including some figurative language
- ■ Notice and remember literary language patterns that are characteristic of traditional literature: e.g., *once upon a time, long ago and far away, happily ever after*
- ■ Recognize some authors by the style of their illustrations, characters they use, or typical plots

> Possible curriculum goals are described in terms of **behaviors and understandings** to notice, teach, and support.

> While **red bullets** indicate new goals for a grade level, keep in mind that all of the goals are important and that children will be challenged to apply each behavior or understanding to more complex texts at each new grade level.

> The **shapes of the bullets** indicate actions for thinking within, beyond, or about the text.

● Thinking **Within** the Text    ◆ Thinking **Beyond** the Text    ■ Thinking **About** the Text

# Using the *Continuum* in Your School

*The Literacy Continuum* is designed to provide teachers, instructional coaches, and literacy leaders with a conceptual tool they can use to think constructively about their work. Naturally, you want to support them in crafting instruction that will link their observations and deep knowledge of their own students with the desired language and literacy learning goals. School leaders are the key to teachers' support systems as they grow in conceptual understanding of their work. Here are some ways to use the continuum to improve teaching and learning in your school.

Teachers, coaches, and literacy leaders use *The Literacy Continuum* to think constructively about their work.

## Planning for and Assessing Teaching

As teachers think about, plan for, and reflect on the effectiveness of providing individual, small-group, and whole-group instruction, they will use areas of the continuum to guide decisions. For example, if a teacher is working with students in guided reading at a particular level, she can use their behaviors and understandings to identify teaching priorities and reflect on student learning following the lesson. The teacher can plan specific teaching moves to support new thinking as she examines the section on interactive read-aloud and literature discussion. The continua for interactive read-aloud, oral language, writing, and phonics, spelling, and word study will be useful in planning explicit reading, writing, and phonics minilessons.

## Linking Assessment to Instruction

Sometimes assessments are administered, and the results are recorded, but then the process stops and the rich information provided is not used to benefit instruction. Teachers may be unsure about what to do with the data or where to go next in their teaching. That's because most assessments reveal what students currently know, not what they almost know or need to learn next. The continuum can be used as a tool for helping teachers identify behaviors students still need to control and then prioritizing those for instruction.

## Link to State and National Standards

This continuum was checked against numerous examples of state and national standards to assure alignment and comprehensiveness. You will find *The Fountas & Pinnell Literacy Continuum* to be much more detailed and more rigorous than most state standards, so it offers a way to make your state goals more specific as a basis for instruction. What really matters is for educators in each school to take ownership of the goals, share them with colleagues, and make them an integral part of teaching.

## Evaluation of Literacy Progress

The continuum can also serve as a guide for evaluating student progress over time. Teachers can evaluate whether students are meeting grade-level standards. Remember that no student would be expected to demonstrate every single competency to be considered on grade level. *Grade level* is always a term that encompasses a range of levels of understanding at any given time.

## Guide to Literacy Teaching in Supplemental Intervention

Some students will need extra support in order to be successful in literacy learning and may participate in supplementary reading or writing help. *The Literacy Continuum* is particularly helpful when the classroom teacher and the interventionist teacher work together to identify the students' strengths and areas of need. In this way, both teachers provide coherence in their instruction because they are working together as partners and are focused on the same goals. Assessment, observation, and the continuum will help teachers identify specific areas in which students need additional help and will guide appropriate intervention.

## Reporting Progress to Parents

The continuum document is extensive and can be overwhelming to noneducators. We do not recommend that teachers share it with parents. Of course, teachers can use the continuum to locate specific information they want to provide about a child's progress, then shape it into language that non-teachers can more easily understand. On a related note, we have always said that a reading level is a teacher's tool, not a child's label. However, parents have a right to know how their child's learning is progressing over time. To convey this information, teachers might show parents a book their child could read early in the year and compare it to one the child is reading at the time of the parent conference. That kind of comparison usually is more helpful to parents than a level which is easily misunderstood. Parents sometimes think that a student should be reading at *one level* all the time, and that is simply not so. In fact, for choice reading, book clubs, and contexts other than guided reading, levels are not significant.

## Foundation for School and/or District Goals

Because this continuum is a detailed description of every aspect of the language arts, you may want to adopt the continuum as your goals for instruction. Alternatively, you may want to review the document for additional or more granular goals for your school or district. Remember, too, that these grade-level expectations are consistent with state and national standards in general. Depending on local priorities, you may want to adjust them lower or higher.

# A Basis for Instructional Coaching

An instructional coach (often called a literacy coach) can use the continuum as a foundation for coaching conversations. It will be useful for coaches to help teachers become able to access information quickly in their copies of the continuum as part of their reflection on lessons they have taught and on their planning. In other words, the coach can help the teachers really get to know the continuum as a tool so they can access the information inside it more easily on their own. Typically, the coach and teacher would use the continuum as a reference before, during, and after the observation of a lesson. The continuum enables the coach to focus the conversation on critical areas of teaching and learning—behaviors to notice, teach, and support to help students read, write, and talk proficiently. It is also an excellent tool for discussing and analyzing texts in a variety of genres and at a variety of levels. The continuum will add specificity to the conversation that will extend teachers' understandings of learning processes and development over time. Ultimately the teacher will be able to use the continuum independently to learn more about teaching.

A literacy coach can use *The Literacy Continuum* to help teachers focus on observable student behaviors and understandings.

## Pre-Observation Conference

- The coach and teacher think about and analyze students' strengths, as well as their learning needs, referring to the continuum as appropriate. The teacher identifies students' strengths and prioritizes a few goals for the lesson.

- They may examine data from students' assessments or the teacher's ongoing observation, again using the continuum expectations as a reference.

- They may look at lesson artifacts—texts the teacher is using or student writing—and consider them in the light of text characteristics for the particular area, thinking about the learning opportunities for students.

## Observation of Lessons

- The continuum is not designed to be used as a checklist. Rather, it is a foundation for discussing and prioritizing critical areas of development.

- The continuum offers a way of sharpening observation. During observation, coaches can keep in mind the evidence of student understanding and shifts in learning. This foundational knowledge will help the coach gather specific evidence of students' learning that can be discussed later with the teacher.

## Post-Observation Conference

■ The continuum will provide a guide as to the appropriateness of texts or tasks in terms of students' current understandings and what they need to learn next.

■ The coach and teacher can use the continuum to analyze the teaching and its effectiveness in meeting the goals discussed in the pre-observation conference.

■ They can discuss examples of behaviors that provide evidence of student understanding.

■ Together, the coach and teacher can use the continuum to help set new learning goals for the students and to begin to plan for teaching.

The ultimate goals of every coaching interaction are to help the teacher expand his knowledge of language and literacy learning and to analyze the effectiveness of the teaching. By talking about the ideas in the continuum and observing students carefully, teachers will come to understand more about the processes

---

### BIG IDEAS FROM *THE LITERACY CONTINUUM*

Across every area of the continuum, several important principles emerge:

- **Students learn by talking.** Talking represents students' thinking. When students engage in conversation that is grounded in a variety of texts–those that students read, hear read aloud, or write–they expand their ability to comprehend ideas and use language to share thinking.

- **Students need to process a large amount of written language.** A dynamic language and literacy curriculum provides many daily opportunities for students to read books of their choice independently, to read more challenging and instructional material with teacher guidance, and to hear teacher-selected and grade-appropriate texts read aloud.

- **The ability to read and comprehend texts is expanded through talking and writing.** Students need to acquire a wide range of ways to write about their reading and also to talk about texts with the teacher and other students.

- Learning deepens when students engage in **reading, talking, and writing about texts** across many different instructional contexts. Each mode of communication provides a new way to process the ideas learned from oral and written texts and from each other.

- **Learning** does not occur in discrete stages but is a **continually evolving** process.

- The same concepts are **acquired** and then **elaborated over time.**

- Many **complex literacy understandings** take years to develop.

- **Students learn by applying what they know** to the reading and writing of increasingly complex texts.

- Learning does not automatically happen; most **students need expert teaching** to develop high levels of reading and writing expertise.

- **Learning is different but interrelated** across different kinds of language and literacy activities; one kind of learning enhances and reinforces others.

---

of learning language, reading, writing, and digital communication. The continuum serves as a guide that becomes internalized through its consistent use. Teachers who use it over time find that the understandings recorded in the continuum become part of their thinking and their teaching decisions.

## A Few Cautions

We need to have a vision of expected levels of learning because it helps in making effective instructional decisions; even more important, it helps us to identify students who need intervention.

At the same time, we would not want to apply these expectations in an inflexible way. We need to recognize that students vary widely in their progress—sometimes moving quickly and sometimes getting bogged down. They may make faster progress in one area than another. The continua should help you intervene in more precise ways to help students. But it is also important to remember that learners may not necessarily meet *every* expectation at all points in time. Nor should any one of the understandings and behaviors be used as criteria for promotion to the next grade. Educators can look thoughtfully across the full range of grade-level expectations as they make decisions about individual students.

It is also important to recognize that just because grade-level expectations exist, not all teaching will be pitched at that level. Through assessment, you may learn that your class only partially matches the behaviors and understandings on the continuum. Almost all teachers find that they need to consult the material at lower and higher levels (one reason that the Guided Reading continuum is not graded).

## The Takeaway

If we look at development over time, it becomes obvious that literacy is a complex process that involves growth in both thinking and action. Readers and writers grapple with many concepts simultaneously. They build in-the-head networks of understanding that continually grow. Yet, their attention is not on what is happening in their brains. They are not exercising skills like muscles. They are reading exciting stories that appeal to their imaginations and inspire them. They are exploring interesting topics, seeking answers to questions, and making discoveries. They are feeling the power of expressing their thoughts in writing to known audiences and sometimes to an audience that is far away. They see themselves as readers and writers, and it's the teacher's job to create the learning opportunities for them to build an effective literacy processing system.

*The Fountas and Pinnell Literacy Continuum* is a practical tool that helps teachers and literacy leaders think about, plan for, and reflect on the literacy instruction they provide to individuals, small groups, and the whole class. It describes the characteristics of texts that students should experience at every grade and the observable behaviors and understandings of proficient readers, writers, and language users that teachers may choose to notice, teach, and support.

In Chapter 10, we shift our focus to how you can develop or refine your schoolwide student assessment system so it will measure proficiency—and students' progress toward it—in ways that are consistent with your school's vision and goals for literacy learning.

## Think About Your School

- What tools are teachers using to inform and guide their work? Whether or not you are using *The Literacy Continuum* in your school, do teachers have tools that enable them to determine specific teaching goals based on solid evidence of what students know and can do?

- What tools do teachers use to document change over time in students' literacy development?

- How well do teachers understand reading as a complex process instead of one that is simple and linear?

## Move Your School Forward

- The instructional coach or professional learning team leader can gather a group of teachers to reflect on how consistent and coherent the curriculum goals are in the school. You may want to establish a *Literacy Continuum* team that can focus on and support its use in the school.

- Make an action plan to achieve coherence in the teachers' goals within and across the grades. Set a timeline to gather together to evaluate progress.

# Chapter 10

# Designing a Comprehensive Literacy Assessment System

*Assess what you value and value what you assess.*
—Grant Wiggins

IN CHAPTER 9, WE discussed the behaviors and understandings evidenced by proficient readers, writers, and language users, and we described a variety of competencies that are evident when children read, talk about, and write about books. In this chapter, we will think together about how to measure the competencies of each child for the purposes of informing instruction, documenting progress across the year and across the grades, and reporting the student's progress to stakeholders.

Assessment begins with the child. In fact, we view the individual child, the curriculum (goals), instruction, and assessment as essential parts of a coherent whole. Each child brings a unique set of lived experiences, interests, and competencies. The instructional program grows naturally out of a precisely built curriculum, and assessments measure progress toward curricular goals. In this way, the assessment system supports both the curriculum and the instructional program, provides continuous and actionable information about student progress toward learning goals, and helps teachers tailor instruction to the unique strengths and needs of individual students.

## Getting Started

As with most initiatives, designing or refining a comprehensive assessment system requires a strong team. If you've already assembled a school-based data or assessment team, you're off to a good start. Probably that team consists of a principal or assistant principal, grade-level teachers, an instructional or literacy coach, an interventionist, and specialists. Although this team may have been assembled for the purpose of analyzing data from your current assessment system, its members should be well suited to the task of identifying what a comprehensive assessment system might look like and determining how your current system stacks up against that vision.

If you want or need to assemble a team from scratch, start with people who have demonstrated interest or experience in assessment-related issues. You might also consider starting with a very small group and growing the team as needed.

## Remember What You Value

Complex decisions are easier to arrive at when you consider them in relation to your school's core values. We have discussed the importance of identifying and recording the values and beliefs that you and your colleagues hold for students and for educators. Before you get deeply into the process of designing or refining your school's assessment system, we urge you and your team to devote all or a portion of your first meeting to looking back at what you value—and to revisit those values often during your work together. This will ensure that all parts of your school's assessment design are aligned with, and firmly grounded in, what you most want for the students and educators in your school.

As with every new initiative, assessment design should begin with a look at what you value most for students and teachers.

## Know What You Want to Know

What do you want to know about each student as a reader and writer? That's a complex question but once it is answered, you'll have a road map for your selection of evaluation tools. With your team, take a moment to jot down at least five things you want your school's assessment system to reveal about each student's competencies as a *reader*. Your list might include some of the following:

- What is the evidence that the student loves to read and write?
- What kinds of texts can she read with high accuracy?
- What is her fluency on a variety of texts she reads?

- How deep is her understanding of texts?

- How accurate is her reading?

- What processing behaviors does she exhibit when reading easy, instructional, or hard texts?

- Can she articulate her understandings in oral language and/or in writing?

- What quantity of reading does she do? How much is voluntary?

- Does she read and understand a variety of genres?

- Does she read at expected grade-level goals?

- Can she think analytically about texts, understanding aspects of text structure?

- What kinds of writing does the student do?

- Does she see herself as a writer?

- Can she write in a variety of genres?

- Does she use conventions appropriately and show improvement over time?

- Is she developing her voice as a writer?

- What craft moves does she show in writing pieces?

- Does she know how to organize her writing to communicate ideas effectively?

- Does she know how to communicate the main points of a story or topic for readers to understand?

- Is she learning to use vocabulary and make word choices to communicate her message?

*"Educators have come to rely mainly on systematic testing of outcomes rather than systematic observation of learning."*
–Marie Clay

## Two Categories of Assessment

With a better sense of what you want to know about the readers and writers in your school, you're ready to think about the categories and types of assessments that can be used to collect the information.

As shown in Figure 10-1, an effective and comprehensive assessment system includes multiple assessment tools that are designed for different purposes. The overall goal is to provide you and the other teachers in your school with varied types of reliable information that will tell you what you most want to know about your students and to inform impactful teaching decisions.

On the next few pages, we describe the components that we believe are most important to include in your school's assessment system. These components fall into two categories: *continuous assessment* and *interval assessment*. Both are essential, both are systematically rather than randomly applied, and both can be built into the school day/week or integrated into the rhythm of the school year.

| TWO ESSENTIAL ASSESSMENT TYPES | | |
|---|---|---|
| **ASSESSMENT TYPE** | **PURPOSE** | **DATA SOURCES AND TOOLS** |
| **CONTINUOUS** | • Provides a constant flow of information about student progress toward learning goals.<br>• Helps teachers systematically tailor instruction to the precise needs of individual students.<br>• Provides information to use in forming and reforming small temporary groups for instruction. | • Observational notes from reading, writing, and word study lessons<br>• Running records at differentiated intervals<br>• Conferring notes<br>• Reading, writing, and word study lesson notes<br>• Reader's notebook entries<br>• Writer's notebook entries<br>• Writing artifacts<br>• Writing rubrics<br>• Word study folders |
| **INTERVAL** | • Helps teachers find reading levels and form small temporary groups for instruction at the beginning of the year.<br>• Helps teachers make decisions about instruction at distinct points in the school year.<br>• Helps teachers assess effectiveness of a quarter, half-year, or year of instruction. | • Benchmark assessments<br>• Running records at differentiated intervals<br>• Writing to a prompt at intervals<br>• Writing rubric<br>• Diagnostic group or individual phonics/word study subtests<br>• State and district standardized assessments<br>• Student interviews or interest surveys |

**Figure 10-1.** A comprehensive and effective assessment system includes different tools for different purposes.

## Continuous Assessment

The most useful assessment data are collected every day by teachers as they build systematic assessment into instructional contexts (soft data). Teachers learn to interpret data quickly and to use it in the context of everything they know about the child. Such data includes:

■ Anecdotal (observational) notes taken as children read, discuss books, write, and talk about their writing in small groups and in conferences.

■ Running records of coded reading, including level of text read, accuracy rate, fluency score on a rubric, and scores on comprehension.

■ Artifacts such as writing in response to reading and fiction and nonfiction pieces developed by engaging in the writing process.

- Entries in a reader's or writer's notebook.
- Writing rubrics for evaluating writing.
- Observations of students' performance in word study activities.
- Teacher-made or acquired assessments of phonics and spelling.
- Student interviews or interest surveys.
- Students' self-evaluations of writing and reading with or without a rubric.

The collection described above includes both quantitative and qualitative information. It forms a pattern of information that is collected as part of the daily classroom literacy time and shows patterns of growth and change. This is the most useful body of information to track progress and inform daily teaching. This type of assessment focuses on the students you are serving right now—today. It gives teachers the data they need to teach responsively, making adjustments to accommodate individual interests and differences and supporting lifts in learning. In addition to the above distinctions, continuous assessments may be administered in group or individual settings and range from standardized to informal forms. We briefly discuss the most useful forms of continuous assessment below.

## The Value of Systematic Observation

Teachers are central to the assessment process and there is no substitute for the rich data they can collect. As they work with students and examine the artifacts of their teaching, teachers provide the most valuable interpretation of assessment data provided that they have the support and professional learning opportunities they need to develop expertise in this area. Teachers need:

- An understanding of the complex processes of reading and writing.
- The ability to observe, document, and analyze reading and writing behaviors.
- The ability to record and interpret data.
- The ability to use data to inform teaching decisions.
- The ability to make moment-to-moment teaching decisions using the observable reading and writing responses of students.

Teachers who recognize the value of precise literacy behaviors are "noticing" teachers. They notice significant evidence of learning and act on it—but this is not an "art" or something teachers are just born being able to do. Graduate courses and professional learning opportunities can support the ability to notice evidence of learning, but it is accelerated by multiple opportunities to carefully observe literacy behaviors and discuss interpretations with colleagues.

### VALIDITY AND RELIABILITY IN ASSESSMENT

An important characteristic of assessment is assuring that it is as close as possible to the skill being assessed. This establishes strong **validity** for the assessment. When an assessment is applied in a standard way, it yields strong **reliability**, which means the results are consistent across items and with different students and different teachers.

An assessment design needs to address the big picture of progress across the year and across the grades. The details of each child's unique path to literacy and the child's evolving identity are equally important in their literacy success. An effective, valid, and reliable assessment system is essential to the well-being and success of each student in your school. It's important to think about them as readers, writers, and language users as they engage in learning about themselves and their world.

When teachers have a clear understanding of behaviors and understandings to notice, they have a lens with which to capture the significant information.

Systematic observation, or "noticing" the precise reading or writing behaviors from the student's view, enables the teacher to uncover the learner's unique strengths. Not only can the teacher gain objective data, but she also can analyze the logic behind the student's responses.

For example, if a young child is reading and stops at a word, that may be a sign that he needs more help to take the word apart letter by letter or part by part. But it is also a sign that he is *monitoring* his reading—not skipping the word (a weak strategy) or substituting something that does not take the print or graphic information into account. He has paused to think and is ready to be taught to search for and use more information. The important thing is that there is evidence of what he can do or almost do. *Partially correct responses provide important information, as responses are not simply right or wrong.*

With another student, the teacher might note the application of some excellent decoding skills on a technical word but also note evidence that there is a lack of understanding either of the vocabulary or of the section of the text. This kind of "eye" builds the ability to teach responsively—that is, directing moment-to-moment teaching decisions to those that will help the individual learner use what he now knows to problem solve or providing quick information to assist the child in moving on.

There are several contexts across reading and writing that are highly productive for observing and gathering information about literacy learning. Students' oral reading is the best source of evidence of the first five systems of strategic actions. Their talk and writing provide evidence of the last seven (Figure 10-2). Additionally, teachers can observe phonics, spelling, and word study competencies while children are reading and writing.

All of these contexts provide teachers with a window into their students' thinking. The closer and more often they observe, the better they will understand what students know and can do as readers, writers, and language users.

## Tools for Continuous Assessment

Observation takes place "on the run" and is recorded through the use of teachers' observational tools and detailed notes. Teachers have several informal assessment tools they can use to assess their students' learning. We will highlight a few that we find the most effective in generating information about students' understandings and growth as readers, writers and language users.

**Running Records of Oral Text Reading**  One of the most powerful assessment tools literacy teachers can use is the running record. It was developed by Marie Clay, who studied the observable behaviors of readers in great detail for

*continued on page 161*

---

### RUNNING RECORDS VERSUS READING RECORDS

A running record and a reading record are essentially the same thing, with one difference: A reading record contains the typed text of the book being read so the teachers can code it, and a running record is basically a blank form. If you are using *Fountas & Pinnell Classroom, Guided Reading* in your school, teachers probably use the preprinted reading records shown in **Figures 10-3 and 10-4** on pages 163 and 164. In this book, we mostly use the term *running record* unless we are referring to a specific form referenced as an example.

## CONTEXTS FOR ASSESSMENT

| CONTEXT | BEHAVIORS AND UNDERSTANDINGS TO OBSERVE | RECOMMENDED OBSERVATION TOOL(S) AND ARTIFACTS FOR ASSESSMENT | WHEN TO CONDUCT OBSERVATIONS |
|---|---|---|---|
| **Oral Reading** | ▪ Significant behaviors such as self-monitoring, word solving, multiple attempts<br>▪ Fluency<br>▪ Accurate reading | ▪ Observational notes<br>▪ Reading/Running record<br>▪ Conference record form<br>▪ Individual Record of Book Making Progress<br>▪ School Record of Book Making Progress | ▪ Guided reading lessons<br>▪ Independent reading conferences |
| **Talk About Reading** | ▪ Understanding of the big ideas of the text<br>▪ Ability to summarize<br>▪ Ability to infer<br>▪ Ability to synthesize new information<br>▪ Ability to notice aspects of the writer's craft<br>▪ Ability to think critically about a text | ▪ Observational notes | ▪ Interactive read-aloud<br>▪ Shared reading<br>▪ Guided reading<br>▪ Independent reading conferences<br>▪ Book clubs<br>▪ Reading minilessons and group share |
| **Writing About Reading** | ▪ Ability to articulate understandings through writing/drawing<br>▪ Ability to summarize<br>▪ Ability to infer<br>▪ Ability to synthesize new information<br>▪ Ability to notice aspects of the writer's craft<br>▪ Ability to think critically about a text | ▪ Reader's notebook entries<br>▪ Writing samples (e.g., written responses to reading, including quick writes, sketches, notes, and so on) | |
| **Writing Process (or the Act of Writing)** | ▪ Ability to initiate writing independently<br>▪ Ability to collect and choose writing ideas<br>▪ Ability to sustain writing for the entire writing time<br>▪ Engagement and enthusiasm for writing<br>▪ Ability to take risks as a writer<br>▪ Ability to plan writing<br>▪ Ability to revise and edit writing<br>▪ Ability to use writing tools (checklists, spelling resources, and so on)<br>▪ Ability to make writing ready for an audience to read | ▪ Writer's notebook entries<br>▪ Observational notes<br>▪ Writing records (e.g., What I Have Learned as a Writer and Illustrator form; Writing Ideas lists; My Writing Projects) | ▪ Independent writing<br>▪ Interactive/Shared writing<br>▪ Writing conferences<br>▪ Writing minilessons and group share<br>▪ Guided writing |

*continued on next page*

**Figure 10-2.** Contexts for Observation

| CONTEXT | BEHAVIORS AND UNDERSTANDINGS TO OBSERVE | RECOMMENDED OBSERVATION TOOL(S) AND ARTIFACTS FOR ASSESSMENT | WHEN TO CONDUCT OBSERVATIONS |
|---|---|---|---|
| **Talk About Writing** | • Ability to self-evaluate writing and talk about what is good about it<br>• Understanding of what is being worked on as a writer<br>• Ability to articulate writing goals<br>• Ability to learn from other writers (mentor texts)<br>• Ability to articulate genre understandings<br>• Ability to use and explain writer's craft<br>• Ability to use and explain conventions<br>• Understanding of the writing process | • Observational notes<br>• Writing folder records (e.g., Writing Goals, My Writing Projects, What I Have Learned as a Writer) | • Interactive/Shared writing<br>• Independent writing<br>• Writing conferences<br>• Guided writing<br>• Writing minilessons<br>• Interactive read-aloud |
| **Fiction and Nonfiction Writing** | • Ability to rehearse writing orally<br>• Ability to sketch and draw to communicate ideas<br>• Ability to gather ideas in notebook<br>• Ability to compose in a variety of genres and forms<br>• Understanding of the characteristics of a variety of genre and forms<br>• Ability to organize writing to communicate a message<br>• Ability to develop ideas and communicate main points clearly<br>• Ability to choose words that clearly communicate ideas<br>• Ability to write with voice<br>• Ability to use conventions (e.g., grammar, spelling, punctuation, and capitalization) both effectively and expressively | • Observational notes<br>• Writer's notebook<br>• Writing rubrics<br>• Writer's notebook entries<br>• Writing in progress (drafts)<br>• Finished writing pieces (published) | • Independent writing conferences<br>• Writing minilessons and group share |
| **Observe Phonics/Spelling Skills While Reading and Writing** | • Knowledge of early literacy concepts<br>• Level of phonological awareness<br>• Extent of letter knowledge<br>• Understanding of letter/sound relationships<br>• Understanding of spelling patterns<br>• Knowledge of high-frequency words<br>• Understanding of word meaning/vocabulary<br>• Understanding of word structures<br>• Knowledge of word-solving actions | • Observational notes<br>• Benchmark assessment system optional assessments<br>• Running/Reading records<br>• Word study folder<br>• Writing About Reading<br>• Fiction and nonfiction writing<br>• Writer's notebook entries<br>• Reader's notebook entries | • Phonics, spelling, and word study<br>• Shared reading<br>• Guided reading<br>• Independent reading conferences<br>• Interactive writing<br>• Independent writing conferences |

*continued from page 158*

many years. Her award-winning research revealed the complex behaviors of children as they learned to read and provided concrete evidence of how their reading behaviors changed over time. She developed a quick, efficient coding and scoring system called "the running record" to capture the individual child's observable reading behaviors so teachers can analyze those precise behaviors to inform instruction.

### An Essential Observation Tool

The running record has become a widely used observational tool that a literacy teacher can use with a child to gain a wealth of information regarding the child's strengths and needs in building an effective reading process. Sitting beside the child, the teacher captures how he reads orally with minimal support, coding the child's reading behaviors as he reads all or a portion of a book. The teacher talks briefly with the child about his understanding and makes a quick teaching point based on the observations. The teacher makes notes about the child's fluency or how the reading sounded, scores the record, and jots down one or two priorities to guide future instruction.

### A Standardized Assessment Used with Seen and Unseen Texts

The running record is a standardized assessment tool for coding, scoring, and analyzing a student's precise reading behaviors as she processes a short book. The coding and procedures are standardized so that if two teachers were to listen to the same student, their records would be the same. A running record can be used at intervals with a set of common books (unseen texts) that are arranged along a gradient of difficulty to document individual progress at two or three points in time (benchmark assessment). It also can be used as a continuous assessment tool to code, score and analyze reading at selected points so as to capture the student's processing and understanding of a text that has been used for small-group instruction the day before (seen text). This procedure enables the teacher to observe how the student works through a text independently, to assess the effects of yesterday's teaching, and to prioritize the emphases for instruction. Teachers' expertise in using this tool can be useful for both continuous and interval assessment.

### Beyond the Numbers: A Look at Processing

On the right side of the reading record, you can see the letters *M*, *S*, and *V*. These codes indicate the sources of information the child used or neglected in attempting to read unfamiliar words. The *M* means the student used meaning, the *S* means the student used the language structure, and the *V* means the student used the letter and sound information. Actually, these categories include a range of information sources derived from the reader's knowledge of the world, vocabulary, graphic information, and phonological information. These category systems provide a systematic way to quickly identify what the reader is attending to and what he is neglecting.

The real value in a running record is the left side of the record, which shows the reader's problem-solving actions. The checkmarks indicate the student was

---

**Using Digital Assessments Effectively** Digital assessments can provide powerful ways to analyze student data. Analytics can show patterns across classrooms and schools as well as outliers that can alert educators to very specific needs and help individual students get additional supports and interventions quickly. Many digital assessments also provide highly visual, easy-to-interpret reports that can facilitate the reporting of student progress to families. Over time, the data that are accumulated about students can provide a nuanced picture of their strengths and progress.

But technology can also overwhelm educators with an avalanche of data. Too many reports, and no time to analyze and reflect on the information they contain, may actually delay and complicate decision-making. And too often digital assessments do not measure student competencies that reflect the shared values of your school. Make it a goal that digital assessments provide actionable information that is meaningful to teachers and families, delivered in the right amounts at the right time, and connected to your school's values.

The running record is a quick, practical, and informative tool for classroom use.

using multiple sources of information and was checking on himself as he read. Notice anything other than the checkmarks, and you get a window into the student's in-the-head processing from his actions. You can infer that when the student read a word incorrectly and then fixed it, he was self-monitoring and correcting.

### A Wealth of Data

The process of listening to a student read a text and having a brief conversation about the reading yields a wealth of information:

- The percentage of words read accurately.
- The percentage of errors (or number of errors for higher levels) that are self-corrected by the reader. A self-correction is not counted as an error when accuracy is calculated.
- A fluency score based on a rubric.
- Anecdotal notes from a comprehension conversation or a comprehension score created through using a standard form of questions and invitations to talk, with the application of a rubric.
- A record of behavior indicating the quality of the student's processing of a text.

To gain a brief understanding of the information a teacher gathers in a very short time, take a look at the records shown in Figures 10-3 and 10-4. The teacher used forms that contain the text of the book each child will be reading.

**Jeimar** Jeimar read a book from the Guided Reading Collection titled *Wise Folk: A Book of Tales*. The text is a Level S fiction book, and Jeimar read it with an accuracy rate of 97%, which is satisfactory and an indication that this may be a good instructional level for him. He made four self-corrections in his reading of 244 words of the story. His score for fluency, however, was 1, indicating that he read primarily in two-word phrases with some three- and four-word groups and some word-by-word reading. There was almost no smooth, expressive interpretation of meaning and his voice did not reflect the meaning. The reading was slow.

Fluency is certainly a matter of concern and needs to be addressed strongly in instruction. It depends on smooth processing and an awareness of how reading should sound. Jeimar's teacher's notes reveal her thinking that he is an inefficient reader who does a great deal of rereading to monitor and confirm. This slows him down and contributes to lower comprehension.

Jeimar's comprehension score is 4, which indicates limited proficiency in understanding the text (comprehension rubric not shown). He could talk about the "facts" in the introduction to the book but had more trouble when asked to think beyond a literal level. The broad question becomes: *What instruction is needed to increase his fluency and comprehension?*

**Kamila** Take a look at Kamila's reading record on page 164. Like Jeimar, she read 244 words of the introduction to *Wise Folk: A Book of Tales*. Her

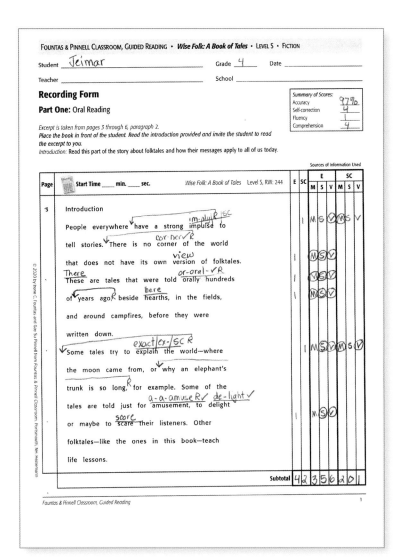

Student **Jeimar**   Grade **4**   Date _____

Teacher _____   School _____

## Recording Form

**Part One:** Oral Reading

*Excerpt is taken from pages 3 through 6, paragraph 2.*
*Place the book in front of the student. Read the introduction provided and invite the student to read the excerpt to you.*
*Introduction: Read this part of the story about folktales and how their messages apply to all of us today.*

Summary of Scores:
Accuracy — 97%
Self-correction — 4
Fluency —
Comprehension — 4

**Part One:** Oral Reading *continued*

**Figure 10-3.** Jeimar's Reading of *Wise Folk: A Book of Tales*

Read mostly with a slow rate with mostly 2-4 word phrases. Does not consistently read punctuation correctly. Read through ending punctuation several times.

accuracy rate was 97%, and she made two self-corrections. It is interesting here that we have two readers at the same level with the same accuracy percentage. Certainly, accuracy tells only part of the story.

Kamila's fluency score was 3, indicating that she reads primarily in larger, meaningful phrases or word groups. She exhibits mostly smooth, expressive interpretation and pausing guided by the author's meaning and punctuation. There are only a few slowdowns in the oral reading. Her teacher noted that Kamila is an efficient problem-solver who uses multiple sources of information to read words accurately. She slowed down only to problem-solve but then gained momentum again. Finally, her comprehension was satisfactory, and her teacher noted that she read with phrasing and expression at a good pace (comprehension rubric not shown). However, it's worth noting that Kamila's record does not yield much information about her processing of the text because she shows so little overt processing behavior. A teacher can infer from the large amount of accurate processing that she is successfully self-monitoring and using all sources of information and will benefit from an increase in challenge.

Student Kamila    Grade 4    Date _____

Teacher _____    School _____

**Recording Form**

**Part One:** Oral Reading

| Summary of Scores: | |
|---|---|
| Accuracy | 97% |
| Self-correction | 8 |
| Fluency | 3 |
| Comprehension | 6 |

*Excerpt is taken from pages 3 through 6, paragraph 2.*
*Place the book in front of the student. Read the introduction provided and invite the student to read the excerpt to you.*
*Introduction: Read this part of the story about folktales and how their messages apply to all of us today.*

Page 3

**Introduction**

People everywhere have a strong *im-pul ✓* impulse to tell stories. There is no corner of the world that does not have its own version of folktales. These are tales that were told orally hundreds of years ago, beside *hear-th ✓* hearths, in the fields, and around campfires, before they were written down.

Some tales try to explain the world—where the moon came from, or why *a* an elephant's trunk is so long, for example. Some of the tales are told just for *a-muse ✓* amusement, to delight or maybe to scare *the* their listeners. Other folktales—like the ones in this book—teach life lessons.

Subtotal: 3 0 2 2 2 0 0 0

---

**Part One:** Oral Reading *continued*

Page 6

One day the family heard a *sound cl-att SC* clatter from the kitchen. The bowl had dropped from the grandfather's *palms A* palsied hands and lay in pieces on the floor.

"Oh, you stupid, *dumb* clumsy old man," said the father to the grandfather. "Just for that, no supper for you."

Subtotal: 2 1 3 3 2 0 0 1

End Time ____ min. ____ sec.  Total: 7 2 7 8 8 0 0 3

*Read in phrases and paid attention to punctuation. Good pace and read with expression. Only slowed to problem solve a couple of words.*

**Figure 10-4.** Kamila's Reading of *Wise Folk: A Book of Tales.*

As you look at scores, you notice that these two readers are similar but exhibit important differences. They were able to benefit from instruction in the same small group. The real value of the record goes beyond the numbers. Attention to their literacy processing systems indicates that they need different kinds of individual interactions with the teacher. There will be different goals for each. It may be that Kamila can go on to a more complex level very quickly while Jeimar needs more work to process smoothly at this level. Looking at the processing in this way helps the teacher to develop the "ethnographic eye."

*Frequency of the Assessment*

Every classroom teacher needs a system for taking running records so that each student's reading progress can be monitored and the teacher can gain the information needed to guide text selection and teaching emphases for small-group instruction. It's important that the teacher have a strong rationale for how often she uses the record. The frequency needs to be manageable. Typically, the teacher takes a running record every week or two on the students who are having reading difficulty so that the teaching can be fine-tuned to meet their needs. For those who are making good progress and reading at about grade level, the teacher might schedule running records about every 4–6 weeks. Students who are reading well above grade level may need a running record about once a quarter. Of course, these are only estimates because we don't know the students. The point is that teachers need to take a running record on every child on a regular basis and have a system and rationales for conducting them.

### Developing Expertise

Taking running records of children's reading behaviors requires time and practice, but the results are worth the effort. Once learned, the running record is a quick, practical, and highly informative tool. It becomes an integral part of teaching, not only for documenting reading behaviors for later analysis and reflection, but also for sharpening teachers' observational skills and their deep understanding of the reading process.

Though many teachers have had some professional development in the use of running records, if they have not used them almost daily, they may have learned to code and score but not learned enough about how to analyze and use the information. Some teachers have not had enough professional development to gain the ease and flexibility that makes the tool indispensable in guiding their instruction. Learning about the development of each child's literacy processing system yields new understandings about how children build a literary processing system and about instruction. It needs to be a lifelong study for literacy teachers.

**Observation Notes** Observation notes in reading and writing complement running records, as they provide another glimpse in time of students' literacy learning. When teachers take observational notes on students' reading throughout the day and across the course of the year, they can identify individual strengths and needs as well as document change in children's learning over time. We recommend that teachers create a flip chart like the one shown in Figure 10-5 (or stick-on labels that can be placed in a folder) to record observations of individual children through the day. *The Fountas & Pinnell Literacy Continuum*, discussed in Chapter 9, is a helpful tool for honing teachers' lens for observing reading and writing behaviors. As they scan the behaviors and understandings listed in the

**Figure 10-5.** A flip chart like this one makes it easier for teachers to record observational notes.

continuum across grades and levels, they begin to internalize the language and learn to put it into their own words in their observational notes.

**Reading and Writing Rubrics** A rubric is a performance-based assessment tool that teachers can use to gather valuable information about a student's performance on a variety of literacy tasks. Generally, a rubric is used to measure one subject area or one task. It can be used to show progress in a very concrete way toward a well-described set of criteria. The criteria categories are listed along the left side, the categories of proficiency along the top, and the cells of the grid provide description of the criteria at the level of proficiency.

Rubrics are tools for both interval and continuous assessment. Teachers can use a variety of ready-made rubrics for reading and writing, such as those available in the online resources for this book, or they can construct their own with each other or with the students. Simple rubrics help students understand the explicit criteria for proficiency. When students are involved in co-constructing rubrics with friendly language, they gain a better understanding of the criteria and how to use a rubric as a tool for self-assessment. Co-constructed (by teacher and students) rubrics also help guide the literacy task from the beginning as they provide a vision for what students are working toward. Figure 10-6 shows a teacher version, and Figure 10-7 shows a student version of the same writing rubric for memory stories. Through inquiry and immersion in mentor texts, students learn to identify the qualities and characteristics of writing across genres. The qualities listed on these rubrics are meaningful to the students because they have studied and identified them in mentor texts. The writing rubrics not only provide a tool for assessment but also capture students' understandings of what writing in a particular genre means.

**Checklists and Guides** Checklists and guides are other forms of rubrics used in continuous assessment because they list the important criteria and guide assessment and instruction for both teachers and students. The Guide for Observing and Noting Writing Behaviors, found in the online resources for *The Writing Minilessons Book* (Fountas and Pinnell 2022), is one such tool. This guide helps teachers observe students for understandings of genre, craft, conventions, and the writing process. The Guide for Observing and Noting Reading Behaviors, found in the online resources for *The Reading Minilessons Book* (Fountas and Pinnell 2019) poses questions to help teachers analyze running records for evidence of systems of strategic actions. Both guides are based on the behaviors and understandings that appear in *The Literacy Continuum*. By directing the teacher to the important behaviors, the teacher learns more about the reading and writing processes and students' development over time. Whether you use these guides or develop your own based on school or district learning goals, it is helpful for school teams to discuss a common vision of what to look for as evidence of growth in literacy learning.

Checklists and guides help teachers mine student work and behaviors for evidence of what the student understands as a reader, writer, and language user.

*continued on page 169*

**What Is a Rubric?** Typically designed as a grid, a rubric lists performance criteria along the *x*-axis and describes performance levels along the *y*-axis. Educators (and students) look across the rubric row by row to identify the performance level that best describes their work or development.

## TEACHER RUBRIC FOR ANALYZING MEMORY STORIES

| | Limited Proficiency | Approaching Proficiency | Proficiency |
|---|---|---|---|
| **GENRE UNDERSTANDINGS** | **THE WRITER:** | **THE WRITER:** | **THE WRITER:** |
| | ▪ is not at all focused on a meaningful memory<br>▪ shares few or no thoughts or feelings about the memory<br>▪ does not reveal something important about self or life | ▪ is somewhat focused on a meaningful memory, but the significance of the memory is evident<br>▪ shares some thoughts and feelings about the memory<br>▪ reveals something important about self or life | ▪ stays focused on a small, meaningful memory and clearly communicates the significance of the memory<br>▪ shares thoughts and feelings about the memory<br>▪ clearly reveals something important about self or life |
| **CRAFT** | **THE WRITER:** | **THE WRITER:** | **THE WRITER:** |
| **Organization** | ▪ does not sequence the events logically<br>▪ does not write an engaging beginning and ending | ▪ sequences most of the events logically<br>▪ attempts to write an engaging beginning and ending | ▪ sequences all the events logically<br>▪ writes an engaging beginning and ending |
| **Idea Development** | ▪ includes few, if any, details about the important events and/or includes many unimportant details | ▪ includes some interesting details about the most important events as well as a few unimportant details | ▪ includes many interesting details about the most important events and omits unimportant details |
| **Language Use** | ▪ does not use time words, such as *then* and *later*, to show the passage of time | ▪ occasionally uses time words, such as *then* and *later*, to show the passage of time | ▪ consistently uses time words, such as *then* and *later*, to show the passage of time |
| **Word Choice** | ▪ uses no interesting words or sensory details | ▪ uses some interesting words and sensory details to enhance meaning | ▪ uses a range of descriptive words and sensory details to enhance meaning |
| **Voice** | ▪ rarely or never writes in the first person<br>▪ does not write with a unique, personal voice | ▪ usually writes in the first person, using pronouns such as *I, me*, and *my*<br>▪ sometimes writes with a unique, personal voice | ▪ consistently writes in the first person, using pronouns such as *I, me*, and *my*<br>▪ writes consistently with a unique, personal voice |
| **CONVENTIONS** | **THE WRITER:** | **THE WRITER:** | **THE WRITER:** |
| **Handwriting** | ▪ does not form and space letters clearly; the reader has difficulty reading them | ▪ forms and spaces most letters clearly; the reader can read them | ▪ forms and spaces all letters clearly; the reader can read them easily |
| **Spelling** | ▪ spells few, if any, high-frequency or other words correctly | ▪ spells some high-frequency words and other words correctly | ▪ spells most high-frequency words and other words correctly |
| **Punctuation** | ▪ omits end punctuation from most sentences; uses only periods<br>▪ omits quotation marks from simple dialogue or uses them incorrectly | ▪ mostly uses periods, question marks, and exclamation points<br>▪ mostly uses quotation marks correctly in simple dialogue | ▪ consistently uses periods, question marks, and exclamation points<br>▪ consistently uses quotation marks correctly in simple dialogue |
| **Capitalization** | ▪ rarely capitalizes the first letter in a sentence, the first letter of a name, and the pronoun *I* | ▪ mostly capitalizes the first letter in a sentence, the first letter of a name, and the pronoun *I* | ▪ consistently capitalizes the first letter in a sentence, the first letter of a name, and the pronoun *I* |

**Figure 10-6.** Teachers can use a variety of ready-made rubrics or construct their own with each other or with the students.

# STUDENT RUBRIC FOR ANALYZING MEMORY STORIES

| | I need help with this. | I need more practice with this. | I can teach someone about this. |
|---|---|---|---|
| **GENRE UNDERSTANDINGS** | | | |
| | ▪ I did not write about a special moment or memory. | ▪ I wrote some things about a special moment or memory, but I did not write why the memory is important to me. | ▪ I stayed focused on a special moment or memory, and I wrote why the memory is important to me. |
| | ▪ I didn't really share my thoughts or feelings about the memory. | ▪ I shared a few thoughts and feelings about the memory. | ▪ I shared many meaningful thoughts and feelings about the memory. |
| | ▪ I didn't really share anything I learned about myself or life. | ▪ I shared a little about what I learned about myself or life, but it is not clear. | ▪ I shared something important that I learned about myself or life. |
| **CRAFT** | | | |
| **Organization** | ▪ I had trouble writing what happened in the order it happened. | ▪ I tried to write what happened in the order it happened, but sometimes it isn't clear. | ▪ I wrote what happened in the order that it happened. |
| **Ideas** | ▪ I did not write many details about the important parts of my story.<br>▪ I wrote about some things that are not important to my story. | ▪ I wrote some details about the important parts of my story.<br>▪ I wrote only one or two details about things that are not important to my story. | ▪ I wrote many interesting details about the important parts of my story.<br>▪ I did not write details about things that are not important to my story. |
| **Sentences and Flow** | ▪ I did not use time words, like *then* and *later*, to show when things happened. | ▪ I used a few time words, like *then* and *later*, to show when things happened. | ▪ I often used time words, such as *then* and *later*, to show when things happened. |
| **Word Choice** | ▪ The words that I used would not help readers imagine what things looked, sounded, smelled, tasted, or felt like. | ▪ I tried using words to help readers imagine what things looked, sounded, smelled, tasted, or felt like. | ▪ I used many interesting words and phrases to help readers imagine what things looked, sounded, smelled, tasted, or felt like. |
| **Voice** | ▪ I did not use words like *I*, *me*, and *my*.<br>▪ I didn't write in a way that you can hear my voice. | ▪ I tried to use words like *I*, *me*, and *my*.<br>▪ I can sometimes hear my voice in my writing. | ▪ I used words like *I*, *me*, and *my*.<br>▪ I can hear my voice in my writing. |
| **CONVENTIONS** | | | |
| **Handwriting** | ▪ I did not write my letters clearly. It is hard for me to read my writing. | ▪ I wrote many of my letters clearly. Other people can read most of my writing. | ▪ I wrote my letters clearly. Other people can read my writing easily. |
| **Spelling** | ▪ I had a lot of trouble spelling words. | ▪ I spelled some words that I know correctly. | ▪ I spelled many words that I know correctly. |
| **Punctuation** | ▪ I did not end most of my sentences with punctuation.<br>▪ I did not use quotation marks correctly. | ▪ I ended most of my sentences with punctuation.<br>▪ I used quotation marks correctly most of the time. | ▪ I ended all my sentences with punctuation.<br>▪ I used quotation marks correctly. |
| **Capitalization** | ▪ I did not write a capital letter at the start of sentences or names. | ▪ I sometimes used a capital letter for the first letter in a sentence, the first letter of a name, and the word *I*. | ▪ I always used a capital letter for the first letter in a sentence, the first letter of a name, and the word *I*. |

**Figure 10-7.** When students co-construct rubrics, the friendlier language contributes to their understanding of the criteria.

*continued from page 166*

They provide valuable information for the teacher to use for instruction and for informing the day-to-day decisions of responsive teaching.

## Instructional Artifacts: A Wealth of Assessment Data

Assessment tools provide the most information when they are used to analyze authentic and meaningful literacy work. Across the instructional contexts, students are also building up a collection of artifacts such as student writing that offer the teacher opportunities for further observation and deeper analysis. These documents "hold still the evidence of learning" so that teachers can recognize, analyze, and reflect on them. Shifts in student learning become visible when such documents are examined over time.

Teaching teams will enjoy and gain professional expertise from sharing artifacts and talking about the evidence they present. Sometimes teachers formally analyze these artifacts with an assessment tool (e.g., Writing Behaviors or the Guide for Observing and Noting Reading) while other times they use artifacts to inform their observation notes and goals for each child in reading, writing, and phonics and word study.

**The Reader's Notebook** Probably, the students in your school regularly make entries in a reader's notebook. This practice adds to self-reflection and student independence and provides an invaluable window on each student's identity and reading life. In addition to being a powerful instructional tool, the reader's notebook offers valuable data for assessment. In general, reader's notebooks provide teachers with the following kinds of information, all of which have bearing on the assessment of the student as a reader.

- The student's personal identity and perspective as a reader.
- The quantity of books the student has read across the year.
- The number of texts read in each genre, growing from fiction/ nonfiction to the full range over time.
- The list of specific texts, the genre, and student comments and opinions.
- Letters and other forms of writing about reading that reflect the student's thinking about his reading.
- The student's ability to think beyond and about a text.
- The student's ability to recognize genre and articulate the writer's choice of genre.
- The student's ability to see the larger messages in a text and to take on language and vocabulary.
- The student's response to principles taught in the reading minilessons.
- Teachers' responses to student letters and other entries.

---

**Assessing Individual Learners** As you support the policies and procedures in your educational system, consider how your assessment design acknowledges the complexity of language and literacy learning. Every child is not only different from every other child, but the learner's development each day and each week is unique. Concepts such as "average" are not helpful when describing individual learners because each learner starts in a different place and brings a composite of different strengths and experiences. The learner changes by the day and by the week and does not fit one prescribed sequence of learning.

This understanding can help you look at the assessment design with an eye to the use of assessment data for the purpose of informing the instruction of individual children and documenting their unique paths of progress over time. Tools such as individual book graphs and data walls are especially useful because they focus on the individual child.

---

## Reader's Notebook

Name: Aastha

School: _____ Grade: ____

When students write in a reader's notebook, they open a window on their identities and reading lives.

**Books I Read**

7  Title: alphabet adventure

Author: Audrey Wood

If you do some thing good you can do something good.

Every one tried to find i's dot and they did so they get to go to school.

Happy ending.

i found his dot and they could go to school.

7    FEB 2 - 2018

I think every letter is helpful because, every letter tried to rescue i. For example i fell down in the water so they made a rope to rescue him and i lost his dot on the top so every letter tried to find i's dot.

flexible    When i lost his dot no one said "why i cann't we go to school"or"i+'s all i's folt"

kind    If they weren't kind they won't try to find i's dot.

**Begin with the Child**  In the late 1980s, author and educator Donald H. Graves asked teachers to engage in a task. He told them to draw three columns. In column 1, they were told to write the names of all the students in their classroom. If they could not name them it was a serious problem. In the second, they were told to write ten things that they knew about each child. If they couldn't, he said, they were failing these students. Lastly, they were told to put a check mark beside the name of each student who knew that the teacher knew those ten things about them. His point was that if this task could not be performed, the teacher did not know the whole learner—the unique child—which should be imperative for every teacher. Every assessment begins with knowing the whole child

The reader's notebook is very useful in the individual conferences that teachers hold with students. Together, they can look at the students' records of reading and discuss the thinking and opinions collected there. It is also an excellent tool for reporting progress to parents. In one document, they can be shown the quantity and quality of their child's reading. Teachers can share copies of the books students have read and written about, as well as discuss progress made during the quarter, semester, or year.

**Individual Record of Book Reading Progress**  This useful tool allows teachers to document individual student progress across the year. Notice the levels A–Z up the left side, the dates along the bottom, and the title and accuracy scores across the top. Figure 10-8 on page 171 shows Elijah's progress from instructional Level J on his benchmark assessment (unseen text) and the levels at which he was reading documented by a running record about every ten days (seen texts used in guided reading instruction). The circles filled in black show that he was having some difficulty at the level and the accuracy level was below 90 percent. By year's end, he was reading at Level O. This same graph can be kept electronically if your benchmark assessment system includes electronic tools.

**School Record of Book Reading Progress**  It is also important to document student progress from grade to grade. Using a similar process of administering a standardized benchmark assessment two or three times per year (unseen text) and using running records with the books used in guided reading instruction (seen texts) between the benchmark assessments, you can see from Figure 10-9 on page 171 that Heather started kindergarten reading at Level B and was reading at Level U by the end of grade 5.

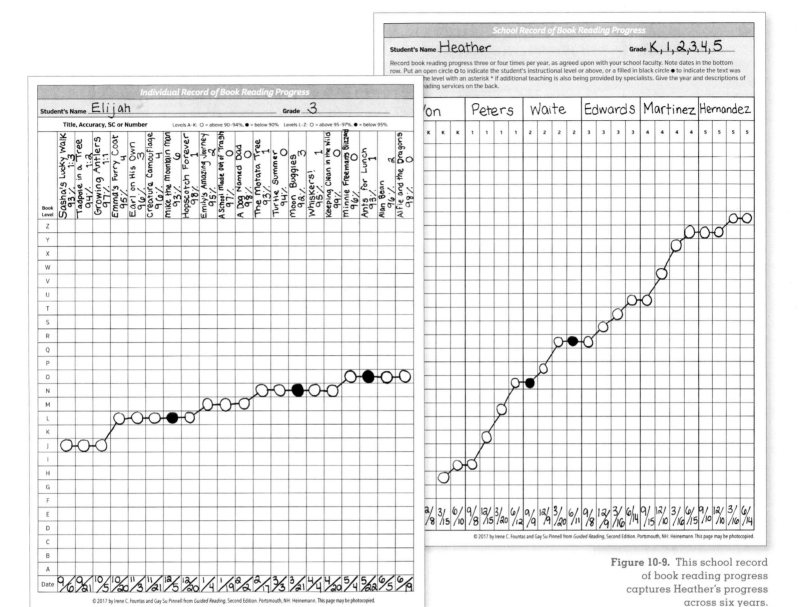

**Figure 10-8.** An individual record of book reading progress for Elijah. Elijah's record of book reading progress shows that he was reading at grade level by year's end.

**Figure 10-9.** This school record of book reading progress captures Heather's progress across six years.

**The Writer's Notebook and the Writing Folder** Using the recursive writing process, students produce writing and drawing as young as preschool (often starting with bookmaking). Whether they are working on making books or writing the first draft of an informational piece, their in-process drafts reflect what they understand about genre, craft, conventions, and the writing process. Students use their writing folders to collect these drafts. Some drafts will turn into published pieces of writing and others will be considered "finished" in draft form. Books and drafts in-process provide the most valuable glimpse into the writer's understandings at a particular point in time. Finished pieces of writing are also a valuable source for self-assessment as students choose pieces that they feel represent their growth and new understandings as a writer. Some teachers choose to collect these in a portfolio to show a writer's growth over time.

Starting in grade 2 or 3, we suggest that students begin to use a writer's notebook. They can collect thoughts, observations, ideas, poems, artifacts such as photos, and memorable language in a writer's notebook that they can carry with them. The notebook serves as a repository to capture ideas that may later lead to pieces of writing. Students also use the notebook to try out ideas for writing pieces they are working on in draft form. They may experiment with different techniques they learn from other writers or sketch out an idea to revise their draft. Their writer's notebook can also be a place to record their writing projects, collect their writing goals, and reflect on their new learning.

Progress over time is visible in the written documents. In general, the writer's notebook and folder provide examples of:

- The student's thinking, perspective, and identity as a writer.
- The quantity of writing that the student is producing.
- Writing that shows the student's ability to revise and edit work.
- Writing that shows the student's ability to write in different genres.
- The student's growth in word choice (from simple to more complex).
- The student's understanding of organization, text structure, and text layout.
- The student's growth in written language complexity.
- The student's ability to write with voice.
- The student's spelling ability.
- The student's abiilty to punctuate and capitalize to communicate meaning.

  - Writing that the student considers to be her best (showing self-evaluation).
  - Response and new learning from writing minilessons.
  - The student's identity as a reader and writer.

Like a reader's notebook, a writer's notebook and writing folder are very helpful tools to use in writing conferences with individual students. They also provide useful tools for showing parents the students' progress in writing.

**Word Study Folder** Many teachers use a word study folder, particularly for students in grades 2–6. In the folder are resources fastened by a brad for student reference (e.g., word lists students use). The pockets in the folder are to

A student's writing brings his thinking, perspective, and identity into focus.

keep current phonics and word study work such as word sorts and word webs. To determine a student's word analysis skills, the teacher's observation of the reader's ability to recognize words or take them apart in reading is of most value. The student's spelling in writing also provides strong evidence of phonics knowledge.

# From Assessment to Responsive Teaching

Assessment that is not connected to instruction will always be superfluous, ineffective, and even a dreaded and annoying interruption. Yet without effective assessment, instruction will be merely guesswork. We propose a seamless cycle from assessment to responsive teaching as shown in Figure 10-10. In this cycle, teachers move from (1) observation of reading, writing, and language behaviors to (2) making inferences about the students' control of strategic actions to (3) prioritizing behaviors and understandings to notice, teach for, and support, and then to (4) teaching for change and growth in strategic actions (Figure 10-11). From there, the cycle begins again.

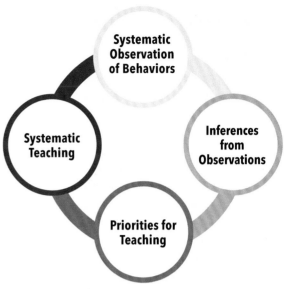

**Figure 10-10.** Assessment to Teaching Cycle.

# Interval Assessments

Interval assessments are administered at selected intervals across the year. Interval assessments are standardized to ensure that the information they provide is as reliable and valid as possible. Below we discuss the most valuable types of interval assessments to include in a comprehensive student assessment system.

## Benchmark Assessments

A benchmark system adds a great deal of value to assessment in literacy learning. Benchmark assessment systems are available for purchase, and some teachers have even created their own by selecting a set of trustworthy texts at each level and creating protocols. For our purposes in this chapter, we will refer to the widely used *Fountas & Pinnell Benchmark Assessment System*. This assessment system is linked directly to *The Literacy Continuum* and to classroom instruction. Benchmark assessments are useful because in a short conference with a student the teacher gains a treasure trove of valid information about the reader.

Benchmark assessments:

- Involve students in reading continuous text while teachers measure factors such as accuracy, strategic actions, fluency, and comprehension.
- Can be administered by classroom teachers who keep data for their own purposes and/or report it schoolwide.

## ASSESSMENT TO TEACHING CYCLE

### STEP ONE
Observe children's reading, writing, and language behaviors.

**Oral Reading:** What you see and hear as a reader processes a text.

**Talk About Reading and Writing:** What you hear as children talk about their reading and writing.

**Writing About Reading:** What you notice about children's thinking in their drawing and writing about a text.

**Writing Process (or Act of Writing):** What you notice about children's engagement in the writing process.

**Writing:** What you notice about children's understandings through drawing and writing fiction and nonfiction.

**Observe Phonics Skills While Reading and Writing**: What you observe about children's word analysis skills as they read and write.

### STEP TWO
Infer from observational evidence what children know and can do.

Observe evidence of children's use of strategic actions:

- Searching for and using information
- Monitoring and self-correcting
- Solving words
- Maintaining fluency
- Adjusting

Observe evidence of children's use of strategic actions:

- Summarizing
- Predicting
- Making connections
- Synthesizing
- Inferring
- Analyzing
- Critiquing

Observe evidence that children are:

- Initiating drawing and writing
- Planning and rehearsing their writing
- Sustaining and producing quantities of writing
- Drafting and revising
- Proofreading and editing
- Publishing

Observe evidence of children's understandings about:

- Genre
- Organziation and text structure
- Idea development
- Language use
- Word choice
- Voice
- Text layout
- Grammar and usage
- Spelling
- Handwriting/word-processing

Observe evidence of children's understandings about:

- Early literacy concepts
- Phonological awareness
- Letter knowledge
- Letter-sound relationships
- Spelling patterns
- High-frequency words
- Word meaning and vocabulary
- Word structure
- Word solving

### STEP THREE
Prioritize the behaviors and understandings that you want you want to notice, teach for, and support.

Think about your observations of the students' reading, writing, and phonics behaviors and compare them to the behaviors and understandings listed in *The Fountas & Pinnell Literacy Continuum* or your school's grade-level expectations.

### STEP FOUR
Teach for growth in strategic actions.

Once you have identified your teaching emphases, demonstrate, prompt for, and reinforce the behaviors and understandings that will expand the students' competencies.

**Figure 10-11.** Assessment to Teaching Cycle

- Offer information that is useful for setting instructional goals at the classroom level and for administrators and boards of education.
- Provide ways for teachers to determine whether they are meeting their own goals and for schools or districts to evaluate the effects of literacy programs.

A benchmark assessment system uses an established set of texts, or "exemplars," that children are asked to read as a teacher listens and codes their oral reading behaviors and calculates accuracy, fluency, and comprehension on a form that includes the typed text. It might sound like the teacher is coding in a typical running record, and there are obvious similarities. (Note: A typical running record is taken on a blank form so it can be used with any text.) But there are important differences as well.

When a running record is used as part of continuous assessment in the classroom, the student has read the text once before in a small-group setting (a seen text). The teacher introduced the book for the group and the students discussed it after reading. For these reasons, the expectation is that the child's performance will be satisfactory; in fact, the assessment serves as a check on the effects of the previous day's instruction.

For a benchmark assessment, the student reads a text she has never seen before (an unseen text) in order to yield an analysis that is as conservative as possible. The assessment is administered using a standardized procedure, with a two- or three-sentence introduction to a short book. A benchmark assessment provides evidence of what students are currently able to do independently and yields the best starting point for instruction for a particular student.

*The Benchmark Assessment System* is used at the beginning of a school year to determine levels that will be productive for instruction (Figure 10-12 on page 177). Some schools also use it to assess progress mid-year and/or at the end of the year. Additionally, it can be useful in finding the appropriate instructional reading level for a student who is new to the school.

*The Benchmark Assessment System* also includes a variety of optional assessments for diagnostic purposes at the primary and intermediate/middle levels. Many benchmark assessment systems other than our own also provide optional assessments that do more than measure reading levels. These might include assessments such as those designed to assess early literacy behaviors, phonological awareness, word parts, or, at the upper grades, analogies or vocabulary in context.

Benchmark assessments should not be administered too frequently. Most schools identify an instructional reading level at the beginning of the year to form groups and begin instruction and then another administration in about April or May to document yearly progress. Some districts conduct a midyear administration to the whole cohort or to those students who were not reading at grade level at the beginning of the year. *The Benchmark Assessment System* is not designed to be used more than about three times per year. It can,

## Fountas & Pinnell

# INSTRUCTIONAL LEVEL EXPECTATIONS FOR READING

| | Beginning of Year (Aug.–Sept.) | 1st Interval of Year (Nov.–Dec.) | 2nd Interval of Year (Feb.–Mar.) | End of Year (May–June) |
|---|---|---|---|---|
| **Grade K** | | C<br>B<br>A | D<br>C<br>B | E<br>D<br>C<br>Below C |
| **Grade 1** | E<br>D<br>C<br>Below C | G<br>F<br>E<br>Below E | I<br>H<br>G<br>Below G | K<br>J<br>I<br>Below I |
| **Grade 2** | K<br>J<br>I<br>Below I | L<br>K<br>J<br>Below J | M<br>L<br>K<br>Below K | N<br>M<br>L<br>Below L |
| **Grade 3** | N<br>M<br>L<br>Below L | O<br>N<br>M<br>Below M | P<br>O<br>N<br>Below N | Q<br>P<br>O<br>Below O |
| **Grade 4** | Q<br>P<br>O<br>Below O | R<br>Q<br>P<br>Below P | S<br>R<br>Q<br>Below Q | T<br>S<br>R<br>Below R |
| **Grade 5** | T<br>S<br>R<br>Below R | U<br>T<br>S<br>Below S | V<br>U<br>T<br>Below T | W<br>V<br>U<br>Below U |
| **Grade 6** | W<br>V<br>U<br>Below U | X<br>W<br>V<br>Below V | Y<br>X<br>W<br>Below W | Z<br>Y<br>X<br>Below X |
| **Grades 7–8** | Z<br>Y<br>X<br>Below X | Z<br>Y<br>X<br>Below X | Z<br>Z<br>Y<br>Below Y | Z<br>Z<br>Y<br>Below Y |

### KEY

- Exceeds Expectations
- Meets Expectations
- Approaches Expectations: Needs Short-Term Intervention
- Does Not Meet Expectations: Needs Intensive Intervention

The Instructional Level Expectations for Reading chart is intended to provide general guidelines for grade-level goals, which should be adjusted based on school/ district requirements and professional teacher judgment.

**Figure 10-12.** A benchmark assessment yields the best starting point for instruction for a particular student.

of course, be used any time for new students who enter the school. Across a district, benchmark records can be transferred with the student's electronic records.

## Writing to a Prompt

You may choose to ask children to write to a prompt at a few intervals throughout the year. This type of writing often is required on state tests, and the students' work products can help teachers assess their ability to apply what they have learned about writing in different situations. Consider the following when you choose a writing prompt:

- Is the prompt open-ended enough to allow children from all different backgrounds and experiences to share an authentic experience or story?
- Are you assessing writing about reading or their ability to compose original fiction or nonfiction?
- Are you asking students to write in different genres at the different times you offer prompts throughout the year? Are these genres represented in the curriculum and instruction?
- Do students understand how their writing samples will be assessed?
- Do the rubrics used in evaluating the prompted writing samples match the ones used or developed in the classroom?

# Evaluating Your Current Assessment System

We have reviewed the components of a high-quality, comprehensive assessment system. Now it's time for you and your team to consider the strengths of your current system and to identify components you'd like to add or drop.

There are many ways to go about this kind of analysis, but we recommend that you start by evaluating continuous assessments that provide the kind of information that is an integral part of instruction (such as running records). Select artifacts for assessment that offer authentic, reliable evidence and can be subjected to systematic analysis using guides or checklists if needed. Then, start a search for interval assessments to fill out your design. You may find that one source of data will address many different questions you have about children as readers and writers and that the evidence will change over time.

Keep in mind that no assessment has value if it doesn't result in improved instruction. It is best to have a design that provides the essential information to inform teaching and document progress over time. You and your colleagues can make thoughtful decisions about your assessment design. Here are some additional questions to pose and discuss.

**Your Budget Will Thank You**
Coherence in assessment practices across schools in your district is critical. When you have provided each classroom teacher a standardized set of leveled books with a standardized protocol to conduct a benchmark assessment two or three times a year, you have made a well informed and economical decision. The books are not consumable, and the teacher can copy the coding forms or go paperless and use a digital tool to capture the information.

Not only do the recording tools offer treasure troves of useful information, but the books can be used over and over by teachers. A child's digital files can be saved in an electronic portfolio and passed on to the next teacher, creating a document of the child's progress across the grades in each school. When a new child enters the school, the classroom teacher can pull out the benchmark assessment and get quick, reliable information to begin instruction. The per-child cost of using such an assessment for all the children in a school, year after year, is minimal.

## Is the Information Accessible?

The system must be practical and usable. The assessments cannot be viewed as separate and burdensome tasks, but as a regular part of daily practice. Of course, you will do some initial assessments to determine strengths and reading levels, and there will be a few periods of focused assessment, but even that should involve students in productive activities such as reading stories and nonfiction books and writing and talking about them. The most powerful kind of documentation that teachers can have is the information collected as an integral part of teaching.

## Are the Tasks Authentic?

Assessment approaches need to be as close as possible to the task being assessed. Children learn to read and write by reading and writing; we need to assess their progress by observing them as they read and write. This process ensures that students' time is not wasted on filling in blanks or bubbles and that it supports the assessment's validity.

Your assessment system needs to include both formal and informal measures of student progress.

When inquiring about validity, we need to ask, does this test really measure what we are trying to assess? Sometimes validity is referred to as *authenticity*. However, it is impossible for all assessment tasks to be completely authentic because generally the task is not one the student has chosen for his own purposes and implements in an idiosyncratic manner. A reliable and systematic approach to assessment inevitably leads to some contrived procedures, but assessments need to be as authentic as possible. Authenticity is an underlying principle of effective assessment.

## Does Observation Play a Key Role?

Systematic observation captures the shifts in responding that indicate instruction is working. For a teacher of reading and writing, observation is an essential daily tool, but it must be done systematically so the important information is documented and collected over time. Consider working with your school's literacy team to create a standard form for recording observations of individual children and a system for organizing them for reflection.

## Are the Assessments Reliable?

The assessment system must be designed to yield consistent information. In other words, each time the assessment procedures are used, they build a database on an individual, one that allows teachers to know the results of their

## STATE TESTS: TO PREP OR NOT TO PREP?

State tests have the greatest significance for educators at the school and district levels because they serve to identify groups of students who are not thriving in the district so that school leaders can address the problems. But within or across a school or a district, teachers and school leaders need to take ownership of *all* forms of assessment. It's a good idea to meet with teachers and study the literacy sections of your state test to determine what the assessment expects readers and writers to know and be able to do. Then discuss what aspects of the format would be unfamiliar to students.

Tests are a genre, and like all genres they are "distinguishable by characteristics of form, style, and content" (Fountas and Pinnell 2001). You'll notice that typically there are certain characteristics that signal both the required understandings and the process of skilled test taking, for example:

- Some specific vocabulary will be used (*selection, summary, answer, which, why*).
- There are questions to answer and sometimes these are in the form of statements.
- The answers come from the print (but sometimes from graphics as well).
- Students are often asked to write what they have learned from print and/or graphics.
- Reading passages usually have few or no pictures.
- There are several kinds of questions—multiple choice, short response, long response.
- For multiple choice, more than one answer may seem to be right. Choose the best.
- For a short response, a very concise answer that stays on the topic and goes right to the question will be best.
- For a longer response, students need to focus on the topic but organize the response in a clear way.
- Students will need to identify genres in reading passages and write in the specific genre they are asked to use.
- Usually, students will need to support their answers with evidence from the text or personal experience.

If you take the time to do this analysis, you can uncover some important skills that can be built into reading and writing minilessons, even from kindergarten. For example, through oral conversation in interactive read-aloud lessons and book clubs, children can support their comments with personal expression or evidence from the text. Reading minilessons on writing about reading help children learn how to respond to a text in short or longer form.

The first requirement for successful performance on state tests is strong reading and writing, and that is built every day across a comprehensive literacy design. But even when those skills are present, students may still need some specific lessons on the test genre. Just remember that if strong reading and writing are not the foundation, then test prep will have a negligible effect.

*". . . we need to know on an ongoing basis that every child is learning by making ongoing assessments and by incorporating that information about each child's learning into daily instruction—a nonnegotiable practice."*
—Lynn Sharratt and Michael Fullan

## ABOUT THE NATIONAL ASSESSMENT OF EDUCATIONAL PROGRESS

A prominent national test is the National Assessment of Educational Progress. NAEP is congressionally mandated to use nationally representative data to identify what U.S. students know and can do in subject areas like mathematics, reading, science, and writing. The sampling procedure is representative of the geographical, racial, ethnic, and socioeconomic diversity of schools and provides a common metric for the states and districts that participate. In the beginning (1964), participation was voluntary but in 2001, the reauthorization of the Elementary and Secondary Education Act required that states receiving Title I funding participate in NAEP assessments in math and reading at grades 4 and 8 every two years. This act had the effect of making NAEP compulsory.

We treat NAEP results with some skepticism. For one thing, the landscape in literacy achievement is constantly changing. Instructional approaches, curriculum materials, and the tests themselves change over time. Scores go up and down over the years. Criticisms have been raised about the interpretation of results because a small mean difference may be only a few points but be considered statistically significant, triggering widespread publicity. Even when a concentrated effort (No Child Left Behind, 2001) was made in early literacy, the result was little difference in scores. Gaps between the scores of students of color and the scores of white students did not appreciably close. A sensible stance is to consider test results, look at real numbers, and draw your own conclusions rather than make a knee-jerk response. Certainly, you would not want to make drastic decisions based on the results of one assessment, no matter what is promised. There are no quick fixes.

teaching. A reliable procedure is applied in a standard way so that it yields consistent results across items and with different readers and different teachers.

## Is the System Multidimensional?

A multidimensional system provides the best chance to collect reliable and valid information on student progress. The system should include both formal and informal measures; for example, you might combine anecdotal records, running records taken on a regular basis, and writing rubrics. It should take into account the analysis of a variety of work samples or artifacts (e.g., lists of books read, writing about reading samples from a reader's notebook, entries in the writer's notebook, and drafts in a writing folder. For early readers, recommend some assessment of beginning knowledge of items related to literacy— the names of letters of the alphabet and awareness of print conventions.

A multidimensional system also allows you to look across curriculum areas to find and use valuable information. For example, the assessment of a student's growth in writing can provide valuable information for helping her learn to read and vice versa.

## Do the Assessments Create a Feedback Loop?

A feedback loop sounds complicated, but it simply means looking at the combined results of assessment and applying the results to instructional design and implementation. The first part of the loop, observational assessment, happens when a teacher works with an individual student. The behavioral evidence gained from observation might result in the teacher checking her assumptions about the student against what he is actually doing. (Clay 1995).

The second part of the loop takes place at the classroom level. In midyear, a teacher might assess all students on one or two similar measures. If children are reading every day and there is little progress in the level of text that they can read, something might be wrong with the way texts are selected for children in the group or stronger teaching with more explicit demonstrations might be required.

The last part of the loop takes place at the school level. The literacy team or a grade-level team could, for example, conduct study of their results using the information across classes to make decisions about further professional development needs or materials they want to purchase.

## Can the Assessments Identify Children Who Need More?

Assessment is critical in identifying students who are not benefiting fully from the classroom program even if it is of high quality. Because intervention will be required for these students, assessment must occur early and be ongoing, so that no student moves on through the system without the level of support she needs to succeed. Chapter 16 contains a thorough discussion of intervention programs and practices that can be applied when systematic assessments reveal the need.

## Are Students and Their Families Involved?

Assessment systems for early, intermediate, and middle-level students can provide opportunities for them to reflect on their own strengths and goals for further learning. Involving families allows them to learn more about their children's strengths and provides teachers with additional reliable and valid information. And families have the right to know whether their children are reading and writing at, above, or below grade level and to hear some simple descriptive

### COMMUNICATING ASSESSMENT INFORMATION TO FAMILIES

Families always want to know how their children are progressing in school, and most look forward to regularly scheduled opportunities to meet with teachers. Yet too often these conferences leave parents dissatisfied with the level of feedback they receive and confused about how the teacher's jargon-laden comments add up to a full picture of their child's learning. As you consider what you and your colleagues value in literacy teaching, learning, and assessment, think about the important role of communicating with families several times a year to discuss student progress.

Report cards are common tools, but we have found that their formats remain static year after year, and the information they contain rarely reflects the richness of the literacy experiences in today's schools. On top of that, the language in report cards is not always understood by noneducators. Consider using a variety of artifacts in conferences such as the reader's and writer's notebooks, and examples of a book the child was able to read at the beginning of the quarter and one that the child is currently reading. Consider also how to involve students in the conference. For example, in advance of a family conference, the teacher can ask the child to select and mark pages in a book she is reading. During the conference, the child can talk about what makes those pages special or important.

Families are highly invested in their children's literacy progress and want to understand from the teachers if their children are progressing as expected and how they can support their learning. Consider how you and your team can engage in a process of identifying the important information families want to know in language that is friendly and clear. We encourage you to invite a parent or two to join the team to gain rich input and valuable critique.

**Manage Your Time** Time can be a
roadblock, and assessment can consume the first two months of school.
With a well-designed system and an
efficient schedule, beginning-of-the-
year assessments can be completed
in two or three weeks, with a teacher
conducting a benchmark assessment
conference with two or three children
per day. The leadership team and
everyone in the school can work to
remove the roadblock. There are ways
to make assessment efficient.

Bring teachers together to design
time-efficient ways to accomplish
benchmark training and to design
ways of recording information efficiently within instructional contexts.
The objective is to use assessment data
to achieve responsive teaching, but
that will not happen automatically.

statements about what the students can do as readers and writers and what
they need to learn next. Reader's and writer's notebooks and samples of texts
that children have read or written over time are wonderful tools to use in self-
assessment and in family conferences.

# Policies and Practices for Making Assessment Work

A school's assessment plan requires dedication to collecting, organizing, discussing, and drawing implications from meaningful data. A collection of data
gives you a window into what is happening in students' minds and it also provides an important way to monitor for equitable student outcomes. Assessment
data can help you identify and respond to students who need intervention. And
then, assessment can help you choose the right intervention and document students' progress. To make assessment work, classroom teachers need the information, and it must be relevant and useful.

## Becoming Data Literate

You can't make good decisions if you are simply swimming in a huge pool of
data. Data literacy involves the ability to *find the story* in the data. It means organizing the set of data so that it provides meaningful soft and hard information. Flying blind through the data does not work. It is not enough to collect
and understand the data. Educators must use skills in inquiry to interpret the
results. Decision-making based on data is not random but takes great focus.
"School leaders are often drowning in data but are unsure which forms of data
will help them create a portrait of student achievement that will motivate staff
to look beyond simple trends and delve deeper into root causes" (Datnow and
Park 2015).

You need to ask how data can serve your school improvement needs. You
cannot make decisions based on a single score, a table or two, or "off the top
of the head" results. Looking at data without a critical eye can lead to overly
simplified solutions. We have known schools or districts that actually reject
materials they have just acquired and that teachers say are working well
because of a single article. We have known schools to adopt one approach
because of a single set of scores in one school. Caution, patience, and an analytical approach are needed when making decisions based on data.

## Data Walls for Progress Monitoring: Making Individual Achievement Visible

In a school where the educators believe they are collectively responsible for the
students, they need to go beyond trends and percentages to address each student's progress over time. When teachers "put faces on the data" (Sharratt and

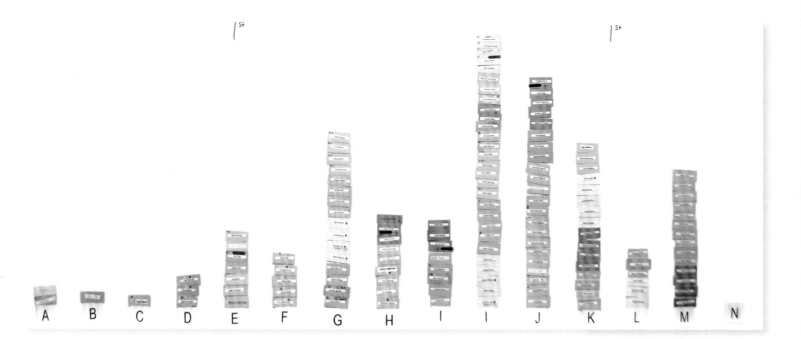

A    B    C    D    E    F    G    H    I    I    J    K    L    M    N

Fullan 2012), they can drill down with a laser-like focus to each child's status, by name, and document her progress over time.

A data wall is a practical tool for putting faces on the data that are used in many schools to help teachers and school leaders maintain focus and keep a close eye on shifts in learning. Data walls are displayed in secure places in the teachers' meeting room or on fold-up boards that can be opened for a group meeting.

Data walls can take various forms—from actual walls to bulletin boards to digital displays. Many kinds of data can be recorded on the wall, but the most useful (and easiest to update) come from running records collected in connection with guided reading instruction. Each student is represented by a sticky note or icon along a continuum of progress and the sticky note is placed at the child's instructional reading level. The icons represent the faces of the students and can be moved at intervals to show shifts. Each grade uses a different color to be able to see the cohort at a glance and each child's name is written on the note. Often, a colored dot is also used to hold additional information such as "English Learner" or "SPED services."

At a glance, the data wall reveals students who need extra attention (for example, assuring *daily* small-group instruction or providing intervention). It allows teachers to view and discuss the progress of the group as a whole as well as engage in collaborative problem-solving to address challenges. It allows school leaders to talk about the progress of the whole school and determine where extra support might be needed. Monthly photographs of the data wall can allow them to compare with previous years to determine improvement over time. The data wall keeps assessment up front in the conscious decision-making of teachers and leaders. Each time the group gathers, teachers physically move the posted notes—a rewarding experience for all. After moving

**Special Education**

● Reading Recovery

● English Language Learner

● Early Intervention Program

 Gifted

 RT I/Tier/Subject

Data walls allow school leaders to talk about the progress of the whole school and determine where extra support is needed. The data wall shown above is made from a large piece of foldable presentation board, making it portable for use in a variety of settings.

the notes to their new positions on the wall, the teachers and leaders discuss progress and problem-solve as a group. It makes the most of the investment of time and resources and creates a sense of community and collective ownership of student outcomes.

## Cautions About Assessment

Reacting to bits of data without thoughtful analysis of the complex nature of learning is unhelpful. The examination of assessment data should not result in a frenzy of changes that are unconnected to your school's strategic literacy goals.

Another approach to avoid is what Bryk (2015) calls "solution-itis," which is the tendency of educators to immediately jump from one "solution" to another in hopes of fixing a persistent, complex problem. What is needed is to maintain objectivity and make thoughtful decisions based on continuous collection of assessment data, always keeping an eye on individuals and teaching. Rather than constantly changing everything, educators can make small changes that "add up" and then evaluate the effects of the change to make decisions. The protocol tool **Developing an Effective Design for Literacy Assessment (08)** on the next page can help your team work through the process of developing an effective design for literacy assessment.

# The Takeaway

Assessment is important work, and it affects students powerfully; therefore, it must be undertaken with an eye to the highest quality. Teachers are the primary agents.

> Whether they use tests, work samples, discussion or ongoing observation, teachers make sense of students' reading and writing development. They read the many different texts, oral and written, that students produce in order to construct an understanding of students as literate individuals. The sense they make of a student's reading or writing is communicated to the student through spoken or written comments and translated into instructional decisions in the classroom (e.g., subsequent assignments, grouping for instruction). Because of such important consequences, teachers must be aware of and deliberate about their roles as assessors.
> —Joint Task Force on Assessment of the International Reading Association and the National Council of Teachers of English, 2010

Teachers are closest to students' learning and can collect data over time; therefore, they are in a unique position to engage in valid and reliable assessment of their students' literacy competencies. The more they invest in the process, the

Designing or refreshing a literacy assessment system is no small task. It requires requires concentrated effort and as much time as it takes to reach consensus. The protocol tool **Developing an Effective Design for Literacy Assessment (08)** will help you and your team step through the process efficiently and productively.

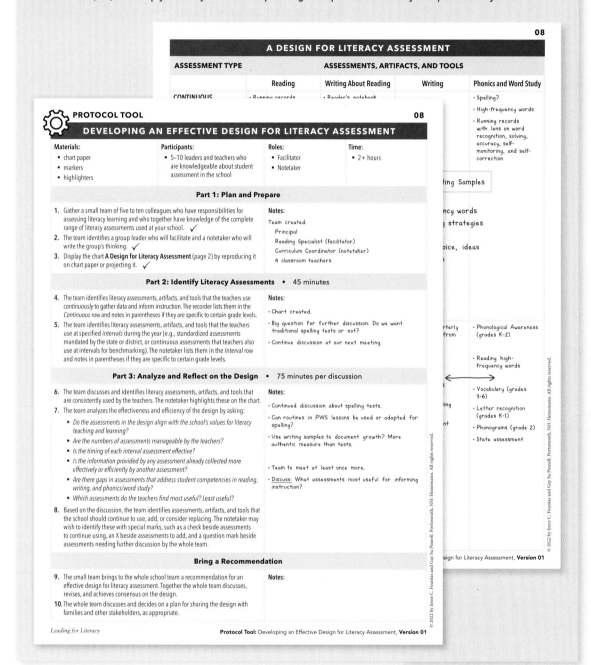

**08**

| A DESIGN FOR LITERACY ASSESSMENT | | | | |
| --- | --- | --- | --- | --- |
| **ASSESSMENT TYPE** | **ASSESSMENTS, ARTIFACTS, AND TOOLS** | | | |
| | Reading | Writing About Reading | Writing | Phonics and Word Study |
| CONTINUOUS | • Running records | • Reader's notebook | | • Spelling?<br>• High-frequency words<br>• Running records with lens on word recognition, solving, accuracy, self-monitoring, and self-correction |

⚙ **PROTOCOL TOOL**　　　　　　　　**08**

## DEVELOPING AN EFFECTIVE DESIGN FOR LITERACY ASSESSMENT

| **Materials:**<br>▪ chart paper<br>▪ markers<br>▪ highlighters | **Participants:**<br>▪ 5–10 leaders and teachers who are knowledgeable about student assessment in the school | **Roles:**<br>▪ Facilitator<br>▪ Notetaker | **Time:**<br>▪ 2+ hours |
| --- | --- | --- | --- |

### Part 1: Plan and Prepare

1. Gather a small team of five to ten colleagues who have responsibilities for assessing literacy learning and who together have knowledge of the complete range of literacy assessments used at your school. ✓
2. The team identifies a group leader who will facilitate and a notetaker who will write the group's thinking. ✓
3. Display the chart **A Design for Literacy Assessment** (page 2) by reproducing it on chart paper or projecting it. ✓

**Notes:**

Team created:
　Principal
　Reading Specialist (facilitator)
　Curriculum Coordinator (notetaker)
　4 classroom teachers

### Part 2: Identify Literacy Assessments　•　45 minutes

4. The team identifies literacy assessments, artifacts, and tools that the teachers use *continuously* to gather data and inform instruction. The recorder lists them in the *Continuous* row and notes in parentheses if they are specific to certain grade levels.
5. The team identifies literacy assessments, artifacts, and tools that the teachers use at specified *intervals* during the year (e.g., standardized assessments mandated by the state or district, or continuous assessments that teachers also use at intervals for benchmarking). The notetaker lists them in the *Interval* row and notes in parentheses if they are specific to certain grade levels.

**Notes:**

• Chart created.
• Big question for further discussion: Do we want traditional spelling tests or not?
• Continue discussion at our next meeting.

### Part 3: Analyze and Reflect on the Design　•　75 minutes per discussion

6. The team discusses and identifies literacy assessments, artifacts, and tools that are consistently used by the teachers. The notetaker highlights these on the chart.
7. The team analyzes the effectiveness and efficiency of the design by asking:
   ▪ Do the assessments in the design align with the school's values for literacy teaching and learning?
   ▪ Are the numbers of assessments manageable by the teachers?
   ▪ Is the timing of each interval assessment effective?
   ▪ Is the information provided by any assessment already collected more effectively or efficiently by another assessment?
   ▪ Are there gaps in assessments that address student competencies in reading, writing, and phonics/word study?
   ▪ Which assessments do the teachers find most useful? Least useful?
8. Based on the discussion, the team identifies assessments, artifacts, and tools that the school should continue to use, add, or consider replacing. The notetaker may wish to identify these with special marks, such as a check beside assessments to continue using, an X beside assessments to add, and a question mark beside assessments needing further discussion by the whole team.

**Notes:**

• Continued discussion about spelling tests.
• Can routines in PWS lessons be used or adapted for spelling?
• Use writing samples to document growth? More authentic measure than tests.

• Team to meet at least once more.
• Discuss: What assessments most useful for informing instruction?

### Bring a Recommendation

9. The small team brings to the whole school team a recommendation for an effective design for literacy assessment. Together the whole team discusses, revises, and achieves consensus on the design.
10. The whole team discusses and decides on a plan for sharing the design with families and other stakeholders, as appropriate.

**Notes:**

*Leading for Literacy*　　　　　　**Protocol Tool:** Developing an Effective Design for Literacy Assessment, **Version 01**

*(partially visible right column:)*
ting Samples

ncy words
g strategies
oice, ideas

rterly
from

• Phonological Awareness (grades K–2)

• Reading high-frequency words

• Vocabulary (grades 3–6)
• Letter recognition (grades K–1)
• Phonograms (grade 2)
• State assessment

sign for Literacy Assessment, **Version 01**

better they can use their records for sharing, determining patterns of progress, conferring with parents, grading, and reporting.

The central purpose of assessment must be to improve teaching and learning. That is the ultimate goal and without it, our investment in assessment cannot be realized. Only with the goal of improving teaching and learning can assessment be a primary factor in assuring that all members of the society will acquire full and critical literacy.

## Think About Your School

- What is working well in your school's assessment design for reading? writing? phonics?
- How has your thinking about assessment shifted in small or large ways?

## Move Your School Forward

- Reflect on what you and your colleagues value in literacy learning and the kinds of formal and informal assessment tools that will provide the most usable information for teaching.
- Assemble a team to design a clear, coherent assessment system and a professional learning plan that assures a high level of expertise, especially in the analysis and use of assessment information. The protocol and planning document shown on page 185 will be helpful.

# SECTION 4

*Implementing a Coherent Design for Literacy Teaching*

# SECTION 4

## *Implementing a Coherent Design for Literacy Teaching*

The role of "instructional leader" is a challenging one for school leaders. It can be difficult to support excellent instruction across the full range of grade levels and areas of the curriculum. Some school leaders have had little experience in some of the content areas or instructional contexts they are expected to supervise. Others have experience at one or two grade levels but not others.

But good news! A school leader doesn't have to know everything to lead improvement efforts and promote effective practices. It is, however, very helpful to know some important things about instruction, in this case, about literacy teaching and learning. Ask yourself these questions:

- When I walk into a classroom, do I attend to the important characteristics of the instructional context the teacher is implementing?
- As I observe a lesson, do I know what to look for in the teacher's actions and in students' responses?
- Do I know how to determine whether materials are appropriate and sufficient for student needs?

The first three chapters in this section provide important information about reading, writing, and phonics/word study contexts to support your knowledge of the elements of a coherent design for literacy teaching and learning. We describe five contexts for reading and five contexts for writing, all of which have different benefits and outcomes and all of which are essential. Then we outline a structured approach to teaching phonics and word study that supports efficient decoding and vocabulary development. The section ends with two chapters that have equity at their heart. Every child—including each English learner and each student who finds reading and writing difficult—has the right to literacy. Your greatest responsibility as a school leader is to create conditions in your school and classrooms that enable every child to be successful in literacy learning. These chapters are designed to help you do just that.

# Chapter 11

# A Design for Teaching Reading: Learning to Read by Reading

*Reading is a message-getting, problem-solving activity which increases in power and flexibility the more it is practiced.*
—Marie Clay

MANY DISCUSSIONS IN THIS book have centered on the importance of creating inclusive learning communities in which every voice in the classroom matters, teachers notice and respond to student needs and interests, and teachers view each student as a competent learner. Students have choice, intrinsic motivation thrives, and the learning opportunities offered each student expand their language and literacy competencies.

In this section, we describe the classroom instructional contexts for teaching reading, writing, and word study. An *instructional context* is a structure for teaching a group of students. Each context has its own set of teaching actions, appropriate materials, expectations for students, and ways of detecting evidence of learning. Across contexts, in a coherent literacy design, teachers have a repertoire of ways to teach responsively and promote self-initiating, independent reading and writing behaviors among students. The graphic *A Design for Responsive Literacy Teaching* (Figure 11-1) illustrates how the instructional contexts for reading, writing, and phonics/word study work coherently across whole-group, small-group, and individual instruction. We have developed a

**A Design for Responsive Literacy Teaching**

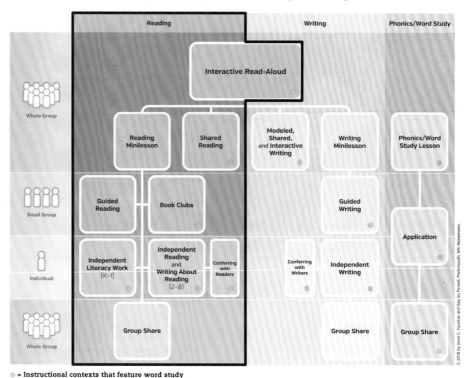

⬤ = Instructional contexts that feature word study

**Figure 11-1.** A Design for Responsive Literacy Teaching

series of tools for your use in supporting teachers' analysis and reflection of each instructional context. We suggest that you share these tools in professional learning sessions so that they become a familiar resource.

You have the responsibility of supporting teachers across grade levels to increase expertise in all these contexts. But no school leader can be an expert on every aspect of teaching in PreK to grade 6 classrooms. It is possible and helpful, though, to know:

- The characteristics of each instructional context.
- Why it is included in a coherent instructional system for literacy.
- The special features of each instructional context.
- How learning is connected across instructional contexts.
- What to look for as you observe and participate.
- How you can support teachers in their teaching decisions.

In this chapter, we describe five instructional contexts for reading that offer a range of rich opportunities for community- and competency-building: (1) interactive read-aloud; (2) shared reading; (3) guided reading; (4) book clubs; and (5) independent reading. Independent reading is the foundation for a readers' workshop structure so that students are engaged in meaningful and productive learning while the teacher works with small groups or confers with individuals. We believe this set of research-based instructional practices implemented across the school will provide a rich, coherent design for

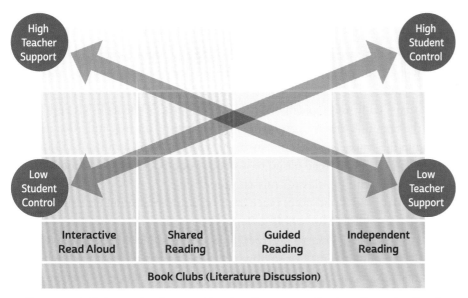

**Figure 11-2.** Relationship Between Teacher Support and Student Control in Reading

literacy learning. The instruction varies: some contexts are whole class, while others are small group or individual. Most contexts are heterogenous; only one (guided reading) brings students together in temporary homogenous groups. The contexts vary from high to low teacher support depending on the reader's control in relation to the text (Figure 11-2).

When the text is one that is beyond what most students could process for themselves, the teacher provides the most support. When the child can process a text independently, there is little or no teacher support. In all instructional contexts, teachers work to support students' independence in processing text.

## Interactive Read-Aloud

We begin with read-aloud, called *interactive* to emphasize the way students experience and use talk in response to reading. In a sense, interactive read-aloud is the heart of the literacy curriculum. Through interactive read-aloud, students engage as a community in thinking and talking about high-quality texts that offer beautiful art, complex language, a variety of text structures, and interesting ideas that engage their intellect and emotions. The complex texts provide learning opportunities for all students and offer a rich context to expand students' thinking within, beyond, and about age-appropriate, grade-appropriate texts. The texts become mentor texts for minilessons in readers' and writers' workshops. In interactive read-aloud lessons, teachers provide the highest level of support. You will find grade-by-grade descriptions of the characteristics of texts for reading aloud and behaviors and understandings to notice, teach, and support in the Interactive Read-Aloud and Literature Discussion section of *The Literacy Continuum*.

During an interactive read-aloud lesson, students engage as a community in thinking and talking about a high-quality text.

## What Is Interactive Read-Aloud?

During an interactive read-aloud lesson, the teacher selects and reads a book to the whole group of students, sharing illustrations and occasionally and selectively pausing for brief, relevant discussion points. Ideally, interactive read-aloud occurs daily and typically lasts 15–20 minutes. Students listen and think about the text, talk about it, and respond to it before, during, and after the reading in the whole group and sometimes with partners or in triads. Occasionally a teacher may read aloud to a small group if a substantial number of students are new to the class or missed the reading.

Interactive read-aloud takes place in the classroom meeting area that the teacher has established for whole-group meetings. Ideally it is located next to the classroom library area on a carpet. Read-aloud books can be displayed, covers facing out, on a rack or shelf where they can be easily accessed when there are connections between texts. Often teachers and students create a class chart of *Books We've Shared* to document their shared literary knowledge.

Teachers read from collections of carefully selected, high-quality fiction and nonfiction texts (mainly picture books) that remain in the classroom all year.

**TEXT SETS**

An important feature of interactive read-aloud is the use of "text sets," books selected to be read aloud, organized into groups of about four or five, and sequenced to build on one another. The books may be connected by genre, author, illustrator, topic or concept, theme, message, or other connection, for example, "the importance of friendship," "humorous stories," or "sharing cultures/folktales." We encourage grade-level teachers to work together in creating text sets and sequencing them. Everyone on a grade level uses the same text sets. As they confer with colleagues, teachers can have lively conversations about the lessons they are teaching and the different responses of students.

Text sets are a rich resource for learning. Understandings accumulate over time and the books are available in the classroom for constant reference by teacher and students. In addition, they are used as mentor texts, forming the base for reading and writing minilessons.

**Figure 11-3.** Example of a Text Set Focused on Earth Science

These texts are often grouped into text sets, described opposite in Figure 11-3. The teacher will also need chart paper and markers for lessons.

## Benefits of Interactive Read-Aloud

When they listen to and discuss books that the teacher has read aloud, students engage as a member of a literate community. The books read aloud become a rich text base, or the shared literary knowledge, that all students share and can use as resources all year. Free from the process of decoding the texts for themselves, students can give full attention to understanding, enjoying, and thinking about the messages and crafting of the text. Interactive read-aloud lessons offer many opportunities for learning (Figure 11-4). This context is the heart of a rich, culturally relevant literary experience.

---

### LEARNING OPPORTUNITIES IN INTERACTIVE READ-ALOUD

***Deeper Understanding of Texts***–*students expand their abilities to:*

- Understand the literal meaning, with important details, of the story or informational text.
- Think beyond the text, for example, making inferences or predictions.
- Think about the text, for example, thinking analytically and critically.
- Expand knowledge of characteristics of various genres.
- Expand knowledge of text structure (simple to complex) in fiction and nonfiction.
- Notice literary aspects of texts (the author's and illustrator's craft in creating fiction and nonfiction).
- Notice underlying structures (compare/contrast, description, chronological and temporal sequence, cause/effect).
- Expand the examples of high-quality, complex, and well-constructed texts that they can draw on to help them understand other texts and support their writing.
- Develop a deep reading of texts.

***Expanded Content Knowledge***–*students:*

- Build background information that can be used to understand more sophisticated texts in small group and independent reading.
- Understand the historical roots of problems of society.
- Gain new perspectives on problems of society.
- Develop respect for people with identities and lived experiences that differ from their own.
- Develop appreciation for and support their world and the environment.

***Expanded Language and Vocabulary***–*students:*

- Build knowledge of language syntax and grammar.
- Expand knowledge of more complex syntax in literature.
- Acquire academic language to talk about texts and content.
- Build vocabulary, especially those Tier 2 words that appear more in literature than in oral language and Tier 3 scientific and technical words.

***Expanded Cultural Knowledge***–*students:*

- Hear and view literature that reflects a wide range of cultures, backgrounds, and lived experiences.
- Experience a text collection that reflects the diversity of society.
- Develop empathy and respect for many different cultures.

***Expanded Sense of Community***–*students:*

- Develop a common language for talking and writing about texts in other contexts.
- Have an accumulating collection of texts that they have shared and discussed with peers.
- Talk with each other about aspects of texts using examples that their peers understand and remember.
- Use shared texts to engage in interesting class discussions.
- Gain social and emotional understanding.
- Have experiences talking with others about cultural, social, and emotional issues.

**Figure 11-4.** Learning Opportunities in Interactive Read-Aloud

## Structure of an Interactive Read-Aloud Lesson

We recommend placing interactive read-aloud within an intentional lesson structure that includes planning and preparation, reading the text, discussing the text, revisiting the text, and options for extending understanding of the text (Figure 11-5).

**Planning and Preparation** During this important step, the teacher selects a text that offers opportunities to teach for understandings that the teacher has identified as goals for the lesson. The texts used in an interactive read-aloud lesson are beyond those that students can read independently. The teacher reads and analyzes the text to determine points at which to stop during reading to invite discussion. Prior to the lesson, the teacher jots notes about each stopping point on a sticky note and places it in the text. The teacher also plans prompts to support the discussion after reading and, if appropriate, extensions of the lesson, such as writing about the reading. We recommend planning for a year of read-alouds in a logical sequence of text sets. This may take some time but will have greater impact and save time later.

**Introducing the Text** The teacher gathers the whole group in the meeting area and very briefly introduces the book, author, illustrator, and any important background material.

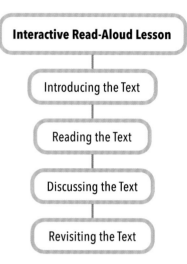

**Interactive Read-Aloud Lesson**

Introducing the Text

Reading the Text

Discussing the Text

Revisiting the Text

**Figure 11-5** Structure of an Interactive Read-Aloud Lesson

**Reading the Text** The teacher then reads the book to the students, stopping occasionally for brief comments by the students. These can be made to the group as a whole or in "turn and talk" to a partner. The time required to read the book varies by the book, but we recommend mostly picture books (even for upper grades) that take no more than 15 to 20 minutes to read. Occasionally, a teacher may read a short novel over a few days.

**Discussing the Text** The teacher invites students to talk about the text, using prompts that keep them focused and encourage thinking beyond and about the text. Discussion usually takes 5 to 10 minutes.

**Revisiting the Text** The teacher may want to revisit the book (on the same day or occasionally on subsequent days) to reread it, or parts of it, so that students can notice more about how it is crafted and expand their understanding of its meaning.

The selected text offers opportunities to teach for understandings that the teacher has identified as goals for the lesson.

**Extending the Text** Occasionally, the teacher may choose to assign an additional activity that extends the students' thinking about a book. Options for extending the text include writing about reading, responding in a reader's notebook, research, inquiry about the topic or author, and an artistic reflection on the book. Most extension activities are accomplished as independent work.

## What to Listen and Look for in Interactive Read-Aloud

When you observe an interactive read-aloud lesson, you will see the teacher demonstrating attention to and appreciation for the text through expressive reading and inviting students' thinking and attention to important language and concepts in the text. The conversation involves give and take, rather than the teacher asking questions and affirming or repeating student comments. Through structures like "turn and talk," there is student-to-student comment about the text. Students are listening actively and talking with each other. They use evidence from the text to support their thinking, and there is evidence that they are deepening their understanding as they benefit from each other's thinking.

The observation tool **Interactive Read-Aloud Lesson (09)** is designed for use in supporting teacher expertise over time through observation and reflection. You can use it (and all the observation tools in this chapter) as your lens for observing and discussing a lesson. We suggest sharing the tool in professional learning sessions, so teachers are familiar with it and use it for their own reflection. A teacher may want to select one box to focus on. The tool should focus your attention on the characteristics of a high-quality lesson. After observing an interactive read-aloud lesson, we suggest you spend time talking with the teacher so you can think together about the teaching and learning. Take a listening and collaborative inquiry

Use the observation tool **Interactive Read-Aloud Lesson (09)** before the lesson, during the lesson, and after the lesson to support your observations and collaborative discussions with teachers.

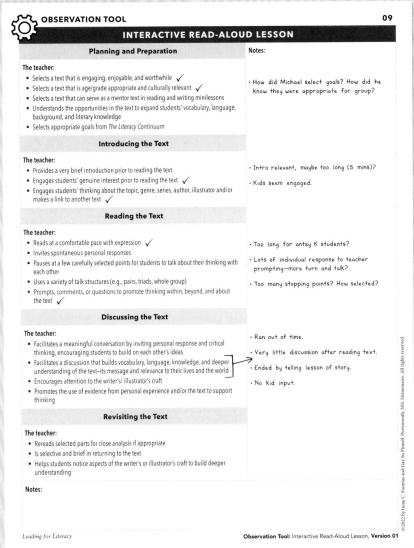

stance, remembering that the teacher is most knowledgeable about the students. Some good questions or prompts might be:

- The students seemed very interested in this book. What are you thinking about their engagement? What kinds of thinking has this text set fostered?
- The student responses seemed to be evidence of deeper comprehension. What are you thinking?
- Let's take a look at *The Literacy Continuum*. What will be your teaching priorities for the next few days?

# Shared Reading

Shared reading provides a second enjoyable reading experience with the same benefits as interactive read-aloud. It has the added advantage of engaging students in processing the print and illustrations with a high level of support from other readers in their classroom community, as well as an element of performance. Shared reading is especially useful in building fluency and provides an opportunity to have enjoyable, successful experiences with texts at or above grade-level difficulty. You will find grade-by-grade descriptions of the characteristics of texts for sharing and performing and behaviors and understandings to notice, teach, and support in the Shared and Performance Reading section of *The Literacy Continuum*.

## What Is Shared Reading?

Shared reading builds fluency and provides enjoyable, successful experiences with texts at or above grade-level difficulty.

In shared reading, students read aloud in unison from an enlarged version of an engaging text (e.g., book, poem, song, speech, play, and so on) that all students can see. Sometimes they read the whole text. Other times they read parts. Students may read a text for several days before going on to a new text. By taking part in multiple readings over time, students notice more about the text as the teacher makes instructional points based on student needs. There is emphasis on participation, enjoyment, and reflecting the meaning of the text through oral reading.

Shared reading generally takes place in the classroom meeting area. Students are seated so that all can clearly see the enlarged text and participate in oral reading. Shared reading lessons are provided daily, when possible, and typically last 5 to 10 minutes. Occasionally, a group will practice a choral reading for a longer period to capture the nuances. The texts that students read are enlarged so that everyone in the class can see. The teacher uses an easel or a document camera for displaying a book and a plain pointer with nothing on the point that would block the view of the print. Often there are small versions of the text available to the students for rereading independently or for a listening center.

Another approach, effective with older students, is to have individual students have their own copy of a text and read parts in readers' theater or read poems chorally. They can use their voices to reflect dialogue, rhythm, emotions, and beautiful language. A small group can perform for the class or just for themselves; there is pleasure in using the voice as an instrument for communicating meaning.

## Benefits of Shared Reading

The benefits of shared reading include all of those listed for interactive read-aloud. The text is often somewhat shorter because it is being read aloud by the students, so there may be fewer opportunities for students to notice literary features such as character development or complex plots. Shared reading texts have the advantage, though, of students' being able to see the print and art and participate in the reading. Many texts have literary language, including figurative language, rhythm, and rhyme. Many of the learning opportunities offered by shared reading are listed in Figure 11-6.

---

### LEARNING OPPORTUNITIES IN SHARED READING

**Deeper Understanding and Effective Processing of Texts**–students:

- Engage in thinking within, beyond, and about a text because they are freed from initial decoding and have the support of other readers.
- Expand their knowledge of genre characteristics.
- Learn to notice text structure and how to express it when reading aloud.
- Notice literary language and how it sounds when read aloud.
- Notice details in the illustrations and talk about how they enhance the text.
- Give close attention to graphics in nonfiction texts and expand comprehension.
- Notice all text features of nonfiction genres.

**Expanded Fluency**–students:

- Vary the voice according to text genre (fiction, nonfiction, poetic).
- Read smoothly in meaningful phrases.

**Expanded Content Knowledge**–students:

- Give close attention to photographs in nonfiction text to study how they provide information.
- Use text structures such as compare and contrast.
- Learn more about how to use features such as labels and timelines.

**Expanded Language**–students:

- Experience the pleasure of well-crafted language.
- Enjoy poetic language.
- Internalize language syntax and grammar by reading it several times in unison with others.
- Use the more complex syntax of written language during repeated readings.
- Practice the use of academic language and colorful vocabulary.

**Expanded Cultural Knowledge**–students:

- Experience reading texts that reflect a global, multicultural society.
- Enjoy rhymes and tales from different cultures.
- Realize that all cultures have typical stories and sayings.
- Read some texts with words other than English.

**Expanded Sense of Community**–students:

- Have an accumulating collection of texts that they have performed with peers.
- Gain social and emotional understanding through a sense of teamwork.

Figure 11-6. Learning Opportunities in Shared Reading

## Structure of a Shared Reading Lesson

A shared reading lesson includes planning and a brief introduction, a first reading of the text by the teacher, rereading the text with students joining in, discussing the text, and revisiting the text to make teaching points (Figure 11-7). Teachers may sometimes extend a particular text with optional learning opportunities.

**Planning and Preparation** The teacher selects a text that has potential for shared or performance reading from a collection of enlarged texts (books or poems) or one that can be enlarged. The teacher reads and analyzes the text to determine voice variations that will be meaningful and selects appropriate goals from *The Literacy Continuum*. The teacher then creates a very brief but engaging introduction and plans some prompts to support discussion after reading. It is efficient to plan for a sequence of several texts over time. Remember that texts may be read for several days before going on to a new text.

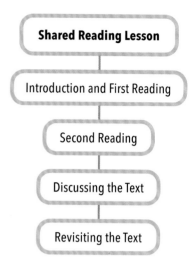

Figure 11-7 Structure of a Shared Reading Lesson

**Introduction and First Reading** The teacher assembles the students in the meeting area; briefly introduces the book, author, and illustrator; and explains any important background material (such as culture of origin). The goal of the introduction is to engage students' interest in the text. The teacher then reads the book or poem to the students. With emergent readers, the teacher points crisply under each word so that children attend to the right part of the print.

As students join in on the reading, the teacher models phrasing, appropriate stress, and meaningful intonation.

As children become more proficient, the teacher may point only to the beginning of each line. The teacher models phrasing, appropriate stress, and meaningful intonation. The teacher may choose to pause briefly at a few points to invite noticings and quick comments about the text, but it is important to sustain the momentum of the reading. It is important for students to enjoy and understand the text.

**Second Reading** The first and second readings are completed on the same day. For the second reading, the teacher invites the students to read the whole text or assigned parts. With the support of the teacher and peers, all students can successfully engage in a complete reading of the text.

**Discussing the Text** The teacher invites students to have a brief discussion or make a few comments about the text. Since texts will be reread over subsequent days, there will be more opportunity for students to reflect on the meaning and messages of the text.

**Revisiting the Text** The teacher may revisit the text after the second reading and on subsequent days to make brief teaching points. In one or two minutes, the teacher may draw attention to text structure, literary language, or features of words. Enlarged texts offer many opportunities for phonics/word study instruction (using highlighter tape, for example, to identify rhyming words, letters, words, and parts of words).

**Extending the Text** As in interactive read-aloud, the teacher may choose to assign an additional activity that extends the students' thinking about a text. Options for extending the text include responding in a reader's notebook, research, inquiry about the topic or author, and an artistic reflection on the book. Most extension activities are accomplished as independent work.

## What to Listen and Look for in Shared Reading

As you observe a shared reading lesson, the observation tool **Shared Reading Lesson** (10) will help you notice some significant teaching moves that make the experience powerful for children. After observing the lesson, you may wish to talk with the teacher about the experience. Take a listening and collaborative inquiry stance, remembering that the teacher is most knowledgeable about the students in the class. Some questions or prompts are:

- I noticed that students were paying close attention when you first read the book and they seemed to be wanting to join right in. What were you thinking?
- Talk about the level of engagement you observed in students during the second reading.

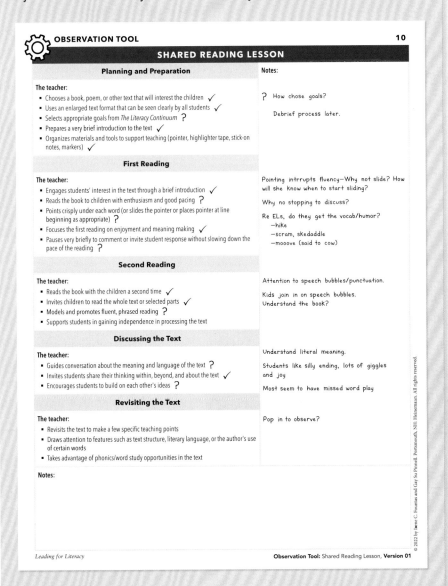

**OBSERVATION TOOL**

The observation tool **Shared Reading Lesson (10)** is designed for use in supporting teacher expertise over time through observation and reflection. It may be helpful to focus on just one box at a time as you work collaboratively with a teacher.

**OBSERVATION TOOL**                                          **10**

**SHARED READING LESSON**

**Planning and Preparation**                    Notes:

The teacher:

- Chooses a book, poem, or other text that will interest the children ✓
- Uses an enlarged text format that can be seen clearly by all students ✓
- Selects appropriate goals from *The Literacy Continuum* ?
- Prepares a very brief introduction to the text ✓
- Organizes materials and tools to support teaching (pointer, highlighter tape, stick-on notes, markers) ✓

? How chose goals?

Debrief process later.

**First Reading**

The teacher:

- Engages students' interest in the text through a brief introduction ✓
- Reads the book to children with enthusiasm and good pacing ?
- Points crisply under each word (or slides the pointer or places pointer at line beginning as appropriate) ?
- Focuses the first reading on enjoyment and meaning making ✓
- Pauses very briefly to comment or invite student response without slowing down the pace of the reading ?

Pointing intrrupts fluency—Why not slide? How will she know when to start sliding?

Why no stopping to discuss?

Re ELs, do they get the vocab/humor?
—hike
—scram, skedaddle
—mooove (said to cow)

**Second Reading**

The teacher:

- Reads the book with the children a second time ✓
- Invites children to read the whole text or selected parts ✓
- Models and promotes fluent, phrased reading ?
- Supports students in gaining independence in processing the text

Attention to speech bubbles/punctuation.

Kids join in on speech bubbles.
Understand the book?

**Discussing the Text**

The teacher:

- Guides conversation about the meaning and language of the text ?
- Invites students share their thinking within, beyond, and about the text ✓
- Encourages students to build on each other's ideas ?

Understand literal meaning.

Students like silly ending, lots of giggles and joy

Most seem to have missed word play

**Revisiting the Text**

The teacher:

- Revisits the text to make a few specific teaching points
- Draws attention to features such as text structure, literary language, or the author's use of certain words
- Takes advantage of phonics/word study opportunities in the text

Pop in to observe?

Notes:

*Leading for Literacy*                        **Observation Tool:** Shared Reading Lesson, **Version 01**

- Shared reading gives the students opportunities to attend to word solving. What opportunities do you see in this text?
- What evidence of learning did you see in the lesson? How do you want to take it further?

# Guided Reading

Guided reading is a small-group instructional context in which a teacher supports each reader's development of a literacy processing system. By bringing together a small group of children who are at a similar point in their reading development and guiding them to process a new text that is leveled on a gradient of difficulty, a teacher is able to provide an incremental amount of challenge at each reader's edge of ability. With the teacher's selective support, the reader learns how to think in new ways about a text and can apply learning to any other text. You will find level-by-level descriptions of readers, the characteristics of texts, and behaviors and understandings to notice, teach for, and support in the Guided Reading section of *The Literacy Continuum*.

## What Is Guided Reading?

For a guided reading lesson, students are grouped according to the teacher's assessment of their reading strengths and the identification of the reading level that will give challenge and opportunities to learn. The teacher works with a small group of students that assessment reveals are alike enough to read the same book and benefit from the instruction. Guided reading supports learners in expanding their processing competencies through highly responsive teaching. The teaching and the matched text support students in building systems of strategic actions which they apply to process increasingly challenging texts. Guided reading is the only instructional context in which leveled texts are used.

Guided reading usually takes place in a corner of the classroom where students can talk in low voices and be heard by the group. Ideally, teachers have a round or kidney-shaped table. The teacher should have his back to the corner so that he can scan the room and the students will be facing the teacher and each other. The group is small, usually three to eight students, assembled according to information from observational notes and assessments. Usually, a teacher can conduct two or three guided reading groups daily, about 15 to 30 minutes each, depending on the grade level. Each student will typically process three to five new, short texts per week.

Teachers use high-quality short fiction and nonfiction texts that are precisely leveled (A–Z), lesson plans or guides, and record-keeping forms to record observations made during the lesson. Also, they need an easel and chart paper as well as magnetic letters or word cards to support the word study portion of the lesson. Books the teacher has selected for the week and materials for the lessons are best arranged on shelves near the small-group area for easy teacher access.

During a guided reading lesson, students are temporarily grouped according to the reading level that will give challenge and opportunities to learn.

## LEARNING OPPORTUNITIES IN GUIDED READING

**Effective Processing of Texts**–*students:*

- Monitor their reading for accuracy and understanding.
- Decode words rapidly and automatically while reading continuous print.
- Take unknown words apart to solve them.
- Use a flexible range of strategies to solve words.
- Use knowledge of language structure to anticipate the sentence.
- Process texts with more complex syntax.
- Demonstrate all dimensions of fluency: rate, pausing, phrasing, stress, and intonation.

**Deeper Understanding of Texts**–*students:*

- Gather information to understand the text while solving words.
- Think about literary aspects such as plot, story problems, and characters while reading the written language.
- Summarize information and ideas while reading nonfiction texts.
- Notice and adjust reading in light of genre.
- Process dialogue with expression.
- Talk about the text after reading it individually, expressing thinking within, beyond, and about it.

**Expanded Content Knowledge**–*students:*

- Bring background knowledge to the reading of a text.
- Synthesize new knowledge acquired from reading.
- Learn scientific or technical words from reading.

**Expanded Language**–*students:*

- Build knowledge of language syntax and grammar by reading it.
- Derive the meaning of new words from contextual information.
- Use new vocabulary in discussion after reading.
- After reading, use academic language to talk about texts.

**Expanded Cultural Knowledge**–*students:*

- Process texts that present facts and ideas from the diverse cultures of the world.
- Search illustrations and written text to understand places and people from different parts of the world.
- Process traditional literature from different cultures.

**Expanded Sense of Community**–*In the introduction and after reading, students:*

- Discuss ideas and new understandings with a small group of peers.
- Talk with others about cultural, social, and emotional issues.

**Figure 11-8.** Learning Opportunities in Guided Reading

## Benefits of Guided Reading

Guided reading provides a setting within which teachers can do the kind of powerful teaching that expands students' ability to read more complex texts. In the guided reading lesson, the reader takes on a more challenging text than she can process independently. The teacher's support, however, makes it possible for the student to read the text successfully with a minimum amount of support. A guided reading lesson offers many learning opportunities (Figure 11-8).

## Structure of a Guided Reading Lesson

Guided reading is highly structured for efficient and intensive teaching. Teachers need to be aware of time and move the lesson along. We outline the shape of the lesson at right (Figure 11-9).

**Planning and Preparation** Having determined the instructional level for each student, the teacher identifies teaching priorities for each student and for the group. Each day the teacher selects a text at the instructional level and makes notes to guide the lesson. Throughout the lesson, the teacher takes notes of observations that will inform teaching in the next lesson.

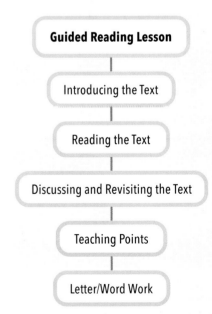

**Guided Reading Lesson**

Introducing the Text

Reading the Text

Discussing and Revisiting the Text

Teaching Points

Letter/Word Work

**Figure 11-9** Structure of a Guided Reading Lesson

**Introducing the Text** The teacher introduces the text in a way that provides just enough information to support students' reading of this more challenging text. The introduction is not long. It sets up the readers to be able to work through the text successfully. It engages students' interest in the text and may explain some background information, draw attention to new or key words that are important for understanding the text, and explain a new idea or concept. But the introduction will leave plenty of problem-solving for the reader to do as he processes the text for himself.

**Reading the Text** Each student reads the whole text individually and silently. (Beginning readers will read in a low voice or whisper until they gain control of silent reading.) The teacher may sample oral reading from some or all the students. Or the teacher of older students may leave them reading silently and move about the classroom to confer with individual readers and return for a brief discussion. As the reading finishes, students may respond in their reader's notebooks or read their independent choice books until everyone is ready for the discussion.

**Discussing and Revisiting the Text** The teacher and students discuss the meaning of the text. The purpose is not to have students retell or prove they read the text but to help them put their thinking into words. As they talk with others, students deepen their understandings. The teacher observes for evidence of students' thinking within, beyond, and about the text.

**Teaching Points** From immediate observations (and from assessment and analysis of reading records taken over time), the teacher makes one or two teaching points (usually going back into the text) that demonstrate, prompt for, or reinforce strategic actions that readers can apply to other texts.

After reading the book, students discuss the meaning of the text as the teacher notices evidence of thinking within, beyond, and about the text.

**Letter/Word Work** The teacher engages students in two to three minutes of preplanned word work designed to help them solve the types of words that they will meet in texts at this level. Word work *does not* take the place of the daily phonics/word study lesson. It is targeted for the needs of students reading at this level.

**Extending the Learning** As an option, the teacher may prompt students to draw and/or write about their reading. This activity offers readers an opportunity to express in writing their thinking within, beyond, and about the text.

**Reflection** After the lesson, the teacher takes a moment to finish making brief notes and plan for the next lesson. She is taking reading records of individual readers on a regular basis and considers these data too. She thinks about whether the book was easy, just right, or hard for the students. This information feeds into the decision about using a more difficult text in the next lesson. (It is not necessary to conduct a benchmark assessment before going up to the next level.)

## What to Listen and Look for in Guided Reading Lessons

During a guided reading lesson, you can observe how a teacher works with a small group of students to expand their abilities to process a new text. The teaching in a guided reading lesson is highly responsive. The teacher is carefully observing how each reader is processing text and is making teaching points—sometimes selected before the lesson but often chosen in the moment based on students' observable behaviors—that strengthen the reader's processing power. Because so many decisions are made before, during, and after a lesson, guided reading offers a rich opportunity for collaborative discussions about a teacher's practice and decision-making. The observation tool **Guided Reading Lesson (11)** can support you in these conversations. After you observe a guided reading lesson, take time to share what you noticed and invite the teacher's thinking. Below are some ideas for conversation openers.

The observation tool **Guided Reading Lesson (11)** is designed for use in supporting teacher expertise over time through observation and reflection. It may be helpful to focus on just one box at a time as you work collaboratively with a teacher.

⚙ OBSERVATION TOOL     11

### GUIDED READING LESSON

#### Planning and Preparation

The teacher:
- Uses assessment data (running records or anecdotal notes) as evidence to support text selection
- Expresses sound rationales for the grouping of students ✓
- Prepares a brief introduction to the text that matches the strengths and needs of the readers ✓

**Notes:** Eric to focus on decision-making during intro and while kids read. Wants to get better at responding to individual needs.

#### Introducing the Text

The teacher:
- Provides a brief, well-placed guide through some, but not every page, of the text ✓
- Helps the readers understand how the book works
- Engages the students in a conversation that sets them up for successful reading of the new text ✓
- Attends to the meaning and the language (including about two or three essential new and important words) in context yawned, mane, darken
- Attends to special print or text features that may be important or new

Nice intro. Made connections, gave kids chance to predict what happens. Kids eager to read.

#### Reading the Text

The teacher:
- Supports the students' ability to self-monitor (or check on) their reading
- Supports the students' ability to search for and use all sources of information (meaning, language, structure, phonological information, and print)
- Helps students learn how to take words apart using several sources of information as they process the text
- Supports the readers' construction of the meaning of the text ✓
- Supports the students' ability to read with phrasing and fluency
- Uses prompts that are not specific to the book but that foster problem-solving by the readers (strategic actions) ✓
- Supports the readers' ability to initiate problem-solving actions as needed as they work through the text
- Helps students learn how to initiate worthwhile independent work if finished before others (e.g., reading, writing about reading)

Good job listening, praising, helping while kids read. A little too quick to tell words. Debrief: Prompt for different strategic actions (find part you know, do you know a similar word).

#### Discussing and Revisiting the Text

The teacher:
- Invites personal response to the text
- Helps readers give immediate attention to the full meaning of the text (thinking within, beyond, and about the text) ✓
- Promotes sharing of thinking and adding to ideas, not teacher-student questioning only ✓
- Helps students think about the big important text ideas and their relevance (the "so what") ✓

Eric prompts, and kids conclude book is fantasy. Nice! Asks kids to explain thinking, expand answers, tell why they think that. Really good discussion.

#### Teaching Points

The teacher:
- Selects from immediate observations one or two teaching points to demonstrate, prompt for, or reinforce strategic actions that readers can apply to other texts ✓

T.P on reading with expression. Gives kids chance to notice punctuation themselves and react with expression. Well done!

#### Letter/Word Work

The teacher:     r-controlled vowells (ar, er, ir, or, ur)
- Preplans work that helps students learn how to take words apart (not words read incorrectly from the book)
- Provides two or three minutes of fast-paced attention to letters, words, and how they work ✓
- Supports flexibility and quick word recognition ✓

Vowel pattern sort. Lesson tightly focused, moves quickly. Lots of noticing—kids discover the lesson principle.

*Leading for Literacy*     **Observation Tool:** Guided Reading Lesson, **Version 01**

- ■ Let's talk about the evidence of learning you saw in this lesson. What are you thinking the readers learned how to do for themselves?
- ■ Let's compare our observations to the behaviors and understandings in *The Literacy Continuum*.
- ■ What do you think these readers need to learn how to do next?
- ■ What do you think are the strengths of each reader in the group?

**Budget for Books** Your leadership role includes the responsible use of financial resources to maximize the benefit to students. There is never enough in the budget to address all the needs schools have, so every decision needs to be a wise one.

In an authentic literacy classroom, the most important resource is books that represent a variety of lived experiences and paper for reading and writing. Books are a long term and economical investment, not a resource that will need to be replaced in a few years. There will always be a need for more beautiful books to create rich classroom libraries, multiple copies of texts for book clubs and guided reading, enlarged print books for shared community print experiences, and beautiful picture books for read-aloud at every grade level.

Work with your team to create an inventory of the books in each classroom and to make a budget plan to invest in adequate resources that can be built on each year. Talk with them about expenditures that can be reduced—for us the first reduction is often the photocopying budget.

# Book Clubs

Students from kindergarten through the upper grades find book clubs to be an enjoyable experience. The context offers a natural extension of the discussion model that students have become familiar with during interactive read-aloud. Students choose a book based on their interest, read it or a section of it as agreed upon, prepare to talk about it with a small group of peers, and discuss it with their group at a scheduled meeting. The teacher meets with the group to help keep the discussion on track and lift students' thinking when needed, but students become increasingly independent as they gain experience. They take responsibility for the discussion and learn to use collaborative language, follow a topic, build on each other's ideas, and disagree courteously. By participating in group discussion, students together build a richer understanding of the text than any one student could get from the reading on their own. You will find grade-by-grade descriptions of the characteristics of texts for literature discussion and behaviors and understandings to notice, teach, and support in the Interactive Read-Aloud and Literature Discussion section of *The Literacy Continuum*.

## What Are Book Clubs?

Students meet in small, heterogenous groups to discuss a book that they have all chosen to read. They sit in a circle and not at a table; the meeting area might work or a quiet corner where they won't disturb others. Each student has a copy of the book for reference. The group members listen to and talk with each other. The teacher is in the circle but intervenes only when needed. Through sharing their thinking, students build a richer understanding than any one of them could gain from independent reading alone, while practicing norms for productive, respectful book discussion. Over time as students become more experienced, teachers move slightly back to signal more independent talk by students. Teachers often schedule book clubs once or twice a month for 15–20 minutes at grades K–2 and for 20–30 minutes at grades 3 and higher. For example, one teacher scheduled one book club meeting each Friday of the month while another scheduled book clubs each day for the first week of each month.

Book clubs require multiple copies of a title so each student has a book in hand. To have one book club, a teacher would need four different titles for students to choose from, with about six copies of each. The books that students can choose from are often related in some way—by genre, form, author, topic, theme—but they may just be a variety of good books that will appeal to students and not be connected in a specific way. Titles may be connected by the focus of text or may be linked to interactive read-aloud text sets. Students may use their reader's notebooks to jot their thinking and/or sticky notes placed at points in the text to prepare for book club.

Teachers typically have a special place in the classroom for the multiple copies of titles, organized into sets. Sometimes teachers are able to sequence book club choices so that they are coordinated with the categories of the books used in interactive read-aloud. After a book has been used for a book club meeting, a copy can be placed in the classroom library because other students might want to read it.

## Benefits of Book Clubs

A book club provides an opportunity for students to participate in the kind of activity many adults love all their lives—thinking and talking about books with other people. Not only does the talk deepen comprehension, but it also increase readers' ability to notice and appreciate important aspects of texts. Beyond age appropriateness, students' reading levels are not relevant. If the book is too difficult for any of the students, they can listen to an audio recording. Book clubs provide many of the benefits of interactive read-aloud with expanded opportunities for individuals to express their individual thinking and, perhaps, take on new perspectives from the rich dialogue. Some of the learning opportunities offered in book clubs are listed in Figure 11-10.

| LEARNING OPPORTUNITIES IN BOOK CLUBS | |
|---|---|
| **Effective Processing of Texts**–*students:*<br><br>■ Read (or listen to) a book with an additional "eye" (what thinking would I want to share in the book club?).<br><br>■ Sustain interest in reading a book over several days (for longer texts).<br><br>**Deeper Understanding of Texts**–*students:*<br><br>■ Notice literary aspects such as plot, story problems, and characters while reading (or listening).<br><br>■ Notice and mark important content and ideas while reading (or listening).<br><br>■ Notice characteristics of the genre to talk about with others.<br><br>■ Talk about the text after reading (or listening to) it individually, expressing thinking within, beyond, and about it.<br><br>**Expanded Content Knowledge**–*students:*<br><br>■ Bring background knowledge to the reading of (or listening to) a text.<br><br>■ Synthesize new knowledge acquired from reading and articulate it to others.<br><br>■ Learn and use scientific or technical terms in conversation about a book.<br><br>■ Discuss graphics with others and the facts and ideas they show.<br><br>■ Understand the historical roots of problems of society.<br><br>■ Gain new perspectives on problems of society.<br><br>■ Develop respect for people with identities and lived experiences that differ from one's own.<br><br>■ Develop appreciation for and support their world and the environment. | **Expanded Language**–*students:*<br><br>■ Expand vocabulary by reading (or listening to) a book and talking about it with others.<br><br>■ Sustain talk with others, sometimes using syntax and vocabulary from a text that they all have shared.<br><br>■ Use new vocabulary in discussion after reading.<br><br>■ Use academic language to talk about texts.<br><br>**Expanded Cultural Knowledge**–*students:*<br><br>■ Discuss illustrations and how they show different people and places in the world.<br><br>■ Process traditional literature from different cultures.<br><br>■ Recognize and talk about different styles in illustrations from different cultures.<br><br>**Expanded Sense of Community**–*students:*<br><br>■ Talk with others about cultural, social, and emotional issues, some of which may be beyond their own experiences.<br><br>■ Use conventions of social conversation (turn taking, "I agree (or disagree) because . . ."<br><br>■ Learn to sustain conversation around a topic.<br><br>■ Show courtesy in conversation with others.<br><br>■ Listen thoughtfully to others.<br><br>■ Learn constructive ways of stating an opinion. |

Figure 11-10. Learning Opportunities in Book Clubs

## Structure of a Book Club

In a book club meeting, students listen to and talk to each other about their thinking. They use social conventions to conduct a lively and respectful discussion that incorporates a variety of perspectives. And they do most of the talking (not the teacher). So, while a simple lesson structure is implemented (Figure 11-11), it is up to the students to bring their thinking to share with others. When students are new to book clubs, the teacher will need to model effective social behaviors and language that is productive in a rich dialogue.

**Figure 11-11** Structure for Book Clubs

**Planning and Preparation** The teacher prepares a "book talk" to introduce each of the books in a set to the whole class. A book talk is a one- or two-minute introduction designed to build student interest in the book and give them an idea of the topic or story. Each student then ranks the books (e.g., on a slip of paper with the titles listed) to indicate their preferences. Using the students' preferences, the teacher forms heterogeneous groups, trying to give each student their first or second choice. The teacher prepares a few prompts with key ideas that may be important for students to discuss but leaves plenty of room for students to drive the discussion with their thinking. The teacher makes a schedule so that students know when they will meet. The teacher plans to make an audio recording of books that children have chosen that may be too difficult for them to read independently.

During book club, students learn to use collaborative language, follow a topic, build on each other's ideas, and disagree courteously.

**Independent Reading of the Book** Students read the book independently (or listen to a recording) during independent reading time. As preparation for their group discussion, students may use a few sticky notes or jot down a few page numbers in their reader's notebooks to identify places they want to talk about or questions they have.

**Book Discussion** Each reader has a copy of the book and has prepared something he wants the group to talk about. The teacher (or a student) opens the discussion with a question such as "Who has something to get us started?" Students take turns talking and responding to the comments and questions of other group members. The teacher may interact with comments like:

- "Let's go back to our discussion of _____."
- "Take us to the part of the book that makes you think that."
- "Who else has something to say about that?"

The teacher may need to facilitate discussions at the beginning of the year, but the goal over time is for students to initiate the talk, respond to others in the group, and add to each other's ideas using evidence from the text or personal experiences to build a rich understanding.

Each reader has a copy of the book and has prepared something for the group to talk about.

**Group Evaluation**  At the end of the meeting, students talk with each other to evaluate the meeting on characteristics such as turn-taking and preparation. Questions they may pose include:

- Did we look at the person who was talking?
- Did we take turns?
- Did we make sure everyone got a turn?
- Did we share our thinking?
- Did we build on each other's ideas?

Students talk about what they will work to improve during future book club meetings.

As you can see, the structure is simple, but the students' thinking—and the conversation—are complex. Book clubs give students the maximum opportunity to share their thinking and unique perspectives with their peers. The teacher's role is supportive. She may need to be sure students are grounding their talk in the text rather than rambling; and she prompts them to give specific textual evidence for their comments, predictions, and opinions.

Young children in their first book clubs are accustomed to looking at the teacher and responding to his directions and questions. Book club is a completely different situation. Students are explicitly taught how to engage in book clubs—how to listen to each other and respond before changing the subject. Every social skill used in book clubs is explicitly taught in whole-class minilessons. It is very useful for students to learn these social skills, which are necessary in many situations beyond the classroom.

# OBSERVATION TOOL

Use the observation tool **Book Clubs (12)** to support your observations and collaborative discussions with teachers. It may be helpful to focus on just one box at a time as you work collaboratively with a teacher.

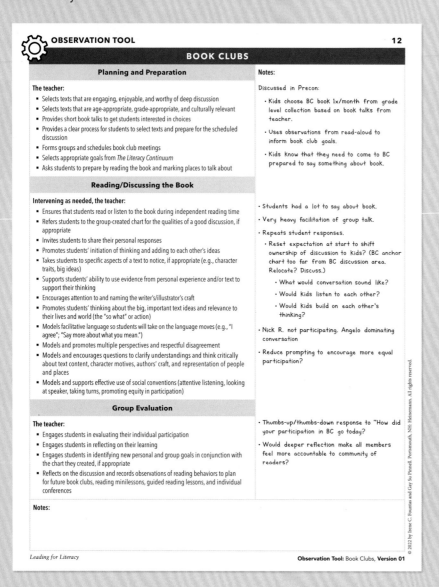

## What to Listen and Look for in Book Clubs

As you observe a book club meeting, you'll want to sit outside the circle but close enough to hear the students. One of the most important characteristics to listen and look for is that the students are doing most of the talking. Other characteristics to notice are listed in the observation tool **Book Clubs (12)**. Use the tool to support productive conversations with the teacher. Take a collaborative stance, remembering that the teacher is the expert about the students and their responses. Prompts and questions that you may wish to use in your conversation include:

- What were you thinking about each child's participation?

- What do you think was the level of interest in this book [topic, kind of story, genre, author]?

- What progress have you seen in your students' ability to have a productive book discussion?

- What are your priorities for this group discussion today?

# Independent Reading as the Foundation of Readers' Workshop

The readers in a classroom community need extensive opportunities to engage in choice, independent reading. The instructional context for independent reading offers children the chance to read, enjoy, and talk about self-selected texts. During independent reading, children have full control of the reading process, although the teacher supports them by offering a rich, well-organized collection of books through which they can browse and select titles that appeal to them and by having brief conversational conferences. An organizational framework, called *readers' workshop,* offers an organized set of language and literacy experiences that support high engagement in reading, student choice, and skilled whole-group, small-group, and individual instruction. Two sections of *The Literacy Continuum,* Interactive Read-Aloud and Literature Discussion and Writing About Reading, are helpful in understanding and supporting readers during independent reading and readers' workshop.

## Readers' Workshop: An Instructional Framework for Independent Reading

Independent reading is an instructional context that is nested within a readers' workshop, an instructional framework that includes minilessons, the small-group contexts of guided reading and book clubs, individual reading conferences, writing about reading, and sharing as a group. We encourage the use of a workshop structure for many reasons that are rooted in theories of effective learning. The children engage in constructive, social, active learning with the support of expert assistance. While engaged in authentic literacy behaviors, they regulate their learning, develop agency, and experience joy and confidence in reading and writing.

During independent reading, children read books of their choosing for a sustained period of time.

The teacher starts a readers' workshop by providing a short minilesson on any aspect of reading that assessment and ongoing observation indicate will be helpful to students. To explain and illustrate the minilesson principle, the teacher often uses a book or text set that students have processed together in interactive read-aloud. Then, students begin independent literacy work with the minilesson principle in mind. Very young students may have several activities, such as rereading easy books they have encountered in guided reading or shared reading, choosing a book from the classroom library, listening to an audio book, or writing. From about second grade, students read independently a book they have chosen from the classroom or school library. They have a reader's notebook in which they collect their thinking and respond to their reading. The teacher conducts brief conferences with students as they are reading. Through an individual conference, a teacher can observe children's understanding of the text as well as support their thinking and help them extend their understandings. During this time, the teacher may also work with small groups in guided reading and book club.

Readers' workshop is, ideally, about 60–90 minutes (more time is needed in the primary grades). The reading minilesson takes about 5–15 minutes, depending on the number of examples and the complexity of the principle. Independent work (reading and writing about reading) takes about 50 to 60 minutes, with group share taking about 2–3 minutes. The reading minilesson and group share take place in the meeting area, while independent reading takes place at students' tables or desks or in areas around the classroom with comfortable seating.

To support independent reading, each classroom library should include hundreds of high-quality books within the reading range of the children in the classroom. The collection can be built over time. (Remember that classroom library books are not organized by levels.) Teachers also need a collection of read-aloud books from text sets that illustrate the principles teachers have chosen for minilessons.

## The Benefits of Independent Reading Within Readers' Workshop

The goal of all reading instruction is competent, voluntary, and high-volume independent reading. Every student needs to live a reading and writing life in school. For us, this means reading with deep understanding and engagement, learning from reading, and expanding the ability to process increasingly complex texts.

**Benefits of Independent Reading**  Independent reading has all the benefits of guided reading, but the ability to read without teacher support is unique and necessary. A high volume of voluntary reading correlates strongly with high test scores (Anderson, Wilson, and Fielding 1988). We believe that, in addition to expecting students to read independently at home, we must find time for independent reading within the school day, because this activity has unique learning opportunities (Figure 11-12).

**Benefits of Reading Minilesson and Group Share**
The reading minilesson and group share are based on principles appropriate to the grade level and the range of texts that students are reading. Reading minilessons and group share offer additional learning opportunities.

**Benefits of Writing About Reading**  Writing in response to reading is a method for exploring and communicating one's thinking. Among the learning opportunities offered by writing about reading, readers can construct knowledge, generate new thinking, clarify their own thinking, and share ideas with other readers. A separate section of *The Literacy Continuum* details the understandings and behaviors related to writing about reading.

Students help co-construct the anchor chart by contributing ideas and observations related to the minilesson principle.

**Reading Minilesson**–students:

- Reengage with rich language and complex structures of mentor texts that are familiar through read aloud.

- Engage in the inquiry process that leads to the discovery and understanding of a general principle.

- Link their previous experiences with texts and their own independent reading.

- "Try out" each new concept before independent application.

- Summarize the new learning and think about its application to their own work.

- Build academic vocabulary.

- Develop a shared language for thinking and talking about books in a classroom community.

**Independent Reading**–students:

- Build reading stamina by processing a large number of fiction and nonfiction texts.

- Exercise choice in the books they read, increasing motivation.

- Greatly expand content knowledge through reading about topics that interest them.

- Greatly expand knowledge of genre characteristics through meeting yearly requirements and also reading widely in the genres of interest.

- Become more aware of their preferences as readers.

- Build self-efficacy as readers.

- Recognize and reflect on the amount and variety of their reading.

- Express their thoughts as they write about reading in a readers' notebook.

**Writing About Reading**–students:

- Express their appreciation and thinking about literature with words or drawings.

- Revisit a text that has been read with the lens of a writer.

- Extend their thinking by revisiting a text.

- Use language structures or vocabulary from the text.

- Articulate new content knowledge gained from reading.

- Express appreciation for the craft of writing and illustrating.

- Write or draw about characters or ideas that inspire them.

- Express critical thinking about the text.

- Analyze the characteristics of texts.

**Group Share**–students:

- Return to a single, explicit principle after applying it to their own reading.

- Share their discoveries about texts with others.

- Use academic vocabulary to share their thinking about books.

**Figure 11-12.** Learning Opportunities in Readers' Workshop

## Structure of Readers' Workshop with Independent Reading

Several of the instructional contexts in this chapter are key parts of a workshop as it moves from a whole-class meeting to individual reading and small-group work and back to a whole-class meeting (Figure 11-13).

**Planning and Preparation** The teacher selects a minilesson *principle* to teach based on ongoing observations and assessments of the students. Mini-lessons can be organized into four categories: (1) management; (2) literary

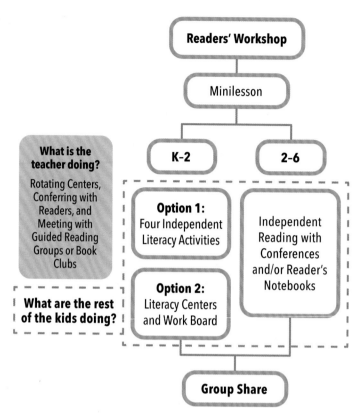

**Figure 11-13** Structure of Readers' Workshop

analysis; (3) strategies and skills; and (4) writing about reading (Figure 11-14). It is helpful when minilessons are further organized into *umbrellas,* which means they are clustered so that students follow a series of lessons that teach different aspects of a similar topic. For example, some umbrellas might be "Using the Classroom Library," "Using the Appropriate Volume of Voice," "Getting Started with a Reader's Notebook," "Studying Biography" (or other genre), and "Nonfiction Text Features." The teacher chooses texts that have been read aloud to the class to use as mentor texts that clearly illustrate the principle.

**Minilesson** At the beginning of the whole-class meeting, the teacher may introduce books that have been added to the classroom library by giving brief (one-minute) book talks. The teacher may choose to talk about the writer, illustrator, and genre; provide a brief "teaser" of the plot or interesting facts; or show a few particularly engaging illustrations or photos. To teach the minilesson, the teacher presents the read-aloud books selected to illustrate the principle. Depending on the principle, the teacher may ask students to attend to some aspect of texts—characters, plot, presentation of content, text structure, and so on. Students have the opportunity to examine the texts, looking across them for characteristics that illustrate the explicit principle. They derive the principle while the teacher writes their comments and adds the principle to the chart. The teacher summarizes and asks students to apply the principle to their independent reading.

## CATEGORIES OF READING MINILESSONS

| | |
|---|---|
| **Management** | Management minilessons focus on routines that are essential to the smooth functioning of the other instructional contexts. These lessons are usually taught close to the beginning of the year and they establish the management system, allowing the entire literacy system to operate in an orderly way and permitting the teacher to put maximum energy into instruction. They include classroom actions such as:<br><br>• Choosing books and putting them back.<br>• Using the readers' notebook.<br>• Learning the routines of book club. |
| **Literary Analysis** | Literary analysis minilessons build students' awareness of the characteristics of various genres and of the elements of fiction and nonfiction texts. |
| **Strategies and Skills** | Strategies and skills lessons reinforce broad principles that every reader in the class needs to learn. While most strategies and skills are taught in guided reading and phonics/word study lessons, bringing them to the students' attention in reading minilessons and asking students to apply them to their own reading can be efficient and effective. |
| **Writing about Reading** | Writing about reading minilessons help students use a reader's notebook to respond to what they read and promote independent literacy learning. Writing about reading lessons range from the very earliest invitations to draw and write about books to the kinds of persuasive and analytic writing that upper elementary students do. |

**Figure 11-14.** Categories of Reading Minilessons

**Grades 2–6: Independent Reading, Writing About Reading, and Conferring** By the middle of grade 2 and beyond, students choose the book(s) they want to read. They then read independently and silently. Students may also choose to write and draw about their reading in a reader's notebook. They may write about any book they are reading or have listened to or talked about, for example, a book they heard during an interactive read-aloud lesson, a text they read aloud with classmates during shared reading, or a book they read and discussed during book club.

The teacher may confer with individual students about their independent reading. During the conference, the teacher talks with a student about a text, may listen to a sample of oral reading, promotes further thinking, may talk about a reader's notebook entry, and provides customized instruction. While

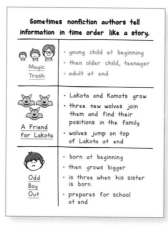

Anchor charts state minilesson principles and become reference tools that help students initiate and regulate learning. (Images from *The Reading Minilessons Book*)

During independent reading, students choose the book they want to read.

students are reading independently, the teacher may also conduct guided reading lessons and/or may hold book clubs.

**Kindergarten–Grade 2: Two Options** In the early grades, children engage in four independent literacy activities or rotate through literacy centers. In the first system (Option 1 in Figure 11-13), children work on the same four literacy activities every day: reading a book, listening to a book, word work, and drawing and writing about reading. They can choose to do them in any order, or the teacher can suggest an order. This system is easy to implement and most useful in the earliest grades.

Teachers can introduce this limited number of activities to the children one at a time. Each activity must be taught, demonstrated, and practiced. If teachers are using *The Reading Minilessons Book* and *The Writing Minilessons Book,* they will find appropriate management minilessons to help students learn each of the routines used in the system.

Teachers start the year by having all students engage in the same activity at the same time. Then, students self-evaluate how they did. Each time a new routine is introduced, teachers start with a short practice period and then gradually lengthen the time. When one routine is established, they introduce another routine. When two or three have been introduced, children can try them one after another in the time period. This process is not lengthy; within a couple of weeks students should be able to handle all four, with refinements coming through minilessons.

The second system (Option 2 in Figure 11-13) is structured around centers and a work board that lists tasks for individuals to complete in order. It is a strong choice for encouraging children to develop independence, self-manage their learning, and work at their own pace when children are taught to use centers productively. A centers and work board system offers a wider range of choice literacy activities to students.

A work board is a colorful and descriptive chart that shows icons indicating tasks for independent reading time (Figure 11-15). Teachers set up the work

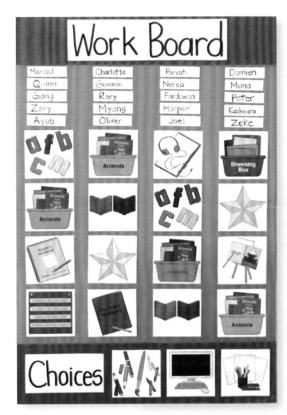

Figure 11-15. Examples of Work Boards

board each week with about four activities, all of which have been carefully taught as routines. The children's names are at the top, and children follow the column of activities below them. Notice that in this system, four different tasks are going on in the classroom at any one time. The teacher may also post options for children to select if they finish all tasks.

Some of this work takes place in centers. A center is a place in the classroom organized for specific learning goals. The center has appropriate materials to enable children to explore, work, and learn independently—as individuals, with partners, or occasionally with small groups. Some permanent centers that are used all year are the classroom library, a writing center, the word work center, and a listening center, as well as centers for computer, poetry, math, and science.

As with the first system, the teacher begins with one activity, and the children practice it and self-evaluate. The scope is gradually widened. When children truly understand the expectations and derive pleasure from the activities (as well as accomplish a great deal of literacy work), it has great benefits. Children become independent, self-regulated learners who help each other. Rather than individual competition, there is collaboration and cooperation in the use of materials and completion of work. Students can give directions and guidance to each other, leaving the teacher more time and attention to work with individuals and small groups. New students entering the classroom during the year have a whole group of friends to help in the orientation.

**Group Share** Students convene in the meeting area, bringing their chosen books and reader's notebooks. They share their discoveries in their own reading relative to the minilesson principle, and the teacher reinforces the minilesson principle.

## What to Listen and Look for in Readers' Workshop

If you want to get a feel for the way things are going in a readers' workshop, it would be a good idea to observe the entire 60–90 minute period. Move around the room during independent reading time and talk softly with some individual readers. The students will enjoy the attention and you can get to know them as readers. You can ask them to share some parts of their reader's notebooks. You may find the observation tool **Readers' Workshop Lesson (13)** helpful in focusing on specific parts of the literacy period, such as the reading minilesson, independent reading, conferring, or group share. At the end of your observation, you may want to take a few moments to reflect with the teacher. You may have talked with several readers, and you can share what you learned from their responses. Some possible conversation openers with the teacher are:

- What did you learn from the student comments in group share?

- How well do you think the students understood and applied the principle?

- Can we look at some entries in reader's notebooks together? I'd like to hear your thinking about what the children have learned and how their writing about reading is improving.

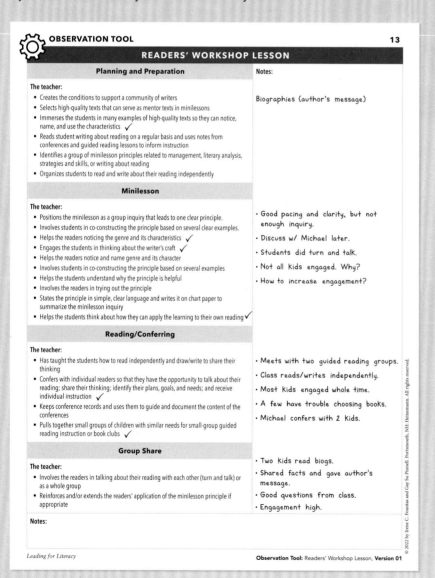

A reader's notebook is a useful tool that can be used by readers to collect their thinking about their reading. The notebook is a place to keep a record of books read, plan for future reading, gather thinking about texts, and engage in conversation with other readers. A reader's notebook that is full of letters, sketches, and other forms of writing at the end of the school year is a treasure. It is a student's reading life all together in a notebook. The dialogue with the teacher is a collection of thinking and a record of conversation between two readers as they think together about texts over a prolonged period of time.

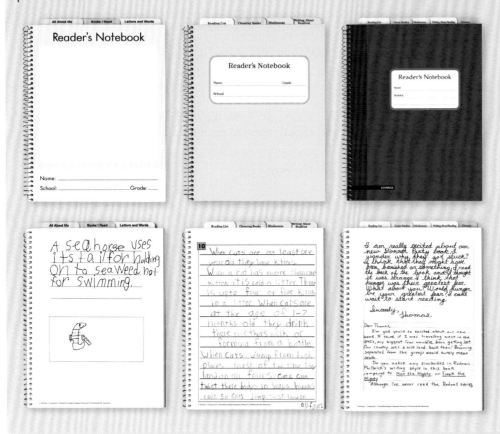

## The Takeaway

In this chapter, we have described five contexts for reading, each of which operates in a different way, has different procedures and purposes, and uses different materials, but all of which work toward the same systems of strategic actions that are described in detail in *The Literacy Continuum* (Chapter 9). In one context, guided reading, leveled books are used to give teachers the opportunity to work with precision to address the strengths and needs of individual children in a small group. In the four other contexts, leveled books are not used. In interactive read-aloud, students engage with texts that are far more complex than they can read for themselves; in shared reading, they are supported by the group, and in book club and independent reading they have choice. All of these contexts, with their varied levels of teacher support, are important elements in a cohesive literacy design for teaching reading. As a school literacy leader, you have the opportunity to support teachers in implementing this dynamic, effective literacy design.

## Think About Your School

- What instructional contexts for reading are teachers using effectively and consistently across the grades?
- Do teachers have the books and materials they need to teach effectively within each of the five instructional contexts? What actions are needed?
- What types of professional learning opportunities would increase teachers' power and effectiveness in each instructional context?

## Move Your School Forward

- Consider holding grade-level meetings that focus on one specific context at a time. Identify strengths and prioritize areas teachers identify as needs.
- Bring together a small group to examine and discuss the instructional contexts that teachers in the school feel the least comfortable with. Identify ways to bring coaching and models of effective practice in every context to teachers to expand their competencies.

# Chapter 12

# A Design for Teaching Writing: Learning to Write from Writers

*Writing workshop is a sophisticated, respectful structure
for teaching writing to students. It values them as learners
and requires a belief that all students can and will learn
to write if given proper and ongoing instruction, and a
block of time to write every day.*
—Janet Angelillo

THE CLASSROOM IS A place where students learn the many ways that writing plays a role in their lives. They learn to write by writing and noticing the decisions that other writers and illustrators make by experiencing and analyzing the craft of mentor texts. They learn to write by engaging in the writing process with the help of the teacher and with the support of their peers.

In this chapter we describe five instructional contexts for writing: (1) modeled writing; (2) shared writing; (3) interactive writing; (4) guided writing; and (5) independent writing. Independent writing is the foundation for writers' workshop structure so that students are engaged in meaningful and productive learning while the teacher works with small groups or confers with individuals. The graphic *A Design for Responsive Literacy Teaching* illustrates how these instructional contexts work coherently across whole-group, small-group, and

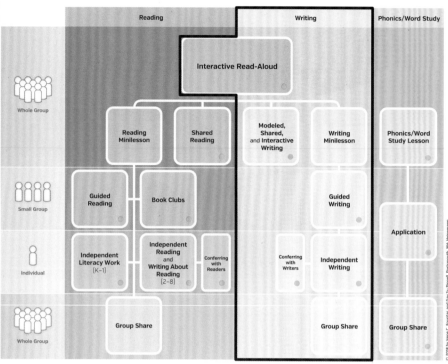

**A Design for Responsive Literacy Teaching**

© 2018 by Irene C. Fountas and Gay Su Pinnell. Portsmouth, NH: Heinemann.

● = Instructional contexts that feature word study

**Figure 12-1.** A Design for Responsive Literacy Teaching

individual instruction alongside the teaching of reading and phonics/word study (Figure 12-1). Modeled, shared, and interactive writing share the same box because, as we will discuss shortly, the three contexts are similar in that the teacher demonstrates all or much of the writing.

Notice that interactive read-aloud crosses over into the writing column. This is because the same texts that are read aloud to students also serve as mentor texts for reading and writing minilessons. Students examine these texts in detail, learning about the author's craft, text organization or structure, figurative language, dialogue, and so on. They form a strong foundation for literacy learning in both reading and writing. Consider the result if students listen to, engage with, discuss, think about, revisit, and analyze almost 200 high-quality texts per year. As part of their whole-group experience, they will form a foundation of shared literary and content knowledge. And if each classroom on a grade level is using these same text sets, then as students move up in the school (or transfer within the district), there is a rich foundation of shared texts that every student knows. The books in interactive read-aloud form a linguistic treasure chest that is available as a resource for readers and writers.

The instructional contexts for writing are like those for reading in that the level of teacher support varies from high teacher support with low student control to very little teacher support with a high level of student independence (Figure 12-2). Deciding which context to use depends on the level of support the students need relative to the challenge of the writing and the teacher's goals for the lesson. Grade-by-grade descriptions of behaviors and understandings to notice, teach for, and support are provided in the Writing section of *The Literacy Continuum*.

## Modeled, Shared, and Interactive Writing

Modeled writing, shared writing, and interactive writing share a common characteristic. In all three contexts, the teacher demonstrates the process of writing a short text in a particular genre, for example, a summary of a book, an

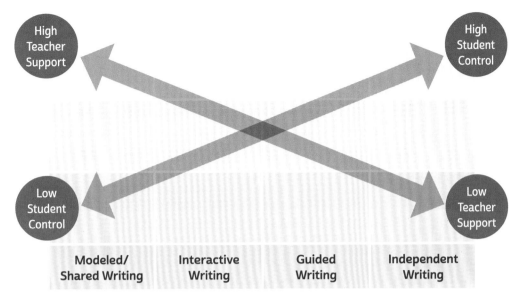

Figure 12-2. Relationship Between Teacher Support and Student Control in Writing

**Central Office Memo**

**Supporting Writing** As part of your role, supporting curriculum coherence within a school and across schools is critical. Writing is a tool for learning and a means to communicate learning across the curriculum, but students also need a focused time each day to study the processes and craft of writing in and of itself to become skilled writers.

Consider the consistency in providing time for writing each day and the school leaders' understanding of the overall goals of the writing curriculum. How do they support teachers in developing the essential understanding that children learn how to write from studying writers and their processes and products to develop their craft? Instead of simply being told, students need to learn how to notice how texts are written and to name the craft moves the authors and illustrators make. This exploration of mentor texts is often a major shift in thinking about the teaching of writing, and the school leader needs to experience the shift in order to be able to support teachers in learning how to think in this way.

effective opening to a story, a letter, or a short book recommendation. The teacher may use the opportunity to demonstrate several parts of the writing process, from thinking of ideas to putting them in writing to revising and editing. The contexts differ, though, in the level of participation by the students.

## What Are Modeled Writing, Shared Writing, and Interactive Writing?

In modeled writing, the teacher composes a piece of writing without soliciting input from the students. The teacher shares the process with the students by "thinking out loud" while constructing the text. For example, with early writers, the teacher may say words slowly, write them letter by letter, draw attention to word spacing, and demonstrate return sweep to the next line. With more experienced writers, the teacher may talk about decisions she is making in terms of word choice, dialogue, or organization as she composes, edits, and revises a piece of writing. The teacher may also bring in some writing she has completed and ask students to notice some aspects of it. Modeled writing may be used as often as the teacher thinks a demonstration is beneficial to students, for example, daily when students are first writing in a new genre, or occasionally to draw every writer's attention to a particular aspect of the writing process or the writer's craft. By modeling all the thinking and writing, the teacher provides the highest level of support to students.

Modeled writing becomes shared writing when the teacher engages students in composing the text. The teacher is the scribe. Freed from the mechanics of spelling, students can give full attention to what they want to communicate in written language. They contribute ideas and may have input into conventions, sound-to-letter work, and spelling of words. The students work as a group *with* the teacher to compose the message.

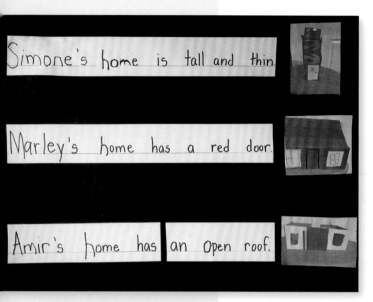

In this example of interactive writing, the teacher chose a few easy-to-hear consonants and a vowel for children to contribute. A few children also were invited to write the letters of their names that they know how to write quickly.

A fifth-grade teacher and her students co-construct a poem using shared writing.

Shared writing becomes interactive writing when the teacher selectively pauses to involve students in the writing at points that have high instructional value. Individual students share the pen and are invited up to the easel to write a letter, a word, a part of a word, or punctuation. It is not necessary for every student to get a turn at the easel in every lesson. The teacher works to keep the writing moving along. Interactive writing is used mainly with younger children in PreK, kindergarten, and grade 1 because of the value it has in focusing their attention on the details of print. It is also productively used with small groups of children at other grade levels who would benefit from this level of support. It is highly effective for English learners as they co-construct the message and can more easily access it to reread.

Modeled, shared, and interactive writing can be used to construct any form of writing, including paragraphs, summaries, lists, recipes, letters, poems, short stories, and memoirs. The teacher may choose any of these types of writing to teach a new aspect of craft, a new text feature, or a new genre. Modeled, shared, or interactive writing takes no more than 10–15 minutes.

Whole-class lessons usually take place in the meeting area, but the teacher may also use modeled, shared, or interactive writing at the table as part of a guided reading or guided writing lesson, or occasionally with an individual student during a writing conference. The teacher may use an easel and chart paper, a computer and connected screen, or a document camera to assure visibility for all students. When writing on an easel, the teacher uses a colored marker (darker colors rather than light orange or yellow), highlighter tape, and correction tape. With younger students, the teacher may also use magnetic letters on a whiteboard, a name chart, and an alphabet chart to teach or reinforce letters and letter-sound relationships.

## Benefits of Modeled, Shared, and Interactive Writing

During a modeled writing lesson, students view the teacher as a fellow writer who engages in the same kinds of thinking and decision-making about genre, craft, and conventions that they do. Observing the writing process in action encourages young writers in their own efforts and often inspires them to take on new challenges in their writing. This is perhaps the most powerful benefit of modeled writing, but many other opportunities for learning are listed in Figure 12-3.

Additional learning opportunities are offered in shared and interactive writing. Once produced, a piece of shared or interactive writing

**Develop Identity and Voice**–*students:*

- Listen to how a writer thinks about her process.
- Listen to how a writer talks about choosing a topic.
- Listen to how a writer uses her own lived experiences as inspiration and a resource.
- Listen to how a writer sees herself and communicates her thinking.
- Listen to how a writer selects a genre according to purpose.
- Learn that a writer can express her own culture and/or language as part of a piece.

**Attend to Process and Product**–*students:*

- Observe a demonstration of how a writer organizes a piece of writing.
- Observe an authentic demonstration by a writer they know.
- Observe a writer who is using foundational conventions like spacing and punctuation (younger students).
- Notice the choices made during the construction, revision, or editing of a written text.
- Hear a writer talk about decisions influenced by genre, audience, and purpose.
- Observe how a piece of writing develops over time.
- Have a classroom resource that they can use as an example for their own writing.

**Engage as a Writing Community**–*students:*

- Share the experience of seeing a writer at work.
- Work together to analyze the decisions of a writer.

**Figure 12-3.** Learning Opportunities in Modeled Writing

**Writer to Writer** Students have an opportunity to talk with the teacher "writer to writer." The teacher's writing will be more mature and skilled than the students' current abilities. The model the teacher provides is not just the writing, however. It is the students' opportunity to understand that writers are people like themselves and that adults also write for many reasons, sometimes for their own pleasure.

might be illustrated by students and remain as a reading resource in the classroom for several months. Students may borrow ideas from the shared writing piece or use it as a mentor text to enrich and expand their own writing. The parts of the text written by children during interactive writing have high instructional value, give children more ownership in the piece, and capture their attention. Other learning opportunities are listed in Figure 12-4.

## Structure of a Shared Writing and Interactive Writing Lesson

Modeled, shared, and interactive writing may be used briefly as part of other lessons. Shared or interactive writing may also be the focus of a lesson. When it is, it follows a structure (Figure 12-5).

During modeled writing, children can observe a writer using foundational conventions such as spacing and punctuation.

| Trash | Treasure |
|---|---|
| wood | treasure chest |
| plastic bottle | iphone holder |
| paper cup | flower pot |
| popsicle sticks | wooden house |
| old sock | puppet |

The teacher can use interactive and shared writing to familiarize students with different genres and forms of writing.

```
┌─────────────────────────┐
│  Shared Writing and     │
│ Interactive Writing Lesson │
└─────────────────────────┘
            │
      ┌───────────┐
      │ Before Writing │
      └───────────┘
            │
      ┌───────────┐
      │ During Writing │
      └───────────┘
            │
      ┌───────────┐
      │ After Writing │
      └───────────┘
```

Figure 12-5 Structure of a Shared Writing and Interactive Writing Lesson

The teacher uses shared writing with fourth graders to capture their ideas about a text.

## LEARNING OPPORTUNITIES IN SHARED WRITING AND INTERACTIVE WRITING

**Both Shared and Interactive Writing**–students:

- Focus attention on composing a meaningful text for a specific purpose.
- Engage in thinking to compose a text with teacher support.
- Participate in the various aspects of the writing process.
- Participate in the writing of different genres that can serve as models for their own writing.
- Record shared classroom experiences–responses to reading, science investigations, art production, and so on.
- Attend to words and parts of words during and after writing.
- Participate in producing a text that has accurate spelling and writing conventions.
- Produce a piece of writing that can be used as a resource for independent writing.
- Use text features as appropriate.
- Reread to remember the composition and to check on the accuracy of the writing.
- Reread in a shared way with others.
- Revisit the text to look closely at the conventions of writing.

**Shared Writing**–students:

- See writing that moves along quickly as the text is composed.
- Observe clear handwriting and effortless spelling of words.

**Interactive Writing**–students:

- Observe and participate in a demonstration of early behaviors (such as directionality, use of space, letters, words, punctuation).
- Increase phonological awareness by saying words slowly to listen for individual sounds or clapping syllables to listen for parts.
- Connect patterns of sounds to letters that represent them.
- Focus attention on applying principles that they are learning in phonics/word study.

Figure 12-4. Learning Opportunities in Shared Writing and Interactive Writing

**Before Writing** Shared and interactive writing emerge from a meaningful experience that provides a purpose and foundation. The teacher engages students in the discussion of a book that has been read aloud, a scientific experiment or other investigation, an exploration of the school or environment, an artistic creation, or any shared experience that lends itself to a record or response in writing. Shared and interactive writing may also be used to support the creation of classroom community routines, for example, how to choose books for independent reading. Before any writing begins, the teacher talks together with the children to decide what to write about, what to say, and how to say it.

**During Writing** In shared and interactive writing, the teacher engages students' thinking to compose a text, thinking about the organization or structure of the text and any features they want to incorporate. The students and the teacher decide the exact wording of the text (or part of it), and the teacher writes. Typically, students reread sentences and then, guided by their discussion, compose, and write more. They may reread to revise or make corrections. The teacher uses correction tape to cover errors or revisions and rewrite over them. The teacher may think aloud to reveal aspects of the writing process to the students.

During interactive writing, the same process is used but the teacher pauses at strategic places to invite the students to "share the pen" and write some of the message. Attention may be given to directionality (left to right and back to left), space between words, hearing words in a sentence, saying words slowly to hear sounds, writing known words quickly, and using conventions (for example, capital letters and punctuation.) The remainder of the group participates while one individual writes quickly; they may trace the letter or word on the carpet or in the air and say the word slowly.

**After Writing** The teacher summarizes the new learning in the lesson and invites writers to apply the principle to their own writing. The writers may revisit the text to revise, proofread, or add material. The teacher may invite the students to revisit the text for further teaching, for example, to notice language, words, or word parts. The text remains displayed in the classroom for a time as a resource, or it may be used as the purpose dictates (e.g., an invitation, a thank-you note, a shopping list, and so on).

## What to Listen and Look for in Shared Writing and Interactive Writing Lessons

Observing shared or interactive writing is an enjoyable experience. If the prewriting experience is meaningful, then students are full of ideas. Group members build on others' ideas and the teacher guides them to a "writable" sentence. In this way, young children learn the constraints that writing places on oral language and the differences between oral language and the more formal written language. All students learn about composing meaningful sentences and using forms of written language such as letters, lists, and summaries. Shared and interactive writing slows down the processing so that the written language and its construction are visible to students. You can look for evidence that:

- The classroom reflects a large amount of shared and interactive writing that the teacher and students have produced so far.
- The teacher has engaged students in a meaningful, shared experience as a base for writing.
- The teacher talks with students to establish a purpose and select an appropriate form.

A student "shares the pen" and writes a word as the teacher uses interactive writing to construct a friendly letter.

The observation tool **Shared Writing and Interactive Writing (14)** is designed for use in supporting teacher expertise over time through observation and reflection. It may be helpful to focus on just one box at a time as you work collaboratively with a teacher.

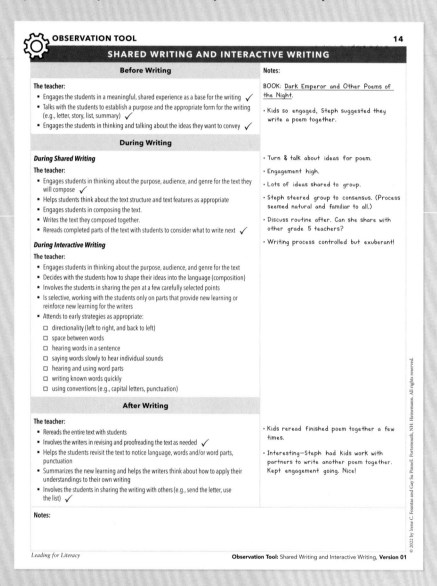

- Students are actively engaged in the composition of the writing, generating ideas, and suggesting sentences and ways of organizing the piece.

- The teacher invites students to reread during the construction of the text to be sure it makes sense and to compose what comes next.

- [For younger students] The teacher teaches explicitly for early behaviors (learning how print works).

- The teacher selects a *few* opportunities to involve students in sharing the pen during interactive writing.

- Student opportunities to write have instructional value and build on what students know.

- Students and the teacher revisit the text to notice language, words and/or word parts, and punctuation.

- The teacher summarizes the new learning and helps writers think how they might apply the understandings to their own writing.

Some indicators to listen and look for are listed in the observation tool **Shared Writing and Interactive Writing (14)**. After observing a lesson, you may wish to talk with the teacher about the experience. Take a listening and collaborative inquiry stance, remembering that the teacher is most knowledgeable about the students in the class. Some questions or prompts are:

- What do you think your students learned how to do as writers today that they will be able to do in their own writing?

- I noticed that _____ offered _____ and seemed to be highly engaged. What were you noticing about their thinking?

- Talk about evidence of learning you observed during the lesson. We can take a look at *The Literacy Continuum* to identify some writing behaviors that we both noticed.
- How do you think shared (or interactive) writing is helping your students as writers?
- Can you share what your writing priorities are for tomorrow?

# Guided Writing

In guided writing, the teacher works with a small group of students who are similar in their writing needs at a particular point in time. For example, some of the students may need help in exploring meaningful ideas for writing, others on writing an effective beginning or ending, and others on using capitalization in their pieces. Guided writing is a good context to use when most of the students have a principle under control but some students still need more support to take on the new learning. Some students may also need more challenge in writing and the teacher can offer it in a guided writing lesson.

## What Is Guided Writing?

A guided writing lesson provides differentiated teaching that addresses the common writing needs of a small group of students. The teacher often provides a brief minilesson or review based on the common need of the group and provides further support through shared or interactive writing. Students can bring their own "in-process" pieces of writing to the table and work on them.

Guided writing usually takes place at a round or horseshoe table with about three to eight students. The teacher may use a chart or easel to compose new writing or share a piece of writing that students can work on as a group. Students can bring their own pieces and the teacher can interact briefly with them as they apply the principle.

Guided writing lessons take place while other students are working on their independent writing and usually last about 10–15 minutes (although students may stay at the table longer to work on their writing, often as partners). They may be held as frequently as the teacher sees the need.

## Benefits of Guided Writing

Guided writing is a way to provide multilevel learning to students. Students demonstrate a wide range of writing competencies (and the gap gets wider as students move up the grades). The responsive writing

*"The child develops as a writer/reader. The notion of reading preceding writing, or vice versa, is a misconception. Listening, speaking, reading, and writing abilities (as aspects of language— both oral and written) develop concurrently and interrelatedly, rather than sequentially."*

**—Bill Teale and Elizabeth Sulzby**

Guided writing usually takes place at a round or horseshoe table with a small group of writers who have a similar writing need at a particular point in time.

**Figure 12-6.** Learning Opportunities in Guided Writing

**Figure 12-7** Structure of a Guided Writing Lesson

teacher's role is to build on strengths and address needs. The teacher can bring more intensity to the instruction in a small group, with all writers participating actively, and with focus on *one* principle, which they apply to their own writing. The learning opportunities offered in guided writing are listed in Figure 12-6.

## Structure of a Guided Writing Lesson

Guided writing groups are temporary and designed to help students gain control of a particular aspect of writing. Guided writing is usually a short "get together" during independent writing time, and it is based on the teacher's analysis of student work, as well as individual writing conferences. Below we describe the structure of the lesson (Figure 12-7).

**Planning and Preparation** The teacher determines the needs of writers by examining student writing that is in progress. The teacher may review drafts of pieces in the students' writing folders and consult observational notes from writing conferences with individual students. The teacher identifies an aspect of writing that a small number of students need to work on and that many other students in the class have under control or are not yet ready for. (If all or almost all students need instruction in a particular area, the teacher prepares a whole-class minilesson.) The teacher consults *The Literacy Continuum* to help in setting priorities and selects the focus of the lesson: one principle of written language. The teacher prepares a brief minilesson based on the principle.

**Minilesson** The teacher teaches a single principle that is based on the needs of a small group of writers at a particular point in time. The lesson is brief and engages students in noticing an important principle that they will be able to apply to their writing. The teacher may remind writers of a piece of shared writing composed during a whole-class lesson or may provide or create a new example. The teacher allows student inquiry to drive the learning by inviting the students to talk about the example and derive the principle.

The teacher provides a piece of writing and invites the students to have a try in their notebooks or with a partner so that they can apply the new understanding. The teacher supports the students' learning with additional teaching and draws attention to effective applications of the principle by members of the group.

**Independent Writing with Conferring** The teacher invites the students to try out the principle using an existing piece of writing or, as appropriate, by beginning a new piece of writing. Students continue to work at the small table as the teacher observes and provides guidance that deepens individual students' understanding of the principle.

**Group Share** The teacher invites students to share what they noticed and learned during the lesson. Students may wish to share specific examples of how they applied the principle to their works in progress. The teacher reinforces the principle and encourages students to share the next steps they will take in their writing.

## What to Listen and Look for in Guided Writing

A guided writing lesson offers opportunities to observe how a teacher selects, plans, and teaches a lesson based on evidence from student data—in this case, the writer's notebook, drafts collected in writing folders, and pieces of writing in progress. Just like guided reading, guided writing offers a rich opportunity for collaborative discussions about a teacher's practice and decision-making. The observation tool **Guided Writing (15)** is designed for use in supporting teacher expertise over time through observation and reflection. After you observe a guided writing lesson, take time to share what you noticed with the teacher and invite collaborative discussion. The following conversation prompts may get you started:

- Let's take a look at some of the writing of the students in the group. What's your thinking about their progress?
- What have you taught your students how to do as writers?
- What do you think these writers need to learn how to do next?
- Let's look at *The Literacy Continuum* for writing behaviors and understandings for your grade level and identify the strengths you see in each writer in this group.

The observation tool **Guided Writing (15)** is designed for use in supporting teacher expertise over time through observation and reflection. It may be helpful to focus on just one box at a time as you work collaboratively with a teacher.

**OBSERVATION TOOL**    15

### GUIDED WRITING

#### Planning and Preparation

The teacher:
- Reads and analyzes student writing on a regular basis to identify behaviors and understandings to notice, teach for, and support ✓
- Forms a small, temporary heterogeneous group of writers with similar needs or interests ✓
- Uses the students' needs as writers (student work, notes, and *The Literacy Continuum*) to identify principles ✓
- Articulates the lesson principle in simple, clear language
- Jots some questions that may be helpful in conferences
- Plans how to engage students in small-group sharing

**Notes:**

FOCUS: Improve kids' word spacing and end punctuation.

- Rick to use GW to bring attention to these expectations.
- Punctuation a new skill for second graders.

#### Guided Writing Minilesson

The teacher:
- Gathers the small group together and explains the purpose of their meeting
- Engages the students in inquiry to construct the principle in simple, clear language ✓
- Uses examples from mentor texts as appropriate (texts from interactive read-aloud, teacher or student writing, modeled or shared writing) ✓
- Involves the writers in trying out the principle (have a try) ✓
- Helps the students understand what is important to know and why it is important ✓
- Summarizes and helps the students think about how they can apply the learning to their own writing

- 5 kids in group at easel where morning message posted.
- Kids look at MM to notice what makes it easy to read.
- Nicely guided inquiry—Rick steers to word spacing and end punctuation w/ short lesson on importance of each.

#### Writing/Conferring

The teacher:
- Confers with individual writers in the small group setting to help them apply the new learning
- Engages students in partner conferences as appropriate
- Makes anecdotal notes to document interactions

- Application: Kids choose recent page of writing from notebooks to review for punctuation and word spaces.
- Lots of chatter at tables as kids talk about what they find.
- Nice: Rick has kids add to their pieces and check new writing for spaces and punctuation.

#### Sharing/Reflecting

The teacher:
- Involves the writers in sharing/talking with each other about what they learned how to do as writers and when they might apply the new learning in their writing
- Invites writers to record what they learned in writing folder or writer's notebook
- Plans future whole-group minilessons, guided writing lessons, or individual conferences based on observations of the group's writing behaviors

- Will Rick follow up with the group? How?
- Debrief: What if he had met with the group twice, teaching one skill each time?

**Notes:**

*Leading for Literacy*

**Observation Tool:** Guided Writing, **Version 01**

**Supporting Students' Writing with Digital Tools** As digital devices, platforms, and products emerge and change, technology offers new ways to write and new forms of writing for students to try. Digital tools also create new ways for students and teachers to reach wide audiences with pieces that have real purposes: blogs, reviews, tweets, emails, podcast scripts, posts, and more. As teachers plan writing instruction, they can use digital tools and resources to expand the students' use of the writing process, e.g., generating and recording ideas, tracking edits, sharing and incorporating feedback, and publishing pieces for an audience. Students gain experience in choosing media elements–videos, images, music, and graphics–that make their pieces more effective. As a school leader, consider how digital portfolios can help students, teachers, and families understand progress in writing over time.

## BOOKMAKING

Bookmaking is a powerful way for children to enter into drawing and writing. It brings together important literacy processes and understandings in an authentic experience. When children make books, they view themselves as writers, illustrators, and readers. They experience feelings of independence and accomplishment at having created something that is uniquely their own, and they build stamina and persistence by working on a book over several days. The books that children create are valuable artifacts for the teacher. They contain evidence of what children know about drawing and writing. By analyzing the craft moves and conventions that children use and comparing those to a curriculum document such as *The Literacy Continuum,* teachers can use the information in the books to decide what children need to learn next.

The No School Day Book

I went to the nurse's office today and I had an ear infection.

Then I went to the doctor's office and I got a sticker. The nurse weighed me.

And the doctor did my blood pressure.

And took my temperature and I got another sticker.

I only needed Tylenol™.

# Independent Writing as the Foundation of Writers' Workshop

Like readers' workshop, writers' workshop is an organized set of language and literacy experiences that put a strong instructional frame around students' independent writing. The teacher presents a writing minilesson, confers with individual writers, and may convene a guided writing group to provide differentiated teaching. Students work in their writer's notebooks and on their own pieces of writing. During the workshop, students are learning how to use their writer's notebooks and a process for producing and refining a piece of writing in a genre they have selected. Writers' workshop creates a space within the school day for students to do what professional writers do: write.

## Writers' Workshop: An Instructional Framework for Independent Writing

Independent writing is a daily, structured time that provides students with an ongoing opportunity to work in their writer's notebooks and develop their own pieces of writing. Students select their own topics, compose the language, and write the words, sentences, and paragraphs for themselves. Independent writing is supported by the instruction and community of a writers' workshop.

At the beginning of the workshop, the teacher provides a short minilesson on any aspect of writing that assessment and ongoing observation indicate will be helpful to students. The teacher has a number of minilessons as priorities for the year, drawn from a document like *The Literacy Continuum* and tailored to the observable needs of the writers. After the minilesson, students move to independent writing with the minilesson principle in mind. The teacher works with individuals or small groups until the end of the period when there is a brief group share.

Ideally, the writers' workshop takes place daily and takes about 45–60 minutes. The writing minilesson takes about 5 to 10 minutes, depending on the complexity of the principle and the examples needed. Students spend most of the time writing. Conferences each take about 3–5 minutes, and group share takes about 5–10 minutes at the end. The writing minilesson and group share include the whole class and take place in the meeting area. Independent writing takes place at students' tables or desks.

The teacher needs an easel, document camera, or computer to project examples as well as markers and highlighter tape. Students need their writer's notebooks (grades 2–8), writing folders with resources and stored work (grades K–8), and writing materials. They may also use digital devices and applications. The mentor texts used as examples in the minilesson are available in the classroom for writers to study.

## The Benefits of Independent Writing Within Writer's Workshop

Clear, well-organized writing is an advantage to individuals all of their lives. The best way to develop this ability is to write every day and learn from examples of effective writing.

**Manage Your Time**

**Structuring Writing Time** Ensuring that students have enough time for writing is the greatest challenge for teachers. Perhaps the teachers have allocated dedicated time for the teaching of reading but often the teaching of writing has received less attention. Giving children the assignment to write is not the same as teaching them how to write well. When they learn how to write well, they will be able to write effectively across the day in a variety of disciplines. The structure of a writers' workshop itself will create a rhythm for the teacher and the students and will become an efficient use of time when the foundational procedures are in place.

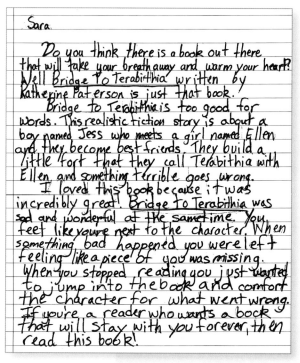

Sara

Do you think there is a book out there that will take your breath away and warm your heart? Well Bridge To Terabithia written by Katherine Paterson is just that book.

Bridge to Terabithia is too good for words. This realistic fiction story is about a boy named Jess who meets a girl named Ellen and they become best friends. They build a little fort that they call Terabithia with Ellen, and something terrible goes wrong.

I loved this book because it was incredibly great. Bridge to Terabithia was sad and wonderful at the same time. You feel like you're next to the character. When something bad happened you were left feeling like a piece of you was missing. When you stopped reading you just wanted to jump into the book and comfort the character for what went wrong. If you're a reader who wants a book that will stay with you forever, then read this book!

After the minilesson on a selected writing principle, the teacher guides students as they apply it to their own writing, as in the sample above.

Writing is a basic tool for learning as well as for communicating with others.

**Benefits of Independent Writing** When students produce a piece of writing that reflects the best of their current abilities, they have concrete evidence of an accomplishment. They can look at the collection of their work across time and self-assess progress. They learn to write in different genres and for different purposes and audiences. Other important learning opportunities are listed in Figure 12-8.

**Benefits of Writing Minilesson and Group Share** The writing minilesson is designed to lift students' writing abilities with every piece of writing they undertake. It is a short, concise, explicit lesson on any aspect of writing. Group share is a way to bring closure to the day's work and for the teacher to gain important assessment information. Opportunities for learning in the writing minilesson and group share are listed in Figure 12-8.

## LEARNING OPPORTUNITIES IN WRITERS' WORKSHOP

*Writing Minilessons–students:*

- Use texts that they read or hear read aloud as mentor texts for their own writing.
- Use the teacher's examples as mentor texts for their own writing.
- Expand their ability to use the writer's craft.
- Through explicit demonstrations and examples, learn more about the conventions of written language.
- Learn to use the steps of the writing process.
- Learn that writers have the flexibility to revise and reorganize texts to accomplish their purposes.
- Develop careful word choice.
- Develop confidence in their ability to use the writing process.
- Self-assess their work in writing and follow their own progress yearly.
- Increase awareness of the role of writing in their lives.

*Independent Writing–students:*

- Build writing stamina and ability over time.
- Receive individual help from the teacher who can answer questions and help in decision-making.
- Apply new learning immediately to an authentic piece of writing.
- Become aware of audiences other than the teacher.
- Expand knowledge of writing genres by selecting and writing them.
- View themselves as writers.
- Build self-efficacy as writers.
- Develop voice in their writing.
- Expand content knowledge through doing research and writing informational genres.
- Keep a record of their productivity in a writing folder (physical or digital) so they can assess the amount and variety of their writing.

*Group Share–students:*

- Are accountable for their use of the minilesson principle in their own writing.
- Share their decisions with other writers in the class.
- Participate as a member of a community of writers.
- Review the minilesson principle to add it to their understandings.

**Figure 12-8.** Learning Opportunities in Writers' Workshop

# Structure of Writers' Workshop with Independent Writing

A writers' workshop helps students develop a rhythm for writing regularly. The structure moves from a whole-class meeting to individual writing and small-group guided writing lessons and back to a whole-class meeting (Figure 12-9).

**Planning and Preparation** The teacher selects a minilesson principle to teach based on ongoing observations and assessments of the students. Writing minilessons can be organized into five categories: (1) management; (2) genre; (3) craft; (4) conventions; and (5) writing process (Figure 12-10). It is helpful when minilessons are further

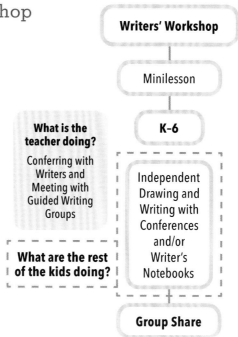

**Figure 12-9** Structure of Writers' Workshop

| CATEGORIES OF WRITING MINILESSONS | |
|---|---|
| **Management** | It is always a good idea to teach management minilessons at the beginning of the year to establish how to engage in the routines of writers' workshop. Students learn how to retrieve supplies and materials and keep them in order. They need to learn how to use a writer's notebook and to keep records and drafts in the writing folder. |
| **Genre** | Students learn the characteristics of effective writing within specific genres, such as functional texts, narrative texts, persuasive texts, poetic texts, and hybrid texts. They learn to write with purpose and voice in specific forms within each genre. |
| **Craft** | Producing an effective piece of fiction or nonfiction writing involves clear organization and well-developed ideas. The writer makes careful word choices and constructs sentences to convey precise meaning. The text is well organized and has voice (reveals the person behind the writing). Writing minilessons help young writers develop their own style. It is important to note that the writing minilessons on craft include inquiry. Students are presented with clear examples from texts that they know well or shown examples which they discuss and connect, identifying feature that show what writers do. |
| **Conventions** | Knowing and observing the conventions of writing make it possible to communicate ideas clearly. Beginners are learning the basics of writing words left to right, leaving space between words, handwriting, and the constraints writing makes in oral language. Older students, however, continue to learn conventions across the years. They learn to accurately use punctuation and capitalization, paragraphing, and refine spelling. |
| **Writing Process** | The same processes are used over and over (some simultaneously) in producing a piece of writing. Young writers grow in sophistication over time by engaging in the steps of this process. They expect to draft and revise writing, and the writing minilesson teaches them the value of the process. Process minilessons usually take place close to the beginning of the year so that students can engage in it right away. |

**Figure 12-10.** Categories of Writing Minilessons

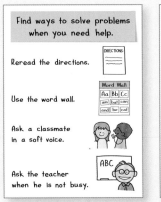

Anchor charts are developed with students as they derive minilesson principles. They serve as a reference tool as students apply the principle in their own writing. (Images from *The Writing Minilessons Book*)

> *"Reading is like breathing in, and writing is like breathing out."*
>
> **–Pam Allyn and Ernest Morrell**

When students produce a piece of writing that reflects the best of their current abilities, they have concrete evidence of an accomplishment.

organized into *umbrellas*, groups of lessons which are directed at different aspects of the same big idea. Sample umbrellas might be "Adding Dialogue to Writing," "Learning About Punctuation," "Working Together in the Classroom," or "Making Powerful Word Choices." The teacher chooses mentor texts familiar to students or prepares other examples that illustrate the minilesson principle.

**Minilesson** To teach management minilessons, the teacher describes and demonstrates routines that promote efficiency and self-regulation during the workshop. To teach genre, craft, conventions, and writing process minilessons, the teacher often presents several texts the students know from their interactive read-aloud experience as examples and asks students to attend to some aspect of writing—details, description, presentation of content, organization such as comparison, and so on. The students think across texts or examples to derive the principle, which the teacher writes on an anchor chart. The anchor chart is co-constructed by the teacher and the students. It states the minilesson principle in clear, concise language and captures students' thinking about examples of the principle in books and application of the principle in new writing.

The teacher summarizes the principle and invites students to "have a try" with a partner by applying their understandings to a new example. The teacher then summarizes the lesson and asks students to apply the principle to their own writing.

**Independent Writing and Conferring** Students may collect ideas, write, draw, or reread entries in a writer's notebook. They might work on a piece of writing. They learn to engage in all aspects of the writing process in order to effectively communicate their message(s) to the intended audience. Pieces of writing that students are currently working on are kept in the student's writing folder. Finished pieces are saved in a hanging folder.

# WRITING IN A WRITER'S NOTEBOOK

A writer's notebook is an organized resource that captures a child's writing life. The notebook is a place for students to gather and record ideas, sketch images, collect memories, organize information for future pieces of writing, and try out new ways to write. Students can even attach objects that inspire writing or represent the seeds of an idea for a piece of writing. Items that students may choose to collect include photos, magazine articles, maps, pamphlets, certificates, or ribbons. A writer's notebook is an important tool that supports the daily writing that students do during writers' workshop.

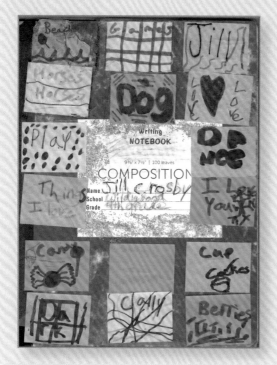

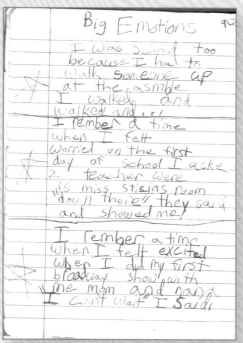

**Daily Notebook Writing**  We suggest that teachers plan for children to spend 10 minutes a day drawing and writing in or reading from their writer's notebooks outside of the writers' workshop time. This special time can be first thing in the morning when the children enter the classroom or at another specific time of the day. There are many advantages for students when they get in the habit of 10 minutes of notebook drawing and writing daily–they will develop confidence and fluency in sharing their thoughts in writing and build a notebook full of meaningful seeds for their writing projects.

The students will learn how to use their notebooks through minilessons the teacher will provide in writers' workshop but will take their knowledge of the process to their daily quick-writing time.

The teacher may confer with individual students about their independent writing. The teacher may discuss a new piece of writing with a student, look for evidence that a student is applying a minilesson principle, and talk with the student about what help is needed or what the student is working on as a writer. While students are writing independently, the teacher may also conduct small-group guided writing lessons.

**Group Share**  Students convene in the meeting area, bringing their writing folders and writer's notebooks. During a group share, the teacher reinforces and assesses new understandings. Students share their work with a community of writers.

During a conference, the teacher may guide a student to begin another action within the writing process.

The observation tool **Writers' Workshop Lesson (16)** is designed for use in supporting teacher expertise over time through observation and reflection. It may be helpful to focus on just one box at a time as you work collaboratively with a teacher.

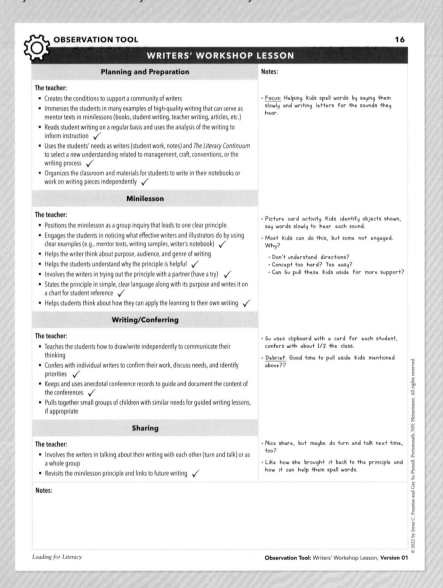

# What to Listen and Look for in Writers' Workshop

Observe the entire writers' workshop if possible. During the workshop, you will observe several components, but you and your colleagues may want to select one area to focus on. The observation tool **Writers' Workshop Lesson (16)** may be helpful in focusing on specific parts of the workshop and then reflecting on the lesson with the teacher. Generally it is a good idea to observe silently, though you may decide to get permission to talk with individual students about their writing. Some possible conversation openers with the teacher are:

- Can you share your insights about _____ as a writer? [Repeat with another student if appropriate and look at the writing folders.]

- Talk about your students. What have you taught them how to do?

- What are your priorities for your next minilesson? Let's take a look at *The Literacy Continuum.*

# The Takeaway

Writing is a basic tool for learning as well as for communicating with others. Writing is multifaceted in that it orchestrates thinking, language, and mechanics. Throughout their lives, students will need to use many genres and forms of writing for a wide range of purposes and audiences.

In this chapter, we have described five contexts for teaching writing, each of which operates in a different way, with different procedures and purposes, but all of which work coherently toward the same effective writing processing system that is described in detail in *The Literacy Continuum* (Chapter 9). All of these contexts, with their varied teacher support, are important elements in a cohesive literacy design for teaching writing. As a school literacy leader, you have the opportunity to support classrooms where students learn the many ways that writing plays a role in their lives and experience the joy of writing within a supportive community of fellow writers.

## Think About Your School

- Are all students becoming stronger and more effective writers each year? What is the best evidence of their progress?
- Are teachers using all the instructional contexts for writing to effectively support students in taking on new learning and applying it to their writing?
- Are some instructional contexts for writing underutilized? What is in the way of teachers effectively delivering instruction in those contexts?

## Move Your School Forward

- If some instructional contexts for writing appear to be underutilized in some classrooms, arrange for the coach to work with those teachers on expanding their practice to include writing in all contexts. If you do not have an instructional coach in your school, you might pair teachers who need extra help in this area with teachers who are making adequate use of all contexts for writing.

# Chapter 13

# Phonics, Spelling, and Word Study for Reading and Writing

*Students need hands-on opportunities to manipulate word
features in a way that allows them to generalize beyond
isolated, individual examples to entire groups of words that
are spelled the same way.*
—Connie Juel and Cecilia Minden-Cupp

NO ASPECT OF LITERACY education has been debated more than phonics, and
we often wonder why it is debated at all. Phonics is a critical part of learning
to read effectively. The more rapidly and effectively children can read words,
the more accurate and fluent their reading of continuous text, making it possible to give greater attention to meaning. Phonics and word study form an
instructional approach designed to teach children to use letter/sound relationships to solve words in reading and spell words in writing. Although phonics
and word study lessons are explicit and separate from the other contexts for
reading, a comprehensive design for literacy learning provides for explicit phonics instruction within all literacy contexts. In this way, students can become
aware of and use what they are learning about letters, sounds, and words in

- easel
- chart paper
- large and individual dry-erase boards and markers
- magnetic letters, magnetic word cards, and magnetic surface
- pocket chart
- foam letters, sandpaper letters
- premade and blank letter, word, and picture cards
- alphabet linking chart [PreK-2]
- consonant cluster linking chart
- name chart [PreK-1]
- sort sheets
- Elkonin box cards
- word wall
- word study folders

Children need many and varied experiences with letters in order to learn their distinguishing characteristics.

daily explicit phonics and word study lessons. But the benefits go beyond a simple chance to apply phonics; they are reciprocal. For example:

- Interactive read-aloud, shared reading, guided reading, book clubs, and independent reading expand vocabulary as students derive new words from context.

- In shared reading, children have a chance to actively apply what they are learning about how print works and make new discoveries.

- In guided reading, teachers can draw attention to letter-sound relationships, syllables, and word parts that make decoding more efficient. Every guided reading lesson includes "word work" instruction that explicitly demonstrates word solving.

- In conferences, writing minilessons, and guided writing, teachers can draw attention to morphology, to more complex letter/sound relationships, and to words with irregular spellings.

Every time students work on print, they build implicit knowledge of how words work. In addition, teachers bring explicit examples to their attention. In all the settings mentioned above, children will encounter some concepts *before* an explicit lesson brings them to close attention in an isolated way. This allows students to make connections as they participate in and apply the concepts. The more you already know about something—even in an implicit way—the more it is possible to increase learning. And the more sense explicit lessons will make to the learner.

It also is important for teachers to notice opportunities to be responsive. Peter Johnston and colleagues (2020) describe how systematic teaching needs to be opportunistically timed to coincide with children's noticings:

> Students develop word knowledge faster because we *systematically* attend to their *actual* conceptual understanding from careful observation. We are well aware of common patterns of development, but we do not constrain children to learning in a fixed sequence. Our teaching of these relationships is *systematically* related to the concepts and strategies they know and are beginning to grasp. Our instruction is also *opportunistic*. When children notice patterns, we capitalize on the fact that they have initiated learning. When explicit instruction is timed to coincide with a feature children notice or a problem they face, learning is more likely to be rapid.

Consequently, the more teachers know about the alphabetic system, and the more they observe students' conceptual progress, the more agile they can be in their instruction.

# What Is Phonics, Spelling, and Word Study?

We see phonics and word study as the development of a broad spectrum of understandings related to words. From a beginning understanding of print, sounds, and letters, children's understanding about words grows to highly sophisticated levels, even into adulthood. What we want is for students to become explorers and discoverers of words. Phonics is not a mechanical process; it is a child's first venture into the fascinating way words work.

## Nine Areas of Learning

An important task in teaching phonics, spelling, and word study is to present lessons that reflect a systematic, organized approach to becoming an expert word solver. The following areas of learning represent a comprehensive inventory of phonics, spelling, and word study knowledge.

**Early Literacy Concepts**  Early understandings about literacy are crucial to children's ability to understand instruction in phonics, reading, and writing. Often, you do not find explicit lessons in concepts such as how to open a book and read; that you read the print, not the picture; left to right directionality; and the use of space to define words. Children who have had very few preschool experiences with reading will develop understandings quickly with explicit teaching and an immersion in shared and guided reading.

**Phonological Awareness**  A key to becoming literate is the ability to hear the sounds in words. *Phonological awareness* is general awareness that words are made up of sounds; it includes the awareness of rhymes (words that sound alike in some way), and segments in words such as onsets and rimes. The individual sounds are called *phonemes*, and students need to be able to identify and distinguish them in words. Hearing the sounds in words (and eventually in sequence) is an essential element in the ability to connect sounds to letters. When children have developed sensitivity to the units of sound, they can map the sound system onto their symbols.

An alphabet linking chart is an indispensable resource in primary classrooms, while a consonant cluster chart is more useful with older children. Both provide links to the connections between letters, sounds, and words.

When learning to build words, children can work with magnetic letters, foam letters, tile letters, or letter cards.

**Letter Knowledge** There are fifty-two symbols, or letters, that represent the sounds (phonemes) of the English language. Children need to learn early how to distinguish one letter from another by looking at the *distinctive features*. Once these forms are learned (and students can hear phonemes in words) the two can be connected. This is known as the *alphabetic principle*.

**Letter-Sound Relationships** The sounds of oral language and the graphic forms are related in simple ways but also in very complex ways. Some letters can be related to several sounds (for example *a, s*). Some sounds can be connected to several letters, including parts of words like *-ough*. Students learn to look for and recognize these letter combinations as units, which makes word solving more efficient. But in the early grades, the simple relationships are learned first.

**Spelling Patterns** Word solving can be accelerated and made more efficient by knowledge of word patterns such as phonograms. Spelling patterns help learners understand the relationship between sounds and letters and discover the larger parts of words. Spelling patterns include phonograms, common affixes, and other word parts.

**High-Frequency Words** Readers and writers need a strong core of known words so that problem-solving can take place against a backdrop of accuracy. Beginning readers take control of a small number of high-frequency words that do not lend themselves to decoding (e.g., *the*). Knowing these words allows their reading to sound more natural. Students use decoding skills to solve many words and also acquire high-frequency words, thus continually adding to their core of learned words that they can recognize without effort. It is useful for older students to consciously work on the ability to spell a large number of high-frequency words (at least 500 by the end of elementary school).

**Word Meaning/Vocabulary** The words a person knows in a language are a *vocabulary,* and this refers to oral language. But we also have a reading and writing vocabulary (which overlap but are different). For comprehension in reading and coherence in writing, students need a large vocabulary of words they know. At more advanced levels, they explore words with multiple meanings, figurative meanings of words, and the use of Greek and Latin roots in deriving meaning. Throughout life, individuals are constantly adding to their vocabularies.

**Word Structure** Words are built according to rules. Looking at the structure of words will help students learn how words are related to each other and how they can be changed by adding letters, letter clusters, and larger word

Sorting activities are not just for primary students. Here, fifth graders sort words according to their Latin roots.

parts. The smallest part of a word that has meaning is a *morpheme*. Morphemes can be "free" in that they have meaning on their own (e.g., *play*) or they can be "bound" because they add meaning (e.g., *-ing*). Studying the morphology of words helps in decoding, in understanding meaning, and in constructing sentences.

## KEY TERMS IN WORD STUDY

Some key linguistic terms are relevant to making decisions about your instructional design for word study, and they can be very confusing. This glossary of key terms offers a quick review.

| | |
|---|---|
| **ALPHABETIC PRINCIPLE** | The concept that there is a relationship between the spoken sounds in oral language and the graphic forms in written language. |
| **ETYMOLOGY** | The history, or origin, of a word and how its meanings have developed over time. |
| **GRAPHEME** | A letter or cluster of letters representing a single sound, or phoneme, for example, *a*, *eigh*, *ay*. |
| **MORPHOLOGICAL AWARENESS** | The recognition, awareness, and use of units of meaning in words. |
| **MORPHOLOGY** | The combination of morphemes (building blocks of meaning) to form words; the rules by which words are formed from free and bound morphemes—for example, word roots, prefixes, and suffixes. |
| **ONSET AND RIME** | In a syllable, the part (consonant, consonant cluster, or consonant digraph) that comes before the vowel is an onset, for example, the letters *cr* in *cream*. In a syllable, the ending part containing the letters that represent the vowel sound and the consonant letters that follow is a rime, for example, *dr-eam*. |
| **PHONEMIC (or PHONEME) AWARENESS** | The ability to hear individual sounds (phonemes) in words and to identify and make particular sounds. |
| **PHONETICS** | The scientific study of speech sounds—how the sounds are made vocally and the relation of speech sounds to the total language process. |
| **PHONICS** | The knowledge of letter-sound relationships and how they are used in reading and writing. Teaching phonics refers to helping children acquire this body of knowledge about the oral and written language systems; additionally, teaching phonics helps children use phonics knowledge as part of a reading and writing process. |
| **PHONOGRAMS** | Graphemes that represent a phoneme or combination of phonemes; the "patterns" in language such as *igh* for /i/ or *at* as in *hat*. |
| **PHONOLOGICAL AWARENESS** | The awareness of words, rhyming words, onsets and rimes, syllables, and individual sounds (phonemes). |
| **SPELLING PATTERNS** | Beginning letters (onsets) and common phonograms (rimes), which form the basis for the English syllable. Knowing these patterns, a student can build countless words. |
| **SYLLABICATION** | The division of words into syllables. |
| **WORD MEANING/VOCABULARY** | *Word meaning* refers to the commonly accepted meaning of a word in oral or written language. *Vocabulary* often refers to the words one knows and understands in oral or written language. |

Look for a part of the
word that can help.

in-side
The word is inside!

Use your finger to help you learn
how to take apart new words.

prob

proba

probably

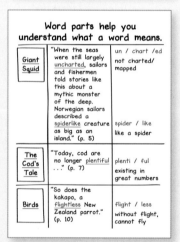

Word parts help you
understand what a word means.

| Giant Squid | "When the seas were still largely uncharted, sailors and fishermen told stories like this about a mythic monster of the deep. Norwegian sailors described a spiderlike creature as big as an island." (p. 5) | un / chart /ed not charted/ mapped |
| | | spider / like like a spider |
| The Cod's Tale | "Today, cod are no longer plentiful . . ." (p. 7) | plenti / ful existing in great numbers |
| Birds | "So does the kakapo, a flightless New Zealand parrot." (p. 10) | flight / less without flight, cannot fly |

Classroom anchor charts like these
are useful references for students
as they apply phonics principles
independently or with partners.

**Word-Solving Actions** Word-solving actions include all of the active strategic moves that readers and writers make using the eight categories of knowledge listed above. We want readers and writers to use everything they know, but to use understandings *strategically* and *efficiently*.

## The Research Base for Phonics and Word Study

We suggest that strong phonics instruction in the early years is necessary *but not sufficient alone* for ongoing literacy progress. Students need strong instruction in how words work across years of education. And it is obvious that they need many opportunities for rich experiences with texts to build content knowledge and comprehension.

We have extensively examined the research related to phonics and word study, including many syntheses of studies. We do not base any conclusion on a single study or a handful of short-term studies involving only a few students. We include here twelve compelling principles from research on effective phonics and word study instruction. These principles, which are supported by research as referenced in the back of this book, are basic to an effective design for phonics and word learning *across the grades*. (You may want to download a more detailed paper from fp.pub/community.)

1. Daily, explicit phonics instruction is effective when taught in a sequence that ranges from simple to more complex in a cumulative process.

2. Effective instruction assures that children develop strong phonological awareness, including awareness of individual phonemes or sounds, in the first two years of schooling.

3. Children need to learn how to look at print and to name the individual symbols.

4. Instruction that includes helping children learn that letters and sounds are connected in a systematic way (the alphabetic principle) is essential.

5. Effective phonics instruction includes synthetic approaches (moving through words sound by sound and/or letter by letter) and analytic approaches (noticing parts and patterns in words and taking words apart).

6. Noticing and seeking word patterns and their relationships to sounds helps readers and writers expand their word-solving ability.

7. Children need to learn the structure of words and to use this knowledge flexibly to take words apart.

8. Readers and writers need a repertoire of known words so that problem-solving takes place against a backdrop of accurate reading.

9. Readers and writers need a flexible range of in-the-head strategic actions to apply as they read or write. These actions include the ability to solve words but also to comprehend and read with fluency.

10. Effective word study instruction includes robust teaching of vocabulary and spelling across the grades.

11. Written language is complex; it is essential for teachers to understand the simple and complex relationships between graphic symbols and phonemic elements, as well as base words, word roots, and etymology.

12. An effective literacy design includes daily explicit phonics instruction and takes place within a comprehensive approach so that learners have ample opportunities to apply their understandings as they engage in meaningful reading and writing.

## Benefits of Phonics, Spelling, and Word Study

Students will benefit from the opportunity to look closely at words and to discover connections and patterns. They will also have chances to make discoveries about words and become fascinated with language. When they are reading and writing, students do not always look closely at words and notice the letters and letter patterns. Teachers need to bring children's attention to these features so they can call them to mind later when reading and writing. Through phonics, spelling and word study, students:

- Participate in a sequence of experiences that build upon one another.
- Notice and use powerful examples of the ways words are connected.
- Establish foundations of knowledge about sounds and letters.
- Systemize knowledge about written language and how it works.
- Give attention to and learn about word structure (syllables, base words, root words, affixes).
- Develop systematic ways of studying the spelling of words.
- Acquire powerful ways for deriving the meaning of words (through morphology).
- Learn about the ways language evolves across history.
- Understand connections between different world languages.

## The Word on Spelling

There are many reasons for students to learn how to spell well. The most important reason is students' need for other people to understand what they write, and spelling errors can make that harder. Families and society expect students to communicate with accurate spelling in their writing so they will leave readers with positive impressions and communicate with purpose and clarity. Spelling needs to be a visible part of word study instruction if students are to apply effective strategies for learning new words and writing most words quickly and accurately. They also need to know about the variety of resources they can check their spelling against when they are unsure.

**Manage Your Budget**

**Ensuring Essential Resources.** At a time when resources are precious few, you need not think about replenishing consumables for learning about phonics and word study. The most useful tools for learning about words are the hands-on manipulatives that offer children the ability to have kinesthetic experiences with words. These include resources such as colorful plastic magnet letters, sandpaper letters, sand trays, dry-erase boards, and pocket charts that can be used year after year.

Consider each classroom in your school and take an inventory of the manipulatives. Notice how they are organized for children to use them independently. Work with your team to create a budget that adds more manipulatives for each classroom until there is an adequate supply for the essential resources or the number of students in the class.

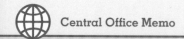
To develop strong spelling skills, students need frequent opportunities to inquire about word patterns and structure and to develop a love of words. When the instruction focuses on helping students learn how letters, sounds, and words work, they learn to take words apart to read them and to construct words letter by letter and part by part to write them. A consistent approach to constructing words as part of the word study teaching and attention to spelling as part of the writing approach across the grades will ensure that all students become competent spellers.

## The Word on Vocabulary

An extensive vocabulary is essential for effective oral and written communication. When teachers plan for vocabulary instruction that is cognitively challenging and when they look for opportunities to expand students' development of vocabulary across the day, students have exposure to relevant, useful words that become part of their oral and written vocabulary and enhance their comprehension of texts.

**Vocabulary Teaching Opportunities** When teachers show a love for the sounds and meanings of language with all its nuances, students become language-conscious and develop a curiosity about words. Opportunities for vocabulary development abound in interactive read-aloud and shared reading as well as wide independent reading. In addition, teachers have opportunities to teach discipline-specific vocabulary related to content-area learning. Students learn about specific word choice and genre-specific words in writing minilessons.

**Teaching for Word-Solving Strategies** Teachers help their students develop ways of learning word meaning—everything from looking at meaningful word parts such as prefixes and suffixes to studying Greek and Latin roots to using context in reading. Often specific reading and writing minilessons, in which the teacher involves the students in inquiry, provide a meaningful context for expanding their word-solving competencies. Phonics and word study minilessons as described in this chapter provide opportunities for children to learn specific principles for solving word meanings and applying their understandings in their reading and writing.

**Studying Individual Words** Teachers who love words also see the value of helping children study deeply one or two individual words a day to stimulate their curiosity and challenge them to expand their language competencies. Vocabulary power is directly related to students' competencies as speakers, readers, and writers and can be an exciting part of in-school and outside-of-school learning.

## Working with English Learners

All languages have different phonological systems, and they may differ slightly (or a great deal) from English. A student may have excellent phonological awareness in her own language but now need to build that awareness in English. Meaningless "training" for long periods of time on English phonology may be confusing or boring. That's why every experience a student has in English needs to be packed with as much meaning as possible.

Teachers can work with students to focus on the letters and accept dialects that vary. They can help students notice how a word *looks*. If students are young enough, they may quickly acquire almost standard English phonology; or, they may always have slight variations that do not get in the way of decoding and comprehending text. If students are older, they can still process and understand the text.

### DEVELOPING EFFICIENT SYSTEMS FOR LEARNING WORDS

Young readers construct their repertoire of known words and flexible ways of solving words, and their progress is usually very rapid. Kaye (2007) analyzed proficient second graders' behaviors across a school year. In her examination of more than 2,500 text-reading behaviors, the 21 proficient readers demonstrated more than 60 ways (both one-step and multistep actions) to solve words—and these were only the behaviors they displayed overtly.

All words read correctly by students demonstrated their ability to recognize words instantly or engage in quick "covert" problem-solving. The proficient second graders usually worked with large sub-word units. They never articulated words phoneme by phoneme. Presumably they *could* "sound out" words when needed because they had excellent knowledge of letter-sound relationships. But they appeared to take more efficient or "economical" approaches, as described by Clay (2001). These readers also were extremely active in their problem-solving: they *never* appealed to the teacher without first initiating an attempt. These proficient word solvers had learned many words; more important, they had developed important systems for learning words.

## Structure of a Phonics, Spelling, and Word Study Lesson

When considering what constitutes effective phonics instruction, two questions often arise:

- Should instruction be explicit or implicit, that is, embedded in the processes of reading and writing?
- Should we teach students directly or allow students to discover or generalize essential concepts for themselves?

A coherent literacy system answers both questions in the affirmative, with a "both/and" (instead of "either/or") approach. A driving goal of our teaching is to help children become active examiners and analyzers of print. We want them always to be searching for connections and patterns, to form categories of knowledge, and to have a store of examples to which they can refer.

Instruction in phonics and word study may take place across all literacy contexts while reading or writing, but here we examine the structure of the minilesson that we recommend daily. Typically, phonics and word study begin with a whole-class lesson that focuses on an aspect of language appropriate for the grade level. The teacher's goal is to communicate a clear, concise principle of language that students need to learn and apply to reading and writing. We recommend placing phonics and word study lessons in an intentional, three-part lesson structure (Figure 13-1), as presented in broad strokes below. For this structure we assume that the Apply activity is performed simultaneously by all students working with partners or in small groups. Depending on the number of sets of materials available, young students could rotate to a word study center.

**Teach** The teacher provides a concise, inquiry-based minilesson based on one specific and clear principle related to what students need to learn at a particular point in time. Often the teacher asks students to study words that exemplify the principle and guides them to construct their understandings and arrive at the principle themselves. For some principles, the teacher may need to state the principle first and then show examples. In either case, the teacher writes the principle in precise language on a chart or easel and students generate more examples. The teacher then describes the application activity.

**Apply** Students engage in an active, "hands-on" application activity independently or with a partner. The application is based on routines that students have been taught and that they know well. They might sort letters, make words, sort words, write, or engage in other active exploration of the lesson principle. Students can work independently or with a partner.

**Share** Students meet for a brief discussion at the end of the period so they can share what they discovered during the application activity. Finally, the teacher returns to the lesson principle, using clear language that students can remember. This provides a useful assessment opportunity.

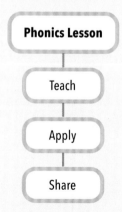

**Figure 13-1** Structure of a Phonics, Spelling, and Word Study Lesson

## The Power of Inquiry

Well-planned and -organized direct teaching of language principles is critical, but lessons also must contain an element of inquiry so students engage in constructing their understandings. The inclusion of inquiry, where possible, rivets students' attention to discovering and constructing understanding for themselves; it makes the lesson enjoyable, even exciting. Students come to seek patterns and discover words, which we hope will be lifetime habits.

# When Can Phonics, Spelling, and Word Study Instruction Take Place?

Explicit attention to phonics, spelling, and word study takes place at several times during the day. Teaching, application, and sharing are provided both during a separate, dedicated time for "out of text" teaching and during "in-text" instructional contexts, such as interactive read-aloud, shared reading, and guided reading (Figure 13-2).

| Out-of-Text Teaching | Lesson Structure | In-Text Teaching |
|---|---|---|
| **TEACH** | | |
| PWS • Lesson (Generative Principle) • Inquiry-Based | • Whole Group | IRA SR • Interactive Read-Aloud • Shared Reading • Modeled/Shared/Interactive Writing |
| **APPLY** | | |
| PWS • Hands-On Practice • Constructive Experiences | • Small Group or Literacy Centers (K–1) • Partners • Individuals | GR BC • Guided Reading • Book Clubs |
| **SHARE** | | |
| PWS • Assessment • Summary • Link to Reading and Writing | • Whole Group | IR • Independent Reading • Independent Writing |

**Figure 13-2.** Systematic Instruction for Phonics, Spelling, and Word Study

Use the **Phonics, Spelling, and Word Study Lesson (17)** tool to support teacher expertise over time through observation and reflection.

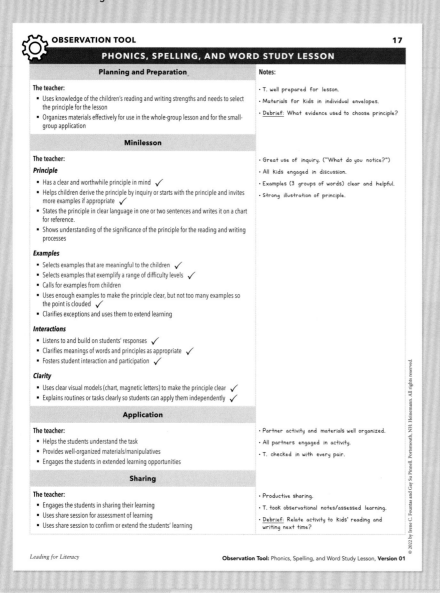

# What to Listen and Look for in a Phonics, Spelling, and Word Study Lesson

Observe the entire lesson, if possible. The observation tool **Phonics, Spelling, and Word Study Lesson (17)** may be helpful in deciding what to focus on during the lesson. You may have the opportunity to reflect with the teacher afterward. If so, here are some conversation openers that may be useful.

- What did you learn about the students' phonics knowledge?

- What do you think the students learned about words that they can apply in their reading? writing?

- Some of the students were excited about noticing connections between words. What have you found to be especially helpful in getting them interested in words?

- What did you observe in the students' application of the principle? What do you think students learned from the application?

- What are your priorities for the next few minilessons?

# The Takeaway

Phonics, spelling, word analysis, and grammar and usage strategies are important, but they are not the end goal of literacy education. Their importance lies in their contribution to students' reading and writing of continuous text. The more that students can solve words, derive the meaning of words, spell words, and parse language syntax rapidly, fluently, and unconsciously, the more likely they are to read and write with competence and ease.

We have described nine areas of learning that offer an approximation of typical learning over time. We've also provided a simple, three-part structure for teaching phonics and word study principles through inquiry-based minilessons. By itself, a phonics or word study minilesson will not help teachers achieve what you want for all the students in your school. Children need to use their developing understandings of words and word-solving *all the time* as they read and write.

A variety of phonics, spelling, and word study lessons can be presented with picture cards, letter and word cards, and a pocket chart.

## Think About Your School

- How do teachers create fascination with and interest in learning about words?

- Is there evidence that children are active examiners and analyzers of print?

- Are teachers helping students learn about words by actively searching for connections and patterns?

- Are teachers explicitly and effectively teaching and facilitating student-centered discovery to support children in taking on the greatest amount of learning possible each day in phonics instruction?

## Move Your School Forward

- Consider sending home to parents an overview of the phonics and word study curriculum, including a rationale for explicit phonics lessons within the literacy block.

- Work with your central office partners to ensure adequate funding for the materials used in phonics instruction and word study. You might want to share with then the list of materials presented on page 240.

# Chapter 14

## Assuring Access and Equity for English Learners

*Schools that affirm and promote English learners' language
and cultural backgrounds, take into account their social
and economic circumstances, adopt a collective approach
to their education, and promote the participation of their
families and communities are in the best position to advance
improvements in their education.*
—Sonia Nieto

FORTUNATELY FOR SCHOOL SYSTEMS in the United States, a group of students
who have the capability and experience to significantly enrich every classroom
they enter are increasing in number: English learners. These students bring new
perspectives, varied life experiences, and rich funds of cultural knowledge to
every teaching and learning opportunity. They have the potential to positively
impact our schools. If our goal is to educate students to become global citizens,
then multilingual students, who already speak more than one language and
have a growing understanding of more than one culture, enjoy a great advantage. Multilingual learners are actively learning to be global citizens because

they are experiencing more than one culture—a home culture and a school culture. And they are learning more than one language—at least one home language and the language of academic English. As they negotiate these cultures and languages, they are gaining valuable perspectives and understandings that will serve them well throughout their lives and careers as citizens of the world. They also help monolingual students (and teachers) understand the world in all its diversity. Simply put, students who know a language other than English are not a *problem* for the school or an individual teacher; they are an *asset*.

# Beyond the Label

English learners deserve a high-quality education that prepares them for college and careers *and* that nourishes their home language and culture. The great diversity among English learners can make this goal challenging to achieve. The moment we begin to consider the education of a linguistically diverse group of learners, we perceive almost immediately the limitations of a label. A label such as *English learners* or *emergent bilinguals* may be useful when identifying the broad needs of a particular group of students, acquiring extra resources to support them, and helping teachers work with them in appropriate ways. But we must take care that the label does not keep us from seeing the individual. Cornelius Minor (2019) cautions that "labels cannot cover our whole humanity. . . . We lose lots of human capital each year because people bearing essential insights and experiences are wearing labels that we've been conditioned to ignore."

Multilingual learners are alike in only one way: they are learning English. Consider all the other ways these children vary:

- Their home languages are different from each other. For example, the home languages of some students are not based on an alphabetic system, as in English. And even among home languages with an alphabetic system, the relationships between sounds and letters vary greatly.

- Even if they speak the *same* language, their family's country or region of origin may vary, which means different understandings of phonology (for example, dialects) and distinctive cultural differences.

- Diverse students come from different cultural backgrounds. Their accustomed ways of behaving and making decisions may vary from one another and from the school culture.

- Even if they speak the same language and come from the same country of origin, they will vary in *length of time* in the United States. Some may be newcomers, while many others will have been born and grown up in the U.S.
- They will certainly vary in the level of English that they currently can understand, speak, and write.
- They will vary in the amount of education they have received. Some students may have had limited opportunities to attend school before immigrating to the United States. Other students, including English learners born in the U.S., may have gaps or significant interruptions in their formal education.
- The number of English speakers and the amount of English spoken in their homes will be different.

EL Connection

**English Learners**
- Long-term English learners (seven years or more in the U.S.)
- Newly arrived (strong foundation and schooling in home language)
- Newly arrived (little or inconsistent education in home language)

## Language Is Identity

As we move past labels to see the individual children in our schools, it's important to remember that a child's language is at the core of a child's identity. Language is more than learning vocabulary or syntax or semantics. Language is intimately connected to culture, personality, and one's sense of self. It's an integral part of who we are as individuals and it connects us with a community, which is critical for our well-being and even survival. We even develop different ways of using language in different contexts—home, neighborhood, solemn occasions like funerals, and formal occasions like speeches and interviews. When someone publicly corrects, denigrates, or makes fun of our language, we feel diminished and with good reason.

As a school leader, you have the opportunity to honor, sustain, and even grow the linguistic and cultural diversity within your school. Our schools, our teams, and our students stand to benefit greatly from our English learners. One of the most important priorities for school leaders is providing effective education for this group of learners that ensures access to grade-level content and equity in learning academic English. In this chapter, we discuss conditions that support English learners at the school level and in individual classrooms.

**Academic vs. Conversational English** It's important to distinguish between a child's ability to engage in informal conversation and the same child's ability to use and understand the academic language of school. Some children pick up conversational English quickly, but that can be misleading. Our most important responsibility to English learners is to help them develop the language competencies they need to access and excel in the academic program.

## Schoolwide Supports for English Learners

English learners and their families are valuable linguistic and cultural resources within the school and classroom communities. By taking the time to discover and learn about these children and their families, schools can use their knowledge and experiences to strengthen teaching and learning for all students.

## A Positive Stance

*Problem* or *promise*? *Lacking* or *lucky*? *Struggles* or *strengths*? *Challenges* or *competencies*? The language we use to talk about students reveals everything about our stance toward their potential as learners. This is never truer than in the language we use to think and talk about the multilingual students in our schools. When you happen upon conversations among teachers about English learners, what does their talk reveal about their perspectives on these students in their classrooms or the stance they take toward these learners in your school? Do teachers perceive these students as having a deficit, with significant barriers to overcome? Or do teachers perceive English learners as possessing assets, rich capabilities, and funds of knowledge on which to draw?

This poster featuring flags from around the world is just one way the school celebrates different cultures and languages.

Our language reveals our mindset.

Recently, a superintendent of a school district located in a wealthy suburb of a large city was interviewed by the local newspaper. The school district had been given a B grade from the state. With good intentions, the superintendent explained that she was very happy with the grade because, in comparison with other wealthy districts in the state, hers had a subgroup (about 5%) of students who were immigrants and didn't yet speak English. The intent was to help the community understand that the teachers had a hard job but were doing it well. However, in the news article, her explanation came across like this: "This group of children is dragging down our scores. Our teachers have a harder job than other teachers." That's not the message that the superintendent intended to convey, of course, but her language unintentionally revealed the district's stance toward English learners.

The language we use and the stance we take are based on the values we hold. As you consider the values of your school, you might ask: Do our values honor multilingualism and encourage students and families to maintain their home languages? Are educators committed to implementing a set of culturally relevant practices that increase *all* learners' access to academic opportunity? Does the culture of our school encourage families and communities to share their funds of knowledge? Do the norms in our school make space for diverse perspectives and experiences?

A positive stance means seeing the advantages that English learners bring to a school. We should see them as people who have something to teach everyone in the school community—both teachers and students alike. For example:

A positive stance means seeing the advantages that English learners bring to a school.

- Native English speakers have the opportunity to learn new language expressions and customs of people who are not just like themselves and thus build important skills for their future.

- Teachers have a chance to expand their pedagogical skills and implement culturally relevant teaching practices.

- Families of English learners can bring richness into the school and classroom by sharing their histories, cultural artifacts, customs, crafts, and areas of expertise.

- The school is more vibrant and interesting to everyone.

Celebrate diversity! Even if your school has a relatively homogenous population of students, they will be living and working in a world that is very diverse. You may need to reach out to your community or partner with other schools to provide students with authentic experiences that promote these values. It is to the advantage of all students to interact and create friendships with people who are different in many ways from themselves. Diversity and inclusivity will be characteristics of a future society and a good place to begin experiencing them is in school.

## Know and Respect the Home Languages and Literacy Practices of Families

Educators in the school have a responsibility to know the nature of the languages spoken by the families whose children attend the school. But that's just the beginning. It's valuable to know as much as possible about each family's culture and experiences—their values, history, religion, and traditions; the places they've lived; and even their stance on the political and social conditions of their country of origin. How much schooling have their children received? Have their children lived in this country their entire lives? Were they born here? Are they recent immigrants or refugees?

The goal at the beginning of the year is to discover as much as you can about the students and their families. Establish intake procedures that respectfully gather all the important information that teachers and specialists need to know to create effective lessons and meaningful literacy experiences for each child in the school, whether they are learning English or have spoken it all their lives.

You may find it helpful to develop a home language or home experiences survey for new families—preferably one that is oral, informal, and brief. Part of the intake questionnaire could ask families to list books and other print and digital resources in any language that they have available to them at home. Identify families' literacy practices at home,

**Celebrating Language Diversity**
Look for evidence that languages other than English are spoken and welcomed in the school, for example, welcome signs, printed forms, labels, and even schoolwide announcements in the various home languages of students.

EL Connection

**Important Information to Learn About English Learners and Their Families**
- Home language
- Home country
- Life experiences
- School experiences and records
- Home language proficiency in listening, speaking, reading, writing
- English proficiency in listening, speaking, reading, writing
- Cultural literacy practices
- Learning preferences
- Special needs
- Interests and talents
- Social-emotional experiences

It is valuable to know as much as possible about each family's culture and experiences.

**Making Information Accessible to Families** Ensure that intake and enrollment procedures are easy to implement across all languages represented at the school. Create multiple ways for families to access key information related to school policies and procedures, including choices they can make for their children and special services available to them. You may wish to create booklets or short videos in the home languages of families. You can enlist members of the language community to help. Remind groups that communicate with families on behalf of the school, such as parent-teacher organizations or after-school clubs, to translate key information into the home languages of students.

Central Office Memo

**Supporting High-Quality Translations** To communicate with families in their home languages, schools sometimes use machine translation software. However, such software may not produce accurate, sensible translations in certain languages. Districts can support schools by hiring the services of professional translators to translate information that is crucial for families to know. Someone in the community may help.

both in English and just as importantly in their home languages. Learn about culturally situated roles that families typically play in their child's education. What are their expectations for their child's schooling? And how are they most comfortable interacting with educators?

Throughout the process of gathering information, reassure families that the information they share will be used only for the purpose of creating the best learning experience for their students. Design intake procedures that respect the rights of parents and students. And be sensitive to how styles of communication vary across cultures and the degree of personal information that families are comfortable sharing.

## Create a Welcoming Environment

As a school leader, you know that a school's environment sends important messages to staff and visitors alike. From the signage along the road, to the organization of the front office, to the bulletin boards in the hallways, to the sounds from the cafeteria—the school environment matters. To English learners and their families, the environment of the school conveys a special message: either that they are welcome here—that this is a community to which they belong—or just the opposite.

A welcoming environment begins with what students and families see, hear, and experience as they enter and move through the school. Consider a large welcome sign in multiple languages near the front doors. Within the office, the school demonstrates its partnership with families by posting the rights of parents in multiple languages, providing key documents in the home languages of families, and displaying cards from local businesses in various languages.

The staff at the front desk are smiling and greet families in their home languages. Ideally, some staff members are fluent in the languages most heavily represented at the school and are always ready to translate for families and students. In the hallways, artifacts from home cultures are on display and maps, photos, and portraits of leaders and "heroes" from around the world hang from the walls. Signs throughout the school are in multiple languages, and diverse languages can be spotted on bulletin boards. Multiple languages are spoken in the hallways and in the cafeteria, by students and educators alike. In the school library, a multilingual section features a robust collection of fiction and nonfiction titles at a wide range of levels and about many different topics. Schoolwide literacy events honor the multilingualism of students in the school and celebrate their cultures by inviting authors, lyricists, poets, journalists, actors, and community leaders who write in and speak their home languages.

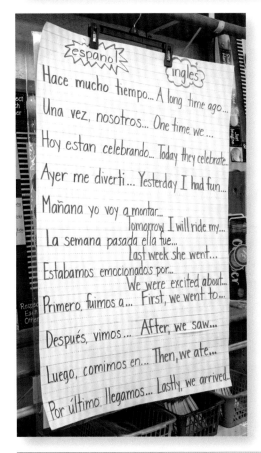

A climate of acceptance within the school helps English learners and their families feel that they belong.

**Digital Literacy**

**Don't Forget the Website** Like the physical environment, the digital environment of a school reflects its values. Incorporate multilingualism into the school's website. Feature English learners and their families prominently in the site's design, and share their stories and accomplishments regularly in blogs, photos, and social media posts.

**EL Connection**

**Home Visits** Encourage teachers to plan home visits to get to know the school's families better. You or one other school leader may wish to accompany the classroom teacher in meeting families away from school. Home visits can be a powerful way to communicate the school's commitment to get to know each family and the home languages and cultures they treasure.

Cultivating a climate of multi-language acquisition and acceptance within the school will help English learners and their families feel that they belong. Precisely because they *are* learning English and because they *do bring* knowledge of another culture, they are immediately and warmly welcomed as valuable contributors to the school community. They know from what they see, hear, and experience throughout the school that they are important and accepted.

## Engage Families

The families of English learners care deeply about them and want them to succeed. Many are immigrants who came here to provide a better life for their children. As you get to know the families of English learners and welcome them into the school community, identify effective ways to engage them regularly in their children's learning and in the life of the school. Begin by learning the best ways to communicate with them: printed material, phone calls or voicemail, text messages, or email. Plan events that are tailored to the needs of families of English learners: for example, a discussion of community resources that families may find valuable or a walkthrough of academic policies and expectations at the school, including how to access students' grades online. Schedule events at times when families are most likely to be able to attend. And ask school and community volunteers who are fluent in the home languages of the families to translate the information presented, as needed.

Another important way to engage families is to involve them in collaborative decision-making at the school level. Publish schoolwide surveys and requests for input from families in multiple languages. Encourage family members to take leadership roles at the school—sitting on a school advisory committee, chairing a committee in the parent-teacher organization, or leading up a schoolwide event, such as a literacy night, for example. Take time to communicate with individual families—using their preferred method of communication—to get their thoughts and opinions about decisions the school is making.

## Know the Linguistic and English Language Teaching Expertise of Your Team

Implementing effective and culturally relevant practices that increase *all* learners' access to academic opportunity is a responsibility shared by all the educators at the school. It's imperative that every teacher, specialist, coach, member of the support staff, and administrator:

- Understands the important role played by home languages and culture in all learning, and especially in the learning of a new language.
- Affirms students' home languages and funds of cultural knowledge as important resources for the entire school community.

- Celebrates diversity within the school.
- Commits to the implementation of sound, culturally responsive teaching practices and materials that prepare students to be global citizens.

Every educator will be at a different point in taking on this responsibility and putting it into practice, which is why it is important to assess the linguistic and teaching expertise of your school team. Take an inventory. Are some staff members fluent in one or more of the home languages represented at the school? Do any of the teachers have training, certifications, or endorsements in teaching English learners? Have any educators studied culturally relevant teaching practices, perhaps within a professional learning community, through in-service training, or at a conference? Do any staff members have connections within the community that could support multilingual families and students at the school?

When you identify expertise on the team, find ways to utilize and expand the expertise. Ask teachers with ESL/ELD training to share one or two effective practices during each staff meeting or present the essentials of second language acquisition during an after-school roundtable discussion. Create protocols for allowing multilingual members of the staff to step out of their roles during the school day to translate for families in the office or in a conference. Encourage reflective practice among grade-level teams and the school's ESL specialist. As a group, they can share, reflect upon, and learn from their experiences teaching English learners.

When you identify areas of needed expertise, provide opportunities for professional learning. Ask district specialists to design and deliver in-service experiences on asset-based teaching practices or attend a staff meeting to share district initiatives that support English learners and their families. Encourage teachers to participate in communities of practice that gather to study, apply, and assess multilingual learning and culturally responsive teaching in their classrooms—and join one yourself! Identify funding to send teachers to professional conferences that offer sessions on teaching English learners. When they return, invite them to present what they learned to the entire team. No single educator can know all there is to know about teaching English learners. But together, in collaboration, a team of educators can become highly proficient at delivering instruction and designing learning experiences that ensure every student's access to academic opportunity and a literate life.

## Classroom Supports for English Learners

When English learners enter the classroom, they have already accomplished a huge amount of learning. They have learned a language for communicating with others. They have acquired a phonological system, a syntactic system, and a semantic system (see Chapter 8) for their home language. They have learned

> "Linguistic capital–the advantages that come with being literate in two languages–offers benefits both to society and to individuals who are bilingual and biliterate."
> —Sonia Nieto

*how to learn* language, a process that they are now applying to learning English. With these accomplishments and abilities, English learners are poised to succeed academically. They deserve expert teaching in every classroom, every day, that builds upon and expands their learning and linguistic prowess and helps them reach their academic potential.

## Authentic Talk Is Valued

When you open the door to a classroom, what do you hear? Is there talk? And if there is, who is doing the talking and what is it about?

All literacy learning is grounded in oral language. The use of oral language helps all students, including English learners, process and deepen their understanding of texts and grade-level content. Talk is thinking. When students are talking, they are learning—communicating and refining ideas, developing their understandings, supporting their perspectives, and making meaning from texts and experiences. The teacher is talking *with* students, not *at* or *for* students.

During effective lessons and application activities, English learners are frequently engaged in collaborative conversations with their peers and the teacher. Their talk is authentic because the activities of the classroom are authentic. Students have a genuine need to produce comprehensible language because they are living a literate life—doing the things literate people want and need to do—within the classroom and the school. They are putting academic language and language structures to use in purposeful ways.

According to Clay (2005):

> Children who come to school speaking any language well have a preparation for literacy learning that is to be valued, whatever that prior language is . . . we need to see them as competent children who speak and problem-solve well in their first culture and who are lucky to be learning a second language while they are young and active language learners. It is surprising how rapid their progress can be.

Every student who speaks a language—any language—is a competent user of language, whether or not the child has full control of English. Students learn language by using it. The classroom provides daily demonstrations of language in use, orally and through texts.

## Home Languages Are Honored

Maintaining a home language other than English is an asset and carries many benefits, including helping students create broader perspectives about the world and the United States, developing a powerful sense of their identity, and opening up additional educational and career opportunities. It is important for family members to speak to their children in their home language. When children develop strong control of their home language, they have built a strong foundation for learning English, too.

As you observe teachers and students in their classrooms, notice evidence that the home languages of children are being utilized and nurtured in teaching and learning.

- Centers, tools, and materials are labeled in multiple languages.

- Anchor charts are highly visual, and the key understandings are translated into the home languages of the students in the class.

- The classroom library includes bins of books written in languages other than English and about many cultures.

- Students who share a home language use the language to exchange ideas, assist one other in comprehending English words and concepts, and deepen their knowledge of grade-level content. When one student in a pair is more proficient in English, the students can move between or mix languages (translanguaging) during turn and talk and other activities to make meaning.

- Cognates are recorded by students, posted in the classroom, and utilized by the teacher, when possible, to help clarify an English word.

## Teaching Is Culturally Relevant

Gay (2010) defines *culturally responsive teaching* as "using the cultural knowledge, prior experiences, frames of reference and performance styles of ethnically diverse students to make learning encounters more relevant to and effective for them." Culturally relevant teaching is effective teaching. By considering the cultural practices, norms, histories, and ways of behaving of the students in the classroom, a teacher can optimize teaching and learning.

Culturally relevant teaching requires, of course, that teachers take the stance of learners. They must learn, over time, the cultures of the students in their classrooms and how those cultures influence how the students behave, respond, and learn. Teachers grow in their cultural competence year over year. Yet they recognize that each student is unique. They must discover how even a well-understood culture influences the individual students standing in front of them.

Classrooms need to contain books and materials that reflect the cultures of the students in the school, and indeed, in our diverse world. All students need to experience a wide range of cultures to help them do the thinking they will need to do as global citizens. Evaluate books carefully, asking: *Does the collection reflect the diversity of the world? Do the books promote kindness, empathy, and a willingness to build community? Are the books and other materials free of stereotypes and bias?*

EL Connection

**What Is Translanguaging?**
*Translanguaging* is an intentional choice by multilingual students to use two or more languages to most effectively communicate a message or accomplish a task. For example, a speaker of Spanish and English may begin communicating an idea in English and then deliberately continue the thought in Spanish because Spanish more effectively conveys a particular part of the idea. Translanguaging is used by multilinguals at all levels of proficiency. Helping English learners understand when and how to use their languages, separately or in concert, is an important instructional goal.

*"When English language learners choose to participate or withdraw, their decisions are connected to the teacher's cultural inclusivity in her approach to teaching and learning. If teachers position ELLs as powerful and provide them with many opportunities to develop their positive identity, the students could more actively participate in their own learning."*

—**Bogum Yoon, *Achieving Literacy Success with English Language Learners***

Culturally relevant teaching is student-centered teaching. When our work is centered on students, our concerns shift away from teaching a lesson or covering standards. Instead, our focus is the learning outcomes for students. Teachers engaged in this work will ask: "Did learning occur today?" and "What can I do tomorrow to help students learn more productively?" The answers to these questions necessarily address the whole child, including how the child's culture impacts learning.

When a teacher commits to inclusive and culturally relevant teaching, the children in the class are represented in accurate, authentic ways. The children see themselves in the books and materials that they use for learning. The teaching in each instructional context honors the histories and values of the cultures of the students. Teachers select books that present multiple representations of a culture, because any single story or issue or perspective runs the risk of perpetuating stereotypes. Application activities and learning experiences are shaped by the cultural norms of the learners. Culturally relevant teaching honors and centers the cultural practices, norms, histories, and ways of being and behaving of children and their families.

Structure, strong language support, and responsive teaching help English learners expand both their language and their content knowledge.

When teaching is culturally responsive and relevant, the cultural knowledge, experiences, practices, and perspectives of students influence most of the decisions that a teacher makes on a daily basis:

- Classroom schedule.
- Ways in which students may respond to questions.
- Books used during each instructional context.
- Types of choices that students can make throughout the day.
- Seating options.
- Ways in which students may exhibit their learning.
- Types of individual and collaborative work.
- Examples used during lessons.
- Books available in the classroom library.
- Ways of representing understandings on charts and in graphic organizers.

## Supporting English Learners in Specific Instructional Contexts

Throughout this book, we have argued for inclusive classrooms that reflect the understanding that it is not the class that learns; it is only the individual students who learn. This means that teachers need to assure appropriate opportunities for unique learners who take "different paths to common outcomes" (Clay 1998). They need to avoid stereotyping or generalizing and understand that different individuals will have different responses to instruction. The teacher who knows each child well will acknowledge and consider the strengths and needs of that child within the individual, small-group or whole-group instructional context. The literacy design we described in Chapter 11 provides a predictable structure, strong language support, and the kind of responsive teaching that maximizes the language and literacy progress of English learners. We will briefly highlight some key characteristics that are particularly helpful to the language learner at all levels.

### Interactive Read-Aloud and Literature

**Discussion** Consider the many benefits of interactive read-aloud and small-group book clubs for children to build knowledge and expand language. The entire context, including turn and talk, gives English learners a supportive structure for taking risks, getting input, constructing meaning, and expanding language. Picture books at every grade level provide additional support, and when audio is made available, they can listen to the text many times.

Do the systems in your school support each proficiency level? Are there levels of proficiency for which teachers need more support or strategies? As you review assessment data across the year, are English learners at each proficiency level showing gains?

| Level 1 | Entering | Memorized phrases, small vocabulary of high-frequency words, a few familiar exchanges |
|---|---|---|
| Level 2 | Emerging | Limited range of sentence patterns, some content words, simple verbal and written interactions |
| Level 3 | Developing | Range of phrase and sentence patterns, mid-frequency words and a few hundred content words, interacts in most everyday social situations, performs academic tasks with modifications |
| Level 4 | Expanding | Wider range of utterances with increased accuracy, hundreds of technical words and some idioms, differentiates between formal and informal registers, performs many academic tasks |
| Level 5 | Bridging | Variety of utterances in connected discourse, thousands of technical and content words, frequently used idioms, participates in extended discussions for a wide range of functions and academic tasks |
| Level 6 | Reaching | Fluently produces grade-level utterances with accuracy, uses grade-level vocabulary, variety of idioms, performs academic tasks independently |

Even after English learners reach intermediate and advanced levels of proficiency, they still deserve to receive expert teaching in more challenging aspects of language.

**Shared Reading** Shared reading texts are meant to be read and reread in unison or in choral parts, providing a very high level of support. English learners can join in on parts that they can say as they follow along the lines of the print. Rereading the text several times gives students the opportunity to acquire sentence stems and frames that they can use again and adjust to communicate what they want. The group carries the reading along in an enjoyable way. Shared reading books often have rhythm and playful language. The learning is rich—vocabulary, phonology and pronunciation, tricky language structures and complex English syntax, and understanding that is developed over several readings. Interactive writing, shared writing, and interactive read-aloud are also particularly supportive and productive contexts for English learners.

**Shared/Interactive Writing** This is an ideal context to build on the children's experience and languages. As the children compose and dictate a text or take turns sharing the pen with the teacher, they construct a text that will be easily read because they helped to create it. The text can be reread many times, and the language and vocabulary become well known to the child.

**Guided Reading** This small-group context enables the teacher to observe and respond precisely to the learners' individual responses. Every part of the lesson, including the book introduction, takes into account the unique learners in the group. Teachers begin with texts containing language that is closer to the language the English learner is learning to speak. There are small shifts in language complexity as the reader moves up a gradient of text. The teacher mediates the text challenges with the child's current repertoire of strengths and needs. From each lesson the child learns something he can do as a reader that he can take to his reading of texts of his choice.

**Guided Writing** The teacher uses knowledge of the children as writers to pull together a group of individuals who need the same kind of support as writers. The child produces his own writing, sometimes using a native language or sometimes translanguaging, to create a piece to share with others.

**Independent Choice Reading and Independent Writing** The child has the support of the teacher in individual conferences for private conversations about a book or the child's own writing. The classroom library ideally includes books at a variety of difficulty levels, books in the child's home language and books that reflect a variety of cultures. The range of books provide mentor texts for the child as a writer.

**Readers' and Writers' Workshop Structure** The reading minilesson provides an explicit statement of understanding that is derived from the child's experiences with familiar books. The child applies the learning to his own book or writing and has an opportunity to share in a variety of talk structures like turn and talk. The anchor chart provides a reference tool for the learner with images that support the language.

## General Teaching Practices to Notice and Support

English learners are well equipped and capable of thinking at high levels about complex topics. The occasional struggle to express their ideas in English does not mean that they are incapable of engaging intellectually with the ideas and content in the lesson, especially when the teaching is scaffolded effectively. English learners need instruction that is modified for them so that they have equal access to grade-level content. In other words, effective instruction for English learners is not merely *good* teaching; it is *different* teaching. These practices and strategies can be applied to all of the instructional contexts listed above.

**Building background** At the beginning of a lesson, the teacher helps students think about what they already know about a topic or concept. They explain and practice key academic vocabulary.

**Making content comprehensible** The teacher uses multiple scaffolds to increase the comprehensibility of a lesson, including:

- The use of visual supports, such as charts, drawings, physical objects, and video.
- Modeling, acting out, and using gestures to clarify assignments, actions, and ideas; restating a concept using different or simpler language.
- Expanding a concept using familiar examples.
- Writing key words and phrases as they are spoken.

**Speaking more slowly** Teachers are conscious of how quickly they speak. They slow down when using words or patterns that may be unfamiliar to students and intentionally pause to give students time to process the language.

**Designing lessons with a predictable structure** The lessons in each instructional context follow a predictable pattern. Because students know what to expect from the experience in general, they can focus on the new content specific to the lesson. They also know when they will have opportunity to share their ideas and can prepare in advance.

**Pairing English learners with students who speak English** Especially when an English learner is new to the school, having a buddy or mentor to turn to when help is needed can go a long way toward helping a child feel welcome and supported and can be the beginning of a strong friendship. Choose mentors or buddies carefully to ensure the English learner will be met with kindness, patience, and respect and that students will learn from each other.

Student buddies/mentors can help English learners feel more welcomed and secure in their new environment.

**Assessing and providing high-quality feedback** Throughout a lesson, the teacher uses a variety of ways to assess students' understanding of the language and content, including oral and written responses, physical gestures, and brief collaborative interactions such as turn and talk. Based on a student's behavior and responses, the teacher provides specific, positive feedback that is tailored to the proficiency level of the learner, for example, reinforcing a lan-

Like all students, English learners need to be known by their classmates as unique individuals.

guage structure that the student has used accurately by modeling the structure in another sentence and prompting the student to produce another example.

**Restating and expanding approximations** When a student uses the wrong structure or incorrect grammar, the teacher restates the student's idea using clear academic language rather than correcting the student's errors. When a student provides a limited response, the teacher elaborates by adding language that supports the student's ideas. The practice validates the student's response and helps develop his language skill.

**Offering language starters** The teacher routinely provides a variety of sentence stems and other language starters to help students engage in productive talk.

## Know Children as Individuals

A final thought: Time spent learning about students is always, always valuable. Teachers who know their students well can deliver the most effective teaching and design the most beneficial learning opportunities. Remember that "English learner" is a temporary description of a child. The long-term outcome is a fluent, multilingual citizen—a lifelong asset that deserves our best teaching.

# The Takeaway

Perhaps nothing is more central to a child's identity than the language she speaks. As a school leader, you have the opportunity—and responsibility—to assure that the cultural and linguistic diversity in your school is respected and celebrated by everyone in the building. At the same time, you want to make it possible for English learners to learn to read and write in their new language so they will be successful in school and in their careers. English learners deserve a high-quality education that prepares them for life *and* nourishes their home language and culture.

Students who are learning English have already learned a lot about language by the time they enter your school, and they are well equipped and capable of thinking at high levels about complex topics. But to have equal access to the grade-level curriculum, they need instruction that is modified for them. Remember, effective teaching for English learners is both good teaching and different teaching. Teachers need to know the strengths and needs of individual English learners, provide a predictable structure, offer scaffolding and strong language support, and teach responsively to maximize the language and literacy progress of English learners. To facilitate healthy discussions about how English learners are supported in your school, use the protocol tool **Supporting English Learners (18)**.

## Think About Your School

- How closely does the school's program of support for English learners align with the school's vision and core values?

- What feedback have you received from families of students who are learning English? What changes might you make in response to that feedback?

- How have you and the teachers in the school systematically observed and documented English learners' progress in language and content learning over time?

## Move Your School Forward

- Find out about upcoming local and national conferences or virtual conference opportunities for educators who work with English learners in a school setting. Depending on available funds, send the EL team leader and a few classroom teachers who are "influencers" in the school. Afterward, have them present new understandings to the rest of the faculty.

- Form a small inquiry group to look at the ways that specialists and classroom teachers engage with one another on supports for English learners. How often do they consult one another? What is the nature and tone of those interactions? What practices can be shared with others?

Use the discussion tool **Supporting English Learners (18)** with your team to discuss and evaluate the amount and types of support that the school currently provides to students who are acquiring English.

### DISCUSSION TOOL · 18

### SUPPORTING ENGLISH LEARNERS

| Necessary Conditions | Strengths | Needs | Follow-Up Actions |
| --- | --- | --- | --- |
| **SCHOOLWIDE SUPPORTS**<br>• The entire school community takes a positive stance toward multilingualism and celebrates the children who are learning English.<br>• Families are respected and engaged as valuable partners in their child's education.<br>• Families are encouraged to continue to support children's use of their home language.<br>• The school environment is warm and welcoming to all.<br>• A range of diverse cultures, languages, and lived experiences are represented in the books and media in the school library.<br>• Translators or translation apps are available to families. | • Warm and welcoming school environment.<br>• School library is extensive and has a range of books that represent various cultures, languages and experiences. | • We don't really partner with parents. How can we get parents more involved?<br>• Not sure we have a "positive" stance toward multilingualism. It isn't negative but it really isn't positive either.<br>• Ways to translate for families (apps, translators, etc.) | • Create a team to brainstorm how we can engage parents more. Make sure this team includes some parents.<br>• Create a team to investigate what languages are represented in the school then create a list of translators and/or translation devices such as apps that are available to use. |
| **CLASSROOM SUPPORTS**<br>• Teachers view English learners as individuals with unique strengths and needs.<br>• Care is taken to pair new students with student mentors for support.<br>• Home languages are honored.<br>• Translanguaging is encouraged.<br>• Teaching is student-centered and culturally relevant.<br>• Students' talk about their learning is fostered and valued.<br>• Teachers use students' home languages when possible.<br>• A range of diverse cultures, languages, and lived experiences are represented in the books and materials in classrooms.<br>• The classroom program provides regular opportunities for students who are learning English to expand both their content knowledge and their language knowledge.<br>• Students who are learning English are supported in all instructional contexts. | • We currently pair new students with mentors.<br>• Teaching is student centered and we are working on being more culturally relevant for all students.<br>• Moving to using books in the classrooms that show a broader range of cultures, languages and experiences. | • Teachers state they are not sure how to support student languages in their classrooms. How can they honor the home language of students while still teaching them English?<br>• Students sometimes miss content knowledge because they are pulled out for language support. | • Professional learning opportunities are needed for teachers to explore how they can better support home languages of students in their classroom while also teaching them English.<br>• Review support services for students and brainstorm ways to support students and also allows them to receive all the instruction in the classroom that other students receive (not miss any content instruction). |

**Notes:**

From this first meeting we have created a starting point. Continued discussion across the year is recommended to continue this discussion and hear progress from the "follow-up actions". Follow-up teams will be formed in the next couple of weeks and are encouraged to meet before our next whole-school meeting next month.

*Leading for Literacy*

**Discussion Tool:** Supporting English Learners, **Version 01**

# Chapter 15

# Intervening for Equitable Literacy Outcomes

*Kids are who they are. They know what they know. They bring what they bring. Our job is not to wish that students knew more or knew differently. Our job is to turn each child's knowledge into a curricular strength rather than an instructional inconvenience. We can do that only if we hold high expectations for all students, convey great respect for the knowledge and culture they bring to the classroom, and offer lots of support for helping them achieve those expectations. Kids are who they are.*
—David Pearson

LIKE MOST EDUCATORS, YOU probably begin the academic year wondering about the children who will enter the building on the first day of school. Who will soar? Who will have difficulties? How will you respond to those who will need extra help in order to succeed? All children want to learn and have the right to learn, including those for whom reading and writing do not come easily. How will you fulfill your responsibility to create effective systems for teaching the children who show up—just as they are—with all their strengths and challenges and uniqueness?

When a child struggles in school, families and teachers feel real pain. They want to help. They want the child to experience the pleasure of reading a book and expressing thoughts in writing. They want the child to be successful, to feel capable, to experience the joy of accomplishment. They want to turn things around. And yet families, teachers, and even some school leaders may not know what steps to take when the stakes are so high.

The fact is, students who have difficulty in literacy learning are more likely to have difficulties throughout school, obtain few academic or career qualifications, receive little work-related training, experience unemployment, and have poor health (KPMG Foundation, 2006). There is strong evidence that if a child struggles with literacy, the gap in academic achievement—recently referred to as an opportunity gap—gets wider as the other children continue to progress. Intervention that assures children make faster progress than their peers is needed to close the gap. Our work must therefore address prevention *and* intervention as part of a comprehensive design for literacy learning.

An integral part of your school vision must be the literacy education of *every* child, including—and especially—those children who find reading and writing difficult. Your entire team of educators at the school needs to take collective responsibility in assuring the success of these children. Achieving equity means providing the amount of support—no matter how much—that every child needs to succeed. "Fair" does not mean giving all students the *same* instruction. It means taking all students from *where they are* to where they need to be.

In this chapter, we describe our views on intervention (which begin with prevention) and discuss the characteristics of a high-quality intervention program.

We suggest that you and your team look back at your school's vision and values and that you review them often during the process of reviewing or renewing your intervention program. This will assure that the decisions you make in this important area are rooted in what you most firmly believe about teaching and learning.

## Why Children Have Difficulty Learning to Read and Write

Children who have difficulty learning to read and write are not all the same. They struggle for different reasons, and the variance grows more pronounced the older they become. Careful diagnosis is required. Examining the behaviors of each learner in detail allows intervention teachers to respond effectively to their students and enable them to use their strengths.

# INTERVENTION POLICIES AND PRACTICES
# THROUGH THE YEARS

The concept of intervention became part of educational thought only in the second half of the twentieth century. The policies and practices of intervention have evolved through the years, from folksy approaches to evidence-based systems mandated by federal law.

## They'll Grow into It

Several generations ago, teachers viewed a lag in literacy development as immaturity. They thought some children simply weren't ready for reading and would need to "grow into it." To determine readiness, primary teachers in the 1950s would examine children's teeth to find out whether the "six-year molars" were beginning to show. Sometimes a child would repeat a year of school but often continued to struggle.

## Wait and Then Remediate

Individual differences in literacy learning were not considered as important as they are today. Plenty of jobs did not require high levels of literacy, so educators tended to wait until the gap was significant and then began to provide limited remedial actions that usually had equally limited effects. Nevertheless, federal funding for remediation firmly established it in schools. While these programs provided some support for students, they did not have promised results. Minority and low-income students were disproportionately assigned to remedial reading in large numbers, giving rise to serious questions related to equity that persist today. Educators still face the difficult question of whether so-called "compensatory" education does more harm than good. Yet, doing nothing is not an option.

## "Teaching to the Test"

The No Child Left Behind (NCLB) Act of 2001 provided new incentives to ensure that every child reaches higher levels of literacy. Little is left of the legacy of NCLB except for an extreme focus on high-stakes testing. The law required annual testing for proficiency in reading, math, and science in grades 3–8 and then again during high school. Failure to show adequate yearly progress (AYP) brought penalties and sanctions. To predict students' performance on end-of-year tests, states and districts administered more tests throughout the year. When students didn't perform well on the predictor tests, states and districts mandated more practice to raise students' scores, which caused teachers to divert valuable instructional time to test prep, often with disappointing results for the children who did not make adequate yearly progress.

## RTI and MTSS

Response to Intervention (RTI) is an instructional framework that is intended to supply each student with the right amount of intervention based on ongoing assessment data, reserving the most intensive services for the children who need them most. Since the 2000s, RTI has expanded from a special education initiative to an approach for monitoring and improving the academic results of all students. RTI consists of levels, or tiers, of Instruction that provide increasingly intensive academic support.

- **Tier 1:** high-quality classroom instruction for every child
- **Tier 2:** targeted interventions with small groups
- **Tier 3:** highly intensive, individualized services

Today, schools receiving federal assistance in literacy are required to implement Multi-Tiered System of Supports (MTSS), which represents a more comprehensive approach that supports both the academic needs and the behavioral, social, and emotional needs of students. MTSS can include behavior intervention plans for students as well as professional learning and support to help teams of teachers solve problems relative to children who have difficulty. MTSS offers an opportunity for your school to include intervention within a more coherent design for literacy.

**Analyzing Subgroups** When a child is not making satisfactory literacy progress, the child has not failed. The educational system has failed the child. The early years of schooling have an indelible effect on the agency, identity, and self-esteem of learners, and these factors set the path for children's success across the grades. Your role in addressing early and highly effective literacy instruction is critical.

As a central office team, identify action steps you can take with school-based leaders to examine evidence of literacy success, grade by grade. Consider the percent of children who exit the classroom program with insufficient literacy competencies. Do you need to talk more about the strength of the classroom opportunities in bringing every child forward? Are there other systemic issues—policies and procedures—that interfere with the success of all the children?

As you study a group of children, analyze the subgroups. If any subgroup is overrepresented in the larger group, you and your team will need to engage in a process to identify and address the systemic issues that may have led to inequitable outcomes for some children. This needs to be a high-priority agenda item for the central office and school-based teams to address together.

On behalf of the National Research Council, the Committee on Prevention of Reading Difficulties in Young Children (ed. Snow, Burns, and Griffin 1998) identified three categories of reading difficulties that may be evident in learners.

> "There are three potential stumbling blocks that are known to throw children off course on the journey to skilled reading. The first obstacle, which arises at the outset of reading acquisition, is difficulty understanding and using the alphabetic principle—the idea that written spellings systematically represent spoken words. It is hard to comprehend text if word recognition is inaccurate or laborious. The second obstacle is a failure to transfer the comprehension skills of spoken language to reading and to acquire new strategies that may be specifically needed for reading. The third obstacle to reading will magnify the first two: the absence or loss of an initial motivation to read or failure to develop a mature appreciation of the rewards of reading."

We would add to these obstacles another factor that is related to all three: failure to acquire the quality of reading with ease and fluency, without which reading can become a tedious task to be avoided when possible. Students may not have the ability to rapidly (and largely unconsciously) take words apart to decode them or may not read print as language they understand. The result is low comprehension and low motivation. All obstacles tend also to affect writing ability.

As you and your teams observe and assess students who are struggling to take on literacy learning, you are likely to notice behaviors that provide evidence of difficulty in one or more of the following areas (Figure 15-1).

## Difficulty Understanding How Written Language Works

Learning how print works is built through hundreds of early experiences with texts, not just with the alphabet and sounds. Through experiences with books, young readers make the first, early connections between spoken language and print. They begin to notice that you read the print, not the pictures, although the pictures are also interesting and provide information about the story or topic. They learn to turn pages and, eventually, to move their eyes left to right across strings of words. They learn that space separates individual written words. All of these understandings seem simple but represent a great deal of learning that is foundational even to the learning of phonics.

## Difficulty Recognizing and Taking Words Apart

The ability to decode words builds over time as readers become familiar with the building blocks of language and learn to use their knowledge "on the run" while reading.

# AREAS OF POTENTIAL READING DIFFICULTY

| | |
|---|---|
| **Understanding How Written Language Works** | ▪ Understanding early concepts such as directionality, word-by-word matching, and the use of space to define words. |
| **Recognizing and Taking Words Apart** | ▪ Hearing and distinguishing individual sounds in words.<br>▪ Distinguishing letters by their features.<br>▪ Connecting letters to sounds and sounds to letters.<br>▪ Blending sounds to read simple words.<br>▪ Noticing parts to take words apart efficiently.<br>▪ Hearing and distinguishing parts in words.<br>▪ Recognizing and taking apart words while reading continuous text. |
| **Comprehending Written Language** | ▪ Understanding that print is language that makes sense.<br>▪ Recognizing and using language syntax.<br>▪ Deriving the meaning of new words and increasing vocabulary while reading.<br>▪ Following the details of a plot or gathering and remembering information while reading.<br>▪ Bringing background information to a text to construct new understandings.<br>▪ Making inferences and predictions while reading.<br>▪ Thinking analytically about the craft of a text.<br>▪ Thinking critically about the content and purpose of a text. |
| **Reading with Phrasing and Fluency** | ▪ Putting words together in meaningful phrases.<br>▪ Reading with ease and automatic word recognition and/or quick decoding.<br>▪ Using punctuation while reading.<br>▪ Using one's voice to reflect the writer's meaning. |
| **Reading with Engagement and Motivation** | ▪ Giving sustained cognitive attention to reading.<br>▪ Choosing books of interest.<br>▪ Reading voluntarily and voluminously.<br>▪ Talking actively about books with others.<br>▪ Making suggestions to others about books to read.<br>▪ Expressing enjoyment in reading. |
| **Writing** | ▪ Writing in a way that is grammatically correct and understandable.<br>▪ Using writing as a tool for thinking and communicating.<br>▪ Using conventions.<br>▪ Understanding the writer's craft.<br>▪ Engaging in various aspects of writing process.<br>▪ Using voice.<br>▪ Identifying audience. |

**Figure 15-1.** Evidence of Difficulties

Decisions about appropriate interventions are rooted in what teachers and school leaders believe about teaching and learning.

**Difficulty Hearing and Distinguishing Sounds in Words** Phonemic awareness, or sensitivity to the sounds in oral language, has been identified as an important element in learning to read. Children who are not aware of individual phonemes in words have difficulty mapping the sounds with their corresponding symbols or letters. Phonemic awareness is built over time as children learn language and find pleasure in it. They become aware of words in sentences or words that rhyme, of syllable breaks, and words that begin or end alike. Eventually, they need to be able to hear individual phonemes in sequence as they occur in words. Phonemic awareness is *oral*, but it is foundational to grasping the alphabetic principle—that sounds and letters are connected in reading and writing. Phoneme awareness is a critical area of early knowledge; however, most children do not need a great deal of instruction in phoneme awareness; research indicates about 21 hours is sufficient, and more does not seem to have benefit (National Reading Panel, 2000). Children who do not attend to sounds need good teaching.

**Difficulty Distinguishing Letters** Only twenty-six letters represent all of the words that can be found in English. And for maximum efficiency, letters are distinguishable from each other by only one or two features (for example, *n* and *m*). Directionality makes a difference (*n, u; b, d*). The young child must learn to detect these slight differences to identify letters. Tactile experiences with letters help. Visual perception may be easier for some than others; if difficulties persist, many confusions may arise.

**Difficulty in Taking Words Apart to Solve Them** Readers learn to distinguish the letters and connect the letters to sounds, but they need to apply this knowledge to solving whole words. Over time, readers learn not only to blend the sounds connected to letters to solve simple words but to recognize frequently occurring patterns—phonograms, digraphs, blends, suffixes, and prefixes. Noticing and using these larger word parts makes word solving more efficient and strategic (Kaye 2008).

**Difficulty Taking Words Apart While Reading Continuous Text** All of this knowledge about letters, sounds, and words is considered foundational to becoming a reader. But the real challenge for young readers is decoding words "on the run" while reading continuous text, and that is sometimes missing from intervention programs. Processing continuous, meaningful text is essential from the beginning so that readers understand the function of the new understandings they are developing about words (Vellutino and Scanlon 2002). Too often, we are in a hurry to teach children the building blocks of language and then find that they do not use them efficiently while reading (or writing).

## UNDERSTANDING AND RESPONDING TO DYSLEXIA

The National Institutes of Health (NIH) describes dyslexia as "a brain-based learning disability that specifically impairs a person's ability to read." Studies are ongoing, but many researchers accept that dyslexia is most commonly due to difficulties in phonological processing, that is, an awareness of the individual sounds of spoken language and linking the sounds to letters or groups of letters. However, there is no single, universally accepted definition of dyslexia nor a definitive set of criteria for diagnosing it (Gabriel 2018).

### Different Methods for Different Students

Students who find reading and writing difficult are different from one another. Children diagnosed as dyslexic will exhibit different strengths and needs, as will any other child experiencing difficulties in literacy learning. When informed that a child is dyslexic, teachers and specialists need to examine the student's particular strengths and gaps in understandings using systematic and careful observation and assessment. It is not acceptable to assume that a single instructional approach, for example, more phonics, will simply "inoculate" students against dyslexia or automatically reverse the factors causing the difficulties.

In its research advisory on dyslexia, the International Literacy Association (2016) states that "students classified as dyslexic have varying strengths and challenges and teaching them is too complex a task for a scripted, one-size-fits-all program (Coyne et al. 2013; Phillips & Smith 1997; Simmons 2015). Optimal instruction calls for teachers' professional expertise and responsiveness, and for the freedom to act on the basis of that professionalism." Knowing that the process of learning to read is complex, educators must keep an open view to best serve each individual child.

### Evaluation and Diagnosis

Educators also need to take care not to rush to label a child as dyslexic until a very careful and thorough evaluation and diagnosis are on record and to be wary of the potential for overcategorization of particular groups who have had less opportunity to engage with literacy than other groups. We believe that we cannot rely on a single group test given at a very young age to accurately diagnose a brain condition, especially if the child has not had rich literacy experiences. Some children may indeed need long-term, expert services tailored to their individual needs through the IEP process. Others, though, might respond quickly to early, short-term intervention.

We think it's wise to look at children early–in kindergarten and grade 1. If they are not meeting expectations, they should be given intensive intervention of a short duration. Then, if they are still having difficulties, they may need long-term specialist help. But it is essential to have skilled early teaching and short-term intervention available so children can quickly enter the world of literacy even if they struggle at first.

**Manage Your Budget**

**Cost Benefits** Think about how you and other leaders in the school can work with your central office colleagues to achieve your goals for intervention in a cost-effective way. The short-term costs of intervention will far outweigh the long-term costs of an entire school career in special education. It will cost more later than it will to intervene early with high-quality instruction. And, of course, the costs to a child's self-esteem are not even measurable. The other cost benefits of early intervention are that the number of children requiring special education services will be fewer and they will receive more attention.

Work with colleagues to collect data showing the many cost benefits of investing in early intervention and of fewer children needing special education year after year. Given the one-year budget cycle of public schools, it can be challenging to build an effective case, but you can look back at data over multiple years to show how early intervention can positively impact children's literacy and their social and emotional health.

## Difficulty Comprehending Written Language

Sources of difficulties in comprehending written language are numerous (Figure 15-2). An early understanding is that print is connected to the language that children speak. (This factor presents an obvious barrier to children who are

Readers must constantly think within and beyond the text.

new to English.) What children read should sound like language and make sense to them. Even when teachers read aloud to them, children don't always realize that the print carries the message. They need the basic understanding that print represents language and the meanings it conveys.

**Vocabulary** Vocabulary is a critical element in comprehending texts (Nagy 1988, 2000). Learning the parts of words also contributes to understanding the meaning of a text. In the beginning, children's oral vocabulary is a contributing factor to comprehension of simple texts; and that is influenced by their experience in hearing written texts read aloud. As they read more, they begin to acquire vocabulary from reading. They use context and word parts to derive the meaning of new words and add them to their vocabularies.

**Background Knowledge** As they read, individuals need to pick up information from the text and come out with an understanding of what happened in the plot of a fiction story or the information in a nonfiction text. A reader should leave a text with these basic understandings, which we could call *literal comprehension*. But readers do much more. When reading an informational text, for example, they bring to bear their own background of information as they read and, in the process, synthesize new understandings. Limited background knowledge becomes an increasing problem if readers do not have a solid experience in acquiring content.

**Higher-Level Thinking** When processing both fiction and nonfiction, readers must constantly think beyond and about the text; that is, they need to make strategic moves such as predictions and inferences that depend on their own thinking as they read the text. Moreover, readers notice how the writer has crafted the text to communicate information to readers. This is true even if the story or informational text is at beginning levels. For example, in fiction this means showing how characters feel and how and why characters change or why they take actions. It means noticing the structure of the plot or the use of language. At the most complex level, it means thinking critically about what is being read. We need critical reading more now than at any time in our history because anything can be published and distributed. Readers are expected to think critically about texts on tests and in their lives as citizens. Comprehension, in all its dimensions, is all important as we think about the reading curriculum, especially for students who find reading and writing difficult.

An overarching principle is that the purpose of reading must be constructing the meaning of the text using language and print. When the focus is on accuracy and decoding alone, young readers may not understand that the purpose of printed language is to make sense and to convey a meaningful message. They may give so much attention to decoding that they have little attention to give to thinking about the meaning and messages of the text. In the pursuit of

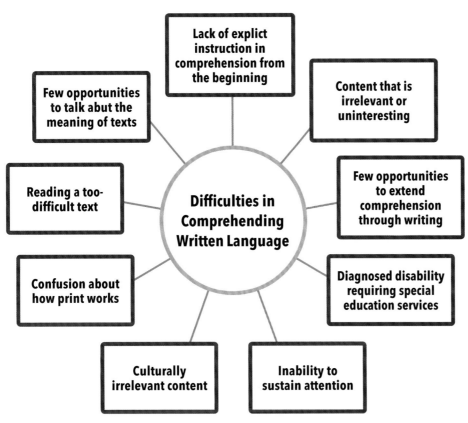

**Figure 15-2.** Difficulties in Comprehending Written Language

accurate reading, it is understandable that teachers focus on helping children with decoding; this tends to happen when the text is too hard for the reader, *even with teacher support.*

Another big idea is that comprehension must be actively taught from the beginning—not by "naming" what the brain is doing but by actively talking about the meaning with the teacher and peers and by writing about the text. In addition, relevance of content and culture makes a difference for the reader, so materials should be evaluated on these criteria.

A pernicious reality is that gaps in comprehension accumulate over time. In the beginning, students rely on background information from their experiences, but very quickly they begin to build such information through reading. At middle and upper grade levels, it is impossible to assess reading comprehension in a neutral way; that is, without taking into account the background information that a student brings to a text. A teacher can assess decoding, but important as it is, we need to realize that students may read at near 100% accuracy and still score low on tests of comprehension. They need a backdrop of voluminous reading, with engagement and comprehension. With every text they engage, from the earliest picture books to upper-level novels, the meaning is paramount. Not only is the deep meaning of texts the focus of high-stakes tests, but it is the critical factor in lifelong literacy.

# Difficulty Reading with Fluency and Phrasing

Fluency depends on rapid and automatic word recognition but also on the individual's ability to understand and use the rules of language syntax in order to comprehend the meaning of a text. Every language has a "grammar," or a set of rules, for the order of words in sentences. In this case the word *grammar* does not mean "standard" or "proper" usage; it simply describes how a language user strings words together in a way that makes sense to other speakers of the language. In English, *dog the ran can* is not a possible sentence. From infancy, children internalize these rules of syntax, and when they begin to read and write, their knowledge of spoken language is a powerful resource (Clay 2014). They can tell, for example, when their reading doesn't sound right or make sense; this awareness promotes close monitoring and higher accuracy.

Fluency is not synonymous with speed; we want readers to move through a text at a good rate (or pace)—not too fast and not too slow—and to reflect other dimensions as well, for example:

- Pausing: reflecting punctuation such as periods, question marks, commas.
- Phrasing: putting words together in meaningful groups (in addition to using punctuation).
- Intonation: changing the tone (higher and lower) of the voice to reflect the writer's meaning.
- Stress: emphasizing selected words to convey meaning.
- Pace: the speed of reading.
- Integration: how all dimensions of fluency work together smoothly.

If the first four dimensions above are evident in the reading, the pace will usually take care of itself. Moreover, skilled readers modify pace, or speed, as appropriate to the genre and meaning of what they are reading. Consider the difference in intonation, stress, and pace for poetry, a bulleted list, or dialogue. It is the integration or orchestration of all the elements in this process of reading continuous text that results in smooth reading and the reader's ability to interpret the author's meaning with the voice. So, integration is the sixth dimension.

Beginning readers are still working to understand and become automatic in using the conventions of print. As they read, they point to help them focus on individual words and support directional movement. As soon as the early behaviors are under control (about the time texts offer dialogue), readers should begin to use phrasing and to notice punctuation. From that time on, they can be fluent readers, provided they are reading texts appropriate for their current abilities (with instructional support). So, unlike other skills, fluency does not need to increase across time, simply to maintain all the dimensions listed above, although students may develop more of a dramatic voice through shared and performance reading.

When a student is reading aloud with good fluency, then the voice will reflect the meaning of the text. We are not talking about speed here or even about the expressive reading a professional performer demonstrates. We're only talking about good, efficient oral reading. Reading fluency may break down for several possible reasons (Figure 15-3). Dysfluency may occur occasionally if the student is highly motivated to read a more challenging text and is willing to persevere because of a fascinating topic; but daily dysfluent reading over long periods of time is not an advisable diet. It can become habitual.

Often, dysfluent reading is an outcome of reading difficulties. Low comprehension and/or vocabulary make it difficult for the reader to use meaningful phrases and punctuation. Some readers cannot make full use of syntax to aid fluency because they do not yet have full control of English rules. Others may be able to read fluently, but the process breaks down when the text is too difficult. Texts should be selected carefully to provide the complexity and challenge readers need, but daily reading at frustration level can create habitual slow reading. Dysfluent reading is a serious impediment to a reader's comprehension of written text and must be addressed in intervention.

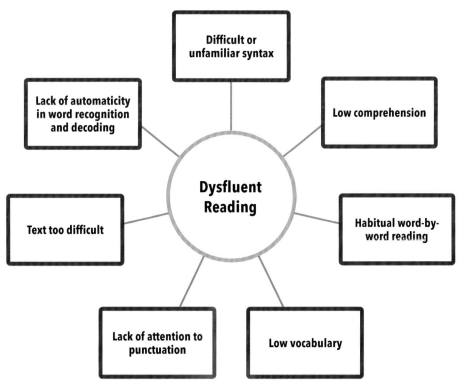

**Figure 15-3.** Dysfluent Reading

## Difficulty Reading with Engagement and Motivation

It is obvious that engagement and motivation play a powerful role in reading growth. To become competent in reading increasingly complex texts, students need to engage in voluminous reading. Part of this reading must include *choice reading* with books that the reader has selected because of interest. That is a very different thing than *compliant reading*. A number of factors can contribute to low motivation and engagement (see Figure 15-4).

As with all learners, students who find reading and writing difficult must be engaged and motivated to grow, and that is the most elusive factor in planning an intervention program. Sometimes, readers are forced daily to read material that is too difficult to achieve competence; there is a delicate balance. We want to challenge students with more complex texts so that they can expand their reading powers, but if texts are too difficult, other problems arise.

Sadly, a student may find what she is expected to read to be unimportant and irrelevant to her life. When students are offered only materials in which they cannot see themselves or their culture, or when materials present characters or informational texts that perpetuate stereotypes, the natural result is that students are reluctant to read.

The material that students read should be worth reading; that is, it should be interesting to them and relevant to the age group and to the different cultures that exist within the school. (Actually, we believe that even students attending a school with a homogenous culture need to read about the diverse

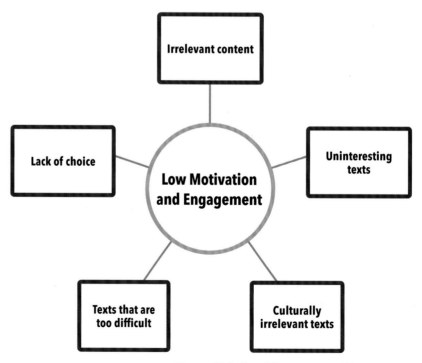

**Figure 15-4.** Low Motivation and Engagement

**Personalized Learning vs. Intervention** In recent years, especially during the Covid-19 pandemic, personalized learning software has come into wider use than ever before as a means of addressing the individual needs of all students. While there is wide variation in the quality of personalized learning products, many do provide beneficial learning opportunities for most students. But personalized learning should not be confused with intervention.

Personalized learning, whether software-based or not, is designed to provide targeted instruction and other learning experiences that correspond to students' unique strengths, abilities, and interests *within the core instructional program* (Tier 1). Intervention programs, on the other hand, generally are designed for students whose short- or long-term needs are not being met by Tier 1 instruction.

It is wise to remember that those students having difficulty in learning to read are the very ones who may find independent work by computer appealing. Personalized learning should be closely monitored and assisted by teachers as needed.

cultures in their country and their world.) Age appropriateness is a very difficult challenge for teachers because often their students are reading far below grade level. In addition, students need to see people like themselves in texts, and they need to see them in admirable roles; of course, texts used in interventions should, in addition to being readable, avoid stereotypes. The best of all possible worlds would include a variety of texts, from traditional literature to informational texts, that reflect the cultures of the world and open them up to students. Even in intervention lessons, students should have the opportunity to expand their knowledge of the incredible diversity of the world.

## Difficulty Writing

Many writing difficulties are highly related to reading difficulties; yet, more is involved. Many adults, when asked, "Are you a reader?" would unequivocally say "Yes." But when asked, "Are you a writer?" the same responders might hesitate. Writing requires individuals to use their literacy understandings to produce language in written form. For many, that is an intimidating task. Writing every day, in classrooms that are alive with text engagement to provide models and inspiration, can nurture writers.

Reading and writing are complementary, yet different, processes. What is learned in reading contributes to writing and vice versa.

In Figure 15-5, you can see a number of parallels with reading and some important differences. Students' ability to spell, arrange words into coherent sentences, and use the conventions of language are processed in reading and produced when the individual writes. The writer's craft is related to the construction of texts and the artistry that readers notice as they hear them read aloud and read for themselves. Talking about books and writing about their

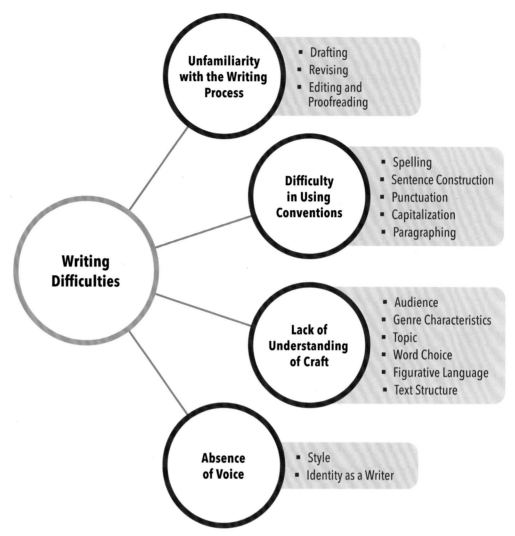

**Figure 15-5.** Writing Difficulties

reading helps students. In addition, writers need a massive amount of practice in working through a process for putting their ideas into finished written pieces. They need to learn to produce and then to revise and polish writing, to organize information in logical ways, to choose words carefully, and to self-evaluate for clear communication. They need to learn how to use writing across the curriculum as a tool for learning and communicating thinking and to spend time writing for a variety of purposes and audiences every day.

Writing is not the "high stakes" subject that reading is (although many U.S. states assess students' writing abilities), but it is an important life skill. The best way for teachers to learn what students can do in writing and to diagnose their needs is to observe them in the process of writing and to examine their drafts and finished pieces. Some students will need assistance in using conventions, while others will need encouragement to develop an identity as a writer. In classroom instruction, whole-class minilessons, small-group teaching, and individual conferences provide support during a time set aside for writing.

Becoming an excellent writer is a skill that will help students in all academic areas as well as most occupations. But considering the ease of writing and "publishing" on the internet, it is even more important to teach clear, logical writing skills and conventions to students.

Because of funding sources and lack of time, most writing intervention takes place in the classroom as teachers work with individuals and small groups (while others are writing independently). Teachers can also provide powerful support by including writing during reading intervention. We have found that text-based writing, called "writing about reading," helps students make a direct connection between writing and reading.

Students use writing across the curriculum as a tool for learning.

## Multiple Characteristics and Causes

Intervention is complicated partly because all of these characteristics and causes interact with one another. For example, a reader who finds reading and writing difficult may avoid it whenever possible and that is interpreted as low motivation. It has been our observation that the feeling of failure can arise as early as grade 1. Frustration can make a reader angry and aggressive, but in our experience, students are more likely to become passive. After all, who wants to pour energy into something she cannot do well? The sense of self-efficacy declines. Even technically proficient readers are sometimes described as "reluctant." A further example: a reader may have failed to develop foundation skills in the early years of school because some condition made it more difficult for her to distinguish letters or hear sounds, or such a gap may be the result of weak instruction. As a result, the reader must work so hard to decode words that she has little attention left to comprehend. Issues of engagement and motivation can interfere with any student's concentration on the meaning of the text.

The causes for low performance in literacy are equally complex. More than one situational circumstance may affect any given learner. In other words, one size does not fit all when it comes to intervention. Teachers need a full toolkit as they begin to work with students who are having difficulty. Different content and experiences will be needed at the beginning and should be adjusted as a student progresses (although, ideally, intervention would not need to continue year after year).

# Benefits of Intervention

The economic impact of illiteracy and low levels of literacy is staggering. The cost to the global economy is over $1 trillion *annually*. Yet despite these statistics we still do not believe the economic impact is the most important reason to provide systematic intervention. Rather, the most important reason is the diminished quality of life that results from low levels of literacy for millions of people around the world. This is what drives us as leaders to intervene on behalf of children who have difficulty learning to read and write. Adults with low literacy rates are more at risk for unemployment, more likely to become trapped in a cycle of poverty, and more likely to experience poor health outcomes.

Intervention, particularly if delivered early and effectively, can prevent these devastating consequences of illiteracy and low levels of literacy. Intervention benefits society, the educational system, and individual children.

- **Benefits to society:** Intervention increases the expertise of citizens and their capacity to contribute throughout society. Highly literate citizens are better equipped to solve systemic problems, participate in civic roles, and perform civic duties.

- **Benefits to the educational system:** Intervention decreases the number of students who need supplementary help and specialized education, as well as the costs associated with these services. We want to equip students with the competencies they need to thrive in a rich classroom environment with strong teaching without the ongoing need for extra help. Intervention reduces the load on the system by reserving the most intensive support for those children who need it.

- **Benefits to individual children:** The greatest benefit of intervention is assuring every child the ability and opportunity to live a literate life. While a high level of literacy does not guarantee a high-quality life, it greatly increases the possibility for both children and their future families. And if children become avid readers, literacy becomes a source of pleasure and personal growth throughout their lives. It gives them access to diverse perspectives and a voice to act on behalf of oneself and others.

# Multi-Tiered Support for Students with Reading and Writing Difficulties

An effective intervention system supports students in all areas of the curriculum, not just literacy, and it consists of multiple tiers of support as shown in Figure 15-6. Each tier is part of a larger framework for providing targeted support to students who need it, when they need it. Special education is available at every tier, but bear in mind that students with an identified disability are considered general education students first and foremost. Federal law requires them to have access to strong classroom teaching *with any additional supports* needed in the classroom. Students with IEPs may require Tier 2 and Tier 3 instruction and interventions at some point, but that would be in addition to strong classroom teaching. And most will never need higher levels of support.

## Begin with Prevention

Our grandmothers used to say, "An ounce of prevention is worth a pound of cure." And it's still true. In literacy learning, two types of prevention will eliminate the need for intervention for most students: early childhood education and good classroom teaching.

**Early Childhood Education.** Universal access to high-quality language and literacy opportunities in early childhood has many benefits and long-lasting effects on the social, emotional, and literacy development of children. There is strong evidence that when children have the opportunity for high-quality language, literacy, and play experiences in preschool and kindergarten, they are less likely to need supplemental interventions, be referred for special education,

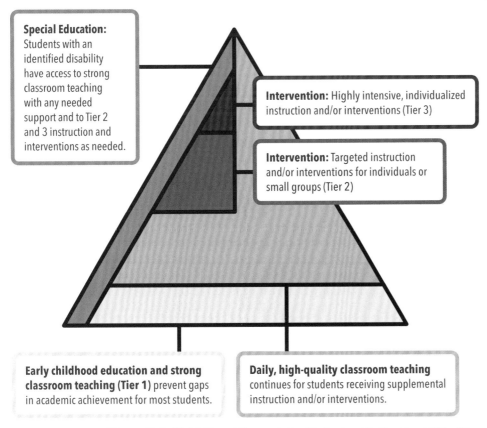

**Special Education:** Students with an identified disability have access to strong classroom teaching with any needed support and to Tier 2 and 3 instruction and interventions as needed.

**Intervention:** Highly intensive, individualized instruction and/or interventions (Tier 3)

**Intervention:** Targeted instruction and/or interventions for individuals or small groups (Tier 2)

**Early childhood education and strong classroom teaching (Tier 1)** prevent gaps in academic achievement for most students.

**Daily, high-quality classroom teaching** continues for students receiving supplemental instruction and/or interventions.

Figure 15-6. Multi-Tiered Supports for Students with Reading Difficulties

be retained, or drop out of school. These positive experiences provide many of the foundational understandings children need to engage successfully with a world of ideas through print. By listening to stories and informational texts, telling stories orally, sharing ideas through drawing and writing, and playing games that expand their oral language and that connect to print, children begin to live a literate life in school. They develop high expectations of print and are able to bring meaning to it and avoid confusion as they move through kindergarten and into grade 1.

Consider the following principles as you and your team strive to provide high-quality early literacy opportunities for young children:

- Create a classroom and school community that celebrates linguistic, cultural, and ethnic diversity by attending to the physical space as well as the policies.
- Learn about each child's history, background knowledge, languages, culture, and experiences.
- Recognize and value each child's unique development and begin with their strengths, taking them on "different paths to common outcomes" (Clay 1998).
- Value dramatic play so that children can draw on their diverse life experiences and engage in literacy opportunities that exist in the real world.
- Create classroom environments that reflect children's languages in instruction and in daily play opportunities.
- Create opportunities to bring in literacy from their homes and from the community.
- Aim to preserve students' home languages and honor their rich cultural background as they learn English.
- Invite diverse community members and family members into the classroom to share as a means of honoring local and family knowledge.
- Teach with high-quality culturally and linguistically diverse literature that respects the variety of languages and histories.
- Help children understand varying points of view and lead them to discussions of how they can to contribute to a better world.

As your team designs early childhood classrooms, it is important to remember that children have learned a great deal before they enter school. Instead of taking the stance that children need to be made ready to learn, create teaching and learning experiences that harness and build on the richness that children bring to the classroom. It is our responsibility to provide the learning opportunities that will foster their growth, not shift blame to the children.

It is our collective responsibility to advocate for high-quality, engaging, diverse early childhood classrooms that give each child the opportunity for success. These environments assure that children have chances to experience the imagination, wonder, and joy of childhood and develop the confidence and agency that every child deserves. And they provide a powerful first layer of prevention against an achievement gap in grade 1 and beyond.

**Good Classroom Teaching (Tier 1)** A second layer of prevention is good classroom teaching that is coherent and continuous across all grades of the school. When daily instruction is responsive, student-centered, and effective, the classroom will produce strong learning outcomes for most children, with only a few needing supplementary interventions to be successful. Even when children do need extra support, they also need the continuation of daily, high-quality classroom teaching (Figure 15-6). If students regularly miss strong classroom instruction because they are pulled out for intervention, they will make less progress and will have gaps in their understandings of grade-level concepts.

Good teaching is especially important in the earliest years of school. Children's early experiences in school often make the difference between being actively engaged in learning or being turned off by learning. Even when children have had limited literacy experiences prior to kindergarten, good classroom teaching can make the difference. Our experience indicates that skilled teaching and rich literacy experiences in kindergarten help most children develop early reading and writing strategies before they enter first grade. Many can read very simple texts before entry. And building on the same elements in first grade turns them into proficient young readers who have the beginning of a self-extending system, one that enables them to learn more about literacy through reading and writing (Clay 2001).

Because no system of interventions—even highly effective ones—can take the place of consistent, responsive classroom teaching, your team will need to examine the results of their instruction on a regular basis to assure classroom teaching is producing good outcomes for all students. If you find that

Teachers need to examine the results of their instruction to be sure the teaching is producing good outcomes for all students.

## RESPONSIVE TEACHING OVERCOMES SOME LEARNING DIFFICULTIES

We need to consider that many children may be confused by the reading instruction they have received. The teaching may lack coherence across the grades or even across contexts within a grade. For example, classroom and specialist teachers may use different language to teach for the same behaviors and understandings. The teaching may focus on plugging gaps in understandings with a series of disconnected skill lessons, what Marie Clay refers to as a "spare parts" model of teaching (1987). Or the teaching may stick to the script of district-supplied plans or programs without meaningful adjustments that prioritize the processing needs of individual children.

As Clay wrote, "the longer the child is in an inappropriate program, the greater the number of times that child will have practiced inappropriate processing, day after day, year after year. Such children are building highly practiced inappropriate response systems. . . . Such children are learning to be [learning disabled] with increasing severity as long as the inappropriate responding continues" (1987). Or as Carol Lyons neatly put it: "many children who are labeled learning disabled are in truth instructionally disabled" (2007).

To make accelerated progress and "unlearn" unproductive behaviors and understandings when processing text, low-achieving literacy learners need intensive, individualized instruction that is responsive to each child's unique profile of strengths and weaknesses (Vellutino 2010). Children with the most need require teachers with the most expertise in delivering effective, differentiated teaching that utilizes a child's strengths and understandings to build a complete, efficient text-processing system in the brain.

a large number of children require interventions to make progress, it can be an indication that regular classroom teaching lacks effectiveness for too many of the children. The good news is that investing in continuous improvement of classroom teaching yields results. Excellent classroom teaching accompanied by effective interventions, when needed, can make it possible for all students to make steady progress and become successful users of literacy.

## Intervention and Special Education

In a team approach, the educators take collective responsibility for the students' achievement, with the classroom teachers and special education teachers working together in the same direction and communicating frequently to bring the children forward. Imagine the impact of a common language, common curriculum, and teamwork on the progress of these children. When classroom teachers and special education teachers work this way, the instruction provided in the classroom and in supplemental services are coherent.

## Meeting the Needs of the Children Who Need Long-Term Special Education Services

The number of children receiving special education services in the learning disabilities category has grown markedly year by year. We have not worked with a school system yet that didn't have more children in special education services than needed to be there. These highly specialized services by highly trained teachers need to be reserved for the children who need them most.

Often the children who are classified early on have reading or writing difficulties that are not reflective of a severe disability. A well-implemented, high-quality intervention program generally leads to fewer students being classified for special education services. We argue for layers of intervention prior to assignment in special education services. The investment of time in early classroom intervention will usually result in some progress and a wealth of diagnostic information about how the child has responded to instruction.

We have observed the unreasonable caseloads of children, each with a different individualized education plan, being served by special education teachers. Often, the children are taught in groups that are far from small, and the frequency of service can be limited by the number of slots available. Often, the literacy instruction provides an overemphasis on certain elements of the reading process without acknowledging its complexity and may be delivered at a slower pace. In contrast to the ways in which good readers are expected to be self-directed and to comprehend what they read, poorer readers are often taught differently, with fluent decoding overemphasized (McGill-Franzen and Allington 1990).

Researchers found that poorer readers were interrupted more often, asked fewer comprehension questions, and assigned more work on skills in isolation. If the children have difficulty, there is an assumption that the difficulty is in the area of phonics. Phonics must be part of every effective instructional program, but readers will need a lot more. Additionally, the students receiving special education services usually include an abundance of children from varied cultural and linguistic backgrounds and more boys than girls.

## Expertise in Literacy Teaching

Special education teachers are an invaluable, expert group of educators to have on any school team. Usually, they are highly trained in observing individual learners closely and tuning in to their differences. But we have found that some have not had the opportunity for training in a variety of literacy approaches that include views of reading as a complex process. Often, we have found they are trained to implement programs—and most often those that are built on a narrow sequence of learning. Marie Clay, herself a special educator and clinical psychologist, argued that teachers need many different ways of interacting with diversity to meet the needs of low-achieving students and that prescriptive, bit-

**The Limits of Labels** Categorizing or labeling a child often changes the nature of the classroom teacher's responsibility for the child's learning. It also influences the teacher's expectations. Too often we have observed the focus on the label instead of the uniqueness of each learner. Our view is that the challenge is in providing instruction that is responsive to the child, not blaming the child for how he or she best learns. Even the child may develop less self-efficacy when the subtle message is that there is something wrong with her abilities.

Two evidence-based interventions that have proven highly effective as a key component of the literacy systems in many schools and districts are Reading Recovery and the Leveled Literacy Intervention system.

### Reading Recovery

Reading Recovery, developed by Marie Clay, is a one-to-one tutoring program for low-achieving first graders that has inspired a generation of educators to intervene at the first signs of difficulty. Research substantiates that children who are significantly behind their peers in first grade are likely to fall further behind as they continue through school. The goal of Reading Recovery is to catch the learner before the gap is too wide and the weight of failure creates low self-efficacy and builds emotional resistance to reading and writing. The positive effect of Reading Recovery is well documented across four outcome domains: alphabetics, reading fluency, comprehension, and general reading achievement. Find the report by What Works Clearinghouse™ at whatworks.ed.gov or readingrecovery.org.

### Leveled Literacy Intervention

*Fountas & Pinnell Leveled Literacy Intervention (LLI)* is an intensive, small-group intervention designed to serve the lowest-achieving students in each grade. Based on the key principles of effective instruction above, *LLI* provides short-term supplementary instruction with the goal of helping students who are not achieving grade-level expectations in reading make accelerated progress. *LLI* has been proven effective in studies of hundreds of students in both rural and urban districts. What Works Clearinghouse™ reviewed the research on *LLI* and confirmed the positive effects on general reading achievement and reading fluency, and Evidence for ESSA gave *LLI* a strong rating. Read the full reports at whatworks.ed.gov and evidenceforessa.org.

by-bit sequential learning models are not effective for many. Teachers need different ways of interacting with children. When special educators have a variety of approaches in their professional training that include instruction with text-based programs, they bring a toolbox of support that will benefit all the children they serve.

# Principles of Effective Intervention

Given what we know about readers who find literacy learning difficult, it is important to design an intervention system that has the best chance for serving all learners. The following principles can offer guidance for your leadership team as you create an effective intervention design for your school or analyze the characteristics of an intervention system you have in place.

1. *Intervention lessons supplement effective classroom instruction.* Students will make less progress and will have gaps in their understandings if they frequently miss strong classroom instruction because they are pulled out for intervention. The positive effects of intervention will be short-lived if classroom instruction is weak. Students need to receive strong classroom instruction *and* additional, supplementary intervention that is highly effective to close the gap.

2. *The student/teacher ratio is low.* A ratio of one teacher to three students in the primary grades and one teacher to four students in the intermediate and middle school grades is ideal. And some students need one-to-one instruction that, if provided very early, can make a significant difference. A low student/teacher ratio allows teachers to provide a large amount of explicit instruction and direct support to individual students while efficiently delivering instruction to all students who need intervention.

3. *Intervention lessons are frequent.* Daily lessons reinforce new learning and help children make accelerated progress. Students gain momentum as they build on what they learned the day before.

4. *Intervention lessons are fast paced.* Struggling readers are easily distracted. Too often intervention means "slowed-down instruction," when instead students need lively learning experiences that allow them to process text with competence. A fast-paced lesson of 30 to 45

minutes with interesting texts, interactive word work, and opportunities for thoughtful writing will keep students engaged.

5. ***Concentrate intervention services in the early years.*** A delay in intervention means much more investment later, as well as the increased likelihood that students will experience confusion, significant gaps in their understandings, and emotional trauma. Of course, an intervention system needs to serve all students who need extra help whenever they need it, but prevention is more efficient and impactful than remediation.

6. ***Interventions are designed to be short-term.*** Interventions are highly effective and impactful so that students do not require extra support year after year, or even the whole school year. The layers within the intervention system are flexible so that teachers can group and re-group students or move from group to individual support.

7. ***Interventions are based on individual assessments that correctly identify students and offer teachers a detailed diagnosis to guide their instruction.*** Only with a precise understanding of a child's strengths and needs can a teacher work responsively with the student. Ongoing individual assessment of student learning relies on regular observation of student behavior, progress monitoring instruments, and an effective system for record-keeping.

8. ***Texts used in intervention lessons are culturally relevant and match the student's instructional level.*** Readers need challenge, but in intervention lessons they must be able to individually process a complex text with proficiency every day. Teachers give support but do not have to read the text to the student. The use of an instructional level text allows the teacher to provide careful scaffolding of a text that contains a productive amount of problem-solving for the reader. Each day the reader learns something he is able to apply to other texts he reads.

Student choice of reading materials is an important factor in intervention lessons.

9. ***Intervention lessons allow for student choice of reading material.*** Research has shown that choice is an important factor in engagement, motivation, and enjoyment during reading. Students participating in intervention lessons deserve the opportunity to choose texts that interest them.

10. ***Intervention lessons feature high-interest, well-crafted texts in a variety of fiction and nonfiction genres that reflect the diversity of our world.*** Readers who struggle need the same variety and quality of texts that proficient readers experience. A top priority is to offer students, from kindergarten throughout the elementary and middle

school years, texts that have stories and topics that are authentically diverse and engaging.

11. *Intervention lessons help students focus on deep comprehension and monitor their reading for understanding.* Some readers who struggle give almost all their attention to word solving. They get in the habit of not thinking actively about the meaning of a text and, as a consequence, have great difficulty when they begin to read more complex texts. Intervention lessons provide supportive teaching that helps students focus on deep understanding of fiction and nonfiction texts, monitor their reading through metacognitive attention as appropriate, and talk and write about their thinking.

12. *Intervention lessons promote smooth, phrased reading.* Many students read in a slow, halting manner that does not reflect the meaning of the text. As students read continuous print in texts that are appropriate for their existing skills (or with instruction just beyond) teachers can actively teach for smooth, phrased reading that is expressive and moves along at a good pace.

13. *Intervention lessons create opportunities for meaningful student talk in connection to texts.* "Talk structures" help students engage in authentic discussion. When students talk about text, they sharpen their thinking, learn to identify the big ideas in texts, and begin to acquire the academic language needed to participate fully in classroom conversations about books.

14. *Intervention lessons provide a dynamic and intensive study of words that grows from phonemic awareness and letter recognition to letter-sound relationships to attention to base words, word roots, and affixes.* It's desirable for students to use the building blocks of language at every step of their literacy journey. Students need excellent word study instruction *in addition* to that provided daily in classrooms. But they need massive opportunities to use their understandings within the context of continuous print as they read and write.

15. *Intervention lessons use writing to support and extend comprehension.* Using writing in combination with reading is highly effective in supporting both reading and writing skills. Children learn conventions of print such as left-to-right directionality, spacing, capitalization, and the use of punctuation; a large core of high-frequency words; how to hear the sounds in words and represent them with letters as they give close attention to visual information; and how to compose ideas that conceptually reflect the texts they have read.

16. *Intervention lessons develop independent, self-initiating, self-regulatory behaviors.* The ultimate goal of an intervention is to equip students to manage their own learning, building the self-efficacy they need to learn more every time they read and write.

The most important aspect of implementing any intervention is to collect and examine the results. You and your team need to closely monitor the intervention, considering the achievement outcomes of students relative to their time in the program. Are the interventions highly effective? Are they efficiently closing the gap between the lowest-achieving learners and students who are meeting grade-level expectations?

# Developing an Effective Design for Literacy Intervention

Your goal is to create a design for intervention that meets the needs of the students in your school. And so, you'll need to examine the options available to you against the student-centered principles previously discussed.

It may be helpful to think of literacy intervention as a system for delivering supplemental instruction that varies in intensity according to children's individual needs (Figure 15–7). For example, the schedule for literacy teaching in your school probably provides time for small-group instruction in reading, which all children need. But some students need it every day, while others benefit from small-group instruction in reading—or in writing—three or four times a week.

Another way to raise intensity is to lower the teacher/student ratio. Over time, research on younger children has shown that successful intervention requires a ratio of no more than 3:1. However, even the lowest ratio can't guarantee success unless teachers are specially trained to work with children who find reading and writing difficult.

Intervention can also be intensified by modifying the design so that teachers move quickly through structured lessons. This stands in contrast to the

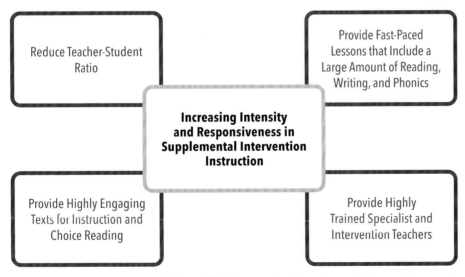

**Figure 15-7.** Increasing Intensity and Responsiveness in Supplemental Intervention Instruction

# PROTOCOL TOOL

The protocol tool **Developing an Effective Design for Literacy Intervention (19)** can help you and your colleagues step through the process of designing or refining your school's intervention system.

## DEVELOPING AN EFFECTIVE DESIGN FOR LITERACY INTERVENTION

| Intervention/Supports | Strengths | Questions and Modifications |
|---|---|---|
| The team agrees that we need a lot more time to discuss each individual intervention before coming to any conclusions. Two additional areas that appear to need further discussion are assessments for students in intervention supports and scheduling of student supports. | • Supports and interventions align with values for literacy teaching and learning. <br> • | • Due to some pullout services, sometimes intervention lessons supplant rather than supplement classroom teaching. |

---

**PROTOCOL TOOL**     **19**

## DEVELOPING AN EFFECTIVE DESIGN FOR LITERACY INTERVENTION

| Materials: | Participants: | Roles: | Time: |
|---|---|---|---|
| • chart paper <br> • markers <br> • highlighters | • Classroom teachers <br> • Special education teachers <br> • Interventionists | • Facilitator <br> • Notetaker | • 2+ hours |

### Part 1: Plan and Prepare

1. Gather a small team of five to ten colleagues, including classroom teachers, special education teachers, and trained interventionists, who together have knowledge of the complete range of interventions currently used at the school.
2. The team identifies a a facilitator and a notetaker who will write the group's thinking.
3. Display the blank chart on the second page of this tool by reproducing it on chart paper or projecting it.

**Notes:**

Team has been identified and first meeting scheduled.

### Part 2: Identify Literacy Interventions • 45 minutes

4. The team identifies Preventive, Tier 1, Tier 2, and Tier 3 supports and interventions currently used in classrooms across the school. The notetaker lists them in the first row and notes in parentheses if they are specific to certain groups of students.

**Notes:**

Chart for Intervention/Supports was begun. Interventions and supports were listed and we began the discussion from the questions in Part 3.

### Part 3: Analyze and Reflect on the Design • 75 minutes per meeting as needed

5. The team discusses the interventions, and the notetaker highlights each one on the chart and makes pertinent points.
6. The team analyzes the effectiveness of each element in the current intervention design by discussing the following questions:
   - *Do the supports and interventions align with the school's values for literacy teaching and learning?*
   - *Does the school provide concentrated intervention services in the early years (K–1)?*
   - *Are most interventions designed to be short term?*
   - *Do intervention lessons supplement effective classroom teaching, not supplant it?*
   - *Are interventions based on assessments that correctly identify students and offer teachers a detailed diagnosis of each child's unique reading/writing strengths and difficulties to guide their instruction?*
   - *Do the students who receive specialized services also have access to strong classroom teaching?*
   - *Are there gaps in the intervention system that should be filled?*
   - *For each element of the intervention design, what is the evidence that the particular support/intervention results in improved outcomes for students?*
7. Based on the discussion, the team places supports/interventions in the appropriate columns on the chart (Strengths or Questions and Modifications). The notetaker may wish to identify these with special marks, such as a check beside strengths in the system or a question mark beside assessments needing further discussion by the whole team.

**Notes:**

We decided the best way to document our discussion was to chart what we consider strengths and what are areas of need.

### Bring a Recommendation

8. The small team brings to the whole-school team a recommendation for an effective design for literacy intervention. Together the whole team discusses, revises, and achieves consensus on the design.
9. The whole team discusses and decides on a plan for sharing the design with the other teachers in the school, families, and other stakeholders.

**Notes:**

"slowed-down" approach that was a feature of traditional remediation. Today's intervention lessons need to be fast-paced in order to keep students engaged and allow substantial time for reading and writing.

Your design for intervention will depend on the sources of funding available to you, the needs of the students in your school, and the ways that teams of teachers are able to work together. Teams can plan a menu of options, including one-to-one intervention and small-group work, reserving the expertise of special education teachers for those students who require ongoing intensive help.

Take a long view to look across the grade levels, identifying the types of interventions that will be needed at each grade. Most important—make sure there is coherence across the kinds of instruction students receive. Take the time to work on a common vision of the kinds of literacy behaviors you want to see in your students. Finally, revisit your design periodically as circumstances change. At some point, you may find that fewer students require intervention because your plan for varied levels of intensity is working or the population of the school has changed.

# The Takeaway

Every child has the right to literacy. Our greatest responsibility as educators is to create the conditions that enable every child to be successful. Children deserve to enjoy a life of good health, safety, and productivity as global citizens, and growing up literate is the passport to opportunity for success in schooling and in life. Your success is measured not by your degree of effort, but by the outcomes it produces for all students.

## Think About Your School

- How has this chapter amplified or changed your views on effective intervention for all students?
- What supports currently are provided in your school to meet the needs of learners who are having difficulty in literacy learning?
- Look at the model on page 295. Are there any areas you and your team would like to strengthen to achieve greater equity for students?

# Move Your School Forward

- If you make changes to your current intervention system, you'll need to plan for what classroom teachers, interventionists, and special education teachers will most need to know about it. When your design is in place, work with the intervention team to discuss what professional learning opportunities should be offered.

- Check with your central office partners to determine what opportunities in the area of intervention are available through the district.

- Convene a small team consisting of interventionists, classroom teachers, and special education teachers to review district-supplied intervention plans and programs and determine how they might need to be adjusted to meet the needs of the students in your school.

# SECTION 5

*Selecting and Organizing High-Quality Texts for Literacy Learning*

# SECTION 5

## Selecting and Organizing High-Quality Texts for Literacy Learning

Every student deserves access to engaging texts of high quality, many genres, exciting and relevant content, and rich text language. Quality matters. Texts must be engaging to students. If you select carefully, you can provide beautiful texts for every instructional context that not only expose students to complex language and rich content, but to beautiful art, too.

Quantity also matters. Every year, each student engages with hundreds of texts, reading forty to fifty of them independently and experiencing many more through hearing them read aloud and participating in shared reading. They discuss books with their friends; they have conferences about books with their teacher to expand their understandings; and they participate in small-group reading of high-quality leveled texts with expert instruction that moves them forward in the development of a reading process. They use beautiful read-aloud texts as mentors for their own writing and extend their abilities as they do so.

Creating high-quality text collections is not just a matter of acquiring the funds; it is a thoughtful, deliberate, and ongoing process. In this section, we suggest practical ways to go about that process. In chapter 16, we describe the rich text base that is essential for every learner. Then in chapter 17, we turn to systems for organizing and sharing text resources in classroom libraries, school libraries, and school book rooms. All play a significant role in students' equitable access to literacy. All work together to provide the text base students need.

# Chapter 16

# A Rich Text Base for Literacy Learning

*When there are enough books available that can act as both
mirrors and windows for all our children, they will see that
we can celebrate both our differences and our similarities,
because together they are what make us all human.*
—Rudine Sims Bishop

As a READER AND writer, you know the power and potential of books to enrich readers' lives. Books entertain, inspire, give joy, offer challenge, nurture hope, and bring perspective. They introduce readers to new voices and new ways of understanding the world. They expand readers' knowledge, deepen their empathy, and call them to take action to make society more equitable and just. Books are essential to living a literate life—for you and for each student in your school.

In order for students to build effective and flexible literacy processing systems, they need to read a large volume of texts. The texts they encounter in their literacy education must be varied, well-written, engaging, socially and culturally relevant, accessible, and *plentiful*. Creating and sustaining a rich text base of high-quality books in the school and within each classroom takes time, planning, and collaboration among the school team but is a critical, "must have" element in supporting students' literacy learning.

In this chapter, we describe the general characteristics of excellent fiction and nonfiction texts for teaching in five instructional contexts (interactive read-aloud, shared reading, guided reading, independent reading, and book clubs), for use as mentor texts in reading and writing minilessons, and for small-group, whole-class, and individual/independent learning. In a multitext approach to literacy learning, teachers will need to choose different books for different purposes, using their understandings of the rationales and text characteristics for each selection.

No doubt there already are large collections of wonderful books and other media in your school and each was carefully and purposefully chosen. But, to remain socially and culturally relevant and to assure alignment with the changing interests of new generations of students, book collections must constantly grow and change. So, this chapter also contains helpful advice and an observation tool for helping you and your team assess how meaningfully the books across your collections represent diverse people and perspectives.

## A Text Base for the Literacy Classroom

Although these pages are about books, we recognize that the text base in schools today will include digital texts, audiobooks, magazines, and a range of other digital resources that students can access on the internet. Literacy learning is enhanced by these different forms. They increase accessibility and serve as important resources for exploration and inquiry projects. But the systematic, highly intentional, structured teaching that is essential for high levels of literacy learning require specific categories of books.

As a school leader, you play a significant role in facilitating the creation of a text base that supports coherent and equitable literacy learning (Figure 16-1). But the effort should be a collaborative one, in which teachers, the school librarian, literacy coaches, specialists, and school leaders have a voice. It also must be a *coordinated* effort if teachers are to accomplish their goals over years of schooling. It might cause a flurry of excitement and good feelings to simply give each teacher a sum of money to purchase books; however, the

### TEXT BASE FOR THE LITERACY CLASSROOM

| Whole-Class Teaching | Small-Group Teaching | Individual/ Independent Teaching |
|---|---|---|
| Books to Read Aloud | Leveled Books for Guided Reading | Books for Choice Independent Reading |
| ▪ Interactive Read-Aloud ▪ Reading Minilessons ▪ Writing Minilessons | Multiple Copies of Books for Book Clubs | |
| Enlarged-Print Books for Shared Reading | | |

**Figure 16-1.** Text Base for the Literacy Classroom

long-term results won't have as meaningful an impact. For example, without collaboration and coordination of the classroom text base:

- It will be difficult to plan a curriculum in which texts build on each other in terms of content and big ideas that build students' background knowledge and serve as a foundation for independent reading and writing.
- It will be hard to get a rich variety of genres.
- There will be duplication of books across the grades (although some duplication can be positive).
- Some voices and perspectives will be underrepresented.
- Student choice may be limited because classroom libraries lack a wide range and variety of relevant books that engage the hearts and minds of the classroom community.

But if teachers work both within and across grade levels, they can create a systematic sequence of rich text resources for each instructional context that really works. Of course, ordering a large number of books takes time and effort. Working by grade level may be the most efficient way to go and putting together grade-level bulk purchases usually results in discounts. As a school leader, you can and should play a key role in coordinating all these efforts to assure the wise investment of financial resources for coherence in literacy learning and improved student outcomes.

## Three General Criteria for Selecting Great Books

We will discuss some very specific characteristics of texts for use in literacy teaching later in this chapter, but let's first take a look at three general criteria that apply to *all* texts. High-quality collections of books for the classroom: (1) reflect the diversity of society and the world, with themes and ideas worthy of reading, discussion, and writing; (2) feature a variety of genres with high-quality language and art to build rich reading experiences that strengthen and expand readers' oral and written language; and (3) contain a wide variety of books for different purposes that can be used in all the literacy instructional contexts.

### High-Quality Book Collections Reflect Our Diverse World

Not only do today's children live in a world that is very different from those of two generations ago, but they live in a world that continues to change exponentially. Today's society is global. Many classrooms include the richness

**MORE BOOKS, BETTER OUTCOMES**

There is evidence that access to a rich, culturally relevant collection of books in schools and in classroom libraries increases student engagement and literacy outcomes. Multiple studies have correlated the number of books in a school to reading achievement (Krashen 2004, McQuillan 1998, Sinclair-Tarr and Tarr 2007). The text collections in the school represent the knowledge base to which students have access. Making a plan to increase the number of books in every classroom is a worthwhile effort that can improve literacy outcomes for students.

**My Rows and Piles of Coins**
by Tololwa M. Mollel
Historical Fiction

This is the story of a young boy in Tanzania in the early 1960s, who is saving money to buy a bike. On one level, the story is about a child saving up to buy something he wants. On another level, it is a story about determination and generosity, and about a family who work together and help each other. The story also reveals something about life in Tanzania during a particular time in history—what a particular community values, and the economic structure of the community. All these details make the book rich with opportunities for students to think and talk.

of students from different cultures and countries. Dozens of different languages may be spoken within a single school—languages that are spoken by students in their homes and their communities. Equally important, students who live in communities with less diversity are part of a world in which multicultural competencies and understandings are increasingly needed and valued.

It is important for students to see themselves and the diversity of people in their world and the range of lived experiences reflected in the books they read and in other materials in the classroom:

> One way to help students develop and maintain positive social identities is to make certain our classroom books reflect the many components of their identities. Of course, we can't be sure we're hitting this mark unless we've taken the time to really get to know our kids as individuals. This may begin with the more visible aspects of their identities, but it can't stop there. Yes, we need books featuring characters who are Black, Latinx, Asian Americans, mixed race, and so on, but our kids' identities extend far beyond their ethnic heritage or racial makeup. Other factors such as family structure, religion, socioeconomic status, health, gender identification, interests, and abilities need to be taken into account as well. Remember, none of us can be defined by a single aspect of our identities; rather, we exist at the intersection of the many social groups to which we belong. (Hass 2020)

All students need to understand, appreciate, and respect perspectives and experiences other than their own. Our friend Rudine Sims Bishop (1990) wrote:

> Books are sometimes windows, offering views of worlds that may be real or imagined, familiar or strange. These windows are also sliding glass doors, and readers have only to walk through in imagination to become part of whatever world has been created or recreated by the author. When lighting conditions are just right, however, a window can also be a mirror. Literature transforms human experience and reflects it back to us, and in that reflection, we can see our own lives and experiences as part of the larger human experience. Reading, then, becomes a means of self-affirmation and readers often seek their mirrors in books.

The classroom can be a safe, inclusive place where readers can seek their windows and mirrors and walk through sliding glass doors. By its very nature, the classroom collection of books should convey some important messages to children:

- Your life has possibilities.
- Everyone has value.
- Everyone has something to contribute.

- Everyone is responsible for assuring that others feel included in conversations and contribute their perspectives.
- All of us are responsible for helping others do their best work.
- We learn and accomplish more when we work together.
- Together, we take care of the places where we live, work, and learn.
- We are kind to others.
- Each of us has qualities and experiences that make us different, and qualities and experiences that make us the same.
- Our differences should be embraced and valued, because they help us learn new things about ourselves, others, and the world.

We do not recommend books with heavy-handed messages designed to overtly teach moral lessons. Didactic texts do not engage students and really don't do justice to the complex ways in which humans behave and interact. You want a collection in which fictional characters speak and behave in believable, authentic ways and the subjects of biography and other informational texts reflect a rainbow of experiences and perspectives. You also want nonfiction books that help students appreciate the wonder, complexity, and beauty of nature.

No single book represents diversity (Everett 2017). Only as students engage with a wide range of texts that authentically represent the lives and perspectives of many different people do they begin to experience real diversity.

The observation tool **Evaluating Texts and Text Collections for Inclusive and Authentic Representation (20)** can help you and your team assess how meaningfully the books across your collections represent diverse people and perspectives. You may wish to work with individual teachers to analyze how specific

## OBSERVATION TOOL

Use the observation tool **Evaluating Texts and Text Collections for Inclusive and Authentic Representation (20)** to evaluate the diversity and inclusivity of classroom libraries.

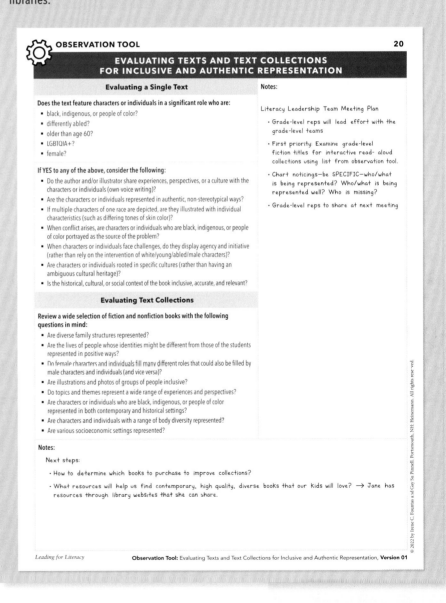

**A Worthy Investment** Financial resources are always a challenge, but the cost of buying a new program every few years is far more expensive (and probably less effective) than a wonderful collection of books that is constantly expanded. A literacy approach that centers on the use of high-quality texts used in a systematic way can be more cost-effective than you might think.

Yes, some books will be read so many times by students that they become worn and eventually need to be replaced. But that is a good expense to have, and book collections should be expanded a little every year to include new or different authors, illustrators, and topics. In general, however, book collections are not consumable materials that only last a year.

Some of the materials teachers and students will need in a multitext classroom do need to be replenished from time to time. Every student will need a fresh reader's notebook and writer's notebook each year, along with a set of pocket folders for writing. And teachers will have to replenish chart paper, markers, pocket charts, and individual whiteboards for word study. These are the basic tools that all readers and writers need, regardless of the teacher's instructional approach, in order for their classroom to be an organized place where high-quality, authentic literacy learning takes place.

books contribute to the diversity and inclusivity of their classroom libraries. You may also wish to bring together a team to think about perspectives, experiences, or identities that are underrepresented in the school's book collections. Together you can make a plan to identify and obtain high-quality books that will offer diverse experiences to readers.

**Books for English Learners** As you think about the text resources in your school, consider the importance of having some books available in the children's native languages so English learners can see how their languages are being honored and promoted (Figure 16-2). It will be very difficult, if not impossible, to acquire books in some languages, but Spanish-language books

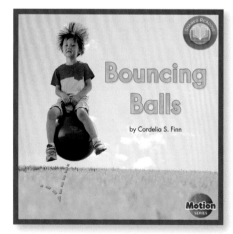 

**Figure 16-2.** Spanish and English book pairing from the *Fountas & Pinnell Classroom™ Shared Reading Collection.*

are quite available and increasingly, so are books in French. Make a concerted effort to obtain a variety of books in the languages represented in your school. You may find that the children's families can refer you to sources.

Look for opportunities to order books that are written both in English and in Spanish (or other language pairs) so the books can be read in both languages. In a shared reading lesson, for example, the whole class can read it with the teacher in English, and then the children who speak Spanish can read it aloud with the teacher in both languages.

## High-Quality Book Collections Feature a Range of Fiction and Nonfiction Genres

Every collection of books in a literacy-rich classroom offers opportunities for students to experience a wide range of fiction and nonfiction genres. By engaging deeply and constantly with a variety of high-quality texts, students build an internal foundation of information on which they can base further learning. They learn how to develop genre understandings and can apply their thinking to any genre. By experiencing this variety, students also develop their preferences and identities as readers.

A genre is a type of text identified by its characteristics and purpose. Prose and poetry are the *ways* that language is used in literature. Both prose and poetry can be either fiction or nonfiction (Figure 16-3). Within those broad categories much depends on the setting and/or purpose of the text. The genres that

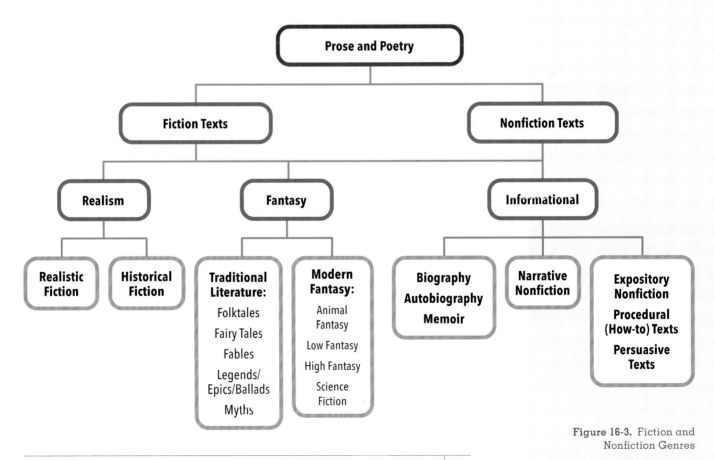

**Figure 16-3.** Fiction and Nonfiction Genres

## WHAT ABOUT DECODABLE BOOKS?

Decodable books are designed to be given to children following phonics lessons. They contain very simple stories that rely on phonetically decodable words and align with phonics principles students have already been taught. Because such texts are contrived to use only certain words, they offer young readers very limited opportunities to understand reading as language or derive meaning from the story.

So, while teachers might choose to use decodable books for particular reasons, we would be cautious about building an entire beginning reading experience around a single type of text. And, if children are reading continuous print every day, as well as participating in a direct, clear, phonics lesson, they quickly will acquire both language patterns and sight words so that both contexts make sense to them.

Instead, as you select books for classrooms or for an intervention program, ask some of the questions that follow.

- Does the book contain a comprehensible, real story or provide interesting information?
- Is the book culturally relevant to children and their families?
- Are easy-to-read word patterns included, along with a few high-frequency words?
- Does the author use repeating word patterns and phrases in a way that increases enjoyment and supports young learners with material that becomes familiar while giving them a deeper understanding of the usefulness of the phonics principles they are learning?
- Does the book use linguistic structures that sound like real language to children, although simpler?
- Is the focus on everyday experiences that will be familiar to beginners and sound real?
- Is the topic interesting and relevant to children and within their capacity to understand at this point in their lived experiences?
- Does the book work as part of a sequence that builds from very simple, one-sentence texts to those with gradually increasing complexity?

have existed through centuries of written language developed because writers needed ways to make their meaning and their message clear. Looking at aspects of genre, we see how the writer's decisions about language, word choice, dialogue, structure or organization, and all other aspects of craft rests on the choice of genre.

**Fiction Genres**  In our book *Genre Study* (Fountas and Pinnell 2022) we have written in detail about the purposes and characteristics of fiction and nonfiction texts, including the particular characteristics and instructional value of the various sub-genres that fall under each of those categories. We've also published two prompting guides for fiction and nonfiction genres that help teachers guide students' inquiry toward explicit understandings of the characteristics of genres.

Both fiction and nonfiction texts come in a variety of types—such as mystery or survival stories—each with its own defining characteristics. The structure of fiction is usually narrative and generally follows a sequence: (1) introduction of characters, setting, and problems; (2) a series of events and rising action; (3) a turning or high point; and (4) the resolution and ending. Along the way, characters may change, grow, or learn a lesson, and relationships may evolve.

The main purpose of fiction, whether realistic or fantasy, is to entertain. Fiction genres can be divided into realism and fantasy. All fiction stories are imagined, but those that fall in the category of realism have settings, characters, and events that could exist in real life. Contemporary realistic fiction stories are in the "here and now" or very recent past. Historical fiction tells imagined stories with characters and settings from the more distant past. Realism allows authors to present a vast and colorful array of human lives and experiences in settings and circumstances that readers may have experienced for themselves. Realism also enables readers to understand the hardships that people endured in the past and continue to face today, develop empathy, and take inspiration from the ways that characters persist and overcome challenges.

Fantasy ranges from the very simple nursery tales, folktales, and animal fantasies that young children enjoy to stories with complex settings and characters and alternate worlds. Traditional fantasy literature ranges in complexity and includes folktales, fairy tales, fables, legends, epics, ballads, and myths. These tales have been handed down through centuries—they originated in oral storytelling and were intended for the entertainment and enlightenment of adults.

Every culture in the world has traditional tales that offer a wonderful way to explore cultural norms and values, and it's important that classroom book collections include traditional literature from many different countries and

## THE IMPORTANCE OF POETRY IN THE CLASSROOM

**Hand in Hand: Poems About Friends**
Poetry
Grade K

Hand in Hand
Poems About Friends

Each poem and song in this collection is about friends: old friends, new friends, furry friends, funny friends.

As you and your team assess the text base of classrooms, you may discover that poetry is underrepresented. Poetry offers special challenges that deter some readers, and consequently, teachers sometimes exclude books of poetry from classroom libraries or text sets and limit the use of poetic texts during their teaching. Yet poetry has important benefits for students as readers and writers. Poems enrich the language of readers and inspire new ways of thinking about the world. As mentor texts, they provide a model for powerful (and often innovative) uses of language to convey feelings and express ideas. In text sets, poetry can provide a fresh perspective on a theme or topic, or in a text set comprising only poetry, students can begin to notice elements of craft that are frequently found in poems. As you assess the variety of genres in classroom libraries, notice the balance of prose and poetry. Promote the inclusion of poetry in text sets and classroom libraries as well as enlarged print poetry books to increase students' understanding of and appreciation for expressive ways of writing.

***Pedal Power***
by June Schwartz
Nonfiction
Level W

In Ghana, the walk to school is often long and hot. A bike can change a child's life–helping to make the journey much faster and easier. This nonfiction title tells about a group of young entrepreneurs who discovered how to make low-cost bamboo bikes that would not only help students but also preserve the environment. The book introduces children to young people who are positively impacting their communities through their initiative and ingenuity.

cultures, including native and indigenous cultures from different regions. Modern fantasy also includes texts that range in complexity, from simple animal fantasy to high fantasy and science fiction. The challenge to the reader is to understand the unrealistic or supernatural elements of the fantasy world and the perspectives of the people within it.

**Nonfiction Genres** All nonfiction texts provide information to the reader, but they do it in different ways. Informational texts may be expository, a categorical structure into which information is grouped logically so that the reader can access what she wants to learn. Expository fiction also includes how-to texts that explain a process or give directions and persuasive texts that use persuasion or argument to sway the beliefs of readers or convince them to take action.

Nonfiction also can follow a chronological sequence, similar to the narrative structure of fiction. A biography is the story of a person's life told by another person, while an autobiography is the story of one's own life. Closely related, a memoir is a poignant memory, often of a shorter personal experience of a place or another person. Memoir is a natural outgrowth of the personal stories that younger writers produce. There is also narrative nonfiction, which is a true story of an event or series of events, usually told in chronological sequence.

Readers learn to recognize and use underlying structures when they read nonfiction. These include description, chronological sequence (time order), temporal sequence (steps in a process that always happens in a certain order), comparison and contrast, cause and effect, problem and solution, or question and answer. Often more than one of these structures appear in the same text. Learning to recognize and use them enhances and is often necessary for comprehension.

**Learning About Genres Over Time** *The Literacy Continuum* (Chapter 9) provides some general guidance for the introduction and use of genres over time in interactive read-aloud so that children establish a strong base in each genre. Books read aloud form the shared literary foundation for all the children regardless of their reading level. Each year, the cognitive "load" becomes more complex. Students are simply enjoying and discussing great fiction and

| Genre/Form | Pre-K | K | 1 | 2 | 3 | 4 | 5 | 6 | 7/8 |
|---|---|---|---|---|---|---|---|---|---|
| **Fiction Genres** | | | | | | | | | |
| Realistic fiction | ■ | ■ | ■ | ■ | ■ | ■ | ■ | ■ | ■ |
| Special types of realistic fiction: adventure, animal story, family, school, humor | | | | ■ | ■ | ■ | ■ | ■ | ■ |
| Special types of realistic fiction: satire, parody; horror; romance | | | | | | | | | ■ |
| Historical fiction | | | | | ■ | ■ | ■ | ■ | ■ |
| Folktale | ■ | ■ | ■ | ■ | ■ | ■ | ■ | ■ | ■ |
| Traditional literature: fairy tale, fable | | | | ■ | ■ | ■ | ■ | ■ | ■ |
| Traditional literature: tall tale | | | | ■ | | | | | |
| Traditional literature: fractured fairy tale | | | | | | ■ | ■ | ■ | ■ |
| Traditional literature: myth, legend, ballad | | | | | | | ■ | ■ | ■ |
| Traditional literature: epic | | | | | | | | | ■ |
| Simple animal fantasy | ■ | ■ | ■ | ■ | | | | | |
| Fantasy | | | | ■ | ■ | | | | |
| Complex fantasy (including science fiction) | | | | | | | ■ | ■ | ■ |
| High Fantasy | | | | | | | | ■ | ■ |
| **Nonfiction Genres** | | | | | | | | | |
| Label book, Concept book, ABC book, Counting book | ■ | ■ | ■ | | | | | | |
| Simple factual text | ■ | ■ | ■ | | | | | | |
| Simple biography | | | | ■ | | | | | |
| Biography | | | | | ■ | ■ | ■ | ■ | ■ |
| Autobiography | | | | | ■ | ■ | ■ | ■ | ■ |
| Memoir (personal memory story) | ■ | ■ | | | | | | | |
| Memoir | | | | | ■ | ■ | ■ | ■ | ■ |
| Simple narrative nonfiction | | | | ■ | | | | | |
| Narrative nonfiction | | | | | ■ | ■ | ■ | ■ | ■ |
| Simple expository nonfiction | | | | ■ | | | | | |
| Expository nonfiction | | | | | ■ | ■ | ■ | ■ | ■ |
| Simple procedural text | ■ | ■ | ■ | ■ | | | | | |
| Procedural text | | | | | ■ | ■ | ■ | ■ | ■ |
| Persuasive text | | | | | ■ | ■ | ■ | ■ | ■ |
| **Hybrid Texts** | | | | | ■ | ■ | ■ | ■ | ■ |

**Figure 16-4.** Genres Across the Grades: Interactive Read-Aloud and Literature Discussion

nonfiction books; but the teacher is engaging in highly intentional instruction to expand their reading life and literacy competencies.

The chart in Figure 16-4, which is drawn from *The Literacy Continuum*, offers general guidelines when choosing titles for a classroom collection of interactive read-aloud and literature discussion books. The chart is not a prescription or a set of hard-and-fast rules. You may, of course, identify texts that are appropriate for younger or older children that don't fit the recommendations. But the chart can help you and your team plan for the range of genres that children need to experience across the grades.

Take a closer look at the chart, and you'll notice some patterns. Younger students take on quite a few genres, but very simple forms of those genres. Some genres are present at every grade, but the examples increase in complexity over time with more forms and topics.

The chart shows genres of text in interactive read-aloud, an instructional context with a high level of teacher support. They also may be used in literature discussions in which students read or listen to the text. The genres of texts in shared reading would be closely aligned. Corresponding genres in guided reading would generally be encountered about three to six months later. In other words, teachers work to establish understanding of the genre through interactive read-aloud and shared reading before students are expected to identify it in guided and independent reading.

**Genre Study** An important instructional approach is called "genre study" (Fountas and Pinnell 2022). In genre study, teachers follow these steps:

1. The teacher immerses students in the genre through reading four or five books that are clear examples and then invites discussion and response.

2. Students work together to share what they have noticed across texts; the teacher acts as scribe to record the list of characteristics.

## DIGITAL LITERACY

**Processing Digital Texts** To become fully literate students need to learn to process digital texts. They take many forms and have many purposes: e-books, magazine articles, websites, blogs, podcast transcripts, email, text messages, posts, and comments. Digital texts open up the world beyond the classroom, piquing students' curiosity and expanding knowledge. They provide increased access and engagement for students and enhance instruction. They offer specific challenges to the reader, such as deciding whether to disregard or follow links and navigating layouts that change based on the device used. As with any text, students must learn to assess the reliability of the source and evaluate the message for bias. Teachers will want to teach explicit reading minilessons to help students explore digital texts and learn how to think critically about the information they encounter. As you reflect on the text collections in your school, notice and evaluate the instructional value that teachers are getting from digital texts and how digital texts are used to enhance students' learning.

3. Students work together to construct a definition of the genre.

4. They add to the list and definition as they encounter more examples.

5. The teacher provides explicit minilessons on each characteristic or "noticing" using the genre examples.

Genre study is an example of using the process of inquiry to immerse students in a type of text so they can study the wide variety of genres that exist. It takes years to internalize deep understandings about genre. Bomer (1995) describes genre as a "road map" to comprehension. Knowledge of genre helps readers know how a text "works" and what to expect. Readers take a different stance toward a text based on genre (Rosenblatt, 1994). In other words, they read and comprehend differently based on their understanding of a genre.

It is obvious that an important goal of the classroom book collection from pre-K to middle school is to provide for the engagement of students in a wide variety of genres, and these texts should be carefully selected to build understandings over time. Students are introduced to genres and study them through interactive read-aloud and minilessons, but they also need the opportunity to experience them in guided reading with the support of a teacher who is helping them take on more complex texts. And they need many opportunities to independently process good books in all of these genres every day. Book club discussions, too, provide opportunities to talk about different genres with others. In all of these instructional settings, genre is an important part of the lesson and the discussion.

## High-Quality Book Collections Contain a Wide Variety of Books for Different Purposes

The instructional design we've described in this book provides for multiple instructional contexts and approaches, each of which accomplishes a different purpose and all of which work together to support students' expansion of background knowledge, language competencies, and vocabulary and the development of effective in-the-head systems of strategic actions for reading and writing. With this design, students become proficient word solvers and process a wide number of texts for themselves in independent reading. They also apply strategic actions to comprehend complex works of fiction and nonfiction that are beyond their present abilities in interactive read-aloud, shared reading, book clubs, and guided reading. The design provides for expansion of comprehending power *ahead* of print processing powers. And that is why so many texts are needed.

| VARIETY IN THE CLASSROOM TEXT BASE | | |
|---|---|---|
| **ELEMENT** | **QUALITIES TO CONSIDER** | **EXAMPLES** |
| **Format** | Size, layout, placement of print, use of art | • Picture storybooks • Picture biographies • Illustrated informational books • Short stories • Easy chapter books |
| **Genre** | Fiction and informational texts with recognizable characteristics | Fiction • Contemporary realistic fiction • Historical fiction • Modern fantasy  Nonfiction • Biography • Memoir • Narrative nonfiction • Persuasive texts |
| **Special Types** | Texts with particular characteristics that are distinguishable within a broader genre | • Mysteries • Sports stories • Survival stories • Romance • Horror • Graphic texts • Two-way books |
| **Content** | Wide range of high-quality content to appeal to as many students as possible and support areas of study | • Social studies • STEM topics • Arts topics • Literary content • "How-to" books |
| **Diversity** | Representation of the diversity of the world in which students live | • Cultural • Regional • Racial • Religious • Linguistic • Gender |
| **Accessibility** | Different media that provide access to a wide variety of texts | • Texts read aloud to students • Audio texts • Book apps |

## Choosing Books for Every Context

A multitext approach to literacy instruction requires selecting the right texts to sustain and expand students' literacy learning in five instructional contexts: interactive read-aloud, shared reading, guided reading, independent reading, and book clubs. A sufficient text base needs to include books—in both print and digital formats—to support all dimensions of students' reading development.

No one feature should be the deciding factor in selecting and using a text with an individual or a group of children at any point in time. Instead, thoughtful analysis of all the characteristics of texts is needed to match books to readers' interests, needs, and ability to read with understanding. And selection criteria should vary according to the purpose and *way* the book will be used in each of the five instructional contexts for reading. (To learn more about the lesson structure of each instructional context for reading, see Chapter 11.)

## Selecting Books for Interactive Read-Aloud

In choosing books for interactive read-aloud, words are not a critical factor because the teacher does the decoding. Consider whether the content will be interesting and relevant to the age group and the themes and ideas within their grasp. Teachers need to select books that have engaging literary language, with sentences that students can understand.

Books for younger children should be straightforward stories and informational texts focusing on a topic that is easy to understand with typical background experience. There may be new vocabulary words, but the teacher is right there to help students understand. Interactive read-aloud is the setting where you stretch students' ability to comprehend texts with more complex factors than they can handle in other settings. They are ideal ways to:

- Build background and content knowledge.
- Enrich vocabulary and encourage academic discussion.
- Support students in learning how to use social conventions in talk with others.
- Deepen comprehension of complex ideas.
- Study genres and discover their characteristics.
- Notice the writer's and illustrator's craft.

**Text Sets** A text set is a collection of two or more texts that can be connected because they have common features. Text sets are used for highly intentional teaching through interactive read-aloud, shared reading, book clubs, and reading and writing minilessons.

Text sets are organized in a way that helps students build specific understandings from book to book. Through text sets, students can gain experience with and develop a deep understanding of a topic, author or illustrator, genre, or element of craft. Text sets can help students:

- Understand how literary elements contribute to a story.
- Get to know the work of specific authors or illustrators.
- Explore content-area topics in depth.
- Experience different aspects of a genre.

*"If a child leaves us having loved one book, we have changed the world."*
**—Pernille Ripp**

- Learn about universal problems.
- Examine history from different perspectives.
- Expand their use of academic language to talk about texts.
- Link or compare content across books.

We advocate for interactive read-aloud lessons that are organized around text sets—about three to five books that are connected in some way. For example, they may be connected by genre, author, illustrator, theme, topic (nonfiction), or poetic language.

Below is an example of a text set for grade 2 interactive read-aloud. As you read the brief plot summaries, think about what connects the five books.

1. *Last Stop on Market Street* (2015). While riding the bus across town, a young boy is encouraged by his nana to notice the wonderful things and people all around him that he takes for granted.

2. *Something Beautiful* (1998). A young girl tells her story of looking for something beautiful in the world around her. Her friends and family help her see that beauty is already all around her.

3. *The Gardener* (2007). When Lydia's father loses his job, she goes to stay with her uncle and helps him at his bakery in the city. While living there, she uses her gardening skills to transform their drab building into a beautiful showcase of flowers.

4. *Jamaica Louise James* (1997). A young girl tells a story about her cool idea to surprise her grandmother for her birthday by beautifying the subway station where her grandmother works.

5. *Wanda's Roses* (2000). A young girl who loves beautiful things takes care of a rosebush and the empty lot where it lives. Even though this rosebush never blooms, the people in the community love her so much that they get involved in cleaning up and beautifying the lot.

Based on the summaries above, you can infer the theme that holds this text set together—the importance of finding beauty in the world. That's a theme that even young children can explore, connect with, and apply to their own lives. When using text sets, the teacher reads aloud one book a day for a week and then revisits all the texts to give children the opportunity to think across them, to talk about how they might be alike, and to discover what children are noticing and taking away from them. Experiencing read-aloud texts in this way builds powerful connections over time. Interactive read-aloud books are a shared classroom resource and need to be placed in a special area of the classroom. Titles can be listed on a *Books We've Shared* chart as students experience them, and this constantly expanding list will help everyone recall the books they have read and discussed. Students may respond to read-aloud books in a reader's notebook.

A mentor text is a book or other text that serves as an example of excellent writing. Mentor texts are used often in both reading and writing minilessons and generally are read and revisited for literature discussion and student writing. In her book *The Writing Thief* (2014), author Ruth Culham says, "By using mentor texts, the reader can virtually position him- or herself to sit beside the author and study how the text is constructed and how it communicates. It is a powerful teaching and learning strategy. . . ."

In each reading context, teachers have opportunities to help students notice the craft so they can apply their knowledge as writers. Every text or poem students experience is an example of the writer's craft. These same texts are revisited in reading and writing minilessons to study author's and illustrator's craft, and students can read them and use them for inspiration in their own writing. The use of mentor texts drives home the point that reading and writing are reciprocal processes.

Books We've Shared

1. My Friend Rabbit (F)
2. Owl Babies (F)
3. Olivia (F)
4. Little Chick (F)
5. My Five Senses (NF)
6. Ocean Babies (NF)
7. Growing Vegetable Soup (NF)
8. Lots of Spots (NF)

Listing the books children have shared helps nourish and sustain the classroom community.

## Selecting Books for Shared Reading

Teachers can select enlarged texts for shared reading using the same general characteristics as those for interactive read-aloud. But the selections should be made with an eye to stories, both fiction and nonfiction, and language that children will delight in speaking out loud. Teachers need a variety of large-print books (big books), as well as poetry books and song charts that everyone can easily view and read together. Teachers also can use as mentor texts large-print books that are accompanied by small book versions for independent reading or a listening center. Students often enjoy reading the big book or small book versions over and over.

Early shared reading texts should feature rhyme, repetition, language play, and rhythm, features that would not be present in books for guided reading. Shared reading books might have idioms and expressions, as well as complex language, but children will be able to process it with the support of the group. Also, enlarged nonfiction texts can clearly illustrate graphics and text features. Enlarged texts for intermediate readers can be used to examine nonfiction text structures or text features. Shared reading texts might include poetic language, stories in verse, plays and reader's theater, speeches, and journal entries, and often books for shared reading have interactive features such as cut-outs, flaps, or pop-ups.

### Illustrators use details to show something about a character.

| Title | What the Illustration Shows | What the Illustration Means |
|---|---|---|
| THE GREAT FUZZ FRENZY | Big Bark thinks he is important.<br><br>Prairie dogs are worried. They are frightened by Big Bark. | Big Bark's body and face show how he feels about himself.<br><br>Prairie dogs' faces and bodies show how they feel. |
| THE PATCHWORK QUILT | Tanya is leaning on Grandma and listening carefully. | Tanya's body shows how she feels about another character. |
| GETTIN' THROUGH THURSDAY | Davis looks at Mom in surprise. | Davis' face shows what he might be thinking. |

Charts like the one above help reinforce the idea that illustrations carry meaning.

## Selecting Books for Book Clubs

Books for book clubs need to be selected for their potential to spark deep, engaging discussion among a small group of students, all of whom will be reading the same text or occasionally a variety of texts on the same topic or issue. Level is not an issue; you want students to choose books they really want to read and talk about (the teacher can provide an audio version to make the text accessible to all students). At the same time, books should not be so far beyond students that they cannot comprehend the ideas or navigate the pictures and graphics. These texts need to be relevant and appealing to students as well as age- and grade-appropriate.

Picture books are published for a variety of ages—some very high-level—and are valuable for discussion at every grade level. Book club selections may be short fiction or nonfiction texts that students can read in one or two days, or they may be chapter books that take about a week to read during independent reading time. It's wise to avoid extremely long chapter books, however, even for older students. They will take students a very long time to finish, which makes it harder to schedule the book club meetings. Fortunately, there are plenty of high-level, challenging texts of shorter length.

For book clubs, we suggest that students choose from four different books that are connected in some way. They might be part of an author study or be related to the text sets in interactive read-aloud, making for more enriching discussions. Teachers need six to eight copies of each book so every student can have a copy. Students can use independent reading time to prepare for their book club discussions, marking places in the text they want to discuss. The books won't be discussed by the class as a whole, but as students talk about their reading during group share, others may become interested in reading these books.

## Selecting Books for Guided Reading

Books for guided reading will be carefully calibrated to *levels* of difficulty and opportunities for the individuals in the group to make shifts in progress. The same text factors apply, but the number of known and new words as well as sentence complexity are critical factors. There must be challenges so that readers can learn from problem-solving, which should be accomplished against a backdrop of accurate reading. The level is a tool designed to help *teachers* do the most skilled teaching they can at the front edge of students' learning. Levels do not describe *children*. Rather they describe the characteristics of a book and its opportunity for children to use their strengths and expand their competencies.

By taking on a more challenging text and processing it with proficiency and enjoyment, students can make important shifts in reading ability. They will "move up" levels, but this is not the best way to think of growth. A "level" stands for clusters of learning goals across all areas of word solving and comprehension. The progress up the gradient is cumulative in that if students can read at one level, they can read books at easier levels as well.

Building the leveled book collection is a challenge because the level is not the *most* important thing about the book. Every book in the leveled book collection should be *worth reading*. Short texts are ideal, so students can process a new text in each lesson. Teachers can use chapter books

**BOOK LOOK**

**Eight Dolphins of Katrina**
by Janet Wyman Coleman
Nonfiction
Grade 4

Did you know that Hurricane Katrina destroyed a dolphin house and sent eight dolphins into the open sea? No one knew how long they could survive or whether their trainers would find them in time to save them. Students will rush to join this book club so they can find out what happened.

**BOOK LOOK**

**Signing with Jim**
by Suzanne Slade
Nonfiction Narrative
Level P

This level P guided reading book is the true story of Jim, a child with Down's syndrome and hearing issues who is entering a new school for the first time and feeling alone and afraid. Jim ends up teaching his entire class how to sign, and the story has relatable themes about appreciating differences and using those differences as opportunities for learning and growth.

on occasion and read them over a few days. The important point is that the reading is not dragged across weeks, chapter by chapter. Of course, students will have their favorites and may respond to some more than others; but all texts should have appeal and engage students' interest. Students should leave the guided reading group knowing that they learned something interesting or enjoyed a story or thought about something in a new way—just as they do after interactive read-aloud or when they reflect on books they choose for independent reading. Books for guided reading have to be good books worth student and teacher time, not simply books to "practice reading words."

The leveled book collection should not be used for students' independent reading, though teachers may add some individual titles to baskets. Remember that students do not choose books by level. For beginning readers, teachers may place some books in a browsing box for rereading, or a student may have a particular use for a book. But, in general, leveled books are organized in a place for teacher access and their exclusive use by small groups is explained to the students. Many schools have a book room that teachers use to access the

## UNDERSTANDING THE TEXT GRADIENT

It is impossible for a teacher to provide high-quality guided reading for students without carefully considering what makes texts difficult or easy for *individuals.* A gradient of text reflects a defined continuum of characteristics against which you can evaluate texts. It becomes invaluable in the process of selecting texts, and it also offers guidance in designing lessons.

*The Fountas & Pinnell Literacy Continuum* lists detailed text characteristics and goals (behaviors and understandings to notice, teach for, and support) for each level of the gradient, levels A through Z. The twenty-six levels encompass progress from kindergarten through high school. There are ten levels across kindergarten and grade 1 and three levels each for grades 2–6, with one level for middle and high school. Within each level, fiction and nonfiction texts are grouped using a combination of characteristics. The gradient is represented in Figure 16-5.

A gradient of text is not a precise sequence of texts through which all students must pass. Books are leveled in approximate groups from which teachers choose for instruction. Teachers who recognize the convenience of the gradient yet remember its limitations will be able to make good choices and test their decisions against children's behaviors while reading and talking about texts.

leveled books they need for one or two weeks. This is an economical system because the books are shared across the school. (See Chapter 17 for information on school book rooms.)

## Selecting Books for Independent Reading

Books for independent reading should be selected according to the typical range of reading abilities and interests for the age group in the whole class so that every student has a range of choices; however, as mentioned above, we have strongly stated that books in the classroom library *should not* be organized or labeled by level. Children do not represent a level. Levels are for books, not for children. In fact, children will be able to read a range of levels. For example, they may be able to read a more difficult book that is of high interest and reflects their extensive background knowledge.

Through shared reading, interactive read-aloud, and guided reading, students will have learned much about their own abilities to process and understand texts, and, they will have formed opinions and tastes. Through minilessons, they will have learned to choose books and monitor their own reading by using a reader's notebook. The books in the classroom library reflect the diversity of students in the school and beyond and include a range of topics that will interest readers in the classroom community. The collection is rich and varied, with a full range of genres, a balance of fiction and nonfiction, and enough books to captivate every student in the classroom.

**BOOK LOOK**

*Moving Day*
by Anthony G. Brandon
Fiction
Grade K

Annie's family is moving to a new home, but Annie insists she won't move. At the end of the story, Annie is surprised with a new puppy to help her transition into the new home. If the new puppy is moving, Annie wants to move, too!

## The Takeaway

Learning deepens when students think, talk, read, and write about wonderful, authentic texts across many different instructional contexts. School leaders play an important role in assuring that classroom libraries contain enough and the right kinds of books to expand children's literacy processing skills and develop in them a lifelong love of reading.

High-quality collections of books for the classroom: (1) reflect the diversity of society and the world, with themes and ideas worthy of reading, discussion, and writing; (2) feature a variety of genres with high-quality language and art

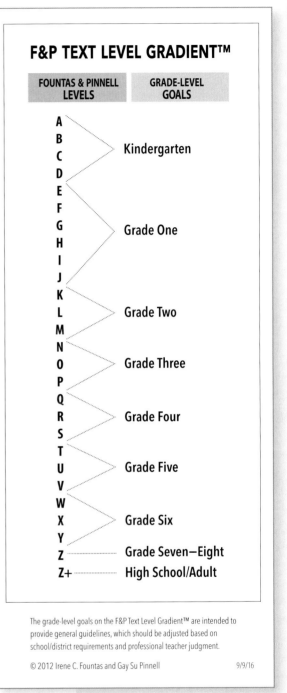

**Figure 16-5.** The Fountas & Pinnell Text Level Gradient™.

to build rich reading experiences that strengthen and expand readers' oral and written language; (3) contain a wide variety of books for different purposes that can be used in all the literacy instructional contexts.

In this chapter, we have advocated for large quantities of beautiful books in every classroom. Maintaining so many texts in so many places requires an organized approach to resource management. In the next chapter, we'll help you set up, house, and maintain the book collections in individual classroom libraries, the school library or media center, and the school book room.

## Think About Your School

As you think about the role of texts in your school, you may wish to reflect on these questions:

- Do the book collections in the school reflect the diversity of society and the world, with themes and ideas worthy of reading, discussion, and writing?
- Does every student have access to an inviting, well-planned classroom library with a collection of engaging, age-appropriate books?
- Do readers experience a variety of genres with high-quality language that builds rich reading experiences and enriches oral and written language?
- Is literacy teaching supported by a sufficient quantity of high-quality texts for each of the five instructional contexts for reading and mentor texts for writing?

## Move Your School Forward

- Organize a team to take inventory of the books available to students in each instructional context for reading and identify needs.
- If you are in the habit of sending out a monthly newsletter to the families of your students, consider photographing a different classroom library each month and treating it as a special feature in the newsletter. Parents will appreciate seeing the places where their children choose reading material, and it will give you a chance to highlight the work of teachers in making their libraries comfortable, inviting, and stocked with carefully chosen books.

# Chapter 17

# Organizing and Sharing Text Resources

*The two most powerful instructional design factors for improving reading motivation and comprehension are student access to many books and personal choice of what to read.*
—Richard Allington and Rachael Gabriel

WE HAVE MADE THE case for a multitext approach to literacy learning and discussed how to select the right books—and lots of them—for five instructional contexts. It is clear from the research that an abundance of books in classroom libraries increases reading achievement and motivation. The number of books in a school has been correlated to achievement on standardized tests and reading comprehension (Krashen 2004). As you read the previous chapter, you may have asked yourself questions like these:

- How many books do we need?
- How will we pay for them?
- Where will we store them?

- How much maintenance will be required?
- Who can help?

In this chapter, we answer those questions and others as we discuss three special places for collecting, organizing, and displaying books. Two of those places—classroom libraries and the school library/media center—are for students, places where they can explore their own identities as readers and take charge of their own lives as literate people. The third place is the shared book room. If you are lucky enough to have one, this room can be the main storage area for leveled books, shared reading books, multiple-copy sets for book clubs, and other shared media in digital and print formats. Additionally, teachers can gather here or work independently to engage in analysis, reflection, and thoughtful decision-making about their work with students. Together, all these places make possible the one essential ingredient in a child's literate life—access to books.

# The Classroom Library

We expect students to read a large number of books they choose themselves—at least fifty per year from about third grade to sixth grade, and more in the primary grades. Ideally, students will choose and read a new book *every day* or, if the book is longer, *every week*. This means that well-supplied classroom libraries are essential. As a school leader, one of the most important things you can do to promote equitable access to books in the school is to ensure that every classroom has a library—at least a small one, to start.

A classroom library is the center of the classroom community, and it is vitally important for building the reading and writing life of every student. A classroom library needs to have a rich, diverse array of books that are well organized and attractively displayed in baskets and bins to enable students to choose books easily; a rug, cushions, a lamp, and plants to make it a cozy and welcoming place; and many of the resources students might need to have stored there or nearby.

*Books in the classroom library should not be labeled or organized by level.* Students will need to choose books for enjoyment and for purpose, using the criteria that all readers apply. They might want to read all the books in a series or by a particular author. They might have favorite topics or genres. They might follow the recommendations of their friends or be captivated by the teacher's "book talks" (Chapter 11). At intermediate and upper grades, students usually have genre requirements, but their choices are their own. The collection of choice reading books in a classroom library is specifically tailored for the grade level and for the particular group of students in the classroom, in terms of interest, age-appropriateness, and experience as readers. At the same time, every classroom library contains books at a variety of difficulty

The classroom library is the center of the classroom community.

levels so that all students can find something they want to read and can read independently.

A great classroom library reflects the culture of students in the school as well as the wider diverse culture of the community, the country, and the world. Many nonfiction books are included on topics that support the social studies and science curriculum adopted by the school or district. But overall, two characteristics are most important when choosing books for the classroom library: engagement and access.

- The classroom library needs to include books that will engage all readers, and that means that there must be a large number of books to choose from, all of which meet a high standard for engagement and interest.

- The classroom library must be accessible to all students, and that requires excellent organization and dedicated space.

**Manage Your Budget**

**Budget for Books** If your school budget doesn't already contain a line item for refreshing and expanding the categories and numbers of books in classrooms and the main library/media center, commit to working with central office personnel to have the line added to next year's budget. Then, consider forming a team that includes representatives from each grade level to make recommendations. With a list in hand, you can shop around for the best prices.

## Role of School Leaders

As a school leader, you can play an important role in helping teachers establish classroom libraries that really work. A classroom library is *not*:

- A two-sided cart with books carelessly tossed on four shelves.
- A crammed bookcase with shelved books, spine out, that children are unable to view.
- A few tubs with miscellaneous books shoved in.
- Some novels with enough copies for every student in the class.
  - A group of twenty or fewer books in one box on the floor.
  - A collection of outdated books, or books that reflect a singular point of view.

When teachers have few resources, have not had the opportunity to learn the wonderful potential of a classroom library, do not have support in acquiring and organizing books, and are struggling with classroom management in general, establishing a classroom library can seem like a mountain to climb. It takes thoughtful effort and time to create a stellar classroom library, but it is within reach (Figure 17-1).

In summary, the classroom library is a place where students can access the resources that will engage and motivate them to read. It offers enormous opportunity for students not only to grow as readers but to develop the habits of literacy that can be a support to them throughout their lives.

## Inside a Great Classroom Library

What's the first thing you notice when you enter a classroom? Most people say it's the classroom library. Maybe this is because the books are so colorful, or maybe it's the coziness of the space, but a classroom library can be riveting. The books and furnishings draw the eye and convey that this is the heart of the classroom. Figure 17-2 describes what you might see as you look at a high-quality classroom library.

The whole ambiance of the classroom library *invites* readers to enter. Ask yourself: *Are you drawn to the area? Is it welcoming and neat? Are the books visible and well organized?* There are many different styles to consider. Teachers may choose to use bright primary colors for a cheerful effect or a neutral palette for a calming effect (Figure 17-3).

---

**A CLASSROOM LIBRARY *IS A* PLACE WHERE STUDENTS:**

Browse well-organized shelves with a variety of books that are attractively displayed.

Thoughtfully choose books they would love to read.

Build a personal repertoire of known texts, authors, illustrators, and genres.

Seek information about a topic.

Share learning with others.

Read for authentic purposes.

Recommend books to others.

Talk about books with friends.

Broaden their points of view by choosing books that allow them to see the perspectives of others, often from places and cultures far distant from their own.

Affirm their own experiences by choosing books in which they see themselves and their lived experiences.

Expand the range of genres and topics that are available to them as readers.

Build stamina as readers.

Grow as a community of readers.

**Figure 17-1.** Great Classroom Libraries

## LOOKING AT THE CLASSROOM LIBRARY

Books are displayed in labeled bins, tubs, or baskets–*genre, topic, author, illustrator, series, theme, award winners, craft element, poetry, ABC books, rhyming books,* and any other label meaningful to students.

A special rack or basket holds books the teacher has read aloud to students.

A chart displays student suggestions or favorites.

Special tubs contain books related to what students are currently studying, e.g., content-area studies, genres, poetry, author studies, illustrator studies, series books, fiction-nonfiction pairs, or current events.

Tubs hold students' reader's and writer's notebooks (although these may also be kept in their personal boxes).

Books are well-organized on shelves appropriate to the height of the students.

A few things make the area welcoming and cozy–a plant or two, a table, a lamp, some cushions, a low chair or chest for the teacher to sit on while reading aloud.

A chart lists books shared with students through read-aloud.

Above all, it contains a generous number of high-quality books.

A rug or shelving defines the area.

**Figure 17-2.** Looking at the Classroom Library and Students' Personal Book Boxes

**Figure 17-3.** Inviting Classroom Libraries

## "MARKETING" THE CLASSROOM LIBRARY

If the classroom is richly supplied, all the books may not be out on shelves at the same time. Many teachers hold back books and, throughout the school year, bring them out as new options, introducing them with fanfare and book talks–just as any store might highlight new arrivals to arouse interest. In fact, the more a classroom library looks like a small, attractive bookstore, the better!

Different teachers will have different styles, but it is important not to have a cluttered cacophony of materials and colors. There should be some adherence to *feng shui* in the harmony and uniformity of the presentation. For example, it will help to have the tubs or bins for books be the same in size and type rather than a hodgepodge of different containers. Of course, all of this depends on budget and what can be acquired, and teachers may have to start with limited supplies and develop the library over time. But neatness, clear labeling, and careful treatment of the books in the library are always important.

## Getting Started

Teachers may need to start with a small collection that they add to over time. We know many who visit garage sales and ask the families of students for contributions of books their children have outgrown. Initially, they may focus solely on acquiring many books. Over time, they sort through the books, eliminating lower-quality titles as the collection grows. If, as a school leader, you have some influence over the school budget, then supplying classroom libraries is a good investment that can both help teachers with management and inspire and support them in creating a vibrant learning community in the classroom. Some simple steps to follow are presented in Figure 17-4.

### GETTING STARTED WITH A CLASSROOM LIBRARY

1. Collect as many books as possible, with the goal of acquiring more.
2. Sort books or let students sort them into categories (genre, author, illustrator, topic, award winners, poetry, series, big idea, or theme).
3. Identify gaps, e.g., the need for more diversity, the need for more variety in specific genres, popular topics that are not represented, etc.
4. Acquire a set of plastic baskets or tubs of uniform size.
5. Identify shelving that is accessible to students.
6. Place books in tubs or bins.
7. Add bins and categories as you need them.
8. Change categories as needed (when studying different authors, genres, or topics, for example).
9. Curate and refresh collections (take away titles and add new ones) in the bins as students read them.
10. Acquire and add multiple copies of titles that are in demand.

**Figure 17-4.** Getting Started with a Classroom Library

You can support teachers through these steps and the process will be rewarding, partly because there is a tangible, beautiful outcome, and partly because as teachers use minilessons to teach children how to use the library (Chapter 11), they will be able to see the literacy community come together in their classrooms.

## How Many Books?

An excellent classroom library contains hundreds of books (and there's always room for more). Start with at least ten titles per child and aim for a total of at least thirty titles per child. That sounds like a lot, but you will be amazed by how many books students can read in a year, and it's important to have a wide range of choice. With careful organization, you can pack a lot of books into a relatively small space. This vision of quantity usually cannot be achieved immediately. Consider a plan that ensures every classroom has a starter collection of high-quality, engaging books, and then systematically build expanded collections across the grades (Figure 17-5).

As Figure 17-5 makes clear, we're talking about a lot of books. But the benefit to students is huge, especially if teachers use them in an intentional way,

## BUILDING COLLECTIONS OF BOOKS IN CLASSROOM LIBRARIES

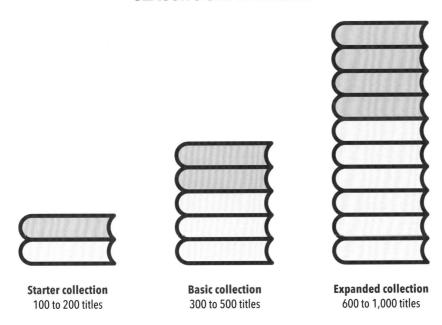

**Starter collection**
100 to 200 titles

**Basic collection**
300 to 500 titles

**Expanded collection**
600 to 1,000 titles

**General principles:**

- Acquire two or three copies of the very popular books.
- Aim for variety rather than multiple copies or many titles in a series.
- Include books of various difficulty levels in each basket.
- Acquire books related to topics, authors, illustrators, and genres that students love.

Figure 17-5. Building Collections of Books in Classroom Libraries

## OBSERVATION TOOL

The classroom library brings students together as a literate community and can make a profound difference in students' lives. Plan a series of walkthroughs that focus on the quality and use of classroom libraries. You may wish to use the observation tool **Evaluating Text Collections in Classroom Libraries (21)** to take notes and facilitate collaborative discussions with individual teachers.

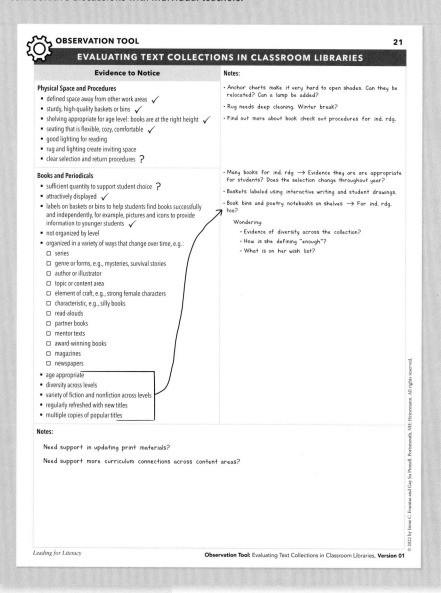

framed by strong instructional use. Remember, these are not *consumable* resources. The only ongoing cost might be a few replacements for worn or lost copies.

## The School Library

Today's school libraries, or "media centers," are gateways to the world. And real-life learning needs to take students beyond the school walls. Not only do school libraries serve as a rich repository of books and other print and digital materials for student choice and investigation, but many offer a range of communication, media, and inquiry tools. And they usually include the help of an expert librarian, or media specialist, who can recommend sources and guide students as they engage in research and inquiry projects. By curating and supporting the use of these resources, librarians create a vital hub of media and information flowing through the school.

We encourage you to advocate for the creation (or expansion) of a school library that is located in a central area of the building. Design it to be a welcoming environment, wherever it is situated. Many books are shelved so that covers are visible to students, as one would find in an attractive bookstore designed to "sell" books, while books in other areas of the library might be organized by series or by popular characters and authors. Primary sources—such as newspapers, biographies, photos of artifacts, meaningful statistical data, and transcripts or audio recordings of public meetings—are available for students to use in their research. Libraries often display seasonal decorations and reading-related works of art. The aesthetics, design, and, most importantly, the content of the school library should reflect the diverse population of the world, and in particular should mirror children's own lives and experiences, as well as open windows and doors to other lives and experiences.

A variety of seating choices are available for younger and older students, as well as a "story time" area where the librarian reads aloud, introduces new books, and tells a story orally. Here, too, children have access to beautiful hardcover picture books that are, at the same time, excellent examples of literary quality and works of art. Such volumes may appear in classroom libraries as well, but usually more paperback books are used because of the cost. A smart board allows the librarian to display and read digital texts and blogs, navigate websites, discuss photos, and share podcasts, interviews, and videos.

With teachers and librarians working together closely, collections of books, primary sources, digital resources, and other materials can be assembled in coordination with the goals of the content curriculum so that students have access to the texts and information they need to pursue inquiry projects. Online resources, too, can be bookmarked to make it easier to do research. The librarian works in collaboration with teachers and is a valuable partner in this work and a key member of the literacy team. The librarian serves as a team member for each grade level and plays an important role in schoolwide initiatives.

The librarian has a working knowledge of age-appropriate materials as well as the types of genres and topics that typically interest students at the various grade levels. The librarian can provide skilled assistance to students in finding what they want and need, and in helping to connect them to books that will inspire and engage them.

> The school library and librarians support teachers by keeping them apprised of new books, suggesting authors, finding resources they need to support curriculum standards, co-planning units of study, and supporting research projects. The librarian is a learning facilitator for a school—helping teachers and students gain access to, evaluate, share, and synthesize information (Mulligan and Landrigan 2018).

Many librarians, or media specialists, today have technical expertise in using a wide range of electronic resources to supplement what is locally available. Often, they have remote access to resources. They make the most of resources in a way that lowers costs.

## OBSERVATION TOOL

Take time to talk with the school librarian about the text collections in the school library. You may wish to use the observation tool **Evaluating Text Collections in the School Library (22)** to think together about the library's physical space and procedures, the quality and quantity of books, and the range of digital texts and primary sources.

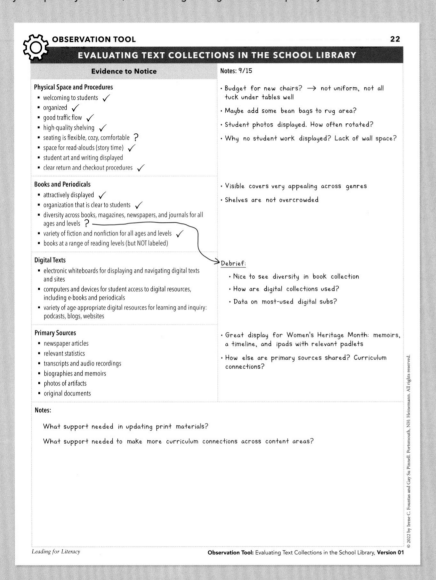

Books "travel" in and out of the library as students and teachers borrow them for projects or supplement the choices in the classroom library for genre, author, or illustrator studies, or simply to offer more options in a popular series. The librarian is an excellent resource for rounding out text sets (Chapters 11 and 16) or providing books when a student wants to read more books by a favorite author.

For all these reasons, even with well-established classroom libraries, the school library remains essential.

## The School Book Room: Access to Shared Resources

Many school leaders choose to create a school book room or other shared space to house multiple copies of leveled books for small-group guided reading lessons that are shared by the team. The shared space often includes other resources, such as enlarged-print texts, multiple copies of books for book clubs, baskets of books related to science, math, or social studies, and baskets of mentor texts. The school book room is a sizeable room in which multiple copies of leveled books are arranged from levels A through Z. This room should not be accessible to students, and in addition to being a place to store shared resources, it can function as a dedicated workspace for teachers. Teachers can plan for one or two weeks of instruction, select and use books for guided reading groups, and return them to the book room.

There are many reasons to create a school book room, not the least of which is making the most of scarce resources. For example, first-grade teachers will typically use levels A through about F as they work with guided reading groups during the first months of the school year. But after that, they usually don't need to use those levels for instruction. At about the same time, kindergarten teachers need books at those levels. This "turnover" works at every grade level. Readers are making steady progress up the gradient of text (Chapter 16) and so the needs change, with instruction focusing on one range of levels at the beginning of the year and on another at mid-year and end-of-year. So, books that are shared get greater use.

We all realize that there are exceptions to the scenario above. New students move into the school; some have more challenges than others; some are advanced. That is why teachers need access to the wide range of leveled books that are available so they can teach at the "edge" of learners' current ability (Chapter 5). A school book room makes that possible.

The school book room not only makes for efficient use of resources; it also creates a space for teachers to gather and talk about books. They are choosing from a common set of texts, and as they discuss their experiences in using these books, they can think more analytically about them and about the students they are teaching. They get to know which books are especially interesting and appealing; they find the challenges and opportunities to learn; they tailor their introductions to achieve maximum efficiency.

We do want to acknowledge that even in schools where space is not a problem, the faculty may prefer to store most resources in their own classrooms, so they are always available to them and to students when appropriate. For example, many teachers want their own shared reading books so children can revisit them often, using them as mentor texts for reading and writing minilessons. Teachers may have room in their classrooms to store multiple copies of books for book clubs. Although we don't think it's a good idea to make books for guided reading available to students before they have read them in the small group, the rest just depends on preference and the amount of classroom space there is for storage.

This school book room provides ready access to a wide range of leveled books.

## Many Advantages and a Few Challenges

Creating a school book room takes true creativity on the part of school leaders, but it is worth doing. There are many advantages and challenges to dedicating a school book room that you can think about to guide your decisions (Figure 17-6).

In this book room, shared reading texts are stored in see-through bags that can also be hung.

## Selecting and Prepping the Space

Before receiving boxes of books, you'll want a room that is prepared to receive them. Identify a space that is fairly central so that teachers can access it quickly if they need to. Space is at a premium in schools, so this is not an easy task. You may need to make some tough decisions. Some school leaders start with any small space that is available, but they try to make plans for expansion. You

## A SCHOOL BOOK ROOM FOR LEVELED TEXTS

| ADVANTAGES | CHALLENGES |
|---|---|
| <ul><li>Creates access to a richer collection.</li><li>Makes a wide range of levels available to teachers.</li><li>Serves as a place for teachers to share information.</li><li>Takes "levels" out of the classroom so students do not focus on them.</li><li>Releases valuable space in the classroom (to be used for classroom libraries and storage of materials).</li><li>Helps teachers stay aware and alert to the texts that support learning across years of progress.</li><li>Makes *The Literacy Continuum* "come alive" as texts are available to illustrate literacy goals over time.</li><li>Supports broader ownership of the learning of "our students."</li></ul> | <ul><li>Requires a dedicated space.</li><li>Takes an initial outlay of money to purchase enough books.</li><li>Requires "set up" organization and ongoing maintenance.</li><li>Means collaboration and cooperation in sharing.</li><li>Requires careful planning and maintenance on the part of teachers.</li></ul> |

**Figure 17-6.** Advantages and Challenges of a School Book Room

don't want this room to be part of the school library unless it is completely separated in a way that allows teachers to have meetings and talk. But, if it is contiguous to the library, teachers may be able to accomplish their own book selection while students are working with the librarian.

## When One Room Isn't Enough

A single book room is the most economical option, and it has advantages beyond sharing resources. Having the full range of reading levels before them always raises teachers' awareness of the paths of progress that students make over time. Teachers at upper grades can see and talk about how far their students have come; those at lower grades can have a vision of where they want them to be. It is the best way to provide a large variety of titles, with more copies of the most popular books.

But in a large school, you may want to have two book rooms, perhaps one leaning toward primary levels and one toward intermediate and upper levels. Teachers could visit either one to find new titles or to get the levels they need.

This clean and well organized book room makes economical use of space.

This option is about as economical as a single school book room, and it makes the location more convenient for teachers. However, it takes more maintenance work, and few schools will have space available for a second room.

## Alternative Storage Options

Whether or not to create a school book room is a team decision, and it depends on the available space in a school. Below are some options for book storage and management in the absence of a school book room. We have seen teachers have success with all of them.

1. Each teacher has a classroom collection of leveled books appropriate to the grade level. They are stored in a place in the classroom for teacher access only. The books represent multiple copies of titles at a range of levels typical for the grade level. The books are handy for the teacher, and the teacher can temporarily place some of the titles in the classroom library baskets.

2. Two teachers can share a collection of leveled books stored in a place convenient for both. The books represent multiple copies of titles at a range of levels typical of the grade level, but since this option is less expensive, it may be possible to have a greater number of titles. It's easy to collaborate and share, and resources are stretched.

3. All teachers at a grade level can share a collection; in this case, more copies of titles may be needed. It also may be difficult to find enough spare space to store the collection in a place that is convenient for all.

The meeting area in this school's book room isn't fancy, but it works.

## Establishing a Meeting Area

In many schools, educators have found a way to create a meeting space within the book room that combines many functions:

- Grade level and staff problem-solving meetings.
- Planning meetings.
- Housing the leveled book collection, with procedures for using and returning books.
- Housing some special volumes that are used for schoolwide initiatives at certain points in the year.
- Housing some text sets for special purposes.
- Showcasing a professional book collection.
- Viewing video and participating in live webinars for professional learning using a computer and large-screen TV

- Housing curriculum and standards documents
- Showing student progress over time on a data wall (Chapter 10)

This room should be professional and inviting. Except for coffee or tea during meetings, it should not be the "lunch" room with microwave and refrigerator, which can get very messy and smelly—not good for books!

## Getting Started with a School Book Room

As a school leader, work with your team to make the decisions regarding resources so there is broad ownership of the plan. You'll want to do some careful planning, especially if this is the first time implementing a school book room. A good time to do this is at the end of the school year. This is a very busy time, but it's wonderful for teachers to come back in the fall to the new book resources. First, reflect on the present situation because it will figure strongly into your planning.

- Add up the number of classrooms and number of students in the school. What is the average class size for each grade level?
- Note the number of teachers who will be sharing the collection.
- Look at beginning-of-year assessment data and end-of-year assessment data to notice typical reading levels for most children at each grade level. This will give you an idea of the number of titles you may need for each level.
- Take an inventory of leveled books you already have. (You can find official F&P text levels for tens of thousands of books at fp.pub/leveledbooks.) If teachers contribute their classroom collections of multiple copies, appropriately leveled for small-group reading, you can make some groups of six to eight copies of each title, and they can go right into the book room. You may have two or three copies of good titles and need just a few more to make "packs" of six to eight for groups to use. We suggest high-quality short texts for guided reading lessons at every level. Longer texts, such as short chapter books, might be appropriate periodically to build stamina, but we strongly recommend short fiction and nonfiction books that can be read in one sitting.
- Be sure to assess the number of books you have for each genre.
- Assess the human diversity and authentic representation featured in the collection.
- Set long-term goals for the number of titles you'll need at each level, but hold these as tentative because your needs may change over time.
- If possible, project your financial resources for the next three or four years.
- Make plans to explore sources of free books or funds that may be available locally (businesses and foundations, bake sales, grants from

parent-teacher organizations, and so on), making sure to evaluate new selections for quality and diversity.

- Set up a plan for ordering a "starter set" of books. Include books in every genre.
- Start work on the location, facilities, and basic materials.

## Growing the Collection Over Time

You probably won't be able to purchase all the books you need in the first year. By committing to create a school book room or central book area, you are embarking on a dramatic change in the intensity and coherence of literacy instruction, beginning in Pre–K or kindergarten and continuing over the grades. Over time, you can expect that the levels students can read with accuracy and comprehension (according to rigorous criteria) will rise. That may mean changes in the number of titles you need at each level.

Based on your budget, consider a "starter set." You might think about twenty titles per grade level, eight copies per level, with perhaps fewer at the very high levels. If the school is larger, you might consider sixteen copies per title, which would increase the price but assure teachers could get the books they need. In the next year, you could consider twenty-five titles per level with the same configuration. An expanded book collection may house thirty to fifty titles per level, varying the number according to the needs of the school.

It's important to use internal resources strategically. You may be able to direct existing textbook allocation and materials budgets toward the purchase of books. There may be donations from a parents' association or a local business. You can also ask for gifts of books, although these are usually more useful for classroom libraries where individual titles are used. If the district makes a large purchase, you may be able to get deep discounts; remember, however, that it's also important for teachers to have ownership in the titles that they acquire for their own book room.

Planning is important. You may be in a situation where no funds are available now. But be prepared to put in your request if and when they become available. If you know what you need and have all the details for a purchase order available, you will be ready and convincing when funds become available. Knowing what you need and why is persuasive!

## Assembling Basic Supplies

There are some basic supplies that will facilitate the use of the book room (Figure 17-7).

**Bins and Baskets** Collect a large number of sturdy magazine boxes, plastic baskets, or bins to house multiple copies

Sturdy bins are perfect for storing books.

Figure 17-7. Supplies for a Book Room

of books from levels A to Z. (You will already have decided the levels at which you need the most titles—at least to start.) It's a good idea to buy sturdy bins or boxes that will last a long time. You may be able to get very sturdy boxes at low prices if you buy in bulk. Also, it's a good idea to have a uniform look to the book room if possible.

For thinner books, a bin or tub can hold multiple copies of more than one title. Place labels on each book indicating the level. Be sure to place this label on the *back* of the book; it should be small and inconspicuous. As far as students are concerned, the level is information for the teacher; and teachers do need a quick way to return books to bins. Place labels on each bin (titles and level). Often, multiple copies of a book are placed in a labeled plastic bag to make it easy for teachers to grab.

Organize bins from levels A to Z on the shelves. Teachers selecting from the shelves will usually be going to different levels and doing it at different times, so there should be no "traffic" congestion unless the room is very small. When teachers look at the wall of shelving, they can instantly identify where they want to go to "shop" for books because they have their ongoing assessment data available at all times. With a plentiful supply of books, they may want to select a couple of options for a group that they think may be ready to go to another level. For younger students (levels A through about G), you may want to have eight-plus copies of books so that teachers can keep one or two copies of the book to place in a browsing box after the group has read it during the guided reading lesson. (These books are returned after a couple of weeks or so.) Beginning readers like to reread a book several times and—if possible—take it home to show off to the family. It's well worth the expense to have this option available.

**Shelving** Use sturdy, practical shelving, ceiling to floor, to make the most of space. Adjustable shelves make it possible to fit the bins exactly. We know some schools that have received donations of shelving from businesses or have purchased them from stores going out of business, but purchase orders do not always accommodate this kind of bargain hunting. You may want to explore whether the school district will build and install some wooden shelves for you, which is a great option. Sometimes, schools are lucky enough to have parents with the skill and time to build and install shelving.

## Establishing Maintenance Systems

A book room in shambles will not support excellent instruction. It's important to develop a checkout system that is easy and convenient for teachers to use. With today's "scan and go" technology, you can easily acquire a "grocery store" system that allows teachers to scan in their own individual codes (from the school ID tag or key bracelet) so that the database can track who has the title at all times. A homier approach is for each teacher to have a tub of clothespins with his/her name on them. When they take a set of books, they simply attach a clothespin to the bin or tub. When they return the title, they remove the clothespin. Some schools also use a checkout card. Everyone must commit to using the same shared system. It is essential that books are returned to the proper place to avoid confusion and lost books.

It's important to set up a good maintenance system from the beginning. Your team will want to have a prominent sign that tells how everyone can contribute to keeping the book room orderly and beautiful to support teachers and students. Figure 17-8 offers one example.

## GUIDELINES FOR USING AND MAINTAINING OUR BOOK ROOM

1. When you take titles for guided reading, please (scan, use clothespin, card, and so on)

2. For K–1 teachers, if you keep a copy for a browsing box, please note on the container

3. Please keep books for a maximum of two weeks and then return them (or check out again if you still need them).

4. Help each other return the books and keep them neatly organized in the boxes.

5. Your team is responsible for checking the order of the room each month (see schedule below).

**Maintenance Schedule:**

**September:** Grade 6 Teachers: _____

**October:** Grade 5 Teachers: _____

**November:** Grade 4 Teachers: _____

**December:** Grade 3 Teachers: _____

**January:** Grade 2 Teachers: _____

**February:** Grade 1 Teachers: _____

**March:** K Teachers: _____

**April:** Principal and Office Staff: _____

**May:** Meeting of all staff to evaluate book room system and plan to order new titles.

**June:** FINAL CHECK AND CELEBRATION LUNCH!

**Maintenance Checklist:**

☐ Go through each bin to be sure books are filed under the right title and level.

☐ Check for and note missing books in the book room notebook.

☐ Put out a notice asking for missing books.

☐ Identify books that are torn or need to be replaced and note in the book room notebook.

☐ Generally, check the book room for order and cleanliness.

☐ Refresh supplies in meeting area.

**Figure 17-8.** Guidelines for Using Our Book Room

# OBSERVATION TOOL

Use the observation tool **Evaluating Text Collections in the School Book Room (23)** to think about how to support, maintain, and grow the collection of texts for guided reading lessons.

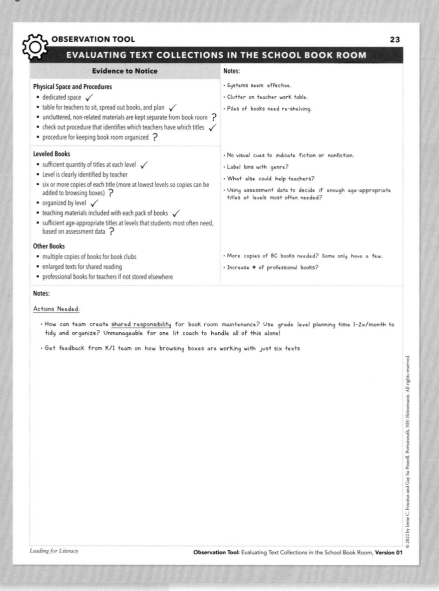

Instead of working by grade level, teachers may want to sign up individually for book room duty. Any system you devise and that everyone is committed to will work. Of course, you may have a paraprofessional or volunteer who can take over the maintenance, but be sure that you can depend on this support.

There will always be problems to be solved. Establishing a strong community in the school will make it easier to approach the problems in a collaborative way (Chapter 3). If there are some titles, for example, that teachers really want to keep in the classroom for a bit longer, it may be possible to acquire some extra copies. Some kindergarten and grade one teachers may want to keep a beloved book all year and make it part of the classroom library. Just keep in mind that the books teachers introduce in guided reading need to be completely new to students.

The maintenance system will detect worn books that need to be replaced, and if the budget isn't available at the time, they can be added to a "wish list" for the next purchasing opportunity.

# The Takeaway

There is no way to overestimate the value of classroom libraries, school libraries, and school book rooms (in whatever formation you choose) in the literate life of children. Access to books is key to their academic achievement and quality of life. Make it a goal to take every opportunity you can to increase access to books in print and digital formats. The realization of that goal depends on the capacity of the school to provide the text base students need—in the classroom, in the school library, and in high-quality instruction in a variety of contexts.

## Think About Your School

After reading this chapter, you may want to join with the school librarian, teachers, and specialists in thinking together about the physical space, procedures, and books of each type used by the teachers in the school. You may wish to consider questions that uncover strengths and needs, such as:

- Does the school library have enough shelving for books to be displayed attractively and stay organized, as well as to allow for growth?
- How well organized are the books for easy access and return?
- How do the print and digital collections compare?
- How do teachers entice readers to try a new book or series in the classroom libraries?
- Are there levels at which there are insufficient numbers of titles in the school book room?
- How can you improve the checkout and maintenance systems to support teachers' selection of texts for guided reading?

## Move Your School Forward

- You may want to create a small team to support classroom libraries across the school. Team members may play a role in helping teachers who may be struggling to set up, organize, or maintain their classroom libraries. Arrange a time for the specialist to meet with individual teachers who might benefit from a consult.
- Consider establishing a small digital team for reviewing the number and quality of digital resources students can access. Have the team report its findings and suggest an improvement plan if they determine one is required.

# SECTION 6 · *Leadership to Sustain Systemic Improvement*

# SECTION 6

## *Leadership to Sustain Systemic Improvement*

In this book we have described some complex systems and ideas: how children learn to read and write; how teachers assess children's literacy behaviors and teach strategically, the creation of a strong and coherent common vision to guide your work, and the materials required to create a rich text base for literacy learning. In this final section, we describe the on-the-ground work that brings it all together and makes your instructional design work a little better every year so you and your colleagues can reach your most important goal: creating a literate life for every student.

No single individual can achieve this goal alone, so on the following pages we suggest building professional capacity through shared leadership and providing new kinds of professional learning opportunities for today's teachers. We also devote a full chapter to the important role of the literacy coach and another to effective supervision and evaluation of teachers.

We recognize that change can be difficult. But a strong commitment to continuous improvement is the engine that moves everyone forward. And so, the last chapter contains a finely articulated rubric that brings together all the big ideas we've discussed in this book. We hope you will find it a practical and helpful tool as you work toward building better systems that produce better outcomes for all students. Nothing else in education is more important or more rewarding.

# Chapter 18

# Building Professional Capacity Through Shared Leadership

*We have long treated teachers as technicians who need to be fixed or filled up with the right knowledge and dispositions, rather than encouraging them to take a lead role in developing their own expertise.*
—Isobel Stevenson and Richard Lemons

A SINGLE LEADER CANNOT create and sustain school improvement, no matter how charismatic, persuasive, and energetic that person may be. A lone school leader attempting to champion improvements and drive change will eventually run out of steam, move on, or settle for less impactful goals that are easier to achieve. To sustain school improvement over time, you will find it beneficial— necessary in fact—to invest in the professional capacity of your school. You can think of *professional capacity* as the level of expertise, decision-making, and initiative among all the educators in your school. It represents the readiness of educators to expand their professional influence through leadership. You build professional capacity by helping your school team grow in expertise, empowering decision-making at all levels, and encouraging initiative among all groups.

# A Culture of Shared Leadership

One of the surest ways to increase the professional capacity of your school is to promote a culture of shared leadership that engages teachers, specialized personnel, coaches, principals and administrators, families, and the community as partners around a set of common aspirational values and beliefs (Figure 18-1). Shared leadership is a powerful approach to leading that can energize school teams to accomplish their common vision and enable teachers to begin to see their work as transformative. School leaders in high-performing schools often advise a rigorous look at every aspect of the school operation to determine the leadership roles that are needed, and to make the necessary changes. That doesn't mean an abdication of decision-making responsibility, but it does mean that the principal and other school leaders have valuable resources of support and information when taking bold action. It is important to solicit information to make good decisions and to let your team know when they will make a decision or when you will make a decision that takes into account their valuable input.

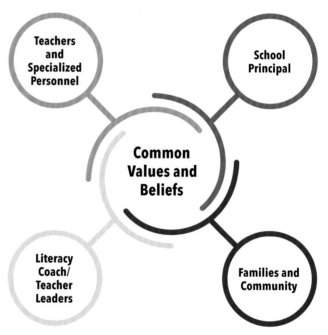

**Figure 18-1.** A Culture of Shared Leadership

## Fostering Leadership Through a Network of Teams

In our work with schools, our primary goal has been to support the system's internal capacity for expanding the professional expertise of administrators, coaches, teacher leaders, and teachers. Investment in the capacity of your team of professionals to develop deep expertise will have the best payoff for student outcomes (Darling-Hammond, Hyler, and Gardner 2017). But how do you go about building up a school of leaders through shared leadership? You foster leadership throughout the school by the way you look at the strengths of your team and encourage individual members of the team to exhibit leadership.

In a culture of teamwork, a network of teams contributes to the improvement goals (see Chapter 4) in a variety of ways. Each team represents an opportunity for teachers, specialists, and other team members to step into a leadership role. Leadership is powered by professional learning. As you support the professional learning of every educator in your school, you build a pipeline of future leaders. Coaches and teacher leaders can play key leadership roles in the school and are an important component in our view of shared leadership. With leadership support and training, they can support a multifaceted design of professional learning (see Chapter 19).

## Powering High-Performing Schools Through Shared Leadership

We have found some commonalities among high-performing schools, and shared leadership is at the heart of these characteristics. Shared leadership in high-performing schools represents a shift from enforcement of top-down decisions to a culture characterized by a collaborative effort among many leaders on the team to identify and solve problems (Figure 18-2). The educators focus on people and processes that add value; paperwork and other details are streamlined.

Working as a team, you can transition from the characteristics in the first column of Figure 18-2 to those in the second. Your school team needs to be flexible and willing to solve problems and make decisions. At times, you may need to deal with challenging issues and tackle difficult problems. For example:

- Serving a population of immigrants who are making cultural, social, and linguistic adjustments.
- Taking an active stance against racism and carrying through with it.
- Reaching consensus about a common vision.
- Using data to evaluate actions.
- Disrupting established traditions when necessary.

Shared leadership will not be achieved overnight but will require time and effort as well as a shift in lens toward continuous improvement. Consider networking with other schools that are engaged in the same journey, so that leaders have a place to touch base. Educators at the building level are in the best position to understand the causes and complexities of problems to be solved. They can work in a collaborative way to test and refine solutions based on hard evidence that they systematically collect (Bryk, Gomez, Grunow, and LeMahieu 2015).

| **FROM** | **TO** |
|---|---|
| <ul><li>Top-down leadership</li><li>Top-down decision-making</li><li>Focus on regulation and minutiae</li><li>Enforced "standardized" curriculum</li><li>Demand for conformity and compliance</li><li>Prescribed way of doing things</li><li>Use of prescribed practice represents compliance, not commitment</li><li>Superficial implementation of adopted curriculum</li><li>Focus on test scores alone</li><li>Looking for a quick fix (e.g., new purchases)</li><li>Closed doors; leaders in their offices</li><li>Rigid roles</li></ul> | <ul><li>A variety of leadership roles</li><li>Collaborative problem-solving and decision-making</li><li>Commitment to making decisions based on the team's shared vision, values, and goals</li><li>Co-construction of norms or working agreements</li><li>Common curriculum based on authentic literacy competencies</li><li>Coherence based on rationales and responsiveness in teaching</li><li>A research-based instructional framework for teaching and learning</li><li>Support for innovation and creativity</li><li>Emphasis on self-reflection and evaluation</li><li>Multidimensional assessment</li><li>Inquiry process on "what works here and under what conditions"</li><li>Focus on continuous improvement in small steps using evidence to plan, test, evaluate, and take action</li><li>Leaders visible around the school rather than solely in an office</li><li>Flexible roles taken by team members</li></ul> |

**Figure 18-2.** Shifts to Shared Leadership for High Performance

# Conditions That Promote Shared Leadership

Schools are traditionally bureaucratic and hierarchical. Jobs are assigned. Individuals are afraid to step out of what they perceive as their assigned roles, and leadership is not typically part of the job description for a teacher. The teacher's assignment is clearly in the classroom, with the implication being that anything outside of that space is "extra." But what if expectations for collegial work were part of the teacher's job description from the point of hire? What if time and resources were allocated to support acts of leadership by teachers? What if teachers had opportunities to grow as leaders and were encouraged to take risks? These are the conditions needed for shared leadership to thrive (Figure 18-3). Expectations would be different, and teachers would see their roles, and their place in the school's organization, differently.

## Expectations

Teachers entering the profession expect to work in a classroom teaching children. Seldom do they expect to contribute in meaningful ways to the work of the whole school. As a school leader, you establish expectations by the way you look at the strengths that teachers possess. Because you value their ideas and perspectives, teachers understand that they are expected to help construct a vision for the school, engage in inquiry to identify more effective ways to teach children, act as a support to colleagues in taking on new learning, and represent the district in an important improvement effort. Your expectations for teacher contributions are set high because you value them as colleagues and leaders.

## Time

The classroom day is long, and teachers need time to prepare for the important work they do teaching children. It can be challenging for them to find time to collaborate with colleagues and to plan for schoolwide or grade-level initiatives. Creating time for teachers to take on acts of leadership will require a careful review of the school day. Are there low-value activities that can be eliminated to create time and space for teachers to share in leadership? We have seen morning announcements and "word of the day" consume half an hour of valuable time. That's 2½ hours a week spent on content that is irrelevant to many children and teachers. Take a careful look at your school's established processes: for example, line-up procedures; cafeteria, bus, and car-line duties; starting and stopping times; recess schedules; use of specialist teachers; periods for art, physical education, music, and library; and faculty meetings. Consider creative scheduling to include time for teachers to work together developing human capital and a sense of collective efficacy.

**EL Connection**

**Engaging Multilingual Teachers as Leaders** As you think about shared leadership in your school, consider the importance of engaging multilingual teachers in acts of leadership. How can you build on the linguistic and instructional expertise of these specialists by nudging them to lead small groups, translate key documents for the whole team to use, liaise with families, offer important cultural information, etc. Multilingual teachers are a unique asset to the school and your proactive stance in supporting their development as leaders will have a lasting impact.

| CONDITIONS THAT PROMOTE SHARED LEADERSHIP | |
|---|---|
| **Expectations** | Expectations are set high for teacher contributions. |
| **Time** | Time is set aside for classroom teachers to perform leadership roles. |
| **Resources** | Resources are carefully managed and allocated to compensate teachers for the extra leadership roles that they take on. |
| **Expertise** | Teachers grow in expertise to take on new roles. |
| **Trust** | Shared leadership takes place within a climate of trust. |

**Figure 18-3.** Conditions that Promote Shared Leadership

## Resources

School budgets are often allocated to match the hierarchical structure of most schools. Jobs performed outside of formally defined roles are usually not compensated, and budgets often have rigid rules. Yet more and more, principals are tapping discretionary funds or finding approved ways to use budgets more flexibly to provide compensation for teachers who take on leadership roles that require considerable time investment outside the school day. You will need a clear policy and guidance for deciding on the responsibilities of those who receive such benefits.

## Expertise

Principals in highly effective elementary schools intentionally develop teacher expertise in leadership (Forster 2020). The best way to learn to lead well is to start with a short-term responsibility, possibly working with a more experienced colleague. Teachers will need opportunities for training. Think of these experiences as building capacity for future leadership. Additionally, teachers may find opportunities for professional growth (such as attending conferences or participating in courses) rewarding. In time, teachers will view the opportunity to lead as a way of expanding their expertise and adding to their qualifications. As teachers grow in expertise and gain experience, their confidence in leadership roles increases.

## Trust

Overcoming the barriers to shared leadership requires an atmosphere of trust, and that takes effort to build. In a culture of trust, teachers support colleagues in leadership roles, being willing to step in to help and to give good advice,

 **CENTRAL OFFICE MEMO**

**Building Leadership Capacity in the System** As central office leaders, an important part of your role is to build the leadership capacity in the system. Invest in the professional capacity of the principals and coaches, and work with the school-based leaders to identify teachers who can take on leadership roles and guide them to take specific actions to accomplish the goals. When you operate with a lens of growing leaders, you provide sustainability for accomplishing your aspirational vision and mission. Consider requiring a goal for identifying and growing one leader in each principal's or coach's yearly school improvement goals.

Work to create a small budget item for honorariums to recognize a few teachers who have taken on the formal role of teacher leader in their school. Work with the school-based leaders to formalize the role of coach or teacher leader as a role in your system and you will have made a wonderful investment that will pay dividends for years.

encouragement, and credit. Trust assumes that people will try their best. Those who step into leadership roles are taking a risk, and for many people that is daunting. As a school leader, you can encourage risk-taking by removing the fear of failure. You will want to cultivate a cultural norm that promotes the belief that we can all learn from failure and trying is worth the risk. After all, there is always a chance that something new won't work perfectly, but analysis by the team can determine how to adjust and try again. And everyone learns from the experience.

# Investing in Teacher Leaders

Teachers have leadership potential. Every day they lead sizeable groups of children and young people into situations that inspire and support their learning. It's our experience, though, that too few teachers see themselves as leaders of their colleagues. Teacher leadership skills are needed more than ever now, as demands on schools and the educational systems increase. People who lead educational systems and who study them suggest that more support and effort is needed than just the principal, keeping the "ship going smoothly," can possibly accomplish alone. There is a need to leverage teacher leadership to make use of the very real talents that exist within any school staff. We suggest that every school already has the resources it needs (or the ability to acquire them) to make a profound difference for its students.

## Fostering Leadership Through the Identification of Teacher Leaders

Given that teachers are such an important asset to your school, consider identifying some teachers as teacher leaders to take on specific leadership roles, for example, assessment leader, data team leader, lead teacher for phonics, or lead teacher for writing. The concept of a teacher leader is not new, and yet teachers who have the ability and interest in assuming active leadership roles are an often-neglected resource in a school. When the person is provided with time, structures, and resources as well as mentoring and high-quality, ongoing leadership training, the impact on the culture of the school is dramatic and the improvement in student outcomes is promising.

The roles of teacher leader and coach are formal roles that teachers who have had informal leadership responsibility may want to pursue (Figure 18-4). In schools that are fortunate enough to have coaches, the coaches are spread thin, and teacher leaders can fill important gaps in supporting the development of other teachers. Teacher leaders are the potential coaches of the future. Creating a formal role of teacher leader provides teachers with another opportunity for professional advancement and returns value to the system by retaining effective teachers instead of losing them to other professions. Teachers who ad-

## INVESTING IN LEADERSHIP CAPACITY

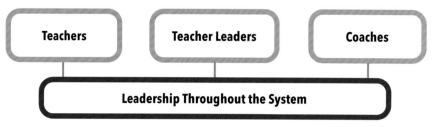

| Teachers | Teacher Leaders | Coaches |

**Leadership Throughout the System**

**Figure 18-4.** Investing in Leadership Capacity

vance up the professional ladder to take on schoolwide or district responsibilities will advocate for the good things that matter because they have grown out of the strong, student-centered culture of your school.

## How Is a Teacher Leader Different from a Coach?

Teacher leaders are classroom teachers and specialists who demonstrate the potential for and interest in taking on additional tasks or roles that leverage their expertise to strengthen the expertise of others. Like coaches, they believe in the commitment and capabilities of their colleagues to refine their craft and demonstrate a genuine dedication to building a collaborative, reflective community. They honor various perspectives and are guided by the evidence that prompts a team to take action toward their mutual goals. With the goal of coherence, teacher leaders are always moving in a direction that is consistent with the shared values and beliefs of the school.

A teacher leader and a coach share many of the same skills and dispositions, but the teacher leader usually has the primary role of teaching students, and the coach has the primary role of supporting the development of teachers. A teacher leader may also support the development of peers in addition to the classroom assignment, and a coach may also teach children in the school to develop increasing expertise and credibility.

In contrast to a full-time coach, the role of a teacher leader can be informal and voluntary as classroom or specialist teachers unofficially take on short- or long-term leadership roles on behalf of the literacy program. Even if the role is unofficial, teacher leaders receive the backing and support of the principal and coach. In some schools, the role is formalized by providing occasional time away from daily teaching and additional compensation for the increased responsibilities. These policies are well established in the policies and procedures of the school. Whether informal

Effective coaches and teacher leaders have built trust with their colleagues and developed strong observational skills to examine teaching interactions.

or formalized, unofficial or established, voluntary or compensated, all teacher leaders need mentoring and special ongoing professional training for leading and teaching adult learners. If we expect teacher leaders to be successful schoolwide leaders, they deserve such support.

## Qualities and Dispositions of Teacher Leaders

A coach and a teacher leader have many qualities in common, including excellence in literacy teaching, a desire to continually learn and grow in expertise, and a commitment to using evidence to inform decisions. These qualities and dispositions enable them to have a significant impact on the school and the system (Figure 18-5).

It seems a tall order, but we would expect that, over time, the experienced staff of a school would exhibit every one of the above qualities. These strong leaders can mentor individuals who are new to the school or the profession. Potential for such qualities figure strongly in the principal's selection of new teachers with the potential of leadership. Having a team of experienced and

| QUALITIES OF EFFECTIVE COACHES AND TEACHER LEADERS | |
| --- | --- |
| The tentative stance of a reflective, continuous learner | A commitment to evidence-based decision-making |
| Evidence of intellectual curiosity and openness to new perspectives | Commitment to working with others to achieve social justice |
| A strong understanding of culturally relevant teaching | A desire to get to know and ascertain the strengths of each team member |
| A deep understanding of the role of data-informed teaching in assuring equitable student outcomes | Strong interpersonal and communication skills |
| Strong observational skills to examine teaching interactions | An ability to help others build self-efficacy |
| Evidence of effective language and literacy teaching | The capacity for building trust, shared ownership, and teamwork in the school community |
| Strong content knowledge, particularly in language, reading, and writing development | A thorough understanding of the structures of school organization |

Figure 18-5. Qualities of Effective Coaches and Teacher Leaders

talented leaders participate in the new-teacher selection process at your school will assure that:

- The candidate understands the expectations clearly.
- The new hire has the good potential to become a strong contributing member of the team.

Individuals who find these qualities attractive will be drawn to your school's goals and vision and will likely be a good fit for your team.

## Acts of Teacher Leadership

Classroom teachers and specialists can perform a number of important roles *outside* the classroom. For example, they can lead efforts to examine data and design research to determine the effectiveness of new practices. They can become resident experts in a particular area and become a resource to colleagues. Teachers with a particular area of expertise can mentor those who find that area difficult or challenging or new. These roles are often temporary, but they play a critical part in the whole school's ability to improve. Acts of teacher leadership will arise naturally and frequently from your collaborative work in the school. To help you identify acts of leadership and opportunities to promote leadership among teachers, consider the following categories.

**Professional Learning Leader** As teachers acquire new learning, they can, in turn, plan an experience to share their learning with others, for example:

- Lead a brown bag discussion of a relevant article or professional book.
- Create a collaborative group online to engage in continued sharing and discussion.
- Invite teachers to share recorded lessons or parts of lessons relevant to a topic and lead a discussion using observation tools.
- Offer an interactive workshop or a study group on a topic.
- Convene a few colleagues to apply for a grant to purchase professional materials or other related learning experiences.

**Leader of Collaborative Inquiry** After identification of a problem, the school team may decide to form a small team to gather more data to explain the cause or identify a possible action. The person who leads an inquiry effort might:

- Convene a team to analyze lessons in a particular instructional context.
- Invite colleagues to submit videos, not for critique but for analysis of how lessons may be made more powerful or to sharpen ability to observe for evidence of learning.
- Work with colleagues to undertake an investigation of research on a topic that informs instruction in a practical way.
- Lead teams to undertake observation across grade levels.
- Record a video of a lesson or part of several lessons and gather a group of colleagues to discuss it.

**Teacher Mentor** Teachers can play an important part in demonstrating and encouraging less experienced team members. For example, a mentor can:

- Assist new teachers in classroom organization and management.
- Demonstrate particular instructional approaches to help teachers begin to take these approaches on.
- Offer examples to help team members take on the analysis of teaching.
- Offer help as a mentor in using tools such as *The Literacy Continuum* or district/state standards in planning for instruction.
- Demonstrate deeper analysis of teaching.

Teacher leaders can play an important role in supporting, encouraging, and mentoring new teachers and less experienced colleagues.

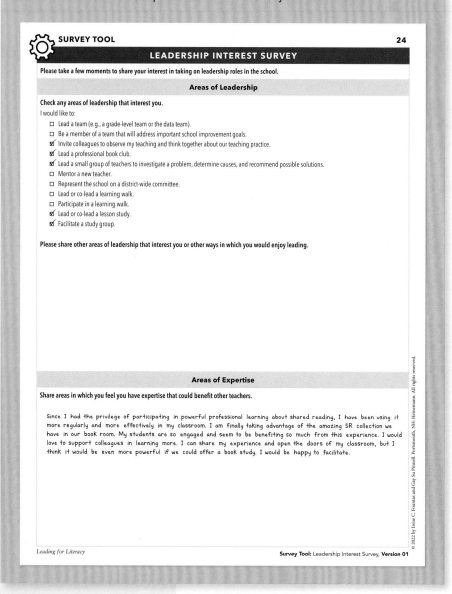

# SURVEY TOOL

Consider distributing this survey tool **Leadership Interest Survey (24)** to teachers with a personal note encouraging them to take a few moments to think of ways they can use their influence, experience, and expertise to strengthen the larger school community. The survey can be an important opportunity to communicate that you and the other leaders at the school value the leadership that teachers can offer beyond the classroom.

## SURVEY TOOL                                                              24
### LEADERSHIP INTEREST SURVEY

Please take a few moments to share your interest in taking on leadership roles in the school.

#### Areas of Leadership

Check any areas of leadership that interest you.

I would like to:
- ☐ Lead a team (e.g., a grade-level team or the data team).
- ☐ Be a member of a team that will address important school improvement goals.
- ☑ Invite colleagues to observe my teaching and think together about our teaching practice.
- ☑ Lead a professional book club.
- ☑ Lead a small group of teachers to investigate a problem, determine causes, and recommend possible solutions.
- ☐ Mentor a new teacher.
- ☐ Represent the school on a district-wide committee.
- ☐ Lead or co-lead a learning walk.
- ☐ Participate in a learning walk.
- ☑ Lead or co-lead a lesson study.
- ☑ Facilitate a study group.

Please share other areas of leadership that interest you or other ways in which you would enjoy leading.

#### Areas of Expertise

Share areas in which you feel you have expertise that could benefit other teachers.

Since I had the privilege of participating in powerful professional learning about shared reading, I have been using it more regularly and more effectively in my classroom. I am finally taking advantage of the amazing SR collection we have in our book room. My students are so engaged and seem to be benefiting so much from this experience. I would love to support colleagues in learning more. I can share my experience and open the doors of my classroom, but I think it would be even more powerful if we could offer a book study. I would be happy to facilitate.

*Leading for Literacy*                    **Survey Tool:** Leadership Interest Survey, **Version 01**

---

**Data Team Leader** Teachers can play an important role in leading a group to use data to inform decisions. Most teachers are not familiar with the data-inquiry process. A teacher who takes on the role of leading a data team can play an important part in focusing the attention of colleagues on evidence. For example, a teacher can:

- Lead vertical or grade-level teams in the collection, analysis, and interpretation of assessment data.
- Convene the team to work for reliability in administering benchmark assessments, assessing comprehension, and evaluating writing.
- Organize and lead an analysis of data at grade level or across grade levels to identify problems and set goals.
- Lead a team in developing rubrics to describe and assess effective teaching in various instructional contexts.
- Work with a group to examine student outcomes with the goal of identifying problems related to equity and set goals to solve them.

You may also wish to survey the teachers in your school to discover who has interest in taking on leadership roles and in what ways they would enjoy leading. You can use the survey we provide at left or create one that matches the leadership opportunities at your school.

## Taking Action to Grow Leaders

Not everyone will want to take a strongly visible role. Some excellent teachers feel uncomfortable in front of a group, which with experience can be overcome. But there are also quiet ways to lead, and you can encourage potential leaders to find and take on what makes them feel effective and powerful. With the many opportunities available, there are roles for every team member.

As principals and coaches, you can work together to grow teacher leaders. A thoughtful plan for professional learning (see Chapter 19) and a trusting relationship go a long way toward developing leadership in your team. For example, you can:

- Identify particular talents in individuals and talk about bringing them to bear on school goals.

- Talk individually with teachers to encourage them to take short- or long-term leadership roles (as opposed to just asking for volunteers).

- Encourage teachers to not only report their progress to the team but to lead discussions and problem-solving sessions related to that progress.

- Bring together teams to work on different problems of practice and ask individuals to serve as team leaders.

- Co-plan and co-deliver a professional learning session with a potential teacher leader.

- Co-plan a professional book club session and have the teacher lead it.

As you and your team take action to expand leadership roles, remember to take small steps and give specific credit, not empty praise. See improvement and growth as continuous. Conceptualize growth of leadership as resting on a set of common values.

The common vision you and the team have adopted operates as a compass for evaluating your efforts and making decisions about future moves, each of which can be evaluated against it. In this way, you assure that you make continuous progress toward the outcomes you want to see for students.

## The Takeaway

As a school leader working for sustained improvement in your school, you will need a deep bench of leaders. Dispersing leadership increases collective efficacy, and teacher leadership holds exciting potential for building the capacity of your school to improve teacher expertise and student outcomes.

**Identifying Leaders in Your School** As you consider the variety of acts of leadership you want to support, focus on the use of technology in professional learning as a key area. Chances are you have a central office person who is leading technological innovation in the system. A resident leader can only add to the impact. It is highly likely you have team members who are engaged and passionate about how technology can support professional learning and student learning. Consider identifying one or two lead teachers or teacher leaders who will share their passion and insights in structured ways with the rest of the team in your school. This is an ever-changing landscape, and specific leadership will keep the whole team on the cutting edge.

Teacher leaders can lead a lesson study, facilitate a study group, or help colleagues use tools such as *The Literacy Continuum* with greater effectiveness in their planning, teaching, and assessing.

Shared leadership breaks down the silos that often exist in schools and fuels the inquiry, communication, and teamwork that solve problems of practice. The team of educators assumes collective responsibility and accountability for the success of their students and their colleagues. Within a culture of shared leadership, expertise can be identified and built across your entire team.

## Think About Your School

As you reflect on this chapter, evaluate the leadership capacity in your school.

- How would the school team describe the current style of leadership in your school? Top-down, principal-driven, shared, or something else?
- Are there acts of leadership already occurring in the school that you can recognize and promote?
- What opportunities do teachers currently have to take on meaningful leadership roles? Make a list and compare to the roles described in this chapter.

## Move Your School Forward

Consider steps you can begin to take to build the leadership capacity in your school.

- Use the survey in this chapter (or create your own) to discover teachers' areas of expertise and their interest in taking on leadership roles.
- Think of a teacher who has demonstrated leadership potential. List two or three steps you can take to nurture this potential, for example, by talking to the teacher about her identity as a leader, pairing the teacher with a mentor and providing sufficient time for acts of leadership, and offering professional learning that builds the teacher's leadership skills.

# Chapter 19

# Reimagining Professional Learning

*Effective professional development is structured professional
learning that results in changes to teacher knowledge and
practices and improvement in student learning outcomes.*
—Linda Darling-Hammond

IT'S HARD TO ARGUE with the premise that today's classrooms hold greater
challenges for teachers than at any other time in our nation's history. The rate
of change in our world has increased with astonishing speed, and schools now
face challenges and questions we could not have predicted just twenty years
ago. How to incorporate technology in seamless ways that accelerate learning?
How to serve ever larger numbers of children who are learning English as a
second or third language? How to guarantee equal opportunity in our nation's
schools regardless of their zip codes? And how best to teach an increasingly
complex array of content and skills in ways that ensure the successful learning
of *all* students? These challenges and others demand a national teaching force
working at the top of its game. Yet, too often, teacher professional development has little or no effect on teaching and learning. And so, at the heart of all
those questions is one more: How can we adequately prepare teachers for their

roles in a fast-changing world and facilitate their high-quality professional learning over time?

Consider one study of three districts that were representative of large public-school systems in the United States and one charter school network. The researchers conducted 100 interviews of staff members and used multiple measures of performance. The title of their 2015 report says a great deal about their findings: *The Mirage: Confronting the Hard Truth About Our Quest for Teacher Development.*

The report reveals that the districts studied spent an average of $18,000 per teacher, per year, on professional development—more than on transportation, food, and security combined. The teachers surveyed reported spending an average of nineteen full school days a year in professional development. Yet the researchers noted little improvement in student outcomes from year to year. Beyond the first few years, it seemed that teachers reached a kind of "plateau" after which there was little growth or change no matter how much professional development they experienced.

There are many reasons why professional development so often fails to achieve desired outcomes. In our work with schools and districts, we have noticed common missteps that tend to impede the professional learning of teachers, including:

- A disconnect between professional learning sessions and what teachers actually need to successfully implement the instructional program in their classrooms.
- Top down "direction" for teachers as they take on a new program.
- A "one-shot deal," meaning that there is no sustained effort or follow up.
- Speakers who know little about the school, its students, or its values.
- Adverse conditions for meeting, such as sessions after school, cafeteria seating, bad acoustics, limited time, and so on.
- Little chance for inquiry or professional conversation (other than asking questions of the speaker).
- Little differentiation to recognize individuals' life and teaching experiences or their knowledge base.
- Lack of dialogue or open sharing.
- Fear of admitting mistakes or exposing lack of understanding.
- No teacher input on the plan for professional learning or the content of sessions.

Remember, every time teachers take on new learning with willing hearts and experience failure, they lose a little faith in the process and become a little more reluctant to take risks in the future. Perhaps that is why there is such a slowdown in improvement after the first few years of an initiative.

Teachers need a new lens to look at their attempts to implement new ideas: mistakes are not failures; rather, they are the learning experiences that lead to progress. The overall goal is improvement in student learning, as evidenced by careful assessment, and that requires improvement in teacher expertise over time.

What is clear is that we need to move beyond "helping teachers," to creating systems for continuous learning in a culture of improvement. We need conditions that lead to greater teacher expertise and satisfaction, and to higher achievement and happiness for students. Like so many of the initiatives and change processes we have discussed in this book, the work of redesigning the professional learning plans in your school needs to begin with what you value.

When teachers work as a team, they take collective responsibility for student achievement.

## Start with What You Value

Gather your colleagues and think together about your school's common values and beliefs about literacy learning and the practices that lead to improved student outcomes. These values will anchor your work in professional learning.

Our own core values in this area (which you can also see on pages 28 and 29 of this book) are as follows.

*Schools are places where all literacy educators:*

1. Are members of a community with a strong belief that their work can transform children's lives through literacy.

2. Work as a team to take collective responsibility for the high achievement of each student in a widely diverse population.

3. Implement a set of evidence-based instructional practices in whole-class, small-group, and individual contexts to assure coherence within and across grade levels.

4. Make sound instructional decisions based on evidence gained from systematic observation and ongoing assessment data.

5. Demonstrate a commitment to their own professional learning and to supporting the learning of their colleagues.

Professional learning opportunities and conversations that support values like these will naturally be rooted in data or evidence that will have demonstrable impact on teachers' instruction and decision-making.

## Determine Your Goals

Establishing a learning environment for teachers is a challenge because it often means changing the culture that currently exists in most schools. You can't grow seeds in concrete, and many efforts fail because the school culture doesn't support it. The conditions for professional learning need to be healthy. It helps to know what you are striving for, even if it takes some time to get there. Think in terms of goals related to the educators' mindsets and observable behaviors as well as the content of the literacy curriculum and related teaching practices. (Figure 19-1).

## GOALS FOR PROFESSIONAL LEARNING

| | |
|---|---|
| **Mindsets** | *People in the school:*<br><br>▪ See professional learning as an opportunity.<br>▪ Consider themselves to be learners through self-analysis of teaching, assessment, observation, data analysis, and information gathering.<br>▪ Think they can learn from their peers and see others as resources.<br>▪ Believe all students can learn and it is their responsibility to find ways to teach them.<br>▪ Have expectations for their own growth and find satisfaction in learning more about their work.<br>▪ Maintain a flexible and open attitude.<br>▪ Have a stake in the achievement of all students in the school. |
| **Observable Behaviors** | *People in the school:*<br><br>▪ Engage in dialogue about their teaching, student behavior, and learning.<br>▪ Open their doors and invite peers to observe their teaching.<br>▪ Engage in collaborative inquiry around student learning outcomes.<br>▪ Hold grade-level and cross-grade-level meetings to plan and share experiences and data.<br>▪ Actively participate in professional learning opportunities.<br>▪ Seek collegial help to solve problems with students.<br>▪ Take leadership roles in planning professional learning sessions. |
| **Content and Pedagogical Knowledge** | *People in the school:*<br><br>▪ Understand what students need to know and be able to do as readers, writers, and speakers at each grade level.<br>▪ Have developed expertise in research-based instructional practices.<br>▪ Understand how to observe and assess students' language and literacy competency.<br>▪ Understand how to analyze the demands of texts and the characteristics of writing.<br>▪ Understand the range and characteristics of genres students need to know as readers and writers.<br>▪ Know how to use precise language that enables learners to act and reflect on their learning. |

**Figure 19-1.** Goals for Professional Learning

## Think "System," Not "Sessions"

With your goals identified, you can now turn to planning for one full year of professional learning. This kind of long-term planning will help you and your colleagues think about a continuum of interconnected professional learning opportunities designed to unfold in a thoughtful and systematic way rather than a smattering of disconnected sessions that don't add up to a coherent program.

As you read the rest of this chapter, keep in mind that you are designing a *system* of professional learning in your school that is based on evidence about teacher effectiveness. Quick bursts of coaching or collaborative problem-solving that spring up organically or in immediate response to an unexpected need certainly have a place in the system. But professional learning that pays off for teachers and students requires careful planning across an entire year, with each individual session building on, and logically flowing from, the one that came before.

---

### THREE GOOD QUESTIONS

Guskey (2017) proposes three important questions related to professional learning that should be asked at the beginning of the professional learning design process:

1. **What do you need to know?** This question almost always has to do with student improvement in literacy learning, but there may be medial goals related to the actions you want to take.

2. **How will you know it if you do?** This question has to do with what counts as evidence. The group needs to decide specifically what they will see, hear, or read that indicates professional learning is paying off.

3. **What else might happen, good or bad?** This question points out that it is important to look for unintended consequences. For example, a session focused on a particular teaching move might cause a teacher to overuse that practice. On the other hand, professional learning experiences focused on fluent reading might also improve students' ability to read with understanding in other content areas. You need to expect the unexpected.

---

## Professional Development vs. Professional Learning

In this chapter we call for reimagining *professional development* as *professional learning* that is designed, developed, and directed by adult learners and in which they are willing, active, and engaged participants. In this view, everyone takes collective responsibility for each other's learning and for the outcomes of every student in the school.

Current literature (e.g., Hicks, Sailors, and ILA 2018) emphasizes professional learning as opposed to the old-style professional development, contrasting the two terms as shown in Figure 19-2. The change of language signals a

*"Effective professional learning is not an adventure–it's a journey. We engage in professional learning with purpose and intent. Although there may be unexpected encounters along the way, we have a clear destination in mind. Specifically, we want to get better at our profession. That's why we call it 'professional learning.'"*

**—Thomas R. Guskey**

| TRADITIONAL PROFESSIONAL DEVELOPMENT | PROFESSIONAL LEARNING |
|---|---|
| <ul><li>Comes from "the top."</li><li>Little or no say in topics on the part of teachers.</li><li>Teachers are seen as receivers of knowledge.</li><li>Performed by "experts."</li><li>Uses traditional formats (workshops, lectures, webinars).</li><li>Sessions disconnected from each other and from the classroom.</li><li>Often presented as "one shot."</li><li>Little attention to implementation.</li><li>Seldom includes concrete follow-up.</li><li>Often based on someone else's judgment of what teachers need.</li><li>Often focused on sets of materials.</li></ul> | <ul><li>Comes from the "top" and from teachers, who have input on the content.</li><li>Recognizes teachers' experiences and abilities.</li><li>Considers teachers active, adult learners who construct their understandings.</li><li>Learning is interactive, and teachers learn from each other as well as the facilitator.</li><li>Engages teachers in collaborative inquiry.</li><li>Is process based, recognizing change is gradual and difficult.</li><li>Allows for co-constructing and reflecting on practice.</li><li>Learning is sustained and extended over time.</li><li>Linked to student outcomes.</li><li>Uses multiple formats and learning structures.</li><li>Always includes follow-up.</li></ul> |

Figure 19-2. Contrasting Professional Development and Professional Learning

shift in stance from top-down, expert-delivered formats to more authentic and personal experiences that engage teachers' thinking and stance as professionals.

In the first column, you see characteristics of the kind of professional development that has become institutionalized. Whole groups of individuals or outside consultants have been employed as "staff developers." Some years ago, you might have overheard teachers saying, "Here come the PD people with their transparencies." Today, just substitute the word *PowerPoint*. As previously reported research indicates, there is little evidence that even a massive amount of traditional professional development results in higher student outcomes.

Traditional professional development is deeply solidified in the policies and organizational structures of many school districts and is reflected in the ways that leaders and teachers talk about professional development. For example:

- "We have two PD days a year. We need to find a workshop leader. Let's take a survey on what teachers want to hear. Or, what do we think teachers need to learn? Or, we'll just ask the speaker what she wants to talk about."

- "Our negotiated contract states that we only have to attend two PD days a year. We are required to sit through 15 hours of PD to gain points."

In the second column of Figure 19-2, you see the goals of today's professional learning. You will notice greater teacher involvement, collaboration, and variety in the way teachers are treated as learners and how they develop a sense of agency in their growth as professionals. They are invited to analyze the results of their own teaching and that of others.

The kind of professional learning we describe here is all too rare, and yet it holds great promise for the sustainability of continuous improvement in schools. The school becomes a "learning organization" (Fullan 2016). Certainly, we have seen schools come alive when school leaders and others work together in this way.

To be fair, teachers often do feel that they need new information or "how-to" sessions to implement the kind of learning experiences they want their students to have. And "experts" may have some good information but generally can't work in a school on a continuous basis to support day-to-day professional learning. That is why the school leader's role is so critical, and why collaborative inquiry is essential. Also essential is a deep understanding of how adults learn.

Professional learning experiences that involve teachers in decisions about the content often lead to better outcomes for teachers and their students.

## A Complex Theory of Adult Learning

Adults and children learn in some of the same ways, but there are also important differences. Most adults have a far greater ability to learn consciously and to sustain effort even when the learning is frustrating. They are willing to perform some tasks they think are tedious or very challenging in the pursuit of new knowledge, skills, information, or personal achievement. Adults who fit that description have a repository of childhood experiences telling them that learning pays off and provides satisfaction. In its most powerful form, learning is inherently enjoyable for children and adults alike.

Some attributes of learning are common to all human beings. As we discussed in detail in Chapter 5 and summarize below, humans learn best when they:

- **Construct their learning.** All learners actively construct their knowledge, bringing their unique experiences and understandings to the process. They develop their understandings from the inside, rather than being told. In this way, they use prior knowledge as the foundation upon which they build new learning.

- **Expand their capabilities with assistance from others.** With the support of a skilled teacher, children can stretch themselves to create new understandings beyond what they could achieve independently. Adults are no different; they benefit from the advice and support of colleagues who may be more experienced or skilled in certain areas of practice.

- **Learn through social interactions.** Collaborative inquiry for students and for adults requires an environment that promotes social

Learning is easier (and a lot more fun) when it takes place in a supportive social context.

interaction. When people work alongside and collaboratively with other people, learning is easier. And when professional learning takes place in a supportive social context, adults feel more comfortable asking for and giving help, and they can build their own understandings on the ideas of other teachers.

- **Learn in emotionally supportive environments.** All learners need an emotionally supportive learning environment if they are to take risks, admit what they don't know and share what they do, ask questions, and make personal connections with their colleagues. An emotionally supportive environment for adult learners is comfortable, free of distractions, uncluttered, and arranged in a manner that is conducive to conversation and collaboration.

- **Are actively engaged.** Some forms of professional "development" require teachers to be passive recipients of knowledge that is delivered to them by an expert other. But teachers, like all learners, need to engage directly in the practices they are learning and need opportunities to participate in small- and large-group activities involving analysis, writing, talking, role-playing, and problem-solving.

- **Take risks and reflect on their learning.** When learners are given the time and opportunity to look back on what they are learning and reflect on how it can be helpful to them in their classroom practice, it instills confidence and sheds light on future learning needs.

Although adult and student learning have a lot in common, teachers are *adult learners*, and their professional development is a form of adult education. This shifts the focus to the needs of teachers and the specific contexts they teach (Knowles 2005).

Let's think of the teacher as a learner who has been wielding working systems (conceptual models) regarding pedagogy from the earliest experiences of schooling (not just their experience in teaching). Sometimes without conscious awareness, a teacher of reading and writing has been assembling and reassembling her theory of:

- What the processes of reading and writing are.
- What literacy learning looks and sounds like in terms of observable student behaviors.
- How to teach reading and writing.
- The kinds of materials teachers should use.

Definitions of the above may vary widely among school staff members, but they seldom surface for examination in schools where educators never engage in inquiry or reflection. Added to that are concepts of organization and management, human interrelationships, and the systems by which schools operate. It's complex.

As adult learners, teachers want to learn, reflect, and be actively engaged in solving their own problems. They bring their beliefs, teaching experiences, and knowledge to their learning. They are likely to be flexible learners because of the many different demands of their roles. They have high expectations for the quality of their professional learning sessions and do not want to waste time if they don't believe it will contribute to their expertise. Adult learners are goal-oriented and have needs and issues that are priorities at a particular point in time. They have many commitments and demands on their time but are motivated to learn for the sake of improving outcomes for their students.

Adult learners want to be responsible for their own learning and to feel a sense of autonomy. Often, teachers resent being told what to learn or do without feeling ownership for the goals. For the experiences to be meaningful, adults need control over their own learning. They bring a wide range of life experiences and many different backgrounds to the professional learning program. They will be more motivated to learn if they believe that the learning will address their perceived needs and apply directly to their practice.

Adults learn what they need to know, but first they need to be aware of those needs and actively involved in planning the professional opportunities they believe they need to improve their practice. The needs of teachers must be balanced with the school and district standards for student learning.

> "To enact change faster and more effectively, to reduce variation in effective teaching in a school or between and among schools in terms of networks, our advice is to use social capital. Use the group to change the group."
>
> —**Andy Hargreaves and Michael Fullan**

## PROFESSIONAL CAPITAL

Hargreaves and Fullan (2012) describe professional capital as "the collective expertise of the people who teach children. That's the investment that holds the most promise if we do it right. This remains the biggest challenge in education. As Benjamin Franklin said, 'An investment in knowledge always pays the best interest.'"

Hargreaves and Fullan have identified three kinds of professional capital:

1. **Human capital**—the expertise of the individuals in the school. They have talent that can be developed and sustained in a dynamic learning community.

2. **Social capital**—closely related to human capital, and referring to the patterns of interaction among people that are focused on student improvement. Social capital is different from human capital; development is a persistent collective effort. There is room for individuality because each person gets feedback and support that builds confidence and effectiveness. Teachers who enter a highly collaborative school are socialized quickly into greater teamwork.

3. **Decisional capital**—refers not just to the individual decision-making that teachers do every day but to the collective responsibility that individuals show in making those decisions. The decision-making is expert-driven and relentless because the stakes are high. It leads teachers not to act on self-interest but to give support to others and to take action in the interest of children. With decisional capital, teachers exercise wise professional judgment. Without it, nothing much happens.

The good thing about professional capital is that it accumulates in the school. With persistent effort, every year gets better. If everyone continues to learn, then the knowledge base increases and teachers have a larger body of support. Your goal as a school leader is to develop professional capital, although you do not bear the full load of the responsibility. The more you can interact with and gain the support of your team, the more you will increase the school's professional capital.

All of this is to say that teachers want to learn and improve their practice on behalf of students. Make the assumption that all teachers care about children, or they wouldn't be teachers. It is not helpful—in fact, it is detrimental—to label them "good" or "bad" teachers. Their teaching simply reflects their current understandings. What they are doing in the classroom is what they understand. All individuals are acting on what they currently know, how they see themselves, and how they see the world. Creating a learning culture instead of an "evaluative" or competitive culture can make an important difference in developing teacher expertise.

## The Role of Motivation in Teacher Learning

What motivates teachers to constantly improve? The first, we hope, is their commitment to the children and their families. Intrinsic motivators go a long way. These are rewards like watching children run to the classroom library to grab a book you've introduced with a book talk or noticing that students' writing shows strong evidence of growth in applying conventions. But teachers, like all people who work for a living, also benefit from extrinsic motivation—the kind that comes from external rewards. We realize that most school districts do not have a specified career ladder for teachers or a way to reward strong performance in the classroom with merit pay. But there are other things you can do. For example:

- Provide a small stipend, if possible, to recognize extra work or special leadership work.
- Elevate the status of teachers as appropriate and to the extent possible. For example, if your district has the job title of Teacher Leader, use it!
- When you conduct your next evaluation of a teacher who has shown sustained improvement over the course of a year, be sure to highlight that fact, both in the post-observation conference and the written documentation.
- If you have a strong story to tell about student achievement at the end of the year, reach out to the local newspaper or television station and suggest they cover the news from your school. Then, recommend that they interview the teachers you most want to recognize.
- After any kind of classroom visit, even if it was only for a few minutes, try to take time to write a short message to the teacher highlighting the strengths you observed. You can write it on a sticky note and leave it in a corner of the teacher's desk to find after you have left.
- Enlist the help of the school's parent-teacher organization to provide a yearly "appreciation breakfast" for all staff.

**Three Tips for Finding Time** Time evaporates quickly in schools, so if you are committed to a culture of collaboration you'll need to designate and protect time for teachers to collaborate during the school day. Think out of the box as you consider your options.

1. **Free up time.** Consider temporarily relieving teachers from regular duties during the school day. Tap an administrator, instructional aide, or another teacher to cover the classrooms of a few teachers who need a quick huddle. Or a single teacher can take two classrooms of children for a read-aloud of a wonderful book or monitor them at recess. Remember, you're not looking for any long-term solutions here, just a chance for a few teachers to put their heads together for a short while.

2. **Buy time.** Hire subs for a period or offer stipends to teachers who want to work together over the summer or after school.

3. **Schedule common planning time.** When making schedules, try to build in common planning time for grade-level teams to meet.

## The Principal as Lead Learner

We advocate for the principal to act as the "lead learner" in the school, working alongside teachers and other leaders individually, in small groups, and as a whole team.

It is true that there simply are not enough hours in the day for an elementary school principal, and that is why a literacy coach and a team of teacher leaders are so important in supporting professional learning. But it is essential for the principal to take the stance of a learner and, whenever possible, participate fully in professional learning sessions. We have seen the positive impact of a principal and/or coach attending seminars with a team of teachers and holding exciting "after meeting" planning sessions. We have seen the power of a principal or literacy coach trying out new techniques and engaging in the analysis. Never once have we seen teachers be amused by or unappreciative of the leaders' efforts to learn alongside them, and it's often the quickest way to foster a "we're all in this together" attitude.

Above all, the principal can take the stance that teachers' time is valuable and that their learning and the acquisition of expertise is a priority and an important goal of the school. Instead of reading announcements, post them; instead of going over a list of events in faculty meetings, devote time to lesson study or data analysis. Engage the staff in collaborative planning and evaluation of their efforts. Hold a meeting at the end of the year to plan for next year's priorities and engage volunteers in using digital tools over the summer to

Digital Literacy

**Rethink Faculty Meetings** You're probably familiar with the concept of a flipped classroom, but have you thought about flipping your faculty meetings? Use email or social media to distribute announcements, directives, calendar items, and the like. Then, use the time you'll save for meaningful professional learning during the face-to-face meeting.

## MANAGE YOUR BUDGET

**Practical Support** Administrators and other school leaders usually have some budget authority and the ability to provide some of the practical underpinnings that are needed to support professional learning. For example, teachers need a comfortable place to gather for face-to-face meetings that is conducive to real conversation and inquiry work with books and artifacts around tables or in a circle to engage in dialogue. Other resources an administrator can provide may include:

- Professional books on topics that are pertinent to the topic teachers are exploring.
- Professional tools to support teachers in implementing practice (for example, flexible lesson guides; general tools such as the *Fountas & Pinnell Prompting Guides* and *The Literacy Continuum* in hard copy or digital form).
- Digital tools such as tablets that make other resources easily accessible.
- Adjustment of schedules to provide time.
- Student materials as needed for a rich text experience in many contexts.
- A systematic way of collecting student assessment data to provide evidence of impact.
- Guides to the structure of some types of learning experiences, such as coaching, lesson study, and peer observation.
- Protocols that are available to help the group gain a practical vision of the content.
- Practical tools to guide classroom observations.

plan for the start of school. Try to share some of the professional reading that you expect teachers to do; participate in a book club or article study.

It's also important for the principal to have a strong presence in the school. Greet children and visitors in the morning. Enter classrooms frequently, but don't sit at the back of the room with a checklist. Move around; sit side-by-side with individual children and, if appropriate, softly ask them to talk with you about their work. Make it clear that you enjoy visiting the classroom and appreciate what readers and writers are doing. Your presence is not a signal to stop work or interrupt the teacher, nor is it a signal for everyone to be "on their best behavior." Students and teachers will get used to you being there and will go about the business at hand. Be ready to help if needed.

# The Role of Facilitative Talk Within a Professional Learning Community

Language plays a powerful role in shaping the professional learning culture and in teacher growth, especially the interactions that take place during professional learning between school leaders and the teachers they support. When interacting with teachers your use of language needs to parallel that of teachers as they support the learning of students. The language you use rests on the

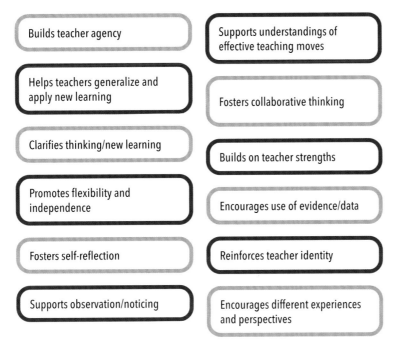

**BENEFITS OF FACILITATIVE TALK**

- Builds teacher agency
- Supports understandings of effective teaching moves
- Helps teachers generalize and apply new learning
- Fosters collaborative thinking
- Clarifies thinking/new learning
- Builds on teacher strengths
- Promotes flexibility and independence
- Encourages use of evidence/data
- Fosters self-reflection
- Reinforces teacher identity
- Supports observation/noticing
- Encourages different experiences and perspectives

**Figure 19-3.** Benefits of Facilitative Talk

principle that an experienced leader—in this case, you—places the learner—in this case, the teacher—on the edge of present understandings and provides a scaffold that allows expansion and growth. Your choice of language positions the teacher as a co-learner who is a co-constructor and co-problem-solver with a shared sense of ownership and commitment to the values of the school. It shapes the teachers' identities as vital, contributing members of the school team, responsible for their own professional learning and supporting the learning of colleagues. See Figure 19-3 above for more benefits of facilitated conversations with teachers.

We believe that the intentional and skilled facilitation of professional conversations by school leaders is the surest way to promote and sustain the learning and expertise of teachers. Let's look at some key characteristics of facilitative talk.

## Collaborative

Facilitative talk fosters collaborative thinking. Your success requires harnessing and developing the expertise and leadership of teachers. This challenge requires letting go of a strict, top-down hierarchy and nurturing and amplifying teachers' voices in educating students. Teachers who feel valued and trusted are more likely to take risks and take on new skills and understandings.

A truly collaborative interaction is conversational and invites multiple perspectives. There is give-and-take; both you and the teacher listen to understand, offer information, and learn from each other. Regardless of their role, pairs or small groups of colleagues think together and dig deep into the acts of teaching and learning for improved student outcomes. A tone of respect and tentativeness permeates the interaction. No one dominates. You pause to listen carefully and with commitment to the teacher rather than simply wait for another opportunity to speak, because a teacher's talk reveals what she currently believes and understands. The conversation is genuine and organic, not artificial or formulaic, nor constrained by a standardized set of rituals. Participants talk about what is real and important to their work and arrive at co-constructed understandings.

## Inquiry-Focused

Facilitative talk promotes genuine inquiry. Picture yourself and another educator wondering and thinking together, focusing on investigating and problem-solving using the literacy behaviors of real students within an instructional context. The goal for both of you is to learn more about responsive teaching, that is, teaching based on detailed knowledge of individual students. You use evidence—both quantitative and qualitative data as well as a combination of the two. You and your colleague are engaging in analysis of the data and the effects of teaching to determine evidence of learning or confusion on the part of the student. The analysis leads to generative thinking; practices that prove to have positive effects on student learning are applied to future teaching.

## Reflective

Facilitative talk supports self-reflection and growth by promoting honest analysis on the part of the learner. For example, you and the teacher can think together and reflect to expand knowledge of teaching and learning. Your goal is to gain as much information as possible about what the teacher understands and believes. Listening to better understand the teacher's perspectives and strengths is an important part of fostering self-reflection. So is the practice of using silence to give space for and time for reflection and processing. Wait time is thinking time. You assume that the teacher is competent and actively identify strengths on which he can build. In other words, your language communicates a belief that the teacher's knowledge, experiences, and unique perspectives are assets. When the teacher feels like your questions are meant to show his lack of expertise, you erode trust.

Instead of repeating dead-end phrases that discourage self-reflection and growth such as "Good lesson" or "You should have . . . ," you invite deeper, nonjudgmental thinking with language such as "Would you like to talk about . . . ?" and "Can you share your thinking about . . . ?" Asking authentic, focused, and open-ended questions rather than testing the teacher encourages thoughtful response and a growth mindset. See Figure 19-4 for more examples of effective facilitative talk.

| EXAMPLES OF FACILITATIVE TALK | |
|---|---|
| **Support Teaching Moves** | ▪ It seemed helpful to the children when_____. <br> ▪ What did you say that shifted the children's thinking? <br> ▪ Where do you feel your teaching was most effective? |
| **Encourage Flexibility** | ▪ That was your plan, but what changed your thinking? <br> ▪ When you saw _____, what choices did you have? <br> ▪ What other decision might you have made? |
| **Promote Independence** | ▪ What are you planning to try next? <br> ▪ What professional resource could help you with that? <br> ▪ What data/evidence will you need to make a plan? |
| **Foster Self-Reflection** | ▪ Why do you think the children were able to figure that out? <br> ▪ What are the biggest challenges you face in teaching small-group reading (writing)? <br> ▪ What was most useful for you in our time together? |

Figure 19-4. Language like the questions and statements above can help move teachers forward in their learning and thinking about teaching.

## One Conversation at a Time

Facilitative talk among educators does not become the norm in a school quickly or without conscious effort. It develops over time, one conversation at a time, as members of the school community work and learn together. Meaningful conversations about teaching and learning rest on the values and vision shared by all educators in the school and require a common understanding of the work that educators are doing together. Facilitative talk emerges from the cumulative effects of hundreds of conversations, starting with the language you take on and use with other school leaders and with the teachers you support.

## The Takeaway

Professional learning is not a "quick fix" or even a fix. It is a *start*, a *condition*, and an *ongoing process*. The sequence of learning over time builds a coherent body of knowledge and a repertoire of skills. In our view, it is the most important part of the literacy leader's job—not necessarily to be the "expert" but to serve as the catalyst for getting it going and keeping it going. The school leader needs to be a co-learner and value the continuous generosity of the team in supporting each other's learning.

**Professional Learning Audit** Think about the funding and policies for professional learning in your district. Consider whether the funding is adequate for the schools to implement high-quality professional development that is coherent and meaningful for the educators. As you review the feedback on the quality from school leaders, identify what you want to continue to build on and what needs to be rethought. Also determine cost factors and whether the funding was sufficient for the goals.

Consider the professional development policies and procedures in place in your system. Do they reflect contemporary views of professional learning for literacy educators? Who has provided input on the policies? Is the professional learning school-based or district-wide? Are special learning opportunities provided for new teachers? How do the policies support effective professional learning? Are there policies that need revisiting? Use feedback to make changes that will serve your educational system well. Get reliable information by asking the school leaders and teachers what is working well and what they would change.

## Think About Your School

- Does the culture of your school create a high level of trust in observing and talking together about teaching and learning?
- How do leaders in your school gain experience and develop expertise in having skilled, facilitative conversations? What opportunities do they have for professional learning?
- How do school leaders—coaches principals, mentors, teacher leaders—view their roles in supporting professional learning?
- How do teachers view their roles in professional learning?

## Move Your School Forward

- Review outlines and presentations for upcoming professional learning experiences to ensure they are in synch with principles of adult learning.
- Make it a point to attend as many professional learning opportunities as possible so you can learn beside teachers and other leaders.

# Chapter 20

# Game Changers: New Practices for Professional Learning

*Professional learning today calls for long-term sustained focus on embedding the practice of learning into the system so that those who have the greatest impact on student learning are continuously developing precision in their work to produce better outcomes for all.*
—Stephanie Hirsh, Kay Psencik, and Frederick Brown

WE KNOW YOU'VE BEEN there: The professional development session you didn't ask for and didn't think you needed in the first place. The one that lasted two full days and consisted only of PowerPoint presentations, one after another in a numbing parade of charts and graphs and bullets. If you're lucky, though, you also might remember a session or two that really made a difference because the content was particularly relevant to a real problem of practice in your classroom or school or because the presenter acted as a facilitator, en couraging you to speak with your colleagues about the content and giving you relevant problems or tasks to work through together so you didn't have time to be bored. Maybe the session format was new to you, or blessedly brief but packed with usable advice and insights from people who knew you and the actual challenges you were facing.

Professional learning sessions do need to provide important content rather than entertainment, but they don't have to be dull or disconnected from classroom practice. In this chapter, we present the characteristics of professional learning experiences that can change the game for teachers and students, discuss various traditional and not-so-traditional structures and formats for teacher learning, and walk you through the important process of evaluating professional learning in your school. We'll also introduce you to several helpful tools for school leaders.

We hope the information you find here will contribute to the building of a professional culture in your school in which teachers are focused on learning, not just on teaching. In this kind of culture, all teachers are collaborative and willing to take risks in the learning environment. They give and receive constructive feedback, engage in dialogue, develop positive and trusting relationships with colleagues, and use a common language to discuss their students and their own goals for professional learning. Let's begin by thinking about what makes professional learning effective.

## Hallmarks of Effective Professional Learning

In their 2017 report, "Effective Teacher Professional Development," authors Linda Darling-Hammond, Maria E. Hyler, and Madelyn Gardner reviewed thirty-five rigorous studies showing that effective professional learning can lead to improved teaching and better outcomes for students. But what makes professional learning effective? The authors identified seven features of effective professional learning, which we have described below.

1. **Content-focused:** Professional learning that focuses on teaching strategies associated with specific curriculum content better supports teacher learning within the context of the classroom. The focus is on discipline-specific content in literacy as well as science and mathematics.

2. **Active learning:** Teachers are actively involved in analyzing, designing, and testing teaching methods. Active participation allows them to experience the same kind of learning experiences they provide for their students and moves away from the traditional model of professional learning that is lecture-based and does not connect directly to the teachers' classroom practice or the needs of their students. Instead, active learning relies on the use of artifacts, interactive activities, and other methods that are more deeply embedded in the real work of real teachers.

3. **Collaboration:** Teachers share ideas and collaborate. Learning sessions are more dialogue than lecture. Effective professional learning allows for the sharing of ideas and collaborative problem-solving,

## HALLMARKS OF EFFECTIVE PROFESSIONAL LEARNING

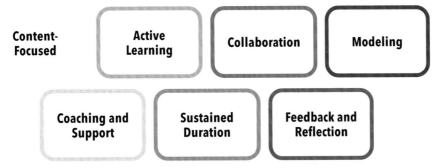

| Content-Focused | Active Learning | Collaboration | Modeling |
|---|---|---|---|
| | Coaching and Support | Sustained Duration | Feedback and Reflection |

Figure 20-1. Hallmarks of Effective Professional Learning

often in embedded contexts (taking place in classrooms within the school day). This kind of collaboration can change the culture of a school and have impact on instruction within a single classroom, across a grade level, or throughout the school or district.

4. **Models of effective practice:** Teachers experience demonstrations or examples (video, live observation, artifacts, lesson plans, schedules) that give them a clear vision of what certain practices look like. Ideally, they look doable! Other useful models include lesson and unit plans and samples of student work.

5. **Coaching and extra support:** Individual, peer, and group coaching are available to support teachers as they try new approaches. Coaches and teachers look at and think together about evidence in terms of student behaviors and their own expectations. Often, effective professional learning focuses directly on the needs of individual teachers. Formal coaching is one example, and so is impromptu sharing of expertise between two teachers.

6. **Sustained duration:** There is adequate time to learn, practice, implement, and reflect on the new approaches that teachers are implementing. The emphasis is on gradual, cumulative improvement rather than sudden change. The message here is that making impactful changes in the quality of teaching is difficult and important work that must be given due time—within an individual session and over the course of an entire year.

7. **Feedback and reflection:** Time is built in for reflection and feedback, which are seen as a necessary part of the professional learning experience. A norm of the culture is that everyone, including school leaders, seeks feedback and

### PROFESSIONAL LEARNING AS INQUIRY

In contrast to traditional views of professional development, inquiry-driven professional learning allows teachers to engage in determining the purpose and direction of their own learning. In this model, the school leader–whether the literacy coach, teacher leader, or principal–contributes expertise by directing the learning toward the school's values and beliefs about literacy teaching and learning. Active inquiry that engages problem-solving is the catalyst that links professional learning and real change that impacts student outcomes (Bransford, Brown, and Cocking, eds., 1999).

engages in self-analysis. It is safe for individuals to critique their own work and results and to seek help.

## A Structure for Professional Learning

The introduction of new ideas or procedures, as well as sharing about how implementation is going, often involve group meetings where the coach takes the lead in presenting information. This is an efficient way to convey information (as opposed to teaching one person at a time). The sessions are usually not long (1 to 2 hours), but they are action-packed. Coaches design sessions that involve teachers in doing some reading and being introduced to resources they can access on their own, viewing brief video examples and engaging in analysis, problem-solving and planning as a group, and planning together for the use of materials and implementation of lessons.

Consider the hallmarks of effective professional learning we discussed and possible structures that reflect meaningful participation of the adults in group professional development sessions. You may want to use a basic structure so there is predictability and a rhythm to most 1- or 2-hour sessions. The sample structure shown below encompasses all the elements of effective professional learning and may help your planning. There can be many variations on this structure and on who leads the session.

1. **Connection:** Link to previous session and/or data.

2. **Outcomes:** Identify desired outcomes of the session.

3. **Content:** Provide video clips, student work, a read-aloud of a children's book, or other samples and forms of input to examine/analyze in relation to a problem of practice.

4. **Collaborative Inquiry:** Partners or small groups engage in thinking and talking about the content related to a problem of practice.

5. **Share:** Group discusses their new learning.

6. **Link to Practice:** Group considers various implications of how the learning may impact their teaching and their students. They may set new goals or priorities for future professional learning.

7. **Evaluation:** Group members pair up and discuss feedback on the session and then the pairs briefly share their feedback orally with the group.

## Gathering Information About Teaching

You can gain information and provide constructive feedback about teaching and learning throughout the school year in a variety of ways that go beyond scheduled teacher evaluations. Your daily presence in classrooms, even for 2 or 3 minutes, provides support for the team and the students while ensur-

**Central Office Memo**

**Supporting Schoolwide Improvement.** As a central office leader, you have aspirational visions for the educational system. Think about the implications of the multi-level, multipronged suggestions for professional learning in this chapter and how they bring together your vision and plans with the day-to-day complexities and realities of teaching and learning inside the classrooms in each school.

When you observe, listen, and learn from the opportunities that await you and your colleagues as you join walk-throughs, instructional rounds, data team meetings, and other forms of professional learning in each school. As you do so, you are disrupting the hierarchical notions that may exist and reinforcing the important concept of collective ownership—of the work and its outcomes.

ing your own continued learning. As a school leader, it's important that you get into classrooms early in the school year and visit often in order to help students and teachers get comfortable with your presence. When you are in the classroom, whether it's for a few minutes or an entire lesson period, you can observe everything from the environment, to teaching moves, to student independence.

In Figure 20-2 we describe a variety of structures and tools for gathering information about the quality of teaching and learning in your school. Every structure and every tool needs to be clearly understood by all members of the team so they are used in a climate of trust and collaboration and teachers can feel included and value them. Otherwise, the good intentions may backfire and result in distrust. The focus of inquiry needs to be established before the visits and needs to clearly define what evidence will be collected and how it will be used.

## Classroom Visits

There are a variety of permutations of classroom visits for the purpose of individual and collective feedback—some scheduled and some not scheduled, some short and some for a full lesson, some including school leaders, and some possibly including district personnel. To be clear, in this chapter we are not concerned with classroom observation solely by the school principal for the purpose of formal performance evaluation. We will discuss that important topic in Chapter 22. The classroom visits explained in what follows are designed to promote a culture of collaboration and professionalism.

We summarize different types of scheduled and unscheduled classroom visits in which you can observe teaching and engage in constructive conversations with teachers and other leaders in Figure 20-2. Together you can assemble a

## OPPORTUNITIES TO GATHER INFORMATION AND PROMOTE LEARNING

### WALKTHROUGHS

- **Unscheduled walkthroughs**
- **Classroom environment walk**
- **Instructional rounds**
- **Learning walks**

- Bring classroom practice into the open (deprivatize practice)
- Scheduled and unscheduled
- Become ubiquitous in the school
- Get to know students over the years
- Accustom teachers to having colleagues in the classroom
- Help visiting teachers sharpen their ability to observe

### OBSERVATIONS

- **Mini-observations with feedback**
- **Peer lesson observations and feedback**

- Can be short or longer; scheduled or unscheduled
- May include oral feedback or brief written messages
- Accustom teachers and students to being observed
- Can lift teachers' understanding of their own work
- Promote collaboration

### COLLABORATIVE INQUIRY

- **Lesson study**
- **Collaborative review of student work**
- **Professional book clubs**

- Can be short or longer; scheduled or unscheduled
- Give teachers the chance to think together
- Can lift teachers' understanding of their own work
- Promote collaboration
- Encourage deep thinking about professional practice

### TOOLS

- **Observation tools**
- **Rubrics**
- **Protocols**
- **Reflection tools**
- **Discussion tools**
- **The Literacy Continuum**

- Support self-reflection and collaboration
- Bring standardized structure to the process
- Guide the observers to key points
- Offer a specific picture of instruction and learning
- Get teachers thinking about their common culture and processes
- Develop a common language and lens for analysis

Figure 20-2. Multiple Opportunities to Gather Information and Promote Learning

# PROTOCOL TOOL

Use the protocol tool **Unscheduled Classroom Walkthrough (25)** to get an overall sense of how a walkthrough might go and as a guide for actions during and after the walkthrough.

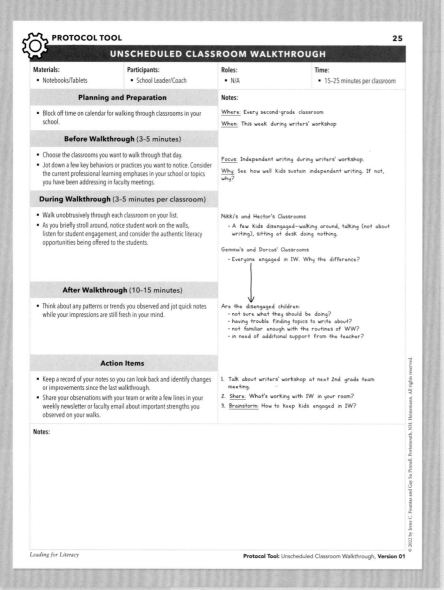

mosaic that gives you a picture of the patterns across teachers and over time as they relate to your team's goals for school improvement. In every context, think about how your facilitative language communicates your support for teacher agency and reflection.

**Unscheduled Classroom Walkthrough by School Leader** When you do a brief walkthrough of the classrooms in your building during literacy time, even for 3 to 5 minutes in each classroom, you will get a real feel for your school. You will likely notice patterns and trends, the level of student engagement, the amount of student talk, the number of children reading books or talking about books, the number of students writing for authentic purposes. When you put time on your daily schedule to walk through classrooms during literacy time, you convey your genuine support for teaching and learning. Your visits will provide feedback on professional learning outcomes and contribute to the direction of future professional learning sessions.

**Classroom Environment Walk** This type of walkthrough is different from others because it takes place when students are not present. The purpose is for participants to freely analyze the physical environment, including whatever student work is visible. When school leaders and teachers spend time together walking through each classroom they engage in meaningful discussion with concrete examples of student work, discuss the reality of the physical space and its organization, and have an opportunity for meaningful collaboration. The classroom environment walk is a concrete, nonthreatening way to include all teachers and get them thinking and talking together about their classrooms. Over time, they will become more comfortable with having each other present in their rooms.

**Learning Walk** Learning walks (Resnick date TK) have been a popular means for generating constructive feedback for individuals and the team, as they support a reflective culture. As a form of collaborative learning, they contribute to a culture of inquiry and provide data for dialogue among the members of a team. Learning walks highlight literacy opportunities for students, reveal common instructional practices, and can serve as the basis for identifying coaching and professional learning needs.

The purpose of a learning walk is to get a picture of what is happening across a school and gain specific evidence to inform school improvement. For teachers, learning walks have the additional benefit of opening a window on the practice of other teachers, perhaps one of the most valuable forms of professional learning that exists.

Most often the professional learning team identifies a focus and specific criteria, and a small representative group conducts the informal walkthrough, possibly repeating it several times to identify change over

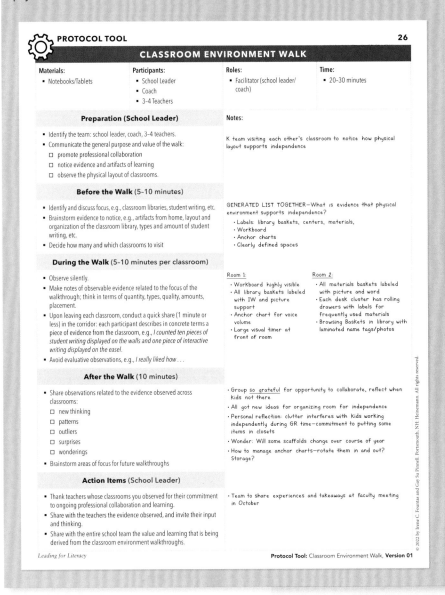

Use the protocol tool **Classroom Environment Walk (26)** to help the team analyze the physical environment and available student work when students are not present.

time. After spending a few minutes in each classroom, the learning walk participants make a few notes so they will have data to inform the discussion. The results are analyzed and discussed with the team on a timely basis so they can identify professional learning needs or set other actions.

Use the Protocol Tool **Learning Walk (27)** to help the team form a picture of what is happening around the school and to gain specific evidence to inform school improvement efforts.

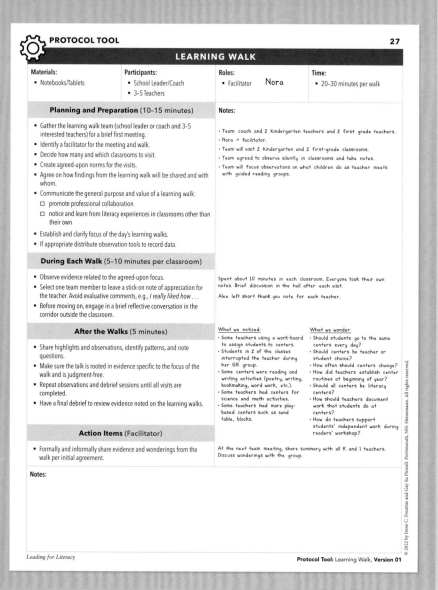

**Instructional Rounds** Instructional rounds can promote a culture of collaboration and continuous improvement in a school. According to Elmore (2002), "The idea behind instructional rounds is that *everyone* involved is working on their practice, *everyone* is obliged to be knowledgeable about the common task of instructional improvement, and *everyone's* practice should be subject to scrutiny, critique, and improvement."

A small group of colleagues, usually about three or four teachers, the coach, and the principal, gather on a regular basis to walk through classrooms. Over time, they develop a community of practice that links their walkthroughs to school improvement plans and goals. Because the rounds model is designed to provide insights regarding schoolwide or district-wide improvement (as opposed to exposing excellent teaching in isolated classrooms), groups often include central office personnel or even the superintendent.

The instructional rounds team visits four or five classrooms on a given day, staying for about 20 minutes in each one. Sometimes teams decide to split into smaller groups. If so, the groups rotate through the designated classrooms. As they observe, group members take notes about what they see and hear. When the observations are complete, the whole group meets to debrief. Individuals share details of their observations and together they build a body of evidence on what they saw and heard in classrooms, any patterns they are able to discern, and how the evidence can be used to improve the problem of practice. Finally, the instructional rounds team members discuss recommendations they'd like to make to school or district leadership and identify what they will look at during their next set of rounds.

Elmore notes that the rounds model helps groups of people who might have

| FOUR TYPES OF WALKTHROUGHS | | | | |
|---|---|---|---|---|
| | **UNSCHEDULED WALKTHROUGH** | **CLASSROOM ENVIRONMENT WALK** | **LEARNING WALK** | **INSTRUCTIONAL ROUNDS** |
| **Purpose** | To notice patterns and trends across the school in level of student engagement, talk, reading, and writing | To analyze the physical environment and notice visible student work | To discover current practices, patterns, strengths, needs, and expertise throughout the school | To analyze data for potential schoolwide problems of practice, identify evidence in classrooms, and implement improvements |
| **Degree of Structure and Formality** | Less structured; informal | Less structured; informal | Less structured; informal | More structured; formal |
| **Participants in the Visit** | School leader | School leaders and 3–4 teachers | School leaders, teachers, and/or specialists | 3–4 teachers, coach, school leader; might include district people |
| **Level of Focus: School, Grade, or Classroom** | Classrooms | Classrooms | School, grade, and/or classroom | School or district |
| **Area of Focus** | Learning environment, literacy opportunities, student engagement, teaching moves | Can vary: classroom libraries, student writing, welcoming aspects, etc. | Specific initiatives, school improvement plans, use of new technology, etc. | Schoolwide improvement based on a problem of practice |
| **Frequency/ Time** | A few classrooms daily  3–5 minutes per classroom | As frequently as teachers feel would be helpful  10 minutes per classroom | Once near the beginning of year and again near middle of year.  5–10 minutes per classroom | Ongoing, in 8- to 12-week cycles  20 minutes per classroom |
| **Examples of Positive Outcomes** | ▪ Presence of school leader felt throughout the school ▪ Convey support of teaching and learning ▪ Open doors on practice ▪ School leaders get to know students over the years | ▪ Meaningful discussions with concrete examples of student work ▪ Chance to discuss the reality of the physical space and how it is organized ▪ Opportunity for meaningful collaboration | ▪ Strengthen culture of trust, transparency ,and collaboration ▪ Teachers become comfortable with school leaders and other teachers in classrooms ▪ Team identifies common areas for professional learning ▪ "Cross-pollination" of effective practices | ▪ Strengthen culture of inquiry, collective efficacy, shared responsibility, and collaborative professionalism ▪ Extends leadership capacity by engaging teachers in inquiry, data collection, analysis, and reflection to support student outcomes ▪ Identify areas for professional learning |

**Figure 20-3.** Types of Classroom Walkthroughs

# PROTOCOL TOOL

The protocol tool **Instructional Rounds (28)** will be a helpful guide as you and your colleagues gather to walk through classrooms on a regular basis.

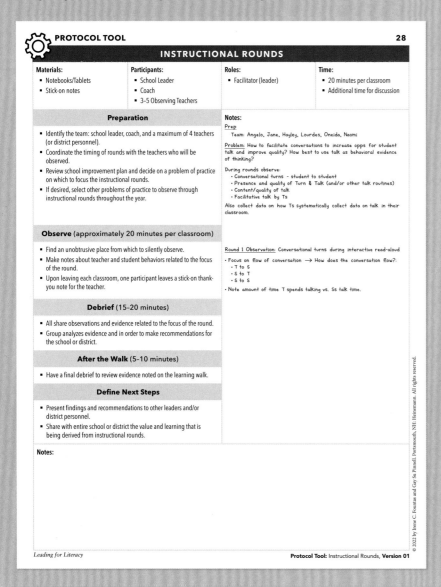

## PROTOCOL TOOL                                          28
### INSTRUCTIONAL ROUNDS

| Materials: | Participants: | Roles: | Time: |
|---|---|---|---|
| ▪ Notebooks/Tablets<br>▪ Stick-on notes | ▪ School Leader<br>▪ Coach<br>▪ 3–5 Observing Teachers | ▪ Facilitator (leader) | ▪ 20 minutes per classroom<br>▪ Additional time for discussion |

**Preparation**

- Identify the team: school leader, coach, and a maximum of 4 teachers (or district personnel).
- Coordinate the timing of rounds with the teachers who will be observed.
- Review school improvement plan and decide on a problem of practice on which to focus the instructional rounds.
- If desired, select other problems of practice to observe through instructional rounds throughout the year.

**Observe** (approximately 20 minutes per classroom)

- Find an unobtrusive place from which to silently observe.
- Make notes about teacher and student behaviors related to the focus of the round.
- Upon leaving each classroom, one participant leaves a stick-on thank-you note for the teacher.

**Debrief** (15–20 minutes)

- All share observations and evidence related to the focus of the round.
- Group analyzes evidence and in order to make recommendations for the school or district.

**After the Walk** (5–10 minutes)

- Have a final debrief to review evidence noted on the learning walk.

**Define Next Steps**

- Present findings and recommendations to other leaders and/or district personnel.
- Share with entire school or district the value and learning that is being derived from instructional rounds.

**Notes:**

Prep
Team: Angelo, Jane, Hayley, Lourdes, Oneida, Naomi

Problem: How to facilitate conversations to increase opps for student talk and improve quality? How best to use talk as behavioral evidence of thinking?

During rounds observe:
- Conversational turns - student to student
- Presence and quality of Turn & Talk (and/or other talk routines)
- Content/quality of talk
- Facilitative talk by Ts
Also collect data on how Ts systematically collect data on talk in their classroom.

Round 1 Observation: Conversational turns during interactive read-aloud
- Focus on flow of conversation → How does the conversation flow?:
  - T to S
  - S to T
  - S to S
- Note amount of time T spends talking vs. Ss talk time.

**Notes:**

*Leading for Literacy*                    **Protocol Tool:** Instructional Rounds, **Version 01**

---

different ideas and interests "to begin the difficult process or forming a coherent view of what constitutes powerful teaching and learning in classrooms. It also forces a certain discipline around the relationship between teachers and those whose job it is to support and supervise them." We particularly like the idea of instructional rounds because, like other forms of classroom visits, that activity regularly throws open the doors on classroom practice so teachers can benefit from the insights of their peers and other members of the school or district community.

## Observation

As a school leader, you are always learning about the teaching in your school as you move through the building and interact with people. But there is no substitute for an informed, structured observation of lessons. Below we describe two types of observations that can be very informative for leaders and for teachers. These two forms stop short of the formal, scheduled observation by the principal that takes place in the context of standardized teacher evaluation. We'll discuss that type of observation in the next chapter.

**Mini-Observations with Feedback** You might consider regular mini 5- to 10-minute mini-observations (Marshall 2018), in which you schedule time each day for quick unannounced visits to classrooms and provide short, timely feedback. Make some quick notes and convey your feedback—or what you noticed—to the teacher using a sticky note, a short conversation at some point in the day, or even an email. When mini-observations become part of the fabric of the school, teachers and students expect your presence and feedback and come to appreciate it.

**Peer Lesson Observations and Feedback** The teachers in your building can provide observation and feedback for each other to promote self-reflection in a nonevaluative context. Peer observation has the added benefit of helping teachers become comfortable with being observed. The peer observation process includes planning, observing, analyzing, and debriefing. The planning includes setting norms for the observation time, for example, if the teacher observer will talk to students, where she will sit, what she will look for, what the teacher wants to focus on for feedback, and when they will debrief. During the observation, peer teachers take notes on what is observed, look for specific evidence, and examine artifacts. To analyze the evidence collected, the teachers highlight aspects of their notes with an eye toward the teacher's specific agenda as well as the wonderings they have that may be opportunities for discussion and teacher growth. The debrief with the teacher is to invite the teacher's reflection, share concrete feedback, and for the teacher to identify actions.

## Collaborative Inquiry

Collaborative inquiry is driven by practice and informed by evidence. The inquiry process, in which educators problem solve to gain knowledge and solve real problems of practice that are relevant to their students and their classrooms, can be a powerful part of professional learning. The analytic thinking that inquiry requires promotes active learning and doing by teachers, who then respond to real challenges in the classroom and improve their instructional practice.

The coach, a teacher leader, or any other interested educator acts as a facilitator and leads and supports a team of at least two, and ideally five to seven, educators as they pursue answers to meaningful questions by analyzing data and other information about a topic of inquiry.

The members of an inquiry group can pursue any question they identify as important in increasing student literacy learning. Their object may be test scores, but it is wiser to pursue more immediate goals such as increasing the amount of independent reading or strengthening student writing in a particular genre.

Collaborative inquiry is not the same as action research. Collaborative inquiry is conducted by a group interested in addressing a school or classroom issue driven by student learning needs. Action research is often conducted by an individual and focused on a single classroom.

On the next few pages, we discuss three processes for collaborative inquiry, each for a different area of study. You will notice differences and similarities among the accompanying protocols. A fourth process (for working through a problem of practice) is discussed on pages 386 and 392, and you will find an accompanying protocol tool as well. All of the protocols in this chapter and throughout the book are available for download at *fp.pub/resources*.

**Where to Find Observation Tools** We have provided many sample observation tools throughout this book, and especially in Section 4, in which we concentrate on observations of teaching. All of these tools are available in the online resources for this book at *fp.pub/resources*.

| | LESSON STUDY | REVIEWING STUDENT WORK | PROFESSIONAL BOOK CLUBS | SOLVING PROBLEMS OF PRACTICE |
|---|---|---|---|---|
| **FOUR TOOLS FOR COLLABORATIVE INQUIRY** | | | | |
| **Purpose** | To learn from decisions made while planning, teaching, and reflecting on a literacy lesson | To develop trust and confidence in the power of thinking together about students | To read and discuss a high-quality book about literacy teaching or learning | To better understand and address a problem or dilemma in the classroom or school |
| **Degree of Structure and Formality** | Less structured; informal | Less structured; informal | Less structured; informal | Less structured; informal |
| **Participants** | School leader or coach 3–6 teachers | Small groups of teachers, usually within a grade | Anyone in the school community | 1 presenting teacher<br>1–4 additional teachers<br>Facilitator if desired |
| **Level of Focus: School, Grade, or Classroom** | Classroom | A few classrooms or a whole grade | School, classroom, or grade | Classroom or school |
| **Area of Focus** | Lesson design | Student work | Professional book | Problem-solving |
| **Frequency/Time** | 90 minutes plus 2 class periods | To be determined by teams (suggest 45–55 minutes per session) | 30–40 minutes per session | 40–45 minutes per session |
| **Examples of Positive Outcomes** | ▪ Classroom-based, teacher-driven inquiry.<br>▪ Deep thinking, inquiry, and focus on art of teaching.<br>▪ Creates collaborative, ongoing process of inquiry. | ▪ Builds deep understandings of the reading and writing process over time.<br>▪ Teachers learn from each other and build collective knowledge. | ▪ Fosters collegiality.<br>▪ Educators can navigate new learning in a supportive and enjoyable environment.<br>▪ Adds to the collective expertise of educators in the school. | ▪ Provides a structure for educators to help one another.<br>▪ Engages educators in efficient, productive learning and problem-solving.<br>▪ All educators in the building can benefit from the small group's decision-making and problem-solving. |

**Figure 20-4.** Four Tools for Collaborative Inquiry

**Lesson Study** With a long history in Japan, lesson study is a professional learning practice in which a small group of teachers work together to develop a lesson plan, teach and observe the lesson to collect data on student learning, and then use their observations to refine the lesson plan carefully and collaboratively. The cycle of planning, teaching, and reflecting can take many different forms and can be used for a variety of purposes.

Lesson studies will leave teachers with banks of usable lessons that are teacher-designed and classroom-tested. That's a nice benefit, but it's not the goal. The goal of lesson study is for teachers to use the process of designing and teaching a lesson to learn from the decisions they make as they plan, teach, and analyze the results.

Lesson study is a powerful way to improve instruction by developing professional knowledge through deep thinking, inquiry, and a collective focus on the art of teaching—not on the performance of individual teachers. We like lesson study because it is a collaborative, ongoing process of inquiry that is classroom-based and teacher-driven. We find that the practice attracts teachers who want to try new things and improve their practice. And, because it is an ongoing process in the school, it creates a consistent buzz from teachers who delight in talking about their craft. Often, the teachers who are most attracted to lesson study eventually become teacher leaders in the school. Here is a protocol you can use to get lesson studies going in your school.

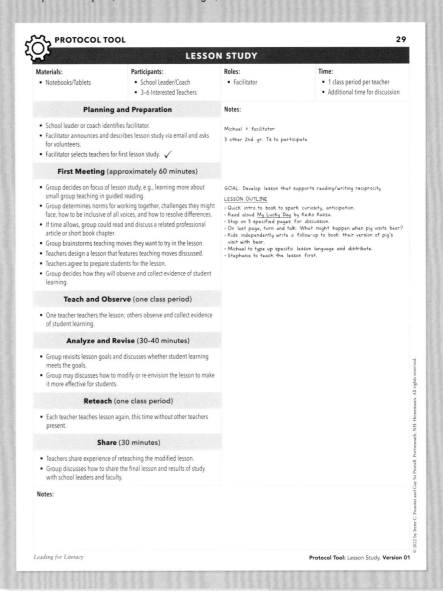

The protocol tool **Lesson Study (29)** will be helpful to teachers as they work together to develop a lesson plan, take turns teaching it, and reflect on the results.

PROTOCOL TOOL                                    29

**LESSON STUDY**

| Materials: | Participants: | Roles: | Time: |
|---|---|---|---|
| ▪ Notebooks/Tablets | ▪ School Leader/Coach<br>▪ 3–6 Interested Teachers | ▪ Facilitator | ▪ 1 class period per teacher<br>▪ Additional time for discussion |

**Planning and Preparation**

- School leader or coach identifies facilitator.
- Facilitator announces and describes lesson study via email and asks for volunteers.
- Facilitator selects teachers for first lesson study. ✓

**First Meeting** (approximately 60 minutes)

- Group decides on focus of lesson study, e.g., learning more about small group teaching in guided reading.
- Group determines norms for working together, challenges they might face, how to be inclusive of all voices, and how to resolve differences.
- If time allows, group could read and discuss a related professional article or short book chapter.
- Group brainstorms teaching moves they want to try in the lesson.
- Teachers design a lesson that features teaching moves discussed.
- Teachers agree to prepare students for the lesson.
- Group decides how they will observe and collect evidence of student learning.

**Teach and Observe** (one class period)

- One teacher teaches the lesson; others observe and collect evidence of student learning.

**Analyze and Revise** (30–40 minutes)

- Group revisits lesson goals and discusses whether student learning meets the goals.
- Group may discusses how to modify or re-envision the lesson to make it more effective for students.

**Reteach** (one class period)

- Each teacher teaches lesson again, this time without other teachers present.

**Share** (30 minutes)

- Teachers share experience of reteaching the modified lesson.
- Group discusses how to share the final lesson and results of study with school leaders and faculty.

Notes:

Michael = facilitator

3 other 2nd gr. Ts to participate

GOAL: Develop lesson that supports reading/writing reciprocity

LESSON OUTLINE
· Quick intro to book to spark curiosity, anticipation.
· Read aloud <u>My Lucky Day</u> by Keiko Kasza.
· Stop on 3 specified pages for discussion.
· On last page, turn and talk: What might happen when pig visits bear?
· Kids independently write a follow-up to book: their version of pig's visit with bear.
· Michael to type up specific lesson language and distribute.
· Stephanie to teach the lesson first.

Notes:

*Leading for Literacy*                        **Protocol Tool:** Lesson Study, **Version 01**

# PROTOCOL TOOL

Use the protocol tool **Reviewing and Analyzing Student Work (30)** to standardize the process of reviewing student work as a small group and ensure that teachers can make the most of their time together.

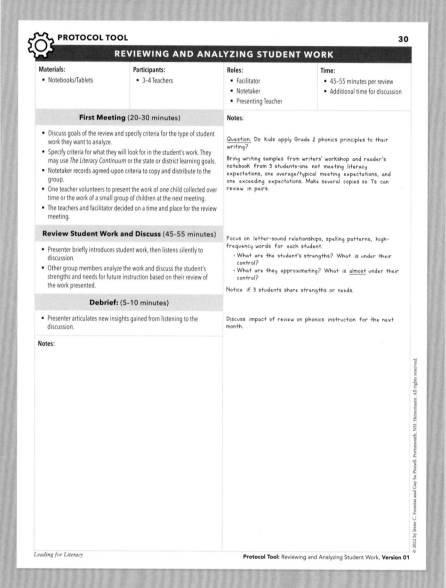

**Collaborative Review of Student Work** The collaborative analysis of student work builds teachers' deep understandings of the reading and writing process over time. When teachers participate in small groups to look at student work, they draw from their knowledge base and examine concrete evidence of the reading and writing behaviors students control, almost control, and do not yet control. And, of course, they learn from each other's insights and build collective knowledge. The collaborative process enables teachers to develop trust and confidence in the power of thinking together about their students.

Almost any kind of student work product—including the drawings and scribbles of your youngest learners—can be mined for understandings about students' literacy processing systems. Running records provide strong evidence of how readers processed and understood a text and give the teacher a window into children's actions in working through the text. For analyzing writing, consider writer's notebook entries, writing about reading in reader's notebooks, or any other writing for a variety of purposes and in a variety of forms that teachers can collect in the classroom. The writing products will reveal evidence of craft but also will provide strong evidence of how children control conventions of writing such as grammar, punctuation, capitalization, and spelling. Their spelling attempts are a powerful window into the letter-sound relationships they control.

There are a variety of ways to engage a group of teachers in looking at student work. We share one example in the protocol here, but teachers will find ways to adapt it for their specific goals. The process can be repeated with different teachers bringing the work and varying the type of evidence they bring. The goal is to think together and develop a lens for looking at the strengths and needs of learners using concrete evidence. All participants benefit by gaining multiple perspectives.

**Professional Book Clubs** Many of you have experienced the pleasure of thinking and talking about a wonderful book with friends. Your memories likely include a comfortable environment for sharing and risk-taking, and of course some enjoyable snacks. Your book club experience likely moved you from a solitary experience and interpretation to a rich discourse that brought multiple interpretations and deeper messages as they were filtered through the personal experiences and knowledge of a unique group of others. The book experience became a more memorable one as it took your thinking beyond the boundaries of yourself.

Consider the opportunities that a face-to-face or even a virtual professional book club can offer you and your colleagues. Identify a book you and others may be eager to read and create a structure to make it happen. You can grow your learning together and build a stronger collegial community in the process of expanding your collective expertise.

When you create a structure for professional book clubs, you help each other navigate new learning in a context that feels enjoyable and supportive. It becomes a form of social and professional accountability, productivity, and enjoyment. Here is a simple protocol you might want to use.

Use the protocol tool **Professional Book Clubs (31)** to provide a structure for helping teachers expand their competencies and and build a stronger collegial community in the school.

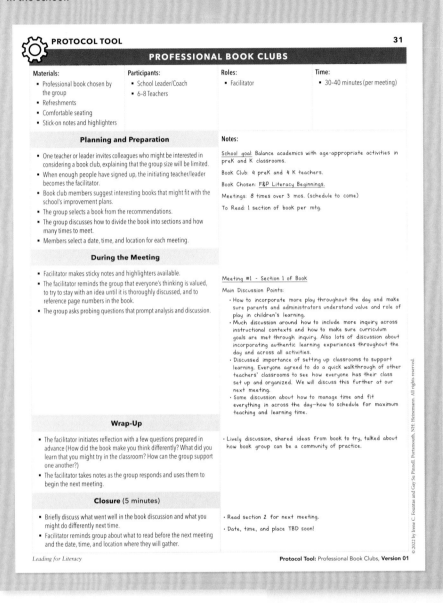

# Tools to Support Walkthroughs, Observation, and Inquiry

While you don't want to be using an obvious "checklist" every time you enter a classroom, it does help to have reminders of what to look for as you walk through or observe teaching. Below we discuss four important tools that we find to be useful for leaders.

**Observation Tools**  Throughout this book, we have provided observation tools that can be used for specific literacy instructional contexts and other purposes, for example:

- Interactive read-aloud
- Shared reading
- Guided reading
- Book clubs
- Independent reading
- Readers' workshop
- Writers' workshop
- Classroom environment
- Student talk
- Modeled, Shared, and Interactive Writing
- Guided Writing
- Independent Writing

Observation tools can be used to help you notice the organization and provisioning of the physical environment, the level of student talk in the classroom, the effectiveness of preparation, and precision in teaching language and also to help the teacher reflect on a lesson or notice literacy behaviors. These observation tools also can be reviewed when you plan a classroom visit; they will help to focus your observation and remind you of characteristics you might forget. They can also be used to help you reflect on what you have just seen. Coaches may make use of the same documents, and as they grow more experienced, teachers can use them for peer coaching or self-reflection.

**Rubrics**  An observation or self-reflection document simply prompts the observer or the teacher to determine whether an important characteristic is present. A rubric, on the other hand, requires a judgment about *the extent* to which it is present. Rubrics present specific descriptions of the presence of characteristics that range from 0 (meaning something like "not present" or "limited") to a higher number like 4, 5, or 6 (describing progress along the way to "fully present"). A descriptive sentence or two is placed under each number.

These specific indicators are useful because they allow you to detect progress. Rather than feeling inadequate because they are so far from "perfect,"

An observation tool helps focus the observation and reminds both the teacher and the leader/coach of areas to discuss later.

**Assuming Coherence** As you think deeply about the essential elements of the educational system, consider the critical role of teacher expertise as it influences student outcomes. Think of the guarantee you can offer families when the quality of literacy opportunities in each classroom, at each grade level, and in each school are the same. The key arbiter of coherence will be the direction and quality of the ongoing professional learning you offer year after year as you build a system of high-performing schools with highly expert teachers who work together on behalf of all the children.

You may need to think out of the box and involve both school leaders and teachers in short- and long-term planning. Work with the union representatives to be innovative in the ways you grow leaders. Be sure to address the time required for professional learning. Identify multiple prongs for collaborative learning by the educators and solicit feedback on the usefulness of the learning and its impact on their students.

You and your team play an important role in looking at how the data can inform the goals of the variety of professional learning activities. The effects of professional learning need to be evident in student outcomes. When you share the inquiry with a broader group you will be able to count on their commitment and shared ownership of the outcomes.

you have concrete evidence as to how teachers are becoming more and more knowledgeable and skilled. You can construct several rubrics that range from "getting started," to much more advanced. The idea is to refine and hone teaching skills over time. While this is important as a goal of supervision, you can encourage teachers to take matters into their own hands. They can use both beginning and advanced rubrics as tools for self-reflection or to discuss in a peer problem-solving group. Rubrics make expectations crystal clear.

There are many generic rubrics that examine various aspects of teaching at a broad, far look. For example, they might help you look at teacher/student interactions or at preparation and execution. We prefer to use rubrics that include specific details, often related to the instructional context. We don't want these rubrics to be so detailed that they overwhelm the supervisor, coach, or teachers, but they should be specific enough that everyone can zoom in on specific goals. With a detailed rubric that has several categories, we suggest teachers and supervisors identify only one category or section of the rubric to work on and discuss. When you and your colleagues develop or use an existing rubric or one you create, you are committing to the criteria for what is effective.

**Protocols** To encourage greater engagement and efficiency at meetings or in a variety of learning sessions, consider using protocols. A protocol is a guide for engagement, and it can be very simple. We have included protocols throughout this chapter as examples of how to engage a variety of team members in efficient, productive learning. When groups use simple protocols such as these,

## PROTOCOL TOOL

use the protocol tool **Working Through a Problem of Practice (32)** with a small group of teachers as they help a colleague understand and address a problem or dilemma in the classroom.

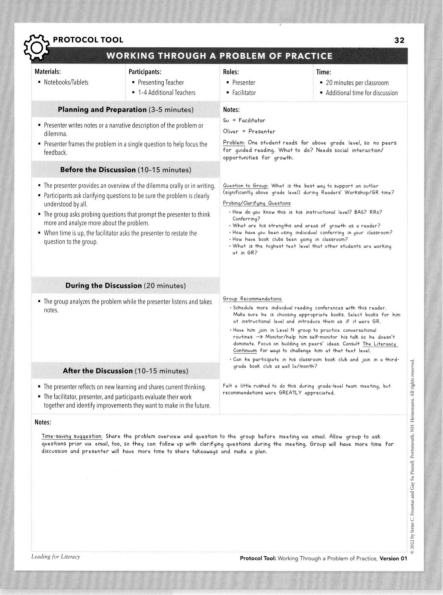

they can work more efficiently and productively than without them. Consider how you might use these structures in your faculty meetings or in professional learning sessions. A caution: protocols that are overused or used in a rigid way can make meetings feel like rote routines and can discourage dialogue.

At left you will find a sample protocol. This one is based on consultancy protocols developed by Dunne, Evans, and Thompson-Grove as part of their work at the Coalition for Essential Schools and the Annenberg Institute for School Reform.

The purpose is to engage practitioners in identifying and articulating a problem or dilemma they are struggling with related to their teaching and student learning. It provides a consistent way for a small group of colleagues to help each other understand a problem or dilemma and think constructively about how to address it.

In advance of the discussion with colleagues it's helpful for the presenting teacher to think about why the problem or dilemma exists, why it feels important that it be addressed, and what has already been done to address the problem.

***The Literacy Continuum*** We have described this powerful tool in detail in Chapter 9. School leaders use it as a means for putting their vision of literacy competence into detailed descriptions that they can apply to their students. Using *The Literacy Continuum* places a "third eye" into your conversation with a teacher and is of invaluable assistance in keeping the focus on learning.

# New Formats for Today's Teachers

Not every professional learning opportunity needs to be formal and carefully structured. Your plan for professional learning should include plenty of other options, including short, focused bursts of professional learning that we call "bite-sized" learning. Sometimes a small but intense learning moment comes out of the blue during an informal conversation between two or more teachers that only lasts a few minutes. Others, like Circle Time for Grown-Ups (see below), can be used at the beginning and end of faculty meetings or as part of professional learning sessions.

Online experiences, social media, and apps offer a great variety of possibilities for short, bite-sized professional learning. For example, a teacher who has found a particularly helpful video of a guided reading lesson might decide to share it with grade-level peers over lunch in the faculty room. Or a school leader might do a quick video call with a small group of colleagues to report on a particularly interesting conversation with a group of students before everyone heads for home. And whole schools can connect with one another for a short time each week via technology. We know of a group of literacy coaches from different schools in the same district who were working together toward

Teachers' expertise expands when they work together to identify goals and plan their teaching.

---

## CIRCLE TIME FOR GROWN-UPS

If you were to visit a school in New Zealand, at some point you probably you would see the school leaders and a group of teachers gathered in a circle of chairs for midmorning tea and discussion while someone else tended to the children outside in the play yard for recess. The circle meeting is a great communication tool that supports collaboration about professional issues, and we have used it with much success in professional learning. Here are some things to know about this practice:

- There are no empty chairs or breaks in the circle: the teachers and leaders sit shoulder to shoulder as colleagues.
- No one is tempted to slip off-task to look through materials or fiddle with technology. All participants are focused on each other.
- Participants can see and hear each other to communicate effectively.
- Participants look at each other to talk instead of facing only the person who is running the meeting.
- The people can turn and talk in pairs or threes for a quick chat and then talk again as a whole group. This allows everyone to share their thinking in a meeting.

A professional learning session may begin in the circle to set a frame for the session, and then teachers can move to tables for inquiry work. At the end of the session, you can reconvene in the circle for sharing and closure.

---

## PERILOUS POWERPOINTS

PowerPoint slides have many advantages in professional learning sessions. We have heard from leaders that the slides help organize their thinking and ensure that they stay on topic and don't forget to say something important. PowerPoint is also a great medium for displaying graphics or other images. And today, even virtual PowerPoint sessions can be more dynamic through new tools that make interaction easier. You can even use the application to poll the meeting participants.

But like the overhead projector and piles of transparencies that may be gathering dust in your school's supply closet, PowerPoint presentations are linear and "set." And it's not easy to shift topics in response to what you might be sensing about the group's needs.

We're not saying you should never use PowerPoint slides. Just be sure to build in breaks for other types of learning, especially group inquiry and collaboration. And bear in mind that too many slides with too much print on them can tempt a presenter to simply read the slides instead of engaging the group in an interactive discussion.

particular goals in coaching. They decided they would "huddle" every Friday, late in the afternoon for 30 minutes, usually by phone so people could share their thinking and progress from home or on the way there.

Blogs, podcasts, and social networking chats also help educators connect with other professional learning communities and receive immediate advice or confirmation anytime, anywhere. These just-in-time, bite-sized professional learning opportunities keep educators thinking and learning together between the scheduled and more structured professional learning opportunities that are available. Guskey (2017) reminds us that "the time and energy teachers invest is too valuable to waste on efforts supported *only* by blogs, twitter chats, or the opinions of charismatic consultants."

There will always be a need for small groups and the whole team to meet in face-to-face professional learning sessions, but these experiences can be augmented by the use of quick meetings and digital tools. School leaders should take advantage of the opportunities that are available. We've discussed many of those opportunities already, but here are a few more you might want to try:

- Reimagined faculty meetings that focus on student learning and teacher inquiry, for example, "flipped" meetings in which educators read or watch content and then attend a meeting live (in person or remotely) to discuss and explore issues collaboratively.
- Brief videos of teachers working with students in the classroom for coaching and self-reflection.

Professional learning moments like this one can happen anywhere and anytime colleagues connect.

- Circle meetings with no barriers between them to engage in dialogue about an issue (see page 393).

- Brown bag lunches to share effective practices.

- Regularly scheduled grade-level meetings on assessment data.

- Spontaneous peer coaching sessions between teachers on specific areas of practice.

- Professional book club discussions (see page 389).

- Children's literature book discussions.

- Peer classroom visits.

- Blogs, webinars, podcasts, short huddles.

- Spontaneous co-constructed meetings in which teachers take the initiative and lead the meetings.

## VIDEO VIGNETTES

During the pandemic, most teachers became more comfortable with using video content in lessons, projects, and homework assignments. And most professional learning experiences occurred through videoconferencing apps and PowerPoint. Now that you're back in the building, you can use that sophisticated video camera in your pocket to improve teaching and learning in the school. Here are just a few of the exciting ways that teachers, school leaders, and coaches are bringing the power of video to professional learning.

- **Embedded video:** Even the dullest PowerPoint presentation comes to life when short videos showing real teaching are embedded in slides.

- **Video coaching sessions:** Coaches can quickly share videos captured during classroom observations to remind teachers of best practices.

- **Pre-session viewing:** Teachers can view and think about video content prior to in-person professional learning sessions. Videos might demonstrate effective interactive read-alouds, show a few different teachers conferring with students, or highlight a particularly strong phonics or word study lesson.

- **Students' oral reading:** Teachers can make short videos of students' oral reading at different times during the year to provide a record of improvement or difficulty that can be reviewed and discussed with the coach.

- **Best-practice libraries:** There are plenty of excellent public-domain teaching videos available for download online, but why not build a library of the examples of powerful teaching and effective lessons happening in your own school? This is not a small project, but it will pay off in teachers' on-demand access to models of effective practice.

# Evaluating Professional Learning

The goals of professional learning are intertwined: to change educator practice and improve student learning. It stands to reason, then, that effective professional learning should include an evaluation of whether those goals were met. There are multiple ways to find out, and all of them start with good questions.

Perhaps the biggest question is: *Does professional learning make a difference?* To find the answer, Guskey (2002) proposes five levels of evaluation, which we have paraphrased below. The kind of evaluation presented here and in Figure 20-5 is designed to answer deep questions about the effectiveness of professional learning based on systematic studies of teachers' behaviors in the classroom and analysis of student outcomes over time. It is an important and complex process that should be part of every school or district improvement plan. The process begins with feedback on the professional learning experience from the people who actually experienced it. Every form of professional learning should include feedback from participants that is directly related to the intended outcomes. If the response is negative, then effective growth or change is not likely to occur.

## Level One: Participants' Immediate Reactions

The goal at this level of evaluation is to solicit immediate feedback on participant satisfaction. The quickest way to collect evidence of satisfaction—or dissatisfaction—is with a simple questionnaire distributed at the end of the session. You probably have filled out dozens of questionnaires like these, and you may have dismissed them as useless or annoying. But if you think of the participant survey in the context of the deeper efficacy study, you will see it as a first-line tool for soliciting the kind of information you can use immediately to improve the very next professional learning experience. Here are just some of the questions you might ask:

- What was enjoyable about the session?
- How well presented was the information? Did it make sense to you?
- What did the presenter do to hold your attention?
- What are the key understandings you will take from this professional learning experience?
- How will the information be useful in the classroom?
- How will you use the information from this session to improve outcomes for your students?
- What are priority topics for your future professional learning?
- How comfortable was the room temperature?
- What changes would you make to the refreshments that were offered?
- How can we improve upon today's professional learning opportunity?
- Please provide any other comments or feedback.

## Level Two: Participants' Learning

This level is all about the learning, and a simple questionnaire won't do the job. You need to measure whether participants have met the specific learning goals. Naturally, that process begins with clearly articulated goals developed during the planning stage. You'll also need a set of indicators you can use to evaluate whether those goals have been met. Some districts rely on paper-and-pencil assessments, and others prefer a more open-ended approach in which teachers are asked to briefly describe (orally or in writing) the understandings they took from the session. If you solicit this information soon after the professional learning experience, you can use it to clear up misunderstandings before teachers begin to apply the new learning in classrooms.

## Level Three: Organizational Support of Participants' Learning

If you are serious about professional learning and encouraging teachers to take on new ideas, then you will need to offer the support and resources they need to apply new knowledge.

Be sure that organizational structures, goals, values, policies, resources, and procedures at the school support all aspects of the professional learning plan. This can't be left to chance. You'll need to ask and answers important questions such as those below.

- Will educators have the physical materials they'll need to change or improve specific practices?
- Do the changes align with the school's and district's values and improvement plans?
- How will successes in individual classrooms be shared and celebrated?
- How will you know you are making progress toward your goals?
- What problem-solving structures are in place?

It may be helpful to think of even a single professional learning experience as a change process you are setting in motion. You need to be sure that changes you'd like to see at the classroom level will be supported, not undermined, at the organization level.

## Level Four: Participants' Application of New Learning

At level four, you endeavor to gain information about how well and to what degree teachers are applying what they learned to their classroom practice. Examining the degree and quality of implementation can leave you with a great deal of information about the effectiveness of the professional learning session(s).

Let enough time pass after the learning experience for teachers to have implemented their new understandings and skills and worked out the inevitable kinks. Then you can begin the evaluation procedures, which may take many forms, including more detailed questionnaires, interviews with participants and the coach or supervisor, oral or written reflections from participants, and classroom observations.

Remember that although this level focuses on teachers in classrooms, you will be using the evidence gathered to determine the effectiveness of the *professional learning experience(s)*, not the teachers. Look for patterns of teacher behaviors across the classrooms, which can help you determine specific areas of learning that did not take hold. These are signs that a specific part of the professional learning experience may have been weak or unclear.

## Level Five: Impact on Student Outcomes

It's not possible to isolate the effects of individual professional learning activities on student outcomes. There are just too many other variables at work. But it *is* possible to collect multiple types of evidence that, together, can support a conclusion about the overall effectiveness of professional learning. A lot of that evidence will be the information you gathered at levels 2, 3, and 4. But it's important that you and your colleagues consider the complexity of level 5 evaluation. If it is based only on test scores you won't have a full understanding of what's moving the needle. And you won't have all the information you'll need to improve your school's plan for professional learning or the effectiveness of individual experiences.

There are many ways to collect evidence at level 5. Guskey suggests looking at school and student records; structured interviews with students, parents, teachers, and administrators; teacher performance portfolios; and in-depth questionnaires. You'll also want to consider how improved teaching may be influencing students' physical and emotional well-being, their confidence as learners, and their daily attendance at school. All of this information can contribute to your understanding of how professional learning is affecting students.

### EVALUATION OF PROFESSIONAL LEARNING

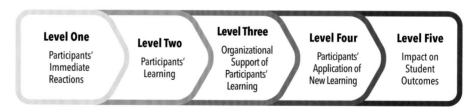

**Figure 20-5.** Five Levels of Professional Learning Evaluation

# The Takeaway

At a time when so much rests on the expertise of classroom teachers, school leaders need to be open to new ways of engaging them as active adult learners. There will always be a need for structured face-to-face sessions, but today's teachers also need frequent opportunities to learn through formats that mirror the ways they have become accustomed to consuming, using, and applying information outside of school.

In the next chapter, we move to a different type of professional learning, the kind that results when teachers and instructional coaches come together to review student outcomes and adjust instructional practice to achieve better results.

## Think About Your School

- Does the school have a professional learning plan?
- How would you describe your school's professional learning plan?
- What changes or additions are you considering after reading this chapter?
- Is there adequate organizational support for your professional learning plan? Will there be support for proposed changes or additions?

## Move Your School Forward

- Bring together a small group of colleagues to help you evaluate the current professional learning plan against the hallmarks of effective professional learning outlined in this chapter.
- Reach out to the district technology team to learn what supports are available as you work to bring more tech-based professional learning opportunities to the school.
- Download the protocols found in the online resources for this chapter and distribute copies to teachers and other leaders as appropriate. Make a plan to implement some of the processes.

# Chapter 21

# Expanding Literacy Expertise Through Responsive Coaching

> *No matter how well-prepared people are in their formative years, few can achieve and maintain their best performance on their own. . . . Coaching done well may be the most effective intervention designed for human performance.*
> —Atul Gawande MD, MPH

IN THE LAST FEW decades, instructional coaches have been placed in elementary schools to help teachers become increasingly proficient at teaching. Many of these coaches focus on literacy teaching, although many others are generalists. In reality, the coach's duties and role can vary widely. Some supervise the implementation of a curriculum or a set of standards. Others act as helpful colleagues who engage individual teachers and small groups in the analysis of teaching. Still others find themselves assisting the principal in a variety of tasks, only some of which involve coaching. Some are part-time and some are full-time. Some are school-based and others are sent out from the central office. Some schools do not have a specific coach but are working toward that goal; still others provide time for more experienced and effective teachers to coach others.

In this chapter, we discuss the powerful role that coaches can play in supporting the professional learning of teachers and sustaining school improvement through responsive coaching. We present a rationale for making a coach a key member of the school team, revisit the qualities of effective coaches and teacher leaders, explain what coaches need to know and conditions that support coaching, and describe the roles and partnerships of coaches with the school-based principal. The information is relevant for all school leaders, with important application for principals who budget and hire for coaching positions. The final sections in this chapter focus on important nuts and bolts of coaching: the stance, skills, and language of a coach and structures and coaching moves that are effective. These sections will have particular relevance for literacy coaches and any school leader who wants to support the work and learning of coaches and teachers. But we first turn to the rationale: *Why coaches?*

## A Case for Coaches

Coaches can play a critical role in raising literacy outcomes for students. There is strong evidence to suggest that coaching as job-embedded professional learning is the key to improvement in literacy instruction. It is most powerful in individualizing professional learning and meeting the needs of a variety of teachers who are collectively responsible for literacy instruction in a school.

Several studies link coaching to teacher efficacy, teacher satisfaction, student achievement, greater use of student data, improvement in teachers' capacity to reflect on their practice, and the development of leadership across the educational system. For example, a team of researchers from the Carnegie Foundation for the Advancement of Teaching designed and implemented a randomized control group study of seventeen Literacy Collaborative schools for three years to examine the effects of their coaches on student outcomes in the primary grades. Using standardized assessments (DIBELS, Terra Nova) across the first three years of implementation, they compared student growth from fall to spring to baseline growth:

- Students in the first implementation year learned at a rate 16% faster than the students in the baseline year before Literacy Collaborative.
- Students in the second implementation year learned at a rate 28% faster than students in the baseline year.
- Students in the third implementation year learned at a rate 32% faster than students in the baseline year.

Further, the study examined the amount of coaching each teacher experienced (high coaching, medium coaching, or low coaching) across nine observation periods. The researchers used rubrics to observe and evaluate the level of

**Don't Just Hire Coaches** Creating coaching positions is simply not enough. In fact, it may be a poor use of the system's limited salary budget if the coaches occupy teacher time without impact. Coaching has to be more than a social structure that teachers enjoy. Data and evidence of improvement are important. Talk with your school-based leaders about the level of training and expertise that has been invested in the coaches and how they will continue their professional learning. You might also create a network of coaches in the district so they can support each other.

As a central office leader, you can support the school-based leaders in maximizing the impact of coaches on teacher expertise and student outcomes. Your strongest support is needed for policies and resources and professional learning that support the coach to develop strong expertise in several key areas. Your informed support, astute observations, and wise guidance can maximize the impact of coaches and the investment in coaches' salaries will be long lasting, and well worth it.

teachers' expertise. The study provided evidence that the more coaching a teacher received, the more improvement in teacher expertise.

A third fascinating finding was the shift in the collaborative culture in the Literacy Collaborative schools. At the beginning of the study there were several silos with little teacher collaboration or interaction with the coach. By the end of three years of implementation, there was a remarkable shift to increased collaborative communication among the teachers at each grade level and across grade levels, and the coach was at the center of communication. This and other studies point to the significant, positive effects that coaches have on teacher expertise, student outcomes, and school culture.

## Qualities of Effective Coaches and Teacher Leaders

As we noted in Chapter 18, a coach and teacher leader have many qualities in common that enable them to have a significant impact on the school and the system (Figure 21-1). The highly effective coach needs the foundational skills of excellent communication and organizational skills, skill in working with adult learners, strong leadership qualities, deep knowledge of curriculum and standards, understanding of social-emotional learning and culturally relevant and sustaining practices, as well as a deep understanding of responsive teaching. The school-based coach creates and maintains respectful, collaborative partnerships with the

### SELECTING A COACH

Your selection of a coach is a very thoughtful decision as it will impact all the teachers on the team for years to come.

#### 1. START WITH A WRITTEN JOB DESCRIPTION

Your first step is to develop a clear understanding of the role and a written job description that can provide clarity to potential candidates.

#### 2. CONSIDER THE ESSENTIAL QUALITIES

Hiring a coach is not as simple as identifying a person whom everyone likes or who is a good classroom teacher. The selection of a coach is tied to dispositions and qualities. Is the person a learner? Does he have strong communication skills? Does she value collaboration? Does he have the capacity to lead?

#### 3. CONDUCT EFFECTIVE INTERVIEWS

Involve a small team to get input, craft questions, and participate in final interviews. Listen for responses that show evidence of the qualities we described and those that show a commitment to equitable practices and a culture of collaboration and teamwork.

## QUALITIES OF EFFECTIVE COACHES AND TEACHER LEADERS

- The stance of a reflective, continuous learner
- Evidence of intellectual curiosity
- Interest in collaborative learning
- Openness to new perspectives
- A tentative and collaborative stance
- Trustworthiness
- Evidence of effective language and literacy teaching
- A strong understanding of culturally relevant teaching
- A deep understanding of the role of data-informed teaching in assuring equitable student outcomes
- Strong content knowledge, particularly in language, reading, and writing development
- Commitment to working with others to achieve social justice
- A desire to get to know and ascertain the strengths of each team member
- Acceptance of good intentions without judging
- Strong observational skills to examine teaching interactions
- A commitment to evidence-based decision-making
- Strong interpersonal and communication skills
- An ability to help others build self-efficacy
- The capacity for building trust, shared ownership, and teamwork in the school community
- A thorough understanding of the structures of school organization

**Figure 21-1.** Qualities of Effective Coaches and Teacher Leaders

teachers and the school principal and keeps the whole team's ownership of student outcomes, as evidenced by data, in the forefront. Finally, the effective coach is positioned as a learner, not the expert, and continually seeks opportunities to self-reflect and enhance his expertise.

# What Literacy Coaches Need to Know

Literacy coaches are knowledgeable but continue to be learners. They have the responsibility for learning from every interaction they have with teachers and students. The concept of co-learners goes a long way to establish trust and mutual respect.

Literacy coaches find themselves at the center of the conversations about language, reading, and writing development in the school. But their constant goal is to make the conversation wider so that teachers talk with and support each other. Their reservoir of knowledge is wide and deep; for example, they:

- Understand screening, diagnostic, and summative assessment tools.
- Are able to collect and interpret data.
- Know theory and research about the nature of the language, reading, and writing process.
- Understand the importance of literacy-rich environments in classrooms.
- Know how to listen with interest and neutrality to gain clarity.
- Know how children change over time as they become literate (a vision of progress).
- Know effective instructional practices (pedagogy).
- Recognize the different characteristics of texts.
- Are familiar with theory and research about the nature of adult learning.
- Understand the role of diversity and equity in adult and student learning.
- Interact in a respectful way with other adults.
- Know how to pose questions in a spirit of curiosity and to open possibilities.
- Carefully observe teaching interactions to identify strengths and notice effective and powerful ones that have impact on student learning.
- Can select and implement observational techniques to detect evidence of learning in students.
- Know how to observe and document teachers' progress over time.
- Communicate with clarity and sensitivity.
- Can think together with colleagues in a way that facilitates new understandings.
- Know how to make statements to clarify, provide, or restate information.
- Have an understanding of inquiry and the process of coaching.
- Possess a repertoire of facilitative language that supports adult learning.

A literacy coach needs deep content knowledge to be able to support teachers in the classroom.

Above all, the effective literacy coach takes a stance that views teachers as developing learners. The coach works to understand what teachers know and the rationales for their decisions and actions. Human beings do not act without some basis. What a teacher says and does tells you about her understandings. The coach does not expect perfection (in herself or others) but looks for evidence of growth or learning and works alongside the teacher as a fellow learner. Together, the coach and teacher engage in inquiry to seek evidence and understanding, using high-quality professional resources in the interactions that act as a "third eye" and a reference (rather than the coach being the "expert" or passing judgment). The coach avoids judgmental language like "good" because the coach is not there to tell the teacher what he did right and wrong but to help the teacher reflect and think analytically to expand knowledge and expertise. With the overall goal of helping teachers develop "learning systems," the coach supports teachers in learning from their own observations of students and analysis of their own teaching and its impact on the learner.

There are some generic or formulaic coaching formats that provide guidelines for interactions (e.g., name three positive things the teacher did and then suggest an improvement). Certain formats may be helpful at some level in some situations. But responsive coaching is more than exercises in paraphrasing, questioning, affirming, or suggesting goals. We know of one large urban district where administrators decided math scores needed strengthening. Because literacy outcomes had been improving slowly over time, the leadership team took all of the literacy coaches and made them math coaches. They thought coaching was a generic skill. The initiative didn't last long.

The most effective coaching is *context specific*. That is, the coach works with a teacher with specific reference to a domain of knowledge and its pedagogy. The literacy coach has very specific *knowledge* about literacy and how it is learned and taught. The best coaching sessions focus intensively on the learning of students in literacy—teachers and coaches are deeply immersed in expanding their own knowledge and skill. Interactions move beyond questioning and conversation to real exploration of rationales and evidence of the effects of teacher decision-making.

## Conditions That Support Impactful Coaching

If you are lucky enough to have a literacy coach in your school, do everything you can to help that person be successful in the role. Principals and other school leaders who have literacy coaches on their team consider themselves fortunate and work to create the conditions in which a literacy coach can succeed. All of the chapters in this book speak to these conditions:

- Educators at the school share a common vision.
- The feeling is communicated that "we are all responsible to help each other do a good job."
- Everyone is a member of the team, and we all work together to achieve our goals.
- Everyone is expected to take the stance of a learner—even the most experienced and expert teachers, the coach, and the principal.
- Instead of "I" and "me," educators use language that emphasizes community and collaboration, like "we," "our students," and "our values."
- Professional learning is seen as something we *get* to do rather than something we *have* to do.

In other chapters, we have emphasized that conditions like these are not built over a weekend or through playing a few team-building games together. They are created by doing some hard work together and seeing success. The payoff is great.

Like all teachers, coaches need the support of professional learning. They need to go further in their understanding of literacy learning but also to understand adult learning and approaches to coaching. Too often, coaches are "appointed" rather than developed. There is an assumption that just being a good teacher is enough qualification to be a coach, and that is simply not true. Even highly expert literacy teachers of children find coaching of adults challenging, and some experience a feeling of failure in the role. The principal can make the difference in the coach's success through a strong partnership and opportunities for professional learning as a coach.

School leaders, including the coach, the principal, and others, play key roles in establishing the school as a learning community. They lead by example because everyone in the school is engaged in professional learning and everyone is coached—even the coach! They work on schedules and space to assure that colleagues have the opportunity to talk with each other and receive coaching. They place value on building relationships and trust. They generate and clearly communicate the core values and vision of the school team and clarify the coach's role within it. The coach is vested with responsibility and trust.

## The Role of Literacy Coach

Every one of us would benefit from working with a coach who can help us achieve our personal best. If you are fortunate enough to have a full-time or part-time coach in your school, consider the many dimensions of the role and how to maximize impact. The coach's role is not to be the implementation police or the fixer of teachers. Instead the coach is a thought partner who brings another set of eyes and ears to collaborate with colleagues and promote their confidence, risk-taking, agency, and pursuit of continuous learning. The coach is a valued member of the school team with a particular role and ideally a person who has had the opportunity for specialized training in working with adult learners.

Of course you may use a different label: instructional coach, literacy leader, and so on. Realizing that there is a need to expand professional expertise in literacy, many schools are currently looking for ways to shift the role of the reading or literacy specialist in the school to take on some responsibilities for coaching and providing other professional development support. Some schools are developing teacher leaders with hopes of moving them into coaching roles in the future (see Chapter 18).

## The Multiple Roles of Coaches

School-based specialized literacy professionals, including coaches and teacher leaders, need to be nimble, making quick adjustments in their role to meet the ongoing needs of students and teachers. As a coach or other literacy educator, you know that you have to juggle multiple responsibilities, often within a single day. The multiple roles of literacy coaches fall into several broad categories (Figure 21-2). An individual who is expected to fill all of the roles inevitably feels some tension, as described in the last column.

We believe that principals must be very careful to protect the role of the coach, with priority placed on the coach's working individually and in groups with teachers and spending enough time with children to maintain credibility and expand teaching skills. Having a deep understanding of the coaching role helps the knowledgeable principal resist assigning non-coaching responsibilities.

It is important that the literacy coach is seen as a key member of the staff but not the "owner" of the program or the initiative. If teachers believe any new initiative belongs only to the coach (or the coach and principal), it is doomed from the start. The coach must be seen as a person who has been granted responsibility to do some work and gain some expertise that will help everyone achieve their shared vision.

## Getting the Role Description in Writing

We counsel prospective coaches not to accept the position of coach unless there is a job description with clear expectations, details about the role, and a scope of responsibilities *in writing*. When the description of the position is thoughtfully written, the school leaders and teachers are clear on the parameters and trust is built. It also enables the coach to refer back to the description when pulled into assignments that are not in the role and do not involve coaching. In urgent situations, people may move out of their assigned roles to do what has to be done. But in general, the job description of a coach needs to specify a high priority for working with teachers.

It needs to be clear in the description of the coach that the coach will provide coaching to all members of the team. No one can opt out or it diminishes the belief that everyone on the team needs to work on their expertise every year. Even the teacher who says "I'm retiring soon" needs to be coached because children are in that class now. All teachers can learn, and as McKay (2012) said, "You don't have to be a bad teacher to get better."

## Communicating the Role of the Coach to Teachers

A clear description of the role of coach helps both teachers and coaches know what to expect. The coach-teacher relationship is built on trust. In our experience, a supervisory role works against the coach's ability to gain the trust of

## MULTIPLE ROLES OF LITERACY COACHES

| ROLES OF COACHES | REASON FOR THE ROLE | POTENTIAL TENSION |
|---|---|---|
| **Teaching Students** | Even full-time literacy coaches also find time to work with students so that they can continue to hone their own skills and maintain credibility with the staff. Some coaches support teachers for about half of the day and go into classrooms to teach for several weeks at a time or provide service to small groups of students the other part of their day. | A coach may struggle to constantly change focus— from teaching children to skilled coaching of teachers. |
| **Coaching Teachers** | It is essential for coaches to work alongside teachers in an intensive way, and that means going into the classroom on a regular basis. Even highly expert and experienced teachers require this kind of support to continually grow. | It is difficult for coaches to juggle the schedule so that time can be reserved for coaching every teacher. In addition, sometimes the coach struggles to generate enough trust to receive a welcome in classrooms. |
| **Coordinating and Communicating** | When events are planned or communication is an issue, it is natural to rely on the coach to act as the organizer or "go between." The coach often runs meetings or provides informative sessions for all the teachers. | Coaches may feel pulled in many directions at once and find it difficult to find enough hours in the day. Sometimes they are involved in minutiae that leave them less time to spend on individual coaching and working with students. |
| **Coordinating Professional Resources** | The coach often brings valuable expertise to the acquisition and organization of professional resources. That means not only the professional tools that teachers use but the rich text base that is essential for implementing an effective literacy system (described in Section 5). The coach can also advise how to organize and share texts and writing materials. | Coaches may be perceived to be the "keeper" of the book room instead of sharing the responsibility with the team. |
| **Partnering with the Principal** | Most principals find the coach to be an extremely valuable partner and resource. In their busy jobs, it's very helpful to have a partner to support improvement in student literacy outcomes. | It is very tempting for the principal to consume a great deal of the coach's time. The coach is often sent to serve on district committees and sometimes represents the school when the principal is unavailable. Because of these tempting assignments, the principal can make it hard for the coach to have time for actual coaching. Too often the coach does not spend most of the time coaching! |

**Figure 21-2.** Multiple Roles of Literacy Coaches

the teacher. The coach is a very important resource for the principal but is not an evaluator. When it is clear the coach is a trusted colleague and a thought partner, teachers are more willing to take risks, share challenges, problem solve, and show vulnerability as they refine their craft.

We suggest that the coach call for a short beginning-of-the-year meeting, with the team sitting in a circle with coffee and refreshments available upon entry. The coach welcomes the team, revisits the school values and beliefs about literacy teaching and learning, reiterates (or introduces if the coach is new) his understanding of the coaching role, and identifies the team's priorities for professional learning based on the data and teacher input. It is a good time to recenter the group's collaborative professional goals, remind and encourage teachers to try to be flexible in scheduling coaching sessions, and answer any and all questions on people's minds. This meeting is effective in fostering a team effort and assuring all are on the same page.

# Coaching Partnerships

Many schools are caught in a command-and-control, bureaucratic culture that makes it difficult to slow things down so teachers and administrators can think and learn together (West 2017). In a collaborative culture, coaches nurture partnerships that influence their thinking and strengthen the learning outcomes of adults in the school.

## Principal and Coach as Partners

The coach and principal work together to clear space for the teachers to learn together. They form a mutual relationship built on a clear foundation of each other's values, beliefs, goals, and understanding of the role of the teachers, the coach, and the principal. They align their understandings of effective instruction and evidence of student learning. The coach and principal collaborate to support the development of expertise in the school and monitor the evidence of student learning. In partnership with the school principal, the coach plays an essential leadership role in facilitating professional learning opportunities that result in improved student outcomes.

Behind every successful coach is a supportive principal. Communication is essential. Both the principal and the coach are informed about schoolwide conditions that affect teachers, and they help each other understand conditions, problems, and progress.

We suggest that coaches and principals have a regularly scheduled meeting on the calendar every two weeks or perhaps monthly so there is regular communication and collaboration about the school goals. The coach keeps the principal updated on progress toward literacy goals, plans for future professional learning, the priorities the teachers are working on, the trends in data, resources needed, and policies that need revisiting. The coach prepares an agenda for each meeting with the input of teachers and sends the agenda to the principal, who can add items. The coach takes notes during the meeting and shares the discussion with the teachers to keep them informed. In essence the meeting is the coach representing the teacher team and problem-solving with the principal as needed. Though the coach shares the kind of work the team is prioritizing in professional development, no teacher names are ever discussed or implied without the permission of the teacher. Since coaching is built on trusting relationships, the teachers need to be able to take risks and rely on confidentiality.

## The Coach-Teacher Relationship

Every teacher needs to feel that the coach has confidence in her ability to grow as a professional and will provide every bit of support to assure success. Just as a teacher would not give up on students, a coach needs to be a relentless supporter of the teacher's growth. You can't teach or coach anyone you think is incompetent. Of course, it will also be important for the teacher being coached to demonstrate a vested interest in refining her craft. As we discussed earlier, the culture of the school will be an important factor in the attitude of the teachers toward opportunities for professional growth.

Successful coaches work hard to build strong relationships with teachers.

Coaching is a relationship. It can be productive, even enjoyable. After all, people thrive when others take their work seriously. But both parties need to work at the coaching. For the development of a trusting relationship, the coach shows grace, humility, sincerity, empathy, and skill. The coach sees the goal of the relationship as developing mutual understanding with the teacher as the judge of the outcome.

The coach and teachers hold each other accountable for face-to-face discussion of any problems or concerns about the relationship. In every professional learning opportunity, including individual or small-group coaching, the coach invites feedback on how it went. In the beginning-of-the-year meeting, it is a good idea for the coach to remind colleagues that if they have concerns about their learning opportunities, they should voice them in the group or privately with the coach so the concerns can be addressed.

## A Coaching Stance

In the remaining sections of this chapter, we speak directly to coaches and teacher leaders, though the information will be edifying for any school leader who supports teacher development. We offer specific information and support related to your stance, levels of support, and practices to help you form collaborative and trusting relationships with teachers that lead to learning and growth.

Your stance as a coach is a critical factor in shaping the teacher-coach relationship. In general, taking a coaching stance means moving away from top-down distribution of information to a collaborative learning relationship (Figure 21-3).

It is true that with teachers who are very new to any process, some of the basics must be established. You would not leave a teacher to flounder around trying to discover everything for herself. Here's where mentorship can play an important role. More experienced teachers can help newcomers with basic procedures and organization, and often, in the process, learn more themselves. Make it clear that orienting new teachers and helping them build strong classroom learning communities is a grade-level priority and responsibility that you and the more experienced teachers share. As noted in Chapter 3, a spirit of

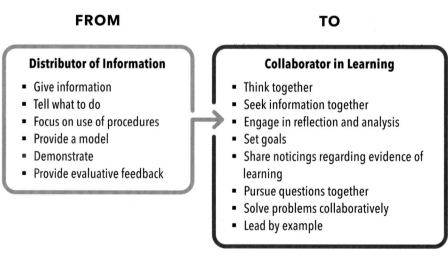

| **FROM** | **TO** |
| --- | --- |
| **Distributor of Information** | **Collaborator in Learning** |
| <ul><li>Give information</li><li>Tell what to do</li><li>Focus on use of procedures</li><li>Provide a model</li><li>Demonstrate</li><li>Provide evaluative feedback</li></ul> | <ul><li>Think together</li><li>Seek information together</li><li>Engage in reflection and analysis</li><li>Set goals</li><li>Share noticings regarding evidence of learning</li><li>Pursue questions together</li><li>Solve problems collaboratively</li><li>Lead by example</li></ul> |

**Figure 21-3.** Moving Toward Collaborative Learning

"our children" or "our students" makes this a moral imperative. The better the teaching in every classroom, the better the outcomes for all students.

Coaching is not about fixing the lesson, fixing the teacher, judging, or telling the teacher what to do. Coaching is about using today's shared example to think forward. As a coach, you help colleagues see where they are in their thinking, articulate where they want to be, and develop a plan to get there. It is important that every coaching interaction is pitched at the "learning together" level. You are a thought partner. When you consult with a teacher, your stance

## FOUR KEY FACILITATIVE COACHING MOVES TO INTERNALIZE

As a school leader/coach, you need to create a learning environment that is emotionally, intellectually, and physically safe for learners. Be aware of your language, your tone, and your body language in your interactions with teachers. Your overall goal in productive conversations is to promote teacher agency and independence. Keep in mind these four key language moves (Figure 21-4), and practice until they become very natural for you. Remember that simply pausing and giving wait time is space for a teacher to think.

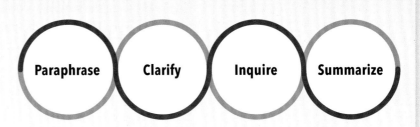

Figure 21-4 Four Key Facilitative Coaching Moves

1. **Paraphrase** by restating the comment in your own words. You will show you are listening carefully and understand what was said. Examples:

   *In other words, . . .*

   *From what I hear you saying . . .*

   *So, you are saying . . .*

   *You seem to be concerned about . . .*

2. **Clarify** by making a comment or asking a question to check your understanding when you might not have fully understood what was said. You will gather more information and learn more about the teacher's thinking. Examples:

   *So are you saying . . . ?*

   *What do you mean by . . . ?*

   *Let me check my understanding . . .*

   *Talk more about . . .*

3. **Inquire** by asking a question that opens thinking through the collaborative exploration of information and ideas grounded in behavioral evidence. You invite the teacher to think in new ways by hypothesizing and analyzing the effects of teaching decisions and calling for analysis and problem-solving. You might also collaboratively consult resources that offer useful information or insights. Examples:

   *What were you thinking when . . . ?*

   *What do you think would happen if . . . ?*

   *How did you decide . . . ?*

   *Talk about another way you might . . .*

   *What would it look like if . . . ?*

   *What might happen if you . . . ?*

   *Is it possible that . . . ?*

   *What was your thinking about . . . ?*

   *Why do you think . . . ?*

4. **Summarize** by identifying the big ideas or insights and next steps. You confirm the shared understandings and priorities for next steps from the conversation and promote reflection. Examples:

   *So, what do you think are the big important ideas from our conversation?*

   *Let's quickly review the important ideas together from our talk.*

   *You indicated that your next priorities are . . .*

requires more listening than telling. It means bringing the individual into the interaction to make decisions and seek solutions. Each time individuals make a decision and analyze its impact, understanding expands. They increase their ability to problem solve, seek help, and take action.

# Levels of Coaching Support

Within any instructional context for literacy, your coaching offers an appropriate level of support so that the teacher can observe more precisely and make more effective decisions within the act of teaching. Always notice the teacher's strengths and seek to understand the teacher's depth of knowledge of literacy content (e.g., the reading process, the writing process) and instructional practice that is responsive to the particular children. While the stance is always "learning together," your level of support is adjusted to the teacher's needs.

## Establishing the Basics

Seek to gain information and support the teacher in getting some basics in place. Such basics might include:

- Assembling a set of organized, high-quality instructional materials.
- Creating a strong, inclusive classroom community.
- Designing a well-organized classroom that supports student independence.
- Knowing how to carefully observe reading, writing, and language behaviors.
- Conducting literacy assessments.
- Providing opportunities to hear the rationales for each instructional context.
- Knowing the instructional routines related to the instructional context.
- Providing opportunities to see demonstrations of the instructional procedure (often through video clips).
- Providing opportunities to try out the instructional procedure, even in a simplified way.
- Providing opportunities to ask questions and get support from others.

All the above are important and you may take the lead in providing this basic support. But once the basics are in place and the routines are established, then your coaching can support the teacher in moving to a new level of understanding.

The basics are not trivial and may take months to establish. Also, with an entirely new approach to literacy instruction, there may be several contexts, each of which has its own basics. The first year may actually be devoted simply to putting the system in place so that it is recognizable. Teachers need maximum support during this time; however, experienced literacy teachers have much to bring to the learning process, and they can help each other.

## Coaching for Shifts in Reading and Writing Behaviors

Even during the beginning phase of implementation, your focus is not solely on the mechanics of teacher actions. As the coach, you can help to establish responsive teaching from the start by focusing conversations on careful observations of student behaviors and evidence of learning. A beginning step might be an assessment system that features analysis of reading and writing behaviors along with a move to specific instructional implications. It helps to introduce teachers to tools like *The Literacy Continuum* and the Fountas and Pinnell Prompting Guides that provide concrete help.

An important part of coaching is helping the teacher connect student behaviors to teaching decisions.

Your role is to help the teacher make connections between observable student behaviors and her own teaching decisions. Responsive teaching means basing decisions on the analysis of student behaviors so that the teacher is assisting the student to work in the "zone" and make shifts in learning. In our experience, teachers can begin to implement instructional procedures fairly quickly after the basics have been established. Then, the coach has the opportunity to corner the conversation by discussing rationales and evidence of student understanding (observation and artifacts). In our view, this focus is more important than making the procedures of the lesson perfect. In this way, teachers begin to see the relationship between their own teaching decisions and that of the students. They become more aware of their language and teaching decisions and how they influence learning.

## Coaching for Analysis and Reflection

When working with experienced teachers, the conversation is seldom at a procedural level, although the teacher can make refinements in technique at any time. Your goal is to help the teacher self-reflect and analyze the progress of each student in a way that moves into planning and decision-making. The cycle becomes automatic as the teacher establishes a continuous process that moves from (1) assessment and observation of reading, writing, and language behaviors, to (2) analysis of the students' control of strategic actions, to (3) planning effective teaching moves, to (4) taking action to notice, teach for, and support specific behaviors and understandings, to (5) reflecting on the teaching and learning (Figure 21-5).

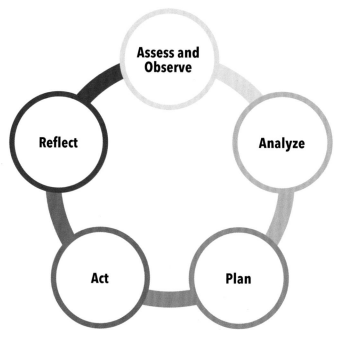

**Figure 21-5.** Responsive Teaching Cycle

# Responsive Coaching Practices That Promote Learning, Inquiry, and Reflection

Responsive coaching means gathering information about the teacher's current theoretical and practical understandings and then shaping the coaching conversation in a way that supports the teacher's ability to think in new ways about teaching and learning. You draw upon an inquiry-based process for coaching, select from a repertoire of coaching moves, and use language that generates reflection and problem-solving, lifts understanding, and promotes learning.

## Coaching Structures

You may provide coaching to individual teachers or small groups of teachers as part of the school's design for professional learning (Figure 21-6). Each coaching structure has its own special impact. Whole-group professional learning sessions with the entire school team create a growing knowledge base that you can draw upon during individual and small group sessions. And while coaching individual teachers and small groups of teachers, you will notice patterns of strengths and needs that inform the content of whole-group sessions. All professional learning and coaching structures have the same goal: to promote a culture of learning, inquiry, and reflection to improve the literacy outcomes of all the students.

**Individual Coaching:** In this structure, you work with one teacher in her classroom. One-on-one coaching usually has the most impact in helping teach-

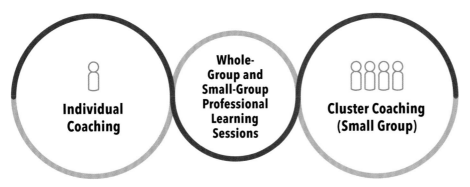

**Figure 21-6.** Coaching Structures in the School's Design for Professional Learning

ers make shifts. Often, teachers will ask the coach to "demonstrate." You can make a decision to demonstrate, but think about it carefully. Like most people, teachers learn more by doing than by imitating. This process may have the unintended result of setting you up as a model, with the teacher avoiding being observed. Further, you cannot be as effective with students that you do not know so the demonstration becomes very procedural. It's helpful to create enough trust (and help the teacher plan) so that lessons can be observed, and you and the teacher can think together about the teaching and learning. One-on-one coaching may involve a particular structure, including preparation, pre-lesson conference, observation, discussion after observation, and follow-up.

**Cluster Coaching:** In this structure, you support a small group of teachers (perhaps grade level) as they observe a colleague's teaching. There can be many permutations of cluster coaching, but the school team may find it helpful if you follow a standard protocol, such as the one we provide here. The purpose is to provide a shared example for all group members to use in order to reflect on their own teaching decisions.

Cluster coaching enables teachers to engage in collaborative inquiry around an observation as you guide the conversation to lift their understandings. Small-group coaching is a little harder to schedule because it means releasing several teachers from their classrooms; however, the observation can be of a single lesson, with a rich discussion taking place over lunch or in a grade-level meeting (as long as it is quite soon after viewing).

Cluster coaching brings teachers into a collegial group with a focus on evidence of student learning and teacher decision-making. Though it certainly does not allow for the precision of individual coaching, it provides an authentic opportunity for collaboration and reflection among teachers with common interests. It helps if the participants use a common tool such as *The Literacy Continuum* to ground the conversation.

The protocol tool **Cluster Coaching (33)** on page 418 will help teachers know what to expect from the experience so they can focus on the new learning.

> ### PEER COACHING
>
> Peer coaching is generally two teachers with similar roles, e.g., classroom teachers, observing each other and thinking together about the teaching and learning. They meet prior to the observations and after. This form of coaching differs from the others in that it does not involve a coach with the specific responsibility of lifting teacher understanding. Peer coaching can be one part of a design for coaching and professional learning in the school. Teachers can support one another in reflecting on and analyzing their practice in light of the new learning they took on with the coach in cluster coaching.

## PROTOCOL TOOL

Use the protocol tool **Cluster Coaching (33)** with a small group of teachers who share common interests to foster collegiality and prepare them for individual coaching.

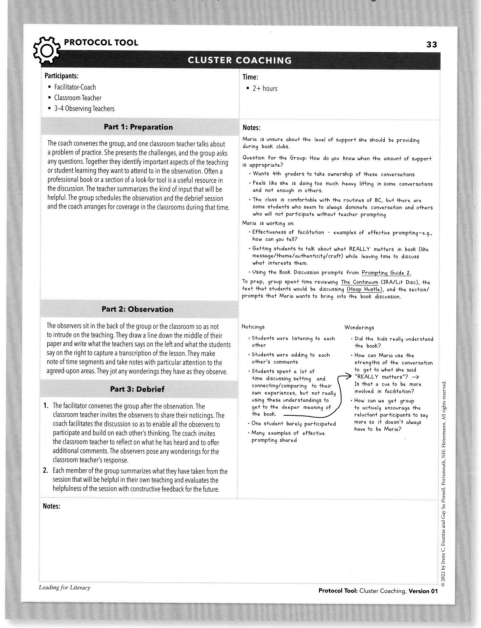

## A Process for Coaching

When working with individual teachers, you can use a structure that helps to frame your coaching not just as an "observation and feedback" event but a co-learning opportunity. We have found this structure to be a helpful way to think about the coaching process (Figure 21-7).

## A PROCESS FOR LITERACY COACHING

| | |
|---|---|
| **Before Coaching** | ▪ Review notes from the last coaching conference.<br>▪ Examine coaching records and reflect on previous work with the teacher.<br>▪ Depending on the instructional context to be observed, look at records of reading levels and/or any writing samples or assessments available.<br>▪ Review professional resources that are pertinent to ground your thinking. |
| **During the Preconference** | ▪ Examine recent data and think together about the students.<br>▪ Ask the teacher about her goals for the lesson (from *The Literacy Continuum*).<br>▪ Become familiar with the materials the teachers will be using.<br>▪ Identify the areas the teacher would like you to notice and think about.<br>▪ Learn what the teacher is working on in her teaching. |
| **During the Observation** | ▪ Create two columns on your page—the left side for teacher language and the right side for student responses.<br>▪ Observe and note student and teacher interactions so you are the memory of the lesson.<br>▪ Scribe significant language from the teacher and students.<br>▪ Note times across the lesson, if applicable.<br>▪ Note questions/wonderings you have.<br>   ☐ What did you see?<br>   ☐ What did you hear?<br>   ☐ What are you wondering about?<br>   ☐ What reading/writing behaviors of students did you notice?<br>   ☐ What reading/writing behaviors of the students were attended to by the teacher? |
| **After the Observation** | ▪ Review observational notes.<br>▪ Think about what was effective in the teaching and why.<br>▪ List any genuine questions/wonderings you have.<br>▪ Brainstorm any big ideas that might be useful to address in the coaching session.<br>▪ Identify 1–3 big ideas you want to discuss with the teacher and prioritize them.<br>▪ Identify professional resources and student artifacts that might be helpful.<br>▪ Think about key understandings so that your talk is grounded in rationales.<br>   ☐ As you begin, what will be your first words?<br>   ☐ How will you move from one big idea to another?<br>   ☐ How will you use the resources you have chosen?<br>   ☐ What language will you use to promote inquiry and address your coaching points(s)?<br>   ☐ How will you address the concerns of the teacher? |
| **During the Post-Conference** | ▪ Share and discuss the coaching points and priorities using professional resources and student artifacts as needed.<br>▪ Address the teacher's agenda (questions/issues raised during the preconference).<br>▪ Make the coaching generative so it can help the teacher transfer the understandings from the discussion about this lesson to future teaching.<br>▪ Summarize new understandings and collaboratively set goals for further learning.<br>▪ Invite the teacher's feedback on the helpfulness of the session. |

**Figure 21-7.** A Process for Literacy Coaching

It is obvious that not all of these elements are characteristic of every coaching interaction but keeping these points in mind will help you structure your time.

## Coaching Moves

A wide variety of coaching moves are available to you. As you examine the moves listed in Figure 21-8, it will become evident that literacy coaching is complex and requires training and ongoing professional support.

### DIGITAL LITERACY

**Expanding Collaborative Inquiry Through the Use of Short Video Clips**  Video has long been used for student learning, but it also has much potential for increasing collaborative inquiry and supporting teacher growth, particularly when the teachers and the coach have a trusting relationship. Video can be a powerful medium for capturing teaching and learning for reflection and analysis. It can serve as the memory of teaching and student-teacher interactions. Even a 2- to 3-minute clip has real value for observing and analyzing teaching decisions. When used for systematic self-reflection related to specific goals, the intentionality of the teacher becomes clear, and the teacher can engage in important self-assessment prior to a discussion with a peer or a coach.

One could argue that video makes teaching decisions too permanent, and video is certainly not as effective as face-to-face coaching interactions, but for expanded opportunities for reflection and discussion they have some advantages. The coach does not have to be present, the lesson can be watched any time, and there is real value in stopping the video clip at any moment to discuss the teaching decision and explore possible "what if" scenarios. The teacher can set goals with a coach, capture 10 or 20 minutes of teaching, take notes, and engage in a follow-up discussion at any convenient time. The frequency of coaching sessions can be increased. The video can be paused, rewound, fast forwarded, or reviewed again with a different lens.

Thanks to advancements in tools and platforms for videoconferencing, the number and frequency of coaching opportunities can be increased. The equipment has become easier to use, less obtrusive, and less expensive. Even a smartphone provides the simplest, most convenient tool to capture audio or video of student-teacher interactions without a lot of effort.

We have used video effectively in ongoing professional learning for coaches for short and longer lesson analysis. For example, we asked the coaches to select 2 or 3 minutes of teaching or coaching from a longer recording and bring to the session to analyze with colleagues. This targeted discussion between two or three coaches together serves as strong evidence for analysis, feedback, and new learning. The clips can also be used for viewing and then role-playing a coaching interaction.

We suggest that teachers or coaches video themselves several times for self-reflection first to get used to the medium and improve recording quality. It can feel awkward at first, and the teacher may become overconcerned with whether they are doing it "right." It's a good idea to focus on one aspect of teaching or learning in early videos. Though there certainly is no such thing as perfect teaching, we suggest that at first teachers or coaches bring clips that they feel went really well or had positive outcomes.

## COACHING MOVES

| | |
|---|---|
| **Gather Information** | <ul><li>Probe the teacher's knowledge.</li><li>Work to understand the teacher's perspective.</li><li>Understand the teacher's rationales for planning and decision-making.</li><li>Gather evidence of the teacher's understanding.</li><li>Review assessment information and artifacts together.</li><li>Ask what the teacher is working on in her teaching.</li><li>Consult professional resources together (e.g., *The Literacy Continuum*).</li></ul> |
| **Open the Conversation** | <ul><li>Get to substantive talk that is grounded in evidence and data.</li><li>Respond to "opening the door" statements in a way that promotes thinking.</li><li>Allow teachers to have input in shaping the agenda so that they take ownership.</li><li>Make sure you understand what the teacher is saying.</li><li>Seek the teacher's opinion.</li><li>Offer evidence from observation.</li></ul> |
| **Enter into Collaborative Inquiry** | <ul><li>Validate and provide confirmation.</li><li>Find a productive way to disagree or give another perspective.</li><li>Promote teacher self-reflection.</li><li>Help teachers draw on evidence that leads to decision-making.</li><li>Help teachers uncover their own thinking.</li><li>Acknowledge teacher's feelings and ideas.</li><li>Facilitate shared inquiry and the use of professional resources.</li><li>Clarify understandings.</li><li>Provide wait time and ample opportunity for teacher to talk.</li><li>Listen actively and accurately to be able to use what is said productively.</li><li>Provide new information or rationales that are helpful.</li><li>Keep the conversation moving.</li><li>Coach in a generative way (points can be applied to future teaching).</li><li>Dig deeper together.</li><li>Summarize big important ideas from the conversation.</li></ul> |
| **Pin down some goals** | <ul><li>Support the teacher in deciding what to change and how to do it.</li><li>Support the teacher in evaluating the effectiveness of teaching decisions.</li><li>Invite the teacher to be more specific.</li><li>Make a plan for tomorrow's teaching together.</li><li>Help the teacher construct a process (not just a response to one event).</li></ul> |
| **Reflect on coaching** | <ul><li>Ask how you were helpful as a coach.</li><li>Identify goals for the teacher and plan for follow-up.</li><li>Look back on progress over time (as represented in notes).</li></ul> |

**Figure 21-8.** Coaching Moves

# The Role of Coaching Language

We have described the coaching stance as one that is collegial—working alongside rather than transferring information from expert to novice. There are times that you will need to deliver information, but the stance is always that of working together. It helps to become aware of the language that sets a collegial, collaborative tone. But first, notice language that, while seeming positive, communicates an evaluative stance (Figure 21-9).

When coaching, you listen actively to your colleagues and use language that communicates respect, opens conversation, and facilitates genuine inquiry. Pause and give wait time, not always trying to fill the silence. The teacher needs to do more of the talking than you do. We know this is not easy because most of us in a leadership position feel the obligation to fill the occasion with talk. But as you work to shape your language, you also influence your thinking, moving toward a more ten-

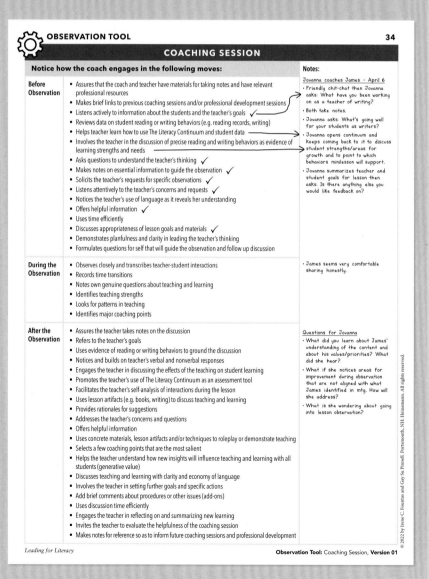

Leading for Literacy

Observation Tool: Coaching Session, **Version 01**

---

## THE LANGUAGE OF COACHING: EVALUATIVE STANCE

- How do you think the lesson went?
- What a good lesson!
- You did a great job!
- I like the way you _____.
- You just left out ___.
- Your pace was good.
- You need to pick up the pace of the lesson.
- You didn't call on _____.
- Do you think your introduction gave them the understandings they need?
- I think you should _____.
- Read this and see if it helps.
- I recommend _____.
- Tomorrow, I suggest _____.
- Have your materials ready, and the lesson will go more smoothly.
- I was impressed with the way you did the word work.
- Great lesson!

**Figure 21-9.** The Language of Coaching: Evaluative Stance

tative, exploratory stance. That tends to take the tension out of the coaching situation and even makes it more enjoyable. Consider your purpose and examples of language that foster a collaborative stance (Figure 21-10).

To help you notice language, moves, the process, and stance as you conduct or observe a coaching session, you might use the observation tool **Coaching Session (34)** to record notes before the observation, during the observation, and after the observation.

## THE LANGUAGE OF COACHING: COLLABORATIVE STANCE

| PURPOSE | EXAMPLES OF FACILITATIVE LANGUAGE | |
|---|---|---|
| **Set an agenda together.** | • What would you like to think together about today?<br>• How can I be helpful to you today? | • How might I be helpful to you in your teaching? |
| **Communicate a tentative stance.** | • This is one hypothesis. Another reason might be . . .<br>• I was wondering if another explanation might be . . .<br>• Let's compare our thinking.<br>• That's one way to think about that. | • Can you help me understand why (student) _____?<br>• I was wondering . . . |
| **Genuinely seek to discover more about the teacher's thinking and practice.** | • Talk about the students you will be teaching today.<br>• What are your goals for your teaching today?<br>• What parts of your teaching are going well?<br>• What was your thinking when . . . ?<br>• What did [student] do that made you think that?<br>• Let's talk about your decision to . . .<br>• Talk about your teaching decisions in the lesson today. | • Were there parts of the teaching that didn't go as well as you hoped?<br>• What made you think you were not clear?<br>• What do you see as important for them to learn next?<br>• Can you share your thinking about _____? |
| **Corner the conversation with evidence.** | • How have you used your information about the children as readers (as writers) to plan for today?<br>• Where will you find evidence of _____?<br>• How will you know if _____?<br>• How will you know your students processed the text well? | • So given what you know about the students as readers, _____?<br>• I took notes to help me remember what I observed. Here's what I noticed.<br>• It seemed helpful to the children when _____. |
| **Use language that supports collegial problem-solving and inquiry and extends thinking.** | • What have you tried so far?<br>• Let's look at the reading records and see what we notice.<br>• Can we look at some of your writing samples to get some ideas for your minilesson priorities?<br>• I have found that children often _____. What do you notice about your students?<br>• What helped you make that decision?<br>• Let's think about _____.<br>• I'm interested in your perspective about participation. Is there anything you are concerned about? | • What else could that mean?<br>• Your observations and mine seem to be similar. Let's look at *The Literacy Continuum* and see where they fit.<br>• What's getting in the way?<br>• What do you think might have happened if you _____?<br>• In my teaching, I try to think about _____.<br>• What else could you try? |

*continued on next page*

**Figure 21-10.** The Language of Coaching: Collaborative Stance

| THE LANGUAGE OF COACHING: COLLABORATIVE STANCE (CONT.) | | |
|---|---|---|
| **PURPOSE** | **EXAMPLES OF FACILITATIVE LANGUAGE** | |
| **Demonstrate your desire to clarify and understand more.** | ■ Let me be sure I understand _____. <br> ■ Can you talk more about that? <br> ■ Can you say that another way to help me understand? <br> ■ When you said _____ to [student], what was your thinking? | ■ Can you share your thinking about _____? <br> ■ What surprised you? <br> ■ What do you see as important for them to learn how to do next as readers and writers? <br> ■ What are you wondering about? |
| **Listen attentively and empathetically.** | ■ So I hear you saying . . . <br> ■ I can understand that his comments would make you think about that. <br> ■ You were noticing that . . . | ■ I noticed that as well! What did it make you think? <br> ■ You are thinking about . . . <br> ■ Is anything frustrating you? Talk about that. |
| **Paraphrase occasionally to show that you are seeking to understand the teacher's precise comments and questions.** | ■ This is what I hear you saying . . . <br> ■ Are you saying . . . ? <br> ■ Are you saying that you are planning _____ in the next few lessons? | ■ Let me summarize what I hear you saying. |
| **Affirm the teacher's thinking and practice.** | ■ I noticed that, too. <br> ■ That was helpful to _____, wasn't it? <br> ■ When you said _____, I noticed that several children _____. | ■ Your wait time seemed to be helpful. Did you notice what _____ did? |
| **Determine actions and next steps.** | ■ What are you thinking you want to do next? <br> ■ What are your next goals for your readers/writers? <br> ■ Based on our discussion, what are you planning to do? <br> ■ What are your highest priorities? | ■ Based on our conversation today, what will you be trying to accomplish in the next few days? <br> ■ What do you need to be able to do this, and is there a way I can support you? |
| **Evaluate time together.** | ■ How did our work together go for you today? <br> ■ Was our conversation helpful? <br> ■ What was most helpful to you in our time together today? | ■ Is there something about our work together that you find especially productive? <br> ■ Is there anything you think we should plan to do differently in our work together? |

## Putting It Together: An Example of Individual Coaching

The most supportive structure for teachers is individual coaching. If a trusting relationship exists between you and the teacher, then the one-on-one setting is a place in which a teacher can feel safe to try out new techniques, to ask questions, to admit confusion, and to learn from mistakes. During the individual coaching interaction, the coach thinks together with the teacher before the teaching, observes the teaching, and thinks together with the teacher for the lift

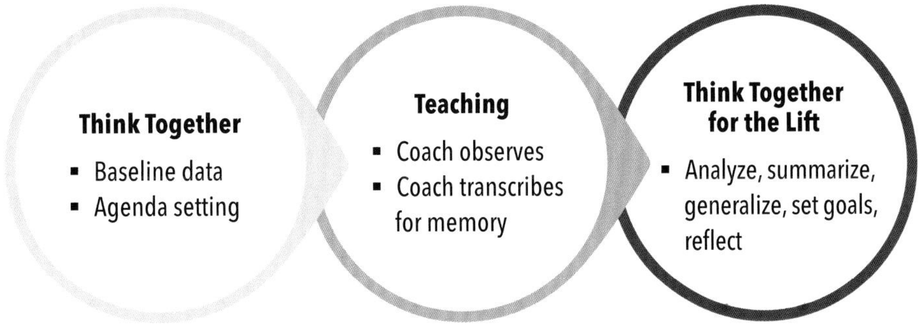

**Figure 21-11.** Structure of Individual Coaching

after the teaching (Figure 21-11). Let's look at some excerpts from a coaching example so you can have a concrete example of the coaching stance we have described.

## Think Together

In this example, the instructional context is guided reading in a third-grade classroom. (See Chapter 11 for a description of guided reading.) Sarah, the coach, begins by looking over her notes of previous work with Maya, the teacher. Maya has assessed her students and formed tentative groups to teach guided reading lessons. She has established a management system for readers' workshop, so students are engaging in independent reading and writing about reading while she works with a small group. Maya has all the components of a comprehensive literacy design in place, although she is still problem-solving the use of time and the schedule with her grade-level colleagues. Sarah has coached Maya individually several times before and has built her own knowledge of the students in the classroom. Together, they have looked at student records of reading and writing about reading and discussed evidence of progress.

In preparation for today's teaching, Maya has selected the book and prepared to introduce it to the students. She has communicated to Sarah the names of the children in the group. She also has prepared to teach the word work component of the lesson, she has some possible teaching points in mind, and she has noted students that she wants to be sure to hear orally reading a segment of the text. Sarah has only a few minutes to chat with Maya before the lesson (Figure 21-12).

Notice that most of Sarah's interactions are designed to provide information that she, as a coach, needs if she is to support Maya. Maya is providing the information. A good

> ### PRE-OBSERVATION CONFERENCE: A FEW MINUTES FOR A BIG BENEFIT
>
> The value of coaching conversations begins with a pre-observation conference. Too often making a few minutes to talk before a lesson observation is a scheduling challenge. Without a pre-observation conference, the learning from the coaching session is diminished. The conversation prior to the observation informs the coach's work and benefits the teacher's upcoming work with the children. It fosters a trusting relationship and positions the coach as a genuine listener.
>
> The preconference conversation comes from a place of co-inquiry and sets the stage for co-learning. The coach and the teacher get on the same page so the coach can have a lens that will be most helpful to her colleague. The teacher can think out loud about his students, his priorities, and his hopes for the coaching session. The teacher shares teaching plans and rationales for the materials selected and identifies evidence that he will look for to determine the success of his teaching. For the most part, the coach listens carefully and affirms the teacher's plans and occasionally asks a genuine question that may result in the teacher thinking in a new way or planning to try something new.
>
> The coach and teachers should make every effort to create opportunities for a preconference session prior to any observation to maximize the benefits of coaching to both parties. When the coach and teacher realize how valuable the time is, they will usually find a way to make it happen.

| COACH AND TEACHER BEFORE THE LESSON | | |
|---|---|---|
| | **INTERACTION** | **COACH'S GOAL** |
| **Coach** | *Hi Maya, I'm looking forward to seeing the children enjoy today's book. What's your thinking about the strengths of the group?* | Establishes ongoing relationship. Seeks information. |
| **Teacher** | I can show you their strengths in these running records. *(Quickly examines and talks briefly about the records of Betsy, Elijah, Fangon, and Moira.)* Here's Victor. I'm thinking he is showing a lot of strength as he initiates problem-solving at difficulty and corrects his own errors. His accuracy is constantly high. He is making really fast progress, and I'm wondering if he is challenged at level P. | Listens to understand. |
| **Coach** | *What is your thinking about his understanding?* | Probes for underlying thinking. |
| **Teacher** | Look at this piece in his reader's notebook. I think he really gets it. Also, his participation in the group is very high. I have to bring the others in to keep him from doing all the talking. | |
| **Coach** | *I'll take some careful notes on his reading today that we can look at later. Let's look together at level P in* The Literacy Continuum. *Talk about the behaviors you think your students control and the few priorities you have in mind today.* | Uses a professional tool. |
| **Teacher** | The group in general controls many of these competencies at level P, but I think they need to dig in to understand the role of nonfiction text features. Today I'm prioritizing bullets related to the interpretation of text features. *(Points to a specific bullet in* The Literacy Continuum: "Infer the meaning of a range of graphics that require reader interpretation and are essential to comprehending the text.") | |
| **Coach** | *Talk about your thinking about the nonfiction features in the book you have selected.* | Invites teacher analysis. Uses a professional tool. |
| **Teacher** | I've chosen *Life in the Redwood Forest*. The author, Joanna Solins, describes the grandeur of these trees, and the special features emphasize their grandeur, especially the sidebar on page 2. It compares the tree with a ten-story building and pictures people holding hands around the massive trunk. This graphic really requires reader interpretation to fully comprehend the text. | Listens for teacher rationales. |

Figure 21-12. Coach and Teacher Before the Lesson

## COACH AND TEACHER BEFORE THE LESSON (CONT.)

| | INTERACTION | COACH'S GOAL |
|---|---|---|
| **Coach** | *Yes. I too was amazed at all the life that depends on the redwoods. The infographic on pages 10 and 11 shows that. This book offers opportunity to interpret such features.* | Shares personal response. Confirms the rationale. |
| **Teacher** | The students also need to be more active in using the glossary and the table of contents to get back to evidence for their statements. *(Points to bullets in* The Literacy Continuum.*)* | Listens to teacher's goals. |
| **Coach** | *Yes, those are two additional bullets in Thinking Within the Text—using organizational tools and using text resources. Are you thinking about setting the students up to notice the glossary and table of contents in your introduction?* | Uses a professional tool. Asks for information. |
| **Teacher** | Yes, I am really trying to set them up to process the text well without my support. We talked about that last time, and I think it has helped. | Listens to teacher's analysis. |
| **Coach** | *What are you working on in your teaching of guided reading lessons? Is there something you want me to notice?* | Inquires about professional learning goals. |
| **Teacher** | When the children have difficulties, I often jump in instead of giving them time to problem solve. Help me think about wait time and my responses at difficulty. Does my language help them work things out for themselves? | |
| **Coach** | *So you are really thinking about how you are teaching them to initiate helpful actions that they will be able to apply to other books they read.* | Confirms teacher's thinking and extends it. |

rule of thumb is to ask only genuine questions, not questions for which you already have answers. The coach is not trying to test the teacher, but to learn as much as possible about her thinking. Some teachers might need more helpful advice than others in planning for the lesson. What you're working to achieve is a situation where the teacher feels free to ask a question about the planning: a sort of "I've been thinking about _____. Can you help me decide?"

## Teaching

As Sarah observed the 20-minute lesson, she scribed the language along with any questions and wonderings (Figure 21-13). She drew a line down the middle of the page, scribing the teacher's language on the left, the children's responses

## OBSERVATION OF THE TEXT AND LESSON

| INTRODUCTION OF THE TEXT | TEACHER'S GOAL |
|---|---|
| Maya begins the introduction to the text by asking what students already know about the redwoods and reading a short author's note. | Activates background knowledge. Shares more information. Activates thinking about the author's purpose. |
| She draws children's attention to the words *giant* and *habitat* and asks them to find the latter in the glossary. | Prompts children to use the glossary. Communicates to students that they can search for word meaning. Untangles a technical word. |
| She asks students to look at the illustration on page 2 and notice the sidebar, asking what information it shows. | Communicates to students that sidebars are important. Communicates that graphics show information in a different and sometimes more interesting way. |
| She points out information in the insets on pages 8 and 9. | Raises awareness that life depends on the trees as shown in photographs. |
| She draws children's attention to the words in bold and asks students where they can find definitions. | Probes to see whether students quickly name the glossary. |
| She gets the students started reading by asking them to read to learn more about the tallest trees in the world and the life they support in the forest. | Sets a purpose for reading. |

### READING THE TEXT

The students begin to read the book silently. Maya samples oral reading behavior of Victor, Fangon, and Elijah and prompts for taking words apart using affixes.

### DISCUSSION AND TEACHING POINT

Maya invites children to share their thinking and to talk about any new information they found in the book.

| | |
|---|---|
| She draws attention to the meaning of the title on page 12 (The Circle of Life). Here is an excerpt. | *This interchange provides evidence that children understand the main thesis of the book—the author's message. Notice that Maya is not asking them to "retell" to prove they have read the text. She is asking for their thinking and the evidence behind it.* |
| **Victor:** *I think it means that the redwoods are useful even when they die because they help the soil.* | |
| **Moira:** *Well, it's kind of like the life cycle of the butterfly. It does something different each time, but it comes around again.* | |
| **Victor:** *It grows and plants and animals live in it. It lives for hundreds of years.* | |
| **Maya:** *What are you thinking about the importance of the redwoods? Do you agree with the author?* | |
| **Elijah:** *I do because even trees grow on it, it's so big.* | |
| **Victor:** *There's something different at every level.* | |
| **Maya:** *Can you take us to a page that helps you think about that?* | |
| Victor and Elijah turn to the vertical infographic on pages 9 and 11 and point out the insets. | |

The lesson ends with a teaching point that draws students' attention to the table of contents, maps, glossary, and other nonfiction text features. Then Maya engages the group in 3 minutes of fast word work on the prefix *un-*.

**Figure 21-13.** Observation of the Text and Observation of the Lesson

on the right, and making time notations at segments in the lesson (Figure 21-14). She put an asterisk next to things she might want to talk about with the teacher.

## Think Together for the Lift

Sarah reviews the notes she took during the observation and identifies some of the big ideas that she wants to address with Maya. She thinks about the evidence that she will present to ground the conversation in rationales and observable behaviors. Her coaching conversation after the observation is focused on analysis, summarizing, generalizing, goal setting, and evaluation (Figures 21-15a and 21-15b).

Sarah and Maya go back to Level P in the guided reading continuum of *The Literacy Continuum* and identify bullet points that describe the understandings for which they found evidence. They identify bullet points that show what is nearly known and could be priorities in future lessons. Finally, they look at tomorrow's book to identify a shape for the introduction and some potential teaching points. A quick conversation about Victor followed.

Providing a full transcript of these coach-and-teacher interactions would take many more pages, but we hope you can gain from these brief excerpts (which are presented in a "neater" form than on-the-run hand notes) a sense of the relationship that has been previously built. For a novice teacher, the conver-

Maya / Guided Reading / Life in the Redwood Forest / Level P
Victor, Moira, Fangon, Betsy, Elijah

| Teacher | Student |
|---|---|
| 8:30   Intro.<br><br>This book is about some very tall trees called redwoods. Do you see the title? | |
| | Fangon: They really made them look tall taking the picture like that.<br><br>Elijah: Life in the Redwood Forest |
| *That's the title. What are you thinking about these trees? | |
| | Fangon: I guess they have all kinds of bugs and things that live in them. Or maybe people live under them.<br><br>Betsy: It's probably more about birds and bugs and things. |
| [Reads aloud the author's note "Awesome redwoods" from the back cover.]<br><br>You said animals live in them and you are right. Look at page 2 and find the bold word habitat. Put your finger under it. You've seen that word before. | |
| | Victor: It's the place where an animal lives and it's necessary.<br><br>Moira: Look. It's so much bigger than a ten-story building like where I live.<br><br>Elijah: And it's really big around. |
| You noticed the illustrations. Most of you probably have not seen the redwoods but you can imagine their size. | |
| | Moira: These little people holding hands show you how big it is. |

**Figure 21-14.** Sample Notations

## EXCERPTS FROM COACHING CONVERSATION AFTER THE OBSERVATION

| | INTERACTION | COACHING GOAL |
|---|---|---|
| **Coach** | *They sure enjoyed learning about redwoods, didn't they?* | Sets the tone for interaction. |
| **Teacher** | I really think they did, and they got it! | |
| **Coach** | *I noticed that Moira compared it to the butterfly life cycle. What are you thinking about some of the others?* | Provides some specific evidence.<br><br>Asks for teacher thinking. |
| **Teacher** | Well, I really was pleased at how they understood the text features. They went right to the glossary and they could use the table of contents. I thought they showed evidence of really understanding those features at this level anyway. | |
| **Coach** | *Your introduction drew their attention to features and there was plenty of evidence that they were getting information from them. Let's take a look at* The Literacy Continuum *to identify some points that match your thinking about what you observed and then identify some priorities for tomorrow. Would you like for us to look at tomorrow's book together?* | Confirms and validates teacher thinking and action.<br><br>Proposes action using a professional tool. |

Figure 21-15a. Excerpts from Coaching Conversation After the Observation

| | | |
|---|---|---|
| **Coach** | *You asked me to look closely at Victor. I agree that he shows a lot of competence. Let's take a look at level Q and come up with a plan.* | Returns to teacher's request during pre-conference and suggests action. |
| **Teacher** | (Examining the text characteristics for level Q). I really think he needs more challenge. | |
| **Coach** | *What have you noticed about his independent reading?* | Probe for more detailed description of evidence. |
| **Teacher** | He has stepped up the volume of reading and seems "hooked" on the Magic Treehouse series. | |
| **Coach** | *What do you think about letting him join another group for a while and seeing how he does?* | Makes a suggestion and turns the decision over to the teacher. |
| **Teacher** | I'd like to do that and will let you know what happens. | |

Figure 21-15b. Excerpts from Coaching Conversation After the Observation

sation might be a little more coach-directed; for a highly experienced teacher, it will likely be a back-and-forth exploration. It helps if you have a repertoire of coaching moves as well as a process in mind so you can be responsive.

# The Takeaway

A coach plays an integral role in the learning life of the school. The coach is a catalyst for inquiry and self-reflection. In each interaction with a teacher, the coach prompts for information and seeks to uncover the rationales in the teacher's decision-making. Trust between the coach and teachers is the important element in helping teachers refine their craft. The coach centers evidence in each conversation and uses genuine wonderings to shift the teacher's thinking. The coach values the unique lived experiences of each teacher and works to understand the perspectives and understandings the teacher holds.

## Think About Your School

Take a few moments to consider the quality of the implementation of coaching in your school. You may wish to consider these ideas and questions as a first step:

- Who gets coached in your school?
- How often is each teacher coached, and what kinds of coaching opportunities do teachers have?
- Are professional learning sessions connected to coaching?
- How often and why does coaching get canceled or rescheduled?

## Move Your School Forward

As you think about the ideas in this chapter, think about the kind of data you can collect and actions you can take to strengthen and promote coaching that leads to improved outcomes for students.

- Meet with your coach to make an action plan for maximizing coaching time in the school. Confront the obstacles together. Once you have a plan, set a time to revisit the results.
- Work with your coach to evaluate your relationship. Take time to assess the effectiveness of your meetings, the clarity of your communication, and the quality of the information you share. Be transparent and honest, with the goal of improving your relationship for the benefit of the teachers and the children in your school. Identify steps you will take to strengthen and improve the relationship, and focus on them one at a time.

# Chapter 22

## Supervision and Evaluation in a Culture of Teacher Growth

> *Evaluation has become a polite, if near-meaningless matter*
> *between a beleaguered principal and a nervous teacher.*
> *Research has finally told us what many of us suspected*
> *all along: that conventional evaluation, the kind the*
> *overwhelming majority of American teachers undergo, does*
> *not have any measurable impact on the quality of student*
> *learning. In most cases, it is a waste of time.*
>
> Mike Schmoker

IN THE INTRODUCTION TO this book, we explained that the information it contains is directed specifically to school leaders—teacher leaders, team leaders, literacy coaches, literacy specialists, principals, and more. In this chapter, however, we turn to the topic of teacher hiring, retention, supervision, and standardized evaluation—responsibilities that generally rest with the school principal. If you're not a principal (or not a principal *yet*), you still may find the chapter helpful for its discussion of the supervisory role, which we view as a coaching role, and the overview we provide of the teacher evaluation process.

For the school principal, effective teacher supervision requires a good understanding of the characteristics of high-quality instruction and a keen ability to observe—to know what to "look for" to make decisions that will support teacher learning. Supervising includes acts of teaching, and doing it well can make a big difference in the professional lives of the teachers on your team.

The responsibility for supervising teachers is a critical factor in providing equity for all the students in your school. Good classroom teaching can overcome many of the disadvantages students bring to school. The stakes are high because, while not *sufficient,* literacy is *necessary* for a successful life. Teacher expertise matters because children, especially those who are more vulnerable, need year after year of good instruction. Uneven and incoherent literacy instruction can confuse and deprive children of the opportunities they should have. They need consistent expert teaching through all the grades, and effective supervision is a key to making that happen.

Your informed leadership can create the positive culture and collaborative team that make supervision effective and supportive. Everyone on the team needs to be committed to the school's vision and to the steps needed to achieve it. That means breaking down the silos and bringing the team together to assure collective responsibility for literacy outcomes. Members need to accept that even the most expert teacher is not enough to ensure years of excellent instruction. And there must be a pervasive sense that to serve all children well, everyone has to be as good as they can be. When educators hold a shared responsibility for all students, supervision becomes a valuable and appreciated part of the collective effort of the team.

In schools like this, the supervisor is present in classrooms for a few minutes almost every day. The classroom doors are open, and teachers and specialists come in and out. Teachers feel supported by the principal and by their colleagues, and collective expertise grows as a result. In addition, structured learning opportunities such as grade-level meetings, data teams, learning walks, individual coaching, cluster coaching, virtual chats, and professional book clubs enhance expertise exponentially.

In this chapter, we discuss the unique supervisory role of the school principal—including your responsibility for hiring and evaluating teachers—through a lens that recognizes continual growth and teamwork. We will describe multiple ways of gathering information so that you can evaluate teachers in an informed way and can offer sound support.

## Supervision Is Teamwork

You may view supervision as something you are required to do, but you can make it a vital part of your school improvement journey. Your ability to bring out the best in every professional, to create a culture of teamwork, and to supervise for continuous growth in teacher expertise are essential to your effectiveness as a leader and to the learning outcomes of students. If students in your school are going to grow and learn, then the adults in the school must grow and learn too. When teachers see themselves as members of an inclusive community, they aim to create similar conditions in the classroom. Continuous professional growth is the expectation of all professionals in the building and this goal is communicated, orally and in written documents, and should be reviewed each year as part of the core values of the school and the system.

Consider the culture in which you supervise the members of the team and think about the person you want to be as a leader and how you are perceived by your team members. Ask:

- How would your colleagues in the school describe you?
- What can they expect from you as their leader?
- Have you communicated to them what you expect from the team?

The success of your leadership in literacy will rest on positive, trusting relationships and teamwork, your clarity in communications, and the deep literacy expertise you create in the school. It will also rest on your belief in every teacher's ability to grow, focusing on each teacher's strengths and building on them. Although expectations should be clear, mandates from the principal tend not to bring out the best in others. Rather, your common vision can inspire others and harness the commitment and expertise of all the educators in achieving their common goals. When you position yourself as a learner, you can relinquish control to the team and gain more strength when your colleagues trust you and come alongside you.

It is important to communicate clearly and often, celebrating the accomplishments of the teaching team, staying true to your common goals, and clearly articulating expectations and processes for decision-making. Teachers need to know when important decisions are being made and how their thinking can inform those decisions in a collaborative way.

## Toward Growth-Centered Supervision

The word *supervisor* comes from the concept of a person in a superior role managing another person. Supervision has traditionally been purely *evaluative*. The principal would observe the teacher in the classroom, write up a report, and deliver the results to the teacher in a conference. The evaluation usually resulted in a satisfactory or better performance rating for most of the teachers but seldom led to significant improvement in instruction or student outcomes. The structure relied on a hierarchy, and the process was full of mandates from above.

Today's vision of effective leadership has led to a shift in the role of supervision. While the principal still evaluates the effectiveness of teachers, effective supervision has become part of a more meaningful, collaborative process that promotes teacher growth.

Think of supervision as something you do *with* the teachers, not *to* them, for the purpose of improving teaching on the way to improving learning.

Growth-centered supervision places the teacher and the supervisor as partners in planning for and reflecting on professional growth every year. The supervisor and the teacher come together around common values, common language, and common tools that center their mutual understandings about effective literacy teaching and how it is evaluated.

Throughout this book we have stressed the leader's role as a trusted colleague who manages, grows, and supports the talent of the team. Instead of trying to lead the school alone, you create partnerships with your school colleagues in the educational process. In this chapter, we attempt to reconcile the role of the "collaborative team members" and that of fulfilling responsibilities as a supervisor.

## The Supervisor's Complex Role

Let's examine several interrelated factors, each of which is relevant to effective supervision (Figure 22-1).

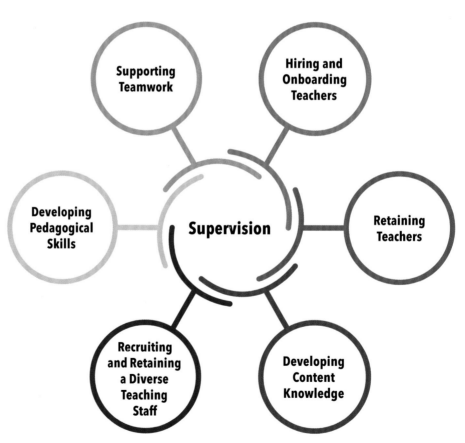

Figure 22-1. Complexity of the Supervisory Role

# Teacher Hiring and Onboarding

It goes without saying that your role as a supervisor begins with recruiting, hiring, and onboarding a diverse staff of outstanding teachers who will readily take to heart and put into practice the shared values of the school. You want to invite into the community of teachers whose practice and experience (even if it's pre-service experience) indicate that they will be a good fit with the team from the beginning. Every person you hire will be an important addition. You may want to consider creating a school-level employment application (in addition to the system application) that reflects your school goals, your vision, and your expectations for teamwork. And it would be ideal to include teachers, (some of whom are teachers of color) on the hiring committee if that is an option.

**Joining a Community of Practice** It is important for new teachers to understand they will join a team in which each member strives to get better at his craft and is committed to helping others grow in service of the children, taking collective responsibility for their students over the years. Strong new hires show the stance of a learner and a deep commitment to inclusivity and diversity. They understand that effective teaching begins with their own expertise and show evidence of a desire to continue learning with colleagues. From the start, they understand that they will not work in a silo, but in a school where teachers feel safe taking risks and de-privatizing their practice to learn from each other.

People feel uneasy when expectations are not clear. You can communicate, warmly and positively, to new team members that there are certain non-negotiables. For example:

- Every person in the building, including the principal and coach, will be coached on a regular basis.
- Staff will not talk in a negative way about families, team members, or the community.
- All staff will participate as team members and contribute to team goals.
- Culture and language of all students, their families, and school staff will be valued.
- Problems will be recognized, examined, and worked on.

**Embracing a Coherent Approach to Literacy** You'll also want to express that the school team has agreed upon a coherent approach to literacy instruction and individuals may not "opt out." While every new teacher deserves time and support in acclimating to the culture and learning from the collective expertise of the team, it is important that each teacher is committed to implementing the school district's literacy approach and contributing to it through their work in the classroom.

# HOW TO FIND GREAT TEACHERS

When it comes to finding and recruiting outstanding teachers, you need to think outside the box. Here are some things you can do:

## ADVERTISE WIDELY

Most districts post job announcements online, but you'll want to reach out to your central office employment partner to be sure your open positions will find a national audience. You might also consider posting on national publications for K–12 teachers and school leaders or using social media to advertise open positions.

## GET SOME GUIDANCE

High school guidance offices sometimes can connect employers with area alumni who attended teacher preparation programs and might be about to graduate. It's not unusual for recent grads to want to work in the same school system they attended as students. You can also reach out to the education departments in nearby colleges and universities.

## TALK IT UP

Teacher hiring typically happens in late spring and summer, after budgets for the new school year have been approved and staff members have announced intentions to retire or transfer. But you can take a page from the business sector and "prime the pump" before you have the go-ahead to hire. You probably won't be able to post jobs publicly until your budget is approved, but that doesn't mean you can't talk with friends and acquaintances about your hiring plans. Word of mouth is often quite effective when it comes to finding talent before they are found by someone else.

## ATTEND JOB FAIRS

See if you can attend a few job fairs in your local community and at surrounding colleges and universities. This may be something your district already does, so you'll want to speak with your hiring partner first. But job fairs can be very effective because you typically have the chance not only to collect a stack of resumes, but to chat briefly with the applicants as well.

## UPDATE YOUR SCHOOL WEBSITE

Teachers who are thinking of applying to a teaching job you've posted are likely to visit your website even before they fill out the application. Make sure the site is friendly and accessible, that the calendar and contact links are up to date, and that visitors will find plenty of beautiful photographs of classrooms, teachers working with children, and children engaged in meaningful work. Check for typos, too, and anything else that might give a negative impression of the school.

Because each child is different and will have a unique literacy journey, the newly hired teacher also needs to understand the complexity of literacy learning and the fact that responsive teaching begins with knowing the children. In a culture of teamwork, the educators become a circle of support for every educator and every child in the community. Though each teacher will certainly have his own style and personality, every teacher will be responsible for interacting with and supporting the other teachers and ensuring that children have the high-quality literacy opportunities that have been articulated in the school's vision. Coherence in the instructional program needs to be evidenced in every classroom.

We have worked with several schools in which the leader crafts a welcome letter that is sent to newly hired teachers. The letter describes the teamwork and collaboration that is valued in the school and serves as a clear communication of the values, beliefs, and goals of the team. It communicates that the teacher will become a member of a team that is collectively responsible for the outcomes of all the students and will not function in the school as an individual teacher responsible only for teaching his own class of students. Many of the letters we've seen also describe *The Literacy Continuum* as a central curriculum document that is used for planning, teaching, and assessing each child's literacy growth, but you can substitute your school or district learning goals. Such a letter provides the newly hired teacher with a clear sense of the vision and culture of the school and how she will play a role on the team. We have provided sample letters to demonstrate the tone and clarity of a communication that is welcoming while also making a clear statement about the expectations of the school for its teaching team (Figures 22-2 and 22-3). Two templates that you can modify and make your own are available in the online resources for this book. Both are also shown on the next two pages.

## Retaining Effective Teachers

We have observed increasing teacher burnout and turnover in schools. We believe that burnout often comes from teaching the same thing, the same way, year after year, and working in lonely isolation. Teachers often cite principal support as one of the most important factors in their decision to stay in a school or continue in the teaching profession. When teachers work in a culture in which they feel valued and respected and benefit from the energy and expertise of their school leaders and peers, they continue to grow and find satisfaction in their roles. If there are teaching challenges, the team is right there to problem solve and support the teacher as needed.

Your ability to create positive working conditions and a collaborative learning culture plays an important role in attracting and retaining highly effective teachers. As a leader, consider what the professional life of each teacher is like in your school. Helping teachers "stretch" their practice, encouraging them to

Dear <u>Name of Teacher</u>,

Welcome to <u>name of school</u> and the <u>name of district</u> School District. We are pleased you are joining our new team. Our team is a passionate group of professionals who are committed to working together to achieve our common goals. In the attached document, we have articulated our values and beliefs about literacy teaching and learning and our expectations of each other as a team of growing professionals dedicated to assuring access and equity in literacy to every child in every class in our school. Please take some time to read and reflect on our common values. You will notice that we will revisit them frequently to talk about and reflect on the implications for our decision-making on behalf of our students. As an active participant in the decision-making process, your voice is valued, and we look forward to your contributions.

We will provide you with all the support you need to be successful and enjoy your work as part of our team. You will be assigned <u>name of teacher</u> as your mentor to assist with your transition to our school. Our team works closely together, so you can expect to feel the support of all your team members. We hope you will seek support with any questions and concerns.

You will have many professional learning opportunities. We encourage team members to visit each other's classrooms for observations, learning walks, peer planning, or any other opportunity for dialogue and support of each other. You will have the opportunity to express your professional learning priorities and will have the support of a coach approximately every two weeks. In addition, you will learn about our workshops, meet ups and grade-level meetings.

You will receive our common curriculum for literacy, *The Literacy Continuum*. Your coach will support you in learning how to use it for planning and for assessing your students' competencies and learning priorities.

In a beginning-of-the-year workshop, you will also be introduced to our assessment system which includes a beginning- and end-of-year benchmark conference to determine students' instructional level for small-group reading in school. Your coach will help you plan and schedule an assessment conference with each child in the first two to three weeks of school.

I know you will find that your colleagues are generous in their support and that we all take responsibility for the success of the students in our school. Our families and our community are our valued partners in achieving this goal.

You have joined a passionate community of educators. Your strengths, experiences, and views will add so much to our team, and we are excited to get to know you.

Warm welcome,

The <u>name of school</u> School Team

**Figure 22-2.** Sample Welcome Letter A

Dear <u>Name of Teacher</u>,

Welcome to <u>name of school</u>. I'm so glad that you are part of this team. From my own experience, I know that it takes time to learn how things are done when starting at a new school and that it can sometimes be difficult to figure out what's important to your new colleagues. I want to help a bit by sharing three values that are important to every educator at <u>name of school</u>.

First, we're learners ourselves. We are constantly learning from each other so that we can become the most effective educators that we can be for our students. Your ideas, experiences, perspectives, and expertise as a teacher will be a valuable part of that effort. I know that we won't get everything right every time. But we'll problem solve together. We'll look at student data, make new plans, try a solution, review the results, and reflect on what we've learned. This learning stance also influences our teaching. We actively learn about each child–strengths, histories, values, perspectives, interests–and use what we learn to make our teaching relevant and responsive.

Second, we believe every child should have the opportunity to grow up literate. We want every child to experience being a reader and being a writer every day, in every classroom. That's why we design our curriculum around books and give every student the opportunity to choose, process, and respond to different texts every day. You will receive a lot of support from me and the other teachers in our building as you build your own classroom library of beautiful and engaging books.

Third, we think of our classrooms as communities. Our classroom communities are inclusive. Teachers and students together take action to ensure that every child is successful. And our classroom communities value the voice and perspectives of every child. Students can take risks, take action to help each other, and take responsibility for their own learning.

This is what we're all about at <u>name of school</u>. And everyone here is committed to helping you be successful in your teaching and professional learning. Again, I'm so glad that you will be part of this team.

Sincerely,

<u>Signature of School Leader</u>

**Figure 22-3.** Sample Welcome Letter B

take risks, offering pathways into leadership roles, and including their voices and perspectives in decisions are all actions you can take to enrich the professional lives of teachers. Creating a collaborative culture that promotes professional growth and opportunities is a very effective way to retain good teachers.

The more you have established a trusting relationship with a teacher, the more effective supervision will be, and the more likely the teacher will be to stay in the building. In order to build this trust and collaborative approach, demonstrate your commitment to the team. For example:

- Attend professional learning sessions whenever possible.
- Be present in classrooms on a daily basis (not just for evaluation).
- Know every student by name.
- Be transparent in decision-making and problem-solving.
- Solicit and be open to constructive feedback.
- Have a good rationale for a decision.
- Fight for resources and flexibility at the central office.
- Become an advocate for students and their families.
- Take a personal interest in each individual on your staff.
- Have lunch with staff members when possible.
- Be sensitive but honest; don't be afraid to be direct.

Strong school leaders regularly solicit and show their openness to constructive feedback.

## MENTORS FOR NEW TEACHERS

Whether a recent hire is new to the profession or simply new to the school, a mentor can provide critical emotional and instructional support for first-year teachers and help in orienting all new hires to the school community.

Many districts and schools have established teacher mentoring programs and requirements. In New York City, for example, first-year teachers entering the system hold an initial certificate. Before they can achieve professional certification, they must receive a full year of mentoring for two periods a week over a ten-month period. A committee, called the New Teacher Induction Committee, interviews mentor applicants and, if they are accepted into the program, matches them with first-year teachers. Mentors must have five years of experience in New York City public schools, demonstrated proficiency in pedagogy and subject-matter skills, strong interpersonal skills, and a commitment to participate in their own professional learning.

Of course, many schools have less formal mentor programs that are also effective for both first-year teachers and those who are new to the school. Teachers are matched with mentors before their first day in the building, and mentors begin by introducing the teachers to the rest of the staff and providing an orientation to the building and to the school's values and norms. During the year, mentors and mentees meet regularly to discuss instructional or classroom management issues, collaborate frequently on problems of practice, and visit one another's classrooms. The mentor consistently provides nonjudgmental feedback after each visit.

If you haven't yet launched a teacher mentor program in your school, we encourage you to do so. Mentors can make the difference between new teachers who start the year adrift on a sea of apprehension and those who feel secure, welcomed, and ready to go.

# A Diverse Teaching Staff

We have a lot more work to do to attract and retain a greater diversity of teachers and school leaders. A diverse classroom team leads to better outcomes for all students. Diversity means great variety not only in race but in languages, socioeconomic backgrounds, and lived experiences. Research shows that when children have a teacher who shares an identity and background similar to their own, they benefit. Black students are more likely to graduate and enroll in college if they have just one black teacher by the end of third grade—and significantly more likely if they have two black teachers in elementary school (Gershenson, Hart, Hyman, Lindsay, and Papageorge 2018).

The entire school community–leaders, teachers, students, and support personnel–have everything to gain from a diverse staff and student body.

We also need to retain teachers who, in addition to all their strengths as educators, contribute diverse voices and perspectives to the team. Educators of color need mentors with similar experiences and identities and need to see teachers of color leading their professional learning. We need to take action to find, train, and retain new teachers of all groups and also support their development as teacher leaders, coaches, and other school leaders.

While you work actively to recruit a more diverse teaching staff, engage the team in work on several other fronts for the short term (Berg 2019). Consider the following suggestions:

- Seek positive role models for students of color.
- Organize visits by accomplished individuals of color from the community and foster positive interactions with students.
- Maintain high expectations as you provide supports and interventions.
- Persevere in providing support to students who are demonstrating difficulties until they are successful.
- Provide culturally responsive and relevant teaching.
- Assume students need to see themselves in the curriculum and in the books they read.
- Recognize the diverse perspectives, communication style, languages, and experiences of students. Tap into them as assets that can advance learning.
- Build trusting relationships with the students and their families. Celebrate the whole child and their families.
- Advocate for equity and equitable outcomes for students.
- Engage as a team in antiracist actions to confront and change the systemic issues that perpetuate racist policies and practices and diminish the lives of children.

# HOW TO RECRUIT AND RETAIN A DIVERSE TEACHING STAFF

Recruiting and hiring bilingual teachers, teachers of color, and those with urban life experience is challenging, not impossible. But it requires a strong commitment and deliberate effort from everyone involved. In addition to the general hiring tips provided in the sidebar on page 438, here are some things to keep in mind:

## CONSIDER YOUR CURRENT STAFF

Closely evaluate the demographics of your teaching staff. What groups are underrepresented? The answer to that question will focus your recruitment efforts.

## MEET WITH YOUR DISTRICT HIRING PARTNER

No doubt, the human resources department in your district has been developing new relationships and recruitment strategies to bring more diverse talent into the district. Be sure to check in with your HR partner to learn how the district team can contribute to your efforts.

## REACH OUT TO THE COMMUNITY

Get involved in community organizations that are for, or led by, people of color. You are bound to meet young people who might be enrolled in a local teacher preparation program or planning to enter one soon. Such relationships might not pay off in time to meet your immediate needs, but you will be building contacts for the future.

## ENSURE REPRESENTATION

Make sure the hiring team in your school includes at least one person of color and that the other members of the team are free of bias and enthusiastically support the goal of diversifying the teaching staff.

## USE ALL THE INFORMATION YOU HAVE

When considering applicants, remember that an applicant's test scores, experiences, and education don't say much about the person's teaching competencies. Often, objective measures say more about the opportunities applicants have had or not had in their lives than their ability to engage and motivate children to learn. The in-person interview should carry greater weight, as should performance-based tasks such as designing and teaching a lesson while the hiring team observes.

## TURN STAFF INTO TEACHERS

Think about the paraprofessionals, administrative assistants, and other non-faculty members of the school staff. Are there individuals of color who might want to consider becoming teachers in the school? Again, this strategy won't help in the short term, but you have to play the long game, too. There might be one or two people who are thinking about it and just need some encouragement. Offer to set them up with a district person who can discuss the best routes to certification, including alternative paths to the profession.

## Content Knowledge and Pedagogical Skills

The role of the school leader has shifted from primarily managing the school operations to engaging closely with teaching and learning. This shift means that it's important to understand the characteristics of high-quality teaching and learning (see Chapters 5 and 6).

As an instructional leader, you need content knowledge related to literacy so that you can use it to make good decisions in supporting high-quality instruction in the school and use it to inform your lens for observing teaching and learning. The more you understand about literacy teaching and learning the better you will be able to support teacher growth and reflection in your supervisory role and the better you will be at making good supervisory decisions.

Literacy learning will have an impact on students' learning in every subject area. In your role as instructional leader in literacy, you will need to continue to grow your expertise year after year. You have absorbed a great deal of information on high-quality literacy instruction from this book and other reading. You will learn more by using the tools we have provided and spending time visiting and observing literacy in classrooms. You don't have to be the most knowledgeable person in the school, but if you show that you are a learner, your effort will go a long way in showing the team your support not only in words but in your actions. Those efforts will expand your overall expertise as a supervisor of literacy teaching.

## Supporting Teamwork

An important aspect of your supervision work is evaluating the degree of teamwork that goes on in the school and how individuals are contributing to the teaching team. To develop a team that works together, focus on relationship-building, trust, and opportunities for collaboration. There is a difference between congeniality and collegiality. Teachers can be very congenial—they probably show kindness to each other, celebrate each other's birthdays with cupcakes, and share materials. But collegiality means much more than that. In a collegial environment, teachers share their teaching, see themselves as continuous learners, and support each other's learning. Instead of criticizing each other, they find ways to problem solve and support one another in achieving the team's goals. They listen to one another and trust each other so everyone can take risks and share with openness. They hold themselves and each other accountable.

Today's school leaders don't just manage school operations, they engage closely with teaching and learning.

Collegiality is a powerful lever in school improvement and is critical to your vision. With energy and tenacity, you need to address the critical components that support a collegial environment. When teachers talk with each other about students, talk together about curriculum, observe one another teach, teach one another—and when teachers and administrators learn together—you create a culture in which collegiality is the norm and every teacher will grow (Hoerr 2005).

With all our suggestions, you will need to consider and honor the agreements made by the teachers' unions in your specific school or state system. In our experience, teachers' unions and associations also hold positive goals for teachers and want them to have every opportunity to grow as professionals.

It is important to show your respect for each teacher's individual style along with the clear expectation that individuals view themselves as team members. And not just team members, but people who are responsible to all the students and to each other for working toward the school's common vision and goals. Though there is no such thing as perfect teaching, you should expect sincerity and openness to continuous growth. We ask you to be brave; the children are depending on your leadership and your actions.

## Supervising for Teacher Growth: Taking a Coaching Stance

The most important skill of leadership is coaching, and we hope you have the opportunity to engage in professional learning that maximizes your coaching expertise. Think about how the information related to coaching in Chapter 21 has strong implications for your interactions with colleagues. When you take the stance of a coach, your priority is to build trusting relationships and help your colleagues build their sense of agency as teachers. Focus on coaching moves that promote independence and reflection through your actions and your language. Provide ample wait time and see opportunities to talk together about teaching as an opportunity to learn together.

A key aspect of your role is to supervise and grow instructional expertise. When you take the stance of a coach, you help every member of your team be the best he can be. As a thought partner, you can help a teacher think more deeply about his work, organize his thoughts, reflect on his teaching, set goals, and develop a plan to meet the goals. With the stance of a coach, you listen more than you talk, ask instead of tell, and focus on developing a rich professional learning community. To be effective, you need to build a trusting relationship in which the teacher feels comfortable taking risks to grow and reflect on his practice.

Consider a variety of contexts for providing teacher feedback. Beyond the few required observations in the teacher evaluation process, consider the multiple avenues for observation and feedback that can contribute to the culture of teacher growth in your school or district. In every context, think about your lens as a coach and how each context can provide an opportunity for you and your colleagues to think together and promote agency, independence, and a reflective stance that will enable teachers to grow.

Focus on the students! When you consider engaging in coaching conversations with a teacher, consider three important categories of knowledge that will be a foundation for effective teaching:

- The readers or writers.
- The text (either reading or their own writing).
- The teaching decisions.

When you share your observations of student behaviors, you bring a "third eye" into the conversation. The teacher has more extensive knowledge of the students, but you can probably make some valuable contributions if you have some very specific "noticings" about individual students. A discussion of students and evidence of their learning keeps the coaching conversation away from praise and criticism and promotes self-reflection and problem-solving (Figure 22-4).

Consider questions such as the following.

*Readers/Writers:*

- What do the readers/writers understand?
- What do they show that they know how to do?
- What do they almost know how to do?
- What do they not yet know how to do?

*Texts:*

- How does the text students are reading support their development of a literacy processing system?
- How engaged are the students in the text they are reading?
- How does the writing about reading task give students the opportunity to develop competencies as a writer?
- What does the written text show that students know?

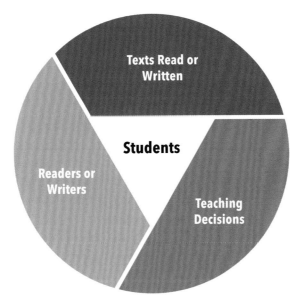

**Figure 22-4.** Student-Focused Coaching Conversations

*Teaching Decisions:*

- What do students need to know how to do next as readers?
- What do they need to know how to do next as writers?

# Standardized Teacher Evaluation

In most school districts, the principal is charged with using a standardized evaluation process. Standardized evaluation is intended to protect teachers by assuring fairness and specificity.

If you are a school principal, you are expected to conduct the required teacher evaluation process in your building, likely one to three times per year for a rotating list of teachers. Think about completing the required standardized teacher evaluations in the most productive way possible and adding on a variety of other opportunities to support teacher growth. We encourage the use of a variety of other professional learning opportunities to create a culture that does not simply measure teachers at a few points in time in the specified categories on the standardized evaluations (often in general ways). Using the same criteria, focus on maximizing teacher growth as a continuous process all year. If you take this approach, the standardized evaluation will go more smoothly and be more productive.

## The Value of Multiple Measures

We have participated in administrative evaluations of our own classroom teaching and observed school principals and other leaders in various time-consuming processes of observing teachers and providing written evaluations. Many tools for the teacher evaluation process have improved over the years to include multiple observations and more teacher input. We have also observed more detailed descriptions of criteria and opportunity for teachers to learn more about the tool and how it will be used. For teacher evaluation to be used to improve literacy teaching, you and your team need a common vision, common understandings, common language, and common tools so that teachers are working toward the same criteria every year. The feedback needs to be substantive and specific, built on evidence and oriented toward growth, not simply a "post-mortem" of the lesson taught.

We expect that the teacher evaluation process in most states and districts will continue to shift so that it can have more of an impact on teacher growth and make the best use of the supervisor's and the teacher's time. Gabriel (2018) referred to teacher evaluation as an opportunity for "joint professional development." Her summary of the purposes of teacher evaluation and the roles of the teacher and the evaluator provides a succinct description of the differences in the two processes.

Perhaps you have spent a great deal of time conducting the teacher performance evaluations. If so, we assume you've poured hundreds of hours into pre-observation conferences, classroom observations, written evaluations, and post-observation conferences for a roster of teachers. Consider whether you have significant evidence of improvement in teaching or improvement in student achievement as a result. Our prediction is that few of you will feel the process has made a significant difference or has had a greater effect than other factors related to teacher growth.

As classroom teachers for many years, we reflected on our performance evaluations and could not link those experiences to significant improvement in our own teaching. Depending on the administrator, the evaluation process felt like an anxiety-producing task or a pleasant interchange without any marked improvement in our teaching.

If it is true that most teacher evaluation processes have minimal influence on improving teaching, think of other approaches to improving instruction that have been implemented in schools. Here are some approaches to improving teacher effectiveness that you may have observed:

- Requiring teachers to use highly scripted programs to standardize instruction.
- Publishing test scores in newspapers.
- Linking student test scores to teacher evaluations.
- Conducting more frequent teacher evaluation cycles.
- Conducting instructional rounds or walkthroughs.
- Providing merit pay to high-performing teachers.
- Developing more rigorous teacher evaluation processes.
- Providing workshops and courses in district and out of district.
- Providing coaching and teacher leader support for professional learning.

Some of these approaches show evidence of positive impact on teacher effectiveness, though some do not. Yet, we believe that significant, continuous improvement in teaching is the single most important factor in student achievement. We propose a variety of professional learning opportunities and evaluation systems that promote growth.

## Setting Professional Goals for Yourself and the Team

We encourage you to consider your own professional goals and share them with your colleagues so they can see that you are a continuous learner who can contribute to the mutual support already present on the team. Consider setting explicit team goals so that you can address and monitor how the team members work together to accomplish the school's vision.

As a supervisor, it is important to set professional goals every year with each teacher. When the teachers share their goals with each other and with the

As established earlier, *usually* the educators in the school are supervised by the school principal. But that is not *always* true. For example, in some places an individual from the central office supervises a teacher, particularly if he works across more than one school.

For example, the English learner specialists may be supervised by the person who directs multilingual learning in the district. Or all the coaches in a district may be supervised by a director of professional development. When the supervisor is not based in the school, the important point is to be clear about who is supervising whom and what the role of the supervisor is and is not. It's also important that the supervisor's expectations are communicated to the school-based principal. The school-based leaders will need to make a concerted effort to be sure the individuals are integrated on the team just like those who are based in the school.

There are also contexts in which an individual is co-supervised by the building principal and someone from the central office. In this case, the co-supervisors and the supervisee need to be sure they are all on the same page in terms of roles and the professional learning and performance goals for the supervisee. To make this work well, clear communication and understandings in writing are essential.

coach, they can focus their efforts. Consider having the teachers share their own professional goals with each other at meetings and make plans to support each other and monitor their progress across the year. They can all benefit from opportunities for dialogue and reflection and from the collective expertise of the team.

# Observation: The Heart of Teacher Evaluation

You are always learning about the teaching in your school as you move through the building and interact with people. But there is no substitute for an informed, structured observation of lessons. Lesson observation is one component of the required teacher evaluation process that has many benefits.

## A Structure for Scheduled Teacher Observation

Below we provide a general three-part structure for your scheduled observations of literacy teaching (Figure 22-5). It's important to formally schedule each of the three parts with the teacher ahead of time.

**Pre-Lesson Conference.** This is your time to be a careful, attentive listener and begin the process of inquiry with your colleague. In a short pre-lesson conference, you get evidence of how the teacher is thinking about the readers/writers/texts/writing and the plan for teaching. You and the teacher might

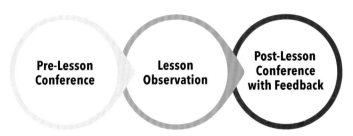

**Figure 22-5.** A Structure for Observing Literacy Teaching

review the observation tools we've provided in this book to identify an area the teacher has been working on. This presupposes the tool has been introduced to the teachers in a professional learning context so that it is familiar.

This is an opportunity for the teacher to articulate her goals and rationales based on her knowledge of the students. Support the teacher's thinking about the children's literacy competencies and her use of evidence to guide her plans for teaching: soft data such as anecdotal notes, student writing, reader's or writer's notebooks and/or hard data such as running records and benchmark assessment data. You also want to find out what the teacher is working on in her craft and particular things she may want you to look for in order to be helpful.

When you ask questions to understand the teacher's thinking, you need not have all the answers and may not have the level of expertise as the teacher, but you are providing a safe context for the teacher to articulate her thinking and reflect on her students and her plans for teaching. Think about the language you might use to gain understanding of the teacher's rationales. We have provided examples of productive language for gaining information during the pre-conference (Figure 22-6).

**Lesson Observation** Sit behind the children as a silent observer and take notes on the lesson. Make a line down the middle of a blank page and make notes on the left side about what the teacher says and on the right side about what the children say. Be sure to notice as many strengths as you can and write notes related to the teacher's requests. Note any of your genuine wonderings in a section on the page.

When you observe a lesson, you bring another perspective to the classroom, and you can think together with the teacher about the students and the effects of teaching on their competencies. The look-for tools can be very useful when you have shared them with the teacher previously, as they allow her to have more agency and to think about the criteria for herself.

## OBSERVING BILINGUAL AND EL LESSONS

For obvious reasons, bilingual teachers and EL specialists usually are supervised and observed by school- or district-level supervisors who speak the language of instruction. In general, a bilingual administrator conducting a formal evaluation of a bilingual teacher during instruction in Spanish, for instance, should have good control of academic Spanish, not just conversational Spanish. Of course, this applies to all languages used during instruction in your school.

Is it ever appropriate for a principal who speaks only English to observe a teacher who is delivering instruction in another language? Maybe. But only if the goal is to observe factors that can be appreciated visually, such as classroom management, levels of student engagement, the classroom environment, or the amount of opportunity children have to talk about their learning.

**Post-Observation Conference** The post-observation conference is a time to reflect together on the teaching and the learning. Your goal is for the teacher to do most of the talking. You can prompt for the analysis of her teaching decisions and their effects on the students using evidence from the lesson. In this constructive conversation, the two of you are inquiring together about a problem of practice that will result in new insights for both of you. Your goal is for the teacher to think in new ways that will benefit all her students in future teaching decisions.

## The Importance of Feedback

Feedback that supports growth and reflection is useful to teachers. Feedback that is negative and judgmental is not. When you and a teacher think and problem solve as colleagues, the whole process feels positive, productive, and free of empty, unspecified praise.

The feedback you give teachers should always be meaningful, useful, and timely. Your coaching language becomes second nature to you. It is important to notice and confirm strong teaching in specific terms, to listen well, to give wait time, and to focus on moving forward. Consider ways to promote agency and independence and support the teacher's ability to learn from teaching.

Unfortunately, some teachers have experienced feedback as an attempt to create a paper trail for dismissal or promotion rather than an opportunity for professional learning. Constructive feedback is more easily received against a background of trust, clear expectations, and shared understandings about the purpose of the observation.

Constructive feedback following an observation should be given right after the observation, usually during the post-observation conference. The conference should take place in a suitable location, preferably in the teacher's space at a table so you can sit shoulder to shoulder or eye to eye. Both the supervisor and teacher need notepads to record the main points. Your two-way conversation is most helpful when you do

| PROMPTS DURING A LESSON OBSERVATION CYCLE | |
|---|---|
| **General** | • What are you working on in your teaching of writing (reading, phonics) this year? How can I support you?<br>• What are you working on in your teaching of guided reading lessons (writers' workshop, phonics lessons, etc.)?<br>• What are you feeling is effective in your teaching of reading (writing, phonics)? |
| **Preparing for Teaching** | • How did you prepare for this teaching (or lesson) today?<br>• Who are the students about whom you have the most concern? What is your plan for helping them?<br>• How do you select principles for your phonics lessons (reading minilessons, writing minilessons)?<br>• Talk about your reading records (writing records) for these students. How have they helped you plan for this reading/ writing lesson?<br>• What information about the students did you use to plan for this reading/writing lesson?<br>• In today's lesson, what are you helping the children learn how to do as readers? writers?<br>• How will you know your teaching was effective? Or how will you assess their learning?<br>• How did *The Literacy Continuum* (or your school or district learning goals) inform your planning? |
| **Assessing Teaching** | • Talk about your students as readers/writers. What have you taught them how to do?<br>• What is your system for documenting student reading progress? writing progress?<br>• How is your assessment system working for you?<br>• What are you learning about your students? |
| **Reflecting on Teaching** | • What do you think was most effective in your teaching (lesson) today?<br>• What do you think you might have done differently?<br>• How will you know your teaching was successful today? |

Figure 22-6. Prompts During a Lesson Observation Cycle

not use words that imply judgement—like *good job*, *excellent*, or *I liked . . . .* Hear the teacher's voice and become a genuine thought partner.

Your goal is to understand the teacher's decisions, not to fix the lesson you have observed. You engage the teacher in a reflective conversation in which she receives confirmation from her self-analysis of what was effective in the teaching. Avoid formulaic feedback such as pointing our three strengths and identifying two areas for improvement. Rather, look at each conversation as an opportunity to engage in inquiry or solve a problem of practice with a colleague that will impact all her future teaching.

Be transparent in communicating what you noticed and what you are wondering about. Aim to get behind the teacher's thinking and understand her rationales for decision-making. You may not know the answers, but when you ask good questions, you create an opportunity for the teacher to articulate and reflect on her teaching—and that tells you a lot about his perspective. The most useful feedback is substantive and rooted in evidence and in the resources and tools you share.

Constructive feedback is more easily addressed when teachers feel there is honesty and openness in a spirit of support not judgment. Think about spending a good amount of the time thinking forward about how the insights can be used to make a difference for all the students in the future. It is important not to overwhelm the teacher and to address the goals the teacher has identified for herself. You might complete a very short summary of your discussion following the debrief and send it to the teacher.

Now let's think about the language you use with teachers during pre- and post-observation conferences and in other settings during the day and year.

## Using Language That Promotes Inquiry and Reflective Practice

Be thoughtful about the language you use across all the contexts within which you interact with teachers. Thoughtful language can support teacher inquiry and reflective practice. As stated earlier, your goal is not to have all the answers. It is to promote your colleagues' ability to analyze and reflect on the effects of teaching on student learning.

As you think together in pre- and post-observation conferences or have conversations after group observations or walks, there will be numerous opportunities for you to prompt teachers to share rationales and analyses of teaching decisions. Remember: you are modeling a reflective process that will permeate the culture of your school.

Your language can impact teachers' expectations for your conversations both within and outside of conferences. Consider the sample prompts from Figure 22-6. Think about what you notice about the specific language in each grouping and its effect on the teacher's sense of agency and ability to reflect on teaching.

# Supervising Teachers Who Resist Change

As a principal who is promoting instructional coherence and continuous improvement, you are bound to encounter someone who finds the expectations challenging for a variety of reasons and shows evidence of resisting change.

## Observable Behaviors Indicating Difficulty

If you have a literacy coach in your school, it might be a good idea to work with him to generate a list of observable behaviors that indicate a teacher is having problems working toward the team's goals. Together, try to think of what you hear teachers say and what they do that implies they are not open to new learning. Some examples are listed in Figure 22-7.

| OBSERVABLE BEHAVIORS INDICATING RESISTANCE TO CHANGE | |
|---|---|
| **WHAT THEY SAY** | **WHAT THEY DO** |
| ▪ I have been teaching twenty years. I do not need to work with a coach. | ▪ Avoid appointments with the coach and/or cancel them. |
| ▪ I already know this. | ▪ Do not participate in discussion with colleagues or share resources and ideas. |
| ▪ I don't have time to meet with a coach. | ▪ Use negative body language (crossed arms, eye rolls, grading papers during professional meetings). |
| ▪ My reading scores are fine. What I'm doing has always worked for me. | |
| ▪ This will only last a short time. | ▪ Do not ask for advice. |
| ▪ I don't have time to read, watch, attend . . . | ▪ Try to involve others in resisting change. |
| ▪ We already tried that, and it didn't work. | ▪ Say they will implement but don't; perform only when the coach or principal is in the room. |
| ▪ This won't work for my kids; they are not skilled (or motivated) enough. | |
| ▪ This is the same as _____. They are just calling it something new. | ▪ Challenge everything others say. |
| ▪ I found something on the internet attacking this approach. | ▪ Comply but not work to internalize new behaviors and/or language. |
| ▪ I don't have the right materials to do that. | ▪ Wait to see if others fail or succeed. |
| ▪ This takes too much preparation/ time. | ▪ Ignore the principal or coach. |
| ▪ Will I have to access that, too? | ▪ Demonstrate caring only about their own classrooms. |
| ▪ Is this required in my contract? | ▪ Complain about too much work or not enough preparation time. |

**Figure 22-7.** Observable Behaviors Indicating Difficulty

If you have been a principal (or coach) for several years, you have probably heard or seen many of the bulleted items in the chart shown opposite. It's useful to think about *why* statements and behaviors like these are seen and heard. And then you need to address the problem quickly, because such behaviors on the part of even two or three individuals can be toxic if they are allowed to persist.

We do not refer here to simple differences in style; for example, some teachers are exuberant and like to sing in the classroom while others might be quieter and more serious. Different personalities can work toward the same goals and give children equally rich experiences. But consider this: In three classrooms, third graders read over fifty books during the year and discuss and write about books daily. In one classroom, third graders spend six weeks on each book and spend most of their time responding to questions on pencil-and-paper forms. Which students will carry a rich experience in literacy learning with them into grade four? As the principal and literacy leader, it is ultimately your responsibility to assure equity and coherence in what is taught and how.

## Confronting Difficulties

A first step might be to try to gain perspective on the teacher's point of view and look for the teacher's strengths. People behave as they do for a reason. For example, an individual might:

- Feel inadequate in facing new pedagogy.
- Decide to "wait it out" because she has experienced so many whipsaw changes in curricula, programs, and personnel over the years. (The teachers in a city school system we know of had a saying: "Nothing lasts more than three years, not even the principal.")
- Have difficulty communicating with the other teachers (or hasn't felt included).
- Believe in her "success" of the past in using specific techniques.
- Distrust the leader and/or leadership team ("in-group").

There can be dozens more reasons. Learning *why* the teacher is reluctant is a first step. Then you will need to balance pressure with support. You can:

- Invite the teacher to have a one-on-one conversation. Tell what you've noticed and ask for his thinking. Take the opportunity to reiterate the team's values and ask how you can support him. With kindness, but clarity, let the teacher know the expectations.
- Provide more support in the form of professional learning opportunities to encourage first steps.
- Interact often to create a trusting relationship.
- Persist in expecting the teacher to take small steps.

There is no guarantee that any of these approaches will result in change or improved behaviors, but you definitely won't get results if you don't try.

## What Else Can You Do?

When you first meet or hire a teacher, make it clear that you want the staff to form mutual expectations and help each other grow and improve. This transparency and clarity will prevent a lot of problems and pave the way for productive work even with teachers who are reluctant to change and grow. Transparency creates trust.

It should go without saying that you need to document opportunities, observations, and interactions so that you have some specific points to make when you have a conference with the teacher. Focus the conversation on something that is doable, and follow up to provide more support as needed. Your persistence in assuring that the teachers make a sincere effort and commitment to the team will be essential. It is your responsibility to address the performance of any team member who detracts from the school's mission and diminishes student learning opportunities.

It is possible that the teacher will decide to apply for a position at another school, and that should not be viewed as a failure on your part. We do caution, however, that passing the problem along to someone else is not always a solution. Other schools may operate in a way that has different expectations, but our hope is that district-level leaders will try to promote coherence across schools. After all, children frequently move from school to school. Vulnerable children benefit from a consistent approach.

It has been our experience that teachers are very different in their reaction to change. Some become excited and want to try a lot of things right away (especially if they have beautiful new books). Others want to take one step at a time, and that's okay. What is not okay is no progress at all, and that should be clear as an expectation. We have seen boxes of new beautiful books that sit in a storage closet and for some reason never reach children. If you have a coach or a very experienced teacher, that person can be extremely helpful in helping everyone take small steps in a positive direction.

# A Systemic Approach to Building Teacher Expertise

Teacher evaluation as a single emphasis will not be adequate for improving teaching quality. A more comprehensive approach that includes attention to the elements of the system is needed, beginning with recruiting high-quality teacher candidates. The evaluation system, with input from teachers and various levels of leadership, needs to include high standards for meaningful student learning along with support structures and aligned professional learning opportunities that assure the continuous improvement of teachers and teaching quality.

# The Takeaway

The supervision of teachers is a complex and time-consuming process, but well worth the effort because of its potential to expand competencies and promote continual growth among the teachers in your school. The most effective supervisors assume a coaching stance in their interactions with teachers, communicating clearly and often, celebrating their accomplishments, staying true to common goals, and clearly articulating expectations and processes for decision-making. When teachers are invited to take an active role in the supervision process, they view the supervisor as a colleague and co-learner, and they are more open to constructive feedback. The principal's role as a supervisor of teachers includes the recruitment, hiring, onboarding, and retention of a diverse staff, including bilingual teachers and teachers of color, as well as teachers with urban life experiences.

## Think About Your School

As you think about the ideas in this chapter, consider the extent to which supervision at your school facilitates the professional growth of teachers. To provide insight, you might reflect on these questions:

- How often am I in classrooms to observe and share in the teaching and learning, with no intention of evaluation?
- What evidence of teacher growth and professional learning can I identify as an outcome of my approach to supervision?
- How is our approach to supervision connected to the vision and values of our school?
- What steps can I take to promote and support a growth-centered approach to supervision?

## Move Your School Forward

Take action on something you learned in this chapter and thought about doing in your school. You might:

- Schedule a meeting with your district hiring partner to see how your efforts to hire a talented and diverse teaching staff can be supported outside of the school building.
- Confer with other school leaders about how you can improve your school's teacher retention rate, using some of the suggestions in this book.

- Confer with other school leaders about how to provide positive, persistent support to teachers who feel challenged by change.
- Address issues of ineffective or mediocre teaching for the sake of the children.
- Take a moment to reflect on each classroom observation cycle you complete, jotting notes on what went well and what you might do differently in the next cycle.

# Chapter 23

# Learning and Leading Forward

*Knowledge emerges only through invention and reinvention,
through the restless, impatient, continuing, hopeful inquiry
human beings pursue in the world, with the
world, and with each other.*
—Paulo Freire

OUR JOURNEY TOGETHER IN these pages is coming to an end, but we could think of this as a beginning. Throughout these chapters, we have done important thinking and decision-making together. We have reflected on the roles and responsibilities of school leaders in helping teachers assure children their human right to literacy. You and your teams have invested in the process of co-creating shared values that center your decision-making and ground your rationales about teaching and learning. We have looked together at how to build and nurture a culture of collaboration, teamwork, and trusting relationships. As Roland Barth (2006) states:

> The nature of relationships among the adults within a school has
> a greater influence on the character and quality of that school and

on student accomplishment than anything else. If the relationships between administrators and teachers are trusting, generous, helpful, and cooperative, then the relationships between teachers and students, between students and students, and between teachers and parents are likely to be trusting, generous, helpful, and cooperative.

We have engaged with the complexities of how children learn through constructive processes, expert assistance, social interactions, emotional support, active engagement, risk-taking, and reflection. We examined essential principles of learning to read and write, that is, reading and writing are complex, reciprocal, and language-based processes and are learned by engaging in real reading and writing. We considered the qualities of a strong learning community and the important role of talk in the classroom.

With these foundational concepts in mind, we turned to literacy teaching and learning and thought carefully about designing assessment, teaching, and intervention systems that are coherent, effective, and grounded in evidence. We looked closely at five kinds of instructional contexts for reading, five kinds of instructional contexts for writing, and workshop structures that create daily opportunities for students to engage in authentic reading and writing. We examined the importance of strong daily phonics instruction to establish the building blocks of written language. We thought together about how to assure equitable literacy outcomes for English learners and students who find reading and writing difficult. We discussed the importance of creating collections of high-quality texts, materials, and resources in your school and classrooms to support literacy learning.

## SYSTEMATIC THINKING ABOUT SYSTEMIC IMPROVEMENT

Sometimes school leaders have reduced school improvement to one aspect of instruction, for example, more phonics or more emphasis on comprehension, and those are often desirable actions, especially when clear instructional needs are evident. But meaningful, sustained improvement will be achieved only when all parts of the system are working together in the same direction. Improvement is complex, multifaceted, and continuous, not simple and quick. For example, the quality of instruction is influenced by the assessments used to guide planning and decision-making; the professional learning of teachers is influenced by the relationships between the members of the team and the design of professional learning; the amount of instructional time for literacy is influenced by the school's common values; the effectiveness of the instruction is influenced by the collection and use of data and evidence; and student learning is influenced by access to high-quality, culturally relevant materials. Systematic thinking is needed to bring about systemic improvement.

In this final section of the book, we have examined the ways your leadership can create and sustain improvements in the educational system by building professional capacity through distributed leadership, promoting professional learning, and supervising for teacher growth. Your thinking around these issues is important because meaningful change in the education system emerges from one's thinking about the role and responsibilities of school leadership. Meaningful change that lasts doesn't happen any other way.

# Keys to Systemic Improvement

Looking across this book, in a variety of ways we have explored twelve big ideas related to the improvement of literacy education in schools (Figure 23-1 and inside back cover). We have clustered them into three categories that we hope will be useful to you as you reflect on and recenter your work as a school leader and engage in dialogue with colleagues. The five concepts in the left circle are integral to the culture of your school and the impact of your leadership. To sustain improvements to the system, a strong culture based on common values and beliefs is essential. To build and maintain a strong culture, you and your team lead through collaboration and teamwork, promote shared leadership by educators in the school, foster continuous professional learning, and nurture family and community partnerships. The five concepts in the right circle are connected to teaching and learning. To improve the systems of teaching and learning within your school, you and your team create a coherent curriculum that builds on the unique perspectives and strengths of each learner through effective classroom instruction. To assure equitable outcomes for all students, strong supplemental interventions are an integral part of the

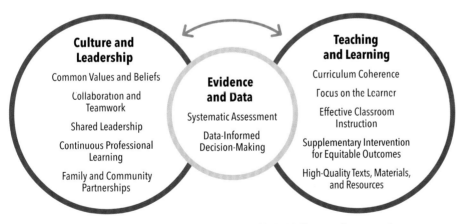

**12 KEYS TO SYSTEMIC IMPROVEMENT**

Figure 23-1. 12 Keys to Systemic Improvement

system, as are high-quality texts and resources for all students. The fulcrum of this work is the collection and use of evidence and data, represented by the two concepts in the middle circle. To make sustainable improvements, the rationales, priorities, and actions of your team will need to be supported by data. Meaningful shifts in culture and leadership or teaching and learning turn on high-quality decisions based on evidence and data.

Notice that the five concepts in the right circle refer to the "bottom line" instructional program in literacy—what teachers and learners do every day. Most efforts at improving achievement start there and stay there. And most fail to make a discernable difference because school teams aren't working from common values and beliefs. Educators aren't pulling in the same direction.

The left circle represents the way to get there with lasting impact and a strong likelihood of success. Common vision, collaboration, shared leadership, continuous learning, and partnerships put a strong frame of teamwork around the improvement effort. People help each other, they take risks together, and they adjust when mistakes are made. Ideas in the left circle have another important benefit. People get better at improvement. They grow as leaders, problem-solvers, and colleagues. They develop expertise and feel they are making a difference.

The middle circle both informs the day-to-day work on the new initiative and gives innovators an important tool to measure its success. It's folly to wait until test scores come out to determine whether you are succeeding. You need feedback along the way so you can make adjustments.

# Systems for Literacy Improvement

Before we part ways for now, we'd like to offer a final tool that brings together the twelve big ideas. The Literacy Improvement Facilitation Tool (LIFT) you'll find on the next several pages is designed as an interactive rubric that can help you and your team reflect on the qualities, strengths, and needs of your school and make a plan to move toward coherent and sustainable literacy improvement (see pages 464–471). While the rubric is written for school-based leaders and their teams, many aspects have important implications for district leaders.

Across the top of the tool, you will notice four categories: 1. Getting Started, 2. Moving Forward, 3. Gaining Momentum, and 4. Expanding Expertise. Each category represents an increasing level of collaboration and a more robust and coherent implementation of your goals within an educational system.

- The first category describes a school where educators work in silos and teachers practice in private behind closed doors. There is little or no collaboration among colleagues nor opportunity to build systemic coherence.

- Move across to the fourth category and you find a description of a school that is a dynamic learning organization, where the collaborative work of educators is continuously improving the coherence of the system and leaders seek opportunities for further innovation.

- The categories in between describe progress as educators take on more collaborative ways of working and prioritize actions that build systemic coherence.

As you read the headings in the left column, you will find aspects of the education system that contribute to the literacy outcomes of children, for example, Common Values and Beliefs, Curriculum Coherence, and Text Resources. They are grouped into four major categories: Culture and Leadership; Evidence and Data; Teaching and Learning; and Texts, Materials, and Resources. The subcategory Effective Classroom Instruction is further divided into Reading Instruction; Writing Instruction; and Phonics, Spelling, and Word Study. The subcategory Text Resources is further divided into types of texts. As you read across the rows, you will find descriptions of how the four categories of collaboration and coherence (1–4 across the top) are manifested in each aspect of the education system. Keep in mind that no box will perfectly describe your school at a given point in time, but consideration of the characteristics can help to center your conversations and thinking.

*continued on page 472*

# LITERACY IMPROVEMENT FACILITATION TOOL (LIFT)

| | **1. GETTING STARTED** <br> Educators work mostly individually without collaborating with colleagues to identify areas of strength and need and have not planned actions to increase systemic coherence. | **2. MOVING FORWARD** <br> Educators are beginning to work collaboratively to identify areas of strength and need and are beginning to plan actions to increase systemic coherence. |
|---|---|---|
| **Common Values and Beliefs** | ☐ Educators have not yet begun the process of identifying or coming to consensus on shared values and beliefs about literacy teaching and learning that will guide their work. | ☐ Educators are beginning the process of identifying shared values and beliefs about literacy teaching and learning. They are working to reach consensus and create a written document that can guide decision-making in their work. |
| **Collaboration and Teamwork** | ☐ Educators work individually most of the time. There is little evidence of meaningful collaboration among colleagues or commitment to building the collective expertise that positively impacts student learning. | ☐ A culture of teamwork is beginning to take hold, with some evidence of collaboration and commitment to building collective expertise. A few small teams are forming to take on work that has positive impact on student learning. |
| **Shared Leadership** | ☐ There is little evidence of shared leadership. Decision-making flows from the top-down. The leaders prescribe ways of doing things, and conformity and compliance are expected. Roles are rigid and hierarchical. | ☐ There is some evidence that school leaders are building a culture of shared leadership by identifying strengths of the team, asking for input on norms and working agreements, and encouraging individual educators to take on leadership roles. They are exploring ways to include multiple perspectives and promote acts of teacher leadership. |
| **Continuous Professional Learning** | ☐ There is little or no evidence of meaningful, relevant, ongoing professional learning. Educators participate in the required professional learning opportunities, although the content may not reflect the strengths and needs of the educators in the school. <br><br> ☐ The professional capacity of the team is limited, and school leaders generally rely solely on outside expertise to provide professional learning opportunities. | ☐ There is some evidence that educators are beginning to take an active role in the direction of their learning to ensure greater relevance to their work and relevant, ongoing learning opportunities. <br><br> ☐ The school has begun to invest in the professional capacity of the team by advocating for coaching positions, making time and resources available for teachers to take on leadership roles, and/or providing some outside expertise to support professional learning |
| **Family and Community Partnerships** | ☐ There is little or no evidence of high-quality communication between the school, families, and the community. Educators have little or no interaction with families. Little effort is made to welcome families into the school or build on their knowledge and perspectives about the children. Families are passive recipients of information about their children's lives at school. | ☐ Some evidence indicates high-quality communication between the school, families, and the community. Educators are beginning to take steps to include families and the community in the education of the children. The school and classroom environments show some evidence that families are valued, e.g., by including artifacts from children's homes and creating signs and important messages in multiple languages. |

**Culture and Leadership**

## 3. GAINING MOMENTUM

There is evidence that educators work collaboratively to build on areas of strength, address needs, and prioritize and take actions that will increase systemic coherence. They have made a few improvements that are small but significant. They are beginning to notice and appreciate the need for innovation to prepare students for their future.

☐ Educators have engaged in a group process to create a written document that describes their shared values and beliefs about literacy teaching and learning. They have begun to use it to guide decision-making in many parts of their work.

☐ There are many examples of collaboration and commitment to building collective expertise. Several teams have formed, and they occasionally report progress toward products or outcomes that have positive impact on student learning.

☐ There are many examples of shared leadership throughout the school. Educators in a variety of roles are helping to construct norms and working agreements and are demonstrating initiative in solving problems of practice through inquiry and collaboration. Leaders provide some teachers with sufficient time and professional learning to support growth in their leadership skills, and teacher leaders are emerging.

☐ There are many examples of educators identifying and participating in ongoing professional learning opportunities that have relevance to their work.

☐ The school continues to invest in the professional capacity of the team by increasing coaching opportunities, making time and resources available for teachers to take on a greater variety of leadership roles, and/or providing more outside expertise to support professional learning.

☐ Many examples of high-quality communication between the school, families, and the community are evident and communication is increasing. Educators are identifying ways to include families and the community in the education of the children and share in the leadership of the school, e.g., by serving on teams. Teachers continue to need structures to learn from families throughout the year, e.g., surveys, interviews.

## 4. EXPANDING EXPERTISE

As part of a dynamic learning organization, the educators consistently work collaboratively and productively to build on areas of strength, address needs, and prioritize actions that increase and sustain systemic coherence. They continue to make many small but significant improvements and consistently seek opportunities for innovation to prepare students for their future.

☐ Educators consistently use the document that describes their shared values and beliefs about literacy teaching and learning as a foundation to guide decision-making in all aspects of their work. They revisit the document regularly to ground their work in their common values.

☐ There is strong evidence that educators consistently collaborate within a culture of teamwork to increase effectiveness, solve problems, measure progress, and support each other's learning. Teams regularly report progress toward products or outcomes that have significant, positive impact on student learning.

☐ Shared leadership is a consistent characteristic of the culture of the school. Collaborative problem-solving and decision-making by teams of educators are evident throughout the school. Decisions flow from the team's shared vision, values, and goals. Groups co-construct norms and working agreements and take action to solve problems of practice through inquiry and collaboration. Flexible leadership roles are taken on by a variety of team members. Teachers are valued as leaders who contribute important ideas, perspectives, and expertise.

☐ Relevant, ongoing professional learning is a consistent characteristic of the school. Educators are fully invested in meaningful professional learning. They take an active role in co-planning learning opportunities that address specific areas of need or problems of practice.

☐ The school builds professional capacity by investing in the expertise of coaches and teacher leaders and by providing relevant outside expertise to support professional learning.

☐ Families and the community are partners in the education of children. They contribute funds of knowledge that educators tap to create more effective and culturally-relevant learning experiences. Educators view families as knowledgeable, helpful partners who are essential in helping students make progress in literacy learning. School-home communication is meaningful and consistent, with translations providing access to families speaking languages other than English at home. Families and members of the community contribute to and lead teams as appropriate.

| | | | 1. GETTING STARTED | 2. MOVING FORWARD |
|---|---|---|---|---|
| **Evidence and Data** | **Systematic Assessment** | | ☐ There is little or no evidence that the school has a comprehensive and systematic assessment design for reading and writing that reflects the educators' values about literacy learning. | ☐ The school has reached consensus on a comprehensive and systematic assessment design for reading and writing that reflects the educators' values about literacy learning. There is some evidence that implementation has begun. |
| | | | ☐ Teachers do not use *continuous assessments* (e.g., running records, student writing, reader's and writer's notebooks, observational records) to inform instruction. | ☐ Teachers are beginning to use *continuous assessments* and are learning about systems for collecting data and using it to guide daily instruction. |
| | | | ☐ Teachers do not administer *interval assessments* (e.g., benchmark assessments, writing prompts) to document change over time in literacy learning. | ☐ Teachers are beginning to administer *interval assessments* to document change over time in literacy learning and use the data effectively. |
| | **Data-Informed Decision-Making** | | ☐ Educators make little use of hard and soft data to inform their decisions. Educators do not yet have a system for collecting, analyzing, and using data to improve student outcomes. | ☐ There is some evidence that educators have begun to use hard and soft data to inform their decisions. Educators are beginning to develop efficient systems to collect, analyze, and use data to improve student outcomes. |
| **Teaching and Learning** | **Curriculum Coherence** (*The Literacy Continuum* or other curriculum document) | | ☐ Teachers have limited or no familiarity with *The Literacy Continuum* as a tool for assessment, planning, and teaching. | ☐ Some teachers are aware of *The Literacy Continuum* and are beginning to use it. Teachers have a tentative plan to use *The Literacy Continuum* but do not yet link assessment data to instructional goals. |
| | | | | ☐ Teachers have not had the opportunity for professional learning that will help them understand and use *The Literacy Continuum* as a tool to observe, assess, plan for, and guide teaching. |
| | **Focus on the Learner** | | ☐ Teachers' observations of student behaviors are random and superficial. They do not yet show understanding of how children develop language and literacy competencies. Teaching does not yet take into account the strengths of each learner. | ☐ There is some evidence that teachers observe student behaviors and are beginning to adjust their teaching to account for the strengths of each learner. They are developing an understanding of how children develop language and literacy competencies. They are noticing how their language influences the learner and are beginning to make more precise choices. |
| | **Effective Classroom Instruction** / **Reading Instruction: Whole Group** | **Interactive Read-Aloud** | ☐ Teachers read aloud texts occasionally, but texts are randomly selected. | ☐ Teachers read aloud regularly and are beginning to use text sets to support making connections across texts. |
| | | | ☐ Teachers generally don't support children in making connections across texts. | ☐ Teachers usually invite students' thinking. The talk is mostly focused on within-the-text understandings but with some evidence of beyond-the-text understanding. |
| | | | ☐ Teachers invite student discussion, but talk is mostly focused on within-the-text understandings. | |
| | | **Shared Reading** | ☐ Teachers currently do not engage in shared reading with enlarged texts or poetry. | ☐ Teachers occasionally engage in shared reading with enlarged texts or poetry but do not revisit for specific teaching opportunities. |
| | | **Reading Minilessons and Group Share** | ☐ There is little or no evidence that teachers regularly teach whole-group reading minilessons and provide follow-up in group share. | ☐ There is some evidence that teachers occasionally teach whole-group reading minilessons. They need more support in selecting minilessons that address the reading needs of most of the readers in the class and providing follow-up in group share. |

| 3. GAINING MOMENTUM | 4. EXPANDING EXPERTISE |
|---|---|
| ☐ A comprehensive and systematic assessment design that reflects the educators' values about literacy learning is in place, and many teachers have learned to use it.<br><br>☐ Teachers use *continuous assessments* and systems for collecting data with increasing regularity. They are using the data to guide daily instruction more frequently.<br><br>☐ Teachers administer *interval assessments* and increasingly use the data effectively to document change over time in literacy learning. | ☐ The school has fully implemented a comprehensive and systematic assessment design for reading and writing that reflects the school's values about literacy learning.<br><br>☐ Teachers consistently use the data from *continuous assessments* (e.g., running records, student writing, reader's and writer's notebooks, observational records) to inform instruction.<br><br>☐ Teachers administer *interval assessments* (e.g., benchmark assessments, writing prompts) at agreed-upon intervals to document change over time in literacy learning. |
| ☐ Many examples indicate that educators use hard and soft data to inform their decisions. Although educators are collecting data, they need to refine their expertise in its analysis and use to improve student outcomes. | ☐ Educators are consistently collecting, analyzing, and using hard and soft data in efficient, effective ways to inform decisions that result in improved student outcomes. |
| ☐ Many teachers are familiar with *The Literacy Continuum* and use it to link assessment data to instructional goals. They confer occasionally with colleagues to expand understanding of the tool.<br><br>☐ Teachers have had the opportunity for introductory professional learning but need more learning opportunities in order to use *The Literacy Continuum* to observe, assess, plan for, and guide teaching effectively. | ☐ Almost all teachers have a deep understanding of *The Literacy Continuum* and use it consistently and effectively to observe, assess, plan for, and guide teaching. They have internalized the student language and literacy behaviors and understandings through daily use. |
| ☐ There is ample evidence that teachers regularly and systematically observe and analyze student behaviors and often use the information to select teaching responses that support the strengths of each learner. They have an understanding of how children develop language and literacy competencies and how their language influences the learner. | ☐ There is strong evidence that teachers systematically observe and analyze student behaviors to inform moment-to-moment, day-to-day teaching responses that confirm and expand the strengths of each learner. They have a deep understanding of how children develop language and literacy competencies and how their precise language (clear statements, prompts, and questions) influences what the learner can do. |
| ☐ Teachers read aloud several times a week, and there is evidence that text selection and discussion are planned. They are using text sets more frequently, making it easier to make connections across texts.<br><br>☐ Teachers usually invite students' thinking within, beyond, and about the text and have established a few talk structures for discussion (e.g., turn and talk). | ☐ Teachers read aloud from high-quality texts daily and interactive read-aloud lessons are planned.<br><br>☐ Teachers consistently use text sets to support strong connections.<br><br>☐ Teachers consistently invite students' thinking within, beyond, and about the text. A variety of effective talk structures are in place to support meaningful discussion that involves all learners. |
| ☐ Teachers regularly engage in shared reading with enlarged texts or poetry and occasionally revisit the texts for specific teaching opportunities. | ☐ Teachers consistently use enlarged texts and poems to engage students in reading complex texts with support several times a week and revisit them for powerful teaching opportunities. |
| ☐ There is ample evidence that teachers regularly teach whole-group reading minilessons that address the reading needs of most of the readers in the class and provide follow-up in group share. | ☐ Almost all teachers effectively use whole-group reading minilessons and group share to support the reading needs of most of the readers in the class. The reading minilessons are carefully sequenced and well designed to support students' learning. |

| | | 1. GETTING STARTED | 2. MOVING FORWARD |
|---|---|---|---|
| **Teaching and Learning** — **Effective Classroom Instruction** — **Reading Instruction: Small Group** | **Guided Reading** | ☐ There is little or no evidence that teachers provide guided reading instruction to small, temporary groups of students based on instructional reading levels and strengths in literacy processing.<br><br>☐ Teachers do not yet understand the structure of a guided reading lesson, how to use facilitative teaching routines, or how to select appropriate texts for groups. | ☐ There is some evidence that teachers provide occasional guided reading instruction and are learning how to form temporary groups based on students' instructional reading levels and strengths in literacy processing.<br><br>☐ Teachers are becoming familiar with the lesson structure and teaching routines and are learning to select appropriate texts for groups. |
| | **Book Clubs** | ☐ There is little or no evidence that students engage in small-group book club discussions led by the teacher.<br><br>☐ Teachers have not established social conventions for students when talking to one another about books. | ☐ There is some evidence that students engage in small-group book clubs a few times a year, but the teacher does not facilitate discussions to lift students' thinking within, beyond, and about the text.<br><br>☐ Teachers are working to establish some social conventions for book discussion. |
| **Reading Instruction: Individual** | **Independent Reading with Conferring and Writing About Reading** | ☐ There is little or no evidence that students have the opportunity to choose books and read independently. Teachers do not confer with readers.<br><br>☐ Students do not write about reading in a reader's notebook. | ☐ There is some evidence that students have limited time (about twice a week) to choose books and read independently. Teachers generally do not confer with readers.<br><br>☐ Students are beginning to learn how to write about their reading in a reader's notebook. Teachers occasionally respond in writing to students' thinking. |
| **Writing Instruction: Whole Group** | **Modeled/ Shared Writing** | ☐ There is little or no evidence that teachers use modeled or shared writing to demonstrate writing in different forms and decision-making about genre, craft, and conventions. | ☐ There is some evidence that teachers occasionally use modeled or shared writing to demonstrate writing in different forms. They do not yet use the opportunity to reveal thinking from a writer's perspective and decisions about genre, craft, and conventions. |
| | **Interactive Writing (PreK– Grade 2)** | ☐ There is little or no evidence that teachers use interactive writing with students in a whole or small group. | ☐ There is some evidence that teachers are beginning to use interactive writing with students in a whole or small group to create texts for real purposes and audiences. |
| | **Writing Minilessons and Group Share** | ☐ There is little or no evidence that teachers regularly teach whole-group writing minilessons and provide follow-up in group share. | ☐ There is some evidence that teachers occasionally teach whole-group writing minilessons. They need more support in selecting minilessons that address the writing needs of most of the writers in the class and providing follow-up in group share. |
| **Writing Instruction: Small Group** | **Guided Writing** | ☐ There is little or no evidence that teachers provide guided writing instruction to small, temporary groups of students based on similar writing needs. | ☐ There is some evidence that teachers provide occasional guided writing instruction and are learning how to form temporary groups based on writing needs. |
| **Writing Instruction: Individual** | **Independent Writing with Conferring** | ☐ There is little or no evidence that students have the opportunity to write in a writer's notebook or write their own pieces. All writing is prescribed by the teacher. | ☐ There is some evidence that students have limited time (about twice a week) to write in a writer's notebook or work on their own pieces of writing. Teachers generally do not confer with individuals. |
| **Phonics, Spelling, and Word Study** | | ☐ Teachers lack adequate knowledge of the alphabetic system and related concepts.<br><br>☐ Teachers do not provide a daily systematic and explicit phonics/word study lesson for 25–30 minutes.<br><br>☐ Teachers may be using a separate phonics, spelling, and word study program, but there is little or no evidence that they link principles to students' reading and writing. | ☐ Teachers have begun to develop deeper knowledge of the alphabetic system and related concepts.<br><br>☐ Teachers provide a phonics/word study lesson about twice a week and are working to make the lessons explicit.<br><br>☐ Teachers use a separate phonics, spelling, and word study program, and there is some evidence that they link principles to students' reading and writing. |

| 3. GAINING MOMENTUM | 4. EXPANDING EXPERTISE |
|---|---|
| ☐ There is ample evidence that teachers provide guided reading lessons to small, temporary groups every day and are becoming more effective at forming groups based on instructional reading levels and strengths in literacy processing.<br><br>☐ Teachers are more familiar with the lesson structure and teaching routines and are better able to select appropriate texts for groups. | ☐ There is strong evidence that teachers provide skilled guided reading instruction systematically and regroup students regularly based on evidence of progress in literacy processing.<br><br>☐ Teachers have internalized the lesson structure, are very familiar with the teaching routines, and can select appropriate texts for guided reading groups. |
| ☐ There is ample evidence that teachers are meeting with students in book clubs more often and have begun to facilitate discussions to lift students' thinking within, beyond, and about the text.<br><br>☐ Teachers are working effectively with students to teach and support their use of social conventions for book discussion. | ☐ There is strong evidence that teachers consistently meet with students in book clubs once a month and have become adept at facilitating discussions to lift students' thinking within, beyond, and about the text.<br><br>☐ Students consistently demonstrate effective social conventions when talking to one another about books. |
| ☐ There is ample evidence that students have time to choose books and read independently several times a week. Teachers are learning how to provide support to individual readers through one-on-one conferences.<br><br>☐ Students write about their reading in a reader's notebook and have learned a few ways to respond. Teachers regularly respond in writing to students' thinking. | ☐ There is strong evidence that students choose books and read independently every day for a sustained time, conferring with teachers on a regular basis.<br><br>☐ Students keep a record of their reading and writing about their thinking in a variety of forms in the reader's notebook each week. Teachers always respond in writing to students' thinking and regularly analyze students' notebooks for evidence of understanding. |
| ☐ There is ample evidence that teachers use modeled or shared writing regularly to demonstrate writing in different forms and occasionally use the opportunity to reveal thinking from a writer's perspective and decisions about genre, craft, and conventions. | ☐ There is strong evidence that almost all teachers consistently use modeled or shared writing to demonstrate writing in different forms and make powerful teaching decisions that reveal thinking from a writer's perspective and decisions about genre, craft, and conventions. |
| ☐ There is ample evidence that teachers sometimes use interactive writing with students in a whole or small group to create texts for real purposes and audiences. | ☐ There is strong evidence that almost all teachers consistently use interactive writing with students in a whole or small group to create texts for a variety of real purposes and audiences. |
| ☐ There is some evidence that teachers occasionally teach whole-group writing minilessons. They need more support in selecting minilessons that address the writing needs of most of the writers in the class and providing follow-up in group share. | ☐ Almost all teachers effectively use whole-group writing minilessons and group share to support the writing needs of most of the writers in the class. The writing minilessons are carefully sequenced and well designed to support students' learning. |
| ☐ There is ample evidence that teachers provide guided writing lessons to small groups every day and are becoming more effective at forming temporary, needs-based groups. | ☐ Almost all teachers provide skilled guided writing instruction systematically. They identify writers with a common need and provide powerful teaching to address it. |
| ☐ There is ample evidence that students write in a writer's notebook or work on their own pieces of writing several times a week. Teachers are learning how to provide support to individual writers through one-on-one conferences. | ☐ There is strong evidence that students write in a writer's notebook or work on their own pieces of writing every day for a sustained time. Teachers provide powerful, systematic support to individual writers through one-on-one conferences. |
| ☐ Teachers are improving in their knowledge of the alphabetic system and related concepts.<br><br>☐ Teachers provide explicit phonics/word study lesson most days of the week.<br><br>☐ Teachers use a systematic and explicit phonics, spelling, and word study program, and there is ample evidence that they are more consistently linking principles to students' reading and writing. | ☐ Teachers possess strong knowledge of the alphabetic system and related concepts to teach students to process texts effectively.<br><br>☐ Teachers provide a daily systematic and explicit phonics/word study lesson for 25–30 minutes.<br><br>☐ There is strong evidence that teachers effectively link phonics/word study principles to students' reading and writing. |

| | 1. GETTING STARTED | 2. MOVING FORWARD |
|---|---|---|
| **Teaching and Learning** — Supplementary Intervention for Equitable Outcomes | ☐ Some intervention exists but it supplants classroom instruction and is haphazardly applied rather than organized and systematic.<br><br>☐ The intervention system is not consistent with research and does not reflect the values and beliefs of the school. | ☐ The intervention system supplements classroom literacy instruction, but the support is generally not applied in an organized and systematic way.<br><br>☐ The intervention system consists of multiple tiers of support, but teachers need to become adept at using different approaches for different students within each tier.<br><br>☐ Special education services are provided at every tier for the students who need them, but teachers and some specialists need support to understand what "access to strong classroom instruction" might look like for different students.<br><br>☐ The intervention system is partially consistent with research and reflects some of the values and beliefs of the school. |
| **Texts, Materials, and Resources / Text Resources** — Texts for Interactive Read-Aloud | ☐ There is little or no evidence that teachers and students have adequate access to high-quality, complex fiction and nonfiction text sets. | ☐ There is some evidence that high-quality, complex text sets for read aloud have been added to classroom resources. |
| Enlarged Texts for Shared Reading | ☐ There is little or no evidence that teachers have high-quality enlarged texts (fiction and nonfiction books, poems, songs) to make shared reading a part of literacy instruction.<br><br>☐ There are no small copies or audio versions of the texts available for individual rereading. | ☐ There is some evidence that teachers have acquired a few enlarged texts.<br><br>☐ There are a few small copies and audio versions of some of the texts for individual rereading. |
| Leveled Texts for Guided Reading | ☐ The school does not yet have a robust collection of leveled books or a dedicated book room for organization, storage, and sharing of leveled texts for small-group differentiated instruction. | ☐ The school has created a dedicated book room, but the number of books at each level is low and the texts may not be of the highest quality. |
| Multiple Copies of Texts for Book Clubs | ☐ The school does not have multiple copies of a sufficient number of engaging texts at each grade level to support book club discussions. | ☐ The school has multiple copies of a limited number of engaging texts at each grade level and teachers are beginning to organize a few book clubs. |
| Classroom Libraries for Independent Reading | ☐ Classroom libraries are small; lack variety of genres, content, and range of difficulty levels; and contain few or no texts that are socially and culturally relevant. | ☐ A plan for identifying ways to expand size, variety, and relevance of texts in classroom libraries has been developed and implementation has begun. |
| Writing Materials | ☐ Children do not have access to a wide variety of tools to support drawing and writing (e.g., paper, writer's notebooks, markers, pencils, etc.). | ☐ Children have access to a limited range of tools to support drawing and writing. |
| Word Study Materials | ☐ Classrooms lack the numbers and kinds of manipulatives and other materials that are needed to teach phonics, spelling, and word study effectively. | ☐ The school has developed a plan to increase the numbers and kinds of manipulatives and other materials needed to teach phonics, spelling, and word study effectively. The plan involves use of district funds, adjustments to the existing school budget, and donations. |
| Digital Connectivity and Expertise | ☐ The school and community lack the digital infrastructure to provide reliable access to the internet to support learning in school and at home.<br><br>☐ Digital learning experiences are limited to the reinforcement of basic skills in a few areas of the curriculum.<br><br>☐ Teachers lack professional learning opportunities to grow their expertise in using digital tools and resources effectively in online and blended environments to support and enhance assessment, teaching, and learning. | ☐ The school is improving its digital infrastructure, and access to the internet is expanding and becoming more reliable. Connectivity in the community may be insufficient to support students' learning at home.<br><br>☐ Digital learning experiences are beginning to move away from the reinforcement of basic skills to more engaging and authentic experiences that support the needs and interests of individual students and groups of students.<br><br>☐ Teachers have limited professional learning opportunities to grow their expertise in using digital tools and resources effectively in online and blended environments to support and enhance assessment, teaching, and learning. |

| 3. GAINING MOMENTUM | 4. EXPANDING EXPERTISE |
|---|---|
| ☐ The intervention system supplements classroom literacy instruction, and the support is increasingly applied in an organized, systematic way that is consistent and coherent with classroom instruction. | ☐ The intervention system supplements classroom literacy instruction, and the support is organized and systematic. It is consistent and coherent with classroom instruction but is more intensive and targeted to what children need to learn. |
| ☐ The intervention system consists of multiple tiers of support for students (MTSS), and teachers are growing in their ability to employ a variety of approaches within each tier. | ☐ The intervention system supports students in all areas of the curriculum and consists of multiple tiers of support (MTSS) and a variety of approaches to meet students' individual needs. |
| ☐ Special education services are provided at every tier for the students who need them, and teachers and specialists better understand what "access to strong classroom instruction" might look like for different students. | ☐ Special education services are provided at every tier for the students who need them, and children with IEPs have full access to strong classroom instruction to ensure the least restrictive environment. |
| ☐ The intervention system is largely consistent with research and reflects many of the values and beliefs of the school. | ☐ The intervention system is strongly supported by research and reflects the values and beliefs of the school. |
| ☐ Classrooms have an adequate supply of high-quality, complex text sets to support interactive read-aloud lessons. | ☐ Classrooms are well supplied with high-quality, complex books to read aloud, and they are organized into text sets. |
| ☐ There is ample evidence that teachers have an adequate collection of high-quality enlarged texts. The school is in the process of acquiring more high-quality books that represent a diversity of lived experiences and a wide range of content. <br><br> ☐ There are small copies and audio versions of a growing number of texts for individual rereading. | ☐ Classrooms are well stocked with enough high-quality enlarged texts (fiction and nonfiction books, poems, songs) for teachers to make shared reading a regular part of literacy instruction. Texts are of high quality and represent the diversity of students' lived experiences and offer rich content. <br><br> ☐ There are small copies and audio versions of each enlarged text for individual rereading. |
| ☐ The school book room is operational, but the text collection is of varying quality and quantities of texts are still insufficient for schoolwide differentiated guided reading instruction. | ☐ The school has a well-organized book room with high-quality leveled books in sufficient quantities for schoolwide differentiated guided reading instruction. |
| ☐ The school has multiple copies of a growing number of texts at each grade level and teachers are organizing an increasing number of books clubs, but not all of the titles are of high quality or represent the diversity of students' lived experiences. | ☐ Classrooms are fully stocked with multiple copies to support student choice. There are sufficient books for all students to participate in one book club per month. The books are engaging, high quality, and reflect the diversity of students' lived experiences. |
| ☐ Classroom libraries are notably larger and contain additional genres, content, and difficulty levels, but the number of socially and culturally relevant texts is still not sufficient. | ☐ Classroom libraries are of adequate size and contain a full range of genres, content, difficulty levels, and socially and culturally relevant texts. Books are organized by category and not by level. |
| ☐ Children have access to an increasing number of tools to support drawing and writing. | ☐ Children have access to a wide variety of tools to support drawing and writing (e.g., paper, writer's notebooks, markers, pencils, etc.). |
| ☐ The numbers and kinds of manipulatives and other materials needed to teach phonics, spelling, and word study effectively are growing substantially in every classroom, although some classrooms are better supplied than others. | ☐ Each classroom is supplied with the numbers and kinds of manipulatives and other materials that are needed to teach phonics, spelling, and word study effectively. |
| ☐ The school provides reliable access to the internet to support student learning. Many homes in the community may have access to broadband connectivity but not all. <br><br> ☐ Digital learning experiences in some areas of the curriculum are engaging, personalized, and authentic, while digital learning is still taking shape in other areas. <br><br> ☐ Teachers have increasing professional learning opportunities to grow their expertise in using digital tools and resources effectively in online and blended environments to support and enhance assessment, teaching, and learning. | ☐ The school and community provide persistent, ubiquitous access to high-speed internet to support learning in school and at home. <br><br> ☐ Digital learning experiences in all areas of the curriculum are engaging, personalized, and authentic. They support higher-order applications of creativity, communication, and collaboration. <br><br> ☐ Teachers have consistent professional learning opportunities to grow their expertise in using digital tools and resources effectively in online and blended environments to support and enhance assessment, teaching, and learning. |

*continued from page 463*

Getting the most from the tool involves a collaborative process of reflection, developing a shared view about the current strengths and needs of your school, and identifying priorities for improvement (Figure 23-2). Used in this way, the rubric becomes a map for your team's journey of systemic improvement and continued innovation to create a school that prepares learners for the future. The rubric can help you and your colleagues realize that the path of improvement is always under your control and that you are taking on only what you can manage at any one time. You set reasonable goals that are achievable within a feasible time frame.

**Figure 23-2.** Making the Most of the Rubric: A Path to Improvement

## Reflect on the Status of Your School

We encourage you to share the LIFT rubric with your school team to foster a reflective process. A reproducible version is available in online resources. (As we learn more about the use of the rubric with increasing numbers of educators, we will make continuous refinements, so the version online will be the most current.) Encourage team members to study the categories and descriptions on the rubric, reflect on the qualities of the systems in your school as they currently operate, and be prepared to share their thinking. You may wish to ask each team member to place checkmarks beside the descriptions that they think most accurately describe your school. Teachers may feel they know some aspects of the system well, for example, the quality of instruction or the use of texts, but are less familiar with others. But every educator in your school can contribute important perspectives and provide insight into the qualities and conditions of the various aspects of the system, so it is important for individuals to first do their own thinking and reflection before putting their thinking together with others.

## Develop a Shared View of Current Strengths and Needs

Bring together the whole group and display the LIFT rubric from the online resources for this book. Ask the group: *Where are we now? Where do we see ourselves as a school in each of these categories?* Invite the thinking of each educator in the school so that you develop an understanding of how the system currently operates. Encourage team members to share the descriptions that they checked on their rubrics. If teachers prefer that their ratings be private, they can still participate in the discussion without identifying their categories. Compare the thinking of the group, and work to reach consensus. On the displayed rubric, place checkmarks beside the descriptions that the team agrees best characterize your school. In this way, the whole team agrees on where they are and can visualize the areas of strengths and needs within your school.

Where do most of your checkmarks fall? Do most of your checkmarks fall within one category of collaboration and coherence (column 1, 2, 3, or 4)? Or are they spread across various categories? If the latter, you're not alone! In all our years of working with schools, we have yet to encounter a school that is beginning at a 1 in every respect. Each school, including yours, has strengths on which to build. You and your school team may have already made significant progress in some areas and be well positioned to make quick improvement in others. Also, we have not encountered a school that has achieved a 4 in every part of the system. There will be areas that haven't been a priority or received careful thought. Factors such as staff turnover will affect the system. Other parts of the system may have received attention and resources but are still in the earliest stages of meaningful improvement.

## Identify Priorities for Improvement

As you and your team look down the rows of the rubric, consider the strengths and needs of your school. Pose the question: *Where do we want to be?* Use the descriptions in column 4 (Expanding Expertise) to help name the outcomes

### FROM "FIND A FIX" TO CONTINUOUS IMPROVEMENT

If you have been a literacy educator for many years, you have probably experienced the search for a "solution" or what Bryk et. al. call "solutionitis." Often the search is in response to the problem of trying to raise reading scores. The solution is seen as a "fix" that might take a year, two years, or three years, but will have some immediate convincing results. Bryk and others (2015) have proposed "improvement science" as an alternate view. The idea is that we do not "find" a solution, implement it, and all will be changed. Instead, we need to view change and development as an ongoing process. Educators study persistent and important problems, conduct a thorough analysis to identify strengths and areas to tackle first, make a plan, take action, and then study the results before implementing a change at scale. Improvement is ongoing and never finished. It drives educators to stay curious and growing. When you use this lens, you can look back each year and celebrate the accomplishments that have been made, but there are always new goals for the future.

you want to work toward. Develop a clear picture of where you want to be in the long term and think about where you can focus your efforts to make the biggest positive impact on the system. Then, as a group, identify your highest priorities for the short term. You may choose to focus on just one section at a time—for example, one category or even a single row—while keeping the whole system in view. Only you and your colleagues can decide what to do first with a clear vision for what you expect to happen over time. It is important that the school team members agree on the priorities so that there is ownership of the improvement efforts.

## Make a Plan to Address Improvement Priorities

The next step is to make a plan to address the priorities that the team has identified. Questions to ask might be: *How do we get to where we want to be? What next steps do we need to take to make progress?* Strong plans will be incremental, feasible within a reasonable timeline, realistic, and practical. The team identifies goals that are "smart": specific, measurable, achievable, relevant, and time-bound. They identify actions, the person responsible for each, a timeline for accomplishing the plan, and the resources they will need. Your plan will often include the formation of small teams that are responsible for taking actions on each priority. If a priority represents a larger system (e.g., writing instruction), individuals or pairs within the small team can work on specific aspects (e.g., effective practices within each instructional context for writing, analysis of a writer's notebook, teaching moves during conferences with individual writers, etc.).

## Take Actions to Make Systemic Improvements

The actions you and your colleagues choose will depend on the status of your school and the improvements priorities you have identified. Actions that help the team make progress on systemic improvements may include:

- Using the tools in this book to strength and support the system.
- Professional learning opportunities to increase understanding of specific aspects of the system that have yet to receive attention.
- Professional book studies to strengthen instructional practices.
- Walkthroughs to increase transparency and build common understandings.
- A collaborative inquiry process.

The last bullet—collaborative inquiry—is a productive process that can help you and your colleagues work towards the priorities you have identified. Let's return to the inquiry cycle we introduced in Chapter 1 (Figure 23-3). And to

## INQUIRY CYCLE

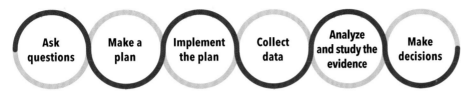

Figure 23-3. Inquiry Cycle

illustrate the process, let's suppose that you and your team have identified as a priority the importance of students engaging in a large quantity of daily independent reading.

**Ask Questions** Take an analytical stance toward the work of improvement. A team will begin its work by asking questions about how the system currently operates. The questions help reveal what information the team needs to learn before making a plan. For example: How many choice books do students read each week in each grade? Is there a sufficient number of engaging books in each classroom from which students can choose? How much time is allocated to independent reading each day at each grade? Do teachers provide instruction that supports students' independent reading?

**Make a Plan** Just as the whole school team makes a plan to address improvement priorities, a small team involved in the inquiry cycle will make a plan that identifies actions, the team member responsible for each, a timeline for accomplishing the plan, and the resources needed. To form a plan, the team considers these questions: *What's working? What's not working? What conditions are contributing to the problem?* and *What resources are needed?* Once colleagues have researched answers to the questions, the team decides what it will try to do. For example, the team might make a plan for creating more sustained in-school time for choice independent reading.

**Implement the Plan** The team knows the action steps, who is responsible for each action, and the timeline for completing the plan. Every member is committed to his responsibilities and to reporting action to the group. The team has regular meetings to monitor progress and quality of implementation and to help each other solve problems. The meetings do not need to be long or comprehensive. They can take the form of quick "check-in" meetings, or "huddles," to assure progress. The tools throughout this book are levers for making improvements and can serve as helpful resources as teams implement their plans.

**Collect Data** Data gathering is a critical part of the process. An essential component of any school improvement is the identification of data that will provide evidence that you are on the right track. Sometimes, these data represent "extra" effort that is collected for team use. But usually, the team will find that evidence emerges naturally from the instructional process, often in

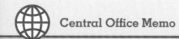
**Take Success to Scale** Many school leaders at the district level are coping with issues of equity across schools. Students who move often within the district, for example, may face a completely different curriculum and expectations as they move from school to school. The lack of coherence across the district puts them at great disadvantage.

One school can sometimes have a "lighthouse" effect in that it serves as a good example and a source of learning for other schools. Consider setting up learning networks across the district to exchange ideas, look at evidence, and offer support for learning. School leaders in each building need to develop their own vision and know their own context. Their paths of progress may be different, so it's not just a matter of visiting and imitating others. But learning networks will make it easier to "scale up" innovations that are showing evidence of success.

*"Simply by sailing in a new direction You could enlarge the world."*

**—Allen Curnow**

the form of soft data such as observations, student notebooks, writing samples, and other artifacts of students' learning. All that is needed is a systematic way of collecting some of it. Increase in independent reading can be documented through student records (e.g., in reader's notebooks) and reading conferences with students.

**Analyze and Study the Evidence** The team will have set a timeline for the plan that includes analyzing the results of the action. Team members can share their own perspectives and observations as well as the evidence they have collected. If the plan's timeline goes for a longer period of time, reflection can take place at several checkpoints. Analyzing an increase in independent reading may be measured in a number of ways, for example, teachers' schedules, records of conferences with individual readers, analysis of student talk about their choice reading, and self-reporting from students.

**Make Decisions** One characteristic of the inquiry cycle is that it is never quite finished! The team will make decisions as to whether to continue, refine, or discontinue the actions, but inevitably, further questions, needs, and priorities will arise. That starts the process over. Think about:

- What did we learn from this action and the evidence?
- Should we continue this action? Did it solve the problem, and would we recommend it to others?
- What else can we do to achieve our overall goals?
- What additional evidence do we need to make a decision?
- What are our next steps?

As we wrote in Chapter 1, a single leader cannot create and sustain school improvement. Meaningful, systemic improvement requires a collaborative process, an analytical stance, and the collective efforts of the whole team working in the same direction.

## Moving Forward with Bold Thinking

Children's success in school is not related to a single factor. The education outcomes of students are the product of many factors and systemic issues and how they work together. Given the competencies that children need to lead fulfilling and successful lives in the future, we are frightened that schools have changed so little over time. Schools *cannot* stay the way they are. Nibbling at the edges of the educational system or focusing every resource on a single aspect of the system will not produce the systemic change needed to ensure all children are prepared for their futures. We all have a collective responsibility to invest and innovate so our schools prepare learners for their future. You and your school teams are creating "future forward" schools with the goal of preparing young students for a future we can only imagine. To reach for the future, we have to be aware of where we have been and to realize indications of progress. You will always be creating new goals and marking progress.

The journey of improvement means moving from a goal of "fixing" education to viewing schools as places of continuous growth. Our schools, including the one you lead, can be dynamic learning organizations that educate children for tomorrow. They are places of generative learning, where children learn how to learn, where teachers learn more about their craft, and where leaders learn more about leading. Think of the educational system, including your school, as a learning system that grows in effectiveness and strength because of the way you think and work. By taking a dynamic stance toward learning, your school becomes a learning organization in which improvements and innovations are a product of how the system operates. When the school is a learning place for adults and children, teachers get better at teaching *by teaching,* students get better at learning *by learning,* and leaders get better at leading *by leading.*

The children in your school deserve visionary school leaders who are bold in their thinking, who embrace innovation, who are courageous in their actions, and who advocate for every single child. Lead for the future, not simply maintain for today. Your school cannot stay the way it is because it isn't educating all children for tomorrow. Schools must think about what it means to be literate in the future. Our schools are places that engage children in real-life learning, authentic problem-solving, robust critical thinking, and deep cultural awareness, where children learn to be empathetic global citizens of the world. We encourage you to be the visionary leader that the children and families of your community need you to be.

As a school leader, you will often need to navigate waters of polarization. May we offer a suggestion? When describing the work of your school, avoid labels. Instead, describe what your school is about. Share the common vision and values that you and your team have co-constructed. Describe the instructional contexts and practices the teachers use and the different types of texts that students engage with daily. Communicate the school's systems for assessing and intervening to assure equity in literacy learning. Explain the improvement priorities that the team has identified. But steer clear of labels. Labels can be misinterpreted and misappropriated. Their original meanings can evolve in ways that no longer represent the culture, values, and practices of your school.

When planning for improvements over time, plant the seeds deep. Take the long view and commit to long-term, systemic improvements. What we've thought about together should result in a short-term plan and a long-term plan. Look back and reflect on each year, but also look forward with your school's shared values in mind so that you don't shift course unwittingly. Think forward with wisdom. Single-year budgeting can lead to short-sightedness and a "fix it quick" mentality throughout the system. Investing in professional, social, and decisional capital can sustain and expand improvement over time.

**Manage Your Budget**

**Budget for the Marathon** Creating innovative, future-focused schools is a continuous, ongoing effort. It's a marathon, not a sprint. As McNulty (2021) reminds school leaders, budget for the marathon. Allocating budget to staff positions or additional curriculum may help you make fast progress but with only limited, short-term impact. As you and your team work for systemic change, think about how your budget can promote real innovation, deliver long-term impact, and sustain continuous improvement. Evaluate innovations against your priorities for improvement and your school's common values. Innovations that align to both are likely to be good candidates for your budget dollars.

We hope the ideas in this book will help to transform your thinking about schools and the educational system, because only transformational thinking at every level of the system will result in innovative schools that prepare students for the future. As you reflect on your school in light of new information, we hope you hold to this perspective: it's not what you do, it's the way you *think* about what you do that makes a lasting impact. The way you think about what you do is essential to sustaining improvement. We don't want children to simply *do* school. Rather our work as leaders is to create schools of thinkers: children as thinkers, teachers as thinkers, and leaders as thinkers. Become a leader of thinkers who builds upon the strengths that you notice in your school.

Schools are the lever for changing the lives of children. May your leadership be the lever for helping teachers assure children their human right to literacy.

# List of Tools

The most current version of each tool can be found in Online Resources, organized by tool number.

# References

Affinito, Stephanie. 2018. *Literacy Coaching: Transforming Teaching and Learning with Digital Tools and Technology.* Portsmouth, NH: Heinemann.

Afflerbach, Peter. 2015. "An Overview of Individual Differences in Reading: Research, Policy, and Practice." *Handbook of Individual Differences in Reading.*

Aguilar, Elena. 2016. *The Art of Coaching Teams: Building Resilient Communities That Transform Schools.* San Francisco: Jossey-Bass.

———. 2020. *Coaching for Equity: Conversations that Change Practice.* Hoboken: Jossey-Bass.

Allyn, Pam, and Ernest Morrell. 2016. *Every Child a Super Reader: 7 Strengths to Open a World of Possible.* New York: Scholastic.

Anderson, Nancy L., and Connie Briggs. 2011. "Reciprocity Between Reading and Writing: Strategic Processing as Common Ground." *The Reading Teacher* 64 (7): 546–549.

Anderson, Richard C., Paul T. Wilson, and Linda G. Fielding. 1988. "Growth in Reading and How Children Spend Their Time Outside of School." *Reading Research Quarterly* 23 (3): 285–303. International Literacy Association.

Ash, Ruth C., and J. Maurice Persall. 2000. "The Principal as Chief Learning Officer: Developing Teacher Leaders." *NASSP Bulletin* 84 (616): 15–22.

Bandura, A. 1993. "Perceived Self-Efficacy in Cognitive Development and Functioning." *Educational Psychologist* 28 (2): 117–148.

———. 1997. *Self-Efficacy: The Exercise of Control.* New York: W. H. Freeman and Company.

Barth, Roland S. 2006. "Improving Relationships Within the Schoolhouse." *Educational Leadership* 63 (6): 8–13.

Bean, R. M., D. Kern, V. Goatley, E. Ortlieb, J. Shettel, K. Calo, B. Marinak, E. Sturtevant, L. Elish-Piper, S. L'Allier, M. A. Cox, S. Frost, P. Mason, D. Quatroche, and J. Cassidy. 2015. "Specialized Literacy Professionals as Literacy Leaders: Results of a National Survey." *Literacy Research and Instruction* 54 (2): 83–114.

Beck, I., M. McKeown, and L. Kucan. 2013. *Bringing Words to Life: Robust Vocabulary Instruction,* 2nd ed. New York: Guilford Press.

Berg, Jill Harrison. 2019. "Leading Together: Following the Lead of Teachers of Color." *Educational Leadership* 76 (7): 87–88.

Biancarosa, G., A. Bryk, and E. Dexter. 2010. "Assessing the Value-Added Effects of Literacy Collaborative Professional Development on Student Learning." *The Elementary School Journal* 3 (1): 7–34.

Bloom, L. 2000. "The Intentionality Model of Word Learning: How to Learn a Word, Any Word." In *Becoming a Word Learner: A Debate on Lexical Acquisition,* R. Golinkoff, K. Hirsch-Pasek, L. Bloom, L. Smith, A. Woodward, N. Akhtar, M. Tomasello, and G. Hollich, eds. New York: Oxford University Press.

Boix Mansilla, Veronica. 2016. "How to Be a Global Thinker." *Educational Leadership* 74 (4): 10–16.

Bomer, R. 1995. *Time for Meaning: Crafting Literate Lives in Middle & High School.* Portsmouth, NH: Heinemann.

Bransford, John D., Ann L. Brown, and Rodney R. Cocking, eds. 2000. *How People Learn: Brain, Mind, Experience, and School.* Washington, DC: The National Acadamies Press. https://doi.org/10.17226/9853.

Britton, J. 1983. "Writing and the Story of the World." In *Explorations in the Development of Writing: Theory, Research, and Practice,* B. M. Kroll and C. G. Wells, eds., pp. 3–30. New York: Wiley.

Brooks, David. 2018. "Good Leaders Make Good Schools." *The New York Times.* (March 12, 2018, Opinion).

Brown, Erin, and Susan K. L'Allier. 2020. *No More Random Acts of Literacy Coaching.* Portsmouth, NH: Heinemann.

Bruner, J. 1983. *Child's Talk: Learning to Use Language.* New York: W. W. Norton & Co.

Bryk, Anthony S. 2010. "Organizing Schools for Improvement." *Phi Delta Kappan* 91 (7): 23–30.

———. 2020. *Improvement in Action: Advancing Quality in America's Schools.* Cambridge, MA: Harvard Education Press.

Bryk, A. S., L. M. Gomez, A. Grunow, and P. G. LeMahieu. 2015. *Learning to Improve: How America's Schools Can Get Better at Getting Better.* Cambridge, MA: Harvard Education Press.

Chingos, Matthew M. 2012. *Strength in Numbers: State Spending on K–12 Assessment Systems.* Washington, DC: Brown Center on Education Policy, The Brookings Institution.

Clay, Marie M. 1987. "Learning to Be Learning Disabled." *New Zealand Journal of Educational Studies* 22 (2): 155–173.

———. 1991. *Becoming Literate: The Construction of Inner Control.* Portsmouth, NH: Heinemann.

———. 1995. *An Observation Survey of Early Literacy Achievement.* Portsmouth, NH: Heinemann.

———. 1998. *By Different Paths to Different Outcomes.* York, ME: Stenhouse Publishers.

———. 2001. *Change Over Time in Children's Literacy Development.* Portsmouth, NH: Heinemann.

———. 2005. *Literacy Lessons Designed for Individuals.* Portsmouth, NH: Heinemann.

———. 2015. *Change Over Time in Children's Literacy Development.* The Marie Clay Literacy Trust. Portsmouth, NH: Heinemann.

Collaborative Inquiry. Ongoing Professional Development. Literacy Collaborative, Lesley University. October 2, 2018.

Coyne, M. D., E. J. Kame'enui, D. C. Simmons, and B. A. Harn. 2004. "Beginning Reading Intervention as Inoculation or Insulin: First-Grade Reading Performance of Strong Responders to Kindergarten Intervention." *Journal of Learning Disabilities* 37: 90–104.

Cromwell, S. 2002. "Is Your School Culture Toxic or Positive?" *https://www.educationworld.com/a_admin/admin/admin275.shtml.*

Darling-Hammond, Linda, Maria E. Hyler, and Madelyn Gardner. 2017. *Effective Teacher Professional Development.* Palo Alto, CA: Learning Policy Institute.

Datnow, Amanda, and Vicki Park. 2015. "Data Use for Equity." *Educational Leadership* 72 (5): 48–54.

Dobbs, Christina L., Jacy Ippolito, and Megin Charner-Laird. 2016. "Creative Tension: Turn the Challenges of Learning Together into Opportunities." *JSD/ The Learning Professional* 37 (6): 28–31.

Donohoo, Jenni, and Steven Katz. 2017. "When Teachers Believe, Students Achieve: Collaborative Inquiry Builds Teacher Efficacy for Better Student Outcomes." *The Learning Professional* 38 (6): 20–27.

Donohoo, Jenni, John Hattie, and Rachel Eells. 2018. "The Power of Collective Efficacy." *Educational Leadership* 75 (6): 40–44.

Durlak, J. A., R. P. Weissberg, A. B. Dymnicki, R. D. Taylor, and K. B. Schellinger. 2011. "The Impact of Enhancing Students' Social and Emotional Learning: A Meta-Analysis of School-Based Universal Interventions." *Child Development* 82 (1): 405–432.

Dweck, C. S. 2016. *Mindset: The New Psychology of Success*. Updated ed. New York: Ballantine.

Elmore, Richard F. 2002. *Bridging the Gap Between Standards and Achievement: The Imperative for Professional Development in Education*. Washington, DC: Albert Shanker Institute.

Eun, Barohny. 2008. "Making Connections: Grounding Professional Development in the Developmental Theories of Vygotsky." *The Teacher Educator* 43 (2): 134–155. DOI: 10.1080/08878730701838934.

Everett, Chad. 2017. "There Is No Diverse Book." *Imaginelit* (blog), November 21. http://www.imaginelit.com/news/2017/11/21/there-is-no-diverse-book.

Fisher, D., N. Frey, and C. Rothenberg. 2008. *Content-Area Conversations: How to Plan Discussion-Based Lessons for Diverse Language Learners*. Alexandria, VA: Association for Supervision and Curriculum Development.

Forster, Jeffrey P. 2020. "What Strategies Do Principals in Highly Effective Elementary Schools Utilize to Foster Teacher Leadership, from Both the Principal and Teacher Leader Perspective?" PhD diss., Auburn University.

Fountas, Irene C., and Gay Su Pinnell. 2009. "Keys to Effective Coaching: Cultivating Self-Extending Teachers in a Professional Learning Community." *The Journal of Reading Recovery* 8 (2): 39–47.

———. 2017a. *Benchmark Assessment System*. Portsmouth, NH: Heinemann.

———. 2017b. *Guided Reading: Responsive Teaching Across the Grades*. Portsmouth, NH: Heinemann.

———. 2017c. *Prompting Guide, Part 1, for Oral Reading and Early Writing*. Portsmouth, NH: Heinemann.

———. 2017d. *Prompting Guide, Part 2, for Comprehension: Thinking, Talking, and Writing*. Portsmouth, NH: Heinemann.

———. 2018. "Every Child, Every Classroom, Every Day: From Vision to Action in Literacy Learning." *The Reading Teacher* 72 (1): 7–19.

———. 2019–2020. *The Reading Minilessons Book: Your Everyday Guide for Literacy Teaching*. Grade K through Grade 6. Portsmouth, NH: Heinemann.

———. 2022a. *The Comprehensive Phonics, Spelling, and Word Study Guide, Second Edition*. Portsmouth, NH: Heinemann.

———. 2022b. *The Fountas & Pinnell Literacy Continuum: A Tool for Assessment, Planning, and Teaching, Second Edition.* Portsmouth, NH: Heinemann.

———. 2022c. *Genre Quick Guide, Grades K–8+.* Portsmouth, NH: Heinemann.

———. 2022d. *Genre Study: Teaching with Fiction and Nonfiction Books, Grades K–8+.* Portsmouth, NH: Heinemann.

———. 2022e. *The Writing Minilessons Book: Your Everyday Guide for Literacy Teaching.* Grade K through Grade 6. Portsmouth, NH: Heinemann.

Frank, Carolyn. 1999. *Ethnographic Eyes: A Teacher's Guide to Classroom Observation.* Portsmouth, NH: Heinemann.

The Free Library. 2014. "Taking Inquiry to Scale: An Alternative to Traditional Approaches to Education Reform." Retrieved Dec. 14, 2021 from https://www.thefreelibrary.com/Taking+inquiry+to+scale%3b+an+alternative+to+traditional+approaches+to . . . -a0344582665.

Fullan, M. G. 2020. *Leading in a Culture of Change.* Hoboken: Jossey-Bass.

Fullan, Michael, and Joanne Quinn. 2016. *Coherence: The Right Drivers in Action for Schools, Districts, and Systems.* Thousand Oaks, CA: Corwin.

Gabriel, Rachel. 2008. "Understanding Dyslexia Laws and Policies." *The Journal of Reading Recovery* 17: 25–34.

Galinsky, Adam, and Maurice Schweitzer. 2015, October. "Building Trust: A Leader's Action Plan." *Nano Tools: Wharton Leadership.* http://wlp.wharton.upenn.edu/nano-tools/nano-tool-2/.

Garet, M., A. Wayne, F. Stancavage, J. Taylor, K. Walters, M. Song, S. Brown, S. Hurlburt, P. Zhu, S. Sepanik, and F. Doolittle. 2010. *Middle School Mathematics Professional Development Impact Study: Findings After the First Year of Implementation* (NCEE 2010–4009). Washington, DC: National Center for Education Evaluation and Regional Assistance, Institute of Education Sciences, US Department of Education.

Garet, Michael S., Stephanie Cronen, Marian Eaton, Anja Kurki, Meredith Ludwig, Wehmah Jones, Kazuaki Uekawa, Audrey Falk, Howard Bloom, Fred Doolittle, Pei Zhu, and Laura Sztejnberg. 2008. *The Impact of Two Professional Development Interventions on Early Reading Instruction and Achievement* (NCEE 2008–4030). Washington, DC: National Center for Education Evaluation and Regional Assistance, Institute of Education Sciences, US Department of Education.

Garman, C. G., and J. F. Garman. 1992. *Teaching young children effective listening skills.* York, PA: William Gladden Foundation.

Gay, Geneva. 2010. *Culturally Responsive Teaching: Theory, Research, and Practice,* 2nd ed. New York: Teachers College Press.

Gershenson, Seth, Cassandra Hart, Joshua Hyman, Constance Lindsay, and Nicholas W. Papageorge. 2018. "The Long-Run Impacts of Same-Race Teachers." NBER Working Paper No. 25254. National Bureau of Economic Research. DOI: 10.3386/w25254.

Gonzalez, N., L. C. Moll, and C. Amanti. 2005. *Funds of Knowledge: Theorizing Practices in Households, Communities, and Classrooms.* Mahwah, NJ: Lawrence Erlbaum Associates.

Greeno, James G., Allan M. Collins, and Lauren B. Resnick. 1996. "Cognition and Learning." In *Handbook of Educational Psychology*, D. Berliner and R. Calfee, eds. New York: Macmillian.

Guskey, Thomas R. 2002. "Does It Make a Difference? Evaluating Professional Development." *Educational Leadership* 59 (6): 45–51.

———. 2017. "Where Do You Want to Get To? Effective Professional Learning Begins with a Clear Destination in Mind." *The Learning Professional* 38 (2): 32–37.

Hargreaves, Andrew. 2003. *Teaching in the Knowledge Society: Education in the Age of Insecurity.* New York: Teachers College Press.

Hargreaves, A., and M. Fullan. 2012. *Professional Capital: Transforming Teaching in Every School.* New York: Teachers College Press and Ontario: Ontario Principals' Council.

———. 2013. "The Power of Professional Capital: With an Investment in Collaboration, Teachers Become Nation Builders." *The Learning Professional* (formerly *JSD*) 34 (3): 36–39.

Harris, J., R. Golinkoff, and K. Hirsh-Pasek. 2011. "Lessons from the Crib for the Classroom: How Children Really Learn Vocabulary." In *Handbook of Early Literacy Research*, S. B. Neuman and D. K. Dickinson, eds. New York: Guilford Press.

Hass, Chris. 2020. *Social Justice Talk: Strategies for Teaching Critical Awareness.* Portsmouth, NH: Heinemann.

Hathaway, Bill. 2020. "A Housebound World Finds Solace in Yale's 'Science of Well Being' Course." *Yale News.* Retrieved August 14, 2020, from https://news.yale.edu/2020/03/25/housebound-world-finds-solace-yales-science-well-being-course.

Hattie, John A. C. 2009. *Visible Learning: A Synthesis of Over 800 Meta-Analyses Relating to Achievement.* New York: Routledge.

————. 2015. "The Applicability of Visible Learning to Higher Education." *Scholarship of Teaching and Learning in Psychology* 1 (1): 79–91. https://doi.org/10.1037/stl0000021.

————. 2016. Mindframes and Maximizers. 3rd Annual Visible Learning Conference held in Washington, DC.

Hattie, J. A. C., and K. Zierer. 2018. *Ten Mindframes for Visible Learning: Teaching for Success.* Routledge.

Hayden, Jeff. 2021. "Why Brilliant Leadership Minds Embrace the Rule of 1 Percent." Inc. Online, 12 Mar. 2021.

Hicks, Troy, Misty Sailors, and International Literacy Association. 2018. *Democratizing Professional Growth with Teachers: From Development to Learning.* Literacy Leadership Brief. Newark, DE: International Literacy Association.

Himmele, Persida, and William Himmele. 2021. *Why Are We Still Doing That? Positive Alternatives to Problematic Teaching Practices.* Alexandria, VA: ASCD.

Hoerr, Thomas R. 2005. *The Art of School Leadership.* Alexandria, VA: ASCD.

Hough, Heather J., David Kerbow, Anthony Bryk, Gay Su Pinnell, Emily Rodgers, Emily Dexter, Carrie Hung, Patricia L. Scharer, and Irene Fountas. 2013. "Assessing Teacher Practice and Development: The Case of Comprehensive Literacy Instruction." *School Effectiveness and School Improvement* 24 (4). DOI: 10.1080/09243453.2012.73.

Immordino-Yang, M. H., and A. Damasio. 2007. "We Feel, Therefore We Learn: The Relevance of Affective and Social Neuroscience to Education." *Mind, Brain, and Education* 1 (1): 3–10. DOI: 10.1111/j.1751-228X.2007.00004.x.

International Dyslexia Association. 2010. "Knowledge and Practice Standards for Teachers of Reading." https://dyslexiaida.org/knowledge-and-practices/.

International Literacy Association. 2016. "Dyslexia." Research Advisory. Newark, DE: International Literacy Association.

————. 2019. "Principals as Literacy Leaders." Literacy Leadership Brief. Newark, DE: International Literacy Association.

————. 2020. "Teaching Writing to Improve Reading Skills." Research Advisory. Newark, DE: International Literacy Association.

Johnson, J., S. Leibowitz, and K. Perret. 2017. *The Coach Approach to School Leadership: Leading Teachers to Higher Levels of Effectiveness*. Alexandria, VA: ASCD.

Johnston, Peter H. 2012. *Opening Minds: Using Language to Change Lives*. Portsmouth, NH: Stenhouse.

Johnston, P., K. Champeau, A. Hartwig, S. Helmer, M. Komar, T. Krueger, and L. McCarthy. 2020. *Engaging Literate Minds: Developing Children's Social, Emotional, and Intellectual Lives, K–3*. Portsmouth, NH: Stenhouse.

Johnston, Peter H., Gay Ivey, and Amy Faulkner. 2011. "Talking in Class: Remembering What Is Important About Classroom Talk." *The Reading Teacher* 65 (4): 232–237.

Joint Task Force on Assessment of the International Reading Association and the National Council of Teachers of English. 2010. *Standards for the Assessment of Reading and Writing,* rev. ed. Newark, DE: International Reading Association.

Kaye, Elizabeth L. 2006. "Second Graders' Reading Behaviors: A Study of Variety, Complexity, and Change." *Literacy Teaching and Learning* 10: 51–75.

Kaye, Elizabeth L., and Mary K. Lose. 2018. "As Easy as ABC? Teaching and Learning About Letters in Early Literacy." *The Reading Teacher* 72: 599–610.

Keene, Ellin Oliver. 2018. *Engaging Children: Igniting a Drive for Deeper Learning, K–8*. Portsmouth, NH: Heinemann.

Killion, Joellen, and Cindy Harrison. 2018. "Coaches' Multiple Roles Support Teaching and Learning." *Tools for Learning Schools* (a newsletter of Learning Forward) 21 (1).

Kim, Robert. 2020. *Elevating Equity and Justice: Ten U.S. Supreme Court Cases Every Teacher Should Know*. Portsmouth, NH: Heinemann.

Knight, J. 2021. "Moving from Talk to Action in Professional Learning." *Making Professional Learning Stick* 78 (5).

Knowles, Malcolm S., Elwood F. Holton III, and Richard A. Swanson. 2015. *The Adult Learner: The Definitive Classic in Adult Education and Human Resource Development*, 8th ed. New York: Routledge.

KPMG Foundation. 2006. *The Long-Term Costs of Literacy Difficulties*. New York: KPMG Foundation, Inc.

Krashen, S. D. 2004. *The Power of Reading*. Westport, CT: Libraries Unlimited.

Ladson-Billings, Gloria. 2006. "From the Achievement Gap to the Education Debt: Understanding Achievement in U.S. Schools." *Educational Researcher* 35: 3–12.

Lyons, C. 2007. "A Tribute to Marie Clay." *The Journal of Reading Recovery* 7 (1): 51–53.

Lyons, C., and G. Pinnell. 2001. *Systems for Change in Literacy Education—A Guide to Professional Development*. Portsmouth, NH: Heinemann.

Mapp, Karen L., Ilene Carver, and Jessica Lander. 2017. *Powerful Partnerships: A Teacher's Guide to Engaging Families for Student Success*. New York: Scholastic, Inc.

Marshall, Tom. 2018. *Reclaiming the Principalship*. Portsmouth, NH: Heinemann.

"Making Time for Collaboration." Adapted from *Learning by Doing: A Handbook for Professional Learning Communities at Work*™ (DuFour, DuFour, Eaker, and Many, ©Solution Tree, 2006, pp. 95–97.

McGill-Franzen, A., and R. L. Allington. 1991. "The Gridlock of Low Reading Achievement: Perspectives on Practice and Policy." *Remedial and Special Education* 12: 20–30.

McKay, C. B. 2012. *You Don't Have to Be Bad to Get Better: A Leader's Guide to Improving Teacher Quality*. Thousand Oaks, CA: Corwin.

McQuillan, Jeff. 1998. *The Literacy Crisis: False Claims and Real Solutions*. Portsmouth, NH: Heinemann.

Minor, Cornelius. 2019. *We Got This: Equity, Access, and the Quest to Be Who Our Students Need Us to Be*. Portsmouth, NH: Heinemann.

Moll, Luis. 1992. "Funds of Knowledge for Teaching: Using a Qualitative Approach to Connect Homes and Classroom." *Theory Into Practice* 31: 132–134.

Mulligan, Tammy, and Clare Landrigan. 2018. *It's All About the Books: How to Create Bookrooms and Classroom Libraries That Inspire Readers*. Portsmouth, NH: Heinemann.

Nagy, W. E. 1988. "Teaching Vocabulary to Improve Reading Comprehension." Urbana, IL, and Newark, DE: National Council of Teachers of English and the International Reading Association (ERIC Clearinghouse on Reading and Communication Skills).

Nagy, W. E., and J. Scott. 2000. "Vocabulary." In M. L. Kamil, P. B. Mosenthal, P. D. Pearson, and R. Barr, eds., *Handbook of Reading Research* 3: 269–284. Mahwah, NJ: Lawrence Erlbaum Associates.

National Center for Literacy Education/National Council of Teachers of English. 2012. "Asset Inventory for Collaborative Teams." Developed by Catherine A. Nelson, Robert Hill, Michael Palmisano, Lara Hebert, and Sharon Roth.

———. 2012. "Framework for Building Capacity." Developed by Catherine A. Nelson, Robert Hill, Michael Palmisano, Lara Hebert, and Sharon Roth.

National Reading Panel (US) and National Institute of Child Health and Human Development (US). 2000. *Teaching Children to Read: An Evidence-Based Assessment of the Scientific Research Literature on Reading and Its Implications for Reading Instruction.* Report of the National Reading Panel. Bethesda, MD: U.S. Dept. of Health and Human Services, Public Health Service, National Institutes of Health, National Institute of Child Health and Human Development.

Neuman, S. B., and D. K. Dickinson. 2011. *Handbook of Early Literacy Research,* vol. 3. New York: The Guilford Press.

Nora, Julie, and Jana Echevarria. 2016. *No More Low Expectations for English Learners.* Portsmouth, NH: Heinemann.

Odden, Allan R. 2011. *Strategic Management of Human Capital in Education: Improving Instructional Practice and Student Learning in Schools.* New York: Routledge.

Palmisano, Michael J. 2013. *Taking Inquiry to Scale: An Alternative to Traditional Approaches to Education Reform.* National Council of Teachers of English.

Phillips, G., and P. Smith. 1997. *A third chance to learn: The development and evaluation of specialized interventions for young children experiencing the greatest difficulty in learning to read.* Wellington, NZ: New Zealand Council for Educational Research.

Pranikoff, Kara. 2017. *Teaching Talk: A Practical Guide to Fostering Student Thinking and Conversation.* Portsmouth, NH: Heinemann.

Pressley, Michael, S. E. Israel, C. C. Block, L. L. Bauserman, and K. Kinnucan-Welsch, eds. 2005. "Commentary on Three Important Directions in Comprehension Assessment Research." In *Metacognition in Literacy Instruction,* pp. 396–410. Mahwah, NJ: Routledge.

Puig, Enrique A. 2019. "Rethinking the Intersectionality of the Zone of Proximal Development: The Challenges of Disruptive and Transformative Change to Improve Instruction." In *Transformative Pedagogies for Teacher Education: Critical Action, Agency, and Dialogue in Teaching and Learning Contexts*, Ann E. Lopez and Elsie Lindy Olan, eds. Charlotte, NC: Information Age Publishing, Inc.

Puig, Enrique A., and Kathy S. Froelich. 2011. *The Literacy Coach: Guiding in the Right Direction*, 2nd ed. Pearson.

Rainville, Kristin N., and Stephanie Jones. 2008. "Situated Identities: Power and Positioning in the Work of a Literacy Coach." *The Reading Teacher* 61 (6): 440–448.

Resnick, L. 1996. *Cognition and Learning*. New York: Macmillan.

Robinson, Viviane M. J., Claire A. Lloyd, and Kenneth J. Rowe. 2008. "The Impact of Leadership on Student Outcomes: An Analysis of the Differential Effectives of Leadership Types." *Educational Administration Quarterly* 44 (5): 635–674.

Rosenblatt, Louise M. 1994. "The Transactional Theory of Reading and Writing." In *Theoretical Models and Processes of Reading*, 4th ed., Robert Ruddell, Martha Rapp Ruddell, and Harry Singer, eds., pp. 1057–1092. Newark, DE: International Reading Association.

Saphier, Jon. 2017. "The Equitable Classroom: Today's Student Body Needs Culturally Proficient Teachers." *The Learning Professional* 38: 28–31.

———. 2018. "What I've Learned: Let's Get Specific About How Leaders Can Build Trust." *The Learning Professional* 39: 14–16. www.learningforward.org.

Sharratt, Lyn, and Michael Fullan. 2012. *Putting FACES on the Data: What Great Leaders Do!* Thousand Oaks, CA: Corwin.

Simmons, Deborah. 2015. "Instructional Engineering Principles to Frame the Future of Reading Intervention Research and Practice." *Remedial and Special Education* 36 (1): 45–51.

Sims Bishop, R. 1990. "Mirrors, Windows, and Sliding Glass Doors." *Perspectives* 1 (3): ix–xi.

Sinclair-Tarr, Stacey, and William Tarr Jr. 2007. "Using Large-Scale Assessments to Evaluate the Effectiveness of School Library Programs in California." *Phi Delta Kappan* 88 (9): 710–711.

Solins, Joanna. 2019. *Life in the Redwood Forest*. Portsmouth, NH: Heinemann.

Souto-Manning, Mariana, Carmen Lugo Llerena, Jessica Martell, Abigail Salas Maguire, and Alicia Arce-Boardman. 2018. *No More Culturally Irrelevant Teaching*. Portsmouth, NH: Heinemann.

Swan Dagen, Allison, and Rita M. Bean, eds. 2020. *Best Practices of Literacy Leaders: Keys to School Improvement*. New York: The Guilford Press.

Taylor, R. D., E. Oberle, J. A. Durlak, and R. P. Weissberg. 2017. "Promoting Positive Youth Development Through School-Based Social and Emotional Learning Interventions: A Meta-Analysis of Follow-up Effects." *Child Development* 88 (4): 1156–1171.

The New Teacher Project (TNTP). 2015. *The Mirage: Confronting the Hard Truth About Our Quest for Teacher Development*. Brooklyn, NY: TNTP.

US Department of Education, National Center for Education Statistics, Common Core of Data (CCD). 2018–2019. "Public Elementary and Secondary School Universe Survey."

Vellutino, Frank R. 2010. "'Learning to Be Learning Disabled': Marie Clay's Seminal Contribution to the Response to Intervention Approach to Identifying Specific Reading Disability." *Journal of Reading Recovery* 10 (1): 5, 23.

Vellutino, Frank R., and Donna M. Scanlon. 2002. "The Interactive Strategies Approach to Reading Intervention." *Contemporary Educational Psychology* 27: 573–635.

Vygotsky, L. S. 1962. *Thought and Language*. E. Hanfmann and G. Vakar, trans. Cambridge, MA: MIT Press.

———. 1978. *Mind in Society: The Development of Higher Psychological Processes*. Cambridge, MA: Harvard University Press.

Wilkinson, Andrew, with Alan Davies and Dorothy Atkinson. 1965. *Spoken English*. Birmingham, UK: University of Birmingham.

Wollman, Julie E. 2007. "'Are We on the Same Book and Page?' The Value of Shared Theory and Vision." *Language Arts* 84 (5): 410–418.

Wren, Sebastian, and Deborah Reed. 2005. "Literacy Coaches: Roles and Responsibilities." *SEDL Letter* 17 (1): 6–12. Southwest Education Development Laboratory/American Institutes for Research (AIR).

# Index